PENGUIN HAN...

THE COOKERY OF ENGLAND

Elisabeth Ayrton was born in Surrey in 1915 and educated at Newnham College, Cambridge, where she read English and Archaeology. During the Second World War she served in Special Operations Executive. She has published three novels, the first of which was centred on cooking as an art and a way of life; many short stories; a book on Doric Temples; and three other cookery books, *Good Simple Cooking*, *Time is of the Essence* and *Royal Favourites*. Since the death of her husband, Michael Ayrton, the artist and writer, in 1975, she has lived in Gloucestershire.

THE COOKERY
OF ENGLAND

being a Collection of Recipes
for Traditional Dishes of All Kinds
from the Fifteenth Century to the Present Day,
with Notes on their
Social and Culinary Background

BY

ELISABETH AYRTON

PENGUIN BOOKS

Penguin Books Ltd, Harmondsworth, Middlesex, England
Penguin Books, 625 Madison Avenue, New York, New York 10022, U.S.A.
Penguin Books Australia Ltd, Ringwood, Victoria, Australia
Penguin Books Canada Ltd, 41 Steelcase Road West, Markham, Ontario, Canada
Penguin Books (N.Z.) Ltd, 182 190 Wairau Road, Auckland 10, New Zealand

—

First published by André Deutsch 1974
Published in Penguin Books 1977

—

—

Made and printed in Great Britain by
Richard Clay (The Chaucer Press) Ltd, Bungay, Suffolk
Set in Monophoto Ehrhardt

To my three daughters,
all good cooks

CONTENTS

A NOTE ON QUANTITIES

Quantities are given in pounds and ounces and in pints and quarts. Metric equivalents are given in all cases as follows:

Solids

Ounces	*Grams (g.)*
1	30
2	60
4	120
8	240
12	360
16	480, or ½ kilo (k.)
1½ lb.	¾ kilo
2 lb.	1 kilo

Liquids

¼ pint	1½ decilitres (dl.)
½ pint	3 decilitres
1 pint	6 decilitres
1 quart	1 litre (l.)

These equivalents have been arranged for easy weighing and measuring and are not accurate to 2 places of decimals. No one wants to weigh out 67·3 grams of flour or measure 3·75 decilitres of milk and, since cooking is not chemistry, there is no need to. The quantities given, either in pounds and ounces or in kilos and grams, will produce almost exactly the same results, though in fact a kilo is 2·2 lb. and a quart (40 fluid oz.) is 1·1 litres.

INTRODUCTION
THE LIVING TRADITION OF THE TRUE COOKERY OF ENGLAND

War was declared between the English and the French over the matter of the fine art of good cooking long before the Middle Ages, and though by the nineteenth century the English were certainly the losers and themselves accepted the French as victors, the war still renews itself from time to time over the years.

'. . . I suppose the Frenchmen never saw the like,' said George Cavendish describing with obvious satisfaction in his *Life of Cardinal Wolsey* the marvellous 'subtleties' which decorated the second course of Wolsey's great feast. He goes on to say that one of the subtleties, in the form of a chessboard, was given to a 'gentleman of France' to take home (rather as though he were a child at a birthday party) 'because that Frenchmen be very expert in that play'.

At this point in the sixteenth century, England was clearly felt to be in the gastronomic ascendant. Some two hundred years later, however, when Parson Woodforde, a great English epicure, described an expensive and elaborate dinner, he commented bitterly, 'Most of the things spoiled by being so Frenchified in the dressing,' the implication being that in this period many Englishmen felt undue reverence for French food. Mrs Glasse in *The Art of Cookery Made Plain and Easy*, first published in 1747, confirms this by the strength of her indignation! 'But if Gentlemen will have French Cooks, they must pay for French Tricks,' she says. '. . . So much is the blind Folly of this Age, that they would rather be imposed on by a French Booby, than Give Encouragement to a good English Cook!' And later, when suggesting that if you have only one pheasant you may roast a chicken with it and no one will know the difference, she finishes her slightly dishonest recipe by saying, 'A Frenchman would order Fish Sauce to them, but then you quite spoil your Pheasants.' A lobster sauce? An anchovy sauce? We should certainly join Mrs Glasse in deploring either.

It is clear, however, that in the eighteenth century English cooks had begun to be fearful of French domination. This arose in great measure because of the culinary advances which had been developing for some time in France but which were first clearly set out by that great chef and gastronome François La Varenne. He published three cookery books while Louis XIV was still on the throne, but the change and improvement which their influence brought about were fully apparent only after the death of the Sun King. The reformed French haute cuisine naturally impressed English visitors, and at the end of the seventeenth century and in the early decades of the eighteenth the English nobility and gentry had begun to believe that French cooking was wholly superior to English. Some even sent their cooks to Paris to be taught, and others imported French chefs, although at that time England was defeating France on the battlefield under Marlborough's generalship. Queen Anne's cook, Patrick Lamb, stood out against this practice and also claimed that English raw materials were the best in the world. He deplored the French 'Quelque Chose', the casual French name for small made dishes, usually sweet, but it nevertheless became fashionable in England, the name being translated as 'Kickshaw'. Like Mrs Glasse and Eliza Smith, he referred to many made dishes as 'French messes', using 'mess' in a pejorative sense and not simply to mean a 'dish' as the term had been used a hundred years earlier, and in 1747 Robert Campbell, author of *The London Tradesman*, declared that 'Fish when it has passed the Hands of a French Cook is no more Fish: it has neither the Taste, Smell nor Appearance of Fish. It, and everything else, is dressed in masquerade, seasoned with slow poisons, and every Dish pregnant with nothing but the Seeds of Diseases both Chronick and acute . . .'

In 1830 the royal seal was set, for the time, on English cooking, when the *Cheltenham Chronicle* reviewed a new cookery book by Richard Dolby, head cook at the famous Thatched House Tavern in St James's Street. The book was an immediate and outstanding success, partly because of the quality of the recipes and partly because it was the first cookery book to be published in simple dictionary form. Many reviewers prophesied that it would supersede all previous cookery books, and the *Cheltenham Chronicle* pointed out that

The present king has dined in his palace during the first three months of his reign, upwards of 21,000 persons including domestics; but what is very extraordinary, the kitchen bills for the same period are less in amount than those of the corresponding quarter in the reign of George IV. His Majesty does not employ in the department of the cuisine at any of his palaces, *one single French cook*. This piece of intelligence, humble though it be, proves beyond doubt not only the excellence but the economy of our native culinary art, as developed in the popular 'Cook's Dictionary' of Mr Dolby, of the Thatched House Tavern. . . . His Majesty's opinion as to who are the best caterers for the table cannot fail to have due weight and the demand (already large) is increased for Dolby's New Family Manual of Cookery.

The war was occasionally taken into the other camp by French borrowing of English terms and dishes. 'Rosbif' was taken to apply to any type of meat, with the result that 'Rosbif de Mouton' was offered on various menus. 'Plum buting' also appeared and seems to have been admired by some French gourmets though fiercely denigrated by the majority.

Not only did the tradition of the true English cooking exist, but it has been continually recorded throughout its history in a field where no one has sought to deny the British a certain pre-eminence, that of literature. In memoirs, letters and novels, the meals described by Pepys, Defoe, Smollett, Thackeray, Charles Lamb, Charles Dickens and Dr Johnson are irresistible. Who has not wished for roast pork after reading Lamb's essay or considered stuffing a leg of mutton with oysters after reading Dickens's letter to the painter Daniel Maclise? Even Keats, most romantic of the English Romantic poets, does not disdain to describe in 'St Agnes Eve' a traditional 'banquet'.

> While he forth from the closet brought a heap
> Of candied apple, quince, and plum, and gourd;
> With jellies soother than the creamy curd,
> And lucent syrops, tinct with cinnamon.

From Chaucer onwards, great English writers have found the food of England worth serious mention, a delight and an inspiration to all right-minded men. The reader of seventeenth-, eighteenth- and nineteenth-century English literature will be able to find here traditional recipes for the dishes which are so frequently mentioned and to make them as Pepys, Sterne, Dr Johnson, Lamb or Thackeray knew them.

The cuisine to which these distinguished Englishmen were devoted is set out in one of the earliest English cookery books, *A Forme of Cury*, put together by Richard II's cook. Probably it goes back still farther. Certainly some

5

recipes show signs of the influence which Roman cookery must have had on the British. Gervase Markham's *The English Hus-wife*, published in 1615, and *The Queen's Closet Opened*, published in 1655, Elizabeth Smith's *The Compleat Housewife*, first published in 1727, and Mrs Rundle's *A New System of Domestic Cookery*, published in 1807, are classics in the field of true English cooking. Mrs Beeton is, of course, a household word, though in fact some of her recipes, by reason of false economies and over-elaborations, are less good than earlier versions of the same dishes included in the books mentioned above. Apart from these, dozens of cookery books were published from the sixteenth to the nineteenth centuries which almost no one reads today, though some of their recipes are quite particular to them in seasoning, flavouring and consistency. Furthermore, there exists in private hands an unknown number of unpublished manuscripts which also contain splendid traditional recipes. I have been fortunate enough to come on four such manuscript cookbooks, from all of which I have permission to include recipes, published here for the first time. *A Book of Choice Receipts* was written out by Thomas Reaveley, who appears to have been a steward on a Scottish estate some time in the late eighteenth century. It is now in the collection of the Edinburgh Public Library. A larger collection, without name or date, was given to me by Mr Richard Gorer. It appears to contain recipes collected from the mid eighteenth century to the mid nineteenth century, judging from the several handwritings and the terms used. The third manuscript comes from Reading Museum and dates from the mid eighteenth century to about 1775, and the fourth, which is anonymous, is from the early nineteenth century.

As an introduction to each department of cookery I have sought to establish a historical pattern, giving a sketch of the social and culinary background, because the method by which food has been cooked, the variety available and the methods of preservation have, in the past, played an important role in the evolution of gastronomy. For instance, the pasty originated as a humble dish which was a convenient method of eating hot meat with the fingers or of carrying a complete meal on horseback or in a boat, but it was so satisfactory that it soon changed its social status and became a delicacy, even a centrepiece, at royal feasts. In the same way, many recipes for potted meats, galantines and brawns were developed not only to preserve meat through the winter at home but also to transport it on long voyages.

Today it is widely believed that dishes are French if they are given French names in restaurants. At the end of a voyage to England or America, and indeed on the aeroplanes and ocean liners which transport the voyager, the names on the menu are, as likely as not, proudly set out in French. Very often these dishes are English in origin and of considerable antiquity. Expecting immediate disbelief, I may cite as examples *blanquette de veau* and *poulet à la crème au riz*, both of which were served in England at an earlier date than they ever were in France. It is of interest that rice seems to have been introduced into England about 1390 but was not used in France for another thirty years. Today, in London, either of these dishes may be eaten as well at Locket's, where they are believed to be English, as at Le Jardin des Gourmets or L'Étoile, where they are assumed to be French, and in all three cases they will be as well prepared as in any of the Paris restaurants given a star by Michelin.

In the nineteenth century and the first years of the twentieth, the vast wealth brought to England by her Empire had begun to spread down the social scale from the upper classes. With the rapid increase of industry and its attendant prosperity and the firm establishment of a prosperous middle class based on ability and not entirely on heredity, changes began in eating habits as in everything else. The middle classes were not only increasingly well-off, they were also full of ambition and, what is more, they were beginning to be accepted by and to marry with the landed gentry and even the lesser nobility.

It was natural and necessary therefore that they should be able to display their increasing grandeur not only to each other, but to those whom they considered a cut above them and to whose level they wished to rise. One of the best methods of displaying their solid and excellent possessions, their houses, their furniture and their plate was the dinner party, to which inferiors could be invited so that they would envy, equals that they might admire and copy, and social superiors in order that such well-endowed hosts might be accepted in their own houses. The arriving guests would see the spacious and well-kept house, the elegant reception rooms, the well-trained staff, the luxurious table appointments, in particular the display of silver; good wine and food would put them in good humour and would show their host's taste and knowledge and the liberality of his expenditure; ladies could be taken upstairs after dinner to the hostess's bedroom and gentlemen to smoking-room and possibly to the billiard-room. Thereafter all would repair to the (with)drawing-room. Thus, by the end of a dinner party, all the best of the host's possessions would have been observed by his guests. Naturally, the food was part of the display, as it had been at the feasts of earlier times, and we find a return to care and elegance in cooking and the use of traditional English recipes, often rather bastardized, in such menus as the following from Mrs Beeton.

Service À La Russe (November)

—

Ox-tail Soup	Soup à la Jardinière

—

Turbot and Lobster Sauce	Crimped Cod and Oyster Sauce

—

Stewed Eels	Soles à la Normandie

—

Pike and Cream Sauce	Fried Filleted Soles

——

Filet de Bœuf à la Jardinière	Croquettes of Game aux Champignons

—

Chicken Cutlets	Mutton Cutlets and Tomato Sauce

—

Lobster Rissoles	Oyster Patties

—

Roast Beef – Poulet aux Cressons	Haunch of Mutton
Roast Turkey	Boiled Turkey and Celery Sauce

Ham

——

Grouse	Pheasants	Hare

—

Salad	Artichokes	Stewed Celery

—

Italian Cream	Charlotte aux Pommes	Compote of Pears

—

Croûtes madrées aux Fruits

Pastry	Punch Jelly

—

Iced Pudding

—

Dessert and Ices

——

It will be apparent that the food is over-elaborate and rather solid, as is always the case with Mrs Beeton's recipes and menus when they are not what she describes as 'plain family fare'. The menu is designed for what was known as 'service à la Russe', which meant that the dishes would be served from the sideboard and handed round to the guests, as formal dinners are presented today. There are altogether thirty dishes on offer, not counting dessert and ices, but whether each guest was to be offered all of them, with a choice of each pair, thick or clear soup, turbot or cod, etc., is not clear, nor can one tell whether there was supposed to be enough of each dish for everyone should the choice fall that way, or how it was decided which would be the most popular. However, the enormous menu involved so much preparation, careful timing and decorative dishing that surely the cook and her staff would have become famous throughout the neighbourhood if all the dishes were success-ful. Mrs Beeton's is the epitome of a menu for a Victorian dinner party of the upper middle class, though it seems unlikely that all the thirty dishes plus dessert and ices were, in practice, served. It is of interest because, although French names are used for eight out of the thirty dishes, none of them is peculiar to French cooking and all have a long English tradition behind them. Ridiculously in an English menu, apple charlotte is referred to as 'Charlotte aux pommes'.

The recipes are all adequate, and those for boiled turkey with celery sauce and for croquettes of game are excellent. On the other hand, Mrs Glasse has a better earlier recipe for turbot with lobster sauce, and Gervase Markham, earlier still, a much better one for pike in cream sauce.

In England after the Second World War, it was very difficult, and indeed it has remained so, to get domestic help. Whoever you were, you had to cook yourself. You still do. And since cooking is undoubtedly an enjoyable activity, and one in which it is easy to shine, this has proved rewarding to many people whose professions are far removed from cooking. Most girls brought up at middle-income levels nowadays grow up able to cook and are familiar at least with holiday cooking: the vast majority have learned to work and play with mother in the kitchen in their childhood. Too many learn from her only how to open a can or two and some packets of frozen food, but some learn early to appreciate and criticize new dishes and when they have their own kitchens work calmly and without fuss.

In general, however, they do not always know whether they are preparing a traditional English dish or a French one, and may well consider only dishes including pasta in some form to be Italian and only dishes cooked in oil and including rice to be Spanish. Many people think that they are cooking in the French manner when they are, in fact, preparing a dish exactly as their ancestors did in London or the Midlands in the seventeenth century. They assume that anything difficult to do must be originally a foreign skill beyond the British and anything but overcooked beef and overboiled cabbage must come originally from the Continent. But let us take a meal provided by a seventeenth-century housewife (albeit one given deathless fame by her husband). In 1660 Mrs Samuel Pepys prepared, with the help of her one maidservant, a dinner which must have involved intensive and complicated preparation. Pepys reports: '. . . my wife had got ready a very fine dinner – vis: a dish of marrow bones, a leg of mutton; a loin of veal, a dish of fowl, three pullets and two dozen of larks all in a dish; a great tart; a neat's tongue; a dish of anchovies; a dish of prawns and cheese.' This served about eighteen people, and we can analyse the cooking required.

The marrow bones had to be baked so that they were ready at the last minute, and were served with 'toasts of fine bread'. The leg of mutton would have been spit-roasted, and so, probably, would the loin of veal. The pullets and larks, perhaps cooked on smaller spits or perhaps baked in a covered pan, and all the birds in their great dish, would have had a fine, rich brown sauce with wine. The great tart and the neat's tongue would have been prepared a day or two earlier, the tongue cooked with vinegar and spices and dried fruit, and set in its own highly flavoured jelly: the anchovies may have been fresh or salted. Mrs Pepys and her maid and perhaps a boy whom the Pepyses seem sometimes to have had to help, would have had to shell the prawns before they could make a rich sauce with cheese, which was considered particularly good with shellfish. Not simple cooking, particularly when all the ingredients you have to deal with are raw and unpackaged and you have an open fire to keep going to produce the temperatures required.

There was many a gourmet living in the English countryside in the eighteenth century who wanted no very plain cooking at his table. Here is the menu for an 'elegant' country dinner given by the Rev. James Woodforde to a party of friends in April 1774:

The first course was, part of a large Cod, a Chine of Mutton, some Soup, a Chicken Pye, Puddings and Roots, etc. Second Course, Pidgeons and Asparagus. A Fillet of Veal with Mushrooms and High Sauce with it, roasted Sweetbreads, hot Lobster, Apricot Tart and in the Middle a Pyramid of Syllabubs and Jellies. We had Dessert of fruit after Dinner, and Madeira, White Port and Red to drink as Wine. We were all very cheerful and merry.

Note that the fillet of veal (a whole fillet) was served with a high sauce, that the lobsters were served hot, i.e. removed from the shells, after boiling, reheated in a delicate cream sauce probably, at that date, flavoured with brandy and mace, put back in the shells, sprinkled with crumbs and browned with a salamander. This was traditional high level English country cooking for a well-to-do gourmet parson in the eighteenth century.

From the time of Chaucer until the end of the eighteenth century the steward or housekeeper in palace or castle, the mistress of the manor, and the rich farmer's wife would have countenanced nothing slipshod in their great kitchens: every dish received exactly its traditional herbs and seasonings and had its proper gravies and accompaniments. *It is when the mistress of a house which cannot support steward or housekeeper leaves the kitchen that the food loses its savour*, and this is what happened to English food in the nineteenth century. It happened for two main reasons: rapid urbanization, which undermined the tradition of good farm housekeeping, so that women with growing pretensions to gentility went out of their kitchens and sat in their parlours; and a vast increase in prosperity for the great landowners and the ruling classes in general, which sent the gentry to Europe in search of education. As a result it became fashionable to import foreign chefs as well as foreign art treasures and Frenchmen such as Carême in the late eighteenth century, Ude in the Regency period, Alexis Soyer in Victorian times, and Escoffier in the Edwardian era became celebrities in England. So great was the victory of national snobberies then that no opera singer could become a star without an Italian name and no wealthy Frenchman would buy his clothes and boots anywhere but in London.

The results were that English urban, middle-class cooking became debased by the frantic but inept imitation of the fashionable and upper-class world which could afford to import its chefs. Only in the deep country, in the London chop-house, and in a few pubs and clubs could plain English fare be found at its best, and only the greatest of British regional specialities continued to be known by English names.

Some of these chop-houses, pubs and clubs still flourish, and the same excellent plain dishes as were on offer two hundred years ago may be found at Stone's Chop House, Ye Olde Cheshire Cheese in Fleet Street, Sweeting's, Sheekey's, or the Trafalgar Tavern. It is, however, essential to know what to choose from a menu, and it appears that most overseas visitors are ill-equipped to make a choice: they have never had steak and kidney pudding (with or without oysters), though they may have had steak and kidney pie; they have never had veal and ham pie with hard-boiled eggs; they have never eaten roast young grouse or venison with Cumberland sauce; they have heard of Yorkshire pudding served with rare roast beef, but have never had it properly made and cooked. Salmon trout, heavily buttered, sprinkled with chopped fresh tarragon and a little fennel, wrapped in foil and gently baked, or small trout wrapped in rashers of bacon and baked with parsley and chives, are new experiences to them. The English roast pheasant, the casserole of partridges with cabbage, the simple kipper or herring, the smoked salmon and the smoked haddock, the Aylesbury duck with apple sauce, are all generously acclaimed as superlatively good, but there is often surprise that we consider them typical of the English tradition in food.

Cookshops, chop-houses, coffee-houses in London and inns in the country have always been taken seriously in England, as the following quotations will serve to illustrate:

Moreover there is in London upon the river's bank . . . a public cookshop. There daily, according to the season, you may find viands, dishes roast, fried and boiled, fish great and small, the coarser flesh for the poor, the more delicate for the rich, such as venison, and birds both big and little . . . Those who desire to fare delicately need not search to find sturgeon or 'Guineas-fowl' or 'Ionian Francolin', since all the dainties that are found there are set forth before their eyes. Now this is a public cookshop, appropriate to a city and pertaining to the art of civic life.

This excellent establishment was thus described by William FitzStephen in the twelfth century. However, five hundred years later, Ward in the *London Spy* described the cheap cookshops near Smithfield:

We soon deliver'd our squeamish Stomachs from the Surfeiting Fumes, that arose from their Rotten-Roasted Diet, which made the Street stink like a *Hampshire* Farmers Yard, when Singeing of a Bacon-Hog.

All is not lost, however. A London spy today would find at least a few traditional English dishes at Wilton's, at the Connaught Hotel, and interspersed among more exotic dishes at Parkes'. Many are available at Locket's, and all have had an unbroken history at least from the early eighteenth century.

Simpson's in the Strand remains the best place for the huge roasts (barons of beef, whole legs of mutton, saddles of lamb, haunches of venison, occasionally a side of veal, possibly a sucking pig to order – two or three different roasts on each day). This is English meat as our forefathers knew it. The French have a saying that a chef who can roast is born and cannot be made: many English cooks have this natal gift, inherited, presumably from long lines of passionately meat-eating forebears. Traditional accompaniments at Simpson's – red-currant jelly, onion sauce, Yorkshire pudding, splendid roast potatoes, are just what they should be, but green vegetables are not of interest, and, indeed, sadly bear out the remark of Walter Page that 'the English have only three vegetables and two of them are cabbage'.

Wheeler's has several restaurants, all specializing in fish of prime quality, prepared and served in ways peculiar to various countries but with the traditional English recipes given pride of place. The original restaurant in Old Compton Street goes back to the eighteenth century and serves excellent whitebait and the best grilled Dover soles obtainable anywhere in the world. Excellent fish, including a splendid fish pie, can also be had at Overton's.

These are all fine eating places, but such high standards are not to be found in every English town any more than they were in past centuries. To have to take 'pot luck', as the phrase implies, is always a risk, and the traveller in the English countryside is not always lucky in the hostelry he chooses unless he has a special recommendation. That this has always been the case the following descriptions of meals provided by inns in the eighteenth century, taken from the *Torrington Diaries* and *The London Spy*, clearly show:

Bedford, June 1st, 1789. My Host, of the true fat Breed, said Dinner was just ready, and instantly brought in a Roasted Fillet of Mutton (a joint not very common) with Cabbage, Cucumbers, and Sallad; and upon this, and Cheese, I fared very well.

For Dinner	10d
Brandy	6
Hay and Corn	4
Servants	4
	2 0

Très bonne Marché.

Grantham, June 7th, 1789. . . . She [the landlady] almost instantly returned . . . placing before us a Round of Beef boil'd, a Leg of Mutton roasted, with Greens, a Rice Pudding, and a Gooseberry-Pie.

Sometimes the traveller was lucky.

Southwell, June 8th, 1789. . . . put up at the Saracens-Head Inn . . . where, to my great contentment, I was instantly Served . . . with Cold Beef, Cold Veal and Gooseberry Tart.

And sometimes he was not.

Wellwyn, May 20th, 1789. Mrs S. Talk'd about Mutton chops: but I stuck to my demand of cold meat, with a gooseberry tart: and was right, for she instantly produced a cold Tongue, and a cold Fillet of Veal: as for her old fusty tart of last years fruit, I open'd the Lid, and closed it tightly down for the next Comer. No Tricks upon Travellers.

Dover, September 22nd, 1790. Never did I Enter a more dirty, noisy, or more imposing* Inn than this York House; for we were charged most exorbitantly, for wine not drinkable, for musty Fowls, and stinking Partridges, never did I leave an Inn with greater Pleasure.

* 'Imposing' is used here in the sense of 'imposing upon the guest'.

However, all over the country today the traveller can find not only good food but good regional English food. It is very important if you are a visitor not very familiar with the country to know the kind of dish you want to eat and not to be put off by a menu which is presented in restaurant French. Very often in English country districts the cook offers pseudo-French food because this is what is thought to be the fashionable requirement; it doesn't mean that he or she can't cook the English specialities of the region, if you ask for them and can allow time for them to be prepared. For instance, if you are driving through Cornwall, you should have no trouble in getting tea at a farmhouse which includes fresh 'splits' with clotted cream and home-made jam, saffron cake and (this last only if you are lucky) Cornish heavy-cake, which is a cross between a biscuit and a pastry mixture, flat, full of currants, the top crisped with sugar and the whole eaten hot with a great deal of salted farm butter. But you should also be able to eat at lunch or dinner a proper Cornish pasty (which never contains mince but always small chunks of meat with rich gravy), mackerel straight from the fishing boats with gooseberry sauce or fennel, lobsters and crabs, generally served with drawn butter, blackberry and apple pie (deep dish) with clotted cream, junket with cream, and some good local cheeses as well as the usual English Cheddar. The Victoria Hotel at Roche in Cornwall, the Nare Hotel at Veryan, and The Cornish Arms at Port Isaac all provide Cornish dishes and will make others if given proper notice. The Suffolk Arms at Malmesbury, the Bay Tree at Burford, the Bell at Aston Clinton, the Walnut Tree near Marlowe, The White Lion at Banbury all regularly offer a few traditional dishes and may be asked to prepare others or to serve a completely English meal.

Finally, here is the Bill of Fare of a Bristol tavern, The Bush, for Christmas in the year 1800. The innkeeper was Mr John Weeks, and the list was handed to or read out to arriving guests, who indicated what they required. Bristol was then at the peak of her maritime wealth, but the extent of the menu was considered unusual and impressive even then. Pineapples were a great luxury and the four mentioned had probably come in on a sugar boat direct from the West Indies.

1 Bustard	Mutton Broth	2 Haddocks
Black cock	Barley Broth	14 Rockfish
Red Game	3 Turbots	18 Carp
1 Turtle 120lb.	4 Cods	12 Perch
1 Land Tortoise	2 Brills	4 Salmon
72 pots of Turtle	2 Pipers	12 Plaice
(different prices)	12 Dories	17 Herrings

Sprats
122 Eels
Salt Fish
78 Roach
98 Gudgeon
1 Dried Salmon
17 Wild Geese
Vermicelli Soup
British Turtle
Giblet Soup
Pease Soup
Gravy Soup
Soup Sante
Soup and Bouille
37 Teal
31 Widgeon
16 Bald Coots
2 Sea Pheasants
3 Mews
11 Veal burrs
1 Roasting Pig
Oysters stewed and
scalloped
Eggs
Hogs' Puddings
Ragouted Feet and Ears
Scott Collops
Veal Cutlets
Harricoed Mutton
Maintenon Chops
Pork Chops
Rump Steaks
Joint Steaks
7 pinbones
Dutch and Hambro'ed
Beef
42 Hares
17 Pheasants
42 Partridges
87 Wild Ducks

Venison
3 Haunch hevior
5 haunches doe
5 necks
10 Breasts
10 Shoulders

Beef
5 Rumps
3 Sirloins
5 Rounds
2 pieces of 5 ribs each

Mutton
8 Haunches
11 Loins
6 saddles
6 chines
5 shoulders

Pork
4 legs
4 loins
4 chines
Spareribs
Half a Porker (cold)
Pinbone steaks
Sausages
Hambro' Sausages
Tripe, cow heels and
Knotlings
5 House Lambs
Veal
17 Wild Turkeys
18 Golden Plovers
1 Swan
5 Quists
2 Land Rails
14 Galenas
4 Peahens
1 Peacock
1 Cuckoo

116 Pigeons
121 Larks
1 Sea Magpie
127 Stares
208 Small Birds
44 Turkeys
8 Capons
19 Ducks
10 Geese
2 Owls
61 Chickens
1 Boar's Head
1 Baron Beef
2 Hams
4 Tongues
6 Chicken
4 Moor Hens
2 Water Drabs
6 Curlews
2 Bitterns
81 Woodcocks
149 Snipe
Bologna Sausages
Dutch Tongues
Paraguay Pies
French Pies
Mutton Pies
Pigeon Pies
Venison Pasty
Sulks
430 Mince Pies
13 Tarts
Jellies
4 Ducklings
11 Rabbits
3 Pork Criskins
Hogs' Feet and Ears
7 Collars of Brawn
2 Rounds Beef
Collared Veal
Collared Mutton
Collared Eels

15

Collared Pigs' Head	Pickled Oysters	Colchester Oysters
Craw Fish	Potted Partridges	Milford and Tenby
Pickled Salmon	Lobsters	Oysters
Sturgeons	52 Barrels pyfleet and	4 Pineapples

The odd numbers of birds and fish are partly due to the numbers brought in direct by local fowlers and sportsmen, partly to what was available in the market and partly because as orders were taken for dishes numbers available were altered. The traveller who lighted unexpectedly here was lucky indeed, since any innkeeper who took the trouble to acquire such an enormous variety for his Christmas trade was unlikely to have accepted poor quality or to have put bad cooking before his customers. Indeed, the variety of pies, pasties, tarts and jellies argues a fairly accomplished head cook. The Bill of Fare has added interest because it reflects the influence of her colonies on English food. Bristol was a sugar port, and we see here turtle soup, expressly called British, Paraguay pies, which were probably parrot pies in which imported parrots may or may not actually have featured, but which were very highly seasoned with pepper and ginger, and pineapples.

Many dishes came to England from the colonies and came to stay. Curries, pepperpot, kedgeree and turtle soup are obvious examples. To this day the Merchant Navy, in the tradition of the East Indiamen, serves a different curry every day for breakfast to all hands, including apprentices; first the porridge or cereal, then a curry, then the bacon and eggs or kippers or some other breakfast dish.

Perhaps the final statement to be made about the great tradition of English classical cooking concerns the banquet. The banquet, already highly evolved in the sixteenth century, was originally only the sweet and dessert course (including subtleties and 'quelquechoses', or 'kickshaws'). The English cuisine excelled at such dishes and considered them the most pleasurable part of the meal. The noble lord, his lady and his principal guests retired from the great hall to the 'chamber' to sit at ease and partake of tarts, fruits and sweetmeats. In the seventeenth century the tradition of moving from the main hall for the sweet course was thought so important that on certain great estates a separate banqueting house was built some little way from the main house. Sir William Petrie erected a banqueting house 'fair and well-builded' in the south-west corner of his orchard at Ingatestone, and at Brocket a 'syllabub house' was built in the park, so that anyone strolling or riding and becoming thirsty could go in and be served with a syllabub by an attendant, a cow being driven up to be milked into the bowl of spiced and sweetened wine on the spot.

It was for the exacting ceremonial dishes and high standards of the banquet that Gervase Markham required the greatest skills and labours from the seventeenth-century English housewife.

Now we have drawn our housewife into these several knowledges of cookery, in as much as in her is contained all the inward offices of Household, we will proceed to declare the manner of setting forth and serving of meat for a great Feast. . . . It is then to be understood that it is the Office of the Clerk of the Kitchen (whose place our housewife must many times supply) to order the meat at the Dresser and to deliver it unto the Sewer, who is to deliver it to the Gentlemen, and Yeomen waiters to bear to the table. Now because we allow no Officers but our Housewife, to whom we only speak in this book, she shall first marshall her sallets, delivering the Grand Sallet first, which is evermore compound; then green sallets, then boiled sallets, then some smaller compound sallets. Next unto sallets, she shall deliver forth all her Fricasees, the simple first, as Collops, Rashers and suchlike, then compound fricasees; after them her boiled meats in their degree. . . . Next them all sorts of Roast meats of which the greatest first, as chine of Beef or Sirloin, the Jigget or legs of Mutton, Goose, Swan, Veale, Pig, Capon and suchlike. Then baked meats, the hot first, as Fallow Deer in Pasty, chickens or Calves Foot pie . . . Then cold baked meats . . . Then lastly Carbanadoes both simple and compound . . . and for made dishes and Quelque choses, which rely on the invention of the Cook, they are to be thrust into every place that is empty and so sprinkled all over the Table; and that is the best method for the extraordinary great Feasts of Princes. . . . I have mentioned nothing but Flesh, yet is Fish not to be exempted; for it is a beauty and an honour to every feast. . . . Now for a more humble Feast, or an ordinary proportion which any good man may keep in his family, for the entertainment of his true and worthy Friends, it must hold limitation with his provision and the season of the year. . . . First, a Shield of Brawn with mustard; Secondly a boiled capon, thirdly a boiled piece of beef, fourthly a chine of beef roasted, fifthly a neat's tongue roasted, sixthly a pig roasted, seventhly chewets baked, eighthly a goose roasted, ninthly a swan roasted, tenthly a turkey roasted, the eleventh a haunch of venison roasted, the twelfth a pasty of venison, the thirteenth a kid with a pudding in the belly; the fourteenth an olive pie; the fifteenth a couple of capons, the sixteenth a custard or Doucets. Now to these full dishes may be added sallets, fricasees, quelquechoses and devised paste. . . . [Thus you shall bring] contentment to the guest and much pleasure and delight to the beholders.

Indeed, we hope so. No doubt the housewife, to whom alone Gervase Markham claimed to be speaking, had a dozen or more women in the kitchen and some boys as well, but even so we can only thank our tutelary gods that we are not called upon to perform the same culinary miracles.

The present book contains recipes from all branches of English cooking,

THE COOKERY OF ENGLAND

and from all periods, from the fifteenth century on. The master cook of the Middle Ages, whose forebears might have looked back and remembered, however remotely, the dishes served during the Roman occupation of Britain, may, at his greatest, have had troops of underlings at his command. His successors may have fought the French in the kitchen no less furiously than on the battlefield. He may have found himself called a 'chef' or subordinated to a chef from France, but his tradition, transmitted with varying degrees of success to the housewife, still survives. What he did, perhaps sporadically, decade after decade, she quietly maintained, despite her lapses in the nineteenth and early twentieth centuries.

All the recipes here have been translated in terms of modern preparation and packaging of ingredients and have been reduced in quantity to serve four, six or eight people rather than the twenty or thirty which the recipe was originally designed to serve. They have been altered very little: seasoning has occasionally been reduced or a difficult herb or spice omitted, sugar in meat and fish dishes has been omitted or much reduced, since it is not in accordance with our tastes today; and quantities of fat have sometimes been reduced, as our ancestors liked the contents of their treasure-chests of pies swimming in butter. In almost all cases the pedigree of the dish is given, and in many cases the original is printed in full.

All the recipes are traditionally English; some are simple; some are rather grand and complicated. If you are English, or American with English ancestry, as you follow them you are preparing food as your ancestors prepared it and sitting down to eat exactly what they ate perhaps three hundred years ago. And this is a satisfaction in itself.

There is no longer gastronomic war between France and England; the French have long been acknowledged to have the victory. But the vanquished have largely recovered. The French cuisine in earlier times had a fierce battle to fight simply because the English were so good that they proved a worthy enemy. Over the years the victory seemed to go sometimes one way and sometimes the other. Gillray, in two cartoons in 1792, shows a starving, if liberated, French citizen eating onions, while a vastly fat Englishman, still enslaved, dines off a huge rib of beef, much in the spirit of George IV when he ordered for breakfast in 1830, some two months before his death, a steak and pigeon pie of enormous size, from which he ate two pigeons and three beefsteaks. Our informant is the Duke of Wellington, himself so insensitive to food that no top ranking chef would stay at Apsley House. The duke added that the king drank three quarters of a bottle of Moselle with his pigeons and steaks, two glasses of port and a glass of brandy.

We no longer take a pride in being great trenchermen, or even hearty eaters. We fear food in a way that would have amazed our ancestors. Little did they know or care what carbohydrates and animal fats may do to an ageing heart. In spite of our greater medical knowledge, however, we can still take pride in serving one excellent meal a day, limiting it to two or three courses and seeing that they are well balanced; and, since most of us work single-handed in the kitchen and have no desire to spend as much time there as Mrs Pepys or as Gervase Markham's ideal housewife, this is enough scope for our abilities.

We have one disadvantage which is also, paradoxically, a great advantage, in the food we cook today. Very few of us can count on any of the home-grown ingredients which were taken for granted by all country dwellers until the First World War. A few great estates still produce most of the game and poultry the family requires and perhaps some veal and pork, but very few indeed could approach the quantities and variety shown, for example, in the household book of the Marquis of Tweeddale at Yester House in the early nineteenth century. This manuscript victual book is arranged to serve as an account book and a diary. The left of every double page is divided into two main headings: 'Account of Meat taken in' and 'Given out to the Cook'. There is a separate column for entering where the meat came from, and all of it came either 'from the farme' or from the gamekeeper. The main columns are subdivided into types of meat – beef, mutton, veal, pork, poultry and game. The right-hand page is headed 'Number in Family and Visitors' and is divided into four columns: 'Family', 'Servants', 'Visitors', 'Visitors' Servants'. Thus for every day it can be seen at a glance how many people sat down to a meal in the dining-room and the servants' hall and what they ate. The way in which the book was used changed. At first detailed menus are given but no details of numbers for dinner; later the members of the family present are named and the number of servants entered, but no details of what they ate.

On 5 January 1817 the following meats were served to the family for dinner:

Breast of Veal
Sur loine of Beef
Mutton Cuttelettes
1 phaisant
1 Hare

and in the servants' hall they ate boiled mutton and roast beef.

On 29 January 1817:

Family	Brisket of Beef	Servants	Roasted Beef
	Saddle of Mutton		Barley broth with beef
	2 Fowls for fillets		Roast Hare
	2 partridges		Mutton
	1 Hare		

For the month 1 January–1 February 1817 the following is entered as the amounts of game and poultry taken in:

Game	111 Hares	Poultry	40 fowles
	88 Rabbits		9 ducks
	45 Pheasants		3 turkey
	7 Partridges		
	1 Snipe		
	2 deeres		

Rabbits and hares were served to the family but recur far more frequently on the menus for the servants' hall, while pheasant and partridge never appear on the servants' menus except, very occasionally, as pies, presumably using up the final odd bits.

On 9 January 1818 the following sat down to dinner:

Family	Marquis and Marchioness of Tweeddale
	Lady Jane Hay
	Lady Julian Hay
	Lord Thomas Hay

Visitors	Lord Balhaven	Servants	6 manservants
	Lady Balhaven		13 maids
	Mrs Campbell		+ 3 servants – 2 men and one
	Sir John Sinclair		maid brought by the visitors.

It was taken for granted at Yester House that all fruit and vegetables were home-grown, and they are not even mentioned. Grain, flour and the resulting breads and cakes are detailed in a separate book; all were produced on the estate. Dairy produce is mentioned but not detailed and came entirely from the farms. Everything, therefore, was grown and reared under the watchful and, no doubt, critical eyes of the bailiff or 'factor' and subjected to the criticism of the steward, the housekeeper, the head cook and finally of the Marquis and Marchioness themselves.

Today we rarely have any idea where the food we buy was grown or reared: occasionally we are told that something is 'local' but in general we know only that meat is English or Scottish or 'imported' and sometimes that poultry or eggs are 'free range'; we are also told the country of origin of our butter. This, of course, means that quality is much more variable than any great household in earlier times had to put up with and we are more dependent on understanding good quality in everything we buy and on taking trouble to look for it. Even the produce sold in different supermarkets varies very much in quality, and where our ancestors might have said that good farming was the basis of good cooking and of eating well, we ought to say that for us good shopping is the basis. However well you cook, however splendid the recipe you follow, the result cannot be good if the meat or bird is tough or tasteless, or the vegetables wilted and stale. It is impossible to take too much trouble over finding shops which sell food of top quality, and it should be remembered that because the joint or fruit is good it is not always more expensive than the same joint or fruit of inferior quality from another shop. It is often worth while to have kippers, smoked haddock and smoked salmon sent direct from Scotland or from an English smokery, and tea and coffee from a City merchant.

Our great advantage over the cooks of the past is that almost all we buy is cut, weighed, cleaned, often partly prepared as in the case of blanched almonds, and with our clean, regulated cookers, running hot water, dishwashers and electric mixers, beaters and mincers, hours of our time are saved.

Let us attend as carefully to the appearance of the meat we buy in the butcher's (beef should always be close-grained and red, not pink; veal and pork white, not pink or grey, with a fine grain; while lamb should be a delicate pink) and to the freshness and ripeness of fruit and vegetables, as we do to the appearance of the finished dishes we present. Let us grow a few herbs in gardens, pots or window-boxes and frequently renew the dried ones which we buy, and let us cook and eat our traditional dishes, remembering that the food of France should be a treat not because it is better than our own but because it is different.

1 · MEAT

The Englishman has always been more than usually carnivorous when he could afford to be. Meat and particularly roast meat with a fine sauce or gravy was what everyone, male or female, noble or peasant, wanted for the dinner and the supper table. Until quite late in the eighteenth century, however, meat, including birds, and a fine bread were the basic foods only of the rich; indeed, in 1719 a French visitor to England, Monsieur Misson,* maintained that he had met there people who ate so much meat that they hardly ever touched bread. The poor, on the other hand, were lucky when they touched anything. Coarse bread was their staple food; the very poor ate it with any kind of grease when butter was out of their reach, or with mustard, treacle, or sprinkled with salt. The rich ate enormously and extravagantly. Great dishes of meat were elaborately and wastefully cut and dressed with rich sauces, spiced, seasoned and sometimes sweetened with raisins or apples; cuts of veal and many kinds of birds were set in jelly, made into pies, surrounded with galantine, set in brawn, stuffed, glazed and decorated. Forcemeats were a speciality of the high cooking of England from the fourteenth till the eighteenth century.

* *M. Misson's Memoirs: Observations in his travels over England*, translated from the French by Mr Ozell, 1719.

Menus for royal banquets in the fifteenth and sixteenth centuries were almost entirely composed of meat and fish; the feast served to celebrate the marriage of Henry IV and Joan of Navarre in 1403 consisted of three courses of meat followed by three courses of fish. Almost all the dishes except the great roasts were extremely elaborate. For the first course the following were brought to the royal table:

1. Fillets of veal in galantine.
2. Viand Royal: a dish of meat made with rice cooked in cream and milk to which honey, dried fruits and many spices and herbs were added. It seems to have come out as a thick, smooth, rather sweet cream; perhaps with small slices of meat in it. This dish took two or three days to prepare, with a master cook and several underlings working on it.
3. Large roasts of beef, mutton and venison.
4. Cygnets – probably skinned, boned, stuffed and roasted and highly decorated.
5. Very fat (this is stipulated) capons.
6. Hot puddings (probably something between a hog's pudding, a boiled sausage and a ballotine), and finally
7. A subtlety; which was a sweet dish to end the course, made of 'sugar plate' pastry, marzipan, fruit paste and spun sugar, in the form of a castle, coats of arms, a historic or mythical scene, a game or any subject having relevance to the occasion: see the contemporary description in the chapter on cold sweets. The subtleties were very carefully modelled and elaborately gilded and decorated, and were intended to be admired rather than eaten.

After all this the next course consisted of venison with a spiced wheat porridge; wine jelly, sucking pigs, rabbits; bitterns; stuffed chickens; partridges; an elaborate cream; a brawn; and another subtlety.

When they had got through those two courses the guests still had another meat course and three fish courses to go. On this occasion the first of the fish courses started like the first meat course, with Viand Royal, presumably made in the same way but with fish, probably sturgeon, instead of meat. The second fish course included porpoise in frumenty (again a wheat porridge but rather different) and ended with a subtlety in the shape of a crowned panther, in compliment to the house of the bride.

The sweet dishes very often contained meat or chicken, chopped or pounded to a paste and mixed with cream, milk of almonds, rose water, honey or dried fruits. The earliest recipes for 'blanc mange', which date from the twelfth century, contained chicken, though the dish was predominantly sweet and not savoury. Every dish, except the pastries and jellies and some of the creams, contained meat, poultry, game or fish in some form, and the distinction between a sweet and a savoury dish was much less clear and important to our ancestors than it is to us. Just as sweets and subtleties often contained meat, so savoury dishes contained raisins or apples in a proportion which would have made them decidedly sweet-tasting, and the pie-filling which we know as mincemeat originally contained finely chopped lean beef or mutton, as did early recipes for Christmas pudding. When Monsieur Misson described his visit to London in his memoirs he also described the 'Christmas Pye' which he said was 'eaten everywhere'. In the English translation of 1719 his reference reads: 'It is a great Nostrum, the composition of this Pasty: it is a most learned Mixture of Neats-tongues, Chicken, Eggs, Sugar, Raisins, Lemon and Orange Peel, various Kinds of Spicery, etc.'

Such a dish as Viand Royal, whether in its flesh or fish form, was intended to taste of its sweetening and spices and to have the texture of its creamy rice rather than of the meat or fish which we today should consider its chief ingredient, and whose flavour we should expect to predominate. An example which has remained with us to the present day of the desire to taste the spice itself rather than to use the spice to bring out the taste of other ingredients is in the flavouring of cakes with chocolate, ginger, saffron, vanilla, carraway seeds, etc.

At Ingatestone Hall in Essex, the property of Sir William Petrie, Secretary of State, a feast was given for Twelfth Night in 1652, 150 years later than the wedding feast of Henry IV. It was not a royal feast, so the dishes would have been less elaborate, and no fish was included. About one hundred people were fed in the Great Hall on the following:

> 9 pieces boiled beef (about 20 lb. to a piece)
> 6 pieces roast beef (about 30 lb. to a 'livery' piece)
> a haunch and leg of pork
> 2 legs of veal
> a whole young pig (not a sucking pig but one 6–9 months old)
> a loin and breast of veal
> 2 rabbits
> 10 beef pasties ⎤
> 2 mutton   „ ⎬ all these were 'very great'
> 4 venison   „ ⎦

3 geese
2 capons
2 partridges
a woodcock
2 teals
12 larks

these would have been laid out
on two vast platters, the larger
birds carved into portions

This works out at about 7–8 lb. meat (including weight of bone) per head.

Apart from these meats and their sauces, dressings, forcemeats and pastry, only bread would have been served, and cheese for the lowest ranks. The Ingatestone Hall bakers made three qualities of bread and baked about 20,000 loaves in a year, though Ingatestone Hall was only a modest 'great house'.

Fortunately for us, the household books of Ingatestone have been preserved. They show that provisioning was lavish but carefully considered, and the servants unusually well fed, and the cooking at all times of a high standard. Nevertheless for the visit of Queen Elizabeth a cook was imported from London, and it is recorded that he asked for ¼ oz. of gold for gilding his subtleties and also for the colourings, which were called 'turnsole' and 'grain', to make his tall, castellated jellies, his marzipan and his 'sugar plate' red and violet.

Meat was the prime purchase and the highest item of expenditure in all well-to-do houses. In inns and cookhouses it was the first demand of the traveller. Birds were always acceptable but were considered lighter fare: at the tables of the great they often appeared as part of the second course, along with fish, various sweet dishes and a few dishes of vegetables.

The 'great meats' – beef, veal, mutton, lamb – were, then, the favoured food of the rich, and the desired food of the poor, but throughout the winter, except in royal households and those of the greatest and most wealthy noblemen, fresh meat was rare except for venison, birds, hares and rabbits which could be hunted or snared, and pigeons, which the big houses kept in their great dovecotes, in enormous quantities.

From Christmas to May
Weak cattle decay

wrote Thomas Tusser in 1580. All but breeding stock were slaughtered in the autumn, salted, potted and cured. There would be no more roast beef, mutton or pork until after the long Lenten weeks, when only fish and eggs could be eaten. Most well-to-do households seem to have had fresh meat on Easter Sunday, sometimes from a bullock or a sheep or two, specially fed through the winter for this purpose.

Not until the late eighteenth century did the overwintering of stock increase as agricultural reforms were introduced, and, as winter-feeding with roots became better understood, feeding and breeding for the quality of the meat became possible.

In the early eighteenth century the country gentleman ate well. By the time Smollett was writing *Humphrey Clinker*, his meat, in both quantity and quality, was generally excellent. Matthew Bramble writes: 'My table is in a great measure furnished from my own ground; my five year old mutton, fed on the fragrant herbage of the mountains, that might vie with venison in juice and flavour; my delicious veal, fattened with nothing but the mother's milk, that fills the dish with gravy.'

There is a clear implication here that venison is to be preferred to mutton, and this probably continued to be the case until the growth of the towns put it out of the reach of so much of the population that it appeared only on the tables of the great, who killed deer on their estates, and of the peasantry, who poached them. Until the Second World War it remained a gourmet's meat, but it was less often served, and in the twenties and thirties of our own century it was unusual to find it in clubs unless a Scottish member donated a haunch or two, and it was hardly ever served in restaurants. From the fifties until today, with the great revival of English traditional cooking, most butchers will get it on order, one or two specialist stores stock it, and many restaurants offer it.

All the meat we buy nowadays has been chilled; most of it has been frozen. It is very good indeed, but we no longer know what fresh meat, butchered and hung for a few days in a cool but not cold chamber, was like, and unless we are farmers of sheep or beef cattle we have no way of finding out. Perhaps we are missing some flavour that our ancestors knew, but, to balance this, the animals we eat are better fed, so that they are neither very fat nor very lean and their meat is rarely very tough.

There is no difficulty in England in getting very good meat if you can afford it. In America this is not the case. Most of the meat obtained in supermarkets seems to have lost both its flavour and its texture, and it is necessary to find a 'meat house' or a very high-class and exceedingly expensive supermarket where the meat is cut for each customer instead of being pre-packaged. Even so, the flavour of both beef and mutton seems reduced. Veal in England is of doubtful quality and outside the towns almost impossible to obtain. Imported Dutch veal is very expensive and very white but rather tasteless. English veal is variable, darker but of a better flavour, though it may be stringy. English pork is very good indeed.

All joints, large or small, hot or cold, roast, boiled or braised, depend for their proper enjoyment not only on perfect cooking but on skilful carving. Far more people cook well than carve well, and this is a development from the rise of the middle class who wished to eat well and ape the gentry but who kept less state and employed fewer and less skilled servants than the great households of earlier times. They employed cooks but not carvers. Today, in general we employ neither, and more of us have learnt to cook well than to carve elegantly.

In the fourteenth and fifteenth centuries the carver's position was high in the hierarchy: the royal carvers were knights who ranked immediately after the nobles. In noble households the Carver was often a Squire. Wyken de Worde published a *Book of Kerving* in 1508 and so descriptive, accurate and urgent are the terms used for the dismembering of every type of game and fish (and even eggs) that it is a great loss that all have long fallen out of use:

The termes of a Kerver be as here followeth:

'Breke that dere'	'strynge that lampreye'
'rere that goose'	'tymbre that fyere'
'lyfte that swanne'	'tyere that egg'
'sauce that capon'	'chynne that samon'
'spoyle that hen'	'splat that pyke'
'unbrace that mallarde'	'splay that breme'
'dismembre that heron'	'tuske that barbell'
'display that crayn'	'culpon that troute'
'disfigure that pecocke'	'trassene that ele'
'untache that curlewe'	'trance that sturgion'
'wyng that quayle'	'under trance that porpose'
'myne that plover'	'tayme that crabbe'
'thye that pygion'	'barbe that lopster'

Somewhat later carving schools were started in Italy, some using wooden demonstration models. In the eighteenth century Lord Chesterfield wrote to his son:

. . . Do you use yourself to carve adroitly and genteely, without hacking half an hour across a bone, without bespattering the company with the sauce, and without over-turning the glasses into your neighbours' pockets?

In this period, it seems that guests were sometimes called upon to carve, and there are instances where carving appears to have been the duty of the hostess. In the nineteenth century the great chef of the Reform Club, Alexis Soyer, in his *Gastronomic Regenerator*, noted that many people when carving complain of the knives and the meat but '. . . it certainly often happens that the greatest gourmet is the worst carver, and complains sadly during that very long process, saying to himself, "I am the last to be served; my dinner will be cold." '

In the middle of the nineteenth century there was a school of carving in Soho where the ladies of London could receive instruction, each bringing with her her own joint or bird. In big houses the butler sometimes carved at a side table, but this does not seem to have been general. Nowadays host or hostess must carve and must recognize carving as a skill to be acquired, but of which the first prerequisite is a truly sharp knife with a blade intended for the meat or game in hand.

Roast and Baked Meats

The upper classes in the wealthy England of the past could afford not only plenty of meat, but the best. This was just as well, since the Englishman has always preferred his meat roast and only the best and most expensive cuts roast well. Cheaper cuts which can be boiled or stewed or braised are uneatably tough, hard or stringy when quick dry heat is applied to them as in roasting or grilling. Almost equally important, the rich supported vast households and the joints they roasted were as large as the animals would provide or as their spits would carry. In a small household this last could be a problem. Pepys, who was very much interested in food and in entertaining, wrote in 1653:

> '. . . found my jacket bore it very well,
> of which I had some doubt . . .'

In the great houses, however, there were spits and jacks of all sizes and several would have been in use at the same time.

A large joint always roasts better than a small one because its size allows time for the outside to be properly crisped, while the inside is just cooked enough but quite undried. The roasts of our ancestors, varying from perhaps 30 lb. ('a livery piece') to 6 lb., were carved to give the best slices to those of highest rank. A piece of the crisp outside, seasoned and 'frothed' and 'tasting of the fire', with several slices from the middle, pink, juicy, and slow cooked because protected by the pounds of meat surrounding them, made a perfect portion for the noble lord. The squires and other ranks could have the dull and probably rather overcooked slices between outside and juicy heart and, to vary them, chunks from the gristly excrescences which occur near the bone of most large joints.

We see the care that was taken over serving the roast in the eighteenth century at a comparatively plebeian dinner at which Dr Johnson was the principal guest. Boswell says:

No man eat more heartily than Johnson or loved better what was nice and delicate. Mr Wilkes was very assiduous in helping him to some fine veal. 'Pray give me leave, Sir: – it's better here – A little of the brown – Some fat, Sir – a little of the Stuffing – Some gravy – Let me have the pleasure of giving you some butter – Allow me to recommend a squeeze of this orange; or the lemon, perhaps, may have more zest.'

The 'taste of the fire' was what the Englishman liked, and when the spit and the jack were in general use this was what he commonly got. Spit-roasting and grilling both ensure this. The *outside* of the joint or bird was of great importance, and all advice on roasting from earliest times until the nineteenth century emphasizes the care which must be taken over basting and the proper protection of the meat by wrapping if the fire was very hot. The removal, late in the cooking, of the heavy wrapping paper in order that the skin might brown and crisp, and the 'frothing' which gave a delicious finish, were no less important. 'Frothing' meant sprinkling the almost cooked joint with flour and then pouring over fat or batter with or without some wine, cider, orange or lemon juice, ale or beer, so that the flour on the hot greasy skin *frothed* and a crisp, finely granulated surface formed as the joint finished cooking.

Robert May, writing in 1660, gives 'the Rarest Ways of dressing all manner of roast meats, either flesh or fowl, by sea or land and divers ways of breading or dredging meat to prevent the gravy from too much evaporating' and lists the following:

Dredgings
1. Flour mixed with grated bread
2. Sweet herbs, dried and powdered and mixed with grated bread
3. Lemon peel, dried and pounded, or orange peel, mixed with flour
4. Sugar finely powdered and mixed with powdered cinnamon and flour or grated bread
5. Fennel seeds, corianders, cinnamon and sugar, finely beaten and mixed with grated bread and flour
6. For young pigs, grated bread or flour mixed with beaten nutmeg, ginger, pepper, sugar, yolks of eggs
7. Sugar, bread and salt mixed

Bastings
1. Fresh butter
2. Clarified suet
3. Minced sweet herbs, butter and claret, especially for mutton and lamb
4. Water and salt
5. Cream and melted butter, especially for a flayed pig
6. Yolks of eggs, grated biscuit and juice of oranges.

Nos. 3, 4 and 5 of the Dredgings are excellent, and so is No. 3 of the Bastings. Roasting hares were often basted with milk with or without egg yolks beaten into it.

Holinshed says that 'the English Cookes, in comparison with other Nations, are most commended for roasted meates', but in the nineteenth century, with the development of the cooking stove and the 'range', spits went out of use and the 'taste of the fire' went with them. Joints of meat were worse cooked than ever before in a country noted for the pleasure it took in the excellence and abundance of its meat. Housewives, cooks, even those who called themselves chefs, put joints to cook in pans containing too much fat of an inferior quality which could only give an unpleasant flavour to the outside of the meat and make it soggy, lacking its crisp light skin. The oven temperatures in coal ranges could not be constantly controlled. Fuel varied, the wind affected the draught. Joints were served overdone or half-raw. Potatoes were packed too closely in the fat round the joint and prevented the sides from browning and were themselves often soggy. On days when the fire roared and the cook was busy, joints were served overcooked, grey and dry and fibrous inside; on days when the fire refused to 'draw' the centre of the meat was hardly warm and the outside was pale and flabby. Some cooks even committed the heinous crime of putting a little water in the roasting tin so that the meat was partly steamed, in fact not roast at all but braised without benefit of vegetables, herbs or seasoning.

This is not to say, of course, that excellent roasts cannot be cooked in ovens, though it must be remembered that meat cooked with dripping or butter in the oven is really being baked and not roasted at all. However, a 'baked' joint, which we refer to as a roast, can be perfectly cooked and should be indistinguishable from one cooked on the spit.

The whole outside of the meat should be rubbed lightly with highly seasoned flour; a little garlic salt may be added to this, and for mutton or pork a little powdered thyme; or sprigs of fresh rosemary may be stuck into the fat of either of the latter. The joint, if it weighs 2½–4½ lb., should then be put in a baking dish on a 2-oz. piece of butter or dripping (but not mutton dripping for beef, or vice versa; pork dripping or cooking fat may be used for any meat). This melts and spreads under the joint. A 1-oz. piece of soft butter (and it should be butter, not cooking fat) should be put on top and spread a little over the surface. Then put the joint into the middle of a hot oven, preheated to 400° F., gas mark 6, and cook for 10 minutes. Reduce heat to 350° F., gas mark 4, and cook as follows:

Beef: 16 or 17 minutes to the lb. for underdone meat (that is, fairly red in the middle). Allow 20–22 minutes per lb. for better done – only a little pink. To cook beef more than this is a desecration and has no place in English cookery.

Baste three times during cooking.

Mutton and Lamb: Real mutton (Southdown, Welsh or Scottish are the best) is very hard to get nowadays, but butchers will often get it for you on request. It should be cooked in the same way as roast beef, but allow 20–25 minutes per lb. A leg of lamb takes a little more cooking than mutton but is smaller and has more bone in proportion to the meat, so allow 20 minutes per lb. and an extra 20 if you don't like it underdone.

Baste two or three times during cooking. 'Froth' just before the meat is done by sprinkling with flour and spooning the hot fat over.

Pork and Veal: Both must be well cooked right through but must not be dry. Allow 25–30 minutes per lb. and 20–25 minutes extra. Baste the veal very often, as it has little fat and may be dry and stringy. A roast of veal is much improved by being stuffed (see the recipe on p. 40). Pork needs little basting because there is generally a good deal of fat and the meat is protected by the thick skin, which should of course have been scored for crackling. Brush the scored skin over with cooking oil (this will make it crisper than any other kind of fat) and then dredge a little seasoned flour on to it; if you grow rosemary, stick some sprigs of it between the meat and the fat.

If you have a modern electric spit, your meat should be even more perfectly cooked than if it is baked in the oven. The times of cooking must be taken from the chart given with the spit, as they vary for different makes, though, in general, they are little different from those given for oven roastings. The meat should be floured in the same way and started at a high temperature to seal the juices; the heat is then reduced after the first cooking.

In *The Art of Cookery Made Plain and Easy* (1747) Mrs Glasse gives the following instructions for roasting beef:

I shall first begin with roast and boiled of all sorts and must desire the cook to order her fire according to what she is to dress: if anything very little or thin, then a pretty brisk fire, that it may be done quick and nice: if a very large joint, then be sure a good fire be laid to cabe [i.e. to make a solid layer of red hot coal or turf]. If beef, be sure to paper the top and baste it well all the time it is roasting and throw a handful of salt on it. When you see the smoke draw to the fire, it is near enough: then take off the paper, baste it well and dredge it with some flour to make a fine froth.

We may thank our scientific forebears that we do not have to 'order' our fires before we start to cook, but our ovens and spit-grills must be preheated to the correct temperature.

When the joint is dished up, if it is perfectly cooked, juice should run from roast beef when it is cut; from mutton and lamb there should be some juice but a little less; from pork and veal there should be none at all.

TRADITIONAL ACCOMPANIMENTS TO ROAST MEAT

With beef: Horseradish sauce
English mustard
Yorkshire pudding
Gravy

With mutton and lamb: Onion sauce
Red-currant jelly
Mint sauce
Savoury herb pudding

With pork: Apple sauce
Pease pudding
Roast apples

Forcemeat may be used to stuff any joint.

A FEW ROASTS REQUIRING SPECIAL TREATMENT

Fillet of Beef

Always expensive but always tender, though with perhaps a little less flavour than rump. There is little waste since it is boneless. A whole fillet usually weighs about 2½ lb. and will serve 8 people, but smaller ones can be bought.

> *For a plain roast:*
> Fillet of beef
> 3 oz. (90 g.) butter
> flour
> seasoning

Trim off all skin and fat. Rub the fillet all over with highly seasoned flour and brush with 1 oz. melted butter. Put the other 2 oz. butter in the roasting tin and lay the beef on it. Put into oven preheated to 400° F., gas mark 6, and after 10 minutes reduce heat to 325° F., gas mark 3. Baste well at this point. Allow a further 20 minutes if the piece of fillet weighs 1–1½ lb. (below ¾ k.), a further 30 minutes if it weighs 1½–2 lb. (¾–1 k.), and 40 minutes if it weighs 2–2½ lb. (1–1¼ k.). Baste twice more. Serve with gravy made in the pan in which it cooked, using stock and a little red wine. Best served with creamed potatoes and a green vegetable or a plain green salad.

The Duke of Wellington's Fillet of Beef

The Duke was not a gourmet, and this is the only dish to which he gave his name. This has been said to be because the finished fillet looks like the leg of a well-polished brown leather boot.

> 1-lb. (½-k.) packet frozen puff pastry
> 2 lb. (1 k.) fillet of beef (all in one piece)
> small tin truffled liver pâté (need not be the most expensive)
> ½ lb. (240 g.) mushrooms
> salt and pepper
> 2 oz. (60 g.) butter
> 1 egg

Pre-heat oven to 425° F., gas mark 7.

Trim fat and skin from fillet. Roll out pastry very thinly to give a piece 1¼ times the length of your fillet and wide enough to wrap round it with a good overlap. Spread the fillet all over with slightly softened butter. Lightly spread some pâté where the meat is to lie along the middle of the pastry and lay a line of mushrooms, caps downwards, along this. Season lightly. Lay the beef on the mushrooms, spread it all over with the rest of the pâté and lay the rest of the mushrooms on it, again seasoning them lightly. Bring up the sides of the pastry to make a neat roll and seal the edges together by moistening with a little milk, making a ridge on top which can be decoratively slashed. Seal the ends tightly. Place on a baking tin on middle shelf of oven for 20 minutes at 425°F., gas mark 7. If browning too quickly, cover with foil.

After 20 minutes, remove the beef, and turn the oven down to 350° F., gas mark 4. Brush the top of the crust with an egg yolk to gild it. Cover lightly with foil and put back for 25 minutes. After a total of 45 minutes you should have really rare beef within the crust. If you like it a little more done, leave it another 10 minutes.

Serve as soon as possible when done (as the beef goes on cooking in the crust if you keep it warm), cutting slices about an inch wide crosswise.

To Bake a Buttock Piece of Beef

(From the Reading MS. 1765)

'Take a thick peice of buttock beef, lay it to soak in a pint of claret wine and a pint of wine vinegar, the beef being first seasoned with peper nutmegg and salt and soe let it lye two days, then take the beef and put it in a pasty well seasoned with nutmeg and salt.'

This is a rather robust early version of the Duke of Wellington's fillet of beef, but it is very good.

> 2½ lb. (1¼ k.) rump steak, cut for roasting
> ½ pint (3 dl.) red wine and ¼ pint (1½ dl.) wine vinegar
> nutmeg, pepper and salt
> 1 lb. (½ k.) short pastry (may be frozen)
> yolk of an egg
> ½ lemon
> 1 tablespoon cornflour

Marinate the beef 24 hours in the liquids and seasoning. Drain well. Roll out the pastry, lay the beef in the middle, season with fresh nutmeg, salt and pepper, and draw up edges of pastry to meet along the top in an ornamental roll. Gild with egg yolk. Put in the oven preheated to 400° F., gas mark 6. Cook for 15 minutes, then reduce the heat to 350° F., gas mark 4, and cook for a further 30 minutes. Cover the pastry lightly with foil if it is browning too much.

Meanwhile reduce the marinade by rapid boiling, thicken with a tablespoon of cornflour, stirred into cold water and added to the boiling liquid, add the juice of half a lemon and check seasoning. Place the beef on a hot serving dish and serve the sauce separately.

To Roast a Tongue

To be eaten hot. This recipe also comes from the Reading MS.

'Boyle your tongue till the skin will come off then stick it with cloves and time put it upon the spit runn the spit through the roote and tye the top and let it roast a quarter of an hour for sauce boyle water and cinnamon 3 or 4 spoonfulls of water is enough then add a little claret sweeten to your taste and thicken it with the juyce of an egg.'

1 ox tongue, boiled and skinned	2 glasses red wine
3 oz. (90 g.) softened butter	2 teaspoons powdered cinnamon
20 cloves	salt and pepper
½ pint (3 dl.) good stock	2 egg yolks, well beaten

Boil and skin the tongue and then stick it with 20 cloves and immediately lay it on a rack in a baking tin and put in an oven preheated to 350° F., gas mark 4, for 20 minutes. Alternatively, put on a spit but be careful not to break: the thin end will have to be tied on. In either case, spread a little softened butter over it.

Remove from the oven or spit and serve at once with a sauce made from the stock and red wine, seasoned with salt and pepper and the powdered cinnamon. Bring to the boil, cool a little, and then rapidly stir in the well-beaten yolks of 2 eggs. Do not let the sauce boil again or it will curdle. Pour it all over the tongue before serving.

Lamb Chops Portmanteau'd

This dish is from the Cotswolds. It was served to gentlemen at hunt breakfasts, the chops no doubt being prepared by the cooks the night before.

Excellent for dinner with a good espagnole or fresh tomato sauce or a green butter, but it must be served immediately the chops are cooked.

> loin chops, 1½–2 in. (4–5 cm.) thick – 1 per person
> 2 chicken livers and 2 medium-sized mushrooms per chop
> 2 oz. (60 g.) butter, melted
> 1 or 2 eggs
> seasoning
> breadcrumbs

With a very sharp knife divide the lean eye of the chop, cutting inwards to the bone. Take off skin and trim off some of the fat. Finely chop the livers and mushrooms, season and sauté together in butter till soft but not brown. Cool and stuff into the incisions in the chops and sew up.

Coat with beaten egg and breadcrumbs, pour a little melted butter over each and bake in a roasting tray at 400° F., gas mark 6, for 5 minutes; then turn and bake for another 5 minutes.

May also be fried.

Roast Saddle of Lamb

1 saddle of lamb   salt and pepper
¼ lb. (120 g.) melted butter   flour

The butcher will prepare the saddle for you in the traditional way.

Rub the saddle with mixed salt and pepper, then dust it with flour and place it in a roasting tray. Pour the melted butter over it. Cook the meat in a preheated oven for 20 minutes at 450° F., gas mark 8, then reduce the heat to 350° F., gas mark 4, and continue roasting for 20 minutes per lb. of meat, basting it frequently. A saddle of mutton or lamb should never be overcooked and must be carefully carved. It is always accompanied by red-currant jelly.

A Crown Roast of Lamb

A dish very much favoured at small Edwardian dinner parties. Your butcher will prepare the crown of lamb if you order it a day or two in advance. The cutlets, well trimmed and joined only by the skin, are turned inside out, and fastened so that the dish looks exactly like a crown.

Place 3 oz. (90 g.) butter in a tin and stand the crown upright. Put in oven at 400° F., gas mark 6, for 10 minutes; then reduce heat to 350° F., gas mark 4, and cook for another 30 minutes. Meanwhile prepare very fine creamed potato, and when you dish your crown fill the middle with it and serve small heaps of spring vegetables round it. Alternatively, the middle is sometimes filled with a macedoine of vegetables, including tiny new potatoes, or with a rich forcemeat. If forcemeat is used, the crown is filled before cooking, and the top should be basted once or twice.

The dish requires (served separately) a very good gravy into which some sherry and a tablespoon of red-currant jelly have been stirred, or an espagnole or good tomato sauce.

Roast Sucking Pig

A sucking pig can generally be ordered from your butcher in the spring and early summer. It should be between 3 and 6 weeks old and as freshly killed as possible. Sucking pigs were much esteemed in England until our own century but now they are rarely served. Dr Kitchiner in his The Cook's Oracle, written in 1817, says that the pig 'requires very careful roasting. A sucking pig, like a young child, must not be left for an instant'. The little pigs, rather horribly reminiscent of spitted babies, were stuffed with a simple sage and onion stuffing, sewn up, and roasted briskly. As the middle always tended to be cooked before the head and tail, a special iron, called a pig-iron, was hung in front of the middle of the pig to keep the heat from it. The crackling was dredged with flour and salt, basted with olive oil and sometimes frothed with flour and the juice of an orange when it was almost crisp. An hour and a half was considered the right length of time for a three weeks' pig.

If you cook a sucking pig on a spit/grill, Dr Kitchiner's instructions apply just as they did to the spit before the open fire. The heat should be reduced after half an hour and a piece of foil wrapped round the middle of the pig and removed twenty minutes before it should be cooked, when the heat can be raised again if you think the crackling is not crisp enough. At this point, also, froth the whole outside by dredging with a little seasoned flour and spooning over it the juices from the drip tray.

If you cook it in the oven, preheat the oven to 400° F., gas mark 6–7. Reduce after 20 minutes to 350° F., gas mark 4, and turn up again for last 20 minutes if you think it necessary. Turn the whole pig over once on to its back after 30 minutes and then back again after an hour.

Traditionally, the little pig was accompanied by any of the following: good gravy to which madeira or sherry is added; red-currant jelly; plain boiled rice; apple sauce; green peas. Creamed potatoes were always served.

If the pig was not stuffed, a savoury pudding (see p. 299) or pease pudding (p. 300) was often served.

Fillets of Pork

Mrs Gerald Leach's recipes for fillets of pork.

For 4

> ½ fillet per person, unless very large
> ½ lb. (240 g.) large prunes, soaked for 3 or 4 hours and stoned (liquid saved)
> 3 oz. (90 g.) breadcrumbs
> 1 tablespoon onion, finely chopped and softened in a little butter
> 1 tablespoon brandy
> ¼ pint (1½ dl.) good white stock (a bouillon cube will do)
> ¼ pint (1½ dl.) double cream   3 oz. (90 g.) butter
> 1½ oz. (45 g.) flour   salt and pepper

Chop each soaked but uncooked prune into about 8 pieces. Mix with the breadcrumbs and the onion in its butter. Season, using plenty of pepper.

Trim the pork fillets and cut across in halves. Split each half longways, and spread the centres with the prune filling, closing like sandwiches. Rub with seasoned flour and place in a flat ovenproof dish. Just melt remaining butter and pour over. Bake closely covered for 20 minutes at 350° F., gas mark 4. Uncover and bake for a further 10 minutes, so that the tops are lightly browned. At this point, pour off the butter and juices into a small saucepan, and while the fillets brown, make the sauce, by stirring into the butter 1½ oz. flour, and adding the prune juice and stock. Boil for 3 minutes, and allow to cool slightly. Stir in the cream and the brandy, and keep warm without further boiling, until the fillets are ready. Pour the sauce round them in their dish and serve immediately.

Papered Fillets of Pork

For 4

> ½ fillet per person, unless very large
> 3 oz. (90 g.) breadcrumbs
> 1 tablespoon finely chopped onion, softened in a little butter
> 1 tablespoon finely chopped parsley
> 1 teaspoon dried rosemary, or very finely chopped fresh

1 teaspoon powdered mace
salt and black pepper
4 oz. (120 g.) butter
a little flour

Cut four ovals of greaseproof paper about 10 inches (25 cm.) at their longest, and 6 inches (15 cm.) at their widest points.

Mix the breadcrumbs, onion, parsley, and rosemary and season lightly with salt and black pepper. Proceed as in the previous recipe, but when the fillets are filled and rubbed, place each on a paper, the centre of which you have spread quite thickly with softened butter and sprinkled with pepper and salt and a very little mace. Fold each paper into a parcel and twist up the ends. Lay in a large baking tray, place in the centre of the oven, and bake for 35 minutes at 350° F., gas mark 4. Serve in their parcels, unless paper has browned so much that they do not look nice. In this case, unwrap into serving dish with all their butter and juices, but it is more pleasing for each to un-wrap his own and get the full aroma.

The parcels may be made with foil, which does not discolour, and cooked for an extra 10 minutes (as the foil slows the cooking), but paper is traditional.

Mitoon of Pork

From a North Country collection of recipes. The suffix 'oon', sometimes used in English cookery, means 'great' or 'large', from the Spanish or Italian, but I cannot trace the exact meaning of the name. The original quantities in this recipe would have served 16 or 20, so it would have been a large dish indeed.

Serves 4–6
8 rashers of bacon (fairly lean)
1 lb. (½ k.) forcemeat (see p. 297)
1 lb. (½ k.) cooked pork, all fat and skin removed, and cut in thin neat slices
1 teaspoon mace
salt and pepper
1½ oz. (45 g.) butter
½ pint (3 dl.) good brown gravy

Heavily butter a soufflé dish or a round casserole. Line it with the rashers of bacon, which should not be too fat. Press down a layer of forcemeat about ½ inch (1 cm.) thick. On this put a double overlapping layer of pork slices and season with mace, salt and pepper. Repeat until all is used and the pot is nearly full, ending with a layer of forcemeat, which you dot with pieces of butter.

Put in the middle of the oven, preheated to 350° F., gas mark 4, and bake for 40 to 50 minutes. Prepare a fairly thick brown gravy. Turn out pork on flat dish, surround with sauté mushrooms, diced carrots, peas or a macedoine of vegetables, and serve the gravy separately.

Roast Breast of Veal, stuffed, with Bacon Rolls

Serves 4–6

2–3 lb (1–1½ k.) breast of veal   ½ pint (3 dl.) stock
6 or 8 rashers of bacon   3 oz. (90 g.) butter
a little flour for gravy   1 medium onion, peeled and quartered

Stuffing:

3 oz (90 g.) breadcrumbs   pepper and salt
1½ oz. (45 g.) suet   a beaten egg and milk to bind
1½ teaspoons chopped parsley   ¼ lb. (120 g.) bacon, finely
a little grated lemon rind   chopped
¼ teaspoon powdered herbs

Ask your butcher to bone and trim the veal for you. Take the bone and trimmings and boil for stock with an onion in 1 pint (6 dl.) water, reducing it to ½ pint (3 dl.).

Prepare the stuffing by mixing the dry ingredients and binding with the egg and milk. Spread the stuffing on the flattened-out meat, roll up and sew the roll to hold stuffing firmly. Place in a roasting tin with the butter and place in the oven preheated to 400° F., gas mark 6, and allow 30 minutes to the pound and 15 minutes over; baste several times; pour off the fat from the roasting tin, keeping back any brown sediment. Add 2 teaspoons of flour; mix well and when brown add the ½ pint (3 dl.) of strained stock and a pinch of pepper and salt; bring to the boil.

For bacon rolls, take a rasher of streaky bacon for each person to be served, remove rind, flatten rasher with back of knife, roll up tightly, thread each roll on skewer, close together, and place beside veal in pan ¼ hour before the cooking is finished. Remove with veal, take rolls from skewer and arrange round meat.

Potatoes may be roasted round this joint and if there is no room for bacon, the skewer may be put on a separate small tin and cooked in the oven above the veal for 10 minutes.

Shepherd's Pie

On the sheep farms of Cumberland tough mutton had to be used up some-how. In a hash (rarely an entirely satisfactory dish anyhow) the meat can be like leather. So the shepherd's wife chopped the cold tough cooked mutton and beat it in a mortar; it was much better; with thickened stock and potato on top it was delicious and very filling. It became a standard dish, made much easier by the advent of the mincer. It is certainly the simple rather than the high cooking of England but none the worse for that.

> 1 lb. (½ k.) cooked meat (any fresh meat or bird may be used but salt beef and sausage meat are not suitable)
> ¾–1½ lb. (½–1 k.) peeled potatoes
> 2 oz. (60 g.) butter
> ¼ pint (1½ dl.) milk
> 1 oz. (20 g.) flour
> seasoning
> ½ pint (3 dl.) good onion-flavoured meat stock
> grated cheese if liked

Mince the meat, removing all fat and skin and gristle first. Cook the potatoes, peeled and cut in halves, till tender for mashing.

Melt the 1½ oz. (45 g.) butter in a saucepan and stir in the flour. To this add, slowly stirring, the milk and meat stock. When smooth and fairly thick and just on the boil, stir in the mince. Stir over very low heat for three minutes, seasoning with salt and pepper to taste. Pour into a flat buttered fireproof dish and leave to get cold. Meanwhile cream the potatoes, season, stir in the rest of the butter and a little milk, and whisk with a fork till smooth. Set aside until the minced meat is cool enough to have solidified and formed a solid surface. If you add the potato to the hot mince it will sink into it.

When cool, spread the potato about an inch thick all over the dish, work-ing lightly with a fork. Dot with pieces of butter, or cover with grated cheese. Cook in a pre-heated oven at 350° F., gas mark 4, for 20 minutes, when the top should be golden brown.

The dish may be prepared in the morning and left for cooking until the evening without harm.

Grilled and Fried Meat

There is little to be said about grilling or frying any form of meat. Grilling is the oldest traditional method in the world and is, of course, the same process as roasting. Man must have roasted lumps of meat on a stick long before he thought of making a pot and boiling them. Almost all meat with the exception, perhaps, of liver, breaded veal or breaded lamb chops or cutlets is better grilled than fried. Sausages are equally good cooked by either method.

The grill can hardly be too fierce: the whole point of grilled beef or lamb is that it should be cut in a slice or chop about 1 inch thick and should be crisp and brown on the outside and for about $^1/_8$ inch inwards; after that it should be pink and juicy right through. This depends on a really hot grill, careful basting with a little butter and the juices from the drip tray, and on turning. Grilled pork or veal should, of course, be cooked more slowly until it is brown outside and white right through the inside.

If meat is to be fried rather than grilled, the pan must be made very hot so that the fat used is smoking. The fat should not be more than ¼ inch (½ cm.) deep, and for preference butter or half butter, half oil should be used. Steaks, chops or veal escalopes should be lightly rubbed with well-seasoned flour, as this helps to seal them and adds to the crispness and flavour of the outsides.

Rissoles, meat balls and croquettes should be deep-fried or fried in at least ½ inch (1½ cm.) of very hot fat, preferably half butter and half oil or a good manufactured cooking fat.

As grilling and frying are the quickest and simplest methods of cooking and familiar to everyone, not many separate recipes are given, but I have included a few traditional dishes which are not very often seen today.

Cutlets Edward VII

Edward VII liked large tender lamb chops trimmed and then dipped in breadcrumbs, then in egg and then in breadcrumbs again. To please him, they had to be grilled very fast so that the golden breaded surfaces showed the darker marks of the grill; inside they had to be pink and juicy but not raw. He liked them served with plenty of iced mayonnaise in a sauceboat and floury potatoes baked in their jackets served on separate plates, without butter, the mayonnaise being sufficient.

Grilled Steaks with Black Coffee

I have one personal recipe for grilled steak:

>   a good fillet or rump steak for each person
>   2 oz. (60 g.) butter
>   ½ pint (3 dl.) very strong, strained, cold black coffee
>   juice of half a lemon
>   1 flat tablespoon cornflour
>   seasoning

Stir into the coffee a teaspoon of salt and a little pepper, and the juice of half a lemon. Marinate the steaks in this for 1 to 3 hours.

Take the steaks out. Spread a piece of softened butter on each and grill in the ordinary way, basting twice with the black coffee mixture. Boil the remainder of this, and thicken with the cornflour mixed into a little cold water.

Dish the steaks and quickly pour the thickened coffee mixture into the drip pan over heat and stir well for half a minute. Pour a little over the steaks and serve the rest separately.

The black coffee brings out the flavour of the meat and makes an inimitable gravy.

Gilded Apples

This is a medieval dish and may indeed have its origin in Roman Britain, since in some early forms it is very close to certain recipes of Apicius. The Harleian MS. 279 of 1430 lists 'Pome dorreng' in the third course of Henry IV's coronation feast, and recipes occur in most cookery books until the nineteenth century.

The 'apples' were always made of finely minced pork or of pork mixed with the white meat of chicken. They were fried crisp in batter (early versions sometimes suggest that they should be spitted and the batter poured over them after they had begun to frizzle on the spits). Half were made with parsley in the batter so that they should be greenish gold, and half were the rich gold of the plain batter. The recipe from the Harleian MS. directs that the meat and spices for the Pommes dorres (the spelling is different from that in the list of coronation dishes) should be mixed with stiffly beaten whites of eggs, then dipped in a light batter and fried, or alternatively lightly floured and boiled for ten minutes in a good chicken broth, lifted and drained carefully. In either case they were to be allowed to get quite cold and then 'endored' which means simply 'gilded', a word still in use in cookery for anything which is brushed over with beaten yolks of eggs. Half the 'apples' were then to be rolled in chopped parsley and all were to be cooked on spits with the warning 'and be well ware that they be not browne' which would have spoilt the colours.

A slightly different recipe, however, suggests mixing the meat with whole eggs and dipping the 'apples' in a light batter, into half of which chopped parsley has been mixed. The batter in this case gives the gold colour and no further gilding or glazing is necessary. This is simpler to make today, and the gilded apples are delicious. They cook extremely well on kebab skewers on an electric grill, if this is available, but are very good carefully fried.

To serve 4 (4 apples per head)

    1 lb. (½ k.) minced cooked pork
      (*or* pork and the white meat of cooked chicken)
    1 teaspoon white pepper
    ½ teaspoon powdered ginger
    1 teaspoon mace
    1 teaspoon caster sugar
    2 teaspoons salt
    4 eggs
    2 oz. (60 g.) flour
    ½ pint (3 dl.) milk
    1 heaped tablespoon finely chopped parsley
    deep fat, or half butter, half oil to give ½ in. (1 cm.) depth, for frying

Mix all the spices and seasoning, including the sugar and 1 teaspoon salt, into the finely minced meat and stir or blend in two whole eggs. Make into round balls about 1½ in. (3·5 cm.) in diameter.

Make a batter by beating the flour with the remaining 2 eggs and adding milk and a teaspoon of salt. Beat very well. Pour half the batter into another bowl and stir in the parsley. Dip each ball, separately, some into the plain and some into the green batter, and fry immediately in smoking hot fat, turning them on all sides if you are shallow-frying. Lift out with perforated slice and keep hot on a dish spread with kitchen paper to absorb any excess fat.

Arrange on a clean dish to serve. Do not keep them waiting after the last are cooked as they should be very crisp.

They are best eaten as a supper dish, accompanied by a fresh tomato sauce and a green salad.

Fillets of Lamb on Croûtons with Spring Vegetables

This recipe and the next are both from the collection of a 'Clerk of the Kitchen to A noble Earl' in the late eighteenth century. The original recipe used the word 'manchet', i.e. fine white bread, where we have become accustomed to the French word *croûton*.

Vegetable quantities are for four. The dish is even better, of course, with fresh asparagus and new peas, as in the original. Other vegetables can be used.

2 fillets per person	pkt frozen sweetcorn
1½ lb. (¾ k.) new potatoes	a small packet frozen peas
½ lb. (240 g.) mushrooms	slice of bread for each fillet
tin of asparagus	½ lb. (240 g.) butter

Any good butcher will cut the small fillets from the loin. Prepare the croûtons by cutting rounds from slices of bread with a pastry-cutter about the same size as the fillets. Next, cook all the vegetables separately, tossing in butter the potatoes, the peas and the sweetcorn when they are drained. Sauté the mushrooms in butter and heat the tinned asparagus. Keep all hot while you fry the croûtons to a light golden colour. Place them ready on a very large flat serving dish and keep hot in the oven. Add more butter to the pan and heat to foaming stage only. It should be about ¼ inch (½ cm.) deep and should not darken. Put the fillets into this and cook gently about three minutes each side. Place them on the croûtons and stir the butter and juices together in the pan and spoon a little over each. Arrange all the vegetables around the fillets in small heaps, one of each for each person. Serve at once.

Scotch Collops

This recipe dates from 1833, and is a rather grand one for a dish which was usually served in much simpler form. It is very good.

For 4

> 4 escalopes of veal
> 1 pint (6 dl.) very well-flavoured thick brown sauce, previously prepared (p. 277)
> ½ lb. (240 g.) small mushrooms, sauté
> 12 small forcemeat balls, previously prepared (p. 297)
> 4 medium-sized gammon rashers
> 3 oz. (90 g.) butter

Cut each escalope into 4 pieces and lightly fry on both sides in the hot butter until faintly brown (about 2 minutes for each side). Put the sauce in a small saucepan and lay the fried veal in it. Add the mushrooms and the forcemeat balls and simmer very gently for 10 minutes. Meanwhile fry the gammon rashers slowly so that they do not become crisp. Pour the collops with their sauce on to a hot flat dish and place the gammon rashers round them.

Veal Fritters

This is an adaptation of a fourteenth-century recipe. The original is very simple and nothing is changed, except that exact quantities are given here.

For 4

    ½ lb. (240 g.) cold cooked veal, minced finely,
        or 6 oz. (180 g.) veal and 2 oz. (60 g.) lean cooked ham
    ¾ lb. (360 g.) fine white breadcrumbs
    3 oz. (1 dl.) strong well-seasoned stock
    pepper and salt
    a little saffron in the original: may be replaced by ½ teaspoon mace or
        a teaspoon grated lemon rind
    a little flour
    2 eggs

Mix together the meat, seasoning and two thirds of the breadcrumbs, and stir in the stock to bind. The mixture should be as firm as sausage meat.

    Flour a pastry or chopping board. Divide the mixture into 6 or 8 small equal heaps and place well apart on the board. Press them flat with the hand and shape into rough ovals, and then press another board on them to flatten. They should be about ¼ inch (½ cm.) thick.

    Beat the eggs, paint each fritter over on each side with egg using a pastry brush. Sprinkle with breadcrumbs and press these down a little. Lift carefully and fry for 2 or 3 minutes in very hot fat about ½ inch (1½ cm.) deep. Serve with slices of lemon or orange.

Rissoles

Andrew Boorde's (1549) recipe adapted. He spells the word Rissheshewes, and it was sometimes spelt resshewes. It probably comes from Norman French *réchauffées*.

For 4

> ½ lb. (240 g.) any cold meat finely minced
> 1 tablespoon finely chopped parsley and chives with a very little thyme
> salt and pepper
> a pinch of mace and a pinch of ginger
> 2 eggs
> ¼ lb. (120 g.) fine white breadcrumbs (or prepared crumbs)
> ½ pint (3 dl.) very good thickened gravy or a good brown, tomato
>   or espagnole sauce

Mix the meat, herbs, spices and seasoning well together, and bind with one well-beaten egg. Shape into balls. Dip into the remaining beaten egg and roll in breadcrumbs, so that each rissole is the shape of a sausage. Fry as for veal fritters, turning once. Serve immediately with separate sauce or gravy.

Scallops of Veal with Cucumbers

This is a recipe of my own adapted from a vast seventeenth-century receipt. As well as the 'cowcumbers' it contained cocks' combs, oysters, and artichoke bottoms, though 'cowcumbers' predominate, and a great many herbs and spices. It was baked as a huge pie, a quart of cream being poured through slits in the lid a few minutes before serving. My adapted recipe is very simple but retains the combined flavours and textures of the veal, cucumber and cream.

> 2 small scallops of veal for each person, cut very thin and flattened
>   (your butcher will do this)
> 1 cucumber
> ½ lb. (240 g.) puff pastry (buy frozen)
> ½ pint (3 dl.) double cream
> flour, salt and pepper
> ¼ lb. (120 g.) butter
> a pinch of paprika

Roll out thinly a small packet of frozen puff pastry, cut into triangular pieces, each side about 1½ inches (4 cm.) long, and bake in a very hot oven (425° F., gas mark 7) for 5 to 10 minutes. These can be made in advance and reheated in a cool oven or the warming drawer.

Peel the cucumber and cut in rings about half an inch thick, which you then halve across. Boil these till tender (about 10 minutes) in salted water. Drain and keep warm, covered.

Coat the veal scallops with seasoned flour and fry in butter, browning on both sides (about 3 minutes a side). Remove and keep hot, covered, in a cool oven. Loosen the glaze and juices in the pan with a spoon, stir in a teaspoonful of flour to make a very little roux, stir in ½ pint of cream, mix in well, and then boil fiercely for a minute or two to reduce and thicken. Season, while it boils, with salt and pepper and a pinch of paprika. Unless it boils, the cream will not thicken to the right consistency.

Arrange the veal fillets on a flat serving dish with the cucumber pieces among them – there should be about four to each fillet. Pour the sauce all over and serve, garnished with the pastry croûtons.

Skuets of Veal
(i.e. Veal on Skewers)

A very early recipe.

For 6

> 1½ lb. (¾ k.) lean veal from fillet or top of leg
> 8 rashers streaky bacon
> 12 button mushrooms
> pepper and salt
> a pinch of mace
> a pinch of ground cloves or ginger
> 3 oz. (90 g.) melted butter
> ½ pint (3 dl.) good veal gravy or a good fresh tomato or brown sauce

One skewer will be needed for each person. They are preferably cooked on a spit-grill, but may be laid on a grid in a baking tray and baked for 6 minutes on each side, turning once, at 450° F., gas mark 8.

Cut the veal into neat 1-in. (2½-cm.) cubes. Cut each rasher of bacon into three.

Mix the salt and spices and rub the veal with this mixture. Thread on skewers, putting a piece of bacon between each cube of veal and a mushroom here and there. Dip each filled skewer in the melted butter so that it is coated all over.

Grill for 10–12 minutes on rotating skewers, beginning at maximum and reducing heat a little after first 5 minutes.

Serve the gravy or sauce separately.

Bubble and Squeak

Dr Kitchiner, writing in 1817,* gives a recipe for this which omits potato. He opens with the couplet:

> When 'midst the frying Pan in accents savage
> The Beef, so surly, quarrels with the Cabbage.

This recipe is exactly the same as that given in the 1819 edition of *A New System of Domestic Cookery* by Mrs Rundell and in 1830 by Richard Dolby of the Thatched House Tavern. Mrs Beeton in 1861 adds an onion. However, almost all later recipes omit onion and include potato in the proportion given for colcannon (p. 357). Bubble and squeak is fried in exactly the same way and is often served to accompany cold meat which is not reheated.

Serves 4

> 16 slices of lean, cold, roast beef
> 1 green cabbage, large enough for 4
> 1 onion
> 1 lb. (½ k.) cooked, mashed potato   } or these may be omitted

Lightly brown in butter neat slices of cold boiled or roast beef which have been lightly dusted in pepper. Keep hot, *covered* so that they will not harden. Meanwhile chop finely a green cabbage, boil it in very little water till tender; drain it well, pressing out all the water. If onion is used, lightly fry it in the pan in which you browned the beef, adding a little more butter if necessary. When soft add the cabbage and potato and cook until it forms a cake. Turn the cake once, fry a little more and then serve on a flat dish with the beef round it and some good gravy.

* *The Cook's Oracle.*

Boiled Meats

Boiling joints of meat was much more usual and much more highly esteemed from the Middle Ages until the early nineteenth century than it has been since. Nowadays many people do not eat boiled meat at all. This is a pity because it can be very good, and by eschewing it we eliminate some great traditional English dishes with their appropriate sauces and garnishes.

Our ancestors were forced to salt down a great deal of meat in the autumn since they could not over-winter most of their stock. Salted meat, except for pork, cannot be roasted or grilled or fried since it becomes like wood. It must be boiled or stewed. We have various comments and records which show that fresh meat was craved, and, of course, in royal palaces and great houses it was available throughout the winter. But some dishes of boiled meat were so good that they remained popular long after the agricultural reforms of the eighteenth century made winter meat less scarce. Boiled meats in the nineteenth century began to be considered a masculine taste, and men often chose them in their clubs or in restaurants. Until the last war English households usually served a boiled silverside of beef with dumplings, slightly salted or fresh, or a leg of mutton with caper sauce, and sometimes a piece of fresh boiled pork, with pease pudding, perhaps once or twice in a month, but almost never at dinner parties, though there are records that dishes of assorted boiled meats were sometimes served at City banquets.

Boiled meat is so different in flavour and texture from roast, grilled or fried that it is very refreshing to be offered it occasionally.

In the Middle Ages, the main cooking stove was a large cauldron which could be boiled over the open fire or buried in coals or turves when it was required for baking.

A boiled joint was prepared in one of two ways. If the meat was salt it was first soaked for 12–48 hours, according to the length of time it had been in the brine. It was then wrapped in a floured cloth or bag and tied in the large cauldron so that it hung to one side. At the bottom of the cauldron a piece of bacon, also wrapped, could be laid, and above this, on a board pierced with holes, a covered jar or two could stand containing fish, potatoes, apples or pears, or stews of cut-up meats. These could be lowered in at the right time to allow them proper cooking. Dried peas or beans or a barley or suet or pease pudding could also be tightly tied in floured cloths and hung like the joint from the handles. The largest cauldrons which have survived would have held a piece of bacon of 3 or 4 lb., a joint of 6 or 8 lb., one stewing jar and 2 or 3 bags of cereal, pudding or vegetables. Large establishments naturally had more than one hearth and more than one cauldron on each fire. In this way a large and varied dinner or several meals could be cooked at once, and at the same time, a great deal of reasonably clean hot water provided.

The meat, tightly and impermeably tied, lost none of its juice or flavour to the water: the adhering flour paste could be wiped off, the joint dried a little by turning in front of the fire (many early recipes recommend this). It was served with a separately made sauce.

Often, however, the joint was soaked for a shorter period, and put un-wrapped into a smaller cauldron of water, with onions, carrots, turnips and whatever other pot herbs were available and a bunch of sweet herbs. Potatoes, when these became common, were added half an hour before the joint was taken up. In a simple household the meat would then be served with its vegetables and the stock from the pot, skimmed and seasoned. In grander houses, it would still be dried before the fire and served with separate sauces as well as some of its own stock; in this free-boiling method some of the flavour was cooked out of the meat and into the water, but there was less danger of the meat itself being too salt. And unless the water, in turn, became unpalatably salt, there was plenty of good broth. A large suet pudding called a 'ball' was very often cooked in the broth and eaten with it but before the meat. In poorer households children were told 'No broth, no ball: no ball, no meat': in fact, you had to eat a plate of the broth before you even got the suet pudding (which sometimes had no suet, being simply flour, salt and water)'. This saying is quoted in *Cranford*, and the implication seems to be that the broth was not much liked: probably very salt and rather greasy.

Fresh meat and large birds were also frequently boiled.

TO BOIL FRESH MEAT

Wipe the meat and cut off any superfluous fat. To a thin piece such as ribs of mutton, allow 15 minutes to the lb. (½ k.) and 15 minutes over; a thick piece such as a leg of mutton or silverside of beef will need 25 minutes to the lb. (½ k.) and 25 minutes over. Pork and veal require 30 minutes to the lb. (½ k.) and 30 minutes over. Very small joints can be successfully boiled but allow no extra time if under 3 lb. (1½ k.).

If necessary, tie the meat in shape. Place the meat in boiling water sufficient to cover, bring again to boiling point and skim. Let it boil for

5 minutes to harden the outside, then reduce the heat and allow to simmer very gently during the rest of the time.

The fairly rapid boiling for the first few minutes hardens the outside and seals in the juices; after that, if the meat is boiled fast it will be hard all through. Carrots, turnips, onions or parsnips may be put in with the meat, if the joint is not very large, but the potatoes, which will be delicious, should be added 30 minutes before the meat will be ready, and peas or broad beans 10 minutes after them. A bundle of herbs such as thyme, parsley and marjoram should be put in; or a bouquet garni. A sprig of fennel gives a subtle flavour. Put in also a dessertspoon of salt and 12 black peppercorns and 2 or 3 cloves.

Silverside of beef or brisket of beef, leg of mutton or well-grown lamb, any lean piece of veal, including breast, any lean piece of venison, or a piece of leg of pork, are suitable for boiling. As, of course, are calves', sheep's and pigs' heads, pigs' trotters, tripe, etc.

TO BOILING SALT MEAT

If the meat is very salt, soak it overnight in cold water and bring very slowly to boiling point in fresh cold water. Pour off the water to get rid of some of the salt and pour on fresh boiling water. Simmer very slowly till tender, allowing 30 to 35 minutes to every lb. (½ k.) according to the thickness of the meat and about 30 minutes over. Skim frequently while simmering.

Boiled pork (salt or fresh) when ready must have the skin removed and the top covered with toast raspings.

The stock is excellent and should be served just as it is or else used in an accompanying sauce.

Boiled Salt or Fresh Silverside of Beef

Ask your butcher for the piece of beef two days before you require it, and ask that it be only slightly salt. If you think it may be too salt for your taste, soak in cold water for 6–12 hours. Fresh silverside may be cooked in exactly the same way, but of course needs no soaking. The water, however, will require salt.

Allow a piece of silverside about 6 lb. (3 k.) in weight for five or six people, as it is delicious cold.

Cook as above, and serve with its own stock or with spiced stock and plenty of dumplings (see p. 96).

Spiced Stock

This was traditional in high-level cookery in the seventeenth and eighteenth centuries.

A few minutes before lifting the meat, pour off about a pint (6 dl.) of the stock into a small saucepan and stir into it half a teaspoon of powdered mace, ½ teaspoon turmeric, a few stamens of saffron and a little white pepper. Taste carefully, for if the beef is fresh it may want salt; if salt, this is unlikely. Stir in some orange zest and about the juice of one orange. Bring to the boil and strain: the liquid should be a clear bright golden colour.

Serve separately, or pour some over dumplings, which will then also appear pale gold.

Boiled Beef in Beer

This is a North Country recipe from the early nineteenth century. The tradition in the household was that the dish had been prepared in the past by their parsimonious ancestors for the hay-making supper for tenants, because part of an old ox which had been kept to work all winter could be used, since the beer helped to tenderize the meat. The tenants liked the taste of the beer and considered the dish a grand one.

4 lb. beef will serve 8.

    1 quart light ale to every 4 lb. (2 k.) beef (to be added after marinating)
    4–12 lb. (2–6 k.) lean beef, well tied (ask for stewing beef)
    2–4 lb. (1–2 k.) onions, peeled and sliced
    large bundle of herbs, sweet
    3 or more cloves
    a little mace
    a little turmeric
    12 or more peppercorns, salt
    ¼ pint (1½ dl.) wine vinegar
    4 oz. (120 g.) dark treacle for every 4 lb. meat

Pile the onions on top of the beef and marinate 12 hours or overnight in all the other ingredients except the ale. Spoon the liquid over the meat from time to time.

Then put the meat, onions and marinade in a very large saucepan and fill up with beer to cover. Simmer very gently for 3 hours, check seasoning and serve with boiled potatoes, red or baked cabbage, and a sweet chutney.

Spiced Beef

In Yorkshire this dish was often preferred to a ham on occasions when a cold collation was required. If there is cause to prepare a large cold buffet today the three great traditional English cold meats given here, Spiced Beef, Boiled Tongue, and Fillets of Pork in Jelly, make an excellent combination and are much less usual than chicken or turkey, a ham and a cold roast. They do, of course, require three very large saucepans or kettles and a fairly large cooker-top to themselves for two or three hours.

Serves 16

       skirt of beef, about 8 lb. (4 k.)
       1 lb. (½ k.) salt
       2 teaspoons black pepper
       1 teaspoon powdered cloves
       1 teaspoon mace
       1 teaspoon powdered thyme
       1 teaspoon cayenne
       1 teaspoon paprika
       3 carrots
       3 onions
       2 leeks if available
       3 sticks celery if available
       a few gherkins to decorate

Get the butcher to bone and trim the beef but not to roll it. Two or three days before the finished dish is required, lay the beef out flat, skin downwards. Rub in most of the salt and sprinkle a snow of remaining salt all over it. Leave overnight and next day drain off all liquid and wipe well, removing all the salt which has not penetrated. Mix together all the herbs and spices and rub into the beef, particularly into the slashes where the bones were removed. Roll up very tightly and tie like a long parcel, the string going round in three or four places. Put in boiling water and boil very gently for 3 ½ hours, together with the carrots, onions, leeks and celery, and the bones and trimmings.

When cooked, remove and drain well, and lay it under a pastry board with one or two weights on top. Leave to get cold. Put the stock to boil briskly so that it reduces to a strong glaze; from the original 3–4 pints of stock only about 1 pint should remain. When the beef is quite cold, pour the glaze over it, decorating the top with a row of slices of gherkins if liked. It will keep perfectly in the refrigerator for a week, or will deep-freeze perfectly and keep for months.

Boiled Ox Tongue

1 ox tongue	12 peppercorns
2 carrots	bunch of sweet herbs
2 onions	1½ pints (9 dl.) good stock
1 turnip	(beef or chicken)

Wash the tongue thoroughly, and soak for one or two hours; if pickled, soak for three or four hours. Put into a large pan of tepid water. Bring slowly to the boil, skim, add carrots, onions, turnip, peppercorns and herbs. The stock from a tongue is apt to be greasy and tasteless. It is better to prepare 1½ pints (9 dl.) of very good beef or chicken stock, highly seasoned. Dissolve a packet of gelatine in this to stiffen the natural jelly.

Cook gently, allowing 30 minutes to each pound, and 30 minutes over. When ready remove skin and small bones very carefully, and press into a large round cake tin or soufflé dish. Pour in prepared stock just to cover. Lay foil on top of tongue and put a weight on it so that tongue is well pressed.

Leave overnight in the refrigerator.

To Boil a Leg of Mutton like Venison

Mrs Glasse suggests that the combination of cauliflower and spinach makes the plain boiled mutton taste like venison. She says: 'This is a genteel dish for a first course at bottom [of the table].' The combined flavours are very good.

Serves 6–8

4–5 lb. (2–2½ k.) fillet end of leg of mutton	
2 cauliflowers	
2 large packets frozen chopped spinach	
2 or 3 carrots	
2 onions	a little thyme, marjoram and parsley
3 bay leaves	8 oz. (240 g.) butter
1 level tablespoon cornflour	½ pint (3 dl.) red wine
a stick of celery	2 oz. (60 g.) flour

Put the mutton in 3–4 pints (1½–2 dl.) of boiling water, with the carrots, onions, celery, and herbs. Allow to boil quite rapidly for 5 minutes, and then simmer very slowly for 2½ hours.

Meanwhile, break 2 cauliflowers into flowerets, boil till just tender and sauté very lightly, without browning, in half the butter. Melt the spinach without water but with a little salt and add 2 oz. of butter as the spinach softens. Mix a level tablespoon of cornflour in a little water and pour this into the spinach when it begins to boil; stir hard and cook for 3 or 4 minutes. You should have a fairly thick purée.

Arrange the spinach in a border on a flat dish. Place the well-drained mutton in the middle and the sprigs of cauliflower on top of the spinach. Carve with a very sharp knife and serve with plain boiled potatoes, and a sauce made as follows.

Ten minutes before the mutton should be ready, pour off a pint (6 dl.) of stock. Skim off as much grease as possible. Make a roux with 2 oz. butter and 2 oz. flour. Stir in the stock and add the wine. Simmer for 5 minutes. Strain and check seasoning.

Boiled Mutton with Caper Sauce

Cook the meat as in the previous recipe, and to make the caper sauce stir 2 tablespoons of drained capers into a pint of white sauce (see p. 277).

Boiled Leg of Pork

Serves 8

Let the piece be at least 4 lb. (2 k.) in weight and have it skinned by the butcher. Follow the general directions for boiling meat on p. 51, and serve with pease pudding (p. 300).

Cabbage and parsnips were also traditionally served with boiled leg of pork.

A little of the stock should be removed a few minutes before the meat is ready and carefully skimmed and seasoned. The rest, when the fat is removed, makes excellent pea soup, using the remains of the pease pudding.

Mrs Glasse gives a splendid recipe for a boiled pork dish designed to be eaten cold. She calls it simply:

A Pig in Jelly

'Cut it into quarters and lay it in your stewpan, put in one calf's foot and the pig's feet, a pinch of Rhenish wine, the juice of four lemons and one quart of water, three or four blades of mace, two or three cloves, some salt or a very little piece of lemon peel: stove it or do it over a slow fire two hours; then take it up, lay the pig into the dish you intend it for, then strain the liquor and when the jelly is cold, skim off the fat and leave the fettling at the bottom. Warm the jelly again and pour it over the pig and serve it up cold in the jelly.'

She really intended a sucking pig, or maybe a pigling of six or eight weeks, but the dish is excellent if made with two fillets of pork. It will serve 6–8 people and is very good for a lunch or supper party.

Fillets of Pork in Jelly

2 pork fillets, well trimmed	1 lemon
1 calf's foot (split by the butcher, well washed)	2 large onions, peeled and quartered
½ bottle red wine	3 hard-boiled eggs
pepper and salt	slices of cucumber
mace	olives ⎫
cloves	pimento, etc. ⎭ for decoration

The fillets should be laid in a fish kettle (since a pork fillet is generally about 12–14 inches long), with a calf's foot and the onions, and simmered in half a bottle of red wine, 1½ pints water (9 dl.), a little mace, 2 or 3 cloves, pepper and salt, the juice of 1 lemon and a piece of its peel, for an hour and a half. They should then be placed on a long dish, while the stock gets cold. Once cold and jellied all fat can easily be skimmed off. Warm again, as Mrs Glasse suggests, and pour half over the fillets and let it fill up the dish round them. Decorate them and the jelly around them with sliced hard-boiled eggs, slices of cucumber, olives, pimento, etc., and allow jelly to set. Heat remainder again until it will just pour and very carefully cover fillets and decorations. Chill slightly and serve.

Mrs Glasse also suggests a much more elaborate jellied pork dish in which the pig is cooked with 2 large eels and a dozen large crayfish, but this I do not propose to attempt.

Boiled Breast of Veal

A very noble lord in the nineteenth century had a passion for tripe. From time to time he demanded the following dish which he said belonged to the same genre and was better when your cook had no real feeling for tripe.

Serves 6–8

3 lb. (1½ k.) breast of veal	a stick of celery
2 or 3 carrots	seasoning
2 large onions	2 lemons quartered
1 turnip	3 slices of bread, without crusts,
a bunch of sweet herbs	toasted and cut in small triangles

For sauce:

1 pint (6 dl.) milk	2 tablespoons finely chopped parsley
3 oz. (90 g.) butter	¼ pint (1½ dl.) cream
2 oz. (60 g.) flour	½ pint (3 dl.) stock from the veal
seasoning	

Put the folded breast into a saucepan of cold water just to cover. Skim it when it comes to the boil. Add the vegetables, herbs and seasoning. Cover closely and simmer gently for 3 hours. Lift and drain.

Place the veal flat on a large dish with the vegetables and pour a good parsley sauce (see below) over all. Place sippets of toast and quarters of lemon round the edge of the dish.

Make the parsley sauce by adding half a pint (3 dl.) of veal stock and a pint (6 dl.) of milk to your roux, which should be made of 3 oz. (90 g.) of butter and 2 oz. (60 g.) of flour. Stir 2 tablespoons of finely chopped parsley into the sauce as soon as it has come to the boil, season, and then add the cream.

CALF'S HEAD

After the Restoration, some of the younger Republicans used to meet once a year at a London Inn, where they celebrated the anniversary of the death of Charles I on 30 January 1649. The main part of the dinner consisted of calves' heads, some crowned with garlands of parsley. The bitterly discontented men drank derisive toasts to the monarchy and eventually went in procession to a courtyard, where they built a great fire. One, masked and carrying an axe, represented Charles I's executioner, a second carried a calf's head on a napkin, and it is only too clear what that stood for. The rest waved handkerchiefs stained with wine to represent blood. The head, amid ribald cries and songs, was thrown into the fire. They called themselves simply The Calves' Head Club and presumably hoped that Loyalists would assume that they met because they considered calf's head one of the greatest dishes of the world.

Until the beginning of the nineteenth century, their descendants ate Calf's Head at home on 30 January every year.

Boiled Calf's Head

Serves about 8–10

1 calf's head, boned and cleaned	a few leaves of sage
1 tablespoon flour	2 or 3 bay leaves
2 large onions	12 peppercorns
2 or 3 carrots	1 dessertspoon salt
a stick of celery	juice of a lemon
sprigs of thyme and marjoram	2 oz. (60 g.) flour

Have the head boned and cleaned by your butcher.

Put the vegetables, seasoning, herbs and lemon juice in a saucepan of boiling water, sprinkle in the flour (which later keeps the head white) and boil for 10 minutes, without the head. Then lower the head into the bouillon. Simmer until perfectly tender (about 1½ hours). Lift out and drain; trim the tongue. Serve the head with a good brown sauce with a few mushrooms in it, a caper or parsley sauce, or a simple vinaigrette. Some of the strained liquor from the head should be used in making whichever sauce is chosen.

If you prefer it, the head may be cut in pieces after cooking and served in a good brown sauce with hard-boiled eggs, mushrooms and olives. There is a fine elaborate seventeenth-century recipe for this which requires cockscombs, kidneys and crayfish in addition.

Tripe and Onions

A Lancashire recipe.

1½ lb. (¾ k.) tripe, dressed	seasoning
1¼ pints (7½ dl.) milk	a little flour
3 large onions	

Take the dressed tripe and cut it into square pieces, place it in a saucepan, cover with cold water, bring to the boil, and throw away the water. Add to the tripe 1 pint (6 dl.) of milk and ½ pint (3 dl.) of water, 3 finely sliced onions, salt and pepper. Simmer for 3 hours, then thicken with a tablespoonful of flour mixed in a little milk and strained into the pot. Re-boil, add extra seasoning, if desired. Serve very hot.

Stewed Meats

To Stew a Rump of Beef

Reading MS., 1765.

'Season your beef with nutmeg mace peper salt and lard it with bacon put it in a pot and lay the fate side downward, put to it a quarter of a pint vinegar ½ pint red wine a pint of water three whole onions stuck with a few cloves – a bunch of sweet herbs two anchovys cover it close and let it stew over a gentle fire – four hours scum of the fate from the liquor and then pouer the liquor put over it in the dish garnish with horseradish and greens scald.'

A very simple rich recipe.

Serves 8

> 3 lb. (1½ k.) rump of beef, cut and tied as for roasting
> 2 rashers bacon
> 2 tablespoons wine vinegar
> ½ pint (3 dl.) red wine
> 3 large peeled onions, with 4 cloves stuck in each
> bunch of herbs or bouquet garni
> 2 anchovies
> seasoning

In a saucepan which fits the beef with an inch or so to spare all round, lay first the bacon and then the beef. Add the onions, herbs, anchovies and seasoning; pour over the vinegar and the wine. Cover with foil and then with the lid, bring to the boil, and then simmer very gently for 3½ hours without uncovering.

Twenty minutes before it will be ready, cook spring greens, broccoli or green cabbage, so that they are very green and still a little crisp. Drain. Keep warm while you lift the beef on to a large flat dish, skim the stock well, check seasoning, and then ladle it over the meat. If the stock has reduced to a very small quantity add some boiling water, stir briskly and re-season. Put the green vegetable in a ring round the dish and serve at once with creamed potatoes and horseradish sauce (see p. 286).

Ragoût of Beef

'Ragoos' or 'ragouts' appeared on the tables of all great houses from the sixteenth century and probably earlier. A ragoût was a thick stew of beef or other meat, poultry or game or vegetables which was enriched either with a 'cullis' (see Sauces) or with a very strong reduced stock and which usually contained mushrooms, artichoke hearts, olives, sweetbreads, cockscombs, etc.

For 4–6

> 2 lb. (1 k.) rump of beef, in one piece, trimmed of all fat
> ½ lb. (240 g.) ox kidney, skinned, cored, and cut up finely
> 1 pint (6 dl.) well-flavoured reduced brown stock (p. 314)
> ¼ lb. (120 g.) mushrooms
> 2 onions, peeled and cut fine
> 12 forcemeat balls
> 2 oz. (60 g.) butter
> a little flour
> salt and pepper
> bay leaves and bouquet garni

Flour the beef and fry it on all sides in the butter in the pan in which it will be stewed. Add the onions and the floured kidney and fry lightly. Add the herbs and seasoning, put in water just to cover and stew very gently for 1½ hours. There should be about 1–1½ pints (6–9 dl.) of liquid at this point. If there is more, pour some off (keep for another dish) before adding your brown stock.

Add the stock and the mushrooms. Cover and stew for a further half-hour. Warm the forcemeat balls in a covered dish in the oven. Remove the herbs and bay leaves and season highly. Put the beef on a flat dish. The stock should be as thick as thin cream. If it is too thin, keep the beef hot while you thicken it with 2 teaspoons of cornflour stirred into a little cold water and added to the boiling stock. Pour over the beef and put the forcemeat balls around the edge of the dish.

Berkshire Jugged Steak

This very simple but very good recipe goes back to the cauldron cookery of the Middle Ages, when the covered jar of steak would have stood on a pierced board and cooked in the great cauldron in which several other dishes were boiling.

Take a piece of rump steak about 1½ inches (3 cm.) thick and 2 lb. (1 k.) in weight, and cut into neat small squares. Place in an earthenware jar or tall narrow casserole. Add an onion stuck with cloves, a little diced celery and carrot, and a teaspoon of mushroom ketchup, salt and pepper to season. Do *not* add water or fat. Cover the jar closely and place in a pan of boiling water or, if preferred, place in the oven and stew for 2 hours.

Stewed Ox Tail

1 ox tail	1 quart (1¼ l.) stock or water
4 oz. (120 g.) butter	pepper and salt
½ lb. (240 g.) onions	2 oz. (60 g.) flour
a bunch of herbs	1 teaspoon paprika, if liked
½ lb. (240 g.) carrots, cut in rings	
½ lb. (240 g.) tomatoes, skinned and quartered	

Ask the butcher to chop the ox tail into joints. Wipe the tail and remove all fat. Dry the pieces and fry in 2 oz. (60 g.) butter until brown; add the stock and salt. Then add the vegetables, including tomatoes, herbs and seasonings. Put into a slow oven (150–200° F., gas mark ¼–½) for 4 hours. Then melt 2 oz. (60 g.) of butter in a saucepan and stir in 2 oz. (60 g.) of flour. When smooth, add up to 1 pint (6 dl.) of gravy from the ox tail (save remaining stock for soup), stirring it in slowly to make a thick, smooth gravy. Add a teaspoon of paprika if liked, and season well. Lift ox tail pieces and vegetables to a serving dish with a perforated spoon and pour the sauce over them. Very good served with dumplings and plain boiled potatoes.

To Dress a Leg of Mutton à la Royale

This recipe (very slightly modified) comes from Mrs Glasse, but there are earlier references to what is clearly the same excellent dish, very good for a large dinner party; the mutton and beef cooked and eaten together are unusual and outstanding. A large fish kettle or an iron or steel casserole which can go on top of the stove is required.

Serves 8

 3–4 lb. (1½–2 k.) leg of mutton (*or* large leg of lamb)

 2 lb. (1 k.) piece of either rump of beef, tied to roast, *or* leg of veal, tied to roast

 2 bouquets garnis *or* sprigs of thyme, parsley, marjoram and a very little sage

 a little flour

 1 large onion stuck with 12 cloves

 3 blades of mace

 12 peppercorns

 ¼ lb. (120 g.) butter

 salt

For the garnish and gravy:

 3 veal or 6 lamb's kidneys

 ¾ lb. (360 g.) mushrooms

 ¼ pint red wine (1½ dl.)

 4 oz. (120 g.) plain flour

 asparagus – about 18 heads (may be frozen or canned)

 2 tablespoons chopped parsley

 1 tablespoon drained capers

 seasoning

 a little lemon juice

Have the mutton skinned, the fat trimmed off, and the shank bone cut off by the butcher.

Flour the mutton and brown it all over in butter in a large frying pan; do the same with the floured beef or veal. Put both into the fish kettle or casserole, add the onion, herbs and spices and 2 teaspoons salt. Pour in water to cover (at least 2½ quarts but not more than 3 (3 l.)). Bring gently to the boil, then lower heat and allow to simmer very gently for 2 hours. The kettle or casserole must be closely covered.

Prepare the kidneys, and half an hour before the mutton should be ready, fry them lightly in butter. Put in a separate 3 or 4 pint casserole. Sauté the mushrooms and put with the kidneys, and then add the wine. Open the meat kettle and take out about a pint of stock and add to kidneys and mushrooms. Cover meat again and gently stew kidneys and mushrooms for 10 minutes. Meanwhile cook or heat the asparagus separately and keep hot by adding a lump of butter, wrapping in foil and putting in the oven or warming drawer.

To thicken the gravy of the kidneys and mushrooms, mix ¼ lb. plain flour with ¼ pint cold water and pour most of the *boiling* gravy on to it. Stir well. Return it all to the casserole, stirring all the time. It will be almost solid. From the mutton and beef ladle more liquid, taking as little fat as possible, and stir into the mushrooms and kidneys until the sauce is slightly thicker than double cream: there should be about 1½–2 pints of it. Taste and season highly, adding lemon juice if you think it should be a little sharper. It should be dark and rich.

Lift the mutton and keep hot.

Carve the beef quickly into neat, thick slices. Arrange these round the edges of a very large serving dish. Pour the sauce with mushrooms and kidneys over; set the leg of mutton in the centre, sprinkle with parsley and capers, and lay the asparagus spears in twos round the dish.

This looks and tastes superb but is difficult to prepare and serve single-handed. I do it like this:

I cook both joints and make the thickened casserole of kidneys and mushrooms the day before I want the dish; I finish the sauce and carve *both* joints, packing the neat slices into two pie dishes, keeping mutton and beef separate. They must be carved hot. I cover the meat in the pie dishes with the stock not used in the sauce, and closely cover with foil.

Before the dinner I cook the asparagus and allow the dishes of meat 30 minutes in an oven preheated to 250° F., gas mark ½–1, and heat the sauce with mushrooms and kidneys to boiling point, and allow just to simmer till wanted.

I arrange the slices of mutton in the centre of a very large flat dish (warmed) and the beef round it, sprinkle the mutton slices with parsley and capers, and pour the kidneys etc. in their sauce over the beef only; some of the sauce should spread under the mutton slices in the centre of the dish. The asparagus heads are arranged on the mushrooms, etc. in groups round the dish.

This takes about 5 minutes: the dishes can be brought straight to table or put back in the oven for a very few minutes.

The dish requires no vegetables but the asparagus and mushrooms. It wants large crusts of French bread, which should really be dipped in the gravy. Otherwise, potatoes in their jackets, without butter, are best.

Pepper Pot

This colonial dish, originally from the West Indies, in its early forms combines meat with shellfish, as island and coastal dishes sometimes do, with great subtlety and success. However, 'Philadelphia Pepper Pot', a famous American speciality, has lost the shellfish, using tripe with veal or lamb. This is an eighteenth-century English recipe.

For 10

    2 lb. (1 k.) leg of lamb, diced (all skin and bone removed)
    ½ lb. (240 g.) gammon rasher diced with the fat (only rind removed)
    1 small lobster or a crab (dressed, taken from the shell, and diced),
      or ¼ lb. (120 g.) shelled prawns, each cut in two or three pieces
    ½ lb. (240 g.) finely shredded cabbage
    1 small lettuce finely shredded
    a handful of chopped spinach or sorrel
    a tablespoon of finely chopped thyme
    3 onions, peeled and finely chopped
    2 or 3 very hot chilli peppers
    1 green pepper, finely sliced
    1 teaspoon cayenne
    1 teaspoon paprika
    12 peppercorns
    salt
    24 very small dumplings (see p. 96)
    tablespoon of lemon juice (or fresh lime if available)
    1 banana for each person
    plain boiled rice

Put the lamb, bacon and onions with the thyme, peppers, green pepper, cayenne, paprika, pepper and salt, to simmer in 3 quarts (3 l.) of water for ¾ hour. Then add cabbage, lettuce and spinach or sorrel and cook a further 20 minutes. Put in the shellfish, stirring gently, and the dumplings. After ten minutes, add the lemon or lime juice, and check seasoning. Add more cayenne if the dish not hot enough.

Serve with plain boiled rice and a banana for each person. The bananas should be peeled and sliced and served in small dishes or saucers. A little lemon juice should be squeezed over them to prevent discoloration. The pepper pot should have a great deal of almost clear, very hot (in both senses of the word) gravy, and the meat and vegetables should not be at all mushy. It is really a soup rather than a stew, and should be served in bowls or soup plates. It is very good for a supper party, as long as the guests are known to like things 'hot'.

Lamb in Claret

Serves 6

2½ lb (1¼ k.) fillet end of leg of lamb
2 onions
2 carrots
2 large glasses red wine
1 clove garlic
salt and pepper
2 rashers streaky bacon
a little parsley
some mixed herbs
piece of lemon peel
a little fat to fry

First cut the lamb into large oblong pieces, ten or twelve. Trim them well, removing all skin and fat. Cut the bacon into the same number of pieces, chop parsley and garlic together finely, roll the pieces of bacon in this, make a slit in each piece of mutton and push a piece of parsleyed bacon into it. Put the prepared meat, sprinkled with salt and pepper, in a casserole and pour the wine over it, add a piece of lemon peel and a bouquet of mixed herbs if possible. Fry the chopped carrots and onions lightly and put in the casserole on top of the meat. Fill up with water just to cover and put in pre-heated oven, 275° F., gas mark 2; cook for 4 hours.

Serve just as it comes from the oven.

About half an hour before serving, mushrooms or dried cepes may be added, or stoned olives, black or green, or a large green pepper, seeded and cut in strips, or ½ lb. (240 g.) skinned tomatoes or 2 or 3 courgettes, cut in halves longways.

Lancashire Hot Pot

The true Lancashire hot pot as cooked in the kitchens of Loughton Hall.

Serves 8

8 very good lean chump chops
3 sheep's kidneys
½ lb. (240 g.) mushrooms
2 oz. (60 g.) butter
2 oz. (60 g.) cooked lean ham
2 lb. (1 k.) potatoes

1 lb. (½ k.) onions
½ pint (3 dl.) stock
pepper and salt
pinch of cayenne
1 teaspoon mace
a little finely chopped thyme

Trim the chops, skin the kidneys, and cut them into rounds about ¼ inch (½ cm.) thick. Peel and slice the onions and potatoes and chop the ham finely. Then arrange everything in layers in the pot, first meat, then kidneys, mushrooms, ham, onions and potatoes, sprinkling the seasonings and herbs over. The last layer must be potatoes. Pour over the stock and put the butter in small pieces on the top. Cover with the lid closely and cook in the oven *very* slowly for about 3 hours. Then remove the lid and allow the top to take a nice rich brown colour. This should take about 20 minutes.

This dish should be sent to table in the pot.

Haricot of Mutton

A very old recipe, though this version comes from a late eighteenth-century collection. At this time it would not have had haricot beans, which had not then been introduced into England. The word 'haricot' had probably been mixed up with the word 'halicot', to chop finely. However, only slightly later recipes have white and red haricot beans.

Serves 8–10
       2½ lb. (1¼ k.) lean mutton (from the leg)
       2½ lb. (1¼ k.) onions
       1 lb. (½ k.) carrots and turnips
       thyme
       1½ pints (¾ l.) stock
       1 lb. (½ k.) haricot beans (dry)
       butter
       a glass or two of red wine
       1½ lb. (¾ k.) peeled, diced potatoes or peeled new potatoes
       piece of fennel
       cup of green or frozen peas
       seasoning

Soak the haricot beans overnight. Drain and cook them in salted water for 1 hour. Drain and reserve.

Chop into ½-inch (1-cm.) dice the very lean mutton. Fry in butter an equal quantity of chopped onion till just browning. Take out and put in the bottom of a deep casserole. Fry the mutton lightly in the onion liquor, then place it on top of the onion. Dice the turnips and carrots, brown in the same pan and add to the casserole, mixing them lightly with the mutton and onions. Add the cooked haricot beans, if these are to be used. Season well and add some sprigs of thyme. Fill up just to cover the meat and vegetables with a good meat stock – not necessarily mutton – and a glass or two, depending on the size of the haricot, of red wine. Cook very slowly in the oven for 2 hours. If no beans are to be used, as in the original recipe, add half the quantity of the meat in potatoes cut in ½-inch dice (or very small new potatoes whole) after 1½ hours. At this point put in a small piece of fennel. 10 minutes before serving, add a cupful or so of green peas.

This recipe was served with the gravy unthickened but slightly later recipes always had the mutton rubbed in flour before frying and some form of gravy browning added. Some had the stock poured off and thickened with roux before putting back over the meat.

In the early nineteenth century the same quantity of beans were added as of meat, and potatoes were omitted. Butter beans can also be used, and these are excellent bought ready in tins and then added only for the last 10 minutes. Green beans, such as lima, are also good.

Kidneys in Onions

A recipe from an inn at Southampton, where the onions were prepared in large trays, cooked in the bread ovens, and served to sailors for their supper. Each man poured some of his tot of rum into his bowl.

Serves 4

4 large onions	1½ pints (9 dl.) good brown stock
4 sheep's kidneys	(see p. 314)
seasoning	a glass of rum

Choose 4 large onions, well shaped. Peel them carefully, cut a slice off the top of each to make a lid. Hollow the onions out till a sheep's kidney will fit into each. Season the inside and put in skinned and cored kidneys, season again and put on lids of onion slices. Place all in a casserole, including the insides of the onions. Add stock to come half-way up the onions and place in a moderate oven to simmer for 1 hour. 20 minutes before serving add a glass of rum. Replace casserole lid and return to oven to cook a further half-hour.

Serve in individual bowls with an onion and some of the gravy and onion pieces in each. Traditionally eaten with a spoon and served with plenty of hot buttered toast.

Stewed Lambs' Kidneys

This recipe comes originally from Warwickshire. It was a great favourite of an erstwhile mayor of Warwick.

Kidneys must either be cooked quickly for a very short time or slowly for a very long one: in between they will be hard.

This recipe is very rich and the sauce is delicious. Serve with large triangular croûtons of very fresh hot toast, at least two croûtons to every portion. Allow 3 lambs' kidneys per person.

For 4

> 12 kidneys
> 2 large Spanish onions
> 4 large cooking apples (which should be as tart as possible)
> 1½ pints good stock
> a little thyme, parsley and marjoram or a bouquet garni
> seasoning
> flat tablespoon cornflour to thicken
> seasoned flour
> 3 oz. (90 g.) butter

Skin the kidneys, cut in halves and remove core, and dip in seasoned flour. Fry the kidneys quickly in about half the butter, put them in a large casserole with lid, add stock and herbs and put in oven to stew gently at 300°F., gas mark 2.

Meanwhile peel and cut up the onions into rings, and the apples each into about 16 pieces. Fry the onions slowly in butter for 5 minutes; then add the apples and fry 5 minutes more.

Add to the kidneys and reduce oven to 250° F., gas mark ½, and leave for 4 or 5 hours. Before serving, thicken the boiling gravy with the cornflour which you have mixed with a little water, and check the seasoning.

To Stew Mutton or Veal in Broth

'Chop ye meat in handsome pieces   put to it as much water as will cover it well   put in a little whole mace pepper and salt, a little nutmeg   a bundle of thyme and savory   an onion   a little ale or strong Beer   an Anchovy, put these in when it is near enough [cooked] and also ye top of a manchet grated or a little flour, some capers shred and some samphire if you have it and a little oister pickle.

Lay snippets in ye dish.'

This is a good, simple stew from Thomas Reaveley's MS. book, Edinburgh, about 1765, which needs no translation. It was thickened either with grated white bread or with flour. The capers are good; the samphire rarely obtainable. Pickled or canned oysters can be used or replaced by mushrooms lightly sautéed.

Blanquette of Veal, 1

A Victorian recipe from a London house.

Serves 4-6

1½ lb (¾ k.) good stewing veal	2 egg yolks
2 oz. (60 g.) flour	2 oz. (60 g.) butter
12 button mushrooms	2 large onions, cut in rings
2 carrots, sliced	a bay leaf, thyme, parsley
4 sticks celery, cut in rings	2 cloves
¼ pint (1½ dl.) double cream	

The veal, which must not have much skin, fat or gristle, should be cut in 1 or 2 large flat slices about ½ inch (1 cm.) thick. Place it in a large saucepan with sufficient cold water to cover it. Add the carrot, celery, onions and the herbs and cloves. Season to taste and cook gently for 1½ hours. 10 minutes before it is cooked, add mushrooms. Strain the meat and remove any skin or gristle. Keep hot with the mushrooms and other vegetables.

Make the sauce as follows. Melt the butter, add the flour, and cook for 3 or 4 minutes over a very low heat. Gradually add 1½ pints of the hot veal stock and allow to simmer for 5 minutes stirring from time to time. Beat the 2 egg yolks and the cream together in a bowl, then stir in ½ pint (3 dl.) of the white sauce. Pour the mixture back into the pan, stir in remainder of sauce and reheat, but do not allow to boil. Pour the sauce over the meat and serve very hot.

Blanquette of Veal, 2
(to use up cold cooked veal)

This is very good when I make it. My mother's rather bad cook used to try and make it; my mother said that her family in Cornwall had always done veal like this, as cold veal was so dull, and she could make it better herself, but the cook would leave.

If the joint is stuffed, the stuffing may be rolled into small balls, fried quickly for 3 minutes and served round the edges of the dish of blanquette of veal.

Serves 4

      about ¾ lb. (360 g.) cold cooked veal
      1 oz. (30 g.) flour
      ¾ pint (4½ dl.) milk
        or ½ pint (3 dl.) milk and ¼ pint (1½ dl.) stock
      1 oz. (30 g.) butter
      salt and pepper
      pinch of mace
      a little lemon juice
      tablespoon chopped parsley

Cut the veal into small cubes, removing skin and gristle. Melt the butter in a saucepan, stir in the flour very gradually over gentle heat until it is a smooth paste.

Take the pan off the heat and add the liquid, mixing well until smooth. Season and cook gently until it has boiled for 3 minutes, stirring all the time. Add the veal and stir for a further 5 or 6 minutes, till meat is hot through. Stir in the chopped parsley and a teaspoonful of lemon juice.

The dish is improved by the addition of ½ lb. (240 g.) mushrooms, sautéed separately.

Serve very hot with small triangular pieces of toast round the dish.

Bombarded Veal

This is a very grand dish for a lordly table. Mrs Glasse gives it without comment on the number of ingredients or the care and time needed to prepare it; nor does she mention, as she sometimes does, the cost. It is, however, the best sort of high cooking; the forcemeats are not overspiced, the various consistencies and flavours complement each other and the dish is extremely ornamental and very easy to serve. I quote her recipe and then give a simplified version which I make myself and which I can promise is worth the not very great trouble it involves. I have omitted the larding of the veal with lemon peel, which is not necessary, but may be done with a larding needle, if liked, and have also omitted the boiled forcemeat.

1747, Mrs Glasse:
'You must get a fillet of veal, cut out of it five lean pieces as thick as your hand, round them up a little, then lard them very thick on the round side with little narrow thin pieces of bacon and lard five sheeps' tongues (being first boiled and skinned) lard them here and there with very little bits of lemon peel, and make well-seasoned forcemeat of veal, bacon, ham, beef suet and an anchovy beat well; make another tender forcemeat of veal, beef suet parsley thyme sweet marjoram winter savory and green onions. Season it well with pepper salt and mace; beat it well, make a round ball of the other forcemeat and stuff in the middle of this, roll it up in a veal caul and bake it; what is left tie up like a Bologna sausage and boil it but first rub the caul with the yolk of an egg. Put the larded veal into a stewpan with some good gravy and when it is [cooked] enough skim off all the fat, put in some truffles and morels and some mushrooms. Your forcemeat being baked enough lay it in the middle, the veal round it and the tongues fried and laid between the boil'd forcemeat cut into slices and fried and throw all over [i.e. scatter the pieces of fried forcemeat over the whole dish]. Pour on them the sauce [in which the veal cooked]. You may add artichoke bottoms, sweetbreads and cockscombs if you please. Garnish with lemon.'

1969, Mrs Ayrton:
Serves 8

> 2½ lb. (1¼ k.) fillet of veal, cut in 10 fairly thick fillets
> 2 pints (12 dl.) very good stock, chicken, veal or beef, which has had all fat removed and which is well seasoned
> 2 small tins of tongue or one larger
> 4 rashers bacon
> 6 oz. (180 g.) white crumbs
> ¼ lb. (120 g.) cooked ham, lean
> ½ lb. (240 g.) mushrooms
> tin artichoke hearts or three large fresh artichokes, of which you will only use the bottoms
> 2 tablespoons parsley, 1 teaspoon thyme, 1 teaspoon marjoram (fresh if possible)

2 lemons
¼ lb. (120 g.) suet
small packet frozen chopped spinach
3 egg yolks
1 teaspoon mace
seasoning
1 medium onion, peeled and finely chopped

Prepare your stock the day before.

Open the tins of tongue and cut the solid meaty part into six thick portions, three from each tin, uncurling the tongue and cutting longways. Chop up the roots of the tongues and the jelly and put into a basin, adding half the crumbs. Mince two fillets of veal with the bacon and ham and add this with half the suet; season and stir well, adding the mace and plenty of pepper. Bind with two egg yolks. This is the pink forcemeat.

In another bowl put the rest of the crumbs and suet and add all the herbs finely chopped, and the onion cut very fine. Lastly stir in the defrosted spinach. One egg yolk will be enough to bind. This is the green forcemeat.

Make the first forcemeat into a ball and work the second round it. Press into a well-buttered round casserole and bake for 1 hour, covered. Lightly sauté the mushrooms cut into large slices. Cook and prepare the artichokes, cutting each large flat *fond* into 4, or open the can, drain, and heat gently in butter. Keep all warm.

Half an hour before forcemeat will be ready, dip the remaining 8 fillets of veal in seasoned flour, place them in warm but not yet boiling stock, which should be deliciously seasoned and ready for the table. Poach the veal lightly in a wide saucepan for 25 minutes or until tender. Just before it will be ready, take up the forcemeat and turn it out of the casserole; carefully cut it in two and lay the halves in the centre of a large flat dish so that the contrasting green and pink of the forcemeats are displayed. Lift the fillets of veal and lay round it, with the slices of tongue between. Pour some of the stock over the veal and tongue but not over the forcemeat. Put mushrooms and artichokes around the edge of the dish or between the meat and the forcemeat. Cover closely with foil and return finished dish to the oven. If temperature is not more than 200° F., gas mark ½, it will keep hot perfectly for at least half an hour while you collect your guests at the table and eat your first course. Have some quarters of lemon ready to put round the dish when you take it in, and serve the rest of the gravy separately.

A Simple Fricassée of Veal

Serves 4–6

 1½ lb. (¾ k.) veal fillet
 1 onion
 2 oz. (60 g.) butter
 1 level tablespoon flour
 1 clove
 1 bay leaf
 sprigs of thyme, parsley and marjoram
 pepper and salt
 ¼ pint (1½ dl.) double cream
 20 triangular croûtons of toast, crisp fried bread or puff pastry, as
  preferred

Cut the meat into ½-inch (1-cm.) cubes, removing all skin and fat, then put them in a saucepan with the onion stuck with the clove, and the herbs and bay leaf, with salt and pepper and water just to cover. Bring to the boil, skim well, then simmer until the meat is quite tender – about 40 minutes.

Melt the butter in a saucepan, stir in the flour, and cook gently for 5 minutes, but do not allow to brown. Remove the onion and herbs from the veal. Stir a little of the stock into the flour and butter, then add to the veal and remainder of stock. Stir for 3 minutes till smooth and creamy. Stir in the cream, check for seasoning, and serve with croûtons and with rice or creamed potatoes.

Ragoût of Veal or Lamb

An early nineteenth-century recipe.

Serves 6

 1 breast of veal or lamb
 1½ pints (9 dl.) good stock
 1 medium onion, peeled and stuck with 20 cloves
 3 carrots, diced
 pepper and salt
 3 or 4 sprigs of parsley and thyme
 1 sprig of rosemary
 2 bay leaves
 2 oz. (60 g.) butter
 flour

¼ lb. (120 g.) mushrooms, sauté
3 or 4 tablespoons cooked peas or broad beans

Cut the meat into 1-inch (2½-cm.) pieces, removing skin, gristle and as much fat as possible. Dip the pieces in flour and fry in the butter till a rich brown on all sides.

Bring the stock to the boil with the onions and herbs. Put in the meat and stew gently closely covered for 1½ hours. Brown the diced carrots in the pan in which the veal was fried, and add them after the meat has stewed for 1 hour. Stir from time to time. After 1½ hours the meat should be tender and the gravy brown and fairly thick. Remove herbs, onion and bay leaves, add mushrooms and peas or beans, check seasoning, cook a further 10 minutes and serve. If the gravy has not thickened in the cooking, it may be thickened with 2 teaspoons of cornflour in the usual manner. If on the other hand it has reduced too much, further stock may be added at any point in the cooking.

Ragoût of Veal

This is a much grander dish than the preceding one and intended for feasts and great dinners. The recipe comes from an eighteenth-century Scottish manuscript. A whole fillet of veal was cut into escalopes and, for the ragoût, a dozen veal kidneys and 2 sweetbreads were used.

The quantities given serve 4, and the dish is memorable.

4 escalopes of veal
¼ lb. (120 g.) forcemeat (p. 297)
1 veal kidney
¼ lb. (120 g.) button mushrooms
¾ pint (4½ dl.) good stock
2 bay leaves
a few sprigs of parsley and thyme
1 medium onion, peeled and finely cut
2 teaspoons flour
2 oz. (60 g.) butter
pepper and salt

Trim the escalopes of veal and flour them. Make the forcemeat into small balls, lightly floured. Skin, core and cut up the veal kidney, brown the pieces in butter and put in a stewpan. Sauté the mushrooms; fry the onion till light golden brown and add to the kidney with the bay leaves, herbs and pepper and salt. Put a small piece of butter into the pan in which kidneys, etc. were fried,

75

work in the flour, and then stir in stock and boil for 2 minutes till smooth and thick. Pour this over the kidneys and stew gently for 30 minutes, stirring from time to time.

After 30 minutes fry the forcemeat balls golden brown in butter and the veal escalopes for 3 minutes on each side so that they are cooked through and lightly browned. While they fry remove the herbs and bay leaves from the ragoût and pour it on to a flat dish. Lay the escalopes on it in the centre and the forcemeat balls around them. Serve very hot.

Curries

Meat, birds, fish, eggs, fruit and vegetables can all be curried, so it is difficult to know in what section to give this dish, but in England, curried lamb, pork or chicken are perhaps the most generally served. The curry came to England, of course, from India, where it had become a fad with the 'John Company' merchants, who vied with each other in eating the hottest possible curries. It was in demand among the passengers on the East Indiamen, and from them the taste spread to the seamen. Finally, it became a tradition, which exists to this day, in the Merchant Navy, where a curry, different on each day of the week, is invariably served for breakfast, following the porridge and preceding the bacon and eggs.

Indian curries vary very much according to the region from which the recipe comes: a Madras curry, for example, is quite different from a Bengal curry. In general, however, the English murder curries, partly because they use stale curry powder instead of freshly ground spices, and partly because a curry, with all its appurtenances, is a meal in itself, and not just a course to be preceded by a starting course, and followed by a pudding. It should always be served with plenty of plain boiled Patna rice, each long grain dry and separate, and little dishes of several of the following should be served with it:

Bombay duck
Mango chutney
Any other sweet chutney
Peeled and sliced apples, well sprinkled with lemon juice
Sliced bananas
Sliced tomatoes
Cucumber, cut in long thin sticks
Melon cut in cubes

All these contrast with the flavour of the curry spices and refresh the mouth from the hot sauce.

Curry Powder

A very good mixture of spices to replace prepared curry powder can be made as follows (quantities are enough for about 1½ pints (9 dl.) of the finished curry, which will serve 6):

1 teaspoon coriander seeds	½ teaspoon dried chillis*
2 teaspoons turmeric	pinch of cardamom
½ teaspoon cummin seeds	pinch of cinnamon
pinch of fenugreek*	12 cloves
½ teaspoon dry mustard*	½ teaspoon cayenne*
1 teaspoon powdered ginger*	
½ teaspoon fresh black pepper or	
12 peppercorns	

Put all the ingredients through a coffee grinder or pound them in a mortar, but they must all be as fine as medium coarse black pepper, and well mixed together.

For the curry

1½ lb. (¾ k.) top leg of lamb or pork, diced in ½-in. (1-cm.) cubes, all skin and fat removed
1 large onion, very finely sliced
1½ pints (9 dl.) good stock
flour
2 tablespoons seedless raisins or sultanas
2 bay leaves
3 oz. (90 g.) clarified butter (p. 126)

Rub the meat in seasoned flour, and fry the onion in clarified butter until soft but not brown. Transfer the onion to a saucepan, and fry the meat in the butter until brown on all sides. Add it to the onion, and pour over the stock. Put in the bay leaves and simmer gently for an hour. After an hour, stir in the prepared spices: first put in half the quantity, taste, and then add more as required. Add salt if necessary, and 2 tablespoons seedless raisins or sultanas. Simmer very gently for a further half-hour. Meanwhile, cook the rice and prepare the accompaniments. Serve the curry in a fairly deep dish, the rice in a snowy pile on a flatter one, and the accompaniments arranged in a circle round them, and let everyone help himself.

---

* If you want a very gentle curry, not at all burning to the mouth, leave out all these.

For really good curried hard-boiled eggs, or for curried prawns, make a thickened curry sauce, as follows.

For 4

> 1¼ pints (7½ dl.) good well-seasoned stock
> 2 oz. (60 g.) butter
> 1½ oz. (45 g.) flour
> spices as above
> salt

Melt the butter in a saucepan. Stir in the flour. When amalgamated, stir in the ground spices and add the stock. Stir well, boil for 3 minutes, add a little salt and taste. Pour this over the warm hard-boiled eggs, which should have been cut in halves crossways, and a small slice cut from the bottoms, so that they will stand in a flat dish. For a prawn curry, gently stir the prawns into the sauce and allow to boil for half a minute only.

Chicken or beef curry may be made in the same way as lamb or pork. Most curries are improved by the addition of raisins or sultanas, which give them a slight sweetness and variety of texture.

Diced cooking apples are also good cooked for 20 minutes with the meat; if they are included in the curry, they should not be served as an accompaniment.

The Hams of the English Counties

The Victorian Englishman who considered himself to live well expected a ham on the sideboard at breakfast and followed his eggs, kidneys, sausages and bacon or fish with a slice or two, and maybe a little cold game as well.

England has always been famous for her hams and almost every county has its own traditional cure.

The basic divergence in curing methods is whether a dry-salt cure or a pickle is used before the ham is smoked. In a few cures the ham is simply hung to dry without smoking. These hams are called 'green'. Apart from this, the variations lie only in the amount of sugar, treacle or honey used with the salt and saltpetre and the different herbs and spices added.

York Hams are traditionally dry-cured with salt, a little saltpetre and a little brown sugar for three weeks and then smoked over oak sawdust for at least two months. Green Yorkshire hams and Green Westmorland hams used also to be obtainable, and very fine they could be. They lay for four days in a special sweet cure which was a mixture of common salt, bay salt, saltpetre and black pepper with treacle poured over all. They were turned and rubbed twice a week for a month and then soaked for twenty-four hours in cold water and hung up to dry. Nowadays they are rarely, if ever, obtainable on the market, though a few may still be cured in this way on farms.

Suffolk hams are sweet-cured but smoked. Honey was considered more penetrating than either sugar or treacle and was preferred for this reason in some districts. It must, of course, have been used in early cures before sugar was available, when a certain sweet flavour to alleviate the general saltness of winter meat was particularly prized.

Bradenham hams, which are the finest Wiltshire hams, are cured according to a recipe dating from 1781. The hams are pickled in a sweet pickle, containing crushed juniper berries and various herbs and spices, and are then hung for several months while their special flavour develops. The pickle produces jet black outside rinds.

In the nineteenth century Gloucestershire and Buckinghamshire hams were considered the best of all because the pigs in these counties fed almost wholly on beech mast which gave the hams a special nutty flavour. Nowadays hams from these counties are difficult to obtain.

In some sea-coast counties hams were smoked over dried seaweed, which was reputed to have given them a slightly sharp flavour and a very firm texture which was considered delicious.

Hams from specific counties cured by the traditional methods can still be obtained in certain London stores, in the best grocers' in the towns of each county, and sometimes in local markets. Some, however, can only be found in private houses where a farmer or landowner cures a few hams for his own use. It should be possible to buy York, Bradenham and Suffolk hams without much difficulty.

Cooked ham bought in a very good store can be tolerable, as long as it has not been canned and is cut, not too thinly, specially for each customer. But it is never as good as ham, or even gammon, which you cook yourself.

TO BOIL HAM OR GAMMON

Allow 30 minutes to the pound and 20 minutes more for pieces up to 5 lb. But a ham of 8–10 lb. should be cooked in 3½ hours. Test with a long skewer.

A sweet-cured or mild-cured ham does not require soaking before being boiled. Consult your grocer as to how salt the cure is likely to have made the meat, and soak for 12–24 hours accordingly.

Put the ham in cold water to cover with ½ lb. (240 g,) of soft dark sugar (or, even better, half dark sugar and half dark treacle) and 20 cloves, bring to the boil and keep gently boiling. It should do rather more than simmer but should not cook at a full, rolling boil. It will be even better if you use half beer, cider or red wine and half water.

Allow the ham to get cold overnight in the cooking liquid. Next day, remove and skin. Finish by dusting with browned crumbs or, even better, stick with a few more cloves, sprinkle thickly with brown sugar and put in an oven pre-heated to 400°F., gas mark 6 or 7, for 10 minutes, when the outside will be coated with a soft golden toffee.

A baked ham can be even better than a boiled one, as all the flavour is con-served. It is not worth while to bake a very small piece, but a piece of any size over 3 lb. (1½ k.) can be cooked in this way. A 4-lb. (2-k.) piece requires about ¾ lb. (360 g.) of flour to make the paste and should be baked for 1½ hours.

TO BAKE A CURED HAM

Soak a half ham or a piece of ham or gammon of 6–8 lb. (3–4 k.) for 6–12 hours. Take it out and dry it. Make a crust with 2½ lb. (1¼ k.) flour and water to mix – no fat – and be sure that the dough is fairly stiff, so that it does not pull easily into holes. Cut it in two pieces. Roll out the first about a quarter of an inch thick, into an oblong longer and wider than the ham, and lay the ham on it. Stick the top of the ham all over with cloves about an inch apart. Then spread the ham with golden syrup or brown treacle and then sprinkle with demerara sugar. Roll out the second piece of crust and place this over the ham. Press the crust gently down over the sticky surface, bring the bottom crust up to meet it and seal the two pieces well together, moulding with your hands so that the whole ham is enclosed. Place it on a baking tray and bake in a slow oven for 3 hours (300° F., gas mark 2). Do not let the crust burn, but it does not matter how brown it gets, as it is only to protect the ham. After 3 hours remove from oven and leave to cool in crust. When cool break off crust and throw away. The ham should be perfectly cooked, firm yet moist and covered with a dark brown glaze from the sugar and treacle. Serve with the cloves in place.

Neat squares of fresh or even well-drained tinned pineapple can be arranged on the ham between the cloves.

Essence of Ham

This extravagant but splendid basis for a rich brown sauce, particularly espagnole, was considered almost essential to really good cooking from the seventeenth to the nineteenth centuries. Here is how they made it in 1833 at the Thatched House Tavern.

2–3 lb. (1–1½ k.) lean raw ham cut into 1-in. (2½-cm.) pieces
3 or 4 carrots, cut into 1-in. (2½-cm.) pieces
3 onions, peeled and sliced
a little butter
1 quart (1 l.) very good brown or white stock
4 oz. (120 g.) mushrooms, coarsely chopped
6 cloves
3 or 4 sprigs each of parsley and thyme

Put the butter in a saucepan and melt gently. Add the ham, carrots and onions and fry, turning, till beginning to brown. Be careful they do not stick. Pour on the stock and add the other ingredients. Cover closely and simmer gently for 2–3 hours. Do not let it reduce by more than a quarter. Strain and keep in refrigerator or deep-freeze to be used in any brown gravy or sauce, or added to the gravy of stews and casseroles.

For immediate use, try the following gourmet's recipe for Braised Cooked Ham.

Braised Cooked Ham

For 4

8 slices of cold home-cooked ham or gammon (each slice should be about 3 in. (10 cm.) square and ⅛ in. (½ cm.) thick, and should be free of all fat)
6 oz. (180 g.) mushrooms, sliced and lightly sauté
¾ pint (4½ dl.) essence of ham (see previous recipe)
2 teaspoons of cornflour
1 glass medium sweet sherry
1 tablespoon very finely chopped parsley

Butter a flat casserole and arrange the slices of ham just overlapping in it; or butter a cocotte dish for each person and lay 2 slices of ham in each. Sprinkle the mushrooms on top. Closely cover with foil. Stand the dish or cocottes in a baking tray with ¾ in (2 cm.) of warm water and bake in the oven at 350° F., gas mark 4, for 30 minutes.

Meanwhile bring the ham essence to the boil, and, unless it is as thick as heavy cream, thicken it by stirring the cornflour into a little cold water, pouring it in and stirring rapidly until the essence is smooth and semi-transparent.

Check the seasoning, add the sherry. Pour this over the ham and mushrooms so that the slices are well covered. Sprinkle thickly with parsley and serve with creamed potatoes. Broad beans are particularly good with this.

Ham in Cream

For 4

8 slices of cold home-cooked ham or gammon (each slice about 3 in. (10 cm.) square and ⅛ in. (½ cm.) thick, and trimmed of all fat)
6 oz. (180 g.) of mushrooms, sliced and lightly sauté
½ pint (3 dl.) good white sauce, rather thick
¼ pint (1½ dl.) thick cream
2 glasses white wine
2 oz. (60 g.) butter
2 tablespoons grated Parmesan cheese

Cook the slices of ham with the mushrooms as in the preceding recipe. Meanwhile make or reheat the white sauce and season highly. When almost but not quite boiling stir in the white wine and finally the cream. Pour over the ham. Sprinkle thickly with cheese. Dot with a little butter and brown for a few moments under a very hot grill. Serve at once.

Ham Stuffed with Apricots

This recipe probably originally came from Oxfordshire, where the famous Moor Park strain of apricots was developed. It is one of the best cold luncheon dishes in the world.

For 8–10, or to serve twice

4–6 lb. (2–3 k.) sweet-cured ham or gammon
½ lb. (240 g.) fresh apricots, not too ripe
¼ lb. (120 g.) fresh white breadcrumbs

3 oz. (90 g.) blanched almonds, fried to a pale golden colour
1 lb. (½ k.) plain flour (for the ham crust)
10–20 cloves
¼ lb. (120 g.) demerara sugar
2 oz. (60 g.) golden syrup or treacle

Cut the bone out of the piece of ham. Make the crust in which it will bake as in the recipe on p. 80, using about 1 lb. (½ k.) of flour for a 4–6 lb. (2–3 k.) piece of ham. Cut the apricots away from their stones and put them in a saucepan with 2 tablespoons of water. Cook for 4 minutes to free the juice a little. Remove from heat and stir in breadcrumbs. Work the mixture together and press it into the hole in the ham. If not firm, tie the ham round with string. Spread with treacle, sprinkle a little sugar, and stick with cloves, lay in the crust and cover firmly.

Bake for 1½ hours (see p. 80). When you have broken away the crust, stick the top of the ham with almonds between the cloves. The apricot stones may be cracked and their kernels used (though not, of course, fried), if preferred.

Ham Mousse

A luncheon dish. This is a very good nineteenth-century recipe for using up cold ham.

Serves 6–8
1 lb. (½ k.) lean cooked ham, finely minced
1 oz. (30 g.) gelatine (powdered)
2 eggs
½ pint (3 dl.) white sauce
¼ pint (1½ dl.) sherry
nutmeg
salt and pepper

Blend the egg yolks with the cooled white sauce. Reheat gently without allowing to boil, as the mixture curdles easily, season with a little salt, plenty of pepper and nutmeg, and add sherry. Dissolve the gelatine in a tablespoon of hot water and stir into the sauce. Then add the minced ham. Remove from the heat, stir well, and when cold, fold in the stiffly whipped whites of the 2 eggs. Place in a mould and set in the refrigerator. Turn out when cold.

Ham Toasts

Cut very small, these were served as a savoury; larger, a late supper dish.

> ½ lb. (240 g.) minced cooked ham
> 4 eggs
> pepper
> 1 tablespoon chopped parsley
> 1 oz. (30 g.) butter
> 4 rounds fresh hot buttered toast

Beat the eggs well. Melt the butter in a thick saucepan. Stir in the minced ham, then add the beaten eggs and the pepper, and stir well. Hold just off heat, and stir until there is no liquid egg visible and the consistency is just solid but creamy. Have ready 4 rounds of hot buttered toast, pile each with the ham and egg mixture, sprinkle with parsley and serve at once.

Ham Loaf

Cold: very good picnic dish. Hot: excellent for lunch if served with a good cheese sauce.

> 1½ lb. (¾ k.) cooked ham with not too much fat
> 3 oz. (90 g.) white breadcrumbs
> 1 tablespoon finely chopped parsley
> ¼ pint (1½ dl.) milk
> 2 eggs
> 1 teaspoon mace
> salt and black pepper
> a little butter

Mince the ham and mix with the crumbs, parsley, mace and seasoning. Stir in milk and the well-beaten eggs. Well butter a basin or soufflé dish and press mixture in firmly and dot the top with pieces of butter. Stand in a baking tray of water and bake in oven preheated to 300° F., gas mark 2–3, for 45 minutes. Turn out carefully if wanted hot, or for a picnic transport in cooking dish and turn out on arrival.

2 · THE TRADITION OF THE SAVOURY PIE

2. *The Tradition of the Savoury Pie*
There are a world of other bak'd Meats & Pies, but for as much as whosoever can do these, may do all the rest, because herein is contained all the art of seasonings, I will trouble you with no further repetitions.

GERVASE MARKHAM

When Gervase Markham wrote this in 1615, it was inconceivable that the table at any feast, or any grand occasion, should be without its pies and pasties.

The meat pie attained its full perfection only in England and held its pride of place from the Middle Ages until the nineteenth century. Originally, no doubt, it was evolved as a splendidly convenient way of eating meat in gravy before the fork was in general use: a cold pie where the stock was jellied was, of course, particularly easy to eat with the fingers. Most, if not all, early pies were 'raised': recipes speak of 'raising' the 'coffin', i.e. the bottom and sides of the pie, and there is never any mention of the use of a pottery dish: usually the only stipulation about the crust is that it should be of 'your finest paste'.

The medieval pie was a feast day dish, and it was expected to be very rich and full of delicious titbits; whatever the main meat or fish ingredients, recipes generally called for at least three or four of the following: cockscombs, artichoke bottoms, truffles, chicken livers, veal sweetbreads, kidneys, oysters, mushrooms, 'raisins of the sun', prunes, dates, currants, apples or pears, and orange or lemon peel, apart from herbs and spices.

Batalia Pye, for which the earliest extant recipe is in *The Compleat Cook* (1655), was very popular and contained 4 game pigeons, 4 ox palates, 6 lamb's stones, 6 veal sweetbreads, 20 cockscombs, 4 artichoke bottoms, 1 pint oysters, marrow of 3 bones, butter, gravy, lemons, mace and seasoning. The name Batalia comes from the French *béatilles*, which meant small delicious ingredients, in fact titbits.

The gravy, generally poured in after the pie was baked, required claret, white wine, and a combination of three or four of the following: rose water, vinegar, gravy, cream and eggs. Very strangely, to our taste, almost all recipes call for 'Sugar: a great store'.

It seems that our forebears customarily accepted and enjoyed a combination of savoury and sweet flavours, and considered that meat and even fish could happily be predominantly sweetened rather than seasoned mainly with salt. Today, we are so convinced that meat must always be savoury that we seldom combine sweetening with it, beyond the point of serving certain fruits with meat and birds, or putting a few raisins or prunes in our forcemeats, a teaspoonful of sugar in certain sauces, and a touch of chocolate in one or two dishes of dark game.

I have faithfully made Gervase Markham's Chicken Pye, and it is very sweet, rather too rich with butter, and all flavour of the chickens is lost. In fact it is very like eating chicken with a slightly sharp but very sweet mincemeat. His recipe, too long to give here in full, includes currants, raisins, prunes, cinnamon, sugar, mace and salt, and for the added liquor white wine, rose water, sugar, cinnamon and vinegar with egg yolks and the pie crust candied over with rose water and sugar.

His Herring Pye I have never dared to try. It consists of white pickled herrings, boiled, skinned and boned, raisins, a few pears, currants, sugar, cinnamon, dates and butter, baked in a crust, to which is added verjuice (i.e. unfermented grape juice), sugar, cinnamon and butter. The crust, here too, is candied over with sugar and the sides of the pie are to be trimmed with sugar.

By the end of the seventeenth century it seems that the division between sweet and savoury became accepted. Pies were still treasure chests of favoured titbits, but the raisins, sugar and rose water were generally omitted. Writing about eighty years later than Markham, Mrs Anne Blencowe in her *Receipt Book* gives two pies which contain no sweetening, and the redoubtable Mrs Glasse, fifty years later still, in the mid eighteenth century, gives fifteen or so pies, of which only the egg pie contains currants and rose water.

Here is Gervase Markham's recipe for a 'Minc'd Pye':

Take a legge of mutton and cut the best of the flesh from the bone and parboyle it well. Then put to it three pounds of the best Mutton Suet: shred it very small, . . . season with Salt, Cloves and Mace: then put in good store of Currants, great Raisins and Prunes . . . a few Dates sliced, and some Orange peel sliced . . . then all being well mixt together put it into a coffin (raised pie crust) or divers coffins and so bake them; and when they are served up, open the lids and strew store of Sugar on top of the meat and upon the lid. And in this sort you may also bake Beef or Veal. . . .

In fact, a very early recipe for mince pies, almost as we know them today. I have made up a small quantity exactly as here, using lean beef rather than mutton, and it was very good indeed, rather sweeter than most present-day recipes. Most, if not all, mincemeat recipes until the twentieth century included a little chopped meat, sometimes raw, sometimes cooked; nowadays it is usually omitted, but some people still prefer to add it.

There is no doubt that late in the nineteenth century the meat or game pie began to lose its importance, and this was partly because the potato, which did not become popular in England until the second half of the eighteenth century though in Ireland it had been a staple food for a hundred years, gradually rendered pastry with meat redundant. True, potatoes were, and still are, very often served with a pie, but the real point of the pie is that it is a complete and self-contained dish, needing no accompaniments.

Recipes for pies from the sixteenth century until today show that there has been a tendency for the amount of crust to diminish and for lighter pastries to be used. Raised pies have become rare: pies are generally made in a dish, and more and more often the dish is not lined but only covered with pastry and the recommended thickness of the lid is much reduced. Only two types of pie remain constant and are to be found in pubs, canteens and grocers' shops all over the country: the factory-made raised pie, always of pork or veal-and-ham-with-egg, and the steak or chicken pie, also factory made.

They are a far and sad cry from the great pies of the past: one of which made the news in the *Newcastle Chronicle* of 6 January 1770:

Monday last was brought from Howick to Berwick, to be shipp'd to London, for Sir Hen. Grey, bart., a pie, the contents whereof are as follows: viz. 2 bushels of flour, 20 lbs. of butter, 4 geese, 2 turkies, 2 rabbits, 4 wild ducks, 2 woodcocks, 6 snipes, and 4 partridges; 2 neats' tongues, 2 curlews, 7 blackbirds, and 6 pigeons; it is supposed a very great curiosity, was made by Mrs Dorothy Patterson, housekeeper at Howick. It was near nine feet at circumference at bottom, weighs about twelve stones, will take two men to present it to table; it is neatly fitted with a case, and four small wheels to facilitate its use to every guest that inclines to partake of its contents at table.

While the Tudors were on the throne of England and for a considerable period after, on Fridays, on certain other Fast Days and throughout Lent no meat was eaten. These, and indeed, for a time, Saturdays as well as Fridays, were made statutory fish days. Fast Days were observed on pain, not only of religious, but of secular penalties also: only children and the sick might have a little meat. Old cookery books make it very clear that the lack of meat pies and pastries was considered a serious deprivation, especially when guests had to be entertained on a fish day. Meatless pies were evolved, some very elaborate indeed, such as Markham's recipe for Herring Pye (described above) and his Ling Pye composed of the soaked jowl of a salted ling (the ling, now not often available, was a very large fish of the cod type, 3–4 feet long), shredded and mixed with chopped herbs and the yolks of a dozen hard-boiled eggs, seasoned with pepper, cloves and mace, and laid in a 'coffin' with 'great store of sweet butter, so as it may swim therein'. The pie is covered and baked and then through a vent hole left in the lid, grape juice, sugar, cinnamon and butter, previously boiled together, are poured. The lid is spread over with the same mixture and then 'scraped over with good store of sugar'. Markham describes it as an extraordinary and special Lenten dish; and so, indeed, it must have been.

Other pies, however, such as Mrs Glasse's Egg Pie and the Kentish Pudding Pies which were proper to Ash Wednesday, are still made in England today, the recipes only slightly altered. Both are given here in the chapters Egg Dishes and Hot Puddings.

In earlier times a pie was often partly cooked with a false lid made of flour and water crust, which was broken away and replaced by the rich pastry lid, just as we replace foil with pastry today. This was necessary where enormous pies were made, since their contents would take so long to cook that any pastry would harden. Such a pie was the Gloucester Royal Pie, part of the city's tribute to the throne from the time of Richard III to Queen Victoria. It was made of lampreys caught in the Severn, crayfish and truffles, with many other ingredients, all set in aspic jelly. The crust was decorated with crayfish set on golden skewers and with a gold crown and sceptre. Four golden lions supported the dish, and there was a banner with the arms of Gloucester. The whole weighed 20 lb.

Since present-day tastes prefer pies made in pie dishes with slightly lighter and thinner crusts than those suggested by the earliest recipes we have, it is, in general, best to cook the contents of the pie in the dish in which it is to be served, with a cover of foil or double greaseproof paper. It is essential that the contents of all pies should be *arranged* in the dish, so that different ingredients are evenly distributed and appear when the pie is opened in separate well-cooked pieces, amalgamated by gravy, sauce or jelly. They must never be a jumbled mass turned into the pie dish from casserole or saucepan.

If the contents of the pie are cooked before the crust is put on, they must also cool before it is added, at least till they are no more than tepid, as otherwise the steam makes the raw pastry soggy and heavy. If possible, leave time for them to cool without removing the foil, so that the condensing steam drips back from it into the pie and none of the flavour or aroma is lost.

The meat, covered with foil, can be cooked very slowly, until exactly tender but holding its shape and consistency, and can be allowed to cool overnight if this is convenient, or for an hour or two. The pastry lid, on the other hand, when put on, can be cooked fast, so that the pastry is light and crisp, and if the completed pie is not to be eaten at once, can later be put into a rather cool oven to heat through for about three quarters of an hour before serving. This does not harm the cooked pastry, which can be protected by foil or greaseproof paper if it seems to be getting too brown during the reheating.

Until the seventeenth century, pastry was almost always made with melted butter and hot water. It was what we call 'raised pie' pastry. In Sir Kenelm Digby's *The Closet Opened* (1669), however, he refers to My Lady Lasson's mince pies and says: 'Her finest crust is made by sprinkling the flower (as much as it needeth) with cold water, and then working the past[e] with little pieces of raw butter in good quantity, so that she useth neither hot water nor melted butter in them. And this makes the crust short and light.' This is the earliest reference I have found to a short crust, made more or less as we make it today.

Early recipes often suggest half suet and half lard for rough puff pastry, but this in general produces a harder crust with a slightly greasy texture, which is less appealing today than one made with half lard and half butter or with all butter.

Pasties, cold pies and raised pies are described separately, as are steamed meat and game puddings with suet crusts. It should be remembered that a suet crust is the easiest and quickest of all pastries to make, and that a steak and kidney pudding is not a 'heavier' or more solid dish than a pie or a casserole of steak and kidney served with a helping of mashed or boiled potatoes. A meat or game pudding can be cooked one day and reheated the next without suffering in any way.

For anyone who wants to prepare dishes for a day or two ahead, pies and puddings are inimitable.

Pastry Making

Do not be afraid of making pastry. It is true that quantities must be fairly accurately measured; butter must never be oiled or even very soft; you must work rather quickly and use your hands lightly and 'rest' the dough as suggested in one or two of the recipes; but on the other hand most pastries take only a few minutes to make and none takes more than half an hour. Pastry making leaves you with some floury working surfaces to clean up, so that it is more worth while to make a pie, an open tart and some tartlets all at the same time.

Again, do not be afraid to buy the excellent frozen pastry on sale everywhere. The puff pastry in particular is so good that it is hardly worth going to the trouble (and it is a trouble) of making your own, except now and again to prove to yourself how good your own pastry is. The short pastry is also very good indeed, but short pastry is, of course, much quicker to make. Frozen pastry keeps for weeks in the freezing compartment of a refrigerator with 3-star marking, and if you always stock a packet you can make a quiche or a cheese or onion tart in ten minutes plus twenty minutes baking time, as a first course or a lunch or supper dish or a jam or treacle tart for pudding, if you have unexpected guests.

Successful pastry depends on careful baking and needs a preheated oven which has reached the right temperature before it is put in. All pastry needs a fairly hot oven, and puff pastry needs a very hot one.

Note the required oven temperature carefully, and preheat to it. Pastry cooked in too slow an oven will sink, and will be heavy and tough. If the oven is too hot it will brown on the outside while still remaining soggy inside.

Almost all open tarts, flans and small tartlets are better if the cases are baked 'blind', i.e. empty, and filled when they are cool. They can then be put back in the oven while the contents cook slowly, if this is necessary. If there seems danger of the pastry edge burning, a piece of foil can be laid over. If tarts are cooked with a filling in place, the bottom is apt to be soggy.

Pies, sausage rolls, turnovers, etc. look much more professional and generally attractive if they are 'gilded' by being brushed over with beaten yolk of egg. Even brushing over with milk improves the appearance.

Always make pastry in a cool place; use cool utensils and very cold water, except of course in the case of choux and raised pie pastry.

The richness of the pastry depends on the fat content. Too little fat will make it dry and crumbly, too much will make it oily and hard to handle.

The quantity of water used is of great importance. Too much will make the pastry hard and leathery. Too little will make it crumbly and incapable of holding its shape. Add water gradually, and mix each spoonful in well before adding more.

The less the dough is handled the lighter the result will be. Always roll pastry lightly. If force is used the paste will be heavy. If rolling is difficult, leave the dough to rest in a cool place, when it will regain its natural elasticity.

A rich short pastry dough cannot be handled easily if rolled out very thin. Roll a little thicker than you want it and lay it in your flan tin and mould it gently by hand over the bottom and up the sides. For the lid of a pie, it must be at least one eighth of an inch thick, and must be laid on and pressed firmly into the supporting strip which is laid round the edge of the pie dish, without stretching and before trimming the outside edge.

Puff pastry, if used for an open tart, often puffs very much when the foil and beans used to weight it are removed so that it may brown. If this happens, the centre can be cut round with the tip of a sharp knife just inside the edge of the flat tin and a layer of pastry lifted off. Underneath the pastry will be white and soft. Cut a little away, being careful not to make a hole right through and put the tin back in centre of oven for five minutes to crisp and brown this exposed centre slightly. Put the removed piece upside down on another tin and put back also. This can be lightly laid on as a lid when you fill the tart, or can be cut in half and the two halves sandwiched with jam or jam and whipped cream, as a separate sweet.

NOTE: The recipe for raised pie pastry is given in the section on Raised Pies (p. 112).

Rough Puff Pastry

Quantities for a small pie or tart, enough for 3 or 4

> 8 oz. (240 g.) self-raising flour
> 4 oz. (120 g.) butter
> 2 tablespoons very cold water
> ½ teaspoon salt

Sift together the salt and flour. Cut the butter into the flour in small pieces no bigger than marbles. Do not rub the fat in. Mix to a stiff dough with cold water. Roll the dough out on a floured board.

Fold the pastry by bringing the side edges into the middle, and then the bottom and top edges to the middle. Press the edges together so that an envelope is formed, keeping the air inside. Leave the pastry to rest in a very cold place for 10 minutes, and then repeat the folding and rolling process. Rest again in a cold place, then roll out. Bake near the top of the oven, 400°F., gas mark 6, for 15–20 minutes.

This pastry is very good for meat pies or sausage rolls when puff pastry takes too much time. It should be used as quickly as possible after being made.

Puff Pastry

> 12 oz. (360 g.) plain flour
> 8 oz. (240 g.) butter
> ½ teaspoon salt
> about 3 tablespoons very cold water

This pastry must be made in a cool place, with cold utensils, and should be handled as little as possible.

Carefully sieve the flour and the salt into a basin. Now cut the butter into thin slices (a ½-lb. (240-g.) piece should cut into eight slices). Fluff up the flour in the basin with a fork, so that it does not lie heavily. Put each piece of butter into it in turn and well coat it with the flour.

Lightly flour a pastry board and roll out separately each slice of butter quite thinly. Place on a cold plate in a pile.

Next form the flour in the bowl into a light dough with very cold water. Use a knife for mixing, and add the water very gradually. Be very careful not to put in too much; the paste must be soft enough to roll easily, but it must not be at all sticky. You will probably find you have to use your hands to form the paste into a ball, but do not handle it more than you need.

Roll out the dough *as thinly as possible*, then cover the centre part of the dough with the rolled out butter; this should use four of the slices, leaving an equal space of uncovered pastry on either side. Fold over the plain pastry on the right side so that it covers the butter, and place the remaining four slices of butter on the piece of pastry you have folded over, and cover it by folding the plain piece of pastry over from the left side. Now roll it out, rolling away from you. Use the rolling pin lightly, giving short rapid rolls, and always rolling forward, not backward. Never roll right off the pastry – stop before you get to the edge. This is important, as the object is to keep the air in the paste, and if you roll off the edge you naturally push it out. Leave the pastry for 10 minutes in a cool place.

The pastry is now a long oblong shape. Cut it in half, put one half aside on a cold plate, and fold and roll the other piece in the same way as you did before – folding from either side to the centre, and then rolling out to an oblong shape. Roll the second half in the same way. Repeat the process of folding and rolling on the first piece; then put it aside and do the same with the other half. Leave for 10 minutes. Then put the two pieces on top of each other on the board and cut through both, making two halves again. Roll each piece out thinly, fold and roll out once more, lay one on top of the other again, roll out finally, and it is ready.

Bake in the oven at 450–500° F., gas mark 8–9, for 15–20 minutes.

This pastry will keep uncooked in the refrigerator for a few days if wrapped in greaseproof paper or foil.

Puff pastry is used for vol-au-vent, mince pies and all fancy dishes where a very light pastry is needed. It is troublesome to make, but no other pastry can quite replace it for party dishes.

Short Pastry

These quantities will make a large pie and a flan or some tarts.

1 lb. (480 g.) plain flour	a good pinch of salt
8 oz. (240 g.) butter	¼ pint (1½ dl.) very cold water

Mix the salt with the flour and aerate it lightly with the fingers. Then rub in the butter lightly with the tips of the fingers, and continue rubbing it in until the mixture looks like fine breadcrumbs and there is no dry flour left in the basin. Add cold water very gradually, until you have a fairly soft dough. The dough should be soft enough to roll easily, but it must not be at all sticky – wet pastry means that it will be hard. You may need a little more or less water. Roll out on a floured board.

This pastry will keep for a few days if it is wrapped in greaseproof paper and left in a cool place. It will keep for a week in a refrigerator but will then be too hard to work and must be left for several hours at room temperature to soften again.

Baking should be in an oven at about 425° F., gas mark 7, for 15–20 minutes.

Short pastry is perhaps the best all-purpose crust.

Flaky Pastry

> 8 oz. (240 g.) self-raising flour
> 6 oz. (180 g.) butter
> 1 teaspoon lemon juice
> ½ teaspoon salt
> about 3 tablespoons water (iced if possible)

Sieve the flour and salt into a bowl. Rub into it 1 oz. (30 g.) of butter and add the lemon juice. Add the water slowly, stirring all the time until a smooth paste is formed. Roll it lightly on to a floured board. Dab the pastry with small pieces of butter with a knife blade. Sprinkle with a pinch of flour.

Fold the pastry towards you and pinch the edges so that it forms an envelope. Roll again, rolling away from the joined edge, and towards the fold so that the air is not forced out. Repeat the rolling and folding three times, until all the butter has been used.

Bake in the oven at 450° F., gas mark 8, for about 15–20 minutes.

This pastry may be used for a meat pie in place of raised pie crust, though it cannot, of course, be 'raised' but is simply used as a lid. It is also excellent for canapés, cheese straws and fruit pies.

Milk Pastry

> ½ lb. (240 g.) self-raising flour   pinch of salt
> 6 oz. (180 g.) butter   about 3 tablespoons of milk to
>   mix

Mix the salt with the flour and sift it. Rub in 4 oz. (120 g.) of butter lightly with the tips of the fingers, until it is evenly distributed. Then add just enough cold milk to form a rather stiff dough. Flour the remainder of the butter and roll, it thinly. Roll out the dough and put the butter on it, sprinkle with a little more flour, fold over and roll out. Then bake at once in the oven at 450° F., gas mark 8, for 15 to 20 minutes.

This pastry is both simple to make and very rich. It is particularly good for flans which are to be eaten cold, since it retains its crispness without becoming hard.

Cheese Pastry

> ½ lb. (240 g.) self-raising flour
> 6 oz. (180 g.) butter
> 2 oz. (60 g.) grated cheese (Parmesan if possible, but Cheddar is good)
> ½ teaspoonful mixed salt and pepper

Mix the salt and pepper with the flour, and rub in the fat with the fingertips until the mixture looks like fine breadcrumbs. Add enough cold water to make a stiff paste. Roll out on a floured board, sprinkle with cheese, fold over, and repeat the process. Bake in oven, 400° F., gas mark 6.

Use for savoury tarts, flans or patties.

Suet Crust

This is the basic recipe for all suet puddings, sweet or savoury.

> ½ lb. (240 g.) prepared shredded suet
> 1 lb. (½ k.) self-raising flour
> 1 teaspoonful of salt
> water to mix

Pour the flour into a mixing bowl. Add the suet and salt and lightly mix all together. Slowly pour in up to ¼ pint (1½ dl.) cold water and mix, add a little more and mix again until the dough is firm and will form a single mass, leaving the sides of the bowl clean. Sift a little flour over it and roll out lightly on a board to about ½–¾ inch (1–1½ cm.) thickness for puddings, thinner for apple dumplings, or in small balls for boiled dumplings for stews.

Suet Dumplings

For 4–6

> ½ lb. (240 g.) self-raising flour
> 3 oz. (90 g.) shredded suet
> 1 teaspoonful of salt
> ¼ pint (1½ dl.) of milk and water

Mix the flour, salt and suet in a bowl and stir in the liquid gradually, making sure that the dough does not become wet and flabby. Shake some flour on a flat surface and roll small balls of dough about 1 inch (2½ cm.) across in it.

Drop these into the simmering stock 20 minutes before the meat should be ready. There should be room for them to cook without touching. If you want more than the saucepan of beef will take, steam for the same length of time in a steamer or in a colander, tightly covered with a lid or with foil, over a saucepan of boiling water.

Lift very carefully as they are apt to break. Arrange round the edges of the beef dish and sprinkle with parsley. Very few people have ever been able to resist dumplings, but they were particularly famous in Norfolk, where in the eighteenth and nineteenth centuries they were served in stews of duck or partridges at the supper tables of sporting gentlemen.

Chicken Pie

This is a recipe from a Somersetshire manor house and goes back to the eighteenth century and probably earlier. It is sometimes made there with double quantities in a very large dish or in two dishes for a luncheon party.

Serves 6 or 7

> 1 chicken, about 3½ lb. (1¾ k.)
> salt and pepper
> 2 or 3 hard-boiled eggs
> ½ lb. (240 g.) mushrooms
> 1 oz. (30 g.) butter
> 1 onion
> beaten egg for brushing over pastry
> 4 oz. (120 g.) lean bacon, in rashers or in 1 piece
> tablespoon chopped parsley
> 1 lb. (½ k.) puff pastry (p. 92),
>   *or* short pastry (p. 93) if preferred
> ½ pint (3 dl.) white stock

Cut the chicken into 8 or 10 small joints, or buy joints of roasting chicken and divide the larger ones. Season these with salt and pepper. Cut the hard-boiled eggs in quarters. Slice the mushrooms, and peel and slice the onion. Chop the bacon and the parsley. Roll out the pastry and lay a thin strip round the edge of the pie dish. Fill the dish with layers of the prepared ingredients, then pour in cold stock, well seasoned, so that it does not quite cover the top layer. Wet the strip of pastry on the dish rim with water. Cover with the rest of the pastry, pressing down and trimming the edges. Brush with beaten egg, and make a hole in the centre. Decorate with 3 pastry leaves and a rose. Bake in a moderate oven for about 1½ hours. Allow 20 minutes at 400° F., gas mark 6, for pastry to cook, then reduce to 275° F., gas mark 1. If the pastry browns too much, cover with foil or greaseproof paper. More hot stock can be poured in through the hole in the pastry before serving.

The crust is here put on the raw ingredients but the contents can be cooked first, covered, for 1¼ hours at 300° F., gas mark 2, cooled, the pastry added and cooked for 20 minutes at 400° F., gas mark 6.

Chicken and Steak Pie

This is a West Country recipe from a nineteenth-century collection.

Serves 6 or 7

1 lb. (½ k.) short pastry	2 oz. (60 g.) butter
1 roasting chicken, about 3½ lb. (1¾ k.)	a little flour
1 lb. (½ k.) good stewing steak	salt and pepper

Joint the chicken (or buy chicken joints) and fry in the butter, browning them on both sides. Cut the steak into small pieces, removing all fat, skin and gristle. Dust with seasoned flour and brown these also. Put the chicken and steak into a stewpan; just cover with cold water, add salt and pepper, simmer until quite tender, about 1 hour.

Thicken the stock with 1 tablespoon flour mixed with a little water and season well. Arrange in a pie dish and leave until cold. Then put the forcemeat balls (see below) on top of the meat, cover with short pastry and bake for half an hour in a preheated oven, 400° F., gas mark 6.

For the forcemeat balls:

2 oz. (60 g.) breadcrumbs	2 bacon rashers
teaspoon dried thyme	salt and pepper
pinch of parsley and sage	2 oz. (60 g.) butter
1 small onion, finely chopped	1 yolk of egg

Finely chop the bacon, add the breadcrumbs, seasoning, chopped parsley, thyme, and sage and finely chopped onion. Bind with egg yolk. Make into small balls, dip in flour and fry in butter, turning on all sides, for 3 or 4 minutes. Leave to get cold.

Game Pie

Serves 4–6

> 2 partridges,
>   *or* 1 and another small game bird *or* 1 pheasant
> 1 oz. (30 g.) butter
> 1 large onion
> 2 rashers bacon
> 1 pint (6 dl.) stock
> ½ lb. (240 g.) lean steak or veal
> sprig of thyme
> bay leaf
> pepper and salt
> 2 hard-boiled eggs
> ¼ lb. (120 g.) mushrooms
> 10 oz. (300 g.) short or flaky pastry,
>   *or*, for a cold pie, 10 oz. (300 g.) raised pie pastry (p. 112)

Joint the bird or birds, cut up the onion and fry in butter with the joints until all is lightly browned.

Cut the veal or steak into 1-inch (2½-cm.) pieces and brown them in the same pan. Cut up the rashers of bacon into ½-inch (1-cm.) strips. Arrange the veal in the bottom of a large pie dish. Place the birds with the onion, bacon, mushrooms (raw) and herbs on them. Season. Just cover with stock, closely cover with foil and simmer in the oven (300° F., gas mark 2) until tender, about 1 hour.

Remove and allow to cool. Put in the hard-boiled eggs. Add a little more stock to bring the liquid within half an inch of the top of the solid meat. Cover with pastry, decorate with a rose and three or five leaves, and bake in a preheated oven at 400° F., gas mark 6, for 20 minutes or till the pastry is well browned. Then reduce the heat to 250° F., gas mark ½, place the pie lower in the oven and leave to cook for a further 15 minutes.

This recipe makes an excellent cold game pie, particularly if 'raised pie' pastry, which is intended to be eaten cold, is used for the lid.

Mutton Pies

These small pies were a great favourite of King George V.

Makes 8–10 pies

2 lb. (1 k.) short pastry (p. 93)
1½ lb. (¾ k.) lean mutton from the top of the leg
1½ pints (9 dl.) good well-seasoned gravy
2 egg yolks
2 tablespoons chopped parsley
2 onions, skinned and chopped very finely

Remove all the skin and fat from the meat and chop it into ¼-inch (½-cm.) dice.

Line deep patty pans or individual soufflé dishes very thinly with short pastry. This is best done by cutting rough circles of pastry and moulding each over the bottom of an upturned tumbler which will just fit inside your patty pans or soufflé dishes, slip off the pastry, press into the patty pan and trim the top edge. Mix the mutton and onions together and fill. Add a little chopped parsley to each. Pour in the slightly thickened gravy, almost to the tops. Cover with rounds of pastry, and crimp the edges together. Make a hole in each with a skewer, gild with egg yolk and cook in a moderate oven, 325° F., gas mark 3, for about an hour. Remove the pies from the tins and serve very hot, each pie sprinkled with chopped parsley. They may be served in their pans if they seem very difficult to get out.

Mutton Pie with Apples

A traditional West Country recipe. Sometimes made with mutton chops and called Squab Pie, as the chops were about the size of young pigeons and the flavour combined with the apples was thought to be similar.

Serves 6 or 7

2 lb. (1 k.) very lean mutton, preferably fillet end of leg
2 lb. (1 k.) cooking apples
1 lb. (½ k.) onions
2 oz. (60 g.) butter
1 lb. (½ k.) short or rough puff pastry (pp. 93, 92)
2 cloves
3 or 4 sprigs of thyme
seasoning
1 tablespoon flour

Cut up the mutton in pieces about an inch (2½ cm.) square, discarding all skin and fat. Cut up the onions. Brown both slightly in the butter in a large heavy saucepan. Add cloves, thyme, seasoning, and the bone from the mutton. Just cover with water and simmer for 1½ hours. Pour off the stock and thicken with 1 tablespoon of flour mixed with a little water. Season and allow to cool.

Arrange the meat and onion in a pie dish in layers with the peeled and cored apples. Cut into thick slices. Pour in the stock, put on crust and bake at 400° F., gas mark 6, for 35 minutes.

Mutton and Turnip Pie

This is a very old recipe from St Germains in south Cornwall. It came to my mother from one of the daughters of a very large but well-to-do hunting family, who said that it was normally put on the table for a Saturday dinner when there had been hunting, with a couple of boiled fowls and piece of bacon at the other end and a great dish of fresh caught pollock or mackerel flanking it. The young sons and daughters who had been riding half the day tried to eat fast enough to have a helping of all three dishes. The pie would have been made in about four times the quantities given here.

Serves 4 or 5
> 2 lb. (1 k.) lean mutton, preferably top of leg
> 2 onions
> 1 lb. (½ k.) turnips
> 1 dessertspoon chopped parsley
> salt and pepper
> 1 oz. (30 g.) butter
> 1 oz. (30 g.) flour
> ¾ lb. (360 g.) rough puff pastry (p. 92)

Cut the mutton into 1-inch (2½-cm.) cubes, removing all skin, fat and gristle, and stew for 2 hours with the onions cut in quarters and the turnips in slices, in water just to cover. Remove from heat and allow to cool.

Arrange in a large pie dish and sprinkle with parsley. Slightly thicken the liquid in which the meat and vegetables cooked by making a roux with the butter and flour and stirring in stock in the usual way. Pour in enough of this for the meat just to appear above the gravy. Do not put on pastry till it stops steaming. Make a pastry rose with 3 leaves to decorate. Bake in a hot oven, about 400° F., gas mark 6, for 25 minutes.

A Wedding Supper all cold

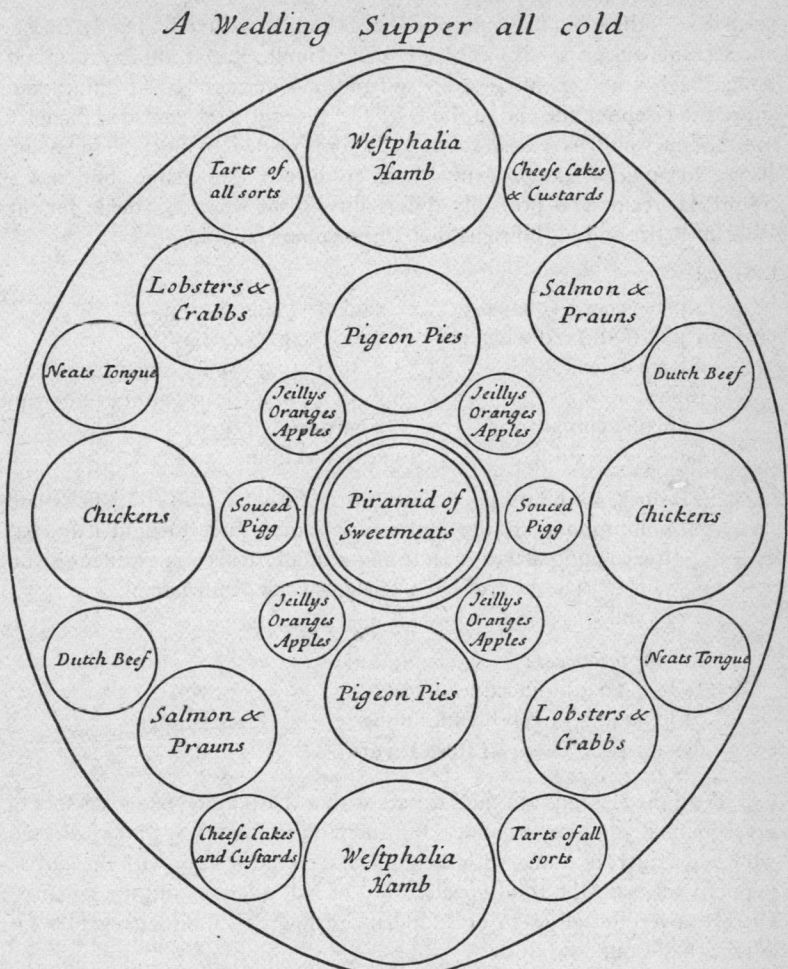

Squab or Pigeon Pie

The household books of Ingatestone Hall in Essex record that, in the week following Easter Sunday of the year 1552, '58 pigeons were taken'. These were from the great dovecote, which still stands. They would have been corn-fed. Nothing but fish, cheese and eggs had been eaten by family, guests and servants during the six weeks of Lent, and on the Easter Sunday roast and boiled beef, veal, capons, mutton and pigeons were served at dinner and supper to celebrate the end of the fast. The pigeons were considered choice meat. Some would have been roasted and some made into pies: the following recipe for pigeon pie probably dates from 150 years later, but was a traditional recipe and probably differs little from what was made for Sir William Petrie and his household at Ingatestone Hall.

Serves 8

4 pigeons or 8 squabs	rind of ½ lemon
1 pint (6 dl.) red wine	2 oz. (60 g.) sultanas
2 large onions	½ lb. (240 g.) small mushrooms
cloves	½ lb. (240 g.) lean ham cut in strips
12 peppercorns	3 hard-boiled eggs
salt	seasoned flour

1¾ lb. (⅞ k.) very good flaky pastry, using 1 lb. (½ k.) flour and ¾ lb. (360 g.) butter and a little lemon juice to bind it (p. 94) (frozen puff pastry – 1 large and 1 small packet – is excellent if you want to save the trouble of making your own pastry)
1 egg yolk

For the forcemeat:

½ lb. (240 g.) minced lean veal	2 egg yolks
½ lb. (240 g.) fresh breadcrumbs	black pepper
dessertspoon chopped fresh thyme	

Cut off all the legs close to the carcases with a sharp knife, using scissors to sever joints if you have difficulty. Put them on to stew in ½ pint (3 dl.) red wine and a quart of water, with the giblets, the onions stuck with the cloves, peppercorns, salt, the thinly peeled rind of half a lemon and the sultanas. Closely cover and allow to boil for half an hour, then simmer gently for another half-hour.

Meanwhile cut the birds in half along the breast bone with a sharp heavy knife: this is not difficult. Rub the halves with seasoned flour, and arrange them in a large pie dish, breasts upwards. The dish should be just large enough to hold them closely packed. Strain the giblet stock, taste and season further if necessary. Pour enough into the pie to come three quarters of the way up the dish. Cover with foil, and cook at 300° F., gas mark 2, for 1¼ hours.

Make the forcemeat balls of equal parts of minced veal and breadcrumbs. Season with finely chopped fresh thyme, black pepper and a little salt. Bind with the yolks of two eggs.

After the pigeons have cooked for 1¼ hours, remove from the oven, lift the foil and arrange the forcemeat balls, mushrooms, quartered hard-boiled eggs and strips of ham between the birds. Cook a further 15 minutes and then allow to cool.

Moisten the edge of the pie dish, put round it a fairly thick strip of pastry and moisten the top of this. Have the rest of the pastry rolled out a little less than a quarter of an inch (½ cm.) thick and at least an inch (2½ cm.) larger than the top of the pie dish. Lift it up, rolling it loosely over your rolling pin to do so, and lower it into position over the pie. Press firmly on to the moistened edge strip, decorate the edge with a fork, and make the centre rose and leaves in the usual way.

Gild with remaining egg yolk, put into the oven preheated to 400° F., gas mark 6, and cook until the pastry is well risen and browned, probably 30 minutes.

This pie can be kept and reheated when required. It should be served very hot, and any extra gravy left after filling the pie should be served separately.

Pigeon Pie

From Yorkshire.

Serves 5 or 6
> 2 pigeons
> ½ lb. (240 g.) rump steak
> 2 rashers lean bacon
> ¾ pint (4½ dl.) good brown stock
> 2 hard-boiled eggs
> seasoning
> ¾ lb. (360 g.) puff, rough puff *or* flaky pastry (pp, 92, 94)

Cut each pigeon into 4 pieces (breast with wings, legs with thighs), the steak into thin slices, carefully removing all skin and fat, and the bacon into strips. Put into pie dish in layers, seasoning each layer, and adding the eggs cut into quarters. Cover with the stock. Put on pastry and decorate with a rose and leaves. Bake in a hot oven at 400° F., gas mark 6, until the pastry is cooked (about 25 minutes). Then cover pastry lightly with foil, place pie low in the oven, reduce heat to 250° F., gas mark 1, and cook for a further 1½ hours.

A Double Crust Pie

    1 lb. (½ k.) suet crust (p. 95)
    1 lb. (½ k.) short pastry (p. 93)
    1 lb. (½ k.) rump steak cut into 6 thin slices
    1 large boiling fowl, jointed
    12 button mushrooms
    a little garlic or garlic salt and a bay leaf
    6 rashers of bacon, diced
    1½ pints (9 dl.) very good, highly seasoned stock, thickened with cornflour to make a good brown gravy

Take a pie dish, grease it well, and lay at the bottom a bay leaf and a very little crushed garlic or garlic salt. Next put in 6 thin slices of rump steak and put the chicken joints on them, seasoning well. Pack in a dozen small mushrooms and add the diced bacon. Fill up with half of the gravy, to which a little tomato purée may be added, if liked, and cover with a very thin suet crust (about ¼ inch, ½ cm.) which should be pressed down flat on to the meat inside the pie dish. Cover the dish closely with foil and bake the pie for 1½ hours at 350° F., gas mark 4. This inside crust keeps in all the flavour and will cook to a very light consistency, while the chicken joints will be tender.

Take out the pie, cut this dumpling crust into squares and pack them down among the chicken joints. Fill up the dish with the rest of the hot gravy, allow to cool a little, put the short-crust pastry over the pie dish in the usual way and return to the oven to bake at 425° F., gas mark 7, for another 30–35 minutes till the crust is crisp and brown. To serve, cut a slice out of the top crust, lift out a square of the dumpling paste, arrange a chicken joint, the piece of beef it cooked upon, some mushrooms and bacon, upon this square of paste, pour gravy round, put a slice of pastry on top. This inside paste, which was sometimes called 'huff pastry', was often used when the meat for a pie was likely to be tough, as it stands long cooking. It also made a very substantial dish, which pleased hungry men, who found that they had dumpling as well as pastry with their meat. In some recipes the inside suet crust was not cut up, but quartered hard-boiled eggs, mushrooms, kidneys which had been sliced and lightly sautéd or sliced sausages and strips of bacon, were laid on top of it and the pie filled up with more gravy. The short-crust lid was then put on and the pie finished in the ordinary way.

Rabbit Pie, 1

This is an early eighteenth-century recipe for rabbit pie from Shropshire. Rabbits were treated with more respect in Elizabethan times (when domestic rabbits were familiarly called 'coneys'), and throughout the seventeenth and eighteenth centuries. They seem to have gone out of favour in the nineteenth century and to have become positively disliked in the First World War and again in the Second, when meat was short. This pie is very rich and splendid. Chickens can be substituted for rabbits if preferred without altering its character unduly.

Serves 6 or 7

1 lb. (½ k.) good short crust (p. 93)
2 rabbits, jointed
½ lb. (240 g.) cooked ham in thick slices

2 onions, skinned and cut finely
4 diced artichoke bottoms
½ pint (3 dl.) red wine

to make 12 or 14 forcemeat balls:
livers of rabbits
4 rashers of bacon
3 oz. (90 g.) cup breadcrumbs

2 egg yolks
thyme, parsley, nutmeg
a little milk

Line your dish with short crust and lay in the ham and the rabbits on it and the onions on them. Sauté the livers, chop fine, and mix with crumbs, herbs, nutmeg, and finely chopped bacon. Mix with egg yolks which have been well beaten with a little milk; season with pepper, salt and nutmeg. Make into balls. Lay them, as the eighteenth-century recipe says, 'here and there in your pie', and put in diced artichokes. Grate a little more nutmeg over the meat, then put in ½ pint (3 dl.) each of red wine and water. Close your pie and bake it 1½ hours at 350° F., gas mark 4–5. If the pastry begins to brown too much, cover lightly with foil. Mushrooms can be substituted for artichoke bottoms.

Rabbit Pie, 2

Serves 3 or 4

2 large onions
1 rabbit
½ lb. (240 g.) lean ham or bacon
2 oz. (60 g.) butter
1½ pints (9 dl.) stock

bay leaf
several sprigs of thyme
salt and pepper
½ lb. (240 g.) flaky or short pastry (see p. 94)

Cut up the onions. Joint the rabbit and cut the ham in thin slices. Melt the butter in a large heavy saucepan and fry the onions, ham and rabbit joints in it for 5 minutes, turning them so that all brown slightly. Sprinkle well with salt and pepper, add the stock and herbs, and simmer gently for an hour.

Leave until cold. Then arrange the meat in a pie dish. Add the stock, which should not quite fill the dish or cover the meat, cover with pastry, and bake in an oven preheated to 400° F., gas mark 6, for 20 minutes till pastry is cooked. Then reduce heat to 350° F., gas mark 4. Lightly cover the pastry with foil or greaseproof paper and cook a further 25 minutes.

Steak and Kidney Pie

The best of all savoury pies: an English dish which is famous all over the world.

Serves 8

¾ lb. (360 g.) puff pastry (p. 92)
2 lb. (1 k.) rump steak
1 lb. (½ k.) ox kidney
seasoned flour
1 large onion
3 oz. (90 g.) butter
4 hard-boiled eggs
½ lb. (240 g.) mushrooms ⎫
  or 18 oysters   ⎬ all optional
1¼ pints (7½ dl.) good brown stock (may be made with a bouillon cube)

You can use a good rough puff or a flaky pastry, put on rather thin and cooked in a very hot oven indeed for the first ten minutes so that it puffs without shrinking at all.

Melt the finely sliced onion in butter and put aside. Cut the rump (it must be rump for the flavour) steak into pieces about 2 inches (5 cm.) square, having removed all fat. Dip in seasoned flour. Lightly brown in the pan in which the onion cooked, adding a little more butter if necessary. Chop, flour and lightly brown the kidney (from which you have removed all skin and fat) in the same pan. Arrange the steak in layers in a large pie dish with a little kidney and some onion on each piece of steak. Mushrooms are an improvement and should be laid in thin slices between the layers of meat.

Stir a little flour into the pan in which the meat and onion browned, and add the stock. Pour into the pie so that the meat is almost covered. Cover the dish closely with foil and cook for 1½ hours in a slow oven, 300° F., gas mark 2. This may well be done the day before you want the pie. In any case, let the dish get cold. Hard-boiled eggs cut in quarters are optional, but if used should be put in at this point, allowing half an egg per person. Oysters, fresh for preference but canned are good, can also be added if liked, but as an alternative to mushrooms. Season well, but use no herbs. Then cover with the crust, decorate and glaze. Bake in a very hot oven, 400° F. (450° F. if puff pastry), gas mark 6–8, for 10 minutes and then reduce heat to 350°F., gas mark 4, for a further 15 minutes or till the pastry is crisp and golden brown.

The steak should be cooked so that it holds its form and is not a series of fibres, and there should be plenty of gravy. If, when the meat is cooking without the pastry, it becomes at all dry, more stock should be added.

Partridge Pie

A rich and well-flavoured pie from *A New System of Domestic Cookery* by Mrs Rundle (1807).

Serves 4

> 4 partridges (or 2 cut in halves if large)
> 1 large slice of fillet of veal (about ½ lb., 240 g.)
> 1 large thick slice of uncooked gammon (about ½ lb., 240 g.)
> 1 pint (6 dl.) good jellied stock
> ½ lb. (240 g.) mushrooms
> 1 tablespoon chopped parsley
> 1 teaspoon chopped thyme
> salt and pepper
> egg yolk to glaze pastry
> 1½ lb. (¾ k.) puff pastry (p. 92)

Cut the veal fillet into four and lay the pieces at the bottom of the dish. Cut the gammon into four and lay on the veal. Put the partridges in a row on the gammon. Put the seasoning, herbs and sliced mushrooms on them and add the jellied stock. Put on a rather thick lid, decorate with rose and leaves, and glaze with egg. Bake for 1½ hours at 350° F., gas mark 4, for the first half-hour, then at 300°F., gas mark 2. Cover the pastry lightly if it gets too brown.

Serve very hot, removing the entire lid on to a separate plate and then lifting out a bird with veal, ham, mushrooms and gravy for each person. Cut the crust in four and place a quarter on each plate.

The same recipe can be made with a poussin for each person.

Rook Pie and Figgy Pastry

A Somerset recipe.

Soak the legs and breasts of six skinned young rooks in salt water overnight. Drain them and place in a pie dish, adding a few pieces of fat bacon cut into chunks. Cover with stock and season with salt and pepper.

For the pastry: Take 1 lb. (½ k.) flour, cut and rub in ½ lb. (240 g.) fat, add pepper and salt to season, then add 4 oz. (120 g.) each currants and stoned raisins. Add sufficient water to make a stiff paste. Turn on to a floured board, roll out to about ¾ inch (2 cm.) thick, and place on pie dish. Cover the pie with greaseproof paper and tie down in a pudding cloth. Place in a large pan of boiling water and cook for three hours. Serve with gooseberry jelly.

This is a curious recipe, which we are unlikely to follow. However, the figgy pastry is very good.

Replace the young rooks with 2 boiling fowls, not too large, jointed each into 6, and a ¾ lb. (360 g.) rasher of uncooked gammon cut into ½-inch (1-cm.) squares. Cover the pastry with two layers of foil, put on very firmly. This is easier than tying down a cloth. Stand in a baking tray of water, so that the water comes about half-way up the sides of the pie dish. Preheat the oven to 300° F., gas mark 2, and cook for 3 hours. Fill up the tray of water if necessary during cooking.

Have ready some extra stock to serve separately.

The gooseberry jelly plus the 'figgy' pastry is rather too sweet, but the pie is really distinctive because the long cooking in the steaming water brings out all the flavour of the chicken and ham, which is set off by the slightly sweet soft crust.

Veal and Ham Pie

This is a traditional recipe which comes from a seventeenth-century cook book. The pie may be eaten hot or cold.

> 1 lb. (½ k.) fillet of veal
> ¼ lb. (120 g.) lean cooked ham, cut rather thick
> 2 hard-boiled eggs
> 1 teaspoon chopped parsley } or a bouquet of 3 sprigs of thyme, one
> ½ teaspoon herbs   } of marjoram and a leaf of sage
> a little grated lemon rind
> salt and pepper
> stock

1 large onion
6 cloves
¾ lb. (360 g.) rough puff or flaky pastry (pp. 92, 94)

Put the veal and the onion, stuck with cloves, in cold water just to cover and stew for 40 minutes. Remove the meat and onion, and reserve the stock. When cold, cut the veal into very thin slices with a very sharp knife, put a little parsley, herbs, lemon peel, salt and pepper on each slice and roll up. Pack the rolls in a pie dish, with the ham cut in short strips and the hard-boiled eggs cut in slices, laid between two layers of the rolls. Reduce the stock from the veal to about half the original quantity, season and pour it into the pie dish. Roll out the pastry, cover the pie, and decorate with a rose and 3 leaves. Bake in an oven preheated to 400° F., gas mark 7, for 25 minutes or until the pastry is golden and crisp. Cover lightly with foil, move to a lower shelf, and leave for a further 10 minutes, to ensure that the inside is really hot.

Very good served cold, when the stock will be found to be lightly jellied.

These quantities will make a pie for four. It is often worthwhile to use double quantities, make up two pies and keep one in the refrigerator to serve cold for lunch two or three days after the first has been eaten hot. The cold pie is best with a plain lettuce salad sprinkled with chives and parsley and dressed with French dressing made with lemon juice instead of vinegar.

Herb Pie

This was intended to be eaten by itself in Lent, but since few of us nowadays have to observe this long fast, it may be served as an unusual accompaniment to a plain roast. Particularly good with a leg of lamb with gravy and red-currant jelly.

Serves 6–8

1 ½ lb. (750 g.) short pastry (p. 92)
½ lb. (240 g.) cooked potatoes (new if possible) cut in ½ inch (1 cm.) cubes
2 medium onions, finely sliced
large packet mixed frozen vegetables, cooked and cooled (or cooked mixed fresh vegetables)
large packet frozen chopped spinach
  or sliced green beans cooked and cooled
2 tablespoons finely chopped parsley
1 tablespoon finely chopped thyme and marjoram
1 tablespoon chopped chives if possible

    4 eggs
    2 oz. (60 g.) butter
    1 pint (6 dl.) milk
    salt and pepper

Line a large pie dish with the pastry, reserving enough for the lid. Be very careful that there are no holes anywhere in the lining.

Lay the vegetables in layers, sprinkling thickly with the chopped herbs and seasoning as you do so. The dish should be almost full. Beat the eggs well with the milk, and season. Carefully pour into the vegetables. They should be almost but not quite covered. Use another egg and a little more milk if necessary. Dot the top generously with the butter. Put on the lid and bake at 400° F., gas mark 6, for 10 minutes. Then reduce the heat to 300° F., gas mark 2, and cook a further 30 minutes. May be kept warm for 20 minutes or so do not allow it to get cold, then re-heat.

The top may be gilded with egg yolk if liked. When the pie is cut in wedges the vegetables should be set into a light but just solid custard.

Raised Pies and Pies Intended to be Eaten Cold

Louis Eustache Ude, a Frenchman who worked for thirty years in England, was cook to the Earl of Sefton, for a time to the Duke of Wellington (whom he left because the Duke was unable to appreciate good food) and for many years steward of the United Services Club. He produced valuable advice on what the English upper classes in the early nineteenth century expected to be given at dinners and banquets. In describing how to arrange a menu for a large formal dinner, he said: 'I have added 2 cold pies, which are likewise served at a large dinner. I like them to be sent to table with the 1st course; and to remain there between the 2 courses. By this means the epicure and dainty eater will always have something before them . . . they may be of game or poultry.'

Perhaps the greatest of all recipes for a raised pie dates from 1765 and comes from Yorkshire. It was collected by Mrs Edden in the twenties in the form in which I quote it here:

Yorkshire Christmas Pie (1765)

'First make a good standing crust, let the wall and bottom be very thick; bone by opening down the back, a turkey, a goose, a fowl, a partridge, and a pigeon. Season them all very well, using ½ oz. (15 g.) of mace, nutmeg, and black pepper, ¼ oz. (8 g.) of cloves, two large spoonfuls of salt, and mix them together. First bone the pigeon, then the partridge, cover them one with the other; then the fowl, the goose, and the turkey, which must be large, covering each bird in turn, so that at the last it looked like one large turkey. Lay the turkey in the pie and fill up the corners with hare or woodcock cut in small pieces. Fill the pie closely and put at least 4 lb. [2 k.] of fresh butter on the top. Cover with a thick lid of paste and let the pie be well baked for at least four hours. This crust will take a bushel of flour.

'These pies are often sent to London in a box of presents, therefore the walls must be well built.

A Standing Crust for Great Pies

'Take a peck of flour, and 6 lbs. of butter boiled in a gallon of water; skim it off into the flour and as little of the liquor as you can. Work it well up into a paste, then pull it into pieces until it is cold, and then make it up what form you will have it. This is fit for the walls of a Turkey Pie.'

The boning of birds and the fitting of one inside another goes back to Roman times, where it was much favoured and it is possible that such a tradition comes straight from the Roman occupation of Britain. Many of the Latin recipes of Apicius show close resemblance to medieval dishes.

Few today would want a pie of the size this must have been, and very few would embark on the boning of five birds. In fact this is not so difficult, as long as a razor-sharp pointed knife is available, but it is a long process and involves a good deal of waste, though skin and meat left on the bones can of course be boiled to make superbly good stock. I would reckon that the boning of the birds would take about two hours and the making of the crust and raising of the pie another two. Such a pie would not have been filled up with gravy. The meat would have been set in butter, as potted shrimps are set, and underneath would have been jelly from the juices. It is interesting that the pie contains no vegetables or titbits: it is solid meat throughout and nothing but poultry and game is used.

Raised Pie Pastry

These quantities are enough for one pie which should be about 6 inches

(15 cm.) in diameter and would serve 6, but it is more rewarding to double or even treble the quantities and chill or freeze one or two pies. Chilled they will keep well for 10 days, deep-frozen for 6 months.

> 1 lb. (½ k.) flour (plain)
> ½ lb. (240 g.) lard (or half lard and half butter)
> 1 teaspoon salt
> ¼ pint (1½ dl.) of milk and water (half and half)

To make the paste, rub 2 oz. (60 g.) of the fat into the flour, with a teaspoonful of salt. Take the rest of the fat and put it on to boil with the milk and water. Make a well in the flour and when boiling pour in the liquid, stirring all with a wooden spoon. Knead well and let it stand for 10 minutes.

The Raising of the 'Coffin': After 10 minutes the pastry should be still warm and pliable. The raising may be done in either of the following ways:

(1) Take a round casserole or a cake tin about the size of the pie you want to make. It must have straight sides and be of sufficient height. Roll out your pastry to about ½–¾ inch (2 cm.) thick, into a large piece which is roughly circular. Stand the round pot or tin in the middle of the paste and work it up to cover the sides of the pot. Turn the pastry-covered pot on its side and roll it a few times to smooth the outside and loosen the pot. Gently work the pot out, and the pie case should remain standing. Fill at once. Trim the top with a sharp knife, roll out, and cut a lid rather too big. Damp the top edges of the pie with a little milk, press on the lid and firmly crimp the edges all round to make a raised ridge. The top can be left plain with 2 or 3 slits or a round hole neatly cut in the middle, or it may be decorated with leaves and a rose.

(2) If you want to raise the pie without using a pot, cut a round for the bottom which is ½ inch (1 cm.) bigger in diameter than you think you require. Roll your paste into long thin snakes, as children do with plasticine or as a potter does with clay for certain pots. Coil the snakes round the edges of the bottom, one on another, until you have walls of the required height. Then carefully work them as smooth as possible outside and in with your fingers, always working the paste upwards. Fill and put on lid as described above.

Bake at 375° F., gas mark 5, for 20 minutes to set pastry; then reduce to 300° F., gas mark 2. Place pie lower in oven and cover lid lightly with foil. Bake a further 1¾ hours.

To glaze: Remove the pie from the oven about 10 minutes before it should be cooked, brush over with beaten egg and return to oven.

You can, of course, line a tin or fireproof dish with the raised pie pastry, and make the pie in the ordinary way, carefully running a knife round the sides when cold and turning out the pie, but 'raising the coffin' is not difficult, and the pastry will be crisper.

Melton Mowbray Pork Pies ·

Famous for generations and entirely different from the bought pies which claim the same ancestry. The many recipes are all very simple, though the earliest I have found, from the fourteenth century, includes raisins and currants.

'Flea [flay] Pyg and cut him in pieces, season with pepper and salt, and nutmeg, and large mace, and lay in your 'coffin' good store of raisins and currans, and fill with sweet butter and close it and serve hot or cold.'

All over the Shires every manor house, farm and inn had its special recipe for Melton Mowbray pork pies, which were originally intended for high teas served to returning members of the hunt.

The pie depends on the flavouring and high seasoning of the jellied stock, and contains nothing whatever but good pork meat and a little seasoning.

Serves 6

1 lb. (½ k.) flour
½ lb. (240 g.) lard
¼ pint (1½ dl.) milk   } for the crust
and water, as on p. 112
2 lb. (1k.) pork from the leg or shoulder
pork or veal bones
a little butter
1 teaspoon salt
½ teaspoon pepper
1 leaf of sage, finely chopped
2 onions
marjoram, sage, thyme, a bay leaf

The pork should be diced in ¼-inch (½-cm.) pieces, some of which may be fat; but there must be no skin or gristle. The butcher may do this if asked, but the meat must *not* be minced. Mix the pork, salt, pepper and sage together for the filling, and pack closely down into the pie to ¼ inch from the top. Put in 2 tablespoons cold water and place on top of the meat about 1 oz. (30 g.)

butter in small pieces. Put on the lid and bake as described in the recipe for the crust on p. 112.

Before you make and bake the pie put any bones from the meat plus a few extra to boil in 1½ pints (9 dl.) water with two onions and a sage leaf, a sprig or two of marjoram, a bay leaf and some sprigs of thyme; or use a prepared bouquet garni. Salt and pepper. Boil for 2 hours, so that it is reduced to a little more than a pint (6 dl.), then cool and skim off all fat. Taste, and check seasoning. The cooling stock should have begun to jell. If it has not, reduce further, but this should not be necessary. Reheat just before the pie will be ready and slowly pour in as much as it will take through the hole in the top crust as soon as it comes from the oven.

Raised Game Pie

A raised game pie should be oblong for preference. An oblong cake tin, lightly buttered, should be lined with the crust of raised pie pastry, about ¼–½ inch (1 cm.) thick, and a piece should be rolled out and cut to size for the lid.

> 1½ lb. (¾ k.) raised pie crust (p. 112)
> ¾ lb. (360 g.) rump steak or haunch of venison, all skin and fat removed, cut into thin slices and dipped in seasoned flour
> 2 pheasants (or 2 grouse and a pigeon), half-roasted as for a salmi, and all the meat cut off
> 2 lambs kidneys, cored, skinned, sliced and dipped in seasoned flour
> ¼ lb. (120 g.) mushrooms, thinly sliced
> 2 hard-boiled eggs, quartered
> 4 rashers of back bacon, cut in dice
> 12 small forcemeat balls, which need not be fried
> salt and 1 teaspoon black pepper
> ½ teaspoon mace
> 2 glasses port
> 1½ pints (9 dl.) very good stock
> salt and pepper

Put the carcases of the birds to boil in the stock as soon as you have taken off the meat. Allow to boil for at least ¾ hour, reducing the quantity from 1½ pints (9 dl.) to 1 pint (6 dl.). Strain, allow to cool slightly, and season highly before pouring into the pie.

Make the forcemeat balls.

Prepare the pastry and line the tin.

Prepare all the meat and pack the pie, with the steak or venison at the bottom, then a layer of meat from the birds, then the quartered eggs and half the mushrooms, a layer of meat, then the kidneys and the remaining mushrooms, then the forcemeat balls and the remaining meat on top, just below the lid.

Fill up first with port and then with stock to within ½ inch (1 cm.) of the top and put on the lid. Reserve the remaining stock to pour in, as in Melton Mowbray Pork Pie, on p. 113.

Bake at 350° F., gas mark 4, for 35 minutes. Then reduce the heat to 300° F., gas mark 2, lightly cover with foil and bake for a further 1½ hours. Serve cold. The eggs and the green forcemeat balls look very ornamental when the pie is sliced across.

A Very Good Pie to be Served Cold

This is my own adaptation of Gervase Markham's Chicken Pye (1615), and Mrs Anne Blencowe's Little Chicken Pye (1694) to a recipe which is easy to make with ingredients available today. It is in the tradition of the great feast day pies, which were treasure chests of different delicacies. It serves 8–10 and requires two rather large pie dishes.

> 1¼ lb. (720 g.) good short pastry
>   or 3 large packets frozen short pastry
> 1 cooked chicken, 3½–4 lb. (1½–2 k.)
>   or 2 of 2–2½ lb. (1–1½ k.)
> 1½ pints (9 dl.) well-seasoned stock which jellies when cold
> 1 large tin of good liver pâté
> 6 hard-boiled eggs
> ½ lb. (240 g.) mushrooms, sliced and lightly sauté
> small tin of tongue
> small tin of artichoke bottoms
>   or bottoms of 3 large fresh artichokes, cooked
> 2 dozen stoned green olives with pimento
> 1 egg yolk, well beaten
> 30 sultanas or seedless raisins
> 2 teaspoons mace
> salt and pepper

This can be made as a raised pie (see p.111), which makes the dish rather more solid though more traditional.

Take all meat from bone. Dice the best in ½-inch (1-cm.) cubes and season with salt, pepper and a little mace. Mince all the rest, and mix with enough warm stock to make a moist but fairly firm consistency. Season highly with half a teaspoon of mace, salt and pepper.

Prepare all ingredients and collect on separate plates. You should have:

    minced meat, seasoned
    diced meat, seasoned
    liver pâté, cut into 12 slices
    hard-boiled eggs, peeled and quartered
    mushrooms, sliced and sauté
    tongue, cut in thin julienne strips (jelly to be stirred into stock)
    artichoke bottoms, cut in halves if small or eighths if large
    olives, halved
    stock, highly seasoned with mace
    salt and pepper
    sultanas or raisins

Line both pie dishes with pastry about ⅛ inch (½ cm.) thick, pressing it well against the sides of the dishes.

Put a layer of diced meat into each dish, scatter with mushrooms and olives. Put a layer of mince about ½ inch (1 cm.) thick and press well down, add a layer of hard-boiled eggs, strips of tongue and artichokes. Put a further layer of mince, press down and add remainder of diced meat, sultanas and raisins, slices of pâté to form a thin layer, and finally the remainder of the ingredients. Pour in slightly warm stock so that it does not quite cover the last layer.

Roll out the remaining pastry and put on lids, brushing the edges of the sides with milk so that they stick, and crimp them firmly together. Cut 3 slits in the centre of the lid to let out the steam and disguise them with a rose and five leaves cut from left-over pastry. The slits should not be completely closed. Brush over the lids and decorations with egg yolk and bake at 400° F., gas mark 6, for 20 minutes. Turn oven to 300° F., gas mark 2, and place the pies lower in the oven for a further 20 minutes in order that the pastry bottoms should be well cooked. If the tops seem to be getting too dark, cover lightly with a sheet of foil.

Remove from the oven and pour through the centre slits (one of which you can enlarge with a sharp knife if necessary) some more stock, which should be just warm, until you think the pie is full. Chill and serve cold. The pies will keep for a week in the refrigerator or may be frozen.

With short crust the pies should not be removed from the dish, but the same filling can be used for raised pies (see p. 112).

Bacon Pie

This is an English eighteenth-century recipe, but there are much earlier versions. It will be seen that it bears the closest resemblance to Quiche Lorraine, except that it is covered.

To serve 6–8

> 12 rashers of bacon (back)
> 1 oz. (30 g.) butter
> 8 eggs
> 1 pint (6 dl.) heavy cream
> ½ teaspoon mace
> pepper and salt
> 1 lb. ½ k.) short-crust pastry

Cut the rind from the rashers and cut them into roughly 1-inch squares. Lightly sauté in a little butter but do not let them get brown or crisp.

Put all the bacon in a pie dish. Beat the eggs, cream, mace and seasoning well together and pour over the bacon, reserving a spoonful to gild the pastry. Put on the crust, being careful not to tip the liquid contents of the dish. Crimp the edges and gild with egg. Bake at 350° F., gas mark 4, for ¾ hour. Allow to get cold for several hours or overnight, when the inside should be a rich savoury creamy custard with a thick layer of bacon at the bottom.

Lightly sauté onions or chopped chives, sliced sauté mushrooms or finely chopped parsley were sometimes added. Early versions suggest lining the dish with pastry as well as covering: this is very good on picnics but is rather solid.

Pasties

Cornish Pasty

For 4

> 1 lb. (½ k.) flour
> ½ lb. (240 g.) butter or margarine
> ½ lb. (240 g.) steak, cut in ½-in. (1 cm.) cubes, all skin and fat removed
> 4 medium potatoes, boiled and diced
> 2 onions, peeled and finely sliced

   salt and pepper
   a little cold water

A rough puff pastry is also good, though the short pastry given here is richer and softer and will hold its shape.

 Rub the fat into the flour, add salt and mix into a stiff dough with water. Divide into four, roll each piece out about ¼ inch (½ cm.) thick and cut into rounds by cutting round 8-inch plates. Cut the potatoes and meat. Season highly the diced potatoes, sliced onions and diced meat, mix well and place a layer on one half of each piece of pastry. Damp the edges of the pastry with milk and fold one half over the other, pinch edges together and crimp them. Cut a small slit in the centre. Glaze with milk, or egg and milk if liked. Bake in a moderate oven for ¾ hour at 350° F., gas mark 4. Then reduce heat to 250°F., gas mark ½, and cook another 30 minutes in order that the steak may become tender.

 Traditionally, Cornish pasties had the initials of each person intended to eat one marked on one corner. In this way, onion could be omitted if someone disliked it, extra meat put in for the master of the house and so on. Fishermen, eating in their boats, would hold the initialed corner and start biting at the other end. If the pasties had to be hastily put down in some emergency, everyone would know his own. Pasties keep hot a long time when well wrapped up.

Other traditional fillings: chopped potato, onion and chopped cooked ham or lightly fried bacon; potato, onion and sliced fried mushrooms; chicken or rabbit with potato and onion and plenty of sage and thyme; mutton with turnips and onions; apples or jam.

Game Pasties

A very grand game pasty as served at the Hundred Club.
'Bone 3 or 4 birds – pheasants, partridges or grouse.

 Season with fresh black pepper, parsley, thyme, marjoram, basil and sage. Take about a pound of a fine forcemeat of chicken, breadcrumbs and sweet herbs, which has soaked for 12 hours in port wine with 2 whole truffles coarsely chopped. Simmer the carcases of the birds in a fine veal consommé with a glass of armagnac and two of port wine. Place birds and forcemeat in an oblong coffin of fine crust and pour the stock all over, almost to cover. Put on a lid of crust and bake. When cold remove the lid and cover the pie with port-wine jelly. When this is quite set, decorate with flowers and stars of truffles, piped anchovy cream and cucumber and glaze in place with a little more of the jelly.'

The pasty, in fact, was no true pasty, in that the sides and bottom were encased in pastry but the top, when finished, was open. It is, in any case, too much for most of us to attempt at home today, but this simpler game pasty is excellent. It comes from a Scottish nineteenth-century manuscript in the Macadam Collection in Edinburgh.

For a large pasty for 6 or for 8 small pasties
> 1 lb. (½ k.) for large pasty, 1½ lb. (1¼ k.) for 8 small pasties, of puff, rough puff, or short pastry
> 1 lb. (½ k.) cooked game, neatly cut in ½–1-in. (1–2 cm.) pieces, without skin or bone
> 1 pint (6 dl.) very good game stock, thickened to the consistency of thin cream and jellied when cold
> 12–16 very small forcemeat balls
> ½ lb. (240 g.) mushrooms, sliced and lightly sauté
> salt, coarse black pepper
> ¼ pint (1½ dl.) claret
> a pinch of nutmeg and cinnamon

Any mixture of game may be used: pheasant, grouse or partridge, with pigeons and hare or venison, or the quantity may be made up with duck, chicken or veal; wild duck is good as long as it is not fishy or muddy in taste.

For the large pasty, roll out and make up the pastry as in the recipe for Venison Pasty, p. 120. Arrange the game meat on the bottom crust. Spread with the jellied stock. Lay on the mushrooms and the forcemeat balls, season and put on the lid. Bake in a hot oven at 400° F., gas mark 6, for 20 minutes and then reduce to 300° F., gas mark 2, and cook for a further 20 minutes, lightly covering the top with foil if it is browning too much.

For the small pasties roll out and make up the pastry as in recipe for Cornish pasties on p. 117. Divide the other ingredients evenly and arrange with 2 forcemeat balls in each. Bake at 400° F., gas mark 6, for 20 minutes and then serve.

Just before the pasties should be ready, make the claret hot, but not boiling, and stir in a pinch of nutmeg and a pinch of cinnamon. As soon as you remove the pasty, carefully open one of the slits in the top and pour in the hot wine. In the case of the small pasties, open a slit in each and pour in a very little of the hot claret.

Serve at once. The pasties are excellent with hot mulled wine, a green salad and cheese for a winter lunch or supper party.

Venison Pasty, 1

This recipe was recorded by Gwillim in 1695. I have clarified it and given exact quantities, but it is unaltered, and very good. This pasty is enough for a supper party of 10 or 12 people. It wants plain boiled potatoes, red-currant jelly, and green salad, and plenty of claret to drink.

> 3–4 lb. (1½–2 k.) haunch of venison cut in very thin slices and cut across so that each is about 4 by 2 in. (9 by 5 cm.)
> pepper and salt
> ½ teaspoon of nutmeg
> ½ lb. (240 g.) butter
> 2 lb. (1 k.) rough puff pastry (p. 92)
> 2 lb. (1 k.) bones from the venison, or veal bones
> 1 pint (6 dl.) claret
> flour

Put the bones in a saucepan with the claret, nutmeg, salt and pepper and a quart of water. Bring to the boil, skim and allow to simmer for 4 hours. At the end the liquid should be reduced by one third.

Divide the pastry and roll it out about ¼ inch (½ cm.) thick into two very large oblongs. Line an ordinary roasting tray about 14 by 8 inches with one half. Lay the pieces of venison, which you have beaten very flat and then rubbed with seasoned flour, in a layer on the pastry bottom. Put a thin slice of very cold butter on each. Then put another layer and end up with pieces of butter. (No liquid is added at this stage.) Put the rest of the pastry on as a lid, sealing it firmly by moistening edges and crimping together. Cut 3 or 4 slits in the top. Put it into a moderate oven, 350° F., gas mark 4, for 30 minutes, or until the top is brown and crisp.

Take from the oven and very carefully and slowly pour through the slits in the pastry about ¾ pint (4½ dl.) of the boiling stock, which will hiss and bubble on the buttered venison, but will keep it moist. Don't let the stock splash on the pastry. Cover lightly with foil. Reduce heat to 250° F., gas mark ½, place low in the oven and cook for 3 hours more.

Go on cooking the stock. When the pasty is nearly ready, strain the stock and season it rather highly. Pour it slowly into the pasty, which should take most of it. Don't let it overflow, and serve separately any that is over. The pasty can be served at once or can be served cold and jellied the next day. Red-currant jelly should be offered with it.

A recipe of the same period but from a different source adds 2 dozen small forcemeat balls (see Pigeon Pie, p. 103) to the venison and a handful of sultanas and some sage, thyme and an onion or two to the stock. With or without these the pasty is very rich and excellent. It can be very gently slid from the tin to a large dish but if it seems in danger of breaking, stand the tin on a dish and do not take the risk.

Venison Pasty, 2

A quick and simple pasty, enough for 3 or 4, or will make 4 small pasties. Good hot or cold.

> 1 lb. (½ k.) venison (best cut from haunch or saddle), diced
> 1 lb. (½ k.) good short pastry (p. 93)
> 2 onions, peeled and chopped fine
> 1 pint (6 dl.) good stock
> ½ pint (3 dl.) port (or any red wine)
> salt, pepper
> 2 teaspoons red-currant jelly
> 2 teaspoons mixed parsley, thyme and marjoram
> 1 egg

Place the diced venison and chopped onions with stock in a saucepan and bring just to the boil; add the port wine, red-currant jelly, salt and pepper to taste, and simmer till tender (about 40 minutes). Strain off the meat and allow to cool, reserving the stock. Roll out the pastry to make an oblong. Place the meat in the centre of one half, sprinkle with the herbs and fold the pastry over. Crimp the edges firmly together, first brushing with milk to stick them. Make a slit near the top. Brush over with beaten egg and bake at 350° F., gas mark 4, for 25 minutes. Meanwhile season and slightly thicken the wine stock, and when you remove the pasty, enlarge the slit and carefully pour in a generous ½ pint (about 3½ dl.). Serve the remainder separately.

Puddings

Steak and Kidney Pudding

Serves 6

> 1½ lb. (¾ k.) rump steak   ¾ pint (4½ dl.) good stock
> ½ lb. (240 g.) ox kidney   1½ lb. (¾ k.) suet crust (see p. 95)
> pepper, salt, flour

Remove all skin and fat from the steak and cut into strips about 1 inch (2½ cm.) wide and 3 inches (8 cm.) long. Trim and cut up the kidney. Beat the steak to flatten. Dip each piece of steak into seasoned flour, put some kidney on each piece, and roll up.

Roll out the crust and line a well-greased basin with it, trimming off the surplus from the edge and rolling out a circle for the top. Put in half of the meat rolls and add the stock: save any stock which is left over to add after cooking. Fill the basin with the rest of the meat. Put on the top, having slightly moistened the top edge in the bowl to make it adhere. Cover closely with foil or greaseproof paper and over this tie a cloth, or cover with a fitting saucer or small plate. Stand the basin in a large saucepan of water, so that the water comes half-way up the bowl, or stand the bowl in a steamer top. In either case, steam for 3 hours, being careful that the water does not go off the boil and that the saucepan does not boil dry. When the level of water gets low, carefully pour in more *boiling* water without removing from heat.

The pudding may be turned out on to a hot dish, or served (which is safer) in its basin with a clean napkin or tea towel pinned round it. Just before serving, make a small incision in the top crust and pour in a little boiling stock. Bring the rest to table in a small jug and pour a little in when you have served the first 2 or 3 helpings. The stock amalgamates at once with the thick gravy in the pudding.

A Pudding of Game

Serves 6

> 1 ½ lb. (¾ k.) suet crust (p. 95)
> ½ lb. (240 g.) rump steak, cut in thin strips, with all fat and skin removed
> 1 pheasant, *or* 2 partridges, *or* 2 grouse, *or* 2 pigeons, jointed
> salt, pepper, flour
> 1 tablespoon finely chopped parsley and thyme
> ½ lb. (240 g.) mushrooms
> 2 glasses red wine
> 1 pint (6 dl.) stock

Line a large pudding basin with suet crust. Dip the steak and joints of the birds in seasoned flour. Put the steak and some of the joints of the birds in the basin, then season, add the herbs, half the mushrooms, and the rest of the birds, and finish with a few mushrooms. Pour in the wine and some of the stock, cover, and proceed as for Steak and Kidney Pudding, p. 121.

One pigeon and one grouse, or one partridge and one grouse or pigeon may well be used.

Rabbit or Chicken Pudding with Mushrooms

Serves 6

>1 ½ lb. (¾ k.) suet crust (p. 95)
>1 or 2 young rabbits, *or* 1 large roasting fowl, cut in joints and dipped in seasoned flour
>3 slices of fat bacon
>sage leaves chopped fine if rabbits are used, *or* some parsley and thyme for chicken
>2 large onions, cut fine
>pepper and salt
>½–¾ lb. (240–360 g.) mushrooms
>a little flour

Line a good-sized pudding basin with the suet crust, put in a layer of meat, chopped herbs and onion, then a layer of mushrooms, and continue until the basin is filled. Sprinkle seasoning and a little flour between each layer. Cut the slices of bacon in thin strips and place them over the top layer of meat. Then cover firmly with suet crust pressed down to join the moistened edges of the lining crust.

Cover with greaseproof paper, twisted well over the edges of the pudding basin and then tie up in a pudding cloth. Stand the bowl in a steamer top and fit over a saucepan of water, or stand direct in a large saucepan with water coming half-way up the bowl. Cover closely and steam for 2½–3 hours. Look at the water level and add a little more hot water when necessary, being careful not to wet the pudding.

Either stand the bowl on a dish with a napkin folded round it, or turn the pudding out – there is always a risk of a meat pudding breaking and it is safer to serve it in the bowl.

Quorn Bacon Roll

This was a substantial but cheap dish for the servants of the hunt and their children. It is not a dish from the manor houses, but it is not to be despised and it is very English.

Serves 4
    ½ lb. (240 g.) plain flour
    6 oz. (180 g.) shredded suet
    8 rashers of lean bacon (back)
    1 teaspoon sage
    1 onion, grated finely
    1 tablespoon chopped parsley
    salt and pepper
    accompanying vegetables
    ½ pint (3 dl.) good gravy

Make suet crust (see p. 95) and roll out ¼ inch (½ cm). thick. The crust contains a higher proportion of suet than is generally used for a pudding crust. Lay on 8 rashers of bacon, sprinkle with sage and grated onion. Roll up, tightly wrap in a floured white cloth and place in a saucepan of boiling water; boil for about 2 hours, never letting it go off the boil. Remove from the saucepan and unwrap the cloth, turn on to a hot dish, sprinkle with parsley, surround with cooked carrots, turnips and potatoes, peas or beans, and serve with gravy.

3 · POTTED MEATS, PÂTÉS AND TERRINES, BRAWNS AND GALANTINES, POTTED FISH

There is no real difference between French pâtés and terrines and English potted meats. The French word *pâté* means 'paste': in fact the meats concerned have been reduced to the consistency of a paste. The English equivalent is *potted meat*: meaning that the meats have been reduced to a form convenient for keeping in a pot; i.e. to a 'paste'. The word *terrine* also simply means the earthenware pot in which, in this instance, the paste is kept, but the French use it only for a pâté which is not completely smooth and in which the best parts of the meat, neatly cut into strips or oblongs, are reserved and arranged at the bottom of the pot and then in layers in the fine pounded mincemeat; olives, pistachios, truffles, etc. are also often added. In England we have no equivalent of the internationally famous and enormously expensive gourmets' dish, pâté de foie gras, but this in its proper form is a specialist's dish, requiring that the geese be forcibly fed so that their livers reach an enormous size, and is not to be attempted at home or by the ordinary manufacturer.

One other word is used in English for this type of cookery, and this is 'cheese': 'head cheese' made from calf's or pigs' heads and 'pork cheese' are really only forms of potted meat (in which the meat is preserved in its own fat), usually made on farms where an animal is killed and parts of the head, belly, etc. were to be used up and preserved for longer than brawn or other dishes would keep.

All pâtés, cheeses, terrines and potted meats were intended to keep for some weeks or months in the larder, covered with clarified butter. In a refrigerator they will keep for several weeks covered only with foil, or in a deep-freeze, in polythene bags, for at least three months.

TO CLARIFY BUTTER

Melt the required quantity of good butter (preferably fresh) very gently in a heavy saucepan or a frying pan. The butter must not colour at all, but should bubble for 2 or 3 minutes. Remove from the heat and leave to settle for a further 3 or 4 minutes. Fold a piece of butter muslin or an old handkerchief so that two thicknesses cover a basin or jar. Pour through it the still warm and liquid butter. Alternatively, place a sheet of kitchen paper in the bottom of a fine sieve or strainer and pour the butter through this. The liquid butter may be reheated almost to boiling and poured straight on to the prepared pots of meat, or it may be stored in the refrigerator for later use. If this is done, it is best to lift out the solid cake of butter when it is quite cold and wrap it in foil for storage, as a little liquid and sediment may have formed under it.

Clarified butter is much better than ordinary butter for frying all breaded meat such as veal escalopes or rissoles.

GENERAL NOTES ON THE MAKING OF PÂTÉS AND TERRINES

If you have part of a cold chicken, its liver, perhaps some calf's liver, and maybe some pork, then you can make an excellent large terrine with what you have in hand. Otherwise buy or reserve what you will need and make say 2 or 3 terrines and 2 or 3 smooth pâtés at the same time for use over the next weeks or months.

Remember to season highly: more than you would for most dishes. All cold food has less flavour than hot, and the dense packed consistency of terrines and potted meats seems to absorb flavours. You will want onions and herbs for some recipes, garlic or garlic salt, mace, nutmeg, turmeric, powdered ginger and thyme; and black and white pepper and salt for almost all. You will need some wine or brandy and probably a good well-seasoned stock made from the meat or bird you are using (see below). Mace and turmeric both bring out the flavour of meat. Mace is particularly good with shellfish. Ginger was often used as an alternative to pepper up to the nineteenth century, but I find that it is particularly good in potted meats as, without being noticeable, it gives them a certain zest. Thyme is very good with beef and all the liver pâtés. The spices of course help to preserve the meat.

Even for a rough pâté or a terrine the meat should be minced twice. For a smooth pâté only liver should be used: meat is too fibrous. The liver should be twice-minced and then put through a blender or pounded in a mortar.

Any plain potted meat or liver pâté can be flavoured with orange zest and a little orange juice or with a very little Pernod or Armagnac, or with mushroom or anchovy essence.

Soak 2 oz. (60 g.) seedless raisins in a tablespoon of brandy and 2 tablespoons of canned grape juice for an hour or so. Mix them with the brandy and juice, into about ¾ lb. (360 g.) raw minced and pounded beef, hare or chicken, season well, and cook in the ordinary way. The resulting pâté is delicious. Such a use of grape juice with finely minced meat comes down to us from Roman times.

All potted meats are excellent as a main dish for lunch or supper, especially if you serve two or three kinds with several sorts of bread and hot toast, and with a green salad. Potted meats and potted fish are of course a traditional starting course, and are also very good for a leisurely holiday breakfast.

Oval or round fireproof casseroles about 3–4 inches deep are best for large terrines; soufflé dishes or oblong cake tins are also good. Individual pâtés can be made in small soufflé dishes or ramekins.

If the potted meat is not to be frozen and is to be kept for more than

3 weeks in a refrigerator or for more than a week in a larder, apart from being covered with clarified butter it must have all liquid pressed from the cooked meat or fish before it is finally potted. A little brandy may be added after the liquid is removed, and some early recipes add claret. The meat or fish must be pressed firmly into the pot to avoid pockets of air. The fat bacon or pork which is generally included in the recipe keeps the consistency soft and moist. If the potted meat is to be used within a week of being made, and to be kept in the refrigerator until this time, or if it is to be frozen only for a month or six weeks, a little strong, reduced stock improves the flavour, softens the consistency, and glazes the potted meat with jelly, when it is turned out. It is essential always to use reduced and highly-flavoured liquids, and never to make the mixture wet as opposed to moist. The insides of moulds and dishes should always be buttered, and then lined with strips of streaky bacon in a lattice work. The fat from this keeps the outside moist. When the mould is turned out, the bacon may be stripped off but it looks very ornamental and is, in fact, delicious.

Potted Meats

All methods of preserving meat, birds and fish without salting or smoking were of the greatest importance until the twenties of our own century. Almost all early cookbooks give recipes for 'potting', which was the term generally used in English cooking, many of them indistinguishable from recipes for French pâtés and terrines, but some, particularly those for whole birds or joints, peculiar to English tables and of an excellent simplicity. For all these the spices with which they were seasoned and the clarified butter with which they were covered and sealed were the chief preserving agents.

These potted meats were particularly prized because they could be eaten in mid-winter, deliciously fresh tasting, and soft in texture, compared with the salt meat which in general was hard and very salty, and the salt fish which was often flabby and tasteless. From the cook's or housewife's point of view they were a blessing in that he or she had prepared them in bulk, in time set aside for the purpose, and so they were ready in an era when no foodstuffs were pre-washed, pre-weighed, pre-packaged, let alone pre-cooked. Perhaps for this reason potted meats, fish and shellfish were often served for breakfast in the great houses and inns.

George Borrow in 1862, in his book *Wild Wales*, describes breakfast at the White Hart Inn:

'What a breakfast! Pot of hare: ditto of trout; pot of prepared shrimps: tin of sardines; beautiful beefsteak; eggs, mutton, large loaf and butter, not forgetting capital tea. There's a breakfast for you!'

Potted meats were also taken by cabin passengers on voyages to Australia and the Indies. Dorothy Hartley* quotes from the journal of one of her aunts who was among the first women to sail to the West Indies. She made the voyage repeatedly and prided herself on the excellent fare she managed to provide through a voyage which would certainly last weeks and which might last several months:

We took goats for milk and hens for eggs, and pigs and sheep, the butcher looked after all animals and they were all eaten by the end of the voyage. Regular diet was salt meat, dried peas and beans, and forms of beans and bacon. We also had boiled salt beef with dumplings, carrots, and root vegetables. Cabin passengers used to take watercress growing in jars, and a few dozen new-laid eggs greased with hot lard and packed in sawdust. The ship provided lemons – against scurvy, and for 'punch'. We took eating apples and conserves in jars. I remember cook used to make a most delicious conserve of fresh apricots and red-currant juice, and we took black-currant cordial. Salves and ointments we always took. I always took a ham as a present to the Captain, as we sat at his table; we cooked it specially with cider and cloves. The cloves helped to keep it. We used to take poultry, potted in tubs and potted trout and salmon done in vinegar, and potted meat in jars. We grew to be very clever. It was our pride. We had apple sauce and onion with the pork. The pig was first to go – the goats and hens last. Cream we boiled with sugar till it was quite stiff; it kept excellently.

Today, the keeping qualities of pâtés and potted meats are less important. It is not always realized how quick and easy they are to make. The butcher's mincer, your own electric mincer, even your ordinary mincer, followed by your blender or your moulin, does in ten minutes the chopping and grinding in a mortar which took kitchen maids and boys a long morning's hard work, while the spices were being ground separately.

Potted Swan

A recipe for Potted Swan is included in Mrs Smith's *The Compleat Housewife or Accomplish'd Gentlewoman's Companion* of 1727:

'*To pot a Swan.* Bone and skin your swan, and beat the flesh in a mortar, taking out the strings as you beat it; then take some clear fat bacon and beat with the swan, and when it is of a light flesh-colour there is bacon enough in it; when it is beaten till it is

---

* *Food in England*, Macdonald, 1954.

like dough, it is enough; then season it with pepper, salt, cloves, mace and nutmeg, all beaten fine, mix it well with your flesh, and give it a beat or two all together; then put it in an earthenware pot, with a little claret and fair water, and at the top two pounds of fresh butter spread over it; cover it with coarse paste, and bake it with bread then turn it out into a dish; squeeze it gently to get out the moisture; then put it in a pot fit for it; and when it is cold cover it with clarified butter, and next day paper it up; in this manner you may do goose, duck, or beef, or hare's flesh.'

Compared with many of Mrs Smith's recipes, this is archaic in style, and is probably a traditional recipe which goes back to the Middle Ages. However, made with beef and translated as follows, it is excellent.

Potted Beef

Makes 2 large pots, about ¾ lb. (360 g.) of potted meat in each:

> 1½ lb. (1¼ k.) best minced raw steak (ask the butcher to put it twice through the mincer)
> ¼ lb. (120 g.) streaky bacon (put twice through your own mincer)
> ½ teaspoon black pepper
> 1 teaspoon salt
> ¼ teaspoon ground cloves
> ½ teaspoon mace
> ¼ teaspoon ground nutmeg
> 1 glass claret
> ¼ lb. (120 g.) butter
> ½ lb. (240 g.) clarified butter

Mix all the ingredients except the claret and the butter very well in a blender or beat and pound them in a basin with a wooden spoon till you have a soft doughy paste. Stir in the claret and about 2 oz. (½ dl.) of water. Butter a casserole and press it in. Put about ¼ lb. butter in pieces over the top. Cover the casserole tightly with foil. Stand the casserole in a baking tray of water and bake for 3 hours (renewing the water occasionally) at 300° F., gas mark 2–3. (Foil adequately replaces the crust recommended for the swan if put on tightly, and there can be no particular merit except economy in baking it with a batch of bread.)

After 3 hours remove from oven and turn out on a dish. Press with a spoon to remove surplus liquor, if any, and press into pots so that they are tightly filled to within an inch of the top. A fairly deep earthenware casserole of any shape will do.

Pour the clarified butter over the tops to a depth of at least a quarter of an inch, and they will keep in a cool larder, with foil over the butter, for a month, and almost certainly for much longer.

If you make the pâté up in two pots, each will serve 6–8 as a starting course, particularly good with tomato salad or with a raw mushroom salad. May be made up without the clarified butter and kept for 2 weeks in a refrigerator and for 2 or 3 months deep-frozen.

Potted Meat

Sir Kenelm Digby's recipe from *The Closet Opened*, 1669, headed *To Bake Beef*, is very close to two eighteenth-century recipes for Potted Meat which I have adapted very slightly for present-day use. Sir Kenelm Digby included herbs and an onion.

Mutton and lamb are not generally considered suitable for potting owing to the very close texture of the meat and the difficulty of preserving its natural flavour.

> 2 lb. (1 k.) haunch of venison, *or* fillet or top leg of veal, *or* a 2½-lb. (1–1½ k.) chicken and ½ lb. (240 g.) gammon rasher, *or* 2 lb. (1 k.) rump steak
> ¾ lb. (360 g.) butter
> 1 teaspoon powdered mace
> ½ teaspoon pepper
> 1 teaspoon salt
> 1 pint (6 dl.) good, well-seasoned stock
> *For venison or steak:* ½ pint (3 dl.) red wine
> *For veal or chicken:* ½ pint (3 dl.) white wine

Cut the venison, veal or steak into 2-inch (5-cm.) pieces, season with mace, salt and pepper, and stew slowly in wine for 1½ hours. Or roast the chicken for 40 minutes at 400° F., gas mark 6, and then take off all meat, discarding the skin, stew in wine and water just to cover for a further 20 minutes, adding mace and seasoning; stew the gammon rasher for 20 minutes in water to which a little brown sugar has been added.

Put all the meat through the mincer twice and then blend or pound it well, working in about ¼ pint (1½ dl.) of the gravy from its cooking. Reheat to boiling point and stir boiling for 2 or 3 minutes. Then put into pots and pour clarified butter over the top.

Covered with foil, it will keep a month in refrigerator or 3 months deep-frozen, in spite of the fact that some of its gravy has been worked into the paste.

Very good served as a main luncheon dish with very hot, fresh toast and butter and a green salad.

It will be seen that no herbs or spices apart from a little wine and mace are used. The potted meats were intended to taste as much like fresh meat as possible to contrast with the salted meats of winter.

Potted Ham

A nineteenth-century recipe from Suffolk.

> ½ lb. (240 g.) onions
> 1 lb. (½ k.) minced cooked ham
> ½ teaspoon cayenne pepper
> ½ oz. (15 g.) curry powder
> 1 teaspoon paprika
> ¼ pint (1½ dl.) cider or red wine

Cut the onions into slices and fry them slowly over low heat until tender, but do not allow them to brown. Put them through the mincer with ham. Add the curry powder, cayenne and paprika. Stir well and add salt if necessary. Stir in cider or wine and simmer for 30 minutes. Allow to cool. Put into a mortar or blender and reduce to a smooth paste. Pack into stone or pottery jars whatever is not for immediate use. Seal with clarified butter to keep for a month in a larder, or put in a refrigerator where it will keep for a month or more; or it will keep for 3 months in a deep-freeze, covered only with foil.

Potted Hare

An Edinburgh manuscript of 1780. Note the free use of fresh herbs, unusual in recipes for potted meat.

'Take 3 lb. [1½ k.] of flesh of hare to 1 lb. [½ k.] of pork or bacon fat and beat them together in a mortar till you cannot distinguish each from other. Season with pepper, salt and a large nutmeg, a handful of sweet herbs [sweet marjoram, thyme, parsley, all shredded fine, double quantity of parsley]. Beat all together till very well mingled, then put in a pot, laying it lower at the middle than the sides and paste it up. Two hours will bake it. . . . When it comes out of the oven, have clarified butter ready, remove the crust and fill the pot an inch or so above the meat while it is still hot.'

Keeps 3 or 4 months.
Can be closely covered with foil instead of a crust for baking.

Potted Tongue

A nineteenth-century recipe. The potted tongue is rather highly spiced and is very good served with hot buttered toast.

> ½ lb. (240 g.) cooked ox *or* sheep's tongue
> 6 oz. (180 g.) clarified butter
> a pinch each of ginger, nutmeg, powdered thyme, mace, black pepper

Mince the tongue and work it to a smooth paste with 4 oz. (120 g.) of the butter, the spices and thyme. Taste and add a little salt if necessary. Press tightly into pots and seal when cold and firm with clarified butter.

Equal quantities of tongue and ham can be used as a variant.

It will keep for weeks in the refrigerator and should be served chilled.

Potted Veal

A seventeenth-century recipe.

> 2 lb. (1 k.) fillet of veal
> a teaspoon each of salt, pepper, mace
> ½ lb. (240 g.) butter
> ¼ pint (1½ dl.) very strong, highly seasoned gravy

'Take fillet of veal, cut it into small pieces, season with salt, pepper and mace. Place it in a pot, lay butter over it and put in the oven to bake. When it is done, pound it in a mortar moistened with a little gravy. Put into pots, press down firmly and, when cold, pour butter over it.'

In fact, prepare exactly as for Potted Venison (see next recipe) but bake for 3 hours, rather than overnight.

Potted Venison

From Nottinghamshire. The venison of Sherwood Forest was famous all over England. The venison in this recipe, baked very slowly all night with a great deal of butter, of which it absorbs a surprising amount, has a particularly fine flavour and consistency.

> 2 lb. (1 k.) haunch of venison
> ¼ pint (1½ dl.) red wine
> ½ lb. (240 g.) butter
> ½ lb. (240 g.) clarified butter
> 2 teaspoons powdered mace
> 2 teaspoons salt
> 1 teaspoon black pepper

Moisten the venison all over with red wine, then rub in powdered mace, pepper and salt, and place in a shallow earthenware casserole. Pour over the rest of the wine and add, cut into pieces, the butter. Cover closely with foil. Place in a low oven overnight, 250° F., gas mark ½. Next morning remove the flesh from the bone and beat in a mortar (or mix in blender or beat in a basin) with 2 oz. (60 g.) clarified butter and, if not highly seasoned enough, add more seasoning. Beat to a fine paste, then press firmly into pots. Stand them in a baking tray, with water to come half-way up the pots. Bake at 250° F., gas mark ½, for 1½ hours. Pour on hot clarified butter, cover with foil and store.

Whole Potted Game

An eighteenth-century recipe. Birds prepared in this way will keep for weeks in a refrigerator and indefinitely in a freezer. They have a rich flavour and a quite outstanding consistency.

This recipe, like the preceding one, is very close to Sir Kenelm Digby's (of 100 years earlier) entitled 'To Bake Pidgeons (which are thus excellent and will keep a quarter of a year) or Teals or Wild Ducks'.

birds	ginger
cloves	white and black pepper
mace	salt
nutmeg	6–8 oz. (180–240 g.) butter per bird

Take any fairly old pigeons, grouse, pheasants, wild duck, etc. Wash very well inside and out and dry carefully. Season highly, again inside and out, with a pinch per bird of each of the following: cloves, mace, nutmeg, ginger (a double pinch), both white and coarse black pepper and salt. Put them breast down in a large casserole or 2 or 3 casseroles if you are doing several birds, and spread about 6 oz. (180 g.) of softened butter on the back of each bird. Cover the casseroles with foil and then with their lids and bake at 300° F., gas mark 2, for 1½ hours.

Take the birds from the casseroles and arrange in smaller pots which fit them closely, one or two birds to each. Allow the butter in the original casseroles to set and then take it off the gravy which will be left underneath. This will be delicious if used with stock or gravy for another dish. Melt the butter again and pour all over the birds so that they are covered up to ½ inch (1 cm.) thick. They should almost fill their small pots so that not too much butter is needed, but you may have to add a little separately clarified butter. The butter used with the birds will have clarified during the cooking.

Allow to set and then cover with foil and store. When you want to serve them, take off all the butter and keep it for cooking any meat dish.

The birds are carved in the ordinary way and served with crusty bread and butter and green salad or some fresh peas, if you keep them until peas are ready in the following year.

To Pot Woodcocks

From the unpublished Reading manuscript of about 1760.

'Draw the cocks and wipe them out with a cloth but not wash them then season them with mace and nutmeg and a little peper and salt then put some butter in the bottome of the pann then lay in the cocks and cover them all over with butter and tye some paper over them or paste soe bake them but not too much but as to be tender then take them out and draw the gravie from them and put them into less [smaller] potts and cover them with the clarified butter. A quarter of an ounce of mace and soe of nutmeg and as much peper as will lay on a shilling when pounded is spice enough for a dozen. Approved.'

One would be hard put to it to find woodcock near Reading now, but quail, young pigeons or spring chickens may be treated in the same way and served one to each person for lunch or supper.

Pâtés and Terrines

Liver Pâté, 1

> ½ lb. (240 g.) chicken livers *or* duck, goose, game, *or* mixed
> ¼ lb. (120 g.) pig's or calf's liver
> 2 or 3 rashers bacon
> a little sherry
> a pinch of salt
> a pinch of freshly ground black pepper
> 1 dessertspoon brandy

Stew the livers very gently in ½ pint (3 dl.) water for 20 minutes, with the sherry and a little salt. Remove and drain, keeping the liquid. Put the livers through a fine moulin (carefully removing all skin, gristle, etc. first). Then put the finely ground livers into the blender or mortar (or a bowl if you have no mortar) and pound them with a pestle or a wooden spoon until quite smooth and blended into a paste. Season with black pepper and add the brandy and a little of the liquid in which the livers cooked – just enough to leave them solid but a little wet. Line a small earthenware casserole with 2 or 3 rashers of rather fat bacon and press the liver mixture well down into it. Cover with another piece of bacon. Put lid on. Stand in a tray of water and cook in oven at 325° F., gas mark 3, for 1 hour. Remove and take off lid. Put a weight on and leave overnight. To serve, strip off all the bacon (unless liked), which will have flavoured and salted the pâté. Serve cold with very hot toast and butter.

Liver Pâté, 2

> ½ lb. (240 g.) livers of poultry or game (calf's or pig's liver is too close
>   in texture)
> 2 oz. (60 g.) butter
> 1 clove garlic
> a sprig of thyme
> 1 tablespoon brandy
> 1 tablespoon sherry
> 3 oz. (90 g.) clarified butter

Melt 1 oz. (30 g.) butter in a frying pan. Put in the cleaned and trimmed livers and fry very gently for 6 or 7 minutes. Remove and put in a blender or mortar (or a bowl if you have none) and pound with a pestle or wooden spoon till smooth. Add the brandy and sherry to the butter in the frying pan and boil for a moment. Then add the garlic crushed with salt, pepper (black if possible) and a pinch of chopped thyme. Stir for a moment and pour into the livers in the mortar. Stir and pound all together and work in one more ounce of unmelted butter. When all is evenly and smoothly mixed, put it in a small earthenware casserole, which it should almost fill. It needs no further cooking. Pour clarified butter over, at least ½ inch (1 cm.) thick. Cover tightly with foil and lid. It will keep in a larder for a month or more, or in a refrigerator for a week without the clarified butter, or it will deep-freeze perfectly. Do not eat for a day or two after making, as the flavour and consistency improve with keeping.

A West Country Pâté

1 lb. (½ k.) cooked hare meat *or* rabbit meat *or* chicken meat, *or* any game meat *or* a mixture
½ lb. (240 g.) pork sausage meat
2 rashers bacon
4 oz. (120 g.) breadcrumbs
livers from the hare, rabbit or birds, or ¼ lb. (120 g.) calf's liver
a little butter
garlic
thyme, fresh or powdered
bayleaf

This recipe is very good flavoured with orange, 2 teaspoons of Pernod (which replaces the aniseed suggested in the original recipe), brandy, anchovy or mushroom ketchup, or raisins and grape juice.

Cook the liver by lightly frying in a little butter. Mince the meat and the raw bacon and the liver and mix well with the sausage meat and breadcrumbs. Season rather highly with pepper and salt. Mince again.* Rub around a suitably sized earthenware casserole with a clove of garlic, and sprinkle with a very little finely chopped thyme. Press the meat down into the dish and put a bay leaf on top. Cover with foil and stand in a tray of water, and cook in oven at 325° F., gas mark 3–4, for about 2 hours. Put a weight on it when cold and leave overnight. Then pour clarified butter over. Store covered in a larder or refrigerator for up to a month, or for at least 3 months in a freezer.

* Stir in flavouring of 2 teaspoons Pernod, or 1 tablespoon orange juice and 1 teaspoon orange zest, or 1 tablespoon brandy, or 2 teaspoons anchovy essence, or 1 tablespoon mushroom ketchup, or 24 soaked seedless raisins and 1 tablespoon grape juice.

Terrine of Grouse

   2 old grouse
   1 onion
   3 oz. (90 g.) diced bacon
   1 pint (6 dl.) stock
   glass of sherry
   sprig of thyme
   1 teaspoon gelatine
   1 bay leaf
   2 oz. (60 g.) mushrooms, finely chopped
   1 oz. (30 g.) butter (plus ½ lb. (240 g.) for sealing tops)

Roast the grouse quickly for 15 minutes, then allow to cool and remove the breasts. Place the carcases in a saucepan. Slice the onion and fry with 3 oz. (90 g.) diced bacon and add this to the saucepan, together with the stock and sherry. Bring to the boil and simmer very gently for 1 hour. Allow to cool, then remove all flesh from the grouse and mince it twice. Strain off 2 cups of stock and add 1 bay leaf, the mushrooms and a sprig of thyme. Boil for 10 minutes, add 1 oz. (30 g.) butter, then dissolve 1 teaspoon of gelatine in it. Cut the breasts of the grouse into thin slices, coat them with the minced grouse, and sandwich them together by twos. Place them in an earthenware casserole and pack in any remaining mince. Pour over the boiling liquid, removing the thyme and bay leaf but not the mushrooms. Stand in a tray of water and cook at 360° F., gas mark 4, for 45 minutes. Press with a weight overnight. Very good and rich. Will keep for 2 weeks in larder if covered with clarified butter, or for 2 or 3 weeks in refrigerator without butter, or may be deep-frozen for 2 or 3 months.

Terrine of Rabbit

   half a rabbit
   1 onion
   tablespoon brandy
   2 oz. (60 g.) fat bacon
   black pepper
   4 rashers bacon
   sage
   bay leaf

Cook the rabbit gently in water with the onion until tender. Remove all the flesh and mince finely. Mince the uncooked bacon and mix with the rabbit. Stir in a pinch of sage and thyme, chopped very finely – just a pinch. Add the brandy, mixing well. Put 2 rashers of bacon over the bottom and up the sides of a small earthenware casserole. Press the mixture well on to these and down into casserole. Put a bay leaf on top and fill up with the liquid in which the rabbit cooked. Stand in a tray of water and cook covered for 40 minutes at 325° F., gas mark 3. Remove and leave overnight with a weight on top. Cover with clarified butter to keep in the larder for up to a month or with foil only to keep in the refrigerator for a month or to deep-freeze for up to 2 or 3 months.

Brawn

Brawns were always made from pig's head, though occasionally other parts of the pig were added. Originally, of course, it was made when a pig or pigs were killed, in cottages, or farms or on great estates, but in the Middle Ages and later it became very much esteemed as a dish for feasts, as it could be set in vast, castellated moulds, turned out and elaborately decorated with piped cream, gilding, etc. The term used was a 'shield of brawn'. The Victorians liked to see it on the cold table less elaborately dressed up, and also, in robust hunting country, on the sideboard for breakfast.

The word 'brawn' in middle English (sometimes spelt 'brawne' or 'braune') simply meant meat, particularly meat from the leg of a boar, though sometimes of leg of mutton or pork and, occasionally, specifically of capon, and it is not always clear whether slices of meat or slices of prepared brawn are meant in early recipes, though in general, it is meat which is meant. 'Brawne with Mustard', mentioned in the menu for the feast for Richard with the Duke of Lancaster at the Bishop of Durham's London Palace in 1387, probably means a prepared brawn, which was always served with a mustard sauce, and 'Broke Braune', at the same feast, means sliced or chopped meat, probably of boar. Several recipes requiring brawn in the sense of fresh lean meat from the leg, generally of a wild boar, are given in the Harleian MSS. of 1450.

For the making of brawn there are innumerable traditional recipes from every part of the country and from all periods. Of the two recipes given here, the one from Lincolnshire cooks the head, feet and hocks immediately, while the one from Ormskirk salts and pickles the head; this was done when the brawn was intended to keep for 2 or 3 weeks. This particular Lincolnshire recipe is for a brawn intended for immediate eating. In a refrigerator, the product of either recipe will keep for 2 or 3 weeks. Brawn is not suitable for deep-freezing as the jelly may partly liquefy when it is defrosted.

Lincolnshire Brawn

½ pig's head (prepared by the butcher)	1 tablespoon dried sage
	20 black peppercorns
2 pig's hocks	20 cloves
2 pig's feet (split)	2 or 3 bay leaves

Wash the head, hocks and feet and then put all the ingredients into a very large saucepan with sufficient cold water to cover and boil until the meat easily comes away from the bone. Remove all the bones and any skin and gristle, and then cut up the meat into small neat pieces about ½ inch (1 cm.) square. Strain the stock and pour it over the meat, mixing it all well together; return to the saucepan and boil it up. It is then ready to be put into basins or moulds, previously wetted. Spoon in the meat evenly so that each basin is at least three quarters full and then fill up with the stock. Any stock left over will make a good basis for soup.

Ormskirk Brawn

Mentioned particularly as a good breakfast dish. A little book called *Breakfast Dishes for Every Morning of Three Months*, by Miss Allen, published in 1896, suggests as the breakfast menu for six people, on 24 March, a Saturday: fried rissoles, chicken patties, corn flour cake, aspic jelly (very savoury), strawberry fool (made with strawberry jam) and brawn. A very curious breakfast for a March morning.

1 pig's head, split by the butcher
6 oz. (180 g.) salt
6 oz. (180 g.) demerara sugar
1½ oz. (45 g.) saltpetre
1 lb. (½ k.) bay salt
1½ lb. (¾ k.) shin of beef (bought 5 days after the pig's head)

Saltpetre and bay salt can be obtained from a chemist.
Sprinkle the head thickly with salt and let it lie for 12 hours. Then rub it well with the saltpetre and sugar. Make a pickle of the bay salt boiled in 4 quarts of water, and allow to get cold. Put in the head, without wiping, and turn it every day for 4 days.

Take up the head, wash it and open it out as much as possible. Put it on to boil with the beef in just enough cold water to cover. Skim twice and cook until the meat leaves the bones. Strain and cut up all the meat into dice, discarding skin, bones and gristle. Season with salt, black pepper, cayenne, and grated nutmeg. Then return the stock to the saucepan, put in the meat, let it boil up well, and pour into wetted moulds.

Galantines

From *A Noble Boke off Cookry ffor a pprynce Houssolde*, c. 1480:

Felettes in galentyne
To mak felettes in galentyne tak of the best of ribbes of pork and fley of the skyn and put the flesshe upon a broche and rost it till it be almost enoughe then tak it of and chope it in peces and put it in a pot with onyons butter and faire grece hole clowes maces quybibes and put it to gedur with a crust of bred and try it through a strener with whit wyne put ther to pouder of peper and put it in the pot and when it boilithe let it not be chargant and sesson it up with poudre of guinger and salt it and serve it.

The origin of the word galantine is obscure, but galantines (often spelt galyntynes) were being made in England as long as we have records of what was served at feasts. Their origin was almost certainly Roman: some of Apicius's recipes could well be called galantines.

They seem in the earliest times to have been a series of variable dishes, generally containing the spice galingale, which was made from the powdered roots of the sweet cyperus. However, in the seventeenth century 'gallantine' seems to have meant a thick sauce for bird or meat, often containing the blood of the bird, thickened with crumbs (or for a swan, with a purée of prunes), highly seasoned and served on separate saucers. In the eighteenth century the present-day dish was introduced into Paris by Prévost, chef to the Marquis de Brancas and afterwards master cook in his own right. The dish he evolved appears to have been very much like some of the 'galyntynes' served at English feasts in the Middle Ages.

A galantine is basically a bird or piece of meat which has been boned but left whole with the skin attached and as much meat as possible adhering to it, and which is then seasoned and filled with minced or chopped trimmings of the meat, and with other mince, as well as eggs, strips of tongue, truffles, bacon, etc. added, the whole highly seasoned, the prepared meat or bird tightly rolled, and tied and boiled, preferably in stock. When cooked and cooled, it is removed, opened from its cloth or basin, glazed with jelly and decorated. Simple farmhouse recipes for galantine suggest mincing meat with bacon or ham, crumbs, herbs, etc., binding with eggs, tying in a cloth, boiling, and afterwards glazing. In other words, the galantine becomes a meat loaf.

A galantine is not intended for long keeping, though it will keep for a week or 10 days in a refrigerator. It is not suitable for freezing.

The grandest brawn of them all was, of course, the Boar's Head, the royal dish, properly made from the head of the ferocious wild boar which the king killed when hunting and not from the head of a plump gentleman who lived in a stye. The flavour of wild boar meat is quite different from that of domestic pork. It is dark, with a game flavour, and so requires the high seasoning which all early recipes suggest. However, it can be very good made with an ordinary pig's head, and may still be highly glazed, decorated, and 'bedecked with bays and rosemarye'.

Boar's Head

'A royal dyshe for the Christmas Feast.'

This comes from Lancashire and dates from the late fifteenth century. It is translated and simplified here, but not altered except that a pig's head must replace the boar's, unless you order a boar's head from France where 'wild' boars are bred in certain areas. The head is not pickled as in many recipes, as it is intended for a specific feast and is prepared only 5 or 6 days in advance. If well pickled with salt and saltpetre it will keep for several weeks, as the salt in the head meat penetrates the filling; but the flavour is not as good and the meat is harder.

To cook a boar's head you will need a very large saucepan or fish kettle and a large pudding cloth.

> 1 pig's head, boned by the butcher
> the tongue, separate, plus another tongue or 2 sheep's tongues
> 2 lb. (1 k.) diced lean pork
> 1 bottle red wine
> 12 peppercorns
> 2 medium onions, minced
> 1 teaspoon powdered ginger
> 1 teaspoon powdered mace
> 3 bay leaves
> 2 teaspoons chopped parsley

1 teaspoon each of thyme and sage, finely chopped
plenty of salt and ground black pepper
bouquet garni
½ bottle sweet sherry or madeira
12 cloves
2 onions, skinned and halved
4 carrots

For the decoration:

macaroni	cucumber
prunes	black olives } optional
hard-boiled eggs	pimento
1 red apple	

For the sauce:

sweet chutney	1 orange
mustard	2 glasses port
red-currant jelly	

For the decoration: The *tusks* may be made from long macaroni, which you hold over steam and curve a little. The *eyes* are made from prunes set in rings of the white of a hard-boiled egg, and held in place by the glaze.

A small red apple should be stuck in the mouth.

Stars of cucumber, slices of hard-boiled egg, stoned black olives, pieces of pimento may all be cut and prepared while the head cooks. They are laid on the first glaze in a pattern and the second glaze sets them firmly in place.

Wash the head very well under a running tap. Put it into a saucepan of boiling water for 3 minutes to scald. Remove, fill the saucepan with water to which the wine has been added, and bring it to the boil. As soon as it is boiling, remove from heat, put in the scalded head, with the tongues and diced pork on top of it. Add 1 tablespoon salt, the minced onions, ginger, mace, peppercorns and bay leaves. Leave to marinate for 3 days in a cool place.

Brain the head but save the marinade. Lift, skin and slice the tongues. Lift the chopped pork with a perforated spoon, and mix it with the minced onion, chopped herbs and ground pepper. Line the cavities of the head with slices of tongue and fill them firmly with the diced meat. Pull the head into shape and sew up the openings. Tie tightly in a cloth. Put back in the marinade and add sherry, bouquet garni, onions and carrots, cloves and a dessertspoon of salt.

Simmer for 5 hours, drain, and allow to get quite cold before untying the cloth. Skim the liquor, which should have made a very strong dark jelly. If not solid enough, boil rapidly to reduce it by a third. Check its seasoning.

Shape the cold head a little with your hand and decorate with prepared tusks and eyes. Stick an apple in the mouth, and brush over one third of the stock to glaze. Add further decorations before this sets, and when set pour over twice more to get a uniform jelly of about ⅛ inch (2 mm.) thickness.

Serve with a sauce: 2 tablespoons of sweet chutney mixed with 1 tablespoon made mustard, 1 tablespoon of red-currant jelly, the juice of an orange and two glasses of port wine all mixed together to make a thick piquant sauce. Mustard or a mustard sauce was traditionally served with all forms of brawn.

Galantine

A nineteenth-century recipe from the collection of a London master cook who used to hire himself out to help prepare the food for ball suppers in the early years of the twentieth century. He had had it from someone else and passed it on to a cook who once worked for my grandmother in Cornwall. My aunt, who was a fine cook herself, had the recipe but never made it. I have made it on several occasions and have here simplified and explained it more fully than the original does. It is a large and very grand cold dish and takes a long time to make and should only be made for a special occasion when you have most of a day to spare the day before it is wanted or the day before that.

a chicken, at least 3–4 lb. (1½–2 k.)   }   enough for 8
    or 2 ducks
    or a small turkey   enough for 8–12
    or 6–7 lb. (3 k.) breast of veal or pork   enough for 15–20
2–3 lb. (1–1½ k.) veal bones and/or calf's foot
¼ lb. (120 g.) calf's liver
1 onion
2 or 3 carrots
bouquet garni
2 lb. (1 k.) raw minced lean veal or pork (for chicken or duck 1 lb. (480 g.) will be enough)
2 egg yolks
parsley and thyme (fresh if possible)
large glass wine (white or red)

small glass brandy
2 crushed cloves garlic
½ lb. (240 g.) cooked ham, cut thick
    and afterwards cut into fine strips
2 hard-boiled eggs
olives or pistachio nuts
truffles if you mean to have them
½ yard (½ m.) cheese cloth or butter muslin

The butcher will bone a large flat piece of breast of veal or of lamb. A bird must be boned at home, but with an exceedingly sharp, pointed knife and plenty of time it is not very difficult.* Mend any tears in the skin by laying trimmed-off pieces over them.

Boil the bones or carcase with extra veal bones or a calf's foot, an onion, a carrot or two, a bouquet garni and a little wine. It must be a very good stock; do not add more than a quart of water to a bird carcase plus 3 or 4 veal bones.

Marinate in a small glass of brandy the lightly fried liver of the bird, the extra liver, some strips of cooked ham, and some halved olives or pistachio nuts; and of course truffles if possible.

Meanwhile, make a fine forcemeat of raw lean pork or veal (the butcher will mince this), season highly, add chopped parsley and thyme and a little garlic and stir in two well-beaten egg yolks to bind. Put the boned meat or the bird on a piece of cheese cloth or butter muslin. If a bird is used, it should be opened out flat. Sprinkle the bird or meat with salt and pepper and spread on it a layer of forcemeat. On this lay half the ingredients from the marinade. Put on another layer of forcemeat and the rest of them, and then a final layer of forcemeat. Pull the edges of meat or bird up, over and round the mixture and sew them into a bird shape or, if meat, into a fairly neat oblong. Wrap tightly in cloth and secure ends by knotting or tying round with string.

When the stock has been boiling at least 2 hours put the parcel into it and let it continue to simmer gently for another 2 hours. Then leave it in the stock to cool for an hour before removing it and gently squeezing out some of the liquid. Leave it to get quite cold, preferably overnight.

Next day take all fat from the jellied stock, which should be quite firm; if it is not, reduce it a little. In any case, heat it gently and add lemon juice,

* Slit the bird along the centre of the back and work the knife under the edges of the slit, cutting as near the carcase as possible. Work over the thighs and up over the breast, turning the bird. Cut out the wing bones and pull the legs inside out to free them.

THE COOKERY OF ENGLAND

salt and pepper, sherry, etc. if it is not already fully seasoned and delicious.

Unwrap the galantine and cut out the stitches. Put it on a dish and pour over some of the stock, cool enough to be almost setting. Decorate with slices of olives, truffles, hard-boiled egg, etc. and then spoon over another layer of jelly to hold them. Put on serving dish and chop up all remaining jellied stock and pile round it.

For a particularly grand variant: Proceed exactly as above, using a small turkey. Order a quail for each person you intend to serve (a 12- to 14-lb. turkey should take 15 to 18). Roast the quail (see p. 207) and when cold fill half your forcemeat and other ingredients into the boned turkey; then put in all the quail, packing them closely, and then the rest of the forcemeat, etc. When serving, carve the galantine first at the breast end, and lift the quail out whole with a spoon, one for each helping. After the quail are finished the remainder is still delicious. Quail can be ordered by post from several quail farms.

A Very Simple Galantine

    1 lb. (½ k.) veal
    1 lb. (½ k.) gammon
    ¼ lb. (120 g.) breadcrumbs
    salt and pepper
    paprika
    1 oz. (30 g.) blanched almonds, split and chopped
    2 eggs
    1 quart (1 l.) good stock, highly seasoned
    olives, gherkins, hard-boiled egg, pimentos, etc., cut in shapes to
        decorate.

Remove the skin, bone and gristle from the veal and gammon and then mince. Mix in the crumbs and seasoning to taste, and add the finely chopped almonds. Beat the eggs slightly and dilute with a little of the stock, then stir into the meat mixture. Form into a roll. Tie in a wet pudding cloth. Boil gently in stock for 2 hours. When cold, lift and pour over some of the nearly-cold stock. Arrange the decorations and when set pour over more stock.

Potted Fish

Various seventeenth- and eighteenth-century recipes for potting whole fish are excellent and make very good starting courses for dinner.

The recipes for potted lobsters and potted salmon which follow both come from the Reading manuscript of 1760. The recipes are quite clear and specific and need no translation or annotation, and are both very good indeed, keeping perfectly, covered, in a refrigerator for three weeks (or indefinitely deep-frozen).

To Pot Lobsters

'Boyle the lobsters till they come out of the shells then take the tailes and clawes and season them with mace, salt and peper then put them into a pott and bake them with sweet butter and when they come out of the oven take them out of the pott and put them into a long pott and clarifie the butter they were baked in with as much more as will cover them very well and set them by for use.'

To Pot Salmon

'Take your fish and wash and scald it very clean then cut it up [i.e. cut it into neat slices] and take out all the bones then season pretty high with cloves mace nutmegs and salt and a little peper let the spice be finely beaten then put it into a pott with butter enough to cover it and bake it and when 'tis baked pour off all the butter and gravie very dry then put it into potts of bigness [i.e. the right 'bigness'] and cover it with clarified butter you should let it draine before you put it into the panns.'

The boned slices should have remained intact and can be carefully lifted into the pots and arranged lengthwise as though the fish were whole, or piled up if the pot is tall and narrow.

Potted Wye Salmon

A traditional recipe for potting salmon, which was very important when there was a glut as the salmon came up the rivers. Nowadays salmon is an expensive luxury but if you have some cold salmon left over after a summer lunch or dinner, it can be pounded and potted, or if you catch or are given a whole salmon you may have a surplus which you will be glad to preserve.

Scale the salmon, wipe it clean but do not wash it. Place on a dish, salt it well and leave till the salt melts. Drain it off and place in an oven tin. Season with mace, cloves, whole peppers and 2 or 3 bay leaves. Cover it with dots or small knobs of butter and place in a moderate oven, 350° F., gas mark 4, and bake. Allow 15 minutes per lb. (½ k.) and 15 minutes over. Drain off the liquor, pound the salmon and place in pots; cover with clarified butter.

Trout may be potted in the same way.

Potted Shrimps

An eighteenth-century recipe from a Suffolk manor. Shrimps, prawns or lobsters, crabs or crayfish may be prepared in this way.

> about 1 lb. (½ k.) shelled shrimps or prawns
>   *or* about 1 lb. (½ k.) lobster, crab or crayfish meat
> ½ lb. (240 g.) butter
> 1 teaspoon mace
> ½ teaspoon powdered ginger
> salt
> cayenne pepper

Very finely chop half the shellfish. Leave the other half whole in the case of shrimps or small prawns, but divide large prawns, lobster, crayfish or crab into shrimp-size pieces.

Mix all together with the mace and ginger. Melt 6 oz. (180 g.) of the butter but do not let it boil. Stir into it the shellfish meat and then add salt and cayenne to taste. Stir over low heat till all the butter is absorbed into the mixture. Remove and press down into jars or moulds. Melt the rest of the butter and pour over tops while the fish mixture is still hot. Leave in refrigerator at least overnight before using. It will keep in the refrigerator for 3 or 4 weeks and will deep-freeze perfectly for months. Turn out to serve, and cut in slices to be eaten with very hot toast.

Shrimp Paste

A nineteenth-century recipe collected by Dorothy Hartley. This was Betsy Tatterstall's shrimp paste as she describes it:

> 1 quart (1 l.) shrimps (*or* ¾ lb. (360 g.) frozen shrimps)
> 1 lb. (½ k.) cooked fish, without skin and bone

mace
cayenne
anchovy sauce
salt and pepper
1 lb. (½ k.) butter

If frozen shrimps are used, the fish can be cooked in a court-bouillon. The colour and flavour, will not be quite the same, though the paste is still delicious.

'Weigh the shrimps and take an equal quantity of fine flaked white fish [cod, haddock, hake or whiting are suitable]. Shell the shrimps, and put heads and shells to boil in enough water to cover. Drain, remove the shells and heads, and now cook the flaked fish in this shrimp water till soft. Let it cool, and pound to a smooth paste with a careful seasoning of powdered mace, cayenne and a very little [½ teaspoonful] anchovy sauce. Now measure, and add an almost equal quantity of butter. When smooth, stir in all the whole shrimps, make all piping hot, press into pots, and cover with melted butter at least ¼ inch (½ cm.) deep.'

The effect was a solid potful of shrimps, cemented together with a soft, delicately seasoned pink butter. It was a great delicacy, and always served on fine white china.

4 · POULTRY AND GAME

The appearance of food is always important, but fashions do change. Today we do not wish to emphasize the fact that the bird we are eating soared in full plumage before it was shot, or swam or strutted, handsome as a lord, before its neck was wrung. Our ancestors thought differently. Indeed they seem to have felt that if a bird was beautiful it must be particularly good to eat. Neither peacock nor swan is really very good: the meat of both is stringy and rather dark, with a slightly coarse flavour which must be masked with high seasoning. Yet both were served at royal banquets because, with skins sewn back over the cooked meat, heads and necks propped up and tails spread, their appearance was splendid indeed. The skinned birds were sometimes roasted whole, in which case the skin was simply laid over the roast, the neck held up by a spike; sometimes they were boned and stuffed with smaller birds and forcemeat and then roasted, which would have made for better eating, and sometimes they were cut up and made into a sort of brawn. In the latter cases the skins were tightly sewn, and the birds, borne in procession into the hall and round the high table, would appear complete. The carver would cut the stitches, lay back the skin and place portions on a serving platter.

At the Vintners' Hall in the City a 'feast of cygnets' is still eaten once a year with traditional ceremony. The cygnets are preceded by six musicians, followed by six Swan Uppers in striped jerseys and white ducks. Two Swan Markers, in red and blue watermen's coats, came after them, and then the cooks carrying the cygnets on great dishes of pewter and silver. Mr Swan Warden (who wears a great swan's feather in his cap) joins the procession and presents the cygnets to the Master Vintner. All is splendid, but the eating would be better if the cygnets could be replaced by fine young geese.

In Norwich, which was famous for swans, the birds were stuffed with finely chopped rump steak, 3 or 4 lb. to a swan: and this was certainly the best part of the dish.

Peacocks tended to be even less good to eat, but they were a splendid spectacle when carried in procession, trains spread and heads set alight so that they resembled phoenixes. In the fifteenth century an Archbishop of York served 100 at a single feast.

Nowadays we hardly ever eat these birds, which are neither poultry nor game, and which we consider too scarce, too beautiful and not well-fleshed enough for the table. We go no further in the decoration of our game than to stick the tail feathers back into the roast pheasant. Nor do we any longer eat many small birds: the lark is safe from us, though we eat (and breed specially) the quail, the ortolan when we can get him and of course the woodcock and the snipe. The wild goose is never as good as the domestic goose, though the wild duck, as long as he is plump and does not taste fishy or muddy, has a special flavour and consistency unlike the domestic duck. In England mallard and widgeon are generally the best.

Our ancestors shot any bird they saw and ate any bird they shot. In general we eat only pheasants, partridges, grouse, teal, snipe, woodcock, the occasional capercailzie, the rare ortolan, the quail, the widgeon, the mallard and a few other wild ducks and geese.

Poultry in England has always been the charge of the mistress of the house. Even in great houses the lady of the house would from time to time visit the hen yard and pigeon cote and discuss with her steward and housekeeper the condition of the birds.

In the orchard at Ingatestone Hall in the mid sixteenth century, 'for the better cherishing of those fowls' there stood in the walled orchard 'a frame made of thin plank, lattice-like with partitions to keep them in, and is placed from the wall at least 16 ft and so continueth his breadth. In this frame both partridges, pheasants, guinea hens, turkey hens and such like do yearly breed and are severally fed and brought up, so as they become tame as other chickens'. And in the same grounds there were stews and ponds where 'the swans do use to breed and have many cygnets which be spent in the house'.

The farmer's wife simply took charge of all the poultry and was expected not only to supply her household but to make her 'pin money' by selling eggs and table birds at market.

The cottager's wife generally let her hens wander in and out of the house at will, and in Wales and some other parts of the country 'hen' was a term of female endearment. 'Come along, hen,' a mother would say to her lagging small daughter.

The provision of game was of course a man's charge, from the king himself down to the poorest and most terrified poacher. For centuries there was a death penalty for poaching deer, even though the beast might be savaging the garden and the strip of field on which the poacher's family depended for their meatless and starvation-level diet. Until 1857 the penalty for poaching remained transportation, and it was then reduced to imprisonment or a hopelessly heavy fine. A labourer who was seen after dark carrying a bundle could be taken to the magistrates and compulsorily searched, and sometimes fined, even when the game he carried was no more than a few roots from the edge of a field. Even when the bird reached the pot the danger was not over. Many a farm-labourer's wife, many a gipsy, has sworn to an untimely visiting keeper that her fine stew of pheasant or partridge contained nothing but a rabbit and a hen dead from extreme old age. Fortunately game has a less distinctive smell when unhung.

The Royal Forests were preserved for the king's hunting alone, and the royal appetite was quickened by the thought that the venison came from the stag the king had killed himself, and the fine dish of birds from those his hawk had brought down. In the reign of Henry VIII, in the year 1536, a proclamation was made 'to preserve the Partridges, Pheasants and Herons from the King's Palace at Westminster to St Giles in the Fields and thence to Islington, Hampstead, Highgate and Hornsey Park'.

Until the late eighteenth century, many of the birds and meats served at feasts and banquets were arranged together on large platters (in the case of the wealthy, of gold or silver) so that their flavours and those of their garnishes and any sauces poured over them must have intermingled. There might well be a dish with a swan or a peacock surrounded by smaller birds, another with two or three geese, a third with a capon or two, with plovers, snipe, teal, woodcock and larks ranged round them. These great platters would be displayed to the high table and then taken to the carver, who filled different platters, held ready by waiting squires and servants, with carved portions from the larger birds and with the small birds whole. These filled platters were offered to the feasters in order of precedence, and records suggest that no one hesitated to take the best on offer. A menu for a dinner at Houghton for James I in August 1617 details for the second course:

> 1 hot pheasant and one for the king
> 6 quails for the king, partridge . . .
> chickens, artichoke pye, curlew roast, pease buttered, rabbits, ducks, plovers, red deer pie, pigs' ears soused, hot herons roast, gammons of bacon, made dish (probably viand royal or a ragoo (sic)), pear tart, palates of grease, dried tongue, turkey pie, pheasant pie, hog's cheek dried, turkey chicks cold.

Either the king's taste in birds was known at Houghton, or, the pheasant and quails being far the best on the first dish of birds, it was assumed that he would help himself to them, since naturally he got first chance.

Urbanization has given wild game an even greater luxury value than in the days of smaller cities and a wider countryside. From most poulterers game must be ordered in advance, and supplies are reduced as it becomes more and more expensive to preserve pheasants, and as grouse and partridges become scarcer and scarcer throughout the British Isles. The English grey partridge is perhaps the best of all game birds, each exactly the right size for one person (no question, as with a small pheasant or some of the wild ducks, of one being too much and half not enough). The larger red-legged partridge, which is preferred in France, is considered by English gourmets to be less good. This bird is not abundant in England, where it was introduced originally by Charles II.

In England game used to be eaten 'high', which means that it was 'hung', that is hung undrawn (once it is cleaned it will not keep) in a cool place with a draught, where neither flies nor cats could get to it. When blood drops from the beak of hanging birds they are ready for eating and can be plucked easily, though some people like pheasant hung a day or two after this occurs, as the flavour is thought to improve.

Nowadays, however, most people prefer game hung only long enough to become tender – 24 hours to 2 or 3 days. If you cook a young bird within an hour of its being shot, it will be perfectly tender, but unless you are camping and literally 'shooting for the pot' this will not often be possible. After about an hour it will not make good eating for another day or two.

Poultry

It has become much more difficult to get a good chicken or duck than any other bird, and this is in a sense a paradox, since chickens in particular are cheaper and more plentiful than they have ever been. Quality, however, has been lost in quantity, and battery-reared birds have neither the same flavour nor the same consistency as those which have run about. It is interesting that in the sixteenth century chickens were fattened in closed sheds, being fed with a corn mash made with milk and raisins which were sometimes soaked in brandy: a candle was kept burning all night to keep them awake and pecking. However, these birds had run free until they were due to be fattened (which took about three weeks), and it seems likely that the Elizabethans preferred them with more actual soft fat than we do today. A good frozen free-range bird is much better than a fresh battery-reared bird, and a fresh free-range bird is better than either. In general, apart from small spring chickens (*poussins*), the bigger the bird, as long as it is young enough to roast, the better its flesh is likely to be. Boiling fowls are generally good if given long slow cooking. It is the 1½ to 2½ lb. roasting chicken or duckling that is so often dry and disappointing with flesh that falls naturally into strings however carefully you cook it.

The free-ranging chickens of England and France are the best in the world, and the dishes traditionally made with them are splendid if properly cooked and seasoned. People sometimes say that they don't care for chicken or that they get very tired of it. Unless they are, for some reason, given it three times a week, this can only mean one or all of the following:

(1) that the chicken dishes have not been carefully seasoned with the proper herbs as well as with salt and pepper;

(2) that the stock used has not been reduced till its flavour is strong, or has not had the fat completely skimmed off;
(3) that the cream, wine or brandy the dish calls for has been skimped;
(4) that the birds have been overcooked and are therefore dry (very easy with chicken). Undercooked chicken is so rubbery as to be almost uneatable and is therefore not often served;
(5) that of all the many traditional chicken dishes only roast and perhaps boiled or fried chickens are being produced.

Farmers' wives realized centuries ago the splendid results which could be obtained by cooking chicken with another meat or even two, and serving them as one dish. In the days of large families, when the farmer's wife was probably feeding 10 or 12 on the main dish, one old hen or a couple of pullets went nowhere. Many vegetables and a piece of bacon were obvious additions, but often a shoulder of mutton or a tongue or some pork were cooked with the chickens, and some very fine dishes became traditional as a result. This did not only apply to chickens. In the North Country, in large families with several children, when a goose was to be roasted they used to pack the legs and thighs of a couple of rabbits inside the goose among the sage and onion stuffing. The children were given these 'inside pieces', which were considered better for them as the rabbit was less rich, and more of the goose was left for the hungry men. Sometimes the rabbit legs were put to roast in the dripping pan under the half-cooked goose. By the time it was done they had taken on its flavour and were handed out with a small slice from the bird to juniors. This roast was referred to as the Six-Legged Goose.

Roast Chicken

Birds suitable for roasting vary in size from a young bird, which weighs about 2½ lb. (1–1¼ k.) and will feed two or three people to a capon or a Christmas cockerel, which weighs 6–8 lb. (3–3½ k.) and will feed 6 or 8 people.

> 1 chicken
> 4 oz. (120 g.) butter
> flour, salt, pepper
> bacon rinds or rasher of fat bacon

Preheat oven to 400° F., gas mark 6. Rub breast and legs of chicken with flour, salt and pepper, and place in baking tray. Spread butter on breast and legs with a knife. Place 3 or 4 bacon rinds or a rasher of fat bacon over the breast. Put on the middle shelf of the oven. Potatoes for roasting may be placed round the bird. After 10 minutes baste and turn down oven to 350° F., gas mark 4. Baste occasionally. A few minutes before the chicken is done, remove bacon from breast to allow it to brown. If you cook the bird with breast uncovered from the start and it begins to darken too much before the bird is done, cover the breast with a piece of greaseproof paper or foil. If you have a spit, the bird will be excellently cooked on it according to the directions given. It usually takes about the same time as in the oven.

A roasting bird of 2½–3 lb. (1–1½ k.) will need 45 minutes.

A roasting bird of 3–5 lb. (1½–2½ k.) will need 45 minutes–1¼ hours.

A roasting bird of 5–8 lb. (2½–3 k.) will need 1¼–2 hours.

It is traditional to serve with roast chicken any of the following:

bread sauce (see p. 281)

bacon rolls

watercress (wash well and arrange 2 or 3 sprigs per person round the bird)

gravy (make as for all roasts, but not very thick for chicken)

small sausages (these and the bacon rolls may be placed in the baking tray with the chicken and potatoes quarter of an hour before bird is ready)

A chicken may be stuffed or not, just as you like. The usual stuffing is (for a 2½–3 lb. (1–1½ k.) chicken):

> 3 oz. (90 g.) fine breadcrumbs
> 2 teaspoons chopped parsley
> ½ teaspoon chopped thyme
> salt and pepper
> 1 egg to bind and a little milk to moisten further if required

Mix all together in bowl. Lift flap of breast at neck end of chicken carcase. Work the stuffing in, mould the breast to a plump shape, pull down flap of loose skin and tuck well under so that stuffing cannot ooze out. It is safest to stitch it with a needle and thread, but not essential.

Boiled Fowl

> 1 fowl
> 1 onion, 1 carrot, both quartered
> sprig of parsley and thyme, or a bouquet garni
> 6 peppercorns
> salt

For the sauce:

3 oz. (90 g.) flour 2 oz. (60 g.) finely chopped parsley
3 oz. (90 g.) butter *or* 2 hard-boiled eggs, chopped
½ pint (3 dl.) milk ½ teaspoon white pepper

Put bird in a pan of cold water with the other ingredients. As soon as it comes to the boil, remove the scum. Then simmer gently until quite tender (about 2–2½ hours). Remove bird and pull off most of the skin, which is glutinous in a boiled fowl and comes away quite easily. Place bird on a large hot dish and keep warm.

For the sauce, melt the butter, stir in the flour, cook gently for three minutes, stirring all the time. Stir the milk in gradually, add salt and white pepper, and stir while it boils gently. Slowly stir in 1 pint (6 dl.) of the stock in which chicken was cooked, boil 2 or 3 minutes and then add parsley or hard-boiled egg. Use remainder of stock for soup. Pour the sauce all over the bird so that it is smoothly coated, and allow the rest of the sauce to surround it in the dish.

To Make a Ffrycacee of Chicken

This recipe, outrageous in itself as in its spelling, comes from the Reading manuscript and is dated 1765.

'Take five chicken cut them in pieces as big as oysters season them with mace, nutmeg and pepper and salt, swett margerum and time, a pint of white wine, two ladles full of strong broth, 2 anchovies, 3 shallots, some balls of forced meat, lemon sliced, let it all stew till they are tender then put them in half a pound of butter and beat it up thick with two yolk of eggs, garnish with fried sippols barbarrys, lemon and oysters.'

It is given here in full because when I reduced it to reasonable proportions I found that it was extremely good and quite different from more modern recipes for a fricassée of chicken.

To serve 6–8

2 chickens of 2½–3 lb. (1–1½ k.) each
2 onions, 2 carrots, and a bouquet garni for the stock
4 tablespoons flour
½ teaspoon ground nutmeg
pepper and salt
5 oz. (135 g.) butter
3 or 4 shallots *or* 2 medium onions

2 teaspoons chopped thyme and marjoram mixed
2 anchovy fillets chopped small
½ bottle dry white wine
1 pint (6 dl.) well-flavoured chicken stock
2 egg yolks

To garnish:
18 small triangular croûtons (sippets) of fried bread
1 lemon cut into 8
½ lb. (240 g.) button mushrooms, lightly sauté (these replace the oysters, but fresh or tinned oysters can be used if preferred)

For the forcemeat balls:
3 oz. (90 g.) white breadcrumbs
2 teaspoons finely chopped parsley
1 teaspoon finely chopped thyme
1 small onion, very finely chopped and just softened in butter
1½ oz. (45 g.) butter
egg yolk

Barberries, which could be replaced by cranberries or frozen bilberries, seem irrelevant to the dish, which does not require an additional flavour.

Cut the meat off the chicken 2 hours before you want to start the cooking of the dish and put it in the refrigerator while you boil the bones, carcases and skin in a quart of water with the onions, carrots and bouquet garni to make a strong stock. After 1½ hours the original quantity should have reduced to about 1½ pints (9 dl.). Strain and put to cool for a few minutes and then skim.

Lightly rub the pieces of chicken with the flour into which you have mixed the nutmeg, pepper and salt. Fry them for three minutes, turning all the time in 3 oz. (90 g.) butter.

Place in saucepan with shallots, thyme, marjoram and chopped anchovies, mix wine and stock and pour over the chicken. Stew very slowly for 45 minutes. While it is cooking prepare forcemeat balls, mushrooms, croûtons and lemon. Make 12 forcemeat balls by mixing all ingredients together, binding with egg yolk, lightly frying in the butter in which the onion was softened.

After 45 minutes lift the chicken with a perforated spoon into an ovenproof serving dish, which should be fairly flat. Pour the liquid into a bowl, melt 2 oz. butter in the saucepan and stir in a tablespoon of flour. Gradually pour the stock back on to this roux, stirring all the time so that the sauce is smooth. Boil 3 minutes. Remove from heat and allow to cool while you beat the yolks of two eggs. Stir these in and beat with a spoon for one minute, holding the pan above the heat but not resting on the stove. Do not allow to boil or it will curdle. It should be of the consistency and almost the colour of a thin custard. Pour over the chicken. Scatter the forcemeat balls over the dish and place the croûtons, mushrooms or oysters and lemon slices all round. Serve immediately.

Rice or creamed potatoes and green beans are very good with the fricassée.

Chicken Dumplings

An old farmhouse recipe from Devonshire. It was written out in a 'commonplace book' in the early nineteenth century with a note that the dumplings had been made in that household 'since my grandmother came', which means that it goes back to the mid eighteenth century, having been brought from another district or maybe from another part of the country on the grandmother's marriage.

This recipe uses cooked chicken, giblets, and stock from a boiled fowl.

½ lb. (240 g.) cooked chicken	1½ pints (9 dl.) chicken stock
1 chicken liver (fried)	2 oz. (60 g.) grated cheese
stewed giblets	1 teaspoon chopped parsley
2 rashers of bacon (fried)	salt and pepper
8 oz. (240 g.) breadcrumbs	¼ pint (1½ dl.) double cream
2 whole eggs	2 oz. (60 g.) flour
2 egg yolks	

Mince together the cooked chicken, liver, bacon and giblets. Mix the mince well and stir in the breadcrumbs, mixing with 2 whole eggs well beaten. Season with salt and pepper and chopped parsley. See that the mixture is fairly stiff and add extra breadcrumbs if too slack. Form into small balls, the size of ping-pong balls. Roll in flour and place close together on the bottom of a large saucepan or wide shallow pan. Cover with stock from the boiling fowl, and simmer very gently for 15 minutes after the stock comes to the boil.

Lift out with a perforated spoon on to a fireproof dish. Keep warm. Beat the two egg yolks well and add the cream. Stir in ½ pint (3 dl.) of the liquid in which the dumplings cooked and gently reheat, beating all the time until the mixture thickens. Do not allow to boil. Pour sauce over dumplings, sprinkle liberally with grated cheese, and brown quickly under a very hot grill, taking care that the sauce does not at any time boil.

Boiled Chicken with Rice and Cream Sauce

This dish is traditional both in England and France (*poulet à la crème au riz*). It is as natural a way to cook a chicken and to use its excellent stock as to roast it or boil it plain. This recipe comes from an eighteenth-century Edinburgh manuscript. Mrs Rundell (1819) gives a slightly different one with a gravy or parsley and butter sauce instead of the cream.

1 fowl	1½ oz. (90 g.) flour
3 onions	½ lb. (240 g.) Patna rice
6 carrots	¼ pint (1½ dl.) double cream
1 bay leaf	½ pint (3 dl.) milk
1 sprig of thyme	1½ oz. (90 g.) butter
1 clove of garlic (if liked)	salt and pepper

Simmer the fowl gently with the carrots, onions, bay leaf, thyme, seasoning and garlic, until cooked (2–2½ hours). Remove the cooked fowl and keep warm, covered with a piece of foil, in a low oven. Strain the liquid, keeping the vegetables on one side. Boil the rice in the strained liquid for 20 minutes, then strain it, reserving the liquid, and keep it hot, covered with buttered paper or foil. Melt the butter in a small saucepan and stir in the flour. Cook for a few minutes, stirring with a wooden spoon, then add ¾ pint (4½ dl.) of the strained liquid and the milk and cream. Stir, and allow to simmer for 5 minutes. If too thick, add a little more milk. Season to taste.

Carve the fowl into joints and pieces, removing all skin. Keep hot while carving and mask with the sauce. Serve the rice and vegetables separately, or arrange them in a border round the chicken, pouring the sauce only over the bird.

Devilled Chicken Legs

The cooked legs and thighs of any of the larger birds, chicken, turkey, goose, duck, are very good devilled and were often served to Edwardian gentlemen for breakfast.

For 4

2 legs and 2 thighs
strip of hot buttered toast for each joint

1 teaspoon dry mustard
½ teaspoon curry powder
½ teaspoon paprika
1 teaspoon salt

pinch of pepper
pinch of cayenne
2 teaspoons French mustard
3 oz. (90 g.) butter (softened)

In a saucepan put all the dry seasonings. Mix together, add French mustard and work into a paste. Add 1 oz. (30 g.) butter and work smooth again. Make slits down the lengths of the joints to be devilled and work a little of the paste into each. Spread the cut, skinless sides, with a little more. Dust the joints with flour, salt, black pepper and cayenne. Place on grill and pour or brush a little melted butter over each.

Grill for 3 minutes, turning 4 ways, so that all sides are grilled. Baste with more butter or with drips from pan 2 or 3 times. The danger in grilling cooked joints is that they will be dry.

Serve at once and very hot, each joint on a strip of buttered toast. A green salad is the best accompaniment.

Chicken in Brandy-Wine

This is what Mrs Hannah Glasse calls 'a very high dish'. Its flavour is really outstanding.

Serves 4

3–3½ lb. (1½–2 k.) roasting chicken
4 oz. (120 g.) lean bacon, cut in ½-in. (1-cm.) strips
1 clove garlic (if liked)
2 oz. (60 g.) butter
12 very small onions or shallots, peeled but left whole
24 button mushrooms
½ bottle dry white wine
1 tablespoon brandy
sprig of thyme
1 bay leaf
½ pint (3 dl.) good chicken or veal stock
2 egg yolks for thickening if required

Cut the chicken into 6 portions and rub the pieces in flour. Melt the butter in a thick, deep flameproof casserole, and fry the bacon and onions until brown. When this is down, add the mushrooms and cook for 2 minutes more. Add the chicken and stir well. Add the garlic and herbs.

When the chicken is lightly browned, pour off the fat from the casserole, pour in the brandy and set it alight. Add the wine with an equal quantity of stock. Cover closely with foil. Simmer gently for 45 minutes in a low oven, 300° F., gas mark 2.

The superb sauce will be very slightly thickened by the floured chicken and reduction during cooking and may be served just as the dish comes from the oven. If, however, a thicker sauce is preferred, the well-beaten yolks of 2 eggs should be stirred in when the dish is off the boil and slowly stirred round for a minute or two without reboiling, which would curdle it. This is how Mrs Glasse would have thickened it: a flour thickening is too heavy for the delicate dish. Almost all sauces until the nineteenth century were thickened with eggs or a panada.

Ayrton Chicken

This is a recipe of my own for dinner parties.

Serves 8

> 1 large roasting chicken (4–5 lb. 2–2½ k.)
> piece of home-boiled gammon, about 3 lb. (1½ k.)
> small tin of tongue
> ¼ lb. (120 g.) flaked almonds
> salt and pepper
> 1 teaspoon thyme, finely chopped
> 2 large onions
> 4 oz. (120 g.) butter
> 2 oz. (60 g.) flour
> ½ pint (3 dl.) double cream

The day before you want the dish, or a day or two sooner, cook the gammon in water with brown sugar and cloves (see pp 79–80). Allow to cool in the liquor. Roast the chicken the day or a few hours before you want the dish, but so that it is only just cooked, barely done, as for a salmi (pp 189–190).

First carve the gammon so that there is a thick slice about 4 inches (6 cm.) square after all fat and skin are removed (shape doesn't much matter) for each person. Lay the slices on the bottom of a slightly buttered, very large flat fireproof dish (about 2–3 in. (5–8 cm.) deep). If necessary use two dishes.

Carve the partly cooked chicken, putting aside the skin, and place a slice of breast and some slices from the legs and thighs on each piece of ham: there should be enough to make a nice helping for each person. Set aside in the refrigerator.

Boil the chicken carcase and bones and skin with the onions, thyme and seasoning for 1½ hours. Leave to cool so that you can take off all fat. Cut the tongue into matchstick strips and scatter these all over the chicken and ham. Fry the flaked almonds very light brown in butter and reserve.

Make a roux with 2 oz. (60 g.) butter and 2 oz. (60 g.) flour, and stir in 1¼ pints (8 dl.) strained chicken stock. Bring to the boil and simmer for five minutes. Season well, allow to cool slightly, and stir in the cream. Check seasoning and pour carefully over the chicken so that all the pieces are covered at least ¼ in. (½ cm.). The sauce should be of the consistency of thick cream. Allow to cool a little and then scatter almonds over the top. Cover closely with foil and reheat without boiling in a slow oven, 200°F., gas mark ¼ for about 30 minutes before serving.

At table carefully lift out the ham slices with the chicken still in place and add extra sauce to each plate.

This dish can't be made with ordinary ready-cooked ham.

Chicken of the Duke of Burgundy

Made in England since the days when Burgundy was an English possession.

Serves 4

    1 young roasting chicken divided into 8 pieces
    flour
    seasoning
    3 oz. (90 g.) butter
    2 onions peeled and finely cut
    ¼ lb. (120 g.) button mushrooms
    large glass cooking brandy
    ½ pint (3 dl.) white stock from chicken, veal or bouillon cube
    ¼ pint (1½ dl.) cream
    ¼ pint (1½ dl.) top of milk
    2 egg yolks

Lightly flour, salt and pepper the chicken, and sauté in the butter which you have made hot in a metal casserole, on top of the stove. (A Dutch oven will do well, or if you have no metal casserole, melt the butter in a frying pan and after browning the chicken transfer it to a glass or earthenware oven dish.) Turn all the pieces in the butter till they are lightly browned on every side. Add the finely cut onions and turn lightly in the butter with the chicken for 2 minutes only.

Cover the dish closely with lid or foil and place in preheated oven, 350° F., gas mark 4, for 35 minutes. Remove from oven, add small mushrooms. Replace and cook for a further 10 minutes. Take out dish, pour brandy over the pieces of chicken, being careful to cover them as much as possible in pouring. Quickly set light to brandy. After a minute blow out, if still burning. Lift pieces of chicken and mushrooms on to a fireproof serving dish and keep hot. Season the butter, brandy and juice in pan with a little salt and black pepper and stir in the stock.

Add the cream, top of milk and egg yolks, well stirred together but not beaten. Stir them well in pan and reheat very slowly but do not allow to boil. Pour over chicken and serve. The burnt brandy and cream give the chicken and the sauce a superb flavour. Serve with plain boiled rice or purée of potatoes and a salad.

Chicken with Almonds

Serves 4

1 roasting chicken	2 tablespoons brandy or sherry
3 oz. (90 g.) butter	2 medium onions
a little flour	½ pint (3 dl.) white stock (can
salt and pepper	be made up from bouillon cube)
4 oz. (120 g.) blanched almonds	

Cut the chicken into 8 portions. Lightly flour, and season with salt and pepper. Melt the butter in a frying pan, and fry the finely sliced onions without allowing them to brown. Remove and place in the bottom of a wide shallow casserole with a lid. Put the joints of chicken in the pan and brown on all sides. Remove and arrange in the casserole on top of the onion. Tip the blanched almonds into the pan and fry gently for 2 minutes, shaking the pan off the heat. Turn into the casserole over the chicken. Stir 1 tablespoon flour into the butter remaining in the frying pan. Work it in well but let it get only slightly brown. Stir in stock, adding it slowly and allowing it to thicken smoothly. Add brandy or sherry. Pour the sauce over the chicken in the casserole, cover closely and place in a preheated oven at 350° F., gas mark 4, for 35 minutes. Serve at once, having checked the seasoning of the sauce, in its casserole.

Chicken with Pineapple

This recipe originally came from Jamaica in the eighteenth century. Pineapples were considered great luxuries, but a few came in on the sugar ships, and though most went to London to the court and the great houses, the merchants of Bristol must sometimes have kept and tried this expensive fruit. Some ship's captain must have described the dish he had eaten on a plantation, and this recipe which is included in a West Country collection, is the result.

It is made exactly as the Chicken with Almonds of the previous recipe, except that pineapple replaces the almonds and a teaspoon of paprika is added when the dish is put into the oven. Half a small fresh pineapple is required.

While the casserole is cooking in the oven, peel and slice half the pineapple, and cut the slices into small wedges, as you would cut a cake. Unless the centre core is very hard, it need not be removed. 15 minutes before the casserole is finished, remove it from the oven, drop in the pieces of pineapple, stir very lightly so that the sauce covers or coats them, cover the casserole again and put it back in the oven for the last 15 minutes.

Chicken Livers on Skewers

Livers of poultry, lambs' kidneys, or cubes of calf's liver were cooked on skewers (called 'skuets') at the court of Richard II. In later times they were generally prepared as small savouries at private suppers and were not offered as a main dish. 'Kebabs' of pieces of lamb or veal are not really part of English traditional cooking.

Serves 4

about 8 chicken livers	1 tablespoon olive oil
2 onions	salt, pepper
8 mushrooms	4 rashers bacon
bay leaves	

Halve the chicken livers and soak them in a little olive oil, seasoned with salt and pepper. Then spike them on skewers, alternately with a small square piece of bacon, a thin slice (not ring) of raw onion, quarter of a bay leaf and a small mushroom. Continue to fill the skewer in this order.

The brochettes may be fried in a frying pan with 2 oz. of butter, being turned so that they cook on four sides, or they may be cooked on the kebab skewers of your spit.

Serve as a savoury, one skewer for each person, or as a light supper dish with boiled rice and a salad.

Also very good made with duck livers, goose livers or turkey liver.

Fried Chicken

Serves 4

1½–3 lb. (¾–1¼ k.) chicken	2 oz. (60 g.) butter
flour	2 tablespoons olive oil
salt and pepper	*or* 2 oz. (60 g.) fat

A very young bird is required of about 1½–3 lb. weight. Cut into eight pieces, and rub each piece with flour, pepper and salt, or buy ready-jointed frying chicken.

Put into a thick frying pan 2 oz. (60 g.) butter and the 2 tablespoons of olive oil or the fat, and heat smoking hot. Fry the pieces of chicken till light golden brown on all sides, turning them so that every part is fried for 2 or 3 minutes in the hot fat; this should take about 10 minutes in all.

The chicken is best if not kept waiting, so before frying it prepare whatever accompaniments you choose, such as small sausages, bacon rolls, mushrooms, sauté potatoes, or fried bananas (cut lengthwise and fried 2 minutes in butter on each side).

A nineteenth-century recipe for a supper dish of fried chicken suggests making a piece of hot buttered toast for each chicken joint, lightly spreading the toast with a smooth liver pâté, placing the chicken on this, and serving with a few green olives and fried button mushrooms.

Spring Chickens (Poussins)

1 per person *or* half a larger bird per person
2 oz. (60 g.) butter for each bird
1 rasher of bacon for each bird

You can stuff the little birds or not, as you like. The following stuffing, which is not too strong for their delicate flavour and texture, will be found very good:

¼ lb. (120 g.) fine breadcrumbs
2 oz. (60 g.) chopped and lightly sauté mushrooms
1 tablespoon finely chopped parsley
1 yolk of egg
pepper and salt

Mix all together and insert in breasts of poussins. Stitch up flap of each breast with needle and thread. If you are serving halves of larger birds, spread the stuffing into the inside half and dot with pieces of butter.

If you are cooking small whole birds they are excellent threaded on the kebab skewers of a spit but should not be stuffed. They will cook in 15 minutes, brushed over with melted butter. The stuffing may be made up into little balls, floured, and cooked in the grill tray underneath the birds.

To cook in the oven, place the little birds, empty or stuffed, in a roasting tray, preferably on a grid though they may lie on the bottom. Cover the breast of each or the stuffed sides of the half birds with a piece of bacon fat. Melt 4 oz. (120 g.) butter in a small saucepan and pour over the birds so that each is well coated. Put into a preheated oven, 400° F., gas mark 6. After 5 minutes, baste with the butter which has run down into the pan. Repeat after 10 minutes, and remove the bacon fat from the breasts. Repeat basting at 15 minutes. After 20 minutes the birds should be nicely browned and cooked exactly enough. Keep hot while you make a rather thin gravy in the pan in which they cooked, after pouring almost all the butter off.

Serve as soon as possible. Fried or straw potatoes or very good creamed potatoes are best with spring chickens, and a plain green salad, particularly if it contains some watercress, is better than a cooked green vegetable. Do not serve sausages or bacon rolls with these; the flavours are too strong for the delicate young chickens.

Chaudfroid of Chicken

An essential dish at all the grander buffets of Edwardian times.

Serves 6

1 boiling fowl 5–6 lb. (2½–3 k.)	6 peppercorns
juice of a lemon	3 pints (1½ l.) of water
1 onion	4 carrots
1 clove garlic (optional)	3 or 4 cloves
sprig of thyme	1 bay leaf
salt	2 oz. (60 g.) tin of liver pâté

Sauce:

1 oz. (30 g.) gelatine	¼ pint (1½ dl.) double cream
pepper, salt	1 packet aspic jelly
1 pint (6 dl.) white sauce (p. 277)	

Place the bird in a large saucepan with the carrots, onion studded with cloves, garlic, bay leaf, thyme, salt and peppercorns, and cover with the water and the lemon juice. Bring to the boil. Remove the scum from the surface, reduce the heat and allow to simmer for 2–2½ hours. When the bird is cooked, remove it from the heat and allow it to cool in liquid. When cold, remove the bird, skin it carefully and spread with the pâté. Place the carrots on one side, and strain the liquid through a fine sieve. Stir the gelatine melted in 2 tablespoons hot water into the white sauce. Allow to cool, then add the cream, and salt and pepper to taste. When tepid, coat the chicken with this sauce. Cut from the cooked carrot a few thin ornamental slices and arrange on the breast and legs of the smoothly coated bird. If you have a little young mint or tarragon, a few leaves of these may also be arranged with the carrot to make a pattern. Canned red sweet peppers cut into shapes may be used, slices of cut olives, slices of truffle or cut pistachio nuts.

Make up the aspic jelly according to the directions using the strained stock, allow to cool but not to set, and pour very gently over the decorated bird, so that you do not disturb the arranged vegetables. Set in the refrigerator or a cool place for several hours or overnight.

Any surplus aspic which has run off the bird or is left over can be beaten up with a fork and arranged in piles round the bird on its dish. Carve in the ordinary way and serve with a good green or mixed salad and potato salad.

This is not a difficult cold dish, but it looks very impressive and complicated.

Chicken in Aspic

Serves 6

> 1 fowl, 4–6 lb. (2–3 k.)
> 4 carrots
> 2 onions
> 4 tomatoes (blanched)
> 2 hard-boiled eggs
> salt and pepper
> 2 packets aspic jelly (to make 1½–2 pints (9 dl.–1 l.))
> peas, cooked ⎫
> mushrooms, sliced and sauté ⎬ optional
> asparagus tips, cooked ⎭

Boil the chicken with the onions and carrots as in the preceding recipe. Allow to cool in the liquor, which may afterwards be kept for stock. Remove the chicken and carve the breast into neat slices. Arrange these over the bottom and sides of a 1½-pint (9-dl.) basin which you have previously rinsed with cold water, or put a small slice in each of 8 or 9 small individual cocottes or small moulds.

Press a few slices of thinly cut blanched tomatoes and rings of hard-boiled egg against the sides of the mould between pieces of chicken. Make up the aspic jelly according to the directions. Cut the rest of the meat from the chicken, remove skin, and dice, so that each piece is about ¼ inch (½ cm.) square. Place a layer in the moulds or basin on top of slice of breast. Pour in aspic just to cover. Next put a layer of the cooked carrots diced, with cooked peas, mushrooms or asparagus tips if you are using these; also a few slices of tomato and hard-boiled egg. Cover with aspic. Add another layer of diced chicken and so on till moulds or basin are full, ending with a layer of chicken. The aspic should just cover.

Leave in refrigerator or cool place to set and serve turned out on a bed of crisp lettuce accompanied by potato salad.

Hindle Wakes

'Hen de la Wake' or 'Hen of the Wake' – i.e. the hen to be eaten during the Fair.

This is a late version of a very old recipe. It was collected near Wigan, about 1900, in its present form. It is a feast-day dish, dating from the Middle Ages, as good to eat as it is gay to look at with its white meat, black stuffing and yellow and green trimmings. To be eaten cold.

Serves 8

 1 large boiling fowl
 ¼ pint (1½ dl.) wine vinegar
 2 tablespoons brown sugar

 For the stuffing:
 ½ lb. (240 g.) fine white breadcrumbs
 1 lb. (½ k.) stoned and soaked (but not cooked) large prunes
 2 oz. (60 g.) blanched almonds, roughly chopped
 salt and pepper
 1 tablespoon finely chopped parsley, marjoram, thyme and chives, mixed
 few sprigs of parsley
 2 oz. (60 g.) suet
 ¼ pint (1½ dl.) red wine to mix

Reserve 6 prunes for decoration. Mix all the other ingredients together and stuff the fowl, both breast and inside. Sew up breast flap and draw together skin at vent. Place in a large saucepan of water to which the wine vinegar and brown sugar have been added. Simmer for 4 hours and allow to get cold in the stock.

While the chicken is cooling, make the lemon sauce.

For the sauce:

2 lemons, and 1 for decoration
1 oz. (30 g.) cornflour
seasoning

2 eggs
1 cup of chicken stock
(cooled and skimmed)

Mix the cornflour with the stock and bring to the boil, stirring in the juice of 2 lemons as you do so. Season and add grated zest of 1 lemon and allow to boil for 2 minutes. Allow to cool slightly and stir in well-beaten whole eggs, holding the pan off the fire. Beat till thick and creamy and on no account allow to boil again. Allow to get cold.

Pour over cold chicken and decorate with grated lemon zest, quarters of lemon and halves of reserved prune and sprigs of parsley.

Carve with a very sharp knife. The white chicken meat and black prune stuffing and the sharp bright yellow sauce look and taste delicious.

A Hen on her Nest

This recipe came from a Norfolk manor house, where it was sometimes served in the nineteenth century 'to please the children'. Originally, however, it was a farm dish, the hard-boiled eggs being served to the children and the chicken to the adults. However, a piece of chicken and an egg with sauce and rice may be served to each person.

Serves 8

1 boiling fowl, about 5–6 lb.
  (2½–3 k.)
8 hard-boiled eggs, cooked in the
  last few minutes of the fowl's cooking
  time, so that they are warm
¾ lb. (360 g.) Patna rice
½ pint (3 dl.) milk
¼ pint (1½ dl.) double cream
1 teaspoon mace

4 carrots
salt
12 peppercorns
¼ teaspoon white pepper
1 teaspoon ground ginger
4 medium onions
1 bouquet garni
4 oz. (120 g.) butter
2 oz. (60 g.) flour

Boil the chicken with the mace, ginger, peppercorns, salt, carrots, onions and herbs in water just to cover for 2 hours. Lift out and put in a roasting tin; spread with 2 oz. (60 g.) butter, which will melt at once on the hot bird. Put in oven for 10 minutes at 350° F., gas mark 4–5, so that it browns lightly, and then keep hot in warming drawer or remove while oven cools and then put back covered with foil. Meanwhile cook the rice in half the chicken stock and hard-boil the eggs.

Make a roux with 2 oz. (60 g.) butter and 2 oz. (60 g.) flour, and stir in 1 pint (6 dl.) of remaining stock and ½ pint (3 dl.) of milk. Allow to simmer 2 or 3 minutes and then pour in cream and season well. Keep hot while you peel the hard-boiled eggs, dish the rice and arrange it in a border round a large flat dish (this is the nest). Put the eggs in the middle, and pour half the sauce over them. Sit the browned chicken on her eggs and serve. Serve the rest of the sauce separately and lift the chicken on to a carving board or another dish to carve it.

Chicken with Mutton

For 8, or to serve twice
>   1 boiling fowl of 3–4 lb. (1½–2 k.)
>   1½ lb. (¾ k.) lean shoulder of mutton, boned
>   1 lb. (½ k.) tomatoes
>   1 lb. (½ k.) onions
>   ½ lb. (240 g.) mushrooms
>   ¼ lb. (120 g.) vegetable marrow (peeled, pips removed and cubed)
>   4 oz. (120 g.) (dry) haricot beans, or dried peas if preferred
>   ½ bottle white wine or dry cider
>   ½ clove of garlic
>   salt, pepper

This dish can be heated up perfectly, or you can often buy half a boiling fowl and can then halve the quantities of all the rest.

It is a very old manor-house recipe from the North of England and originally did not include tomatoes, which were not known, but is much improved by their flavour and colour. Early versions have turnips and carrots or any vegetables available.

Put the fowl in a deep and large casserole and the mutton cut into four large pieces around it. Add the skinned tomatoes and peeled and sliced onions and mushrooms and cubed marrow, also the crushed garlic and plenty of salt and pepper. Pour over the white wine and leave overnight. Leave the dried peas or beans soaking separately. In the morning, drain the peas or beans and add them to casserole and fill up with water to cover the whole. You will need a really large casserole or Dutch oven.

Put in oven at 200° F., gas mark ¼. Leave all day in oven.

To serve: In the evening, lift out the fowl and divide it into joints, removing the rather glutinous skin. It will almost fall apart without being carved. Arrange the pieces with the mutton carved into thick slices on a large shallow dish, with the vegetables around it in a border. Stir and season the stock and pour all over, serving the surplus in a separate jug. The stock can be thickened if preferred.

Requires only plain boiled potatoes as accompaniment.

Supreme of Chicken with Fillets of Pork or Veal

This splendid and luxurious recipe is extracted from a very elaborate Victorian dinner-party dish, which was highly decorated and handed round so that each guest could take a garnished portion. It is unexpected and very good and not difficult or time-consuming in the form given here. It serves 6 and leaves the legs and thighs of 2 chickens for devilling or for a pie or casserole. The meat may be prepared in the morning of the day on which the dish is wanted.

> 1 lb. (480 g.) fillet of pork, cut into 6 slices, *or* 3 escalopes of veal cut in halves
> 2 plump young roasting fowls (free-range) about 2½–3 lb. (1–1½ k.)
> 4 oz. (120 g.) butter
> 4 oz. (120 g.) fine white breadcrumbs
> salt and pepper
> 2 oz. (60 g.) plain flour
> 3 eggs
> 2 oz. (60 g.) grated Parmesan cheese
> 6 croûtons of thin crustless white bread, each about the size of the fillets. (These may be fried in butter before you start frying the meat, and kept hot.)
> 18 button mushrooms
> ½ pint (3 dl.) double cream
> 18 stoned green olives cut in halves (may be stuffed or plain)
> 1 teaspoon ground mace

With a sharp pointed knife, cut the breasts of the chicken away from the carcase, so that each bird gives 3 slices, one across the front (with wishbone) and one from each side.

Mix the flour with a little pepper and salt and rub the chicken and pork or veal fillets in it. Beat the eggs well, dip all the fillets and roll in crumbs, pressing these on firmly.

Fry the croûtons and set aside in a warming drawer. Sauté the mushrooms and keep warm.

Heat the butter in a very large pan or in 2 pans but do not let it colour. Fry all fillets on both sides, very gently, so that they are crisp and golden brown: about 4 minutes on each side. Just before they are finished sprinkle with Parmesan cheese and turn to cook for ½ minute and then repeat for second side. Remove pan from heat. Arrange croûtons on a large flat dish, lift fillets and place a pork or veal fillet on each croûton and a chicken fillet on that. Place 3 mushrooms on each. Keep warm in low oven while you reheat the butter in which they cooked and stir in to it the cream with a little salt and pepper, the mace and the olives. Put a spoonful of sauce on top of the mushrooms on each piece and serve the rest separately.

Chicken with Beef Steak

A West Country dish: traditional and still made.

Serves 8

> 1 roasting chicken, 2½–3½ lb. (1¼–1¾ k.)
> 1½ lb. (700 g.) best rump steak, trimmed and divided into 8 small
>   steaks
> ½ pint (3 dl.) double cream
> 1 tablespoon mixed parsley and chives chopped finely
> 3 lb. (1½ k.) potatoes
> seasoning
> butter for roasting chicken and grilling steak
> butter and milk for creaming potatoes

Roast the chicken and allow to cool slightly. Meanwhile cook, carefully mash and cream with butter, milk and seasoning 3 lb. potatoes. Keep hot. Now cut all the meat from the bones of the chicken, removing all skin. Dice the meat, mix in the parsley, chives, seasoning and cream. Keep warm.

Grill the steaks in the ordinary way. Arrange the potato in a border round a flat dish. Pile the diced chicken in the middle and lay the steaks on the potato round the dish. Serve at once. Spoon the chicken mixture over the potato and steak on each plate.

Chickens with Tongues

Mrs Glasse's recipe of 1747 says this is 'A good dish for a great deal of company'. The flavours of the chicken and the tongues are very good together, and the white cauliflower and chicken, red tongues and bright green spinach or broccoli look very gay, partly masked with the creamy sauce. Colour in food was given great importance from the Middle Ages to the nineteenth century.

A description of the same dish is given in the Reading manuscript and dated 1765; it seems likely from the very slight differences that the anonymous writer of the manuscript saw *The Art of Cookery made Plain and Easy* but did not possess the book. She took some trouble to fit it in on a relevant page by writing sideways. She halves Mrs Glasse's quantities.

To serve 12 or 14

    12 breast portions of roasting chickens
    6 sheep's or pig's tongues (these must be ordered in advance)
    2 cauliflowers
    4 packets frozen chopped spinach or broccoli spears
    2 oz. (60 g.) flour for sauce
    1 pint (6 dl.) milk
    ¼ pint (1½ dl.) double cream
    3 oz. (90 g.) butter
    1 onion stuck with cloves
    2 carrots, sliced
    1 tablespoon finely chopped parsley
    salt and pepper
    a little lemon juice

This is a very good dish for a dinner party as the tongues, chicken joints and sauce can be cooked and kept hot for an hour or so or cooked in the morning and reheated. Only the vegetables must be cooked at the last minute. The dish is very quick and easy to arrange and simple to serve, but looks extremely elaborate and is very good to eat.

Wash the tongues and trim the root ends slightly; put in a saucepan with the onion and carrots and seasoning, just cover with water and simmer very gently for 1½ hours; try with a fork and if not quite tender cook for another 20 minutes. Meanwhile put all the chicken portions in a very large saucepan with water just to cover, season with salt only, bring to the boil and skim and cook gently for 30 minutes. When the chicken is cooked, remove from stock, drain and take off as much skin as possible. Wrap all the joints together in foil and set aside. Put the skin back in the stock and boil fast for another 20 minutes or so to reduce. When the stock is reduced a little, make a pint of good white sauce with the butter, flour and milk (see p. 277) and stir in about ½ pint (3 dl.) of the hot stock, after skimming off as much fat as possible. Season rather highly and stir in the cream. Set aside this sauce, which should be of the consistency of very thick cream. Lift and drain the tongues, discarding the water in which they cooked. Skin them and cut each in half lengthways, squeeze a few drops of lemon juice over each and wrap in foil which you have spread with a little butter, to reheat later in a cool oven.

30 minutes before dinner is to be served, put on the stock and when boiling drop in the chicken portions. Allow them to wait in the stock, off the heat, until 10 minutes before dishing up. Then bring the stock to the boil again and allow to boil for only 2 minutes.

Divide the cauliflowers into flowerets and cook as usual. Cook the spinach or broccoli according to directions. Put the parcel of tongues in the oven for 30 minutes and reheat the sauce just to boiling point.

On a very large dish arrange the cauliflowers in the centre: put the chicken joints round the cauliflower with half a tongue, root outwards and cut side down, between each and a small heap of spinach or 2 or 3 broccoli spears spaced evenly round the edge. Pour the sauce over all but the spinach or broccoli, sprinkle with parsley and serve.

Roast Duck

Aylesbury ducks, large, heavy, their snow-white feathers indicating a light-coloured flesh, have always been thought the best ducks in the world for the table. However, only the very largest will serve more than 3. For four, you will need 2 and will have some cold duck for another meal.

For 3

        1 duck
        flour, salt and pepper
        2 oz. (60 g.) butter or fat
        sage and onion stuffing (p. 296)
        apple sauce (p. 280)

175

Place the duck in a roasting tin and rub over the breast and legs with flour, salt and pepper. Press the butter or cooking fat in small pieces on breast, legs and body. Put in the oven preheated to 400° F., gas mark 6. After 20 minutes, remove and prick the skin over the thighs and body with a sharp pronged fork or pointed skewer. Prick so that you pierce only the skin, not the flesh beneath, in a dozen or so places. This lets the fat run out so that the skin is thin and crisp when done and the flesh not too greasy. Put back in the oven cooled to 325° F., gas mark 3. After another 20 minutes, remove, lightly prick again, and if the breast is getting too dark, cover it with greaseproof paper or foil. After a further 20 minutes, the bird should be cooked.

It is traditional in England to stuff a duck with sage and onion stuffing and serve apple sauce separately. Walnut stuffing and prune stuffing (p. 296) are also excellent. If you do not wish to stuff the bird, stew some whole stoned apricots or peaches in a little water with very little sugar. When the duck is removed to the serving dish and the fat poured out of the roasting tin, before starting the gravy place the drained cooked apricots or peaches in the tin and turn them about over a low heat. Lift them out with a perforated spoon and arrange round the duck, one for each person.

Stir flour into the liquid in the tin and make gravy in the normal way. It will be flavoured with the fruit and the slight sharpness brings out the flavour of the duck. A tablespoon of brandy or sherry is an improvement.

Duck with Orange Sauce

Richard Dolby served duckling with the juice of a Seville orange in the sauce and the grated rind thrown over at the Thatched House in St James's in 1830. Sweet oranges, being less bitter, are in general to be preferred.

Serves 3

1 duck, 2½–3 lb. (1¼–1¾ k.)	6 oranges
giblets, cooked, with their stock	mint
a little sherry	1 oz. (30 g.) flour
salt and pepper	

Peel and cut an orange into thick slices and place these inside the duck. Remove the inside pith from the orange peel, cut it finely and boil in a cup of water for 10–15 minutes. Roast the duck as in previous recipe and keep hot. Take the liver from the cooked giblets and crush it with the orange peel on a board or in a mortar. Work till it is a smooth paste (if it is easier you can put liver and peel through a fine vegetable moulin). Stir in a tablespoonful of sherry. Pour off almost all the fat from the pan in which the duck roasted, so that only its juice is left, and work in the flour. Add the paste of orange peel and liver, work in with the flour and fat and then strain in the giblet stock. Stir over a low heat for 3 minutes. Pour the sauce over the duck and serve with a salad of thinly sliced oranges sprinkled with fresh mint.

Duck in Port

This nineteenth-century recipe comes from the Cotswolds. It is probably the most delicious simple way of cooking a duck, and it is typical of English high cooking at its best.

For 3

    1 duck
    30 large stoned black cherries *or* 6 small cooking apples, peeled and cored, *or* 6 small peaches, stoned and blanched
    ½ bottle good port
    a little butter and flour
    pepper and salt
    ½ pint of very good veal or chicken stock

Put the fruit into a basin to macerate for 24 hours in the port, which should not be too sweet. See that the fruit is almost covered. Cover tightly with foil and put a plate on top of this.

The next day, rub the duck with seasoned flour, place it in a baking tray on 1 oz. (30 g.) butter in an oven preheated to 400° F., gas mark 6–7. Drain the fruit and heat the wine almost to boiling point. After 15 minutes, baste the duck with wine and continue to baste every 5 minutes till it is all in the tray with the duck. Then put the fruit round the duck and baste two or three times more, a tablespoonful at a time, with very good veal or chicken stock. The duck should be cooked in 1 hour. Serve at once with the fruit around and all the gravy from the tray, which you should stir well, poured over.

Ducks à la Mode

The following is a recipe recorded by Mrs Glasse in 1747. I give it in her own words, but add one or two notes.

'Take two fine ducks, cut them into quarters, fry them in butter a little brown, then pour out all the fat, and throw a little flour over them; add half a pint of good gravy, a quarter of a pint of red wine, two shalots, an anchovy and a bundle of sweet herbs; cover them close and let them stew a quarter of an hour; take out the herbs, skim off the fat and let your sauce be as thick as cream. Send it to table and garnish with lemon.'

Should serve 6–8

2 large ducks	¼ pint (1½ dl.) red wine
3 oz. (90 g.) butter	bouquet garni, or fresh herbs
2 shallots *or* 1 onion	lemon for garnish
4 or 5 anchovy fillets	
½ pint (3 dl.) very good brown stock	

Cut the ducks down the backs and then across with game scissors, or joint them in the ordinary way. They are better if lightly floured before browning and again after, as Mrs Glasse suggests. An onion may replace the shallots. For the 'bundle of sweet herbs' use a prepared bouquet garni or a bundle of four or five sprigs of thyme, parsley, one sprig of sage, and two or three of marjoram. I don't think a quarter of an hour is long enough to stew the ducks; I stew them for 30 minutes. Many of Mrs Glasse's recipes give very short cooking times. Thicken the sauce in the usual way to the consistency of cream, and season well. She doesn't mention pepper and salt, but assumes it. Better seasoned at the end, as the anchovies make it fairly salt. It is very good indeed.

A Duckling with Green Peas

It is traditional to serve green peas with roast duck, but in the eighteenth century and earlier they were cooked together, so that the duck flavoured the peas and took on some of their flavour. This is again Mrs Glasse's recipe. For flavour it is inimitable.

For 3

> 1 duckling or very small young duck
> ¾ lb. (360 g.) shelled fresh peas or 2 large packets frozen peas
> 1 small onion, finely chopped
> ½ pint (3 dl.) very good stock
> 1 lettuce, cut up fairly finely
> 3 oz. (90 g.) butter
> a little flour for thickening

   sprigs of thyme, marjoram, parsley and several of mint (*or* a bouquet
      garni and a teaspoon of additional mint)
   3 oz. (1 dl.) double cream
   pepper and salt
   1 saltspoon each ground mace and nutmeg
   12 croûtons of fried bread

Rub the duck with flour, salt and pepper. Melt 2 oz. (60 g.) butter in a deep
saucepan and brown the bird all over, then pour off all the fat and put in the
stock, onion, peas, lettuce, herbs, salt and pepper. Closely cover and stew
gently for 35 minutes. Shake or stir the peas lightly from time to time. After
35 minutes stir in the mace and nutmeg, cook for 1 minute, add 1 oz. of butter
into which you have worked a dessertspoon of flour, stir well, and then add
the cream. Place the duck on a hot dish, remove the herbs and pour the peas
and gravy all over. Surround with croûtons, and serve very hot.

Roast Duck with Cucumbers

This is adapted from Mrs Glasse's 'To dress a Duck with Cucumbers', 1747.

   a pair of ducks
   3 cucumbers
   2 large onions, peeled and sliced
   ½ lb. (240 g.) Patna rice
   ½ pint (3 dl.) very good stock
   pepper and salt
   3 oz. (90 g.) butter
   ¼ pint (1½ dl.) claret
   1 oz. (30 g.) butter into which 1 oz. (30 g.) flour has been worked
   1 tablespoon chopped parsley

First peel the cucumbers, cut in halves lengthways, remove pips and cut the
remainder into ½-inch (1-cm.) cubes. Mix them with the onions, pour the
claret over and leave them to marinate for 2 hours.

   Roast the ducks according to the recipe on p. 175. When they are in the
oven, put on the water for the rice; drain the cucumbers and onions, reserving
the wine, and brown them a little in 2 oz. (60 g.) butter. Sift a very little flour
over them and stir in after 3 or 4 minutes. Season well, put in the butter
worked with flour (this is a very old way of thickening a sauce) and pour on
the stock and reserved red wine. Stew very gently for ¼ hour. Put the rice

into the boiling salted water. Keep the cucumbers warm while you drain the rice and toss in the rest of the butter. Lift and carve the ducks and arrange in the centre of a flat dish with a border of rice all round. Pour the cucumbers in their sauce over the ducks but not over the rice. Sprinkle the rice with chopped parsley. Does not require potatoes or a green vegetable but only good crusty bread.

Roast Guinea Fowl with Green Grapes

Serves 3

1 guinea fowl
2 rashers fat bacon
½ lb. (240 g.) green grapes

¼ pint (1½ dl.) white wine
2 oz. (60 g.) butter
stock made from the giblets

Place the trussed and drawn bird in a roasting tray with two slices of fat bacon over the breast. Press 2 oz. butter or cooking fat in pieces down on to it. Place in the oven preheated to 400° F., gas mark 6. Cook for 35–45 minutes according to weight, basting every 10 minutes, as guinea fowl is inclined to be dry.

Meanwhile blanch and stone the grapes. Make the gravy in the usual way for roasts, but use ¼ pint (1½ dl.) of giblet stock and ¼ pint dry white wine, then add the grapes and let them simmer for 2 minutes in the clear well-seasoned gravy. Serve in boat with ladle so that everyone may ladle out a few of the grapes with the sauce.

Braised Guinea Fowl

Serves 3

1 guinea fowl (need not be young)
2 medium onions
sprig of thyme, parsley and marjoram
2 sticks celery
½ lb. (240 g.) green grapes
¼ lb. (120 g.) mushrooms
1 oz. (30 g.) melted butter
½–¾ pint (3–5 dl.) stock, *or* stock and white wine
1 oz. (30 g.) flour

In a large, deep casserole with a close-fitting lid, place the onions cut into rings, the herbs, and the celery cut finely. On this bed of vegetables place the bird, rubbed over with flour, salt and pepper, and brushed with melted butter.

Put enough stock or stock and white wine just to cover the vegetables. Closely cover the casserole and put in the preheated oven at 350° F., gas mark 4. After 1 hour remove the lid, baste the bird with stock, add the peeled and stoned grapes and the sliced mushrooms, and continue to cook for 20 minutes without the lid, raising the temperature to 400° F., gas mark 6, so that the bird browns a little. Remove from the oven and arrange the vegetables in a ring on a flat dish with the bird in the middle. To thicken the sauce, mix the flour with a little water, stir in a little boiling stock, pour back into the casserole and boil for 3 minutes. Pour the sauce all over the bird and vegetables and serve very hot with plain boiled potatoes.

Roast Goose

A goose is generally stuffed with a sage and onion stuffing (pp 296–297), but a prune stuffing (p. 296) is particularly good.

Rub the goose all over the breast, thighs and legs with flour, pepper and salt. Place in the roasting tray in a preheated oven at 400° F., gas mark 6. After 30 minutes remove from oven and prick with a sharp fork or skewer all over the breast and thighs, and between the thighs and the carcase where there is a lot of fat. Prick very lightly so that you only pierce the skin and not the flesh beneath. Reduce the heat to 350° F., gas mark 4, and replace in the oven. Remove and prick again after 1 hour. A goose of 7–8 lb. (3–4 k.) will require 1½ hours cooking; of 9–11 lb. (4–5 k.) 2 hours cooking. If breast is becoming too brown, cover with foil or greaseproof paper.

Serve with apple sauce (see p. 280).

Michaelmas Goose

Helen Edden* points out that the custom of eating goose at Michaelmas seems to have arisen from the practice among the rural tenantry of bringing a good stubble goose to propitiate the landlord when paying their rent. As the old rhyme has it:

> And when the tenants come to pay their quarter's rent
> They bring some fowls at Midsummer,
> A dishe of fishe in Lent;
> At Christmas a capon, at Michaelmas a goose
> And somewhat else at New Years tide
> For feare their lease flie loose.

* *County Recipes of Old England*, compiled by Helen Edden.

This recipe for a green goose or stubble goose roast dates to 1741. Gervase Markham in 1676 says that a green goose (i.e. a goose which has grazed all the year on pasture) should have a sauce of sorrel and sugar mixed with a few scalded bilberries and served on sippets. But a stubble goose (i.e. one fattened for its last few weeks on the corn stubble) may have various sauces, of apples, onions, barberries, etc.

'Make the stuffing with 2 ozs. of onion, half as much green sage, chop them very fine, add 4 ozs. of breadcrumbs, pepper and salt to taste, and to this add the minced liver, parboiling it first. Mix with a whole egg, well beaten. Stuff the goose but not too full, and truss into shape for roasting on the spit. An hour and a half to two hours will roast a fine goose in front of the fire, or in the oven.'

1 goose	1 egg
2 oz. (60 g.) finely chopped onion	salt, pepper
1 oz. (30 g.) finely chopped sage	flour
4 oz. (120 g.) breadcrumbs	3 oz. (90 g.) butter for basting
the liver, minced	

A Michaelmas goose is much less fat than a Christmas goose and does not need pricking. It should be basted while cooking and 'frothed' with flour, pepper and salt 10 minutes before its cooking is finished.

Serve with apple sauce into which 20 raisins have been stirred and to which some lemon juice has been added.

Roast Turkey

Turkey is inclined to be dry, so it must be well and richly stuffed, so that the fat from the stuffing works through from inside. It must also be well basted and covered with fat bacon and greaseproof paper or foil.

Make sure that the size of the bird you choose will go into your oven. Most modern stoves easily take a 15–16 lb. bird, if you want one so large. Larger birds can, of course, have the legs removed and cooked separately.

Stuffings (see Sauces and Stuffings, p. 272) can be prepared the day before the bird is to be cooked – the dry mixture can be got ready the day before that if more convenient. A hen turkey has more meat to the amount of bone than a turkey cock.

Two kinds of stuffing, or even three, are good. Put one in the breast, moulding it into a good shape. Sew up with needle and thread the loose skin underneath, so that the stuffing is held firmly in place. Put the other stuffings in from the back, pressing them well forward.

Chestnut stuffing is traditional, and mushroom or oyster forcemeats are good used with it, as are also mixed herbs, sausage or celery forcemeat. For recipes see pp 296–299 of 'Sauces and stuffings'.

Use any two or three, taking the mushroom and oyster as alternatives.

When the turkey is stuffed and sewn, place it on a large baking tray. Put 2 rashers of fat bacon over the breast. Spread ¼ lb. (120 g.) softened butter fairly thickly all over the rest of the bird.

Allow 15 minutes to the pound, so that a 10-lb. bird will take 2½ hours. A 16-lb. bird will probably be ready in about 3½ hours rather than the full 4 hours, and should be tested with a skewer after this time. Preheat the oven to 300° F., gas mark 2, and keep it at this temperature until three quarters of an hour before the bird should be done, basting every 30 minutes, and using more fat if necessary. Three quarters of an hour before serving turn the oven up to 400° F., gas mark 6, remove the bacon rashers, baste well, and allow the breast to brown to a rich mahogany. Cover with foil at any time during cooking if the bird seems to be getting too dark.

Sausages may be served with a turkey, and Bread Sauce is a usual accompaniment. Cranberry Sauce is also excellent (p. 283).

Turkey Roast with Honey

Traditional in the north. The Romans cooked various large birds, such as flamingos and herons, in this way, and it is possible that this use of honey goes back to Romano-British times.

> 1 lb. (½ k.) medium thick honey for a bird of 15–20 lb. (7–9 k.)
> ½ lb. (240 g.) butter

Melt the honey and butter together in a saucepan and stir till amalgamated. Place the turkey in a baking tray and pour the honey/butter mixture all over it. Allow to stand for an hour or so and from time to time spoon over it the honey which has run down into the tray.

Roast at 400° F., gas mark 6, for the first 30 minutes. At the end of this time the honey should have made an almost black crust all over the bird. Baste with what has run off, and reduce the heat to 350° F., gas mark 4. After a further 30 minutes, baste again, cover the black turkey with foil and continue to cook as in previous recipe. Take off foil quarter of an hour before serving so that the skin may crisp. The honey seals the bird so that the flesh is very white and moist and the black sweet skin crisp and delicious. A few potatoes put round the bird will be deliciously candied.

183

Game

The term 'game' merely means wild animals and birds killed for eating (or killed for sport and eaten afterwards). The following are the English birds and animals to which the term is applied, with the dates between which they are in season. It is now possible to buy some of them deep frozen from certain large food stores at times when they are technically out of season, or, of course, to acquire them in season and keep them in your own deep-freeze.

Pheasant	1 October	– 1 February
Partridge	1 September	– 1 February
Grouse	12 August	– 10 December
Black game	20 August	– 10 December
Capercailzie	20 August	– 10 December
Ptarmigan		
Wild duck, Widgeon, Teal	September	– May
Snipe		
Woodcock		
Buck venison	June	– September
Doe venison	October	– December
Hare	August	– March
Quail	Any time	
Pigeon	Any time	
Rabbit	Any time	

If you order a bird from your butcher or poulterer, you can ask for it 'well hung' or 'fairly fresh'. On the whole 'well hung' game is an acquired taste, and if you have not been brought up to it you will probably prefer it fairly fresh.

In France and most other parts of the world where the same or slightly different birds are found, they are not eaten 'high' but hung for only 24 hours or so. Birds must be hung in a cold place, where air circulates freely.

All young game birds are best plainly roasted in a fairly sharp oven. Old birds are cooked in casseroles, braised, or made into game pies or puddings.

LENGTH OF TIME FOR HANGING GAME

Pheasant	5–14 days. 3 days if you do not like it high
Partridge	as pheasant
Grouse	3–14 days, but should be plucked after 3–5 days

Black game	7–14 days
Capercailzie	7–14 days
Ptarmigan	3–14 days
Snipe, Quail, Woodcock	generally cooked undrawn (woodcock always)
	hang 24 hours to 2 days, never longer
Wild duck, Widgeon, Teal	1–2 days
Hare	4–7 days
Venison	7–14 days, according to weather
Wood pigeon	Fresh
Rabbit	Draw immediately and eat in 1–3 days

GOOD COOKING OF GAME

All young game birds are best plainly roasted and served with their proper accompaniments (see the table on p. 188). A chart of roasting times is given according to the size and the type of meat of the different birds, since it is pointless to give a separate recipe for roasting each kind of game bird when the same principles apply to all.

All game birds should after hanging (see the table above) be drawn and trussed for the table, except in the case of woodcock, snipe, quail and plover: these are usually cooked without being drawn, which improves the moistness and flavour. All the recipes given are suitable for pigeons but be careful of their age and quality. A piece of butter about ½ to 1 oz. (15–30 g.) should be put inside any drawn bird whether stuffed or not to help retain moisture.

The bird should be placed in a roasting tray; a little flour, salt and pepper rubbed lightly into breast, legs and thighs; and small pieces of butter, cooking fat or pork or poultry dripping (*never* mutton dripping; beef is better than mutton, but not really suitable) dotted about over the bird. Better still, warm the fat, but do not make it really hot, and paint over the whole bird with brush or knife: about half an ounce on the tiny birds, an ounce on a partridge or bird of that size, and two ounces for a pheasant. Butter is much the best fat to use as it gives the right crispness and a delicious flavour to the whole outside of the bird. All game birds require frequent basting with the fat from the pan.

A thin rasher of fat bacon may be placed over the breast of any game bird with advantage, as it prevents it from drying. It should be removed when the bird is half cooked, so that the breast may brown. Game birds may be larded with a larding needle, but this is not really necessary.

Game birds are always cooked in a hot, quick oven. A crisp, brown outside is desirable, but the meat should never be overcooked. The oven should be preheated to 375–400° F., gas mark 5–6, for all birds except the very small woodcock, snipe, etc., where the oven should be 450° F., gas mark 8. The smaller game birds should always be served on a slice of soft toast, or lightly fried bread, which will acquire a delicious flavour from the juice running out of them.

If you have a grill with a spit, you will get particularly good results from roasting birds in this way. Rub the outside with pepper and salt and brush over with melted butter. Put extra butter in the grill pan and baste the birds from time to time as they turn. Spit-roasting was of course traditional in English cooking until the middle of the nineteenth century. All the birds listed in the Christmas menu of the Bristol Inn given on p. 14 would have been spit-roasted, though occasionally small birds, quails, thrushes, larks, etc., were put in flat pans in the bread-baking ovens.

In the case of the modern grill, birds smaller than partridges can be cooked on the kebab skewers rather than on the main spit. If you are roasting two birds together on the spit, spike them on with breasts towards the middle and spike a smallish, firm, peeled onion between the breasts. This flavours them slightly and means that the breasts are not pressed too hard together, which would prevent the skin from crisping.

It is essential to screw the prongs which hold the birds in place very tightly, so that they are gripped too firmly to swing as the spit turns. Spit-roasting time is much the same as oven-roasting time, but different makes of grill vary, and directions are always given.

Place slices of bread or toast in the grill pan under the birds on the spit.

GRAVY FOR GAME

This is always made in the same way. Put the giblets from the bird on to simmer in half to one pint (3–6 dl.) of water, with a little salt, for at least three quarters of an hour before the bird will be wanted. With the small undrawn birds this will not, of course, be possible, and you will want a little stock (not mutton) or a bouillon cube, for the gravy. Remove the bird from the roasting pan, when cooked, and keep hot. Drain off surplus fat, if any. Place the pan over low heat and stir in a heaped teaspoonful of cornflour: gravy for game should be clear, and for this cornflour must be used, but ordinary plain flour – 2 level teaspoonsful will make a quite good though cloudy gravy. Slowly add the giblet stock, pouring through a strainer. Half a pint should give the right consistency. Season rather highly with salt and pepper. A glass of any red wine, or a little brandy or sherry in place of an equal quantity of stock, is an improvement for all game, as it brings out the rich flavour; but it is by no means necessary.

Certain recipes for game call for espagnole sauce, the 'parent' brown sauce, to which reduced game stock is added. These will be explained as they occur.

Sarah Clayton left a manuscript collection of recipes dated 1730. Among them is a 'Sauce for all sorts of Wild Fowls'. This is excellent and may be used as an alternative to the usual gravy:

'Let your sauce for your fowl be made of half a pint of Claret, a ladel full of strong broth or Gravey one Anchovy a little whole pepper one shallot let these Stew over a Chafing Dish of Coals then Strain your Sauce and beat it up with a little freash butter and pour it thro ye bellies of your wildfowl.'

½ pint (3 dl.) claret or other red wine
½ pint (3 dl.) strong brown stock
2 strips of anchovy, well drained, *or* a teaspoon of anchovy essence
12 peppercorns, *or* ½ teaspoon ground black pepper
1 shallot *or* 1 small onion
1 oz. (30 g.) butter
1 dessertspoonful flour

Cook slowly for 1–1½ hours, simmering only. Add a little more wine and water if necessary. Strain. Stir in the butter into which you have worked the flour. Beat well to avoid lumps and to thicken. Best served separately rather than 'poured through the bellies' of the birds.

ROASTING TIME FOR GAME

	Electric ° F.	Gas	
Pigeon ½–1 lb. (¼–½ k.)	375–400	5–6	20–25 mins.
Rabbit 2–3 lb. (1–1¼ k.)	350–375	4–5	40–50 ,,
Grouse	375–400	5–6	15–20 ,,
Partridge	375–400	5–6	15–20 ,,
Pheasant	375–400	5–6	30–35 ,,
Plover	375–400	5–6	15 ,,
Snipe	375–400	5–6	15 ,,
Teal	375–400	5–6	15 ,,
Widgeon	375–400	5–6	15–18 ,,
Woodcock	375–400	5–6	15–18 ,,

TRADITIONAL ACCOMPANIMENTS FOR ROAST GAME

Game	Preparation	Potatoes	Other Vegetables	Accompaniments and Sauces
Grouse, Partridge, Pheasant,* Black game	Prepare as for pheasant (p. 199). Insert a piece of butter inside the bird and follow instructions for pheasant. See times on chart, p. 187. For grouse and partridge place a piece of buttered bread or toast under each bird when starting to cook. *Pheasants may well be stuffed with any good mild forcemeat. A chestnut stuffing is good.	Game chips, roast or creamed.	Cauliflower, onions, celery, green beans, watercress, brussels sprouts with chestnuts.	Green salad, fried breadcrumbs, bread sauce, thin brown gravy. With pheasant, chipolata sausages or forcemeat balls.
Wild duck, Widgeon, Teal Pigeon	Prepare as for pheasant (p. 199). Insert piece of butter. Roast for ¾–1 hour.	Game chips, roast or creamed.	Celery, green peas or beans, orange salad, or watercress.	Cherries stewed without sugar or bottled, thin gravy or orange sauce.
Snipe, Plover, Woodcock, Ptarmigan	Do not draw before cooking. Place a slice of toast under each bird during cooking to catch the trail. Roast 15–20 minutes.	Game chips, roast or creamed.	Orange salad, green salad.	Serve on the pieces of toast with additional thin gravy.
Roast venison	See separate instructions (p. 208).	Roast or boiled.	Any green vegetable, carrots, onions, celery.	Clear brown gravy and red-currant jelly, forcemeat balls.
Roast hare	See separate instructions (p. 192). Stuff with any good forcemeat.	Baked in jackets or roast.	Carrots, onions, or any green vegetable.	Red-currant jelly, brown gravy, chestnuts, forcemeat balls.
Roast rabbit	As for hare, but allow 40–45 minutes (p. 192).	Boiled or creamed.	Onions, cabbage, cauliflower,	Onion sauce, red-currant jelly.

Wild duck 1¼–2¼ lb. (½–1 k.)	375–400	5–6	30 ,,
Ptarmigan	375–400	5–6	20 ,,
Hare 3–4 lb. *(1½–2 k.)	375–400	5–6	1–1½ hrs.
Black game: hen 1½–2 lb. (¾–1 k.)	375–400	5–6	45 mins.
cock 3–4 lb. (1½–2 k.)			
†Capercailzie 2½–3 lb. (1–1½ k.)	375–400	5–6	1–1¼ hrs.*
Venison	350–375	4–5	20 mins. to the lb

GENERAL RECIPES FOR GAME

Separate recipes applying to individual birds and to hare and venison are given, but the recipe for salmi of game, casserole of game and spatchcocked game apply to any suitable game birds, or a combination of birds may be used. Recipes for game pie and pudding and venison pasty are given in the chapter on savoury pies.

Salmi of Game

A dish very popular with gentlemen in Victorian and Edwardian times.

The birds need not be quite young, though they must not be old and stringy.

2 wild ducks, a partridge and a pigeon, etc. may be used together if you are using birds from a shoot and want to feed 6 or 8 people. 1 wild duck and 1 pheasant or 2 partridges, if you are buying from a poulterer, will be enough for 4 or 5.

The following is a very simple recipe for a salmi such as has been served in the shooting season in small country houses all over England for two hundred years. A salmi can, however, be extremely elaborate, including truffles as well as mushrooms, and demi-glace sauce as well as espagnole.

the bird or birds	1 orange
1 onion	1½ oz. (45 g.) flour
1 carrot	salt and pepper
2 oz. (60 g.) butter	¼ pint (1½ dl.) red wine
¼ lb. (120 g.) mushrooms	juice of ½ lemon
2 large tomatoes	

Roast the birds according to the General Notes for Roasting, pp 185–187,

* Oven heat may need reducing after 30–40 minutes.
† Not good eating: tends to be very tough and to taste of turpentine.

but allow only two thirds of the time. Remove from the oven and allow to cool. The roasting may be done the day before the dish is wanted. Cut up the bird into neat joints and pieces, discarding all skin. Put the skin and carcase in a saucepan with cold water just to cover and boil for 30–45 minutes. Meanwhile, peel and finely slice the onion and carrot and fry brown in the butter. Add the cut tomatoes and fry lightly, removing the skin as it comes free. Stir in the flour gradually and add the stock from the carcases slowly, stirring until it boils and thickens. Season with salt and pepper. Allow to simmer on very low flame, stirring from time to time, for 10 minutes, and while it simmers grate the orange rind and stir in. Arrange the pieces of the bird in a rather flat casserole. Lightly fry the mushrooms and add. Strain the sauce through a fine strainer into clean bowl. Stir in the wine, the lemon juice and the juice from the grated orange. Season more if necessary and pour over the bird and mushrooms. Cook very gently, well covered with foil or lid, either in a low oven, 300° F., gas mark 2, or on top of the stove over very low heat for 20–30 minutes until the pieces of bird are tender. Serve with triangular croûtons of fried bread or pastry around it.

Casserole of Game with Beans

Served as a luncheon dish at the Garrick Club in the nineteenth century. A noble member is supposed to have said, 'It's the beans make the bird.' 'You mean,' replied another, 'It's the bird makes the beans.'

bird or birds	¼ lb. (120 g.) mushrooms
2 onions	2 oz. (60 g.) butter
2 carrots	1 oz. (30 g.) flour
salt and pepper	½ lb. (240 g.) haricot or
thyme, parsley, marjoram	butter beans
2 oz. (60 g.) bacon	1 tablespoon chopped
¼–½ pint (1½–3 dl.) red wine	parsley and chives

Old game birds may be used.

In the evening before the dish is wanted, place the bird or birds whole in a deep casserole with 2 cut onions, 2 carrots, salt and pepper, herbs tied together, and the bacon cut in pieces. Pour over the red wine and leave to marinate. Put the beans to soak in boiling water.

In the morning fill the casserole up with water to cover the birds, cover the casserole closely and put in a very low oven, 150° F., gas mark ¼, and cook for 3½ hours. Drain the beans, bring to the boil in a separate casserole of salted water and place in the oven. From time to time check that they have not absorbed all the water and add a little more if necessary.

After 3¼ hours, add the mushrooms to the casserole and a quarter of an hour later remove the birds and carve and joint, discarding skin. Keep the joints and pieces of birds hot. Make a roux in a saucepan with 1 oz. (30 g.) butter into which you stir 1 oz. (30 g.) of flour and cook for 3 minutes. Then stir in stock from the casserole and boil for 2 or 3 minutes. Check that the beans are soft, having absorbed most of the water. Drain, season and lightly stir in the rest of the butter. Place the beans on a hot dish and the carved birds on them, and pour the sauce over all. Sprinkle with chopped parsley and chives.

Grilled or Spatchcocked Game

A London clubman's dish.

> young bird or birds, ½ or 1 per person, according to size
> 2 oz. (60 g.) butter
> pepper and salt
> watercress ⎫
> bacon ⎪
> mushrooms ⎬ any of these as garnishes, if liked
> croûtons ⎪
> tin pâté de foie ⎭

All small young birds, including poussins and ducklings, may be cooked in this way, which is quick and delicious. It is essential that the bird should be really young and quite small.

Take a sharp, heavy knife and cut the drawn but untrussed bird right through the breast bone so that the bird can be opened out flat, the two halves joined only along the back. Lay on the preheated grill, rub with salt and pepper. Brush all over on both sides with melted butter and grill 6–8 minutes on each side. If it begins to brown too much, turn the grill down and baste with a little more butter. Serve at once, on a hot dish garnished with watercress, grilled or fried mushrooms, rashers of bacon, and croûtons of fried bread.

For a grander dish, two minutes before the spatchcocked bird is cooked, see that it is inside-upwards and spread both halves with the contents of a tin of pâté de foie. Grill another 2 minutes.

Special Roast Grouse

1 grouse (for 1 or 2 people)	sprig of thyme
salt and pepper	round of toast
flour	butter
strips of bacon	

Rub the bird all over with salt, pepper and a very little flour. Wrap a rasher of bacon round the breast. Put a sprig of thyme and a lump of butter inside the bird and set it on a large thin piece of toast. Spread 2 oz. (60 g.) softened butter over it and roast in a very hot oven for 15–20 minutes according to size. Grouse should be served slightly underdone.

It may be served whole on the toast or it may be carved and the meat off the legs chopped and mixed with a little of the gravy. Save the grouse liver, fry it slightly, mix it with the chopped legs and gravy, and spread the whole on the toast on which the bird cooked. Place the carved breast on this and serve.

Cold roast grouse is considered a particular delicacy for luncheon or supper. It should be very underdone, served with a watercress salad.

Roast Hare

1 young hare	½ pint (3 dl.) stock
½–¾ lb. (240–360 g.) forcemeat	salt and pepper
¼ lb. (120 g.) rashers of fat bacon	juice of ½ lemon
¼ lb. (120 g.) butter	1 tablespoon red-currant jelly
flour	1 wineglass red wine

Only a young hare is fit for roasting. If the hare is older, have the saddle cut separately and roast only this, jugging the remainder. Stuff the roast with forcemeat (p. 296).

Tie slices of fat bacon on the hare. Make the butter hot in a roasting pan before putting in the hare, cover with well-greased paper or foil, and put in the oven at 350° F., gas mark 4, for 1 hour. Baste it well during the cooking, otherwise it will be dry. Use more butter if necessary. When nearly done, remove the bacon, froth the hare with flour, baste well and put back till nicely browned. Keep warm on serving dish.

Pour off the fat from the tin, and mix in a tablespoon of flour; add ½ pint of stock, and season with salt and pepper. Stir while it boils gently for five minutes; add lemon juice and 1 tablespoonful red-currant jelly and the wine and bring to the boil. Strain and serve. Chestnuts made into a purée or served with brussels sprouts (see p. 352) go very well with roast hare.

Jugged Hare

This recipe comes from the eighteenth century but, judging from earlier collections, goes back almost without differences to medieval times.

It is important that the hare should be truly 'jugged', that is cooked in a deep covered casserole or pot which stands in a larger vessel of boiling water. You may need a fish kettle for size and depth. In this way the hare cooks evenly and without drying and is done in about 3 hours. This method, of course, goes back to the days of cauldron cookery, when there would have been puddings, joints, and so on cooking separately in the same boiling water. However, if you cook a hare in a casserole in the oven or stew it gently in a saucepan on top of the cooker, it will be clear that though both are good neither is the equal in flavour or consistency of the properly 'jugged' hare, since they must have liquid added at the beginning of the cooking.

> 1 hare, or half a hare or the saddle only
> ½ lb. (240 g.) fat bacon in one piece
> 2 large onions, quartered
> 4 or 5 carrots
> bunch of thyme, marjoram, parsley, or a bouquet garni
> a little mace, 6 cloves, 12 peppercorns
> 1 teaspoon salt
> 1 glass of port
> ¼ pint (1½ dl.) red wine
> 1 tablespoon red-currant jelly

1 hare is enough for 8 or 10, the saddle is enough for 4. Ask the butcher for the blood if you intend to use it. The quantities above are for half a hare – reduce slightly for the saddle alone.

Cut all the best parts of the meat into 1½-inch (4-cm.) pieces and divide the legs and thighs as separate portions. (This will usually be done by the butcher.) Peel and cut up the vegetables and cut the bacon into ½-inch (1-cm.) cubes. Fry the bacon for 3 or 4 minutes in a large pan, then add the meat and vegetables and brown as evenly as possible, stirring well. Put into casserole with herbs, mace, cloves, salt and peppercorns. Add no stock or water. Cover tightly with foil and then with the lid. Stand in boiling water which comes at least half-way up the pot and cover the vessel. Keep boiling, renewing the water if necessary, for 3 hours. Meanwhile boil the bones, carcase and trimmings of the hare in 1½ pints (9 dl.) of water, with salt and pepper, for about 2 hours.

Lift and open the pot with the hare, which will be thick but not dry, and lightly stir in the red wine port and red-currant jelly. Add a little more salt and pepper and check for flavour.

At this point the blood of the hare may be added if liked and stirred well in, and the dish reheated a little. On no account must it boil or the blood will curdle. Many of the earlier recipes omit the blood, preferring to stir in ½ pint (3 dl.) of the stock made from the bones. This is really preferable, because the casserole can then simmer for 5 minutes which improves the richness of the added wine, but some people think that a jugged hare must have its blood in the sauce as it gives a distinctive flavour.

The dish should only have enough sauce to coat and moisten the meat and vegetables: it should not be of the consistency of a stew. The remaining stock from the bones may be made into excellent soup.

Red-currant jelly and forcemeat balls may be served with the hare. It is very rich and requires only potatoes mashed with a little butter and a lettuce and watercress salad with French dressing.

The Royal Recipe for Hare

This recipe is best of all for wild boar, but it is also excellent for hare or venison. It comes from the collection of Norman Douglas. The original recipe has 2 oz. (60 g.) pine nuts rather than almonds, but either are very good.

   1 saddle of hare

The meat is marinated in the following marinade for about 12 hours:

½ pint (3 dl.) dry white wine	1 stock celery, sliced
2 carrots ⎫	1 bay leaf
2 medium onions ⎬ finely sliced	3 cloves
1 clove garlic ⎭	sprigs of parsley and thyme

Turn the saddle of hare in the marinade several times and spoon the vegetables and liquids over it.

Melt in a large saucepan or Dutch oven 2 oz. (60 g.) butter. Remove the hare and the vegetables from the marinade and brown all slightly in the butter. When brown, set on a low heat and gradually spoon all the marinade liquor over the hare and vegetables, a little every few minutes, covering it in between. Very slowly simmer for about an hour to 1¼ hours.

Meanwhile, prepare the sauce.

> 1 oz. (30 g.) caster sugar
> 1 tablespoon wine vinegar
> 2 oz. (60 g.) blanched and halved almonds
> 1 oz. (30 g.) stoned raisins ⎤
> 1 oz. (30 g.) currants   ⎦ soaked in a little water
> 2 oz. (60 g.) bitter chocolate, finely grated

Put the sugar into a saucepan with a teaspoonful of water and caramelize over heat. Add a tablespoon of wine vinegar and bring to the boil. Leave to cool.

When the hare is done remove from the pan and keep hot. Strain into the sugar/vinegar sauce half of the liquid in which the hare was cooking. Add the blanched and halved almonds, raisins, currants and bitter chocolate. Stir for 2 minutes. This sauce is wonderful with the strong hare or venison meat, as the chocolate brings out the flavour without being really discernible. It can be served separately and the hare carved at table, or the hare may be carved in slices in the kitchen and the sauce poured over. Be careful to keep it very hot.

Plain rice or boiled potatoes are best with this dish and red wine, rough cider, or beer should be drunk with it. It calls for something more definite than water.

Stewed Hare

This is an adaptation of two recipes of 1430 and 1450 from the Harleian MSS., 'Harys in Cyveye' and 'Hare in Wortes'.

> 1 hare   2 oz. (60 g.) butter
> bunch of mixed herbs   thickening of butter and flour
> 2 onions (each stuck with 3 cloves) ¼ pint (1½ dl.) red wine
> ½ teaspoon black pepper   glass of port
> strip of lemon peel

Instead of red wine and water, rough cider or ale may be used. Both give an excellent flavour.

Wash the hare and cut it into small joints, flouring each piece. Brown lightly in butter. Put into a saucepan with herbs, onions, cloves, pepper and lemon peel. Cover with the red wine and water, and let it simmer until tender – about 2 hours. Take out pieces of hare, thicken the gravy with the butter and flour, and add the port wine. Let this boil for 10 minutes, then strain over the hare and serve very hot. Red-currant jelly and forcemeat balls should be served with this.

In the first of the fifteenth-century recipes, saffron is added but does not much affect the flavour. In the second, finely shredded cabbage (white cabbage is best) with chopped parsley and chopped leeks are added. They should be put in about 20 minutes before the hare should be cooked ('And if she be an olde hare, lete her boile well, or thou cast in thi wortes').

This makes an excellent dish, reminiscent of Partridges Stewed with Cabbage. The not very precise fifteenth-century recipe suggests adding borage, violets, betony and young nettles to the cabbage, but the cabbage, leeks and parsley seem enough in themselves.

Ortolans

Ortolans have become no more than a mythical delicacy, since they are un-obtainable today. Our ancestors took them for granted as delicate small birds, to be served at feasts along with larks and quail. They are a kind of bunting and used to be netted and fattened for the table when they arrived in migration from the north. Mrs Glasse (1747) and Mrs Russell (1819) both give rather casual directions for roasting them on the spit. Other early cookery books imply that any recipe for quails will be even better with ortolans.

Roast Partridge from the West Country

> 1 partridge for 1 or 2 people
> ¼ lb. (120 g.) calf's liver
> small onion, finely chopped
> parsley, thyme
> fat bacon
> butter
> salt and pepper
> 4 cooking apples
> 1 glass brandy
> 2 oz. (60 g.) breadcrumbs
> ¼ pint (1½ dl.) double cream

Fry the calf's liver with the liver of the partridge and a little finely chopped onion. Mince and mix with the breadcrumbs and chopped parsley and thyme, season and stuff the bird from the tail end with this forcemeat. Wrap the bird in bacon and put in a roasting tray. Peel and core the apples and place them round the partridge. Brush the apples and bird over with melted butter. Cook for 15 minutes in a preheated oven, 400° F., gas mark 6. Pour a small glass of cooking brandy (or Calvados) over the bird and set it alight.

If the bird is for 2, split it in half through the breast bone with a sharp, heavy knife and spread the inside of each half with the stuffing, on which you put bacon and butter. Lay in roasting tin stuffing side up. Cook the apples in butter for 10 minutes before putting in partridge halves and then cook for only 10 minutes more, as the halves take less time than a whole bird.

Remove bird and apples to a hot serving dish and keep hot. Put the roasting pan over low flame and stir the cream into the juices. Allow to bubble, stirring all the time. Pour over the bird and apples, and serve at once with creamed potatoes and a plain green salad.

Casserole of Partridge with Cabbage

Enough for 4 or 5
> brace of old birds
> 4 onions
> 4 rashers of bacon
> 2 carrots
> pepper and salt
> sprinkling of chopped parsley and thyme
> 1 savoy cabbage (each quarter should be about the size of a partridge)
> ¼ pint (1½ dl.) red wine or rough cider
> 1 oz. (30 g.) flour
> 1 oz. (30 g.) butter

Place an onion inside each bird and a rasher of bacon over each. Put them in a large casserole with sliced carrots and onions cut into rings, the remaining bacon diced, pepper and salt, and the parsley and thyme. Pour over the red wine or cider. Leave overnight.

In the morning, pack the quarters of cabbage round the birds and fill the casserole up with water, just to cover all. Put in the oven at 250° F., gas mark ½. Leave to cook very slowly for 4 hours.

Lift the cabbage and vegetables carefully on to a large dish and put birds in the middle.

Thicken the gravy slightly by making a roux with the butter and flour in the usual way. Pour over the birds and cabbage.

Serve very hot with plain boiled potatoes or rice. Both cabbage and partridges benefit from being cooked together.

The birds, when served, will need dividing rather than carving.

Stewed Partridges

This recipe comes from a Norfolk farm. It may also be made with pheasants, and about half of a young vegetable marrow, peeled, seeded and cut in inch cubes, may be added.

Serves 4 or 5

brace of partridges	4 cloves
2 oz. (60 g.) butter	6 peppercorns, salt
4 large slices lean ham	1½ pints (9 dl.) stock
1 clove of garlic	1 glass port or 2 glasses red wine
4 tomatoes skinned and halved	pinch of sugar
pinch of thyme	triangles of toast
½ lb. (240 g.) small mushrooms	

Cut up the birds into joints or halves, brown in the butter, then put them into a stewpan with the slices of ham cut up, the clove of garlic, tomatoes, mushrooms, cloves, thyme, sugar, peppercorns, salt, wine and enough stock to cover them. Simmer the birds very slowly for 2 hours, when they will be tender enough to melt in the mouth, yet not in the least stringy or overdone. Serve them on a dish, heaped up with the vegetables and ham, surrounded by the gravy, which has been freed from fat, thickened and made very hot. Place triangles of toast round the dish.

Cold Partridge with Rum

A dish occasionally served in Edwardian days to gentlemen who were breakfasting late after a night at cards. It is very good indeed for lunch.

1 roast partridge per head	lettuce hearts
large glass of rum	watercress
lemon juice	French dressing

Roast the partridge; carve it into joints immediately it is done and while still warm put into a pie dish containing a large glass of good rum. Cover the dish but turn the pieces of bird from time to time and leave till next day. Drain them if very wet, sprinkle with a little lemon juice and serve on a salad of lettuce hearts and watercress, with French dressing offered separately.

Roast Pheasant

brace of young pheasants
2 oz. (60 g.) butter
2 rashers fat bacon
2 shallots or 1 onion
bunch of watercress

a little flour
pepper and salt
2 oz. (60 g.) very fine
   breadcrumbs

Put 1 oz. (30 g.) butter and a shallot or half an onion inside each bird, and wrap the fat bacon around the breast of each. Put them into a roasting tray, cover lightly with foil, and roast in a preheated oven, 400° F., gas mark 6, for 30 minutes. Remove the birds from the oven. Uncover them, dredge lightly with seasoned flour, baste them well, and return to the oven to brown for ten minutes. By roasting covered, you prevent the breasts from drying. If you prefer to roast uncovered, flour lightly at the start and baste well every 10 minutes. Cook on a spit for same length of time as in oven, fastening the birds breast to breast with a small onion between to hold them apart and add flavour. Fix very firmly so that they will not swing while turning. Brush all over with melted butter and baste from time to time.

Serve garnished with watercress and accompanied by fried crumbs, red-currant jelly, forcemeat balls (p. 97), small bacon rolls, and bread sauce (p. 281).

For the crumbs, pour a little of the fat from the roasting birds into a small frying pan a few minutes before they should be cooked, make it smoking hot and drop in the crumbs, shaking and turning them quickly until they are light brown and dry and crisp.

Braised Pheasant

An eighteenth-century Scottish recipe which is very simple but outstanding. Grouse were treated in the same way. The birds were intended to be served in the casserole in which they cooked, one for each person, with no accompaniments except bread. The chutney both sweetens and sharpens the sauce and improves the consistency.

199

> 1 pheasant (enough for 3 or even 4)
> 3 medium onions
> 3 oz. (90 g.) butter
> 2 tablespoons of good, sweet tomato chutney
> 1 glass of red wine
> 1 pint (6 dl.) of very good stock
> pepper and salt
> 1 dessertspoon cornflour to thicken gravy

Peel and cut up the onions and brown lightly in the butter, being careful not to burn. Remove to the casserole, and brown the pheasant on all sides in the butter. Put on top of onions. Add chutney, wine, stock and seasoning. Closely cover and simmer 1 hour in the oven at 300° F., gas mark 2–3. Reduce heat if it bubbles fiercely. Take out, check seasoning and serve on a flat dish with gravy and onions poured over. The bird will almost fall apart but will have a very rich flavour. If you prefer a thicker gravy, pour off stock into small saucepan and bring to boil. Mix the cornflour with a little water, pour in some of the stock, stir well and pour into the remaining stock in saucepan. Boil for 3 minutes and pour over bird.

PIGEONS

Pigeons were extremely important items of food in the Middle Ages, and up till the early twentieth century. Nowadays, they are kept more in the north than the south of England, and more by 'fanciers' for racing than for food. In the country, wild pigeons are shot and the best of the bag eaten, but few households keep them in cotes and kill them regularly for the table. However, they are readily available from most poulterers, though they may have to be ordered in advance.

In the Star Chamber Accounts of 1519 and 1520, they cost a penny each. In 1590 wild birds cost 2½d. each, and house pigeons 6d. At Ingatestone Hall, 20 pairs of pigeons formed part of the supper at Catherine Tyrell's wedding in 1552, and the total killed that year from the great pigeon cote in the yard, between Easter and Michaelmas, was 1,080.

Young pigeons, about a month old, are called squabs, and are considered a great delicacy if roasted exactly as partridges for 10–15 minutes only, or grilled.

Jugged Pigeons

This recipe is from *The Art of Cookery Made Plain and Easy*, but derives from medieval and probably from Roman cookery. The stuffing is typical of the latter. It is given here because it is very simple to make, and so extremely good that it is unforgettable. The pigeons must be plump and well covered, but need not be quite young.

For 4

    4 plump pigeons, drawn and trussed
    2 sticks of celery
    butter
    flour

    For the stuffing:
    their livers, *or* ¼ lb. (120 g.) chicken livers
    yolks of 4 hard-boiled eggs and 1 whole raw egg, beaten
    pinch of grated nutmeg
    pinch of grated lemon peel
    2 teaspoons finely chopped parsley
    2 oz. (60 g.) prepared grated suet
    2 oz. (60 g.) fine white breadcrumbs
    salt and pepper
    butter
    flour

Mince the livers and pound well. Pound the hard-boiled egg yolks and mix with the livers and pound again. Stir in all the other ingredients, using the beaten egg to bind them. Stuff the pigeons' breasts, and put any surplus stuffing in from the vents. Sew up the breasts and draw the skin over the vents so that the stuffing cannot escape. Dip each bird in cold water and then rub with a little salt and pepper. Put them, pressed tightly, into a jug or a deep casserole, with the celery and a piece of butter the size of a walnut (no water). Closely cover the jug or casserole with a double thickness of foil and stand it in a very large bath or saucepan with cold water to come three quarters of the way up the jug of pigeons. Boil 3 hours, filling up with boiling water when necessary. Place the pigeons on a hot dish. Remove the celery from the jug. Make a roux in a small saucepan from ½ oz. (15 g.) flour and ½ oz. (15 g.) butter, stir in the liquor from the jug and boil for 2 minutes. Pour it over the pigeons. It should be just enough to glaze and surround them in the dish.

Serve at once with slices of lemon for garnish. Red-currant jelly is very good with them.

Old grouse are excellent jugged in the same way.

Spatchcocked Pigeons

Very young birds, a little older than squabs, are required. They need a good sauce. The Prince Regent's Sauce (p. 289), or Hollandaise (p. 285) or Mushroom Sauce (p. 287) are all good with the crisp little pigeons.

For 4

> 4 young pigeons
> 4 slices of buttered toast without crust
> salt and pepper
> 1 teaspoon of mace
> 4 oz. (120 g.) softened butter
> 2 oz. (30 g.) fine white breadcrumbs

Cut the pigeons in half with a heavy knife along the breast bones, and open and spread out. Spread all over both sides with almost melted butter, and then roll in the crumbs and sprinkle with salt, pepper and ground mace. Reserve some of the butter and crumbs. Place the slices of buttered toast under the wire grill tray and a pigeon on the tray above each, cut side downwards first. Grill under a hot grill for 4 minutes each side, basting occasionally with more butter. Turn, baste again and sprinkle cut side (now uppermost) with remaining crumbs. Grill a further 4 minutes. The toast will have absorbed a great deal of butter, and will be sprinkled with the crisp fallen crumbs. Serve a pigeon on each piece, with the chosen sauce.

Pigeons Transmogrified

This is Mrs Glasse's recipe. The pigeons emerge looking like large, smooth, very light and fluffy dumplings, and as she says, 'They will eat exceeding good and nice, and will yield sauce enough of a very agreeable relish'.

For 4

> 4 young pigeons, drawn and trussed
> 1½ lb. (¾ k.) puff pastry (frozen is excellent)
> salt and pepper and a little flour
> 1 pint (6 dl.) good brown gravy, slightly thickened, to which a glass of
>   brandy has been added.

Lightly rub the pigeons with the seasoned flour. Roll out the pastry about ⅛ inch (⅓ cm.) thick. Cut it into four and completely wrap each bird, moistening the edges of the pastry to seal them together. Tie each rather tightly in a cloth, gathering the corners and tying round with string, or slip into a plastic bag and wind the closing wire so that the bird is held closely. If bags are used, they should be carefully slit when taking the birds out, as the pastry is very soft and must not break.

Put the bags into a very large bath or saucepan of boiling water. There must be plenty of water. Boil for 1½ hours. Lift very carefully, unwrap them and slide them on to a hot serving dish. Pour over the gravy and serve.

When the dumplings are opened, delicious gravy will run out. The birds are buttery from the rich pastry and perfectly cooked. Some people like the soft pastry and eat it, but many eat the bird and leave the paste, as one would the paper in which a bird might be baked. The point of the puff pastry is the amount of butter it contains.

Squabs

For 4

>8 squabs
>8 thin rashers of streaky bacon, rind removed
>8 large young vine leaves (optional)
>3 oz. (90 g.) melted butter
>4 slices freshly made hot buttered toast
>hollandaise sauce (p. 285)

Squabs are not always available in England, but may sometimes be ordered. They are best of all wrapped each in a thin rasher of streaky bacon, and outside that a large young vine leaf, tied in place with thread. Allow two per person, thread them on a spit, or arrange on an oven tray. Pour plenty of melted butter over to cook quickly (oven temperature 400° F., gas mark 6) for 7 minutes. Cut the threads and remove when serving, but serve wrapped in the bacon and leaves on slices of fresh hot buttered toast with hollandaise sauce.

Pulpatoon (Pupton) of Pigeons

A famous seventeenth- and eighteenth-century dish which seems to have disappeared completely from English tables in the nineteenth century.

This is Patrick Lambe's (master cook to Charles II, James, William and Mary, and Anne) recipe for a 'Pupton of Pigeons' (1710).

'For a little Dish you may take six pigeons, or more according to the Bigness of your Dish, truss them, singe and blanch them; then fry them in a liftly Butter or Hog's Lard, being first larded with small Lardons; then put them in stewing with a little Broth or Gravy; when they are almost tender, put to them two sweet breads cut in large bits and fry'd, a handful of Morils and Musgrooms well pick'd and wash'd and twelve chestnuts blanched; Put all this together then take a Sauce-pan with a quarter of a pound of Butter, a small handful of Flower, and two whole Onions; brown it over the Fire with a pint of Gravy, put in your ingredients aforesaid having first seasoned them with Pepper, Salt and Nutmeg.

'Let it stew so that most of your ragoo sticks to your Meat, then set it off the Fire a-cooling. Take a patty-pan or Sauce-Pan and butter the Bottom and Sides; then cut four or five Slices of Bacon as long as your Hand and as thin as a Shilling; place them at the Bottom and Sides of your Pan at an equal Distance, then place iver it a Quantity of the forc'd Meat, for which you have a Receipt under Letter F, half an inch thick, as high on the Sides of your Pan as you think will hold your Pigeons and Ragoo. Then pour in your cold Ragoo and Pigeons, placing them with the Breasts to the Bottom of the Pan, because the Bottom side is turned up when it goes to Table; then take out your whole Onion, Bacon and Cloves that was in your Brown, and squeeze in a whole lemon, place your pigeons with the Breasts to the middle of the Pan and your Ragoo btwixt your Pigeons at an equal Distance. Cover it all over with the same forc'd Meat an Inch thick, and close it well round the Sides, smooth it well with your Hands and with Egg, strew on it a little grated Bread, bake it an Hour before you have Occasion to use it; then loose it from the Sides of your Patty-Pan or Saucepan, with your Knife, put it on your Mazarine or little Dish, wherein you intend to serve it, and turn it upside down clearly; if it is well baked it will stand upright, like a brown Loaf. Squeeze over it an Orange, lay round it fry'd Parsley; the Sauce in the middle. So serve it for First Course. Note, That we make Puptons of Quails, Partridges, Turtle Doves, Buntings and Larks the same way; only adding to the last two some yolks of hard-boiled eggs.'

Eliza Smith in *The Compleat Housewife* (1727) gives a very much shorter recipe, very difficult to follow, but obviously deriving from Patrick Lambe's.

The suffix 'oon' (from Spanish or Italian) implies 'large' and 'deep' (see 'mitoon of pork'), and the pulpatoon was essentially a large dish. Patrick Lambe specifies that his recipe is for a small one. It was probably introduced in England in the sixteenth century, was extremely popular at the tables of the great throughout the seventeenth century and into the eighteenth, and then seems virtually to have disappeared, without any recognizable modification taking its place.

It was in its essentials a pie in which a forcemeat crust took the place of pastry. Adapted as follows it is quite unlike anything else and so good that its disappearance is extraordinary. It can be prepared ahead and reheated, and it freezes perfectly.

For 8

4 pigeons cut in halves, *or* halves or quarters of chickens
6 rashers of thin back bacon

For the forcemeat :
¾ lb. (360 g.) very finely minced veal (the butcher will mince it)
½ lb. (240 g.) fine white breadcrumbs
2 tablespoons finely chopped parsley
2 small onions, finely minced
2 tablespoons shredded suet
salt and black pepper
1 teaspoon of finely chopped thyme
juice of ½ lemon
2 egg yolks, well beaten
¼ lb. (120 g.) butter
1 oz. (30 g.) extra breadcrumbs
1 tablespoon of finely chopped parsley

For the ragoût :
1½ pints of a very well seasoned brown stock
4 sheep's kidneys
1 onion, finely cut
¼ lb. (120 g.) mushrooms, lightly sauté
some olives *or* artichoke bottoms
12 chestnuts, fresh or canned
salt, pepper
1½ oz. (45 g.) flour
3 oz. (90 g.) butter

Peel, core and cut up the kidneys and stew gently in the stock with the onion for 35 minutes. After 20 minutes put in the birds, which should be about two thirds cooked when the rest is done. Lift out the birds and set aside. Make a roux with 1½ oz. (45 g.) flour and 2 oz. (60 g.) butter and thicken the ragoût. Stir in the sauté mushrooms and the chestnuts. Cook a further 5 minutes, add the olives or artichoke bottoms, and season highly. Pour off ¼ pint (1½ dl.) of the sauce to serve separately. The ragoût should be as thick as thick cream.

Meanwhile, mix all the ingredients for the forcemeat (except the extra ounce of breadcrumbs and the parsley), work it together, and turn it on to a floured board. Sprinkle with further flour and lightly roll ½–¾ inch (1–2 cm.) thick.

Butter a large soufflé dish and line it with the bacon rashers. Cut a circle of forcemeat and press into the bottom over the bacon and a long strip to work round the sides. Make sure they seal together. Lay the birds on the forcemeat, breast down, and pour the ragoût over them. Roll out remaining forcemeat to form a lid and put it on, sealing it well to the sides. Sprinkle the top with a few more breadcrumbs and dot with butter. Bake for 15 minutes at 400° F., gas mark 6, and a further 45 minutes reduced to 350° F., gas mark 4.

Remove from the oven and very carefully turn out on a warm, flat dish, when it should look like a brown loaf. Sprinkle the top with finely chopped parsley. Serve with the reserved gravy. Needs plain boiled potatoes and a sharp green salad.

QUAILS

It is now easy to order quails direct from a quail farm or to get a poulterer to do so. Probably the wild birds which our ancestors ate and which the Romans particularly prized had a better flavour, but they are now impossibly scarce. There are hundreds of traditional ways of cooking and serving quail. I shall give only two, both of which are traditional in England. Quails are always eaten fresh and, unlike woodcock and figpeckers, are drawn. Usually they are stuffed. I am not here giving any of the recipes which require boning, as it is difficult to get this done by the poulterer and very tiresome to do yourself.

Quails with Grapes or Cherries

2 quails per person
large glass of brandy

about 8 grapes per bird
1 vine leaf per bird, if possible
½ rasher fat bacon per bird
2 oz. (60 g.) breadcrumbs
2 rashers lean bacon
2 oz. (60 g.) mushrooms
1½ oz. (45 g.) butter
salt and pepper
1 oblong of lightly fried, thin cut, bread for each 2 quails

Chop the quails' livers and mix with fine breadcrumbs and a little finely chopped bacon and mushrooms, moisten this with a little of the brandy and stuff the birds with the mixture.

Soak the washed vine leaves in the brandy for a few minutes, then wrap the quails in them and tie with string. Save the brandy. If you have no vine leaves, wrap the birds direct in fat bacon, cut thin and then beaten thinner; otherwise put the bacon round the vine leaves. Have ready about 8 grapes per bird, skinned and seeded. Put the birds into a fireproof dish with plenty of butter and put in a hot oven, 400° F., gas mark 6, for 7 minutes. Take them out, turn down the oven to 300° F., gas mark 2, put the grapes in a dish with the birds, and pour the remaining brandy over. Cook another 5 minutes. Prepare fried bread while they finish cooking.

Take out and quickly remove the wrappings from the birds and place each two on a slice of fried bread, serve them with the grapes and pour over all the brandy and the juice which has come from them and from the fruit. Cherries, either fresh or bottled, may be used in the same way as the grapes.

It is probable that this dish, also served in France with very slight differences, comes direct to Britain and to Gaul from the Roman occupation. The Romans were very fond of quail and they habitually cooked birds and meat in grape juice (i.e. 'must') reduced (*de frutum*) or made from dried grapes (*passum*); grapes or damsons were often added, and Apicius recommends wrapping birds before cooking to preserve their flavour.

Plain rice is the best accompaniment to this dish.

Roast Quails, plain

Wrap the birds in vine leaves if possible and in fat bacon as well, as in the previous recipe.

Put into a fireproof dish with plenty of butter and cook 10 minutes in a preheated oven, 400° F., gas mark 6. Baste twice. Take them out and place a slice of bread from which you have cut the crusts under each 2 birds, baste and sprinkle all with salt and pepper. Put back in oven for a further 5 minutes. Serve just as they are, without removing the vine leaves or bacon, which will be delicious. The croûtons on which the birds sit should have absorbed all the butter and the juices.

Roast Snipe

| 1 bird per person | 1 oz. (30 g.) butter per bird |
| 1 piece of toast per bird | ½ rasher of bacon per bird |

Roast without drawing. The head is traditionally left on, the very long beak being passed through legs and body as a skewer. Brush all over with melted butter. Roast in the oven at 400° F., gas mark 6, placing each bird on a piece of toast (which catches the juices), and laying a small slice of bacon over the breast of each. They will take 15 minutes.

Very good spit-roasted, in which case brush over with butter, sprinkle with salt and pepper and place toast in drip tray under grill.

Two recipes for Roast Venison

Meat beloved of English kings, but inclined to be hard and dry unless very carefully cooked, when the flavour is very subtle. The two following recipes give the best methods.

1. Marinate the venison (3–4 lb. (1½–2 k.) piece of saddle or haunch) for 24 hours in the following marinade (which will afterwards make the sauce):

½ pint (3 dl.) red wine	2 tablespoons olive oil
1 carrot ⎱ sliced	clove of garlic
1 onion ⎰	2 teaspoons brown sugar
sprig of thyme	6 oz. (180 g.) butter or
bay leaf	cooking fat for roasting
few peppercorns	a little flour
2 tablespoons vinegar	

Boil all together for 20 minutes. Leave to get cold and lay the venison in the marinade in a cool larder. From time to time turn it and spoon the mixture over it.

Remove the meat from the marinade and roast in a preheated oven at

350° F., gas mark 4, allowing 15 minutes to the lb. Use plenty of butter or cooking fat and baste frequently.

When cooked, remove the meat from the pan and keep hot. Pour off any surplus fat from the pan. Work in 1 oz. (30 g.) flour and gradually stir into it the marinade liquor, pouring through a strainer. Stir well, check seasoning and allow to simmer for 5 minutes.

2.   1 lb. (½ k.) flour and a little more
        2 oz. (60 g.) softened butter
        ½ pint (3 dl.) stock or bouillon cube
        pepper and salt
        red-currant jelly

Make a thick paste with the flour and ½ pint (3 dl.) of water, allowing enough to cover the meat entirely. Roll out to about ½ inch (1 cm.) thickness. Rub the joint with salt and pepper and spread over it about 2 oz. (60 g.) of softened (but not melted) butter. Encase the joint in the paste and seal up everywhere. Place on a roasting tray in a preheated oven at 450° F., gas mark 8, for 10 minutes. Then reduce the heat to 325–350° F., gas mark 3–4, and cook for 30 minutes to each lb. of meat and 30 minutes over.

Make a thick clear gravy, as in the recipe for all game gravies (p. 186) but using butter in which to work the flour and adding meat stock or a bouillon cube.

Break the crust from the venison and discard, carefully adding any liquid to the gravy. Place the joint on a hot dish and serve at once with the gravy and red-currant jelly.

Wild Duck (generally Mallard)

Enough for 2

It used to be said that a wild duck should do no more than 'see the fire' but that the fire should be very hot. They were always served very underdone. Mrs Glasse says that '10 minutes at a very quick fire will do them, but if you love them well done, a quarter of an hour'.

On the whole, they are now generally liked a little more cooked. 20–25 minutes in an oven preheated to 450° F., gas mark 8, is just about right, and the same length of time on a spit.

Froth the skin with seasoned flour and serve with a sauce made of the juice and zest of an orange and ¼ pint (1½ dl.) of good brown stock, thickened with cornflour.

Widgeon and teal (1 per person) are cooked in exactly the same way but ¼ hour is enough for the widgeon and 10 minutes for the teal.

All are good with watercress.

WOODCOCK

'Dishes of woodcock were sent up to the dinners of the Lords of the Star Chamber, and the accounts for them show that prices for these little birds rose from 1/- per bird in 1534 to 2/- in 1605' (André Simon).

Woodcock Roast

Woodcock are not drawn, and the head is sometimes left on, the long sharp beak being turned backward. The birds should each be placed on a slice of crustless, very light toast, so that nothing that drips from them is wasted. Fat bacon should be placed over their breasts and they should be cooked in a hot oven, 400° F., gas mark 6, for 15 minutes. Remove from oven, empty the woodcock, and keep them warm and spread the intestines (called the 'trail') on the croûtons, discarding the gizzards. Sprinkle with coarse black pepper and a very little brandy. Put the birds back on their croûtons, return for two minutes to the oven, and serve very hot with sprigs of watercress.

5 · FISH

Fish, a rich source of protein in diet, has curiously lost importance in England since religious observances have declined. It is a gourmet food at its highest levels (salmon, soles, lobster, turbot, halibut, oysters, prawns) and a cheap and sustaining food at the lower levels (fish and chips where the fish is generally rock salmon or cod, kippers or bloaters, eels, whelks).

Certain fish such as plaice and mussels and frozen prepared fish dishes such as fish fingers, fish cakes and fillets of cod or plaice for frying, bridge the gap, but many middle-class households serve fish rarely and some never, and many households would never propose it for a dinner-party menu. This is not altogether strange when one considers that the Catholic church throughout Europe forbade meat to be eaten on fast days but allowed fish (as it still does, though with lesser penalties), so that meat became, *ipso facto*, the food of feasts and all celebrations, fish, since there was clearly no sin of indulgence or gluttony in eating it, naturally being regarded as inferior. Certainly during the long fast of Lent, there was time to become heartily tired of it. In the sixteenth century in England the state joined the church by directing that only fish be eaten on Saturdays, in order to encourage the fishing industry and because of scarcity of cattle and the high price of meat. Fridays and

Saturdays both became fish days and in 1563 an attempt was made to make Wednesdays fish days as well. The household books of Ingatestone Hall in Essex show that when the Bishop of Norwich came to stay on a Friday and Saturday with Sir William Petrie, no meat could be served him, although the larder contained 2 joints of veal, 1 of mutton, 6 pigeon pies, 3 kid and 1 lamb pasty and 25 pieces of beef.*

In 1561 Queen Elizabeth, on a royal progress into Essex, arrived at Ingatestone Hall on a Saturday, a fish day. One main meal only could be served to her therefore, and no meat at all. The royal fish, sturgeon, was procured and appears in the accounts: '2 firkins of sturgeon at 23/4 the piece, 46/8d: carriage from London 5d.' Apart from this there are listed: 'Soles, flounders, plaice, gurnards, conger and other sea fish, (besides certain sea fish given to my master) £4 3s.'

On fish days one main meal only seems to have been allowed, whether the fast was religious or secular. However, those who were hungry in the evening seem to have been permitted what was called 'Drinking at night' or simply 'Drinking', at which a light meal with eggs, butter, bread and occasionally fish were served. This is referred to both in the Ingatestone household books and in those of Lord Cecil.

Penalties for breaking the fast rules were severe. Charles Wriothesley in his *A Church of England, 1485–1559* says that on 18 March 1552 a 'wyfe' of Hammersmith brought 2 pigs 'to London' to a carpenter in Smithfield, and, this being Lent, the Lord Mayor and Aldermen ordered that the woman and the carpenter should ride 'on 2 horses with panelles of strawe about the markettes of the Citie' each wearing a garland of the pigs' 'pettie toes' on their heads and with the rest of the two pigs hanging round their necks.

In 1563 the fine for non-observance of a secular fish day was £3 or three months' imprisonment. It was, however, possible to obtain a special licence to eat meat on these days. 'Lords of Parliament and their wives shall pay for a license 26/8d yearly to the poor men's box in their parish, Knights and their wives shall pay 13/4 and lesser persons 6/8d.'

This expensive freedom to eat meat did not, however, include beef at any time or veal between Michaelmas and 1 May. The sick could get from their local clergy, permission to eat meat on both secular and religious fish days.

It seems probable that if the church had considered fish the luxury and had deprived good churchmen of it on fast days while leaving them meat, and if the state had wished to encourage the consumption of meat and to preserve

* *Tudor Food and Pastures*, by F. G. Emmerson, Ernest Benn, 1964.

fish, a different attitude to these two major protein foods might have prevailed.

However that may be, good fresh fish, or even fish properly chilled or frozen, carefully cooked and always accompanied by an appropriate sauce is food for gastronomes, and since fish is firmer fleshed and better flavoured if it comes from a cold sea, the fish from around the English coasts is unbeaten anywhere. The soles of Dover and the salmon of Scotland are generally acknowledged to be the best in the world.

Nowadays freshwater fish is so neglected, except among anglers who naturally cook and eat what they catch, that except for trout and an occasional pike or carp it is scarcely eaten at all. Since the transport of fresh fish inland was difficult and much sea fish had to be salted (shellfish were potted), our ancestors kept 'stews' or fishponds well stocked with fish for the house, and recipes for cooking carp, tench, roach, bream, dace, barbel, gudgeon, loach, char and chub abound in early cook books. The ravenous pike had to be kept in a separate pond, which had to be of some size in order that he should grow.

Andrew Boorde, in his *Compendyous Regyment or a Dyetary of Helth* of 1562, claims: 'Of all nacyons and countres, England is best served of Fysshe, not onely of al maner of see-fysshe, but also of fresshe-water fysshe and of all manner of sortes of salte-fysshe.'

Sauces are particularly important with fish; if it is fried or grilled it tends to be dry unless eaten with a separate sauce, such as hollandaise, béarnaise or tartare, or at least with plenty of butter. If time is short or a hollandaise base seems too elaborate, a seasoned butter, particularly anchovy, improves out of all knowledge almost any grilled or fried fish. Green butter, parsley butter, or butter into which a little mushroom ketchup has been worked are also good. Gooseberry sauce is a Cornish speciality with mackerel. Baked or poached fish should, of course, have a sauce of its own liquor thickened with a roux or reduced and seasoned. The large white fish are often improved in appearance and made more interesting in texture by the addition of prawns, shrimps, finely cut lobster or oysters to their sauce. Soles are served with dozens of different sauces, garnishes and accompaniments, but if too elaborate these are apt to mask the superb flavour and firm texture of a really good Dover sole. Boiled fish should always be gently poached in a court-bouillon (that is, in water to which white wine or lemon juice, seasoning, a bouquet garni or a few sprigs of fennel and parsley and, in some cases, the trimmings from the fish, have been added). No fish requires fast boiling in plain water.

The Young Cook's Monitor* says: 'A cod's head could be bought for 4d but the spices and condiments to dress it not under 9/–.' This is not so absurd as it at first appears. Fish, plain boiled, can be insipid and its white appearance is not inspiring, but given proper 'spices and condiments' it takes on subtle flavours and a richer, creamy appearance, and decorated and freshened with the finely chopped bright green of parsley and a slice or two of translucent lemon, becomes a pleasure to see, and seeing, after all, is an important part of eating.

Sea Fish

TO POACH LARGE FISH, WHOLE OR IN THE PIECE
(COD, HAKE, LING, HADDOCK, TURBOT, HALIBUT)

Never allow fish to boil rapidly; always poach gently.

Put the fish into a court-bouillon, which is simply a prepared broth of water, salt, onions, carrots, parsley, thyme, a little lemon juice or wine vinegar, a bay leaf or two and a dozen peppercorns. There should be enough liquid to cover the fish, and it should be boiled for 30 minutes or so and then strained before the fish is put in. Sometimes ¼ to ½ pint (1–3 dl.) of white wine is added; occasionally claret or burgundy or champagne are used. Mushrooms, carrots, onions and celery finely chopped are sometimes left in and served with the fish. For certain dishes the trimmings from the fish are added to the liquid with the raw vegetables and strained from it so that the fish is cooked in a fish stock.

However simple your broth, if it only consists of water, salt, pepper, a chopped onion and a carrot or two and a few herbs, your fish will be infinitely better than if simply cooked in water to which salt is added.

A prepared bouquet garni of dried herbs in a little muslin bag is excellent when no fresh herbs are available, and packets of these may be bought at most good grocers.

For all these fish allow about 20 minutes to the lb., and test with a skewer to see if the flesh comes easily from the bone near the centre of the piece. A thick piece of turbot or halibut (which have very dense flesh) sometimes requires about 30 minutes to the lb. All poached fish depend very much on the sauce served with them, some of which should be poured over them and decorated with chopped parsley, hard-boiled eggs or capers. Without this,

* By M.H., published in 1683 by William Dawning in Great St Bartholomew Close.

poached fish, however good, does not present an attractive appearance.

Cheese sauce (if you are using this, sprinkle the finished dish with grated cheese and brown for a moment under the grill), shrimp, prawn or oyster sauce, lobster sauce, egg sauce, parsley sauce, caper sauce, the fish sauce from the Reading MSS. are all good. Recipes are given in the chapter on Sauces, but when they are to be served with poached fish, all should be made with half milk and half the liquor in which the fish cooked.

COD, HAKE AND HADDOCK

Cod, in particular, is a difficult fish, because unless it is carefully seasoned, well sauced, and provided with interesting garnishes it is insipid and of a cotton-wool texture. Poached, and served with a white sauce or even a parsley sauce, it is nothing but a slightly disguised boredom, but cooked in a court-bouillon with saffron and mace or with onions and fennel, and served with a sauce containing oysters or prawns, it is excellent, since the flaky flesh really absorbs the flavours of the herbs and the shellfish in the sauce give a contrasting texture.

From the Middle Ages till the nineteenth century cod was highly esteemed, because in good houses it was always cooked with spices and vegetables, partly, no doubt, because it was often none too fresh. Its great size made it invaluable to the vast Tudor household, and it was a staple on fish days. The ling, a larger and longer member of the cod family, commonly attaining the length of 7 feet where a cod seldom exceeded 3 feet, seems to have been preferred, particularly when salted. *The Babees Book* says of it: 'Ling perhaps looks for great extolling being counted beefe of the sea, and standing every fish day (as a cold supporter) at My Lord Maior's table; yet it is nothing but long cod. When it is salted it is called Ling . . . the longer it lyeth . . . the better it is; waxing in the end as yellow as gold noble.'

Ingatestone Hall, on a Lenten Thursday, prepared for dinner: 'a jowl of ling, half a hakerdin [halibut], 2 mudfishes [plaice], 40 white herrings, 50 red herrings, 2 cakes of butter.' And for supper, 'A tail of ling, 3 mudfishes, 30 white herrings, 2 cakes of butter, 6 eggs.'

Butter at this time was plentiful and cheap and was used both for frying the fish and as a sauce. A 'cake' of butter weighed generally about 4½ lb. 'Eggs and cheese', known as 'white meat', were sometimes allowed on fast days and always for children or the sick.

Nowadays the ling is rarely differentiated by fishmongers from cod. Small ones are said occasionally to be offered on the Yorkshire coast.

Golden Cod

Equally suitable for hake or large haddock.

This is an early recipe for ling, 'yellow as a gold noble', adapted to use today with cod. It is unusual and very good indeed.

For 4

1 1-in. (2-cm.) thick slice of cod for each person
3 onions, finely chopped
salt and pepper
2–3 oz. (60–90 g.) fine ground oatmeal

1 carrot
1 large parsnip, finely chopped
mixed herbs, finely chopped
2 oz. (60 g.) butter
1½ pints (9 dl.) court-bouillon
saffron

First prepare the court-bouillon from the trimmings of the cod, an onion, the carrot, some herbs, and a good pinch of saffron, using about 1½ pints of water.

Rub each slice of fish well with a piece of the cut onion, then with salt and pepper, and finally coat as thickly as possible with oatmeal and quickly fry golden (but not cooked through) in butter (do not allow the butter to get too hot and darken). Pack the fried slices into a large flat fireproof dish. Fry the remaining onions and the parsnip together till golden brown and pack round and over the fish, sprinkling in chopped mixed herbs and seasoning. Pour over the strained court-bouillon, which should be clear gold from the saffron, cover and bake 40 minutes at 350° F., gas mark 4.

The parsnip may be omitted, if disliked, but should be replaced with carrot, as the dish requires a slightly sweet ingredient of a gold-red colour.

Stewed Cod

Equally suitable for hake or large haddock.

This is an eighteenth-century recipe from Norfolk.

2 lb. (1 k.) cod
½ pint (3 dl.) white wine
1½ pints (9 dl.) court-bouillon made from trimmings and herbs with onion and carrot
1 finely chopped onion
2 blades of mace

½ teaspoon grated nutmeg
seasoning
12 oysters (canned will do)
bouquet garni
1½ oz. (45 g.) flour
2 oz. (60 g.) butter

Place the cod in a saucepan with the court-bouillon and the wine, onion, mace, nutmeg, bouquet garni and seasoning. Simmer very gently for 35 minutes and test with a skewer. If it moves easily from the central bone, it is done. Lay it on a serving dish and keep warm while you make a roux from the butter and flour and pour on the strained liquor from the fish and the liquor from the oysters, stirring to make a smooth sauce. When finished add the oysters, pour all over the cod, and serve.

The oysters may be replaced with prawns or shrimps.

Roast Sea Bream

This is a very old Cornish recipe.

For 4

1 large bream	3 oz. (90 g.) prepared suet
1 tablespoon parsley, finely chopped	a little salt
4 oz. (120 g.) breadcrumbs	a little milk to mix

Have the bream cleaned and scaled. Stuff it with 2 oz. (60 g.) suet, parsley, breadcrumbs and salt, well mixed with a very little milk. Put in a baking dish, sprinkle with remaining suet and salt. Bake in the oven until a golden brown, basting from time to time. Serve with parsley butter (p. 302) and boiled potatoes.

If the fish seems at all dry in the cooking, baste with more suet or a little butter. The suet, being oilier than butter, enriches the plain stuffing and crisps the skin.

A bass may be cooked in the same way.

JOHN DORY

A very delicate fish, which, if carefully cooked, can be as excellent as a good mullet. Particularly fine in Devonshire, as the best of all are caught off Plymouth, but they stand up well to chilling and may be confidently bought from most good fishmongers.

Poached John Dory

1 small fish per person
½ lb. (240 g.) veal forcemeat *or* parsley and thyme stuffing
salt

217

> 8 peppercorns
> English or hollandaise sauce
> 2 glasses white wine
> bouquet garni

The fish should be cleaned but the head and tail should be left on. Stuff it with veal forcemeat (p. 296), or a stuffing of parsley and thyme (p. 297) if liked, in which case, sew up the belly closely after inserting the stuffing. However, the Dory is very good without stuffing.

Bring a pan of water to the boil (there should be just enough to cover the fish). Add salt, the peppercorns, white wine and bouquet garni. Put in the fish and keep just simmering for 15–20 minutes, according to size. Lift the fish, draining well, and serve immediately with English sauce or hollandaise sauce (pp. 281, 285).

Fried John Dory

Have the fish filleted, allowing 2 fillets per person. Dip the fillets in coating batter (see p. 412) and fry till crisp in a mixture of half oil and half butter. Serve immediately with hollandaise or tartare sauce (pp. 285, 291).

John Dory Braised with Tomatoes

For 4

> 8 fillets of John Dory
> ½ lb. (240 g.) tomatoes
> salt, pepper, sugar
> 1 large finely sliced onion
> seasoned flour
> a pinch each of mace and ginger
> butter

Blanch the tomatoes and lay them, halved, in a buttered fireproof dish. Sprinkle salt and pepper and a pinch of sugar over them. Add the onion, and lay on it the fillets of fish lightly rubbed with seasoned flour to which a pinch of powdered ginger and a pinch of mace has been added. Dot thickly with pieces of butter and bake at 400° F., gas mark 6, for 15 minutes. Put a little more butter on the fillets after 7 or 8 minutes. Serve with creamed potatoes or plain boiled rice.

Baked Fillets of Haddock, Hake, Cod or Bream with Bacon

This is a traditional Lancashire dish. The fishermen's families simply laid rashers of bacon on top of the fillets and baked the whole dish so that the bacon was crisp, but a grander recipe from a manor house follows.

Serves 6

2½ lb. (1 k.) fillets of fresh
    haddock, hake, cod or bream
6 rashers back bacon
6 oz. (180 g.) herb forcemeat
2 oz. (60 g.) breadcrumbs

butter
flour
salt and pepper
a little milk

Butter a large shallow fireproof dish and lay in the fillets, which should have been well rubbed with seasoned flour. Pour in a very little milk and sprinkle the fillets with crumbs. Cut the rind from the rashers and cut each in half. Flatten with a knife, lay on each a little forcemeat and roll up; each rasher makes one lean and one streaky roll if back bacon is used. Put the rolls, standing on end, all round the sides of the dish. Dot the dish all over with butter and put in the oven at 400° F., gas mark 6, for 25 minutes. Traditionally served with green peas.

Finnan Haddock

A traditional Scottish dish for breakfast or supper. Fillets of smoked haddock may be used, neither the flavour nor the texture will be as good.

For 2

1 medium-sized smoked haddock
2 eggs
¾ pint (4½ dl.) milk

1 oz. (30 g.) butter
freshly ground black pepper

Add ¼ pint (1½ dl.) water to the milk and poach the haddock gently in this liquid for 20 minutes, turning it once if the liquid does not quite cover. Add no salt. Lift out the fish, remove the backbone, fins and tail, and divide into two portions. Keep warm while you poach the eggs in the milk in which the fish cooked. Place an egg on each portion of haddock, pour over a little of the milk, sprinkle with freshly ground black pepper, place pieces of butter here and there, and serve at once with plenty of hot toast and butter.

Kedgeree

A famous breakfast or supper dish in England in the eighteenth and nine-teenth centuries. The name comes from the Hindi, and the parent Indian dish is quite different.

For 4

> 6 oz. (180 g.) long grain (Patna) rice, cooked so that each grain is dry and separate
> about the same quantity of cooked smoked haddock, all bones and skin removed, and finely flaked
> 2 hard-boiled eggs, chopped finely
> 1 tablespoon finely chopped parsley *or* parsley and chives
> a little salt and plenty of freshly ground black pepper
> 2–3 tablespoons butter

Lightly mix the rice, fish and eggs. Melt the butter in a saucepan without allowing it to colour. Stir in the kedgeree and stir and toss till hot through; or put in a covered dish with plenty of butter in a low oven.

To serve, pile the kedgeree in a flat dish, place a few pieces of unmelted butter on the pile, sprinkle with parsley or parsley and chives, and serve very hot with hot toast and butter.

Mousse of Smoked Haddock

For 6

> 1 large smoked haddock, cooked in water, all skin and bone removed
> ¼ pint (1½ dl.) rather thick basic white sauce
> ¼ pint (1½ dl.) double cream
> 2 glasses white wine
> ½ packet of powdered gelatine
> stiffly beaten whites of 2 eggs
> pepper and salt

Flake the fish and put it through a fine mincer or pound it in a bowl or mortar so that it is almost a paste. Stir it into the hot white sauce. Melt the gelatine in a little water. Stir it into the hot white wine and when melted stir into the haddock mixture. Stir in the cream. Season highly with pepper and little or no salt (the haddock is salty). Beat in the stiffly beaten egg whites, which should hold a peak: make sure they are well beaten in. Turn into small moulds or one large one and chill at least 2 hours or overnight.

Serve turned out on to a bed of lettuce, with a thin half slice of lemon on each mousse and brown bread and butter.

Arbroath Smokies

These are a Scottish delicacy, much finer in flavour and texture than ordinary smoked haddock. Small fish are used and lightly smoked without splitting. They are very good as a starting course for dinner or as a main dish for lunch or supper.

They are best prepared in one of two very simple ways:

> 1 smokie per person
> (1) 1 oz. (30 g.) of butter per smokie *or* (2) 2 tablespoons of single cream per smokie
> freshly ground black pepper

Bring enough water to the boil in a frying pan just to cover the smokies. Put them in and simmer for 2 minutes only. Lift them out and:

(1) Lay them in a flat fireproof dish, spread them lightly with the softened butter, cover with foil, and bake for 10 minutes in an oven preheated to 350° F., gas mark 4; *or*

(2) After simmering for 5 minutes, pour out the water from the pan, put back the smokies, pour the cream over them and simmer very gently, shaking them and turning each over, for 5 minutes, or until quite tender. Lift on to a serving dish and pour all the cream over.

In either case, serve well sprinkled with fresh black pepper.

HERRINGS

Like the mackerel, the herring has always been food for the poor and did not often feature at the high tables of the great except in Lent. Nevertheless, it need be no pauper's dish if cooked with butter and with care, as fishermen and seacoast manors and farms have always known.

Fried or Grilled Herrings with Mustard Sauce

For each person, dip 2 herrings, cleaned and gutted, in seasoned flour, or better still in seasoned oatmeal, and fry in foaming butter (or brush with melted butter and grill) for about 4 minutes on each side. Serve with mustard sauce (p. 288) and plain boiled potatoes.

Stuffed Herrings

This recipe comes from a little book of Victorian breakfast dishes. Menus for breakfasts for a year are given, and the herrings were included with scalloped tomatoes and scotch woodcock for breakfast on 15 February.

> 1 herring for each person
> 2 oz. (60 g.) veal stuffing *or* herb forcemeat (pp. 296, 297) for each
>   herring *or* a mushroom stuffing
> seasoned flour
> butter

Get the fishmonger to open the herrings down the back and remove the backbone as well as cleaning and gutting them. Take off the head and tail. Put in the stuffing and roll up. Stand them closely packed in a well-buttered fireproof dish. Sprinkle seasoned flour over, dot with pieces of butter and bake for 15 minutes at 400° F., gas mark 6.

SOFT ROES

These are herrings' roes and were traditionally served on toast as an after-dinner savoury or in larger portions for breakfast. They were also served with crisp bacon, and in the seventeenth and eighteenth centuries were baked with herbs and seasoning as a side dish.

Soft Roes 'en Caisse'

This recipe was apparently very popular at the Thatched House Tavern with gentlemen, who ordered it for supper. Richard Dolby directs that the dish should be lined with a paper case, but this does not seem to serve any particular purpose.

Serves 4–6
> 8–10 soft roes
> 2 oz. (60 g.) butter
> 2 oz. (60 g.) white breadcrumbs
> 1 tablespoon finely chopped parsley
> 2 teaspoons lemon juice
> 3 oz. (90 g.) maître-d'hôtel butter (2 shallots minced fine or a small
>   onion, 2 teaspoons chopped parsley required for this)
> pepper and salt

A layer of herb forcemeat (p. 297) may be laid under the roes, if you want to make the dish more substantial.

Butter a shallow fireproof dish well. Lay the roes carefully in a clean frying pan, sprinkle with a very little salt and pour boiling water over them to cover. Poach very gently for 3 or 4 minutes till set. Lift them with a perforated slice and lay them, well drained, in rows in a buttered dish. Cover with the crumbs, mixed with parsley, salt and pepper. Dot with remaining butter and bake for 15 minutes at 400° F., gas mark 6. Meanwhile prepare the maître-d'hôtel butter by stirring the shallots and parsley, with pepper and salt, into 3 oz. (90 g.) butter over a low heat until it is melted. Do not let it boil or colour. When the roes are done, stir lemon juice into the maître-d'hôtel butter and pour it over the browned top. Serve at once with slices of fresh hot toast (unbuttered).

It is good as a supper dish with plain boiled potatoes and with green salads served on separate plates.

Soft Roes on Toast

For a savoury, half a roe per person. For breakfast or lunch, 2 or 3 roes.

butter	hot fresh toast
salt and pepper	a little chopped parsley

Melt the butter in a frying pan so that it is about ⅛ inch (½ cm.) deep, and when it is liquid but not foaming, lay in the roes, season and cook very gently, turning once, for 3 or 4 minutes. Lift on to hot buttered toast and sprinkle with parsley.

For *Devilled Roes*, stir a little made mustard, a pinch of cayenne pepper and a teaspoon of paprika into the butter before putting in the roes, and sprinkle with paprika instead of parsley when serving.

Soft Roes with Bacon

John Simpson, cook to the Marquis of Buckingham, seems first to have made use of very small silver 'skuets' to serve various hot savouries.

1 small skewer per person	salt and pepper
1 rasher streaky bacon per person	1 strip hot buttered toast
½ a soft roe per person	per person
butter	

Scald and lightly cook the roes as in recipe for Soft Roes en Caisse. Lift, drain and divide each roe into six. Cut the rind from the bacon, press each rasher out as thin as possible and divide into three. Roll a piece of roe in each piece of bacon. Carefully put on to skewers, and grill under a very hot grill, turning several times until bacon is well crisped outside. For larger skewers for a main course, make larger rolls and put button mushrooms between them. Each skewer may be laid on a long strip of hot buttered toast to serve.

MACKEREL

A very good fish, not generally appreciated and always fairly cheap. It is best of all eaten on board the fishing boat, straight from sea to pan and from pan to mouth. However, it chills well and is worth buying from the fishmonger.

Grilled or Fried Mackerel

Split the fish wide open down the belly so that it lies flat. The backbone may easily be removed with a sharp pointed knife or it may be left. Rub with well-seasoned flour or with fine oatmeal. Fry in foaming butter for 3 or 4 minutes on each side, or place a long thin slice of butter on each side of the backbone and grill for about the same length of time. Baste with butter when the fish is turned over. A sprig or two of fennel laid on the fish as it cooks is delicious.

In Cornwall, mackerel is traditionally served with gooseberry sauce (see p. 284) when goos berries are in season, and this is perhaps the best of all accompaniments. However, any savoury butter (see pp. 301–303) is good, and so is hollandaise or tartare sauce (pp. 285, 291).

Freche Makrelle

A recipe from a manuscript at Holkham.

'To dight a freche makerelle tak and draw a makerelle at the gil and let the belly be hole and wefche him and mak the sauce of water and salt and when it boilithe cast in mynt and parsly and put in the fifshe and ferve it furthe with sorell sauce.'

A really fresh mackerel cooked and served like this is superb, as good today as it was almost 500 years ago when the clerk at Holkham wrote out this simple recipe.

    1 mackerel per person
    fresh mint and parsley
    ½ lb. (240 g.) fresh sorrel leaves
    2 tablespoons cream (for the sauce)
    flour, butter, salt, and black pepper

Ask the fishmonger to clean the mackerel through the gills: if he demurs, then in the ordinary way but making as small a slit in the belly as possible. If the fish is cleaned through the gills, it remains firmer when boiling.

Bring water, with 2 teaspoons salt to the pint, to the boil; add 6 sprigs of parsley and 4 of mint to each 2 pints. Put in the mackerel and let them poach very gently for 15 minutes. Drain and serve on a flat dish, putting a piece of butter on each fish and sprinkling with parsley.

Sorrel Sauce: Boil the washed and stalked sorrel leaves for 5 minutes, using only a tablespoonful of water. Put through a moulin or blender. Melt 1 oz. (30 g.) butter in a saucepan. Stir in ½ oz. (15 g.) flour. Add the sorrel purée gradually to this and bring to the boil. Season highly with salt and black pepper. Stir in cream and serve very hot in a sauceboat.

RED MULLET

Sometimes called 'the woodcock of the sea' because it should not be drawn, but when cooked should keep its 'trail' as should the woodcock. It is the most delicate of sea fishes, nearest, perhaps, in flavour to a really fine lake perch. The mullet has always been much prized in England, and many old recipes suggest cooking it with red wine and onions and making a robust red sauce. This was partly, no doubt, because of its colour, but undoubtedly the wine enhances the flavour of the little fish rather than swamping it. The grey mullet should be cooked in just the same ways, but is perhaps even more delicate if cooked with a dry white wine.

Arundel Mullet

A seventeenth-century recipe.

    1 mullet per person (unless   2 onions, very finely sliced
       very large)   a bunch of sweet herbs
    salt and pepper   a little nutmeg
    lemon juice   4 or 5 chopped anchovies
    2 glasses of wine

Simmer the mullet in salted water just to cover for 10–15 minutes. Pour away half the liquid and add a squeeze of lemon juice, a little black pepper, the wine, onions, herbs, nutmeg and anchovies. Simmer all together for another 15 minutes, and serve in a shallow dish with the sauce poured over. It should be eaten from soup plates, using bread to sop up the sauce.

Baked Mullet

A Cambridge recipe. Red or grey mullets are equally good cooked in this way.

> 1 mullet per person (or 1 for 2 if very large)
> 1 tablespoon chopped shallots
> 1 tablespoon chopped parsley
> 1 teaspoon anchovy sauce
> 1 dessertspoon Worcester sauce
> 3 glasses port
> 3 oz. (90 g.) butter
> ½ lb. (240 g.) tomatoes stewed in ½ pint (3 dl.) water and then sieved
> 1½ oz. (45 g.) flour
> milk
> 1 tablespoon double cream

Butter a flat casserole well, sprinkle with half the parsley and shallots. Put in the mullet, sprinkle with the remainder, and add the anchovy and Worcester sauces and the port. Bake covered for 15 minutes at 350° F., gas mark 4, and then uncovered for a further 10–15 minutes.

Meanwhile make a roux with 2 oz. (60 g.) of butter and the flour; add the tomato purée, the cream and a little milk to make the consistency that of very thick cream. Season well and keep warm. When the mullets are done, lift them on to a flat serving dish and pour the liquid from them into your sauce, stirring well. Pour over the mullets and serve. The original recipe suggests a garnish of truffles and lobster.

Red or Grey Mullets in Paper

An early nineteenth-century recipe.

Serves 6

> 6 mullet   mace
> 3 oz. (90 g.) butter   salt and pepper
> thyme   chopped parsley

4 oz. (120 g.) mushrooms, sliced
6 oz. (180 g.) prawns
½ lb. (240 g.) tomatoes

1½ oz. (45 g.) flour
a glass of sherry
a little cream

Cut a circle of greaseproof paper for each fish. Butter the paper thickly, and sprinkle with salt and pepper, a very little thyme and a very little mace. Lay the fish on the papers and place a few pieces of sliced mushroom and 4 or 5 prawns on each. Fold over papers and secure by rolling the edges of the papers together. Lay the parcels on a flat dish and bake at 350° F., gas mark 4, for 20 minutes. Meanwhile make a tomato sauce as in the previous recipe and add a glass of sherry. Season well, and when the fish are ready add any liquor which has come from the parcels to the sauce. Stir in a dessertspoon of chopped parsley. Serve each fish in its paper and the sauce separately. This is worth doing because when each person unwraps his parcel the odour is delicious and all the flavour has been preserved by the closely wrapped cooking.

Broiled Pilchards

A Cornish recipe of 1753.

'Gill them, wash them, dry them, season with salt; then broil them over a gentle fire and baste them with butter; when they are enough, serve them up with beaten butter, mustard and pepper; or you may make a sauce of their own heads, squeezed between two trenchers, with some beer and salt.'

Both these sauces are excellent and are also good with mackerel.

2 or 3 pilchards per person according to size, cleaned by the fishmonger, and lightly rubbed with seasoned flour
6 oz. (180 g.) butter
2 teaspoons made mustard
black pepper
  or ¼ pint (1½ dl.) beer
salt
flour

Grease a frying pan with butter and make hot, lay in the fish, add a little more butter, and baste them as it melts. Fry gently, turning them once. They will take 6 or 7 minutes to cook.

Have ready 4 oz. (120 g.) butter into which you have worked or blended 2 teaspoons of made mustard and ½ teaspoon of black pepper. The butter should be beaten till soft and creamy. Serve with the fish.

Alternatively, cut off the heads, place them between pieces of foil on a pastry board and press with a rolling pin. Scrape resulting paste and liquor into a roux made of 1 oz. (30 g.) flour and 1 oz. (30 g.) butter. Stir in the beer and season well. The addition of a little anchovy sauce is an improvement. Boil for 3 minutes.

Star-Gazing Pasties (with pilchards)

This is a Cornish recipe, made by generations of fishermen's wives, though rarely seen today. Strictly speaking, it is a derivative of Star-gazing Pie, but in the pasty the pilchards look out horizontally. The pasties are very good made with herrings or small mackerel. The pie was made in a large deep pie dish into which the fish, standing on their tails, were wedged with sliced cooked potato, chives and herbs and strips of bacon. Large spoonfuls of scalded cream were put between the fish and a very thin crust put over all, the heads of the fish being gently worked through, so that they gazed at the stars. Miss Dorothy Hartley points out that this pie probably originated for reasons of economy. It was wasteful to cover the inedible fish heads with good pastry but if they were cut off the oil they contain and their flavour were lost to the fish, so the whole fish were used and covered except for the heads. I do not suggest making this pie as it is greasy and the potatoes, cream and pilchards are not a happy alliance.

The pasties, however, if you like pilchards, herrings or mackerel, are worth making. Gooseberry sauce or a sweet chutney are good with them.

To make 12 small pasties
> 12 pilchards, small herrings or mackerel, cleaned and washed, with heads on but tails cut off
> 2 lb. (1 k.) short or rough puff pastry (pp. 93, 92)
> 2 finely chopped onions
> 2 tablespoons chopped mixed green herbs
> 2 oz. (60 g.) butter
> a little flour
> salt and pepper

Line a very large plate with pastry about ⅛ inch (¼ cm.) thick, but leave the rim clear. Lay the fish, lightly floured and seasoned, each with some onion, herbs and a small piece of butter in its belly, so that the heads stick out on to the rim of the plate and the tail ends meet in the middle. Lay over them a pastry lid, cut rather large so that the pastry can be pressed down between each fish on to the bottom layer, but leave the heads clear. Bake for 35 minutes at 350° F., gas mark 4.

Serve by cutting between each fish, which should be whole and completely enclosed in pastry except for its head.

Huge pilchard pasties were sold on the stalls of Truro market in my grand-mother's day. They were made oblong, the width of a fish, and perhaps 3 dozen fish in length, and were sold by the fish, the vendor simply cutting the pastry between.

Nombles of Porpas

This very early recipe comes from *A Noble Boke of Cookry ffor a pprynce Houssolde*, a manuscript dating from about 1480 from Holkham. It is very early to get such clear and careful instructions.

'*To mak nombles of porpas or other fish*

'To make nombles of porpas or other good fisshe and ye may cut som of the fisshe smalle and put it in the pot and draw a liour with cruste with the same blod and some of the brofe and red wyne and put all to gedur in a pot and put thereto pouder of peper clowes and canelle and set it on the fyere and sesson it up with pouder guingere Venygere and salt, and ye may mak nombles of congure codlinge or other good fisshe in the same manner and serve it.'

The nombles themselves are excellent made with cod or hake as follows.

For 6

2½ lb. (1–1¼ k.) cod or hake

2 glasses red wine

2 pints (1 l.) court-bouillon made with skin and trimmings of the fish, an onion, a carrot, a stick or two of celery, a bouquet garni, a piece of fennel if possible, all boiled for 30 minutes (this is the 'brofe' of the recipe)

pepper

½ teaspoon powdered ginger

salt

a pinch of cloves (powdered)

1 dessertspoon of wine vinegar or 1 teaspoon lemon juice

panada of ½ lb. (240 g.) white breadcrumbs boiled 2 minutes in milk ('draw a liour with cruste': all early broths were thickened with bread rather than flour. 'Liour' means a 'binding')

1 round of hot toast per person

butter

Stew the cod or hake gently in the strained court-bouillon for 30 minutes and then lift the fish, remove all skin and bones and flake it back into half the liquor. Stir in the panada (from which all surplus milk should have been pressed). Stir all together and add pepper, cloves, salt and ginger and wine vinegar or lemon juice. The result should be about as thick as scrambled egg. Add more of the liquor if too solid. Serve on thickly buttered hot toasts, a round for each person. The original recipe would almost certainly have been served on trenchers of bread.

We have to omit the blood with which the porpoise nombles were thickened, but made as above they are delicious, as ginger brings out the flavour of fish if carefully used.

'Nombles' or 'mumbles' of rabbit, hare or chicken were also made. 'Mumbled rabbit' is still served at Beaulieu today.

SOLES

Perhaps, especially from our cold waters, the best of all sea fishes. Although there are hundreds of sauces and garnishes for soles, the fish itself is simply grilled, fried, steamed or poached: a sole is always skinned by the fishmonger. Plaice, the least interesting in flavour of the flat fish, or lemon sole, may be used in any of the following recipes, but the results will not have the same distinction, though the price will be much improved.

Grilled Sole

Dip soles in seasoned flour, brush with melted butter and put under a hot grill for 4–6 minutes each side according to size.

Fried Sole

Dip soles in seasoned flour and then in beaten egg and fine breadcrumbs. Press the breadcrumbs well on and put into foaming hot butter or half corn oil and half butter. They should be fried quickly for 3 minutes on each side to brown and crisp the crumbs and then more slowly for another 3 or 4 minutes to cook them through.

Traditional English garnishes for grilled and fried soles were chopped parsley and slices of lemon. For a grilled sole sweet herbs were sometimes sprinkled over the fish before grilling and the whole brushed over with black butter.

This last was sometimes garnished with capers and sometimes with strips of smoked salmon.

Steamed or Poached Soles

Always poach or steam in a court-bouillon made from the sole trimmings with an onion, carrot, sweet herbs, and a glass or two of white wine.

If poaching, lay the soles in the court-bouillon in a fish kettle or a saucepan which will take their length and poach just at boiling point for 15–20 minutes. If steaming, lay them on the perforated grid of the fish kettle above the court-bouillon and steam for 20–25 minutes.

The following are traditional English ways of serving poached or steamed Dover soles: all the sauces should be made with half milk and half court-bouillon with some additional cream.

1. Covered with cheese sauce, finished with grated cheese and lightly browned under the grill.
2. Covered with a well-seasoned cream sauce into which a few finely sliced and sauté button mushrooms have been stirred.
3. Covered with cream sauce into which prawns have been stirred, and decorated with more prawns and plenty of asparagus tips.
4. Covered with oyster sauce.
5. Covered with lobster sauce and decorated with claw meat.
6. Covered with a white-wine sauce and garnished with soaked, stoned prunes and stoned green olives.
7. Covered with a sauce of white wine and cream into which stoned and peeled green grapes have been stirred.
8. Covered with a good cream tomato sauce and garnished with halves of skinned and grilled tomatoes.
9. Covered with a white-wine sauce and garnished with small artichoke bottoms, with an oyster or a prawn on each.
10. Covered with a cream sauce, into which a very little powdered ginger, a mere pinch, and rather more powdered mace has been stirred. Finally, sprinkled rather thickly with fresh parsley. Taste the sauce to make sure it has enough salt and pepper. The spices give it a very slight and subtle flavour which enhances the flavour of the sole.
11. Covered with a cream and white-wine sauce into which some fresh tarragon, a sprig of thyme, a little parsley and a few chives have been stirred. About a tablespoon of these fresh herbs is enough for ½ pint (3 dl.) of sauce.

12. The same, using fennel instead of tarragon, and a little lemon juice in the sauce.

All the seasoned butters (see the chapter on sauces), hollandaise sauce, lemon sauce, and tartare sauce are excellent with grilled or fried sole. Perhaps hollandaise is the best accompaniment of all.

Mrs Glasse's Fricasee of Soles

This eighteenth-century recipe is very good and can be made successfully (though the pieces of fish are less firm) with lemon soles, which are always cheaper, or with fillets of a large thick plaice, which must be cut into twelve pieces because of the shape of the fish. 'To fricasey soals white,' says Mrs Glasse, 'cut the flesh longways and then a-cross, so that each soal will be in eight pieces.' The fishmonger will do this. Ask for heads, skins and trimmings.

Serves 3 or 4

2 medium soles	¼ lb. (120 g.) mushrooms,
their trimmings	finely cut
1 onion, finely cut	1½ oz. (45 g.) butter
parsley, thyme, and a very	1 oz. (30 g.) flour
little fennel	¼ pint (1½ dl.) cream
2 blades of mace	a pinch of nutmeg
8 peppercorns	1 tablespoon finely chopped
salt	parsley
½ pint (3 dl.) white wine	

Put the fish trimmings, onion, herbs, mace, peppercorns and a little salt into a pan with a pint (6 dl.) of water. Allow to boil briskly and cook until it is reduced by half. Strain, add the wine and mushrooms and put in the soles. Stew gently for 10 minutes and then lift the pieces of sole and lay them in a small buttered fireproof casserole. Keep warm while you make a roux of the butter and flour and pour on to it the liquor in which the fish cooked, stirring while it boils for 2 minutes. Allow to cool for half a minute and stir in the cream and nutmeg. Pour it over the soles, sprinkle with parsley, and serve.

Soles in Coffins

This Victorian luncheon party dish is elaborate and absolutely delicious, as the flavour and consistency of the sole is not lost. I suppose the play on the word 'soul' made a useful ice-breaking joke at a formal meal. In fact, this whole recipe is a kind of elaborate joke, since all these expensive ingredients in their rich sauce are served in the ordinary potato, whose contents, smoothly mashed, are also served, but outside their skins.

1 large potato for each person – baked in its jacket, all the inside carefully removed by cutting a slice from the long side. Reserve the soft potato. Keep potatoes warm, wrapped in foil so that they do not dry

1 pint (6 dl.) very good béchamel sauce, into which a tablespoon of grated Parmesan cheese and ¼ lb. (120 g.) softened butter should be whipped, holding the sauce away from the fire. Keep sauce warm

2 fillets of sole for each potato, rolled and poached in white wine for 10 minutes. Keep hot

half a lobster (2 frozen crayfish tails can well be used) cut in ½-in. (1-cm.) pieces and dropped into the wine in which the sole fillets are poaching for 5 minutes. Keep hot

8 or 9 cooked shrimps or prawns for each potato – frozen are good. Keep hot

¼ lb. (120 g.) button mushrooms, sliced very fine, lightly sautéd in butter, and kept hot

slices of truffle for the top, if you can run to them

a little double cream should be available to cover the fillets if there is no remaining sauce

butter and milk

Pour the sauce into your prepared potatoes, so that they are about one third full. Stand the carefully drained fillets in the sauce, 2 to each potato. Add the lobster, shrimps, or prawns, and mushrooms. Cover with any sauce which is left or with plain cream. Arrange on a large flat fireproof serving dish and put in an oven preheated to 400° F., gas mark 6, for 5 minutes.

While the sole heat, blend the insides of potato with butter, milk and plenty of pepper and salt, make very hot and pipe or arrange in small heaps round the coffins. Put 2 or 3 slices of truffle on each coffin and serve at once.

The potato coffins can be replaced by coffins of puff pastry, previously baked and turned out, but this detracts from the interest of the dish.

Sturgeon (The Royal Fish)

Sturgeon are very rarely, if ever, caught nowadays from any English river, though up to the eighteenth century they were caught quite plentifully in the

Tyne and the Severn and sometimes in the Thames. At one time, the sturgeon was called the royal fish and might only be served at the king's table and to some who had his permission to eat it. Nowadays it is occasionally imported, and this is the traditional way to cook and serve it.

2–3 lb. (1–1½ k.) sturgeon
2 tablespoons wine vinegar
½ lemon
3 bay leaves
2 teaspoons horseradish
  (dried or fresh)

12 peppercorns
1 teaspoon mace
2 teaspoons salt

Put the piece of sturgeon, not less than 2–3 lb. and up to 8 or 10 lb. (4–5 k.), well washed, in a large casserole or fish kettle with a lid. Add the wine vinegar, the juice of half a lemon and 2 or 3 curls of rind, 3 bay leaves, 2 teaspoons of grated horseradish or a piece of fresh root broken up, a teaspoon of powdered mace or 2 blades, a dozen peppercorns and a dessertspoon of salt. Pour water to cover the fish. Cover closely with foil and then with the lid and cook in a slow oven, 300°F., gas mark 2, for 1½ hours. Remove and test the fish with a skewer. If quite done, soft but firm, drain carefully and serve on a large flat dish with the following special sauce.

3 anchovy fillets, chopped, pounded and more or less dissolved in a ¼ pint (1½ dl.) of water
2 tablespoons mushroom ketchup
2 glasses of dry white wine
all the flesh of a small lobster, removed from shell and claws and finely chopped
¼ lb. (120 g.) shelled prawns or shrimps
1½ oz. (45 g.) flour
seasoning
2 oz. (60 g.) butter
1 tablespoon chopped parsley
juice of half a lemon

Melt the butter and make a roux with the flour. Add the anchovies, ketchup, white wine and seasoning, and stir till thick and smooth. Thin with water or more wine until the consistency of thick cream. Stir in lobster and prawns or shrimps. Simmer 3 minutes, stirring. Add a squeeze of lemon juice, check seasoning, pour over the sturgeon, and sprinkle with finely chopped parsley. Serve remainder of sauce in a sauceboat.

This sauce transforms a large piece of poached cod or haddock.

Mrs Glasse also suggests spit-roasting a piece of sturgeon of 8–10 lb. (4–5 k.) (after soaking it for 8 hours in water), basting it all the time with butter, and sprinkling it with flour, nutmeg, mace, pepper and salt, and throwing on chopped sweet herbs and breadcrumbs. It would take 2–3 hours to cook, and if very thick might not be done in the middle. She suggests very much the same sauce with this, except that she adds 'walnut pickle' and a dozen oysters.

TURBOT

Turbot is an excellent, large, solid fish of which Victorian and Edwardian gentlemen were particularly fond, enjoying the glutinous skin and fins. Mrs Beeton says that, when a turbot is served, it is polite to ask guests if they are 'fin fanciers'. Specially shaped turbot kettles could be bought for cooking whole, large fish.

However, the turbot was often filleted for dinner parties or cut crossways in thick, neat slices which could be boned and skinned. These were then poached in a court-bouillon, usually with white wine, drained and served with a rich cream sauce containing lobster, prawns or oysters, each sauce-coated fillet being garnished with more of the shellfish, and with croûtons of puff pastry (which go particularly well with the solid fish).

Nowadays we buy large fish by the piece. About 2½ lb. (1–1¼ k.) cut across the fish will serve six and should be poached very gently in a court-bouillon for about 35 minutes and served with a good rich sauce and any of the garnishes mentioned above; or perfectly plain, sprinkled with parsley and accompanied by hollandaise sauce or simply melted butter.

Brill and halibut may be cooked in the same ways as turbot.

Braised Turbot

A nineteenth-century recipe.

For 6

> about 2½ lb. (1–1¼ k.) turbot cut in a thick slice with the bone removed; ask fishmonger for bone and trimmings
> 6 scallops *or* ½ lb. (240 g.) frozen prawns
> 2 onions, peeled and sliced
> 1 carrot
> a bunch of parsley and a sprig of thyme

a little tarragon and a bay leaf
2 glasses white wine
12 small button mushrooms, sautéd
6 small artichoke bottoms (canned will do) or 2 large fresh artichoke
   bottoms, cooked and cut in quarters
butter
½ pint (3 dl.) good béchamel sauce, rather thick
¼ pint (1½ dl.) double cream
salt and pepper

Boil the fish bone and trimmings in 1½ pints (9 dl.) of water for 30 minutes, with a little salt; strain off the stock.

Put the onions, carrot, all the herbs and the wine and fish stock, with salt and pepper, into a large casserole, fish kettle or Dutch oven. Put the fish on a grid over the vegetables so that the liquid comes only a little way up the sides. If you have no grid, arrange the fish on a bed of vegetables. Cover closely and bake at 300° F., gas mark 2, for 35 minutes. Then test the fish to see if it comes away easily from the bone.

Meanwhile, stew the scallops gently for about 20 minutes, drain and cut each into four. Shake over them a little salt and pepper, butter a piece of foil and wrap the scallops in it and keep hot. If scallops are not liked, replace with prawns, which can simply be warmed in a little butter. Sauté the mushrooms. Cook and cut the artichokes if fresh, or drain and heat in butter if canned, and keep these hot also.

Lift the turbot carefully on to a large flat dish and keep warm while you make the sauce by straining off the liquor in which the turbot cooked, and stirring it into the prepared béchamel sauce. Add the cream and check the seasoning. Unwrap the scallops and pile them at each end of the dish. Pour the sauce over them and over the turbot. Arrange the mushrooms and artichokes along the sides of the dish and 2 or 3 on the top of the turbot.

This is a very grand dish, and if made with scallops has a special character.

Whitebait

A deep fryer and basket are essential for this dish.

about 2 lb. (1 k.) for 4 or 5 people
4 oz. (120 g.) flour
salt and pepper
corn oil or a good compound cooking fat to fry

Wash the whitebait and dry them in a tea towel. Shake seasoned flour over them and shake the fish in the cloth so that all are floured. Have the oil or fat really hot and smoking (about 400° F.). Put in the first fish, half-filling the basket. Shake the basket a little as the fish fry. Lift the fish and drain well. Allow fat to become a little hotter and dip the fish again for 1 minute. This second dipping makes them much crisper. If possible, serve direct from pan to plate, but if not keep hot in oven on a large flat dish with a paper napkin, putting each lot of fish beside and not on top of the previous ones. Serve very quickly as their crispness soon goes.

Should be eaten with very thin brown bread and butter and lemon.

Shellfish

Scalloped Crab

An eighteenth-century recipe from Dorset. This is a very good starting dish for a dinner party or a main dish for supper. Six scallop shells or small ramekins or soufflé dishes are wanted.

Serves 6

1 large dressed crab and 1 smaller	cayenne pepper
2 oz. (60 g.) butter	½ teaspoon mace
4 oz. (120 g.) fine white breadcrumbs	2 anchovies
salt and black pepper	2 teaspoons lemon juice
	2 oz. (60 g.) finely grated cheese

Melt the butter over a low heat and stir in the meat of both crabs, finely chopped, including the claw meat. Reserve small claws to decorate.

Add breadcrumbs, salt, pepper, mace and a pinch of cayenne, stirring all gently together. Add lemon juice and the 2 anchovies, chopped and pounded. Stir till hot, being careful to prevent the mixture sticking to the bottom of the saucepan. Heat your grill and fill the 6 small dishes with the mixture, putting the rest in the larger crab shell. Sprinkle all with grated cheese and brown under grill. Keep hot in oven until wanted but not for more than 20 minutes or so.

Serve the crab shell in the middle of a flat dish with the small dishes round it. Each should be garnished with a crab claw. Each person should take a small dish and should replenish it from the crab shell.

LOBSTER

Peacock, in *Crotchet Castle*, a satire on the Gothic novel, written in 1831, makes the Rev. Dr Folliott say to a Scotsman: 'Every nation has some eximious virtue; and your country is pre-eminent in the glory of fish for breakfast . . .

'Chocolate, coffee, tea, cream, eggs, ham, tongue, cold fowl – all these are good and bespeak good knowledge in him who sets them forth: but the touchstone is fish: anchovy is the first step, prawns and shrimps the second: and I laud him who reaches even to these: potted char and lampreys are the third . . . but lobster is, indeed, matter for a May morning and demands a rare combination of knowledge and virtue in him who sets it forth.'

And a willing cook, unless we are to assume that the lobster was cooked the night before and served cold. The implication is that it was brought in by the fishermen at dawn, to the kitchen door soon after, where it was met by the cook, dropped alive into boiling water and served with drawn butter at an early (and surely very expensive) breakfast.

Lobsters in England have always been treated with the respect due to their natural flavour and consistency, and have most generally been served cold with a salad or hot with drawn butter.

However, Victorian and Edwardian dinner parties demanded that they should be elaborately served, and several very expensive recipes result. A few, however, are worth trying if a good lobster comes your way or may be made with frozen lobster or crayfish tails with success, though the flavour and appearance are not as good as with fresh lobster. One or two of the following recipes make a single fresh lobster go a long way.

Lobster with Cheese Sauce

Much liked in gentlemen's clubs in Edwardian days. Two lobsters cooked like this, with crusty bread and a bottle of dry white wine, make an excellent supper for four.

> 1 lobster for 2 people
> Prepare in advance: 1 pint (6 dl.) court-bouillon made from water with ¼–½ pint (1½–3 dl.) white wine, onion, carrot, parsley, thyme, a sprig or two of fennel, a sprig of tarragon, salt and 8 black peppercorns
> 1¼ pints (7½ dl.) good white sauce, made with ½ pint (3 dl.) milk
> ¼ lb. (120 g.) grated cheese – Parmesan and Gruyère or Emmenthal mixed, if possible

½ pint (3 dl.) court-bouillon and ¼ pint (1½ dl.) cream
butter
salt and pepper

Ask the fishmonger to split the lobster. Remove the flesh from the half-shells and take out all possible claw meat. Cut into ½-inch (1-cm.) dice. Put all this into the hot court-bouillon and allow just to come to simmering point. Then stand aside to keep hot without cooking further.

Meanwhile make the sauce, pouring ½ pint (3 dl.) of the court-bouillon into the roux before adding milk. When thickened, stir in the cheese (reserve a little for the top of the dish), then the cream and finally drain the chopped lobster and lightly mix in. Check the seasoning and fill into the half-shells. Sprinkle with remaining cheese, dot with butter and place near the top of an oven preheated to 400° F., gas mark 6, for 5 or 6 minutes so that the top browns and the sauce is really hot. Do not allow the sauce to boil, but just to reach boiling point. If the top is not nicely brown when the sauce is really hot, put the shells under a hot grill for a minute but watch them all the time.

Lobster in Cream

If the croûtons are made ahead of time, the lobster cut up and the sauce mixed ready to pour into the pan, this superb Edwardian recipe can be well and elegantly cooked in a chafing dish at the table.

Serves 3–4

12 croûtons of puff pastry	1 tablespoon sherry
1 cooked lobster cut into neat pieces, with claw meat	salt, pepper
	1 teaspoon paprika
butter	2 egg yolks, well beaten
1 glass of brandy	½ pint (3 dl.) double cream

Roll, cut and bake croûtons to a golden brown and set aside to be reheated, or keep hot if you are going to cook the lobter immediately. Make a frying pan hot and just grease with butter. Put in the lobster, pour over the brandy and set alight (this gives the dish its inimitable flavour). Mix egg yolks, cream, sherry, and salt and pepper, and stir quickly into the lobster. Shake above the heat, stirring gently all the time until the sauce thickens. Be very careful that it doesn't boil or it will curdle. Serve at once in small dishes with 3 or 4 croûtons stuck round the edges of each.

Lobster Pancakes

A Yorkshire recipe.

Serves 4
>   12 thin pancakes
>   1 cooked lobster, diced
>   ¾ pint (4½ dl.) béchamel sauce, into which a teaspoon of paprika and
>   a tablespoon of tomato purée have been stirred
>   ¼ pint (1½ dl.) double cream
>   salt, pepper, paprika
>   2 oz. (60 g.) butter

Have ready and hot some thin pancakes made without sugar and a cooked and
shelled lobster. Cut the lobster in small pieces, toss these for a minute or two
in butter and paprika. Mix ¼ pint (1½ dl.) sauce with the pieces of lobster,
stuff each pancake with the mixture and roll up. Lay the pancakes on a hot
dish and keep warm while you stir the cream into the remaining sauce, check
seasoning, and bring just to the boil. Then pour over pancakes and serve
immediately.

An added gloss to this dish is to sprinkle the sauce-covered pancakes with
finely grated parmesan cheese and brown for half a minute under a preheated
grill before serving.

Lobster Patties

Traditional at Victorian ball suppers and on all grand buffets.

>   1 lb. (½ k.) puff pastry (frozen is excellent) will make 24 small patties.
>   Bake and allow to get cold. Vol-au-vent cases may be used

For about 24 patties
>   1 lobster cooked and diced neatly and the coral reserved
>   ½ pint (3 dl.) very thick béchamel sauce
>   2 egg yolks
>   ¼ pint (1½ dl.) double cream
>   butter
>   1 glass of sherry
>   ¼ lb. (120 g.) mushrooms, diced and very lightly sautéd
>   seasoning

Stir the lobster and mushrooms into the warm (but not boiling) béchamel sauce and add the cream and egg yolks, beaten together, the sherry, and pepper and salt to season rather highly. Fill the patties, putting a touch of the lobster coral on top of the filling before putting on lids. Heat through in a moderate oven at 300°F., gas mark 4, for 5 or 6 minutes.

Lobster Pie

A very rich Cornish dish, probably going back to the Middle Ages, made in the manor houses, and on some of the farms which also maintained a fishing boat, when lobsters were plentiful. It would be made only for some special occasion. The earliest recipe I know calls for 6 to 8 fine lobsters and directs that a large coffin of fine paste should be raised.

Serves 8

        all the meat from 2 cooked lobsters, including claws
        ½ pint (3 dl.) scalded cream
        pepper and salt and a little powdered mace
        1–1½ lb. (½–¾ k.) short or rough puff pastry
        ½ lb. (240 g.) butter
        6 hard-boiled eggs, quartered
        6–12 oysters, fresh if possible but a can will do

Reserve the small claws and whiskers of the lobster, and keep the head cream and coral separately.

Line a large pie dish with pastry, reserving enough for the lid. Put in all the lobster and season with salt, pepper and mace. Put a third of the butter, cut in pieces, on the lobster. Lay the quartered hard-boiled eggs on this, season, and put on another third of the butter. Then put on the oysters and pour in their liquor. On this put the remaining butter. Put on the lid and stick the small claws through it at each end, turning out over the end of the dish. These are for decoration only. Bake for 30 minutes at 400° F., gas mark 6.

Warm the cream till hot but not boiling, stir in the coral and head cream and a little salt and pepper, and when the pie is done, remove from oven, lift the crust gently just enough to pour in the cream mixture. Replace crust and put back in the oven for 5 minutes.

Stewed Lobster

This very highly seasoned dish was sometimes made for Victorian gentlemen in their clubs for a late supper after much drinking. It was prepared at the table over a lamp.

For 2

1 cooked lobster (meat removed and cut in cubes, coral reserved separately)	1 tablespoon soy
	1 tablespoon port
	pinch of cayenne
1 oz. (30 g.) butter	salt
2 tablespoons strong stock or gravy	plenty of hot buttered toast

Have ready all the meat from a lobster neatly cut into small cubes and slices. Put the butter into a small copper pan or chafing dish. Add the coral and stir in 2 tablespoons of strong clear stock or bouillon, 1 tablespoon of soy, a little salt, a pinch of cayenne and a tablespoon of port. Put in the lobster and stew quite rapidly for 3 or 4 minutes. Serve in shallow bowls, to be eaten with spoons, accompanied by plenty of very hot buttered toast.

MUSSELS

Collected and eaten on the shore since the Stone Age. If actually eaten on the rocks they are delicious roasted on stones made hot in a fire: as soon as a shell opens, a piece of butter is put in and the mussel tipped into a large spoon or straight into the mouth when cool enough.

Basic preparation at home is simply to wash and scrape the shells well and drop into a boiling court-bouillon made with water, a glass or two of white wine, an onion skinned and cut, a clove of garlic, a bouquet garni and 12 peppercorns. Boil briskly for 5 or 6 minutes, shaking from time to time, then all the mussels will be open.

Never use any that are open before cooking or any that open during the first 2 or 3 minutes of boiling: they are dead or dying and should be removed and thrown away.

BOILED MUSSELS

Cook as above. Strain off the court-bouillon carefully through a fine strainer, as there is generally sand or grit from the mussels. Pour the mussels into bowls and the strained stock over them, sprinkle with parsley and serve at once.

Buttered Mussels

This is a translation of a fourteenth-century recipe which begins: 'Take muscules and sith them and pike them oute the shell . . .'

For 4–6
>   1 quart (1 k.) or more of cooked, shelled mussels (p. 242)
>   3 oz. (90 g.) butter
>   2 teaspoons very finely chopped shallots
>   1 clove of garlic, finely chopped
>   1 tablespoon of parsley, finely chopped
>   1 tablespoon of fine breadcrumbs
>   salt and pepper

Take the hot, cooked mussels from the shells and toss them in butter with very finely chopped shallots, a clove of garlic, a tablespoon of chopped parsley. After 2 minutes lightly mix in a tablespoon of fine breadcrumbs and a little salt and pepper. Stir 2 minutes more and serve immediately, a small bowl for each person.

Mussel Pie

For 4–6
>   1½–2 pints (1 k.) cooked and shelled mussels
>   ½ pint (3 dl.) of their liquor, strained
>   1 glass white wine
>   2 small onions, very finely chopped
>   1 tablespoon of chopped parsley
>   2 oz. (60 g.) butter
>   pepper and salt
>   ½ lb. (240 g.) fine white breadcrumbs

Butter a flat fireproof casserole and lay in the mussels. Pour over the wine and sprinkle with the onions and parsley, pepper and salt. Cover with the breadcrumbs so that the top is even. Pour over some of the liquor in which the mussels cooked, so that the crumbs are damp but not swimming. Dot with plenty of butter and bake 20 minutes at 350° F., gas mark 4. If not quite crisp and brown on top, hold for a minute under hot grill. Serve at once.

Mussels in Rolls

Splendid for lunch in the garden or as a supper dish. There are several versions from the sixteenth century onwards. This is from Scotland about 1840.

For 6

> 6 crusty rolls
> 1 pint (½ k.) of mussels, cooked and shelled
> ¼ pint (1½ dl.) of well seasoned béchamel sauce with a pinch of mace added

Pull all the crumb from the rolls. Butter the insides. Stir the hot mussels into the hot sauce and fill the rolls. Butter the outsides of the rolls and stand in the oven at 300° F., gas mark 2, for 10 minutes. Serve with sprigs of watercress.

If you want to prepare the rolls ahead of the meal, proceed as above but wrap each in foil and leave in the oven for 20 minutes to ensure their being hot right through. Then unwrap and put back for 5 minutes more to crisp the outsides.

Mussels in Murphies

This is an Irish peasant dish. The filled potatoes were wrapped in a cloth and carried to the men in the fields.

> a large potato baked in its jacket per person
> a dozen or so cooked and shelled mussels per person (keep these warm in some of their own stock)
> 1 oz. (30 g.) butter for each potato
> salt and pepper

Simply cut the ends off the potatoes, scoop out the insides and mix with the butter, salt and plenty of pepper. Replace some of the mixture, well season the mussels, and put them in. Push in some more potato, put back the cut-off end and put back in oven for 5 minutes to get really hot again.

Serve with the lower half of each potato wrapped in foil, so that it can be held, and eat with a teaspoon.

OYSTERS

Oysters were so plentiful up to the beginning of the nineteenth century that Sam Weller could say: 'Poverty and oysters always seem to go together ... the poorer a place is, the greater call there seems to be for oysters ... here's a oyster stall to every half dozen houses [in Whitechapel]. The street's lined vith 'em. Blessed if I don't think that ven a man's wery poor, he rushes out of his lodgings and eats oysters in reg'lar desperation.'*

In 1700, 200 cost 4s., and in 1840 they still only cost about 4d. a dozen. They were sold in the Fish Market at Billingsgate, which had grown in importance at the end of the seventeenth century. They were also sold on stalls and barrows, often apparently in association with gilt gingerbread. Smollet in *Humphrey Clinker* claims that the connoisseur preferred his oysters to have a green colour, which he took to indicate freshness, and that to this end they were sometimes kept for days in 'slime pits' covered with 'vitriolic scum'. If this can be accepted as fact, many a death must surely have followed from eating them. However, about 1850 they seem quite suddenly to have become scarcer, partly from disease and partly because the beds had been over-dredged. In spite of cultivation, they have remained a luxury ever since.

Colchester 'natives' are esteemed as among the best oysters in the world, and to do anything but serve them on the shell with lemon, pepper and fresh brown bread and butter is almost sacrilege. However, certain ways of serving oysters hot are delicious, and various interesting recipes survive from days when they were cheap and plentiful. They used to be included in many pies and made dishes and frequently as garnishes and in sauces: today, as with truffles, we cannot always afford or even obtain them easily. At Wheeler's they are offered fried, with a cheese sauce or au gratin. We give here four traditional English recipes:

OYSTER LOAVES

'Take a new manchet and rasp it and take out the crumbs then take some of the fforced meat and rubb all the manchet round within then put in the Oyster in a little juice of lemon peper and salt then beat yolks of eggs and wash over the loaf then fry them browne in butter.'

This is from the Reading MSS. of 1760. It makes a splendid supper or luncheon dish for two people if one dozen oysters are used.

    12 oysters
    1 French loaf (about 12 in. long)
    lemon juice, pepper and salt
    yolks of 2 eggs

* *Pickwick Papers*, Charles Dickens, 1837.

For the forcemeat (this recipe is also from the Reading MSS.):
2 oz. (60 g.) prepared suet
¼ lb. (120 g.) cooked minced veal or pork
dessertspoon chopped thyme and parsley
salt and pepper
1 egg
¼ lb. (120 g.) fine white crumbs
2 tablespoons well-seasoned stock (a chicken bouillon cube will do)

Mix all well together.

Rub the French loaf all over lightly with a grater so that the outside is roughened. Cut off one end and with a long knife scoop out all the crumb. Work the forcemeat into a lining inside the loaf, open the oysters and mix their liquor with a teaspoon of lemon juice and some salt and pepper; beard them. Hold the loaf upright, open end upwards. Pour in the liquid and then the oysters. Spread the cut-off end with forcemeat and press back into place. Brush the whole loaf over with the beaten egg yolks. Fry in hot (but not coloured) butter all over till a fine golden brown. Then put in the oven pre-heated to 350° F., gas mark 4, for 10 minutes to heat through. Serve at once accompanied by a plain green salad with a rather sharp dressing. Cut the loaf in half across and give half to each person.

Scalloped Oysters

Dr Kitchiner's recipe from the *Cooks' Oracle*, first published in 1817.
3 or 4 shells or small flat ramekins are required.

Serves 3 or 4

18 oysters	pinch of cayenne*
3 oz. (90 g.) butter	teaspoon lemon juice*
½ lb. (240 g.) fine white crumbs	pinch of mace*
salt and pepper*	

Open and stew the oysters in their own liquor very slowly for 2 or 3 minutes; if there is very little liquor add a tablespoon of water. Lift out the oysters, beard them and set aside, reserving the liquor. Melt 2 oz. (60 g.) of butter and stir in three quarters of the crumbs and all the seasoning. Mix well and add two thirds of the liquor in which the oysters cooked. Butter the scallop shells

---

* Dr Kitchiner, though he suggests them, implies that these conceal the true flavour of the oysters, but it seems to me that they enhance it and improve the dish.

and sift some of the dry crumbs over them. Lay in 2 oysters, put a layer of prepared and seasoned crumbs, put 2 more oysters, more crumbs, remaining oysters and finish with a layer of crumbs into which you pour the reserved liquor, a little into each shell. Sprinkle with remaining dry crumbs, dot with pieces of butter and cook for 5 or 6 minutes at 400° F., gas mark 6, near the top of the oven so that they brown nicely. Serve at once.

Fried Oysters

In the seventeenth and eighteenth centuries great dishes of fried oysters with slices of lemon used to be served. Nowadays they are useful as a savoury, when two per person, served on a strip of toast, are enough. They make an elegant starting course, when three or four per person should be served on a small plate, with two small rolls of bacon, three triangles of fried bread, a slice of lemon and a sprinkling of chopped parsley.

> 2–4 very large oysters per person
> flour seasoned with salt and pepper
> 2 oz. (60 g.) fine breadcrumbs
> 1 egg, well beaten
> 2 oz. (60 g.) butter
> 1 oz. (30 g.) olive or corn oil (not groundnut)

Simmer the oysters in their liquor for two or three minutes. Drain and beard them. Dip them first in the seasoned flour and then in egg and breadcrumbs. Have the butter and oil smoking hot (the oil crisps the outsides and prevents the butter from darkening). Drop in the oysters and brown quickly. They should only be a minute in the pan or they will become hard and tough.

Oyster Patties

Like Lobster Patties, traditional at all grand Victorian supper parties.

For 24 patty cases
> 2 dozen oysters
> ¼ pint (1½ dl.) rather thick béchamel sauce
> 2 oz. (½ dl.) double cream
> salt and pepper
> 1 glass white wine

Beard the oysters and poach for 2 minutes in their own liquid and the wine. Pour all the liquid into the sauce, stir in the cream and season highly. Put a spoonful in each case, then an oyster, another spoonful of sauce on top, and then the lid. Heat at 300° F., gas mark 2, for 5 minutes and serve.

Scallops

A seventeenth-century recipe, as served by Oliver Cromwell's wife, Elizabeth (commonly called Joan). This lady was laughed at for her meanness, but seems, in fact, to have kept a good table.

> 2 scallops per person
> ¼ lb. (120 g.) fine white crumbs
> a pinch each of ginger, cinnamon and nutmeg
> 2 glasses white wine
> 2 oz. (60 g.) butter
> pepper and salt

Boil the scallops gently for ten minutes or so. Drain and slice and add nutmeg, ginger, cinnamon, salt and pepper. Butter the shells and strew with breadcrumbs. Put in the seasoned scallop slices, add a little more butter and a thick covering of breadcrumbs and pour a little white wine into each shell. Finish with dabs of butter and cook in the oven at 400° F., gas mark 6, for 10 minutes.

The original recipe suggests the use of vinegar as well as wine and the addition of sugar 'if they are sharp, for this fish is luscious and sweet naturally'. In fact they are better without either.

Fried Scallops with Bacon

A traditional dish at high tea on the Yorkshire coast and elsewhere in the north.

> 2 rashers of lean bacon per person
> 2 or 3 scallops per person
> ¼ lb. (120 g.) of fine white breadcrumbs
> 2 eggs
> deep fat to fry

Have the scallops removed from the shells and separate the coral from the white. Dip each portion of both first in breadcrumbs, then in beaten egg, then in breadcrumbs again. Fry in a basket in smoking hot fat (about 400° F.) for 3–4 minutes. Drain and serve at once with the crisply fried rashers. Sprinkle with parsley.

A chilled tartare or hollandaise sauce served separately makes this an epicure's dish.

Freshwater Fish

'To Broyle a Carp'

A Northamptonshire recipe from 'Mrs Ann Blencowe', 1694. Lady Blencowe was the daughter of a distinguished Whig mathematician and cryptographer, John Wallis. She married Sir John Blencowe, who was an M.P. and a judge, when she was nineteen. Her spelling is distinctly personal, even for her time, but most of her recipes, though often cryptic, are very good.

'. . . scarbanada it on bothe sides, wash it over with butter and season ye scarbanada with time, Nutmeg and salt. Then put it on your Gridiron and boyle it sloly over charcoals. Keep it basting. You may broyle some Collops of Gammon with it. Sett upp on ye coals in a stewing dish a quarter of a pint of Claret a little Oyster Licker, Minced Oysters and hard eggs with a hanfull of prans. When your Carp are Broyled dish them up and Garnish them with fryed Collops of Gammon and pour on your licker being thickened with a ladelfull of Brown Butter.'

Most good fish shops will get a carp of 2–8 lb. (1–4 k.) given two or three days' notice, and will scale and clean it.

Serves 8

a carp of 3 or 4 lb. (1½–2 k.)	small tin of oysters or 6 fresh
powdered thyme and nutmeg	oysters
black pepper	3 hard-boiled eggs
salt	¼ lb. (120 g.) frozen prawns
flour	½ pint (3 dl.) of chicken or veal
10 oz. (300 g.) butter	stock (may be made from a
½-in. (1-cm.) thick gammon	bouillon cube)
¼ pint (1½ dl.) claret	lemon juice

Cut six 2-inch (5-cm.) slits transversely on both sides of the fish, through the skin but not too deep, from below the head to 2 inches from the tail (carbonadas). Rub thyme, salt and nutmeg into these. Rub a little flour all over the fish, with further salt and black pepper.

Lay it on a baking tray in which you have melted ½ lb. (240 g.) of butter, and spoon it well over him. Place in the oven preheated to 400° F., and bake for 30 minutes, basting frequently. If the fish is not well basted, the flesh becomes woolly, but if it is, it is very delicate. Then cover and cook for a further 10–15 minutes. Test with a skewer through one of the 'carbonadas' to see if it is done.

While it is cooking make the sauce and prepare the gammon. Cut all rind and fat from the gammon rashers and cut each into three. Lay them in the butter round the carp (not covered by the foil), and cook for 10–15 minutes, turning once.

Make a roux with the remaining butter and 1½ oz. (45 g.) flour. Stir in the claret and the liquor from the oysters, canned or fresh, and then add the chicken stock, so that the sauce takes the consistency of thin cream. Add the hard-boiled eggs, finely chopped, the oysters, chopped (rather than minced), and the prawns, halved. Stir lightly and season with salt and plenty of black pepper, and a squeeze of lemon juice to taste.

Dish the carp as Mrs Blencowe suggests. This is a very handsome dish, and the gammon and the strongly flavoured sauce enhance the rather un-emphatic flavour of the fish.

I do not suggest, in these days when we do not breed them in our own fish ponds, that we should serve carp very often, as they must be fairly large and fairly elaborately cooked to be good. But they are well worth ordering and preparing occasionally.

Stuffed Carp

Serves 8–10. Also traditional. Prepare exactly as previous recipe but stuff the carp as follows, using a fish of at least 4 lb. (2 k.).

> *For the stuffing:*
> another small carp or a trout
> panada of ½ lb. (240 g.) of fine breadcrumbs soaked in ¼ pint (1½ dl.) boiling milk
> salt, black pepper
> 2 teaspoons finely chopped parsley
> ¼ lb. (120 g.) mushrooms, finely sliced and sautéd in butter
> a little fennel and tarragon, fresh or dried
> ¼ lb. (120 g.) butter
> 2 eggs

Poach the little carp or trout for 10 minutes in salted water while you prepare the crumbs. Lift the fish, remove all the flesh from the skin and bone and flake finely. Work it into the butter and blend with all the other ingredients, including the panada. Finally, blend in 2 eggs, and when quite smooth fill the large carp and sew up the belly.

Make any surplus forcemeat into balls, flour and fry lightly in butter and put round the fish after the sauce has been poured over it.

Minnows

The minnow is the freshwater equivalent of the whitebait.

Izaak Walton gives a recipe for 'Minnow Tansies' which embodies spring in the water meadows of England. He says that you are to take all the minnows you have caught, head, tail and clean them by the stream. On your way home you are to pick cowslips or primroses or both. As you go through your herb garden you pick a few new shoots of tansy. You take 2 new laid eggs, ¼ lb. (120 g.) butter, salt and pepper. Crush the tansy stalks in a bowl so that a very little juice and flavour is left when you remove them; put in the egg yolks and beat them well; add a tablespoon of cowslip flowers or of primrose petals or a mixture, and a little salt and pepper, and stir all together. Drop in the little fish, lift them out individually with flower petals adhering to them, fry in hot butter, and eat at once. You will be eating the English spring, if by any lucky chance you can manage to fish in a little stream and walk home through flowering fields in April.

Pike

Also called Jack or Luce.

This predator among freshwater fish has lost its reputation since the eighteenth century. Until then the pike was regarded as a very noble dish, perhaps partly because it is the largest of English freshwater fish, for it is true that its flesh is apt to have a cotton-wool consistency with many needle-like bones. The roe of a pike is unpleasant and even slightly poisonous and should never be served. Nowadays pike is chiefly used for quenelles, for which the light, slightly dry flesh and delicate but definite flavour are inimitable. But if the pike is not too large, about 2 or 3 lb. (1–1½ k.), and is cut through into cutlets which are well salted, left in the salt for 15 minutes and then washed, or if the whole fish is washed through with salt water and carefully scaled and cleaned, it can be served in several delicious ways. It is more highly esteemed today in France than in England, and this is a pity, as there are several very good traditional recipes for serving it.

At a great feast for the investiture of George Neville as* Archbishop of York and Chancellor of England in the sixth year of the reign of Edward IV (1466), pike and bream (of which there were 608) were the only fish served, as being truly delicacies.

The following is Izaak Walton's own recipe from the *Compleat Angler* (1653):

'First, open your Pike at the gills, and if need be, cut also a little slit towards the belly. Out of these, take his guts; and keep his liver, which you are to shred very small, with thyme, sweet marjoram, and a little winter-savory; put to these some pickled oysters, and some anchovies, two or three; both these last whole, for the anchovies will melt, and the oysters should not; to these, you must add also a pound of sweet butter, which you are to mix with the herbs that are shred, and let them all be well salted. If the Pike be more than a yard long, then you may put into these herbs more than a pound, or if he be less, then less butter will suffice: These, being thus mixt, with a blade or two of mace, must be put into the Pike's belly; and then his belly so sewed up as to keep all the butter in his belly if it is possible; if not, then as much of it as you possibly can. But take not off the scales. Then you are to thrust the spit through his mouth, out at his tail. And then take four or five or six split sticks, or very thin laths, and a convenient quantity of tape or filleting; these laths are to be tied round about the Pike's body, from his head to his tail, and the tape tied somewhat thick, to prevent his breaking or falling off from the spit. Let him be roasted very leisurely, and often basted with claret wine and anchovies, and butter, mixt together; and also with what moisture falls from him into the pan. When you have roasted him sufficiently, you are to hold under him, when you unwind or cut the tape that ties him, such a dish as you propose to eat him out of; and let him fall into it with the sauce that is roasted in his belly; and by this means the Pike will be kept unbroken and complete.

'Then to the sauce which was within, and also that sauce in the pan, you are to add a fit quantity of the best butter, and to squeeze the juice of three or four oranges. Lastly, you may either put it into the Pike, with the oysters, two cloves of garlick, and take it whole out, when the Pike is cut off the spit; or, to give the sauce a haut gout, let the dish into which you let the Pike falle be rubbed with it: The using or not of this garlick is left to your discretion.

'This dish of meat is too good for any but anglers, or very honest men; and I trust you will prove both, and therefore I have trusted you with this secret.'

*Kettner, 1877, *A Book of the Table*, p. 183.

It is unusual though not impossible to get a pike of more than 3 feet long, and it would tend to be rather coarse, but a pike of about 12–18 inches can be ordered from a good fishmonger (who may take a few days to get it) and is excellent treated just as Izaak Walton suggests, spit-roasted on a modern spit. It should not need splinting, but two wooden splints held in place with fine string can be used and should not burn, as the grilling must be slow with plentiful basting. Under a low grill such a fish should take about 40–45 minutes.

Baked Pike

This is a nineteenth-century recipe from the Wye Valley.

Pike are very good stuffed with a forcemeat of veal. Cynics sometimes say that the stuffing is the best part of the dish, but this shows little appreciation of the subtle flavour and texture of the fish.

2–3 lb. (1–1½ k.) pike	2 glasses of claret
garlic	juice of 2 oranges
3 oz. (90 g.) butter	flour, seasoning

For the forcemeat:

½ lb. (240 g.) veal very finely minced (lean pork or chicken may be used)

parsley, thyme, a sprig of fennel, finely chopped

1 finely chopped onion

3 oz. (90 g.) breadcrumbs

1 egg to bind

Mix all the ingredients for the forcemeat together, season rather highly and fill the belly of the fish, which should have been washed but not scaled. Rub the fish all over with flour, salt and pepper, and lay it in a flat fireproof dish which has been rubbed with a clove of garlic. Put in the butter and the claret and bake at 350–400° F., gas mark 4–6, for about 35 minutes, basting from time to time. Test with a skewer. The flesh should move easily from the backbone. Take the dish from the oven and pour the orange juice over the fish and mix it a little with the wine and butter, adding a little more salt and pepper. Serve immediately.

Quenelles of Pike

The word quenelles is thought by some to come from the Anglo-Saxon word 'caill' which meant 'pounded', and by others to have the same derivation as 'coney' from the Latin *cuniculus*, i.e. the little soft rissoles are 'little rabbits'.

Quenelles are very fine smooth light rissoles made from chicken, veal, game or fish, the best of all fish for quenelles being pike because of its slightly dry texture. They take time and trouble to make. They are a testing dish for a cook and one that is sometimes ordered by a patron or prospective employer when trying out a new cook. They are a very great delicacy and once the trick of flavouring, consistency and shaping is learned, may be made from chicken or veal or salmon as well as from pike. They are particularly well set off by croûtons of puff pastry, and always need a rich but subtle sauce. Garnish fairly elaborately as they should be seen as an impressive dish.

Serves 8–10

1 lb. (½ k.) cooked pike, skin and bones removed, pounded with 1 teaspoon salt, a little pepper, and a pinch of nutmeg

a court-bouillon made from the skin and bones with an onion, a carrot, 2 glasses of white wine, salt and pepper and 1½ pints (9 dl.) water, boiled for 30–40 minutes and then strained

8 or 9 oz. (240–270 g.) of panada of fine white breadcrumbs: for this take 6 oz. (180 g.) of crumbs, pour over them ¼ pint (1½ dl.) of boiling milk. Leave 5 minutes to absorb and then blend or stir until smooth. Stir again for a minute or two over low heat to dry out a little and then leave to get quite cold

½ lb. (240 g.) butter

2 whole eggs and 2 yolks

Work ½ lb. (240 g.) butter till it is soft and blend the fish, panada and butter together till quite smooth. Drop in two whole eggs and two more yolks and blend again. If made in an electric blender the mixture should not need sieving, but it must be extremely white and fine.

The quenelles may be cooked in special quenelle or dariole moulds standing in the court-bouillon, which should cover the tops, or they may be moulded in a serving spoon, using another to mould the tops, and placed on a very clean buttered omelette pan and the boiling court-bouillon poured gently over them to cover. Poach very gently for 15 minutes. Drain and keep warm, closely covered with foil, for not more than an hour.

There are various traditional ways of serving them in England, of which the three most attractive are:

(1) Fry croûtons of bread to a light golden brown and place a quenelle on each. Pour over them a cream sauce made of half good white sauce and half thick cream, well seasoned, and garnish with finely chopped parsley and chopped hard-boiled eggs.

(2) Serve in a fireproof dish with a cheese sauce which contains prawns or finely chopped lobster. Triangular pastry croûtons should be stuck by each corner all round the edge of the dish.

(3) Serve in a very good fresh tomato sauce to which ½ lb. (240 g.) finely sliced and lightly sautéd mushrooms have been added. Garnish with pastry croûtons, and sliced truffles if possible or stoned and halved black olives if not.

Collops of Pike or Carp

From a Scottish nineteenth-century kitchen.

Cut the pike through crossways into 1½-inch (4-cm.) thick slices. Cut out the backbone from each collop and fill the hole with veal forcemeat (see p. 296). Bake in a buttered dish, covered, for 20 minutes at 400° F., gas mark 6. Serve very hot, pouring over a sauce of ¼ lb. (120 g.) melted butter to which the juices from the pan plus the juice of half a lemon have been added.

SALMON

The brown trout and the rainbow trout are also freshwater fish. The sea trout is usually called 'salmon trout' by fish mongers. These are all of the *Salmonidae* family.

Before the pollution of our rivers, salmon was so plentiful that London apprentices are supposed to have insisted that their articles should stipulate that they should not be given it more than three times a week. However, this may be apochryphal, since in the fifteenth century a salmon seems to have fetched 3–5s. in the market (probably about 3d. per lb.) which would have made it more expensive than mutton, which sold at about 1½d. a lb.

Nowadays salmon is extremely expensive, and the chilled Pacific salmon or Canadian salmon has not as fine a flavour or consistency as salmon from Scotland or from the Wye or the Severn. (Soyer, when chef at the Reform Club in the nineteenth century, used to have his salmon sent up from the Severn by train in the morning, met at the station and prepared for that night's dinner.) Imported, chilled salmon will suffice for more elaborate recipes. Really first-class English salmon requires only to be poached, baked in foil or paper, or grilled, and served hot or cold with an appropriate sauce.

Baked Salmon

Serves 4–5

a piece of middle-cut salmon,	flour, pepper and salt
about 1½–2 lb. (¾–1 k.)	a sprig or two of tarragon
2 oz. (60 g.) butter	a bay leaf

Butter a large sheet of foil. Dust the salmon with flour, pepper and salt, and lay on the foil. Put the tarragon and bay leaf on it and dot with the rest of the butter. Wrap into a close parcel. Lay on a baking tray and bake for 30–35 minutes at 350° F., gas mark 4. Open the parcel a little and try with a skewer to see if the fish comes cleanly from the bone. If not, cook for another 10 minutes. If the salmon is to be eaten cold, leave it in the foil overnight and it will be very moist with a splendid flavour the next day.

Baked Rolled Salmon

This recipe is dated 1870. You require a piece of salmon from the tail end about 8 inches long (probable weight about 2 lb. (1 k.)). Get the fishmonger to cut this into two long fillets and to skin them.

Serves 6

2 salmon fillets
6 oysters, or a small tin will do
1 tablespoon finely chopped parsley
¼ lb. (120 g.) fine white breadcrumbs
pinch of nutmeg and of mace
pepper and salt
¼ lb. (120 g.) butter
yolk of 1 egg, well beaten
glass of white wine
¼ pint (1½ dl.) double or scalded cream

Mix the oysters and their liquor with the parsley, breadcrumbs, spices and seasoning, and work in 3 oz. (90 g.) of softened butter and the egg yolk. Spread the fillets with this mixture but not right to the edges. Roll up very tightly and tie round with string or thread near top and bottom. Put the fillets upright in a casserole. Pour in the wine and a ¼ pint (1½ dl.) of water, and put the rest of the butter in dabs on top of the fillets. Cover closely with foil and bake for 45 minutes at 400° F., gas mark 6. Serve the rolls lying flat on a dish, with their own liquor over them. Each will serve 3 people. Stir ¼ pint (1½ dl.) of double or scalded cream into the liquor in the casserole after the rolls have been lifted, heat for a moment and then pour over them.

This recipe is also excellent made with fillets of fresh haddock or of halibut.

Salmon Pie

This recipe comes from a lady whose grandmother cooked for a great house on the Dee where salmon in season was so plentiful that no one would eat it when served plain.

Serves 8

1 lb. (½ k.) puff pastry	½ lb. (240 g.) butter
2 lb. (1 k.) middlecut salmon	seasoning
meat of a small cooked lobster, chopped fine	teaspoon mace
	court-bouillon
2 anchovies, chopped fine	6 glasses white wine
4 hard-boiled eggs, quartered	

Poach the salmon in a court-bouillon which contains 2 glasses of white wine. When cooked (30 minutes) remove and allow to cool. Roll out your pastry and allow it to rest. When the salmon is cool but not quite cold, remove the skin and carefully divide the fish into eight neat slices, cutting through the bone. Keep the shape of the piece.

Butter a large pie dish and lay the salmon in as though it were still in one piece. Press two quarters of the hard-boiled egg and a piece of butter between each slice.

Melt the remaining butter and stir it into remaining white wine (4 glasses), ¼ pint (1½ dl.) of the liquor in which the fish was cooked, the lobster, anchovy, seasoning and mace. Pour this over the salmon.

Put on the crust and bake at 400° F., gas mark 6, for 20 minutes. Then reduce the heat to 350° F., gas mark 4, place the pie lower in the oven and cook a further 10 minutes so that salmon is heated through. Serve at once. Cut the crust right across in narrow segments, which will roughly coincide with the slices of salmon, which should be lifted out whole.

Poached Salmon

Serves 6

> 2 lb. (1 k.) middle-cut salmon (English if possible)
> court-bouillon made of trimmings from the fish, parsley, thyme,
> fennel (if possible), an onion, a carrot, some white wine, salt and
> pepper, a bay leaf, a tablespoon of olive oil

Boil the court-bouillon for 30 minutes, put in a tablespoon of olive oil (this helps to keep the skin of the fish from breaking and the outer flesh from flaking). Put in the fish. Poach very gently for 35 minutes. Try with a skewer to see if the flesh easily leaves the bone. Lift out with a perforated slice and serve at once, if it is to be eaten hot, garnished with thin slices of cucumber and accompanied by a hollandaise sauce (p. 285). If it is to be eaten cold, it should be allowed to cool to blood heat in the bouillon and then lifted and left to become quite cold in the refrigerator. Serve chilled but not icy cold, with mayonnaise and a cucumber and lettuce salad.

Salmon Roast on the Spit

A seventeenth-century recipe. The salmon cooks very well on a modern electrical spit.

For 6

> 2–2½ lb. (1 k.) piece of middle-cut salmon
> 6 cloves
> dried or finely chopped fresh rosemary
> ½ lb. (240 g.) butter
> 1 glass white wine
> 1 glass orange juice and a few slivers of peel
> 6 thin slices of orange
> flour, pepper and salt

Spit the piece of salmon lengthways and tie round with ½-inch tape in two or three places to prevent breaking. (Cut the tape 10 minutes before it will be cooked and remove, so that the bands it leaves may brown.) Dust it with flour, pepper and salt, stick the cloves in here and there, and sprinkle with the rosemary. Spread with the softened butter. The grill should be at a medium heat and the fish should be basted with butter every 10 minutes and grilled for 35 minutes. Test with a skewer that flesh moves easily from bone. When you remove the tapes, pour over the wine and orange juice and peel, and stir them into the butter and juice from the fish as they run off it. Use up any remaining butter.

Carefully take fish from spit on to a hot dish. Lay the slices of orange along it to garnish, and serve the butter sauce from the tray separately.

SALMON TROUT (also called Sea Trout)

Even better than salmon, because the flesh is more delicate. Several early recipes exist for baking and roasting on the spit, but it is clear that these fish were often regarded simply as small salmon.

Baked Salmon Trout

This seems to me the simplest and best method of cooking a salmon trout, whether it is to be eaten hot or cold.

Serves 6–8

> salmon trout of 2–4 lb. (1–2 k.) weight
> butter
> parsley, thyme, fennel, tarragon and chives
> flour, salt and pepper

Put a large piece of butter and some sprigs of parsley, thyme, fennel, tarragon and some chives in the belly. Rub the fish all over with seasoned flour. Butter a large sheet of foil and lay on the butter some more of the same herbs. Lay the fish in the middle and wrap up in a long, neat parcel. Lay it in a baking tray and cook at 350° F., gas mark 4, for 30 minutes. Undo the paper so that the fish is exposed and the skin can crisp a little. Bake a further 10 minutes and test with a skewer to see if the flesh moves easily from the bone. To serve, lift out carefully on to a flat dish, remove the herbs and pour all the butter and juices over it.

Salmon trout is best of all with a hollandaise sauce (p. 285). It is delicious cooked in the same way but stuffed with a forcemeat of ¼ lb. (120 g.) fine white breadcrumbs, some of all the herbs mentioned above finely chopped, 2 anchovy fillets, pounded to pieces, a nob of butter, pepper and salt and a little milk, all well mixed and pushed into the cavity of the belly. Lay the fish on its back on the buttered foil, fold the skin well over the stuffing and wrap tightly, and there is no need to sew it up. Finely chopped almonds or sliced and sautéd mushrooms or a few sliced green olives are delicious added to the stuffing.

Salmon Trout in Cream

An Edwardian recipe from Northumberland. Six large fish were used for a dinner party for thirty, which preceded a ball.

Serves 6–8

> a salmon trout, 2½–3 lb. (1¼–1½ k.) (have the fish skinned as well as cleaned)
> ¾ pint (4½ dl.) of heavy cream
> flour, salt and pepper
> a cucumber cut in neat ½-inch (1-cm.) cubes
> 2 glasses of dry white wine or champagne
> butter

Brush the fish all over with cream, using a pastry brush and making as much adhere as possible. Then sprinkle all over with seasoned flour. Put in a well-buttered fireproof dish. Cook in an oven preheated to 350° F., gas mark 4, for 5 minutes. Then turn the fish over and cook another 5 minutes. Add the wine and cook for 10 minutes. Finally, pour over all the remaining cream and cook a further 20 minutes. Try the fish very gently with a skewer to see if the flesh moves freely from the bone. Gently mix the sauce around it with a fork, adding a little salt and pepper if necessary.

While the fish cooks, poach the cucumber cubes in salted water to which you add a knob of butter. Lift, drain well, and keep hot.

Drop them into the finished dish, return to the oven for 2 minutes only and serve.

Stuffed Salmon Trout in Pastry

This fairly elaborate recipe is traditional. A seventeenth-century recipe prepares a whole salmon in this way; a nineteenth-century one uses a salmon trout, and another uses small trout, one for each person. The salmon is too large for most of us today, and the trout have too much pastry in proportion to the fish; the salmon trout is ideal for six to eight people and the dish, once made, is never to be forgotten.

> a salmon trout, 2½–3 lb. (1¼–1½ k.), skinned but with tail left on
> 1½ lb. (1¼ k.) puff pastry (frozen will do)
> 2 oz. (60 g.) breadcrumbs soaked in boiling milk (panada)
> 2 oz. (90 g.) butter

chives ⎫
tarragon ⎬ fresh if possible; finely chopped, but reserve 3 or 4
parsley ⎪ sprays of tarragon and a few chives whole
thyme ⎭
salt and pepper
1 teaspoon mace
¼ pint (1½ dl.) double cream
slices of lemon
4 oz. (120 g.) frozen prawns or shrimps

The pastry: Roll out very thin, to an oblong shape a little longer than the fish and three times as wide. Leave to rest.

The stuffing: Press the crumbs a little to get rid of the surplus milk. Mix in a tablespoon of parsley and a dessertspoon of tarragon, chives and thyme. Work in the softened butter. Season well with salt, pepper, and mace and blend or beat well.

Pack into the fish and fold the skin well over. Brush over the whole fish with cream, sprinkle with salt and pepper and lay on its back the sprigs of tarragon and the chives. Put the fish in the middle of the pastry. If the stuffing was too much to go into the fish, pile the remainder against it where it thins to the tail. Fold the pastry up and over on both sides of the fish, leaving the head and tail exposed, and make the join into an ornamental roll down its length. Press it in tightly at the head and tail to seal well. If you prefer, the head and tail may be cut off and the fish completely enclosed, but to leave them out is traditional. Place carefully on a large baking tray and bake in an oven preheated to 400° F., gas mark 6, for 20 minutes, after which time the pastry should be golden brown and fully risen and crisped. Reduce the heat to 350° F., gas mark 4, and place the salmon trout lower in the oven. Cook for a further 25 minutes. If the pastry begins to darken, cover it lightly with foil.

Serve on a large flat dish garnished with slices of lemon, and 4 small heaps of prawns or shrimps which have been sautéd for 1 minute in butter. Serve by cutting across to sever head and then across in 1½-inch (3–4-cm.) slices, using a sharp knife which will cut right through the backbone.

TROUT

'Well, sir, and what say you to a fine fresh trout, hot and dry, in a napkin?' asks Peacock's Mr MacQuedy, talking, as in the case of lobsters, about fish for breakfast.

Grilled Trout

A trout which is to be grilled is improved by being lightly coated with seasoned flour or seasoned fine oatmeal and then wrapped either in rashers of bacon, vine leaves or the outside leaf of a leek: all of these protect the delicate skin and give it a delicious flavour. The leaves can be removed for the last two minutes to brown the skin if necessary, but usually it becomes crisp enough through the leaves. If you prefer to cook it with no wrapping, a very little powdered or finely chopped thyme sprinkled over it is delicious. Trout is excellent grilled or fried with mushrooms (ideally, of course, it should have been caught in the stream at the bottom of the field where the mushrooms were picked).

Make the grill very hot and pour or brush about ½ oz. (15 g.) of butter over each fish just before they go under the heat. Turn once and grill each side for about 4 minutes.

Fried or Grilled Trout with Almonds

Traditional and elegantly simple.

> 2 oz. (60 g.) blanched split almonds per trout
> butter
> salt and pepper
> flour
> lemon juice

Rub the fish with seasoned flour and fry in plenty of butter, turning once. They will need 3 or 4 minutes on each side if of average size. Two minutes before they are done, tip in the almonds, and stir them about so that they brown on every side, being careful that they do not darken too much. Squeeze a little lemon into the butter and almonds in the pan when you have lifted the fish and pour all over them. If the fish are to be grilled, treat them as described in the previous recipe and fry the almonds separately in a small pan.

Trout in a Blanket

> 1 trout per person
> 1 large thin pancake for each trout
> 1 tablespoon finely chopped parsley with a little fennel and thyme added
> salt and pepper
> 6 oz. (180 g.) butter

These quantities are for 6 trout.

Work the green herbs into ¼ lb. (120 g.) of the butter. Make the pancakes, which should have a diameter equal to the length of the fish, and should be very thin and crisp. Dip the trout in seasoned flour and grill with the remaining butter. They should be grilled unwrapped, as their skins must be very crisp. Spread each pancake generously with the green butter. Roll up a fish in each and lay them side by side on a flat dish, heads all one way. Return to oven for 3 minutes and serve very hot, spooning any of the green butter which has run out over each roll as you do so.

Trout in Aspic

This is an extremely ornamental Victorian dinner-party recipe. Our ancestors were obliged to go through the long process of making their own aspic jelly and clearing it with eggshells. We can use a prepared packet, and lose nothing, for with the wine it is very good.

Serves 6

6 trout, filleted by the fishmonger
½ bottle of claret
1 pint (6 dl.) packet of aspic jelly
lemon
¼ lb. (120 g.) mushrooms, finely sliced and sautéd and allowed to
    get cold
2 hard-boiled eggs, cut in neat slices
12 stuffed olives, cut in halves
3 anchovies cut in halves
salt and pepper

For the salad:
3 avocado pears
½ lb. (240 g.) very good cooked green peas
hearts of lettuce or very crisp pale inside leaves
French dressing

Poach the seasoned trout fillets in the red wine and allow to get cold. Have ready a small mould or soufflé dish for each person. Make up your aspic jelly with the wine in which the fish cooked, making up the required quantity with water. Add a squeeze of lemon juice, taste for seasoning and allow to cool but not to set. Rinse the moulds with cold water. Pour in a little jelly, lay on this a slice of egg, two olive-halves and two slices of mushroom. Allow this to set in position. When firm, roll the fillets of trout carefully round the insides of the moulds and fill with all the remaining ingredients, ornamentally arranged. Slip slices of egg between the fillets and the sides of the moulds. Fill up with the jelly and allow to set firmly in refrigerator.

Arrange the lettuce on a large flat dish and turn the moulds out carefully (warming the bottoms in hot water if necessary). Cut each avocado in half, peel the halves, squeeze lemon juice over them to preserve their colour, and arrange round the moulds, filling the centres with peas and putting more peas in small heaps between. Serve a very good French dressing separately.

The Victorians could not, of course, have served avocados, but they are particularly good with the wine jelly and the delicate fillets of trout.

Trout with Cream and Fennel

> 1 trout for each person
> flour, salt and pepper
> 6 sprigs fresh fennel, or 2 teaspoons dried
> ¼ pint (1½ dl.) cream for 4 trout
> 2 oz. (60 g.) white breadcrumbs
> 3 oz. (90 g.) butter
> ¼ pint (1½ dl.) milk

Lay the trout, rubbed in flour, salt and pepper, in a well-buttered flat fire-proof dish with the fennel on top of the fish. Pour in the milk. Cover with foil and bake at 400° F., gas mark 6, for 20 minutes.

Remove from the oven and take out the sprigs of fennel. Stir cream into liquor, add a little black pepper. Sprinkle the top of each fish with crumbs, put some dabs of butter on them, and brown the whole dish for three minutes under a hot grill so that the crumbs are just browned and the cream sauce begins to bubble.

Trout in Paper

A very good starting course, accompanied only by thin hot toast or brown bread and butter.

> 4 trout
> 6 oz. (180 g.) butter
> sprigs of parsley, thyme and fennel
> flour, salt and pepper

For each trout cut a circle of greaseproof paper with a diameter two inches more than the length of each fish. Lightly rub the fish with seasoned flour and put a piece of butter, and a sprig each of parsley, thyme and fennel in the belly of each. Butter the middle of the papers and lay the trout on them. Put a long slice of butter on each trout, fold over the paper, and crimp the edges together, so that each trout is in a close parcel. Bake at 400° F., gas mark 6, for 20 minutes.

Serve the parcels, as the aroma on opening is delicious. The trout may be cooked in foil instead of paper, but in this case allow five minutes more and serve unwrapped directly on to plates with all their butter and juices, but with the herbs removed.

General Fish Dishes

Fish Cakes

Traditional in England since Victorian times, but I have found no earlier recipes. They are often made simply by mixing cooked flaked fish into mashed potato, forming the mixture into cakes, dipping them in egg and breadcrumbs and frying them. The results are extremely dry and stodgy. The fish *must* be mixed into a fairly stiff white sauce, well flavoured and seasoned before the potato is added.

For 8–12 fish cakes

> ½ lb. (240 g.) cooked fish (any kind) without skin or bone and well flaked
> 6 oz. (180 g.) fairly thick white sauce, preferably made with fish stock and, in any case, highly seasoned
> ½ lb. (240 g.) cooked potato mashed with plenty of butter and a little milk
> 1 egg (2 may be needed if small)
> 3–4 oz. (90–120 g.) breadcrumbs (fresh or prepared)
> a little flour
> butter and cooking oil (half and half is best) to fry

Mix the fish into the sauce and stir in the potato so that you have a stiff smooth paste. All three should be cold when you mix them. Divide into 8–12 even sized pieces. Roll in flour, then dip in beaten egg and roll in crumbs, shaping the fish cake into a small flat cake about an inch (2 cm.) thick. Drop into smoking hot frying oil and butter at least ½ inch (1½ cm.) deep, or deep fry. As soon as both sides are golden brown lift, drain and put in a fireproof dish in a low oven, 300° F., gas mark 2. They will require 5 or 6 minutes to heat right through.

Mrs Glasse's White Fricassée of Fish (1747)

This recipe is extremely simple, extravagant and excellent. I had never been given such a fricassée until I made it myself, but once served it will be asked for again.

Serves 6

2½ lb. (1–1¼ k.) haddock or halibut or turbot, lemon soles, large plaice or whiting*

nutmeg

mace

salt

black pepper

bouquet garni or parsley, thyme and tarragon

½ pint (3 dl.) double cream

1 oz. (30 g.) butter worked with ½ oz. (15 g.) flour

2 glasses dry white wine

sliced, sautéd mushrooms, prawns, shrimps or diced lobster as additions

12–18 croûtons of puff pastry

The fish must be skinned, boned and cut into pieces, 2 by 1 inches (5 by 2½ cm.).

Put all the pieces in a large shallow saucepan with ½ pint (3 dl.) of water, a pinch of nutmeg, a pinch of mace, salt and black pepper and a bouquet garni or some sprigs of parsley, thyme and tarragon. Cover the pan and let it poach gently for 5 minutes. Remove the herbs and gently stir in the cream, the flour worked into the butter, and the white wine. Shake the pan well and stir all the time, being careful not to break the pieces of fish. The sauce should be very white, and of the thickness of heavy cream. Sliced and sautéd mushrooms, prawns, shrimps, or diced lobster may be added, and the dish served with croûtons of puff pastry.

It is excellent made in the same way with fillets of Dover or lemon sole, skinned and cut crossways, each fillet into three. But in this case, poach only for 3 minutes before adding the cream and other ingredients.

* Mrs Glasse suggests skate but this is too glutinous for present-day tastes.

FISH PIE

The medieval fish pie was a great 'coffin' in which pieces of fish with shellfish and other delicacies were baked with herbs, spices, wine, vinegar and rosewater, and usually sugar as well as salt. Today a fish pie is generally a very simple dish of flaked cooked fish in a white sauce topped with browned potato. Made carefully, however, it can be very good.

Fish Pie, 1

Serves 4–6

> 1 lb. (½ k.) cooked flaked cod, haddock or hake
> 1 pint (6 dl.) white sauce
> about 1 lb. (½ k.) cooked potatoes, smoothly mashed with plenty of butter and a little milk
> butter for the top
> cheese for the top, if liked

If you are buying the fish for this specially, choose haddock, poach gently with an onion and a bouquet garni in half milk, half water for 25 minutes, and make up the white sauce from this (strained) stock. If you are using cooked cold fish, make the sauce half from milk and half from the liquor in which it originally cooked. If this is not available, make an ordinary white sauce, flavour with onion, season it highly and add a teaspoon of anchovy essence if possible.

Mix the fish into the sauce. Prawns or shrimps, oysters, canned or fresh, or sliced sautéd mushrooms may be added to the mixture with advantage but are not essential. Check seasoning. Put into shallow buttered fireproof dish. When cool, lay the mashed potato evenly all over the dish. Put it on lightly in separate spoonfuls so that it does not sink down into the sauce. Smooth it over, roughen it with a fork and generously dot with butter. If liked, the potato may be covered with coarsely grated cheddar cheese or finely grated parmesan before the butter is put on. Bake at 350°F., gas mark 4, for 20 minutes, and then increase heat to 400°F., gas mark 6, for a further 10 minutes to brown the top well; alternatively, brown under the grill.

Fish Pie, 2

Use the same fish mixture as in the above recipe, but put into a buttered pie dish and cover with Cheese Pastry (see p. 95) for a substantial dish or with puff pastry if something lighter is required. Individual pans lined with puff or short pastry and filled with the same fish mixture to which shellfish and a little cream have been added and then covered with pastry lids make a delicious hot starting course for a dinner party.

Fish Pottage *(Two Recipes)*

The first recipe, most elaborate for such a simply named dish, was collected in the year 1709 and is quoted here mainly as a curiosity but also because a 'pottage', whether of meat or fish, was a kind of feast-day stew, an excellent dish, of which the distinctive characteristic was a conglomeration of delicious ingredients chopped or mashed, in a highly spiced broth, which was poured over the central whole meat or fish.

This recipe comes from a great house on the Norfolk coast and is quite impossible today, both in terms of time and of the numbers and cost of the fish required.

The second, much simpler recipe is from Yorkshire in the second half of the eighteenth century. I have adapted it very slightly for use today.

1709: 'Take 4 flounders, 4 mades, 2 tench, 2 eels, 4 whitings, put all these into a stewpan with some water and an onion stuck with cloves, one bunch of sweet herbs, let these boil to mash, only one tench take out when enough for the middle of your dish. Add a large crust of bread and when boyled to mash, strain all through a sieve. Take ½ a 100 crawfish, let them all be spawned if you can, boil them and add a hen lobster, take the meat out of the tails of crawfish and lobster, then put the remaining part in a mortar, beat them well and add some of the strained liquor to them. Strain all this back into the fish broth, which should look red, set it over the fire, then take a quart of oysters, mash them to pieces, put in the tails of the crawfish and lobster, mince in some pieces of the eels, add half a pint of shrimps, the oyster liquor, shake in a little flower, browne half a pound of good butter – [the cook's hysteria is clearly mounting] – a little beaten pepper, half a pint of white wine, give them all a good boyle, when of a good thickness and seasoned to your taste, put your tench whole in the middle of your dish and pour your pottage over it. Garnish it with the bodys of your crawfish stuffed with forced meat, fried oysters and slices of lemon. To these you must add a little strong gravy, if you please, and a sprig of penny royal.' By this time I would have added anything.

About 1780: I cannot recommend this recipe too highly.

Serves 6–8

3 red mullet
1 lb. (480 g.) fresh haddock, filleted
1 small lobster (or 2 or 3 frozen crawfish tails)
1 small crab
½ lb. (240 g.) shelled shrimps or prawns
3 onions

sweet herbs or bouquet garni
2 glasses of white wine
a little mace
seasoning
2 oz. (60 g.) butter
2 oz. (60 g.) flour
saffron
18 triangular croûtons of crisp fried bread

Get the fishmonger to give you trimmings from the mullet and haddock. Have the lobster split and cracked and the crab dressed.

Put all the fish trimmings and shells into 3 pints (1½ l.) of water with one onion peeled and quartered, the herbs, mace and seasoning. Boil briskly for 30 minutes, then strain. This may be done ahead of time if more convenient. Into the resulting broth put the white wine and remaining onions finely cut, and on them lay the haddock fillets and on them the mullets. Poach very gently for 30 minutes. Meanwhile cut up the lobster meat into neat slices. Lift the mullets carefully on to a very large flat serving dish and keep warm. Take out the haddock fillets, remove all skin and flake the flesh. Make a roux with the butter and flour and thicken the broth with this. Then return the haddock flesh to the broth, add the lobster, all the crab meat, the prawns or shrimps and add a good pinch of saffron. Simmer for 2 or 3 minutes. Add further salt if necessary and some fresh black pepper, and ladle over the mullets. Arrange croûtons all round the edge of the dish and serve immediately.

Fish Puddings

Individual fish puddings were sometimes served at Victorian ladies' luncheons and often to invalids. They are very light, and ornamental as a starting course for a dinner party. Six small soufflé dishes are required.

½ lb. (240 g.) cooked haddock, cod or hake without bones or skin
¼ lb. (120 g.) fine white breadcrumbs soaked in milk
1 onion, peeled and very finely chopped
2 oz. (60 g.) butter
a pinch of nutmeg and of mace

salt and pepper
3 eggs, yolks and whites whipped separately
1 tablespoon finely chopped parsley
1 pint (6 dl.) very good shrimp, oyster or lobster sauce with plenty of
  cream (p. 292)
3 shrimps or prawns to decorate each pudding

Stir the cooked fish and the soaked breadcrumbs together, blending or
beating till they are fairly solid. Beat in the softened butter, the onion, spices
and seasoning. Beat or blend in the egg yolks and finally the whites, which
should be not quite stiff enough to hold a peak. Make sure the ingredients
are evenly mixed. Butter the soufflé dishes and fill two-thirds full with the
mixture. Cover each with foil and steam on a grid in a fish kettle or on the
bottom of a very large pan with a cover or in the oven standing in water in a
baking tray (300° F., gas mark 4) for 30 minutes.
    Meanwhile make the sauce and keep warm.
    Turn the puddings, which should be risen to the tops of the dishes, on to a
warmed flat dish or direct on to small plates, one for each person. Pour over
the sauce and put 3 shrimps or prawns on top of each pudding.

Water Sootje or Souchet or Souchy

This very simple dish of fish stew was introduced into England from Holland
in the time of William and Mary. This recipe is from Greenwich, where
people used to go on purpose to eat whitebait while sitting at ease and
watching the traffic of the river. The Water Souchy was kept ready and was
served to them while they waited for the whitebait to be fried. The fish used
were mostly the odd small ones taken from the whitebait nets and any others
available. If of any size they were cleaned and cut up and prepared as follows:

1 lb. (½ k.) small herring, fresh sardine, whitebait or whiting
a large bunch of parsley
1 lemon
salt, peppercorns

Rinse the fish well and throw them into a large saucepan with plenty of water
which should more than cover them. Add ½ oz. (15 g.) of salt to every quart
of water and a dozen peppercorns. Take a really large bunch of parsley with
its roots, wash it well and chop it finely, roots and all. Add to the pan and
simmer for 1 hour. Strain, reserving the liquor, into which any nice pieces of
the fish and a sprinkling of fresh parsley should be thrown back. Add the juice

of half a lemon and put a thick slice of lemon in each serving of this clear green fish soup. Drink with hot toasted brown bread well buttered while waiting for a great mound of crisp fried whitebait.

A very simple, watery dish, but Francatelli adapted it for Queen Victoria and the Prince Consort, who liked simple food, and it became the following, which is extremely refreshing and stimulating to the appetite:

Fillets of salmon or trout, or perch, or pike are laid closely in a large buttered pan which may be set on the stove. They are well seasoned with salt and pepper and a little powdered mace, and about three small or two large fillets are allowed for each person to be served.

Meanwhile, make a court-bouillon in which the trimmings of the fish and half a bottle of white wine are included. While it boils, finely chop a large handful of parsley and finely shred some parsley root. The parsley root is very important to the flavour. A quarter of an hour before the dish is to be served the strained court-bouillon is poured over the fillets, the parsley and parsley root thrown in (reserving a tablespoon of parsley) and the dish allowed to boil fairly briskly so that the fillets are inclined to flake.

To serve, lift the fillets into shallow bowls, which are then filled up with the piping hot broth poured through a strainer. Sprinkle each with the reserved parsley and drop in a slice of lemon. The dish should be eaten with a spoon and accompanied with good hot bread or toast and plenty of butter.

6 · SAUCES AND STUFFINGS FOR ENGLISH DISHES

'Cook, see all your sauces be sharp and poynant
in the palate, that they may commend you . . .'

BEAUMONT AND FLETCHER

'The English have but one sauce.' A libel, of course, today and a libel in fact
since the fourteenth century. It arose from the sticky white sauce with which
late nineteenth- and early twentieth-century innkeepers and boarding-
house landladies used to smother badly cooked cauliflower or macaroni (with
a little cheese added). Even at that time it was a libel, since both served bread
sauce with chicken and onion sauce with mutton, and these, if well made, are
excellent white sauces.

An unexpectedly large number of very early recipes for sauces exist, and
one or two are still in use almost unchanged. 'Eigre-douce' (sour-sweet) is
described in a manuscript of the time of Edward I and is nothing but mint

sauce as we know it today. Sauce Madame, also mentioned and occurring in several later manuscripts, was 'a sage and onion stuffing for goose, stewed into sauce with wine'. In the Ashmole MS. of 1439 and the Harleian MS. of 1450, recipes for various sauces are given, mostly so strongly spiced and seasoned as to conceal all the flavour of the meat they were intended to 'sauce'.

A thick, smooth golden sauce for which the Ashmole MS. gives a recipe was called sauce gauncile: 'Take floure and cowe milk, safrern wel y-grounde, garleke and put into a faire litel potte and sethe it over the fire and serve it forthe.' A different hand added 'peper, salt'.

'Black Sauce for Capons', also of 1439, contained their livers, aniseed, ground ginger, cinnamon, bread, verjuice (in this case probably crab-apple juice) and the fat from the capons. If one had managed to get this down one would certainly not have tasted anything else on one's plate.

Recipes of 1450 give a sauce for roast crane in which the liver is to be minced with powder of ginger, vinegar and mustard; and for a pheasant, 'his sauce is to be sugar and mustard'.

Some 165 years later, Gervase Markham, writing in 1615, gives a dozen or more sauces, and it is clear that at this time the term 'sauce' often meant what we should call a garnish. 'To sauce' a dish was not invariably to pour a liquid over it, but to add accompaniments which enhanced it. Markham sometimes uses the term 'gallantine' (always mysterious) for a sauce made with blood. He gives a recipe which he calls 'Gallantine, Sauce for a Swan':

To make a Gallantine, or sauce for a Swan, Bittern, Hern, Crane or any large Fowl, take the blood of the same Fowl and being stirred well, boil it on the fire, then when it comes to be thick, put into it Vinegar a good quantity, with a few fine white bread-crumbs and so boil it over again; . . . season it with Sugar and Cinnamon and then serve it up in Saucers as you do Mustard, for this is called a Chauder or Gallantine and is a sauce almost for any Fowl Whatsoever.

Some of Markham's more acceptable sauces are as follows:

To make sauce for a pig, some take sage and roast it in the belly of the pig; then boiling verjuice [i.e. juice of unripe grapes, or of crab apples, very like a wine vinegar] butter and currants together, take and chop the sage small and mixing the brains of the pig, put it altogether and so serve it up.

This would make a smooth thin sauce, slightly sharp but sweetened by the currants and well flavoured with sage. Brains lightly stewed can be worked quite smooth and are occasionally used in certain sauces today.

The best sauce for green geese [i.e. grass-fed young geese] is the juice of sorrel and sugar mixed together with a few scalded Feberries [the berries of the berberis] and served upon sippets . . . or else feberries mixed with verjuice, butter sugar and cinammon and so served up on sippets [i.e. poured over small slices of bread or toast instead of thickening].

To make sauce for a loin of veal . . . take all kind of sweet pot herbs and chopping them very small with the yolks of two or three eggs [hard-boiled], boil them in vinegar and butter with a few bread crumbs and a good store of sugar; then season it with cinnamon, and a clove or two crushed . . . and pour it on to the Veal with the slices of oranges and lemons about the dish.

Another seventeenth-century sauce for veal was made from quinces cooked to a soft pulp in water to which crab-apple juice was added. It was put through a sieve and claret, sugar, lemon juice, nutmeg, cloves, pepper, salt, and a little wine vinegar were added. I have tried this, since we grow many quinces, and it is good but extremely sharp, rather like a very highly spiced chutney. Extra sugar improved it, but the veal could not be tasted at all.

For a sauce for venison, Markham suggests:

Take vinegar, breadcrumbs, some of the gravy which comes from the venison and boil them well in a dish; then season it with sugar, cinnamon, ginger and salt.

Another recipe of much the same date refers to 'the old sauce for venison' which consisted of currants boiled in water, to which wine, sugar and cinnamon were added.

By 1747, however, when the final edition of Mrs Glasse's book was published, sauces had become very much as we serve them today.

For a goose, make a little good gravy and put it in a basin by itself and some apple sauce in another.

For a turkey good gravy in a dish and either bread or onion sauce in a basin.

To fowls you should put good gravy in the dish and either bread or egg sauce in a basin.

For ducks a little gravy in the dish and onion in a cup is liked.

Pheasants and partridges should have gravy in the dish and bread sauce in a cup.

Gone is the sugar and mustard with pheasant of 200 years earlier.

For a hare she suggests:

Take for sauce a pint of cream and half a pound of fresh butter . . . keep stirring till the butter is melted and the sauce is thick. Then take up the hare and pour the sauce into the dish.

This is too rich for our tastes today, and does not seem to have any relevance to the dark, strong-flavoured meat of a hare. But her next sauce is very much what we serve:

Another way . . . is to make good gravy thickened with a little piece of butter rolled in flour . . . you may leave the butter out if you don't like it and have some currant jelly warmed in a cup of red wine and sugar boiled to syrup; done thus: take half a pint of red wine, a quarter of a pound of sugar and set over a low fire to simmer for about a quarter of an hour . . .

She suggests currant jelly or a syrup of red wine, vinegar and sugar for venison. For lamb and occasionally for pork she suggests mint sauce, and for a roast sucking pig a sauce made from its gravy with beef gravy added, thickened with butter rolled in flour and with ketchup, chopped sage (which has been roasted inside the pig), the brains of the pig and the yolks of two hard-boiled eggs, all beaten up together and worked into this. She says this is a very good sauce, and it probably would be. She also suggests bread sauce with a few currants in it.

Her fish sauces are all rich with butter. She suggests lobster sauce with salmon, turbot, cod or haddock; a shrimp sauce made simply from clear beef stock, thickened with butter and flour and with the shrimps boiled in it; her oyster sauce is more elaborate and her recipe is given, as is her excellent recipe for anchovy sauce.

A very elaborate sauce for carp, dated 1760, was said to have been preferred by Lord Halifax to any other:

Take 12 anchovy fillets, a quarter pint of clear stock, half a pint of white wine. Beat together until the anchovies are dissolved. Then add the blood of the carp which must be saved by bleeding it into 4 spoonfuls of elder or tarragon vinegar. Thicken it with butter and serve the carp on toast.

This seems to revert to the fierce sauces of the sixteenth century and would have concealed the taste of the fish entirely, though its blood would have given a fishy flavour and with the butter would have made the sauce very thick.

Robert May's book, *The Accomplish't Cook*, published in 1660, suggests in a Christmas bill of fare 'A jegote of Mutton with Anchove Sauce' and a 'pig sauced with tongues'; I give an eighteenth-century recipe for tongue sauce later, though Robert May here uses 'sauced' to mean 'enhanced' by the tongues, rather than that they were made into a sauce. Patrick Lambe in his *Royal Cookery or The Compleat Court-Cook* of 1710 gives an elegant recipe for salmon cooked 'in champaign wine' which has a fine sauce made as follows:

... a piece of fresh butter, a little grated Bread [this always replaces the flour of modern recipes as a thickening agent] some Truffles and Mushrooms: then pour over ½ a bottle of Champaign Wine and set the saucepan on a stove with a well kindled Fire. When the liquor is wasted to the degree that it ought, bind it with a Cray fish Cullis, dish it up handsomely and serve it warm for the first course.

A cullis was, in fact, a basic sauce considered essential by all the foremost cooks from the fifteenth to the seventeenth centuries for royal and noble dishes. It was used to thicken and bind gravies and stocks or highly seasoned and flavoured as a sauce. The word comes from a French root, *coulisse*, which means something that slides or slips smoothly. It meant, in the high cooking of England, a rich stock which had been reduced until it had the thickness and slippery texture of melted jelly and which was usually further thickened with a panada. Therefore a veal knuckle or calves' feet were often included in the first boiling and in all cases a large quantity of meat and/or birds was used to give a relatively small quantity of stock. There were various fish cullis and vegetable cullis which were used to thicken herb, vegetable or fish soups.

Cookbooks intended for the housewife of manor or farm, as were those of Markham and Mrs Glasse, give no recipe for cullis but thicken and bind all sauces with butter and breadcrumbs and egg yolks. It may be inferred that in the great kitchens which catered for the nobility several kinds of cullis (which was always prepared separately from the main dishes) were made daily by assistant cooks and kept on hand. Cullis was exceedingly extravagant since its principle was reduction of great quantities to small, but it would have given a splendid flavour, strength and smoothness to dishes in which it was incorporated.

By the early nineteenth century sauces were usually made and seasoned much as we make them today. In Richard Dolby's book, *The Cooks' Dictionary*, of 1830, several recipes are given specifically made on a roux of butter and flour, and are mentioned as suitable sauces for all sorts of dishes. One is a straightforward butter sauce and another a good strong brown sauce for meat or game.

The traditional recipes which follow should make it clear, once and for all, that the Englishman has always appreciated sauces and gravies and has devised excellent recipes for many varieties. Indeed his fondness for a delicate sauce has sometimes led him to excess. In the nineteenth century a retired

major living in the country gave a dinner consisting entirely of sauces, arranged in a sequence of fish, meat, game and sweet, unaccompanied by any
solids except a little bread, and Hayward in his *Art of Dining* (1852) quotes
Mrs Piozzi* as saying that Dr Johnson had been known to call for the butter-
boat containing the lobster sauce during the second course and pour the whole
of its contents over his plum pudding.

Sauces for Meat, Poultry and Game

Basic Brown Sauce

As dispiriting a name as white sauce but inescapably useful. All the best
brown sauces depend on using very good stock which has been strengthened
(see Brown Stock, p. 314) and reduced. Only reduction by boiling can give
the sauce its proper coating consistency.

For 4 to 6
>   2 oz. (60 g.) butter
>   1½ oz. (45 g.) flour
>   ½ pint (3 dl.) very good brown stock, reduced from its original
>   quantity
>   squeeze of lemon juice

A strengthened first stock is best of all but any strong well-flavoured stock
will do.

Melt the butter, stir in the flour and allow to colour but not to burn. This
takes 4 or 5 minutes, stirring over a fairly low heat. Stir in the stock, bring
to the boil and add salt and pepper (unless the stock is already highly
seasoned) and a little lemon juice.

Add a glass of claret or of port, a pinch of mace, a dessertspoon of red-
currant jelly, a teaspoon of anchovy essence and of Worcester sauce, and you
have a sauce almost exactly like Reform Sauce and very good indeed with
hare or venison, steak or chops.

White Sauce

A depressing name for a sauce which is really only the basis of many dishes

---

* Born Hester Lynch (1741–1831), married Henry Thrale and then Gabriele Piozzi.
  Dr Johnson had more or less lived with the Thrales, and the widow's second marriage
  almost broke his heart.

and more complicated sauces and which should never be served without the most careful seasoning and the addition of herbs or stock. It is anathema if it is made thick and paste-like and poured over an innocent cauliflower.

Larousse points out that, whereas in France béchamel sauce was originally made by adding cream to a thick velouté sauce, in our own time it is made exactly as white sauce in the recipe given here.

>1 oz. (30 g.) butter
>1 oz. (30 g.) flour (plain flour is better than self-raising for this)
>1 pint (6 dl.) milk
>½ teaspoon salt
>pinch of pepper

Take a small heavy saucepan, aluminium rather than enamel. Melt the butter over low heat, not allowing it to brown. Stir in the flour, being careful that it does not colour and stirring till the roux is absolutely smooth and no separate flour or melted butter is visible. Add the milk a very little at a time, stirring each addition in until it is smoothly taken up by the roux. When all the milk is taken up, add salt and pepper and simmer gently for 3 minutes, holding the saucepan just above the heat and stirring hard, so that the bottom does not catch.

The sauce may always be made with half white stock and half milk, and the addition of cream is always an improvement.

For Parsley Sauce: add 1 tablespoon finely chopped parsley to 1 pint (6 dl.) white sauce, season rather highly, using plenty of pepper.

For Egg Sauce: add 1 or 2 hard-boiled eggs, finely chopped, to ½ pint (3 dl.) white sauce. Season highly.

Espagnole Sauce

Made in England in the eighteenth century but used as a base for other sauces much less than it is in French cooking. It is very well worth making in quantity and keeping in the deep-freeze in small containers. The first part of the cooking should in any case be done on the day before the sauce is to be served.

This recipe requires 3 pints (1½ dl.) of strengthened brown stock in all; it should give about 1–1½ pints (½–1 l.) when finished. As it takes a long time to make and is used in several dishes, it is worth making this large quantity and storing it in a refrigerator for up to 2 weeks or deep-freezing it indefinitely.

Take 1 quart (1 l.) of strengthened brown first stock (see p. 314), which need not be clarified. Thicken with a brown roux made of 4 oz. (120 g.) butter and 4 oz. (120 g.) flour. Bring to the boil and add

> a finely chopped carrot
> a finely chopped onion
> 2 rashers finely chopped streaky bacon } lightly fried till just brown
> a sprig of thyme
> a bay leaf
> a glass of white wine
> salt and pepper

Some recipes use 3 oz. (90 g.) of chopped raw ham instead of the bacon, as giving a better flavour. Originally Spanish ham was preferred. This gave the sauce its name.

Simmer the sauce very gently for 1½ hours, and strain. Add a further pint (6 dl.) of the brown stock and cook a further 2 hours. (All the time the sauce is reducing, and therefore strengthening, it should simmer covered.) Stir well, and then allow to get cold.

The next day skim off any fat and add 2 tablespoons of tomato purée (tinned or fresh). Cook very slowly for an hour and then strain. Check seasoning and set aside to be reheated before serving.

Half a pint of this sauce is required for a perfectly traditional Reform Sauce.

The tomato purée is sometimes omitted if it is not considered that its particular flavour marries well with the garnishes of an intended dish.

Alboni Sauce

In spite of its Italian name, even the French always attribute this sauce to the English kitchen.

This is a very fine, very strong sauce for wild meats. It was primarily meant for venison but is very splendid for wild boar (now obtainable from France), roast saddle of hare or true mutton (not lamb). The juniper berries and the pine kernels give it a slightly resinous forest taste when combined with the rich wine-flavoured basic sauce.

For 4–6

> 1 large glass white wine
> 1 tablespoon finely chopped shallots
> bay leaf, sprig of thyme and parsley
> pinch of cayenne

Put all these ingredients in a pan and reduce the wine by fast boiling for 2 or 3 minutes until only a third remains.

> ¼ pint (1 ½ dl.) good brown sauce (p. 277)
> ¼ pint (1 ½ dl.) very strong reduced game stock (canned can be used)
> 10 crushed juniper berries

Add these to the reduced wine and boil for 5 minutes, stirring occasionally; strain.

> 1 oz. (30 g.) of pine kernels, lightly browned in a little butter
> 1 tablespoon of red-currant jelly

Stir these into the sauce, and serve very hot.

Apple Sauce

For 6

1 lb. (½ k.) apples	sugar
curl of lemon peel	½ oz. (15 g.) butter

Peel and core the apples and cut into thin slices. Put them into a saucepan with 1 tablespoonful of water and a piece of lemon peel and stew gently until they become pulp. Sweeten to taste, but not too much as apple sauce is better a little sharp. Put through a moulin or blender. Return to the saucepan with a nut of butter and heat up before serving. The sauce may be prepared ahead and kept warm at the side of the stove or in a warming drawer without harm. The addition of butter is optional.

The quantities given should make enough to serve cold with cold pork or birds after the hot roast.

Sauce for Boar's Head

The following is a Hanoverian sauce for boar's head, though some form of mustard sauce had been served in England with boar's head or any brawn since the Middle Ages. It is very good with any brawn or with cold lamb, veal or pork.

'Grate the rind of a Seville orange or lemon on to 1 tablespoon of caster sugar. Squeeze the juice over, add half a tablespoon of dry mustard, 2 tablespoons of olive oil and 2 tablespoons of port wine. Mix and beat all very well together and serve a little on a saucer for each person.'

Bread Sauce

For 6

1 small onion	½ pint (3 dl.) milk
3 or 4 cloves	1 oz. (30 g.) butter
3 oz. (90 g.) fresh breadcrumbs	pepper and salt

Peel the onion and push the cloves into it. Simmer gently with the milk and a tablespoonful of water for 20 minutes. Remove the onion, or, if you like it, remove the cloves and chop and crush it well into the milk. Add the breadcrumbs. Stir well. Add butter and seasoning. Stir again, and leave on the side of the stove at least 5 minutes for the breadcrumbs to swell. Then beat well with spoon for a minute, and if too thick add a little more milk and another nut of butter. Reheat and serve.

Butter Sauce and Lemon Butter Sauce
(Sometimes called English Sauce)

This particular eighteenth-century recipe is from a Scottish manuscript. The sauce is really a form of hollandaise but a little less rich and of a slightly more liquid consistency. It is very easy to make and very good indeed with fish, asparagus and cauliflower. There are dozens of recipes for this sauce: all vary slightly in method, but this gives an excellent result.

For 6

8 oz. (240 g.) butter
1½ oz. (40 g.) flour
¼ pint (1½ dl.) boiling salted water
1 egg yolk
2 teaspoons lemon juice for Lemon Sauce

Melt 3 oz. (90 g.) of butter and stir in the flour. Add the boiling salted water and whisk well. Beat the egg yolk in a tablespoon of cold water and add to the mixture, keeping it off the boil and stirring it well. Cut the remaining butter into small pieces and, holding the saucepan just above the heat or standing it in another of boiling water, stir them in two or three at a time. The sauce must on no account boil. Stir in lemon juice when all the butter is absorbed if a sharp sauce is wanted.

For Fennel Sauce simply add finely chopped fennel and only a very little lemon juice. Particularly good with mackerel, grilled herrings or grilled trout.

Parsley Sauce made in this way is also very good with grilled meat or fish.

Anchovy Sauce is made in two ways: either by flavouring the butter sauce with a teaspoon of anchovy essence added to the original roux, or by making anchovy butter (see p. 302) and making the sauce with this. Either method gives a very good sauce. A little more anchovy essence can be added at the last minute if required.

Cambridge Sauce

For all cold meats: a fine sauce for nineteenth-century dons and deans.

For 4–6

>2 yolks of hard-boiled eggs
>3 anchovy fillets
>2 teaspoons capers
>2 teaspoons chives, finely chopped
>2 teaspoons chervil and tarragon finely chopped
>1 teaspoon made mustard
>1 tablespoon wine, cider or tarragon vinegar
>3 tablespoons olive oil
>2 teaspoons finely chopped parsley
>¼ teaspoon cayenne
>salt and pepper

Pound all the solids except the parsley and cayenne together very well, working the anchovy fillets into very small pieces. When reduced to a paste add the vinegar and oil a little at a time beating as for mayonnaise. When thick put through a strainer, stir in the parsley and cayenne, and sieve. The sauce keeps very well for 2 or 3 weeks in the refrigerator if a larger quantity is made up.

Caper Sauce

Traditional since medieval times with boiled mutton, but good also with boiled fish or occasionally with a boiled chicken.

For 4–6, take half a pint of white sauce (p. 278), using half milk and half the stock in which the mutton, fish or chicken was cooked. Season and add a tablespoon of well-drained capers. Do not boil after they are added or the sauce may curdle.

Chaudfroid Sauce

To mask a cold chicken or pheasant, or cold veal cutlets.

For 1 large or 2 smaller birds
¼ pint (1½ dl.) aspic jelly (may be made up from packet)
½ pint (3 dl.) well-flavoured white sauce
2 tablespoons cream
salt and pepper

Make up the aspic jelly according to directions on packet. While still hot add the sauce, mixing thoroughly. Bring just to the boil; cool slightly. Stir in the cream and season. Use while still warm before it thickens and sets.

Cheese Sauce

For fish, macaroni, cauliflower.

For 6

2 oz. (60 g.) butter	¼ lb. (120 g.) grated cheese,
2 oz. (60 g.) flour	Cheddar or Parmesan
1 pint (6 dl.) milk	salt and pepper

Gently melt half the grated cheese with the butter for the roux. Be careful that the cheese does not stick or solidify. Stir in the flour. Add the milk and the other half of the cheese and bring to the boil, stirring all the time. Boil for 3 or 4 minutes. Season highly with pepper and carefully with salt.

Cranberry Sauce

For 6
½ lb. (240 g.) cranberries
3 oz. (90 g.) sugar
2 level teaspoons cornflour

Boil the cranberries with 3 tablespoons of water for 5 minutes, rub through a moulin and reheat with the sugar. Mix the cornflour with 1 tablespoon of cold water, stir in the purée of cranberries, and boil gently for 5 minutes.

Cumberland Sauce

This is a simple recipe, but very good.

For 4

    2 oz. (60 g.) red-currant jelly   ½ oz. (15 g.) butter
    juice and finely grated peel   ½ oz. (15 g.) flour
      of an orange   ¼ pint (1½ dl.) good,
    1 teaspoon of lemon juice   well-seasoned brown stock

Gently melt the red-currant jelly and stir in the orange and lemon juice and orange peel. Make a roux of the butter and flour, add the stock, bring to the boil, stir in the melted jelly, boil 2 or 3 minutes and serve.

Devilled Sauce (or Sauce of the Devil)

Much favoured by Victorian gentlemen, with cold meats or plain grills.

For 4–6

    2 glasses white wine
    1 tablespoon white wine vinegar
    1 medium onion or 2 shallots very finely chopped
    bay leaf, sprig of thyme, sprig of parsley
    ¼ teaspoon white pepper
    salt
    ½ pint (3 dl.) brown sauce (p. 277)
    2 tablespoons tomato purée
    ½ teaspoon cayenne pepper

Put the wine, vinegar, onion or shallot, herbs, white pepper and salt into a saucepan and boil quickly to reduce by two thirds. Remove from heat, add the brown sauce and return to heat, stirring until it comes to the boil. Stir in the tomato purée. Boil for 2 minutes. Season with the cayenne pepper to the desired devilish hotness.

Dr Kitchiner's Recipe for Gooseberry Sauce (1817)

The best sauce in the world for mackerel, and very good with pork.

For 4–6

    ½ pint (3 dl.) green gooseberries, topped and tailed and stewed
      (or 1 can)
    ¼ pint (1½ dl.) melted butter
    a pinch of powdered ginger
    1 tablespoon of caster sugar

Sieve the gooseberries and stir into the melted butter. Add ginger and sugar and boil for 2 minutes. Taste. They should be sharp but not really sour. Not as good with canned gooseberries but still worth making.

Ham Sauce

For steaks, grilled chops or veal. A very fine nineteenth-century sauce. It may be used with a hot boiled ham, in which case the strips of ham are omitted and ¼ pint (1½ dl.) of Madeira or brown sherry added to the sauce, which makes it very slightly sweet.

A tongue sauce was made in exactly the same way using strips of tongue instead of ham.

For 4–6

  2 oz. (60 g.) lean cooked ham cut in tiny strips
  3 finely chopped shallots *or* a tablespoon of chopped chives
  1 oz. (30 g.) butter
  ½ pint (3 dl.) good brown sauce (p. 277)
  juice of half a lemon
  freshly ground black pepper
  2 teaspoons finely chopped parsley

1 small glass of brandy, sherry or Madeira enriches and strengthens the flavour but it is very good without.

Lightly fry the shallots or chives in the butter for 3 minutes to soften them but do not allow them to brown. Add the ham and fry a minute or two more. Stir in the brown sauce and bring to the boil, add the pepper and lemon juice and boil for 3 minutes. Add the alcohol, if used, and the parsley, boil 1 minute more and serve. Allow to cool, and reheat before serving if more convenient, but only let it just come to the boil.

Dutch or Hollandaise Sauce

This is a traditional recipe for a sauce which is indispensable in its own excellence and which can have chives, parsley, fennel or tarragon added to it. It is good with boiled, grilled or fried fish, with grilled meats and chicken. It is called Dutch sauce in early recipes but is so well known as hollandaise that there is no point in anglicizing it. It requires careful making but does not take more than 10–15 minutes.

For 4–6

2 tablespoons lemon juice or wine vinegar	½ lb. (240 g.) butter salt and pepper
2 egg yolks	

Boil the vinegar or lemon juice to reduce its quantity almost to nothing (about 3 minutes). Cool slightly, add a small piece of butter, and stir in the well-beaten yolks of 2 eggs, salt and pepper. Stir with a wooden spoon with the saucepan standing in a pan of boiling water, as the sauce must thicken but not boil. As you see it begins to thicken, slowly add the remainder of the butter, which should have been softened slightly by being worked with a wooden spoon. Add it a small piece at a time, beating the sauce as it is added. If too thick, stir in 1 tablespoon of cold water. When all the butter is absorbed and the sauce is thick and creamy, keep warm in its saucepan by standing in hot water until it is wanted. It should never boil at any time during its making after the vinegar is reduced.

Horseradish Sauce, 1

If you can grow or buy a root, it is much better than the prepared sauces and creams.

For 6

¼ pint (1½ dl.) white sauce	seasoning
2 tablespoons finely grated horseradish	2 tablespoons cream

Stir the horseradish into the sauce and simmer, stirring, for 3 minutes. Cool a little and add the cream and seasoning. Good hot or cold.

Horseradish Sauce, 2 (to serve cold)

Serves 6

2 tablespoons finely grated horseradish	1 tablespoon caster sugar salt and pepper
1 egg yolk	2 tablespoons fairly thick or well-whipped cream
1 tablespoon wine vinegar	

Put the grated horseradish in a bowl. Pour over vinegar. Add egg yolk and beat briskly. Add sugar, salt and pepper. Finally stir in cream.

Benton Sauce

Mrs Rundle (1807) (spelt Rundell in later editions) has a recipe for Benton Sauce which I have found nowhere else and which is very good.

    2 oz. (60 g.) horseradish, finely grated
    1 teaspoon made mustard
    2 teaspoons caster sugar
    4 tablespoons vinegar

Stir well and allow to stand an hour or two.

Mint Sauce

First mentioned in a manuscript of the time of Edward I under the name 'Egire-doace' (sour-sweet). It was described as a sauce of vinegar, honey and sweet herbs.

For 4–6

    1 tablespoon very finely chopped mint
    3 tablespoons vinegar (white or red wine or cider vinegar is much
        better than malt vinegar)
    2 teaspoons caster sugar

Heat the vinegar and dissolve the sugar in it. While still warm (but not hot) add the mint and leave to steep for at least an hour before serving with lamb.

Mushroom Sauce

This recipe comes from Wiltshire and is so good that once eaten it will never be forgotten.

For 6–8

    ½ pint (3 dl.) white sauce   a few chives, finely chopped
    ½ lb. (240 g.) mushrooms,   a sprig of thyme and parsley
        very finely chopped (with stalks) salt and pepper
    ¼ pint (1½ dl.) cream   a trace of garlic salt and a
    3 oz. (90 g.) butter   suspicion of crushed,
    1 onion, finely chopped   fresh garlic

Very gently melt the onion in the butter and when soft stir in all the chopped mushrooms. Stir in the herbs and seasoning and stir and turn until quite soft – about 5 minutes. If any butter is not absorbed, drain off. Warm the white sauce, stir in the mushrooms and herbs and bring to the boil. Just before the sauce boils, stir in the cream. For a smooth sauce, strain before adding cream, but the chopped mushrooms are delicious. Very good with roast chicken or with veal.

Mustard Sauce

For 4

  1 oz. (30 g.) flour   ½ pint (3 dl.) milk
  1½ teaspoons dry mustard   salt and pepper
  1½ oz. (45 g.) butter

Into the butter for the roux stir the dry mustard and the flour. Add the milk, stirring all the time. Bring to the boil and boil for 3 minutes while continuing to stir. Season rather lightly with salt, but add only a little pepper.

Onion Sauce

For 4–6

  2 oz. (60 g.) butter   3 medium onions
  1½ oz. (45 g.) flour   salt and pepper
  ¾ pint (4½ dl.) milk

Peel the onions and cut in quarters downwards. Stew them for 20 minutes in the milk. Pour into a bowl, and in the saucepan in which they were cooked make your roux as for white sauce. Add the onions in the milk slowly to it, stirring well, season and simmer for 2 or 3 minutes. If too thick stir in a little extra milk.

Orange Sauce

For duck, wild duck, wild geese.

For 4–6

  ½ pint (3 dl.) good brown or espagnole sauce (p. 278), rather thick
  2 glasses red wine
  thinly peeled rind of a large orange and the juice of 2
  salt and pepper
  cayenne

Put the orange peel to marinate in the wine for 2 hours.

Bring the sauce to the boil, strain off the wine and discard the peel and stir into the sauce. When boiling again, remove from heat, add the orange juice and season highly with salt and pepper, but add very little cayenne.

Port Wine Sauce

A traditional Edwardian recipe which probably originated much earlier, very good with grouse, partridge or wild duck.

For 4

    2 wineglasses of port
    a sprig of thyme
    a bay leaf
    a teaspoon of chopped chives *or* shallots
    juice of an orange
    juice of half a lemon
    ½ teaspoon grated orange zest
    ¼ pint (1 ½ dl. good brown sauce (p. 277)

Boil the port with the thyme, bay leaf and chives or shallots to reduce to half the quantity of the wine. Add the orange and lemon juice and the zest, stir in the sauce and simmer for 3 minutes. Strain and serve.

The Prince Regent's Sauce

A fine sauce invented for the Prince Regent. To be served with roast chicken or supremes of chicken, pheasant or guinea fowl, or for sweetbreads. It is well worth while to make four times this quantity and store it in 3 or 4 containers in a deep-freeze. It defrosts and warms perfectly.

For 6–8

    3 tablespoons butter
    ¼ lb. (120 g.) lean ham, diced
    1 onion, peeled and cut in quarters
    1 chopped shallot
    1 large glass dry white wine, boiled to reduce by one third
    ¾ pint (4½ dl.) reduced chicken stock
    ½ pint (3 dl.) good brown sauce, reduced by boiling

Cook the ham and onion in the butter, without colouring. After 5 minutes stir in the shallot and cook a further 2 or 3 minutes. Add the reduced wine and half the chicken stock. Cook over low heat for 10 minutes. Put through a moulin but do not force too much of the ham through. Add the reduced brown sauce. Reduce the remaining chicken stock to half by rapidly boiling separately and stir this in. Boil the whole to reduce a little further. It should almost coat the spoon. Check for seasoning. Pour through a strainer and serve.

Reform Sauce

Invented for the Reform Club by the great chef Alexis Soyer. This is a shortened and simplified version of his sauce, but it retains its essential character. Serve with lamb cutlets, fillets of beef or escalopes of veal.

For 4–6

> ¼ pint (1 ½ dl.) espagnole sauce (p. 278)
> ¼ pint (1½ dl.) jellied brown stock *or* canned consommé
> juice of 1 lemon
> 2 teaspoons red-currant jelly
> 1 glass red wine
> black pepper
> ½ tablespoon cayenne pepper
> 1 tablespoon tomato purée
> white of 1 hard-boiled egg, cut into tiny strips
> 3 or 4 lightly sauté mushrooms
> 2 oz. (60 g.) cooked ham, also cut into tiny strips

The hard-boiled egg, mushrooms and ham decorate the sauce and enhance its consistency but can be omitted.

Bring the espagnole sauce to the boil and stir in the consommé and juice of lemon, red-currant jelly and wine. Add about ½ teaspoon of freshly ground *black* pepper, a good pinch of cayenne, and the tomato purée. Boil for 3 or 4 minutes.

Add the tiny strips of white of egg, ham and mushrooms. The sauce may be reheated but do not boil again.

Roebuck Sauce

Traditional with venison and also with good hare.

For 4

> 2 oz. (60 g.) butter

2 tablespoons chopped onion
2 tablespoons diced raw lean ham
a bunch of sweet herbs tied together
2 tablespoons wine vinegar
¼ pint (1½ dl.) espagnole sauce (p. 278)
1 small glass of port
1 tablespoon red-currant jelly

Brown the onion and ham in the butter and add the vinegar and herbs and reduce vinegar till almost dry. Stir in the espagnole sauce and simmer very gently for about 10 minutes. Take out the bunch of herbs and stir in the port and red-currant jelly.

Tartare Sauce

For 4

1 teaspoon mustard
1 teaspoon vinegar
¼ pint (1½ dl.) mayonnaise
2 teaspoons each chopped pickled gherkins, onions and capers

Mix the mustard to a paste with vinegar. Add this slowly to the mayonnaise, beating well. Stir in gherkins, onions and capers, which must be very finely chopped.

Tomato Sauce, 1

For 4–6

1 oz. (30 g.) butter
1 oz. (30 g.) flour
½ pint (3 dl.) good stock
1 onion
1 carrot

1 rasher bacon
1 lb. (½ k.) tomatoes
pepper and salt
sugar
2 tablespoons cream

Cut the onion and carrot into thin slices. Cut the bacon in pieces, put all into a saucepan with the butter, and fry gently. Add the tomatoes, cut in quarters. Fry for 4 minutes. Stir in flour, then add the stock. Bring to the boil. Season with salt and pepper and sugar. Cover and simmer gently for 30 minutes, stirring occasionally. Put through a fine moulin or sieve. Reheat and add the cream.

Tomato Sauce, 2

For 4–6

¼ pint (1½ dl.) white sauce
½ lb. (240 g.) tomatoes

2 tablespoons cream
a few grains cayenne

Slice the tomatoes and stew them gently in a very little water until soft. Put through a moulin or sieve, fine enough to keep the pips from going through. Stir into them the white sauce, bring to the boil, add the cream and cayenne, and serve.

Special Sauces for Fish

Oyster Sauce, Mussel Sauce, Shrimp Sauce and Lobster Sauce

Add 12 cooked oysters (bearded and with their liquor), *or* 18 cooked mussels, *or* ¼ lb. (120 g.) shrimps (cooked and picked), *or* the chopped meat and coral of a small lobster to:

½ pint (3 dl.) white sauce (p. 278) and
½ pint (3 dl.) fish stock; and season carefully

(For the stock, boil ½ lb. (240 g.) of any white fish or fish trimmings in 1 pint (6 dl.) of salted water with a little parsley, tarragon if possible and half a small onion for half an hour; strain.)

Mrs Glasse's Oyster Sauce (1747)

This recipe has been adapted for present-day use.

For 4

12 oysters (bearded) with their liquor
2 blades of mace
12 peppercorns
½ pint (3 dl.) good reduced white stock
2 tablespoons white wine
3 oz. (90 g.) butter*
1½ oz. (45 g.) flour
salt

* This quantity of butter makes a buttery sauce. Mrs Glasse uses ½ lb. (240 g.), which is too much.

Put the oysters and their liquor in a saucepan with 2 tablespoons of water, the mace and peppercorns. Simmer for 5 minutes. Lift out the oysters and reserve and let the liquor boil quite briskly for another 5 minutes. Meanwhile make a roux with the butter and flour, and stir in the stock and wine. Strain the reduced oyster liquor into this sauce and add the oysters. Add salt if required.

Serve with any grilled fish or with boiled turbot, halibut or cod. If using for boiled fish, ½ pint (3 dl.) of the court-bouillon in which it cooked can be substituted for the stock. Mrs Glasse specifies 'gravy', and the character of the sauce is altered if fish stock is used, though both forms are very good.

Anchovy Sauce

This, again, is Mrs Glasse's recipe adapted. A different version of anchovy sauce will be found under Butter Sauce (p. 282).

'Take a pint of gravy,' says Mrs Glasse, 'put in an anchovy, take a quarter of a pound of butter, rolled in a little flour, and stir all together till it boils. You may add a little juice of lemon, ketchup, red wine and walnut liquor just as you please . . . in short, you may put as many things as you fancy into the Sauce.'

I like it like this:

For 4

> ½ pint (3 dl.) veal or chicken stock or fish stock
>   (or a chicken bouillon cube)
> 1 oz. (30 g.) butter
> 1 oz. (30 g.) flour
> 6 anchovy fillets (well pounded)
> 2 teaspoons lemon juice
> ½ teaspoon black pepper

Make a roux with the butter and flour, stir in the pounded anchovies and cook for a minute. Add the stock, bring to the boil and boil for 3 minutes. Stir in lemon juice and pepper and check if the anchovies have made the sauce salt enough.

Sauce for Carp, Trout, Perch, Tench, or any freshwater fish

This is a very rich and yet delicate sauce, particularly good with trout.

> 2 tablespoons finely shredded raw carrots
> 1 tablespoon finely shredded raw parsley root
>   *or* ½ tablespoon finely chopped fennel
> 1 dessertspoon finely shredded orange peel
> 2 glasses white wine
> 3 tablespoons court-bouillon
> ¼ pint (1 ½ dl.) hollandaise sauce (p. 285)

The vegetables may be shredded on the coarsest part of a grater: the carrot and orange look like tiny goldfish in the creamy yellow sauce and the parsley root gives a special flavour which brings out that of the fish. Have the hollandaise ready.

Boil the vegetables and peel in the wine until all the wine is absorbed: this takes a minute or two only. Pour the court-bouillon over them and boil until that is almost absorbed – 2 or 3 teaspoons of liquid should be left. Allow to cool and stir the hollandaise into the saucepan so that all the flavour is retained from the bottom. Stir and lightly beat all together but do not reheat. Turn into a sauceboat and serve.

Fish Sauce

This is a sauce intended for any plainly boiled, baked or grilled fish. It comes from the Reading MSS (about 1760).

'Take a few cloves and some whole mace and just make it boyle a little in 3 or 4 spoonfulls of water then strain it out and put it into some fresh oysters with their licquor and some mushrooms pickled, with a little of the pickle and thicken it with a good lump of butter mixt with flower and grated nutmeg and keep it stirred and stirr into it 2 or 3 spoonfulls of claret or white wine or both if you please.'

This is extremely good but must have half a dozen fresh oysters or it loses distinction. The mushrooms may be fresh, and lightly sautéd, with a little soy and Worcester sauce added instead of their pickle.

For 4–6

> 6 cloves
> 2 blades of mace
> 6 oysters on the shell

¼ lb. (120 g.) mushrooms,
  sliced and lightly sautéd
1 teaspoon soy sauce
1 teaspoon Worcester sauce

1 oz. (30 g.) flour
nutmeg
1 oz. (30 g.) butter
1 glass of wine, white or red

Boil the cloves and mace in ½ pint (3 dl.) water for 3 minutes. Strain, reserving the liquor. Into this spiced water drop the oysters and their liquor, the mushrooms, and the soy and Worcester sauces. Make a roux in a small saucepan with the butter, flour, and a little nutmeg. Stir in the other ingredients and the wine and boil for 2 minutes. If too thick, thin with more wine or with water.

There will be almost ¾ pint (4½ dl.) of sauce using these quantities.

Sauce for Fish in Lent or at any Time

'Take a little Thyme, Horse-radish, a Bit of Onion, Lemon Peel, and whole Pepper; boil them a little in fair Water; then put in 2 Anchovies, and 4 Spoonfuls of White Wine; then strain them out and put the liquor into the same Pan again, with a Pound of fresh Butter; and when 'tis melted, take it off the Fire and stir in the yolks of 2 Eggs well beaten, with 3 Spoonfuls of white Wine; set it on the Fire again, and keep it stirring till 'tis the Thickness of Cream, and pour it hot over your Fish; Garnish with lemon and Horseradish.'

This is really a form of hollandaise sauce and is very good indeed. I translate it into practical modern terms as follows:

2 or 3 sprigs of thyme or a pinch of dried thyme
1 teaspoon dried horseradish
1 teaspoon finely chopped onion
a curl of lemon peel
4 peppercorns
4 anchovy fillets
white wine
½ lb. (240 g.) butter
2 egg yolks

Boil together the thyme, horseradish, onion, lemon peel, and peppercorns in a medium-sized saucepan in ¼ pint (1½ dl.) water for 5 minutes. Then add the anchovy fillets and a glass of white wine and boil again for 5 minutes, reducing a little. Strain all the solids from the liquor, put this back in the pan and stir in the butter, cut into pieces. Melt it but do not let it boil. Take it from the heat and stir in the well-beaten egg yolks and 2 tablespoons of white wine. Stand the pan in a larger one of very hot, not quite boiling water. Keep this on a low heat and stir and beat constantly until the sauce is creamy and thick. Do not let it get anywhere near boiling or it will curdle.

Forcemeats, Stuffings, and Savoury Puddings

FORCEMEATS AND STUFFINGS

Forcemeats and stuffings have always been very important in the highest levels of traditional English cooking. Forcemeat means only 'forced' or 'minced' meats, and meat here is used as in medieval times to mean food in general. Forcemeat (minced food), therefore, could be used as a stuffing or served separately, usually in small balls. The meat which is stuffed flavours the stuffing, the herbs in the stuffing flavour the meat. The poor housewife would rely on it to eke out the meat and help to fill the hungry children, who got plenty of stuffing but only a small slice of meat.

Any of the following forcemeats are excellent in turkey or chicken. The chestnut stuffing is traditional with turkey and is very good with pheasant. All of them can be made into small cakes, baked or fried, and served around a joint or bird if you prefer not to stuff it.

The following basic recipe comes from an unpublished eighteenth-century manuscript in Reading Museum.

'For Forced Meat

'Take twice as much beef suite as veal or porke, seasoned with salt peter time and parsley 3 eggs the crumbs of a manchet chopt small all together . . .'

This forcemeat is intended for any roast and is a very good basic stuffing which can be varied by using different herbs.

For a joint of 3–5 lb. (1½–2½ k.) or a large chicken or duck, take:

    ½ lb. (240 g.) good sausage meat or minced veal or pork
    ¼ lb. (120 g.) suet (MS has quantities reversed – twice as much suet
        would make a very greasy stuffing unless a great quantity of crumbs
        were used)
    salt and pepper (no particular point in saltpetre)
    2 teaspoons finely chopped thyme, fresh if possible
    1 tablespoon finely chopped parsley, fresh if possible

¼ lb. (120 g.) white breadcrumbs (a manchet was a fine white loaf)
¼ pint (1½ dl.) good stock, well seasoned
yolk of an egg to bind

Mix all together with the stock, and stir in the well-beaten egg yolk.

For pork or goose, substitute a teaspoon of sage for the thyme.

For variety add chopped mushrooms or walnuts, or a few raisins, sultanas or chopped prunes. For duck add a little grated orange peel and mix with orange juice instead of stock.

The sausage meat, veal or pork can be omitted and the forcemeat made only with 6 oz. (180 g.) of the crumbs, suet and herbs.

Mixed Herb Forcemeat

8 oz. (240 g.) breadcrumbs
3 oz. (90 g.) shredded suet
2 oz. (60 g.) lean ham or bacon
2 teaspoons finely chopped parsley
2 teaspoons powdered herbs *or* 4 teaspoons finely chopped fresh
    herbs (marjoram, thyme, sage, bay leaf)
salt and pepper
2 eggs

Mix together the breadcrumbs and suet. Add the ham, finely chopped, the herbs, parsley, salt and pepper. Bind with the well-beaten eggs.

Oyster Forcemeat

12 oysters cooked, or 1 small tin oysters
1 oz. (30 g.) finely chopped suet
4 oz. (120 g.) breadcrumbs
salt and pepper
2 tablespoons cream
2 eggs

Mix the breadcrumbs with the suet, add the liquor from the oysters, a good sprinkling of salt and pepper, the cream and the oysters cut in small pieces. Mix well with the beaten eggs. Stir in a double saucepan over boiling water for 5 minutes. Leave until cold, then use.

297

Sausage Forcemeat

> 1 lb. (½ k.) pork sausages *or* sausage meat
> 2 tablespoons fine breadcrumbs
> 1 teaspoon finely chopped fresh herbs or a good pinch of dried ones
> 1 tablespoon stock or gravy

Remove the skins from the sausages. Mix thoroughly with the other ingredients, moisten with the stock and use.

Mushroom Forcemeat

> 4 oz. (120 g.) breadcrumbs
> 1 teaspoon finely grated onion
> a sprig of thyme or marjoram or a pinch of dried herbs
> ¼ lb. (120 g.) mushrooms, chopped coarsely but uncooked
> a sprig of parsley
> 4 oz. (120 g.) bacon fat
> salt and pepper
> 2 eggs
> 2 oz. (60 g.) butter

Mix all the ingredients together and stir in the well-beaten eggs and the butter melted but cooled. Beat well with a fork and stuff the bird.

Celery Forcemeat

> ½ lb. (240 g.) finely chopped celery
> ¼ lb. (120 g.) shredded suet
> 1 tablespoon chopped parsley
> grated rind of half a lemon
>
> ½ lb. (240 g.) breadcrumbs
> 2 oz. (60 g.) ham
> good pinch of dried mixed herbs
> salt and pepper
> 2 eggs

Use the white heart of the celery. Mix all the dry ingredients together and blend with the well-beaten eggs.

Chestnut Stuffing

> 2 lb. (1 k.) chestnuts (as large as possible)
> ½ pint (3 dl.) milk
>
> 1½ oz. (45 g.) butter
> salt and pepper

First cut a small slit or prick a hole with a skewer in the skin of each chestnut. Then put on a large baking tray in an oven preheated to 350° F., gas mark 4. Leave for ¼ hour.

Remove and as soon as you can handle them, peel, scraping off the inner skin where it adheres. There is no need to keep them whole. Put all the skinned chestnuts into the milk, bring to the boil, being careful that the milk does not boil over, and simmer very gently, stirring and mashing for 2 or 3 minutes. Remove and put through a fine moulin or into a blender, with any of the milk which has not been absorbed. Melt the butter in a saucepan and stir the resulting purée into it. Season to taste. When cool and solid, stuff turkey, pheasant, chicken or veal.

If you prefer a chestnut purée to serve separately, thin the purée to the desired pouring consistency with more milk.

To stuff a bird with whole chestnuts, proceed as above but when skinning the chestnuts keep them as whole as possible. Sprinkle them with a little salt and pepper and put into the carcase of the bird from the tail end, pushing 3 or 4 nut-sized pieces of butter in with them.

Savoury Pudding

Made on the big farms of Cumberland and Northumberland in the nineteenth century, as the farmers' ancestors had made it for generations. It sometimes had prunes or raisins in it. To cat with pork or goose.

Serves 8 or 10

    1–1¼ pints (7½ dl.) milk
    ¼ lb. (120 g.) fine oatmeal
    ¼ lb. (120 g.) breadcrumbs
    2 eggs
    3 oz. (90 g.) flour
    ¼ lb. (120 g.) suet, finely chopped
    1 tablespoon chopped sage, thyme and parsley
    pepper and salt
    ½ lb. (240 g.) onions, very finely chopped

Heat the milk and pour it over the breadcrumbs and oatmeal. Let it stand for 10 minutes, then beat in the eggs. Mix the suet, herbs and seasoning with the flour, add the onions, and mix into oatmeal mixture. Beat thoroughly, adding a little extra milk if necessary. Bake for about 1 hour, and serve with pork or goose in the same manner as a Yorkshire Pudding.

Pease Pudding, 1

> Pease Pudding hot:
> Pease Pudding cold;
> Pease Pudding in the pot,
> Nine days old.
>
> (Nursery rhyme)

Traditionally served with pork since the Middle Ages, pease pudding has never gone completely out of favour though it is served more rarely nowadays. It is as good with roast pork as with boiled. Originally the peas were probably tied in a floured cloth and hung to cook in the cauldron in which a large piece of pork was boiling.

The oldest and simplest method is to soak ½ lb. (240 g.) dried green peas overnight. Boil them with sprigs of mint, thyme, parsley and marjoram or with a bouquet garni, until soft, with the skins loosening. Drain very well and put through moulin or blender with 1 oz. (30 g.) or so of butter. Add salt and pepper and press the pudding down tightly into a well-greased basin. Cover tightly with foil and steam for 1 hour (unless you prefer to tie it very tightly in a floured cloth and boil it briskly for 1 hour: in this case be sure the water doesn't go off the boil).

Turn out carefully as it is rather soft and serve in spoonfuls with the meat.

Pease Pudding, 2

This is a more elaborate recipe which makes a much firmer pudding and came from Welbeck Abbey, Nottinghamshire.

½ lb. (240 g.) dried green peas	salt and pepper
1 large onion	1 oz. (30 g.) butter
sprig of parsley, thyme, mint	1 tablespoon flour
marjoram and savory *or* a good pinch	¼ pint (1½ dl.) milk
of dried sweet herbs *or* a bouquet	1 egg
garni	

Soak the peas overnight. Then put them in a saucepan with the onion peeled and sliced and the herbs and enough boiling water to cover well. Boil until the peas are quite tender, then drain and rub through a sieve or moulin or put through blender, and season with salt and pepper. Melt the butter in a saucepan, add the flour and stir over gentle heat until it is a smooth paste, add the milk gradually and continue stirring until it has boiled for 5 minutes.

Add this sauce to the pea purée and mix thoroughly. When it has cooked a little allow it to cool, stir in the well-beaten yolk of an egg, and finally the white beaten to a stiff froth. Turn into a greased pie dish and bake in a moderate oven (350° F., gas mark 4) for 30 minutes.

Turn out to serve: it should cut in neat slices. It may also be made in individual moulds or ramekins and turned out.

Savoury Butters

How to make sundry sorts of most daintie butter, having a lively taste of sage, cinnamon, nutmegs, mace etc. This is done by mixing a few drops of the extracted oils of sage, cinnamon, nutmegs, mace etc. in the making up of your butter: for oyle and butter will incorporat and agree very kindely and naturallie together.

DELIGHTES FOR LADIES, Sir Hugh Platt (1600)

In 1600, the stillroom was an essential part of any well-run household and the mistress of the house or the housekeeper would prepare vegetable oils and distil rosewater (of which gallons were used in cooking, particularly in pies), orange-flower water and lavender water (the latter for the toilette only), as well as many herbal medicines for men and beasts. However, the savoury butters which Sir Hugh Platt suggests do not require the extracted oils of herbs and spices, but may be extremely quickly and easily made with the finely ground or chopped herb or spice worked directly into the butter. Sage alone is too strong and bitter for our taste today, but a little used with parsley and/or chives is very good. Cinnamon butter is good and mace butter is very good with fish. Nutmeg is rather strong and hot. I give a selection of butters below but, of course, all sorts of variations can be made according to taste.

When making up the butter, the herbs or spices should be as finely chopped, ground and pounded as possible, and the butter should be just softened, though not at all melted, so that the flavouring will work in easily. The flavoured butter should then be chilled and should always be served very hard and cold with grilled steaks, chops, fish or jacket potatoes on hot plates, so that it is just beginning to melt as it is eaten.

All butters keep well in small jars in the refrigerator for a few days or so, and will deep-freeze for 2 or 3 months.

Anchovy Butter

For 3 or 4

> 2 oz. (60 g.) butter
> 2 anchovy fillets *or* ½ teaspoon anchovy essence
> a pinch of cayenne

Work the butter until it is soft. Pound the anchovy fillets and cayenne into the butter and make into pats or balls. Serve with any grilled or fried fish.

Cheese Butter

To a tablespoon of creamed butter add a tablespoon of very finely grated Gruyère or Parmesan cheese, a little made mustard, and a pinch of cayenne pepper. Work all well together. Serve as canapés on small squares of toast, or on biscuits, or with potatoes baked in their jackets.

Cinnamon Butter

> 2 oz. (60 g.) butter   a few drops lemon juice
> 1 teaspoon powdered cinnamon   a pinch of paprika

Work the cinnamon, paprika and lemon juice into the slightly softened butter. Chill and serve with grilled fish or potatoes in their jackets, or spread it on toast, but in this case do not sprinkle with sugar, as is usual with cinnamon toast, but with a little salt and freshly ground black pepper.

Chives in Butter, Parsley Butter and Tarragon Butter

> 2 oz. (60 g.) butter
> 1 tablespoon finely chopped and pounded fresh chives, *or* 1 dessert-
>   spoon finely chopped tarragon

Simply work together the chives, parsley or tarragon and the butter. The chive butter may be served with any grill, and is best of all in spring, when chives are young and juicy. Tarragon butter is very good with grilled fish, but a revelation with plain roast or fried chicken. Parsley butter is good with all fish

Devilled Butter

For 3–4

> 2 oz. (60 g.) butter

SAUCES AND STUFFINGS FOR ENGLISH DISHES

1 small teaspoon made mustard
½ teaspoon curry powder
½ teaspoon lemon juice
a little cayenne
a little paprika

Work all well together. Chill and serve with potatoes baked in their jackets, on canapés, or with chops, cutlets or grilled kidneys.

Green Butter

For 3–4

2 oz. (60 g.) butter
a pinch of salt
1 leaf spinach ⎫
3 sprigs parsley ⎪
2 sprigs mint ⎬ put all through a parsley chopper together
2 leaves sage if liked ⎭

Put the butter in a bowl. Add the chopped herbs (the spinach leaf gives green colour). With a wooden spoon beat them until the butter is soft and the herbs evenly worked into it.

Make into pats or balls to serve, and chill a little. Very good with plain grilled steaks, or with potatoes which are to accompany cold meat.

Horseradish Butter

Per person
This is intended to replace horseradish sauce with cold beef or with smoked trout.

To 1 oz. (30 g.) creamed butter add a teaspoon of very finely grated horseradish and a pinch of salt, and drop in half a teaspoonful of lemon juice. Beat up well.

Salad Dressings

Lettuce is much used in Salets in the Summer tyme, with vinegar, oyle and sugar and salt, and is formed to procure appetite for meate, and to temper the heate of the stomach and liver.

COGAN, *Haven of Health*

Gerard mentions more than thirty salad herbs as being in general use in the sixteenth century:

thyme	orach	endive
violet	dock	sorrel
Spanish nut	water pimpernel	rampion
a kind of floare de luce	borage	purslane
onions	birnet	samphire
leeks	sage	watercress
chives	nasturtium	bugloss
garlic	winter cresses	hop sprouts
turnip tops	rocket	muskrose
lettuce, cultivated	tarragon	rosemary
and wild	other cresses	
beet	Succorie	
spinach	dendelion	

Various dressings were favoured with all sorts of combinations of these, but oil and vinegar were almost invariably used, generally with the yolks of hard-boiled eggs. Even salads which were mainly or entirely for show seem generally to have been dressed. In general, the proportion of vinegar used was greater than is usual today.

Dr Kitchiner's Salad Dressing (1817)

2 hard-boiled egg yolks	1 teaspoon salt
1 tablespoon double cream	1 teaspoon made mustard
2 tablespoons olive oil	1 tablespoon vinegar

Pound the yolks into the cream, and then mix all ingredients well together.

Dr Kitchiner gives 3 tablespoons of vinegar, which is much too much, but with 1 the dressing is excellent. He also gives water as an alternative to cream, melted butter to olive oil and sugar to salt. I do not like to think what the resulting dressing would be like if all these alternatives were used.

The Thatched House Tavern's Salad Dressing (1830)

yolks of 2 hard-boiled eggs
1 teaspoon mixed pepper and salt
1 teaspoon dry mustard

6 teaspoons wine vinegar
12 teaspoons olive oil

Pound the yolks of eggs, pepper, salt and mustard together to make a smooth dry paste. Stir in the vinegar and then the olive oil. Beat hard for a minute. Alternatively, put all ingredients together into a blender. The dressing should be of the consistency of thin cream and will need no further shaking or stirring even if left to stand.

English Vinegar Dressing

A nineteenth-century recipe.

1 shallot, finely chopped
1 dessertspoon each parsley, chives, mixed tarragon, thyme and chervil, finely chopped
1 teaspoon salt and pepper mixed
3 tablespoons wine or cider vinegar
4 tablespoons olive oil

Put all the herbs and salt and pepper in a bowl. Pour on the vinegar and mix well. Gradually stir in the oil and beat very well and serve. Of course, all ingredients may be put together into a blender.

Mayonnaise

2 yolks of egg
¼–½ pint (1½–3 dl.) olive oil
1 tablespoon wine or tarragon vinegar *or* ½ tablespoon lemon juice
1 teaspoon salt
½ teaspoon pepper

Very quick and easy to make in a blender, when all ingredients may be put in together. If an electric beater or simply an egg whisk is being used, it is rather long and slow to make and the oil must be added drop by drop.

There are good prepared mayonnaises on the market, but none is as good as a home-made mayonnaise. The quality of the olive oil is very important. A good Italian oil, particularly from Lucca, is the best of all. Mayonnaise keeps very well for a fortnight in the refrigerator, but will need beating when taken out.

If making by hand, first beat the egg yolks well with the pepper and salt and then stir in a little of the vinegar, add a drop of olive oil, beat well, add further oil, a little more vinegar and so on, till all the vinegar is used. Then continue to add the oil a few drops at a time, always beating, until the mixture begins to thicken and becomes a pale primrose colour. It should be as thick as very thick cream, stiff enough to pile lightly with a spoon.

Simple Salad Dressing

This is what I generally use myself.

> 3 tablespoons good Italian olive oil
> 2 teaspoons wine or tarragon vinegar
> 1 teaspoon lemon juice
> ½ teaspoon salt
> ½ teaspoon black pepper
> ½ teaspoon caster sugar
> 1 teaspoon made mustard (optional)
> a touch of garlic (optional)

Mix all the dry ingredients with the vinegar and lemon juice. Add the oil slowly, beating hard. Or mix all together in a blender.

Sidney Smith's Potato Mayonnaise

> 'Two large potatoes, passed through kitchen sieve
> Unwonted softness to the salad give:
> Of mordant mustard add a single spoon
> Distrust the condiment which bites too soon;
> But deem it not, thou man of herbs, a fault
> To add a double quantity of salt;
> Three times the spoon with oil of Lucca crown,
> And once with vinegar, procured from Town;
> True flavour needs it and your poet begs
> The pounded yellow of two well-boiled eggs;
> Let onion atoms lurk within the bowl,
> And, scarce suspected, animate the whole;
> And lastly, in the flavoured compound, toss
> A magic teaspoon of anchovy sauce:
> Then, though green turtle fail, though venison's tough,

And ham and turkey are not boiled enough,
Serenely full, the epicure may say,
Fate cannot harm me—I have dined today.'

Kettner in 1877, in his *Book of the Table*, called Sidney Smith (1771–1845) the 'witty canon', and his poetic recipe, much quoted but rarely understood, has sometimes been taken to be a joke because it was assumed to be a recipe for potato salad, which, of course, it is not. It is an excellent mayonnaise or thick dressing, based on potato: try it with tomato salad or with a cold salmon trout or salmon or with any grilled fish.

3 oz. (90 g.) sieved mashed potato (without butter or milk)
2 yolks of hard-boiled eggs
1 teaspoon dry mustard
1 teaspoon salt
3 tablespoons olive oil

1 tablespoon wine vinegar
½ teaspoon anchovy essence
½ teaspoon onion juice from pounded onion *or* ½ teaspoon of onion salt

Beat all the dry ingredients into the potato. Stir in the oil and vinegar in alternate small quantities. Beat well again, add the onion juice and anchovy and give a final beating. Or put all ingredients together into blender. The sauce should be very smooth and of the consistency of very thick cream. It may be thinned with a very little extra vinegar and additional olive oil if necessary.

Sweet Sauces

Butterscotch Sauce

For ices and puddings.

For 4–6

½ lb. (240 g.) white sugar
½ lb. (240 g.) brown sugar
¼ pint (1½ dl.) cold water
1 tablespoon hot water

2 tablespoons golden syrup
1½ tablespoons butter
½–1 teaspoon vanilla essence

Put into a saucepan the sugar, syrup and cold water and boil until it is brittle when a little is dropped into cold water. Draw off the heat, mix in the butter, hot water and vanilla.

Fruit Sauces

For hot steamed puddings or for ice cream.

For 4–6

A purée of soft fruit, such as blackcurrants, raspberries, gooseberries, loganberries, blueberries or blackberries, is sweetened to taste and thickened with cornflour which has been stirred into very little cold water and added to the boiling purée in the proportion of 2 teaspoons cornflour to ½ pint (3 dl.) purée. The mixture must boil for at least 3 or 4 minutes to cook the cornflour.

Hard Sauce

Traditional English pudding sauce: recipes go back to the early eighteenth century.

For 4–6

4 oz. (120 g.) butter	1 tablespoon brandy
3 oz. (90 g.) caster sugar	

With a wooden spoon, or using a blender, cream all together, till the brandy is taken up and the sugar and butter are evenly amalgamated. Roll into balls about half the size of ping-pong balls and serve with Christmas pudding or on plain suet pudding with or without dried fruit.

Jam Sauces

For hot steamed puddings or ice cream.

For 4–6

Melt ¼ lb. (120 g.) of any jam. Stir in 2 teaspoons of lemon juice. Serve very hot. The sauce may be strained if preferred or thickened with a teaspoon of cornflour mixed in cold water, added to the jam and boiled 2 or 3 minutes:

Traditional Sweet Sauce for Hot Steamed Puddings

For 4–6

1 oz. (30 g.) butter	½ pint (3 dl.) milk
½ oz. (15 g.) flour	1 oz. (30 g.) sugar

For flavouring, boil a bay leaf with the milk (removing it before serving), add vanilla or the grated rind of a lemon or orange, or 2 oz. (60 g.) of cooking chocolate dissolved in a little water.

Melt the butter without allowing it to colour and stir in the flour. Slowly add the sugar and the plain or flavoured milk, bring to the boil and boil for 3 minutes, stirring.

Custard Sauce for Puddings

Make as above and when it has finished boiling immediately stir in 2 egg yolks. Beat well and do not allow to boil again. This is a very much better sauce than any packet custard.

Plum Pudding Sauce

Dr Kitchiner's recipe, 1817; very good with any steamed pudding.

For 4–6

>   1 glass sherry
>   1 glass brandy
>   1 dessertspoon caster sugar
>   4 oz. (120 g.) just-melted butter
>   1 teaspoon of lemon zest
>   a little grated nutmeg

Stir the sugar and lemon zest into the brandy mixed with the sherry and slowly stir the warm butter into the mixture. Keep warm over hot water and stir well just before serving in a sauceboat with ladle. At the last minute sprinkle a little grated nutmeg over it.

7 · ENGLISH SOUPS

'We hope,' says Dr Kitchiner in 1817, after sundry awful warnings about the dangers of dirty earthenware soup pots and badly tinned copper pans, some rather sharp comments on over-spicing, and some very sensible recommendations as to the length of time soups need to boil, 'we have now put the common Cook into possession of the whole arcana of Soup making – without much trouble to herself, or expense to her employers, it need not be said in future that an Englishman only knows how to make Soup in his Stomach, by swilling down a large quantity of Ale or Porter, to quench the thirst occasioned by the meat he eats. John Bull may now make his soup "secundum artem" and save his principal viscera a great deal of trouble.'

This egregious piece of prose is characteristic of Dr Kitchiner's self-opinionated book, *The Cooks' Oracle*, which was, in fact, a best-seller in the field of cookery for many years after its publication. Nevertheless Dr Kitchiner is presumptuous: he presumes that the great houses of the nobility, the farms and the cottages did not know their business and had never known it; that they had not been making soups from every bone and carcase, every surplus vegetable, since the Middle Ages and long before that.

Soup has always been important in England, as it is in all cold or temperate countries. The agricultural labourer coming in from milking on a cold winter's afternoon could fool himself that he was properly warmed and fed if he had a bowl of boiling broth with salt and a few vegetables in it, even if it was mostly hot water. 'When the meat's short we puts plenty of pot herbs [i.e. carrots, onions and turnips],' an old Cornishwoman said to Sir Arthur Quiller Couch, 'and when the pot herbs is short we puts plenty o' salt. Salt and water's never short in these parts.'

From Cornwall also comes the tragic recipe for famine soup for children. It was called 'Sky blue and Sinkers' and was made by mixing a little flour with skimmed milk and pouring it into a large quantity of boiling water and allowing it to boil for a minute or two. Meanwhile a piece of barley bread was put into a bowl for each child and the boiling liquid poured on to it. The bread rose to the surface and then sank so that only the liquid, the pale blue of watery milk, was visible.

Soup was the standby of the poor. Only the open fire and one cooking pot were needed: any meat could be fished out and given to the men of the household, and the women and children filled up with broth and vegetables. The wife of the rich landlord carried soup to the sick wife of the poor tenant. Its general nutritive value, in terms of calory content, was overestimated. Jonas Hanway, in 1767, proposed a soup which would provide food 'for 5 stout men, or 10 common persons, including women and children':

1 lb. lean beef	3 large leeks
1 pint split peas	2 heads celery
12 oz. mealy potatoes	salt
3 oz. ground rice	9 pints of water

J. C. Drummond points out that this would give between 3,000 and 3,500 calories, which is just about what one 'stout man' would require for a day's manual labour.

Sometimes, however, the food value of soup has been forgotten or ignored altogether. The great chef Alexis Soyer, visiting the Crimea in order to attempt to improve the feeding of the army in the field and of the sick in the hospitals, found that the huge joints issued to the hospital kitchens were labelled by each sergeant in charge of a mess, suspended in huge vats, fished out at a certain hour, no matter when they had been plunged in, cut up and served to men too ill to eat solid food at all, while the broth, after being used for several days, was simply thrown away. Many men who might have recovered starved because they could not eat. Miss Nightingale and her nurses prepared broths from what they could beg or steal from the army cooks and cooked arrowroot and rice in their own rooms for the sick men. Soyer changed all this almost within hours. The indignant mess sergeants found themselves required to add pot herbs, salt and pepper, and even on occasion rice and beans, to the liquor in the vats, to use fresh water, to cook all joints for a specific length of time, to skim fat and to serve each man with a can of broth and vegetables which he might sup even if he could not manage the chunk of meat which was his essential ration. The furious and omnipresent Soyer for several days rushed round the hospitals tasting the broth himself.

Returning to happier circumstances and richer soups, the traveller, arriving cold and wet at an inn, would sup a bowl from the great cauldron on the hearth along with his pint of ale while he waited for his meat to be cooked and the hunting party coming home hungry before dinner was ready might be given bowls of soup and bread while they waited. Soup was the proper beginning of all English dinners. 'Soup of the evening, beautiful soup,' sang the mock turtle movingly.

Hayward in *The Art of Dining*, 1852, shows how seriously soup, and above all turtle soup, was taken by the English gourmet:

Turtle soup from Painter's in Leadenhall-street is decidedly the best thing in the shape of soup that can be had in this, or perhaps in any, country. 'The first judge in Europe' asserts that Painter is the *only* turtle artist in Europe. The chief rule to be observed in making the ordinary soups is to use none but the very best meat and vegetables, and carefully to clear the meat of fat. The grouse-soup at Hamilton Palace was made on the principle of a young grouse to each of the party, in addition to six or seven brace stewed down for stock. It has very recently been asserted in Blackwood that Scotland stands pre-eminent in soups, and this boast is not entirely without plausibility.

Real turtle soup, richest of all, introduced from the Indies, was for the Lord Mayor's Banquet. At a fund-raising banquet for the building of the Crystal Palace, which was given in the Guildhall at York in 1850, Prince Albert and two Lord Mayors, of London and of York, were present. Soyer designed and prepared the banquet, and it opened with turtle soup and two other soups named for royalty, of extreme complexity and richness. At certain City banquets it was assumed that the diners would take several plates of turtle soup, which was served in five different ways: thick, clear, calipash, calipee, fins.

A really fine turtle soup required most of two days to be prepared and needed, apart from the turtle, a leg of veal, chickens, ham, beef stock, cloves, cayenne, allspice, mace, pepper and salt, eggs and Madeira. It is not to be attempted at home, but Lusty's canned turtle soup is good enough to give some idea of what this soup should be.

Mrs Glasse (1747) gives a full description of how to turn a live turtle of about 60 lb. weight into soup 'the West-Indian way'. She says that 'the callepy', or undershell, and the callepash, or back, should be made into thick soups, more or less stews, with forcemeat balls made from the minced turtle meat and veal; the fins should be served in a separate broth with plenty of Madeira; the lights, etc. make a fourth soup or stew; and the liquor in which the head and bones stewed makes a clear soup. Whether she ever really dealt with a vast live turtle in her own kitchen, there is no means of knowing.

In the sixteenth century Andrew Boord in his book *Dyetary of Helthe* gives the following description of soup: 'Pottage is made of the lyquor in the whych flesshe is sodden in, with puttyng to chopped herbes and oatmeal and salt.'

Many 'pottages', however, before the nineteenth century, contained a whole bird or piece of meat, which was served in the dish of soup, being pulled and cut apart by the diners. Later the broth was eaten first and the bird or birds served separately. The grouse soup served at Hamilton Palace and mentioned by Hayward always contained a whole *young* grouse for each person, and was in our terms a stew rather than a soup.

The traditional soups of English cooking are real turtle, mock turtle, oxtail, game soup, pea soup, hare soup, gravy soup, asparagus and mushroom soup, but many others, such as chicken, artichoke, spinach or tomato can be as good.

In general, soups divide as follows:

1. Clear soups
2. Thick soups based on purées
3. Thick cream soups based on roux
4. Broths
5. Fish soups.

1 pint (6 dl.) of soup is enough for 2–3; 1½ pint (9 dl.) for 3–4; and 1 quart (1 l.) for 4–6.

STOCK

For good cooking it is essential to have good and well-flavoured stock in the refrigerator at all times. Bouillon cubes and canned consommés are better than nothing but they are not the same. Although stock is more difficult for us today than it was for our forebears, because we have smaller families and so serve fewer large joints, and because we spend less time in the kitchen, we can keep it much longer, once it is made, than was possible without refrigeration. Reduced stock can be deep-frozen and will keep for at least 2 months.

All bones and carcases should be boiled up with herbs or a prepared bouquet garni and any pot herbs available, i.e. carrots, onions, leeks or celery; turnips and potatoes are apt to turn the stock sour very quickly. If no bones are available, buy beef or veal bones from the butcher, who will split them for you.

Any stock can be strengthened by the addition of lean beef for brown stock or joints of chicken or pieces of veal for white, after straining from the bones, and boiling for a further two hours, so that it not only gains from the added meat but also reduces in quantity. If it is already strong and well flavoured, reduction by boiling by about one third of its original quantity may strengthen the stock enough without the need for further meat.

Such stock is the basis of most good thick soups, unless these are to be entirely vegetable, and of all broths, and above all, of all gravies and of many sauces and casserole dishes.

This recipe from the Reading manuscript of 1760 gives an excellent strengthened broth or stock.

To make Strong Broth

'Take 2 pound of buttock beef sliced and beat and fry it in a pann brown put good broth to it season to your palet with peper salt parsley onion a little cloves and mace boyled over a gentle fire till it hath the collour of strong bear.'

Use 1 lb. (½ k.) of buttock beef to 2 pints (1 l.) of beef stock. This gives an excellent strengthened but unclarified stock. For a white stock, use a whole small chicken or a pound of veal or half a boiling fowl.

CLEAR SOUPS OR CONSOMMÉS

For a proper clear soup, or consommé, a 'first stock' is required, which is then clarified and strengthened at the same time.

First Brown Stock (Basic Recipe)

2 lb. (1 k.) shin of beef	1 teaspoonful of salt
2 qts. (2 l.) cold water	20 peppercorns

2 medium-sized carrots
2 medium-sized onions
2 bay leaves

dripping or butter
bouquet garni

Wipe the meat and remove all skin and fat. Cut the lean into small pieces; scrape the bones. Heat a little dripping and fry the pieces of meat and the bones quickly until all are a good brown colour. This improves the flavour and the colour of the stock. Strain off any surplus fat, as grease must be avoided. Add cold water and leave to soak for half an hour. Bring slowly to boiling point; add the salt and remove any scum. Add the peppercorns and bay leaves, and simmer for 3 hours; then add the prepared vegetables. Simmer the stock for 2 hours more and then strain into a bowl and leave standing overnight to allow time for any fat to solidify. Remove all traces of fat the following day.

First White Stock (Basic Recipe)

Use a knuckle of veal and a chicken carcase, with skin, instead of beef. Omit the frying of the meat and bones; otherwise follow the method given above, but 4 hours boiling is enough.

Strengthening and Clarifying (Basic Recipe)

1 qt. (1 l.) first stock
4 oz. (120 g.) lean, juicy beef
1 egg white and shell (crushed)
1 small onion

½ teaspoonful of salt
6 white peppercorns
1 piece of celery
1 large carrot

Shred the beef finely and soak it in ¼ pint (1½ dl.) of cold water to extract the protein for 1 hour. Discard the liquid and put the beef with all the ingredients, including unbeaten egg white and crushed shell, into a large, deep pan. Whisk steadily over gentle heat with a balloon whisk or a fork until boiling point is almost reached. Stop whisking and allow the stock to boil up two or three times, removing the pan from the fire for 2 or 3 minutes each time it boils. Leave the covered pan in a warm place and allow the stock to infuse for about 15 minutes. Strain the stock twice through a very fine strainer. (The egg shell and partially coagulated egg white act as a filter.) Reheat the strained stock but do not allow it to boil, as this makes it cloudy. Season, and serve very hot, or chill 2 or 3 hours in a refrigerator or cold larder and serve cold and jellied, or use for sauces or other dishes as called for.

A white first stock is also clarified with a piece of beef and with egg white.

Artichoke Soup, 1

1 tablespoon lemon juice	1½ pints (9 dl.) white stock
2 lb. (1 k.) Jerusalem artichokes	1 pint (6 dl.) milk
2 oz. (60 g.) butter	¼ pint (1½ dl.) double cream
1 medium-sized onion	Parmesan cheese
salt and pepper	toast croûtons

Put the lemon juice into a basin of cold water. Wash the artichokes; peel and put them at once in the acid water in order to keep them white. Melt the butter in a saucepan, and as soon as it is hot drain the artichokes well and add them to the butter with the onion peeled and sliced. Sprinkle with salt and pepper, and cook gently for 5 minutes, turning them: they must not brown at all.

Add the stock gradually and simmer gently until the artichokes are quite soft. Do not drain. Rub through a fine moulin or blender, return to the saucepan, and add the milk. Season well. Bring just to boiling point, stir in the cream and serve very hot with small squares of toast and finely grated Parmesan cheese.

Artichoke Soup, 2

This gives a thicker soup.

Serves 4–6

2 lb. (1 k.) Jerusalem artichokes	½ pint (3 dl.) milk
1 tablespoon lemon juice	salt and pepper
1½ pints (9 dl.) white stock	¼ pint (1½ dl.) double cream
1 medium-sized onion	Parmesan cheese
2 oz. (60 g.) butter	toast croûtons
2 oz. (60 g.) flour	

Peel the artichokes, putting them at once in water as above. Boil them in the stock with sliced onion for 30 minutes. Drain and sieve, reserving the liquor. Make a roux with the butter and flour and stir in the liquor. Add the sieved artichokes and the milk. Season and stir in cream. Serve as in previous recipe.

Asparagus Soup

This is an eighteenth-century recipe from a manuscript in the Macadam collection, Edinburgh. It may be made with the thin green asparagus which often sells cheaply. The peas or spinach improve the clear green colour.

20 asparagus heads
   or 2 large bundles of small
   green 'grass'
½ lb. (240 g.) green peas
   or spinach
1½ pints (9 dl.) white stock

1 teaspoon sugar
1 oz. (30 g.) butter
1 oz. (30 g.) flour
¼ pint (1½ dl.) milk
¼ pint (1½ dl.) double cream

Wash and prepare the asparagus, discarding all but the top 2 or 3 inches of stem, as the lower part is apt to make the soup bitter. Reserve ½ inch (1 cm.) tips for garnish and cook them separately for 10 minutes. Cut the remainder into 1-inch (2-cm.) lengths, cook in the boiling stock with peas or spinach, sugar and seasoning until tender. Rub through a fine moulin without draining. Make a roux with the butter and flour, add the asparagus purée and bring to the boil, stirring in the milk. To serve, stir in the cream, and add the asparagus tips, a few to each bowl.

Barley Cream Soup

This is an eighteenth-century recipe which brings out the delicious and very subtle flavour of the barley.

4 oz. (120 g.) pearl barley
1 quart (1 l.) white stock
¼ pint (1½ dl.) milk
¼ pint (1½ dl.) double cream
1 oz. (30 g.) butter
salt and pepper
chopped parsley

Blanch the barley for a minute in boiling water, drain, simmer in the stock for 2 hours. Pass through a fine moulin, add the milk, cream, seasoning and the butter cut in small pieces. Reheat and serve sprinkled with chopped parsley.

Bean Soup

For 4–6

1 lb. (½ k.) dried haricot beans
   or butter beans
1 onion
6 cloves
1 carrot

salt and pepper
1–3 pints (6 dl.–1½ l.) stock
2 rashers fat bacon
   or 1 ham bone
1 pint (6 dl.) milk

> bouquet garni
> butter *or* sprigs of thyme, parsley and marjoram
> 1 teaspoonful chopped parsley
> croûtons

Soak the dried beans in cold water overnight, then cook them in any good stock made up with water to 3 pints, together with the onion studded with the cloves, the carrot, bacon or ham bone, herbs and seasoning. When tender (2–3 hours) sieve without draining and dilute the purée with the milk. Season again to taste with salt and plenty of pepper. Add a nut of butter at the last moment, and garnish with croûtons and chopped parsley.

Iced Beetroot Soup

For 6

> 2 large beetroots
> 1½ pints (9 dl.) clarified first white stock
>   *or* 2 tins of jellied consommé (if consommé is used add ½ pint (3 dl.) of water)
> salt and pepper
> 1 teaspoon wine vinegar
>   *or* lemon juice
> 1 pint (6 dl.) aspic jelly
> chopped parsley or chives
> ¼ pint (1½ dl.) fresh cream, whipped to hold a peak (sour cream may be used if preferred)

Cook the beetroots in the oven, like potatoes baked in their jackets, for 2 hours. Peel and then grate them into the stock or consommé and simmer very gently for 10 minutes. Season highly and stir in a teaspoonful of wine vinegar or lemon juice; make up mixture and pour all through a fine strainer into a large bowl. Put to set and chill in refrigerator.

This soup should be served chilled piled in spoonfuls in shallow bowls. It is a beautiful bright red and very refreshing. Sprinkle the jelly with chopped parsley or chives and place a large spoonful of whipped cream on each bowlful.

Carrot Soup

This very good soup comes from a house in Devonshire.

Serves 4–6

1 lb. (½ k.) carrots	a little sugar
2 oz. (60 g.) butter, and an extra piece	3 oz. (90 g.) rice
	1 pint (6 dl.) milk
1 onion	1 glass of fairly sweet sherry
1½ pints (9 dl.) stock	croûtons
seasoning	1 tablespoon chopped parsley

Slice the carrots and cook them gently in the butter, together with the sliced onion, for 2 or 3 minutes. Add the stock, and season with salt, pepper and a pinch of sugar. Add the uncooked rice. Cook gently until all is tender. Rub through a sieve or moulin without draining and dilute the purée with the milk. Check the seasoning. Add a nut of butter and a glass of sherry at the last moment. Garnish with croûtons and chopped parsley. The sieved rice thickens and binds the purée.

Celery Soup

1 or 2 heads of celery	1½ oz. (45 g.) flour
1½ pints (9 dl.) white stock (may be made with a bouillon cube)	1 pint (6 dl.) milk
	pepper and salt
bouquet garni	croûtons
1½ oz. (45 g.) butter	

Wash the celery thoroughly, and cut up the sticks. Cook in the stock with the bouquet garni until tender – about 40 minutes. Then rub through a fine moulin without draining. Make a roux with the butter and flour and add the purée and milk gradually. Stir until boiling and add seasoning. Serve garnished with croûtons of toast.

Chestnut Soup

Mrs Glasse's recipe of 1747 for chestnut soup begins: 'Take half a hundred chestnuts . . .' She adds a quart of beef broth, some ham, veal, a pigeon, herbs, onions, carrots and mace. She cooks two more pigeons in the soup, lays them in a dish on each side of a crisp-fried French loaf, pours the broth with the chestnuts over them and serves. She adds a note that a French cook would beat a pheasant and a brace of partridges to pieces and add to the broth but she clearly feels that this is extravagant and unnecessary. Many eighteenth-

319

century soup recipes make it clear that a whole bird was served in the soup for each person.

My own recipe for chestnut soup is lighter:

2 lb. (1 k.) chestnuts	1 oz. (30 g.) flour
1 onion	1 oz. (30 g.) butter
cloves	pepper and salt
1 quart (1 l.) of white stock	a little milk if required
or bone stock	¼ pint (1½ dl.) double cream

Prick the chestnuts well and roast at 400° F., gas mark 6, until the shells crack. Remove the shells and inner skin; pound the chestnuts lightly. Put into a deep pan with the onion, cloves and well-flavoured stock, and simmer until tender, about an hour. Put through a moulin without draining, make a roux with the flour and butter and gradually stir in the chestnut purée. Bring to the boil and boil 2 or 3 minutes, stirring. Season highly with pepper and a little salt. If too thick, dilute with milk. Add the cream just before serving.

Clear Chicken Soup

A nineteenth-century Scottish manuscript has a note that 'for a dinner the cook should clear the soup in the usual manner [i.e. with beef and eggshells – see p. 315] and should serve in it tiny stripes of tongue, very small quenelles of chicken, asparagus tips or little flowers cut from cooked young carrots and turnips, but for the household the broth is good as it comes and may have small dumplings, peas and sliced young carrots served in it'. It is, in fact, good enough for most of us.

1 old boiling fowl	a bouquet garni or a bunch of
1 blade of mace	sweet herbs
2 onions, peeled and quartered	2 or 3 sprigs of thyme (or a
2 carrots	teaspoon of powdered thyme)
1 leek	12 peppercorns
2 stalks of celery	salt

Put all this into 2 quarts (2 l.) of water. Bring to the boil and simmer 4 hours. Strain. Allow to get quite cold and remove all the fat. Dice all the best of the chicken meat and serve in the soup with tiny dumplings (see p. 96) which may be dropped into the soup to boil for five minutes when you reheat it to serve. Check seasoning. Any remaining chicken meat, having been boiled so long, is not worth saving.

Cream of Chicken Soup

Make exactly as in the previous recipe until the point where all the fat has been removed from the cold stock. You will then need:

2 oz. (60 g.) flour
2 oz. (60 g.) butter
¼ pint (1½ dl.) milk
¼ pint (1½ dl.) double cream

Make a roux with the butter and flour, being very careful that it does not colour at all. Gradually add all the stock and the milk. The soup should be a little thicker than single cream and very white. Stir in the cream, check seasoning, and add whatever garnish is preferred. Some of the chopped white meat of the chicken may be stirred into the soup.

Some traditional English garnishes are: 2 tablespoons very finely chopped sorrel or parsley; 2 or 3 tablespoons of very finely chopped watercress or cooked asparagus tips; 3 or 4 tablespoons of mushrooms stewed in milk, drained (use their milk to replace milk given in ingredients) and chopped.

Cock-a-Leekie

This is a traditional recipe from the eighteenth century. Almost all early recipes contain prunes, though one or two have raisins instead. There should be a very little but quite definite sweet element in the soup.

For 8–10

1 old fowl
2 lb. (1 k.) shin of beef
3 dozen leeks
3 quarts (3 l.) cold water

½ lb. (240 g.) prunes (no need to soak first)
1 teaspoonful pepper
2 teaspoonsful salt

Cut the beef into small pieces. Soak the leeks, wash them well and cut in thin slices, using as much of the green ends as possible. Put all except the prunes into a large pot with the fowl. Boil gently for 4 hours, then add the stoned prunes and boil for 1 hour longer. Take up the fowl and cut up the best parts in small pieces, return them to the soup; take up the beef and remove any stringy, fat or sinewy pieces, returning the rest. Serve very hot with plenty of fresh bread.

An Eighteenth-Century Garden Soup

This is a very delicate soup which tastes of summer.

Serves 8

On the day before the soup is required, take:

2 lb. (1 k.) veal bones or a knuckle of veal ⎫ these can be bought
a few lamb bones   ⎬ all at the same time
½ lb. (240 g.) shin of beef   ⎭ from the butcher

Stew all these gently with:

2 large onions	1 teaspoonful mace
12 peppercorns	12 cloves
1 dessertspoonful salt	

for 5 hours in about 2½ quarts (2¼ l.) of water. Strain, allow to cool over-night and remove all fat.

Three quarters of an hour before serving, on the next day, bring to the boil and add:

1 large lettuce	2 heads of endive
12 leaves of sorrel	20 spring onions or shallots

all washed and finely chopped.

Boil briskly for half an hour in the stock and then add as many heads as possible of small green asparagus and a tablespoon of finely chopped parsley and thyme. Boil for 10 minutes to cook the asparagus and serve very hot.

We float a large spoonful of cream stiffly whipped with chopped chives on top of each bowl of this soup. We often make it with a good chicken stock to which a couple of rashers of bacon have been added.

Gravy Soup

This was a Victorian speciality. It was considered particularly nourishing for invalids but was also favoured as a good soup to precede an elaborate dish of a white fish such as turbot or soles. A glass of sherry may be added just before serving, if liked, and tiny forcemeat balls or vermicelli were often served in this soup.

For 8

2 lb. (1 k.) shin of beef, cut in 2-in. (5-cm.) pieces

2 lb. (1 k.) knuckle of veal, chopped by the butcher
3 rashers lean bacon
2 oz. (60 g.) butter
1 onion, peeled and stuck with cloves
2 carrots
4 or 5 sticks of celery
a bouquet garni or some fresh herbs, especially thyme
3 bay leaves and 2 blades of mace
12 peppercorns
salt
a curl of lemon peel

In the bottom of a very large saucepan melt the butter and lightly brown the beef and the bacon. Add the veal and all the remaining ingredients. Fill up with 2 quarts (2 l.) of water, bring to the boil, and simmer for 6 hours.

Pour off the stock and discard the meat bones and vegetables. Allow the stock to get quite cold and then remove all the fat. Pour it through a fine strainer into a saucepan. Bring to the boil, check seasoning, and serve.

Hare Soup

Enough for 8–10

half a hare cut in joints
1 lb. (½ k.) lean beef (shin will do)
   cut in 2-in. (5-cm.) pieces
1 teaspoon allspice
1 teaspoon mace
6 peppercorns
salt
a few sprigs of parsley and thyme

4 onions
4 carrots
2 or 3 rashers of bacon
½ pint (3 dl.) port wine
1 dessertspoon lemon juice
1 tablespoon red-currant jelly
about 2 dozen small
   forcemeat balls (p. 296)

Put the hare and the beef in a very large saucepan in 2 quarts of water with all the ingredients except the wine, lemon juice and red-currant jelly. Boil fairly briskly for 2 hours, when it should have reduced to about 3 pints (1½ l.). Strain the soup, return to its saucepan and bring again to the boil. Take the best of the hare meat from the bones and return to the soup. Add the wine, red-currant jelly (stir until dissolved) and lemon juice, check the seasoning, and serve with the forcemeat balls floating on the top.

Kidney Soup

1 lb. (500 g.) ox kidney	2 oz. (60 g.) cornflour
2 oz. (60 g.) butter	2 oz. (60 g.) butter
1 small onion	seasoning
1 quart (1 l.) bone or brown stock	1 glass of sherry
1 small carrot, finely cut	croûtons
bouquet garni	

Remove all fat from the kidney, wash, dry and cut into slices. Fry quickly in hot butter with the onion; drain and add to the stock with the vegetables and herbs. Simmer for 2 hours, then strain, reserving the liquid, and cut the kidney into dice. Make a roux with the flour and butter and stir in the liquid. Boil for 2 or 3 minutes. Add the kidney, seasoning and sherry, and serve very hot with croûtons of toast.

Cold Leek and Potato Soup

4 leeks	1 teaspoon salt
2 small onions	1 pint (6 dl.) milk
1 oz. (30 g.) butter	seasoning
3 large potatoes	½ pint (3 dl.) whipped cream
1 quart (1 l.) chicken stock	chopped chives

Slice the well-washed whites of the leeks and the onions, and fry in butter without allowing them to brown at all. Peel and slice the potatoes, then add them to the other vegetables, with the chicken stock and salt. Boil for 30–35 minutes. Rub the mixture through a moulin or blend; return it to the heat, and add the milk. Season and bring to the boil. Chill and fold in the whipped cream. Leave in refrigerator at least 2 hours and serve sprinkled with chopped chives.

White Lentil Soup

½ lb. (240 g.) lentils (soaked overnight)	1½ pints (9 dl.) of water
1 ham bone *or* rasher of fat bacon	1 oz. (30 g.) each of flour and butter
1 blade of mace	1 pint (6 dl.) milk
6 peppercorns	¼ pint (1½ dl.) double cream
1 sprig of parsley	½ teaspoonful sugar
1 stick of celery	seasoning
1 sliced onion	

Put the lentils, ham bone or bacon, flavourings, vegetables and water to cook until tender (2–2½ hours). Remove the ham bone or bacon and rub the remainder through a sieve without draining. Make a roux with the butter and flour. Stir in the milk and then add purée of lentils and bring to the boil. Cool slightly, add the cream and sugar, reheat without allowing to boil, season and serve.

'A Soop Meagre'

From an early nineteenth-century unpublished manuscript. The name Joannes Askew is written on a blank page in the middle of the book in a different hand from the four separate hands in which the recipes are written. The medicinal prescriptions are in two different hands again. Several whole pages and the tops of others (presumably with headings) have been torn or cut out.

'Take spinnage, sorrel, chervil and lettuces chop them smale then brown some butter and put in your herbs, keep them stirring that they do not burn, then have ready boiling water, and put to it a very little pepper, some salt and an onion stuck with cloves and a French roll cut in slices, and some pistachio nuts blanched and shred very fine and let all boil together. then beat up the yolks of 6 or 8 eggs with a little white wine and a piece of lemon, mix with your broth and toast a whole French roll and put it in the middle of your Dish and your soop over it if you choose you may garnish your dish with poached eggs and spinnage.'

Translated, this is a supremely fresh-tasting light summer soup. Quantities given are enough for six. The garnishing of a poached egg and some chopped spinach in each bowl is not really to our taste today. The first French roll mentioned is purely to thicken. Early recipes often use bread rather than flour for thickening, but the delicate green soup is smoother if flour is used. The second roll should be a small French loaf cut in slices, which are toasted crisp. One should then be put in the bottom of each bowl and the soup poured over. All the herbs must be fresh for this country garden soup.

> ½ lb. (240 g.) leaf spinach, washed and chopped very fine
> 6 or 8 leaves of French sorrel or a handful of young wild sorrel leaves
> 1 tablespoon chopped chervil or parsley
> 3 lettuces, washed and chopped small

6 oz. (180 g.) butter
salt and pepper
1 onion stuck with cloves
2 oz. (60 g.) butter
2 oz. (60 g.) flour
2 glasses white wine
2 oz. (60 g.) pistachio nuts, chopped fine (they can be replaced with finely chopped blanched almonds)
yolks of 3 eggs
2 tablespoons double cream
1 tablespoon finely chopped mixed parsley and thyme for garnish
1 small French loaf, sliced and crisply toasted

Wash, chop finely and mix together the spinach, sorrel, chervil or parsley and lettuces. Melt the butter in the bottom of a large saucepan and turn all the leaves about in it, letting the butter just begin to colour, but only just. Fill up with a quart (1 l.) of boiling water and simmer gently for 30 minutes after adding the onion and salt and pepper.

Pour the soup into a large bowl, remove the onion and cloves, and make a roux in the saucepan with the butter and flour. Gradually pour and stir the soup into it and add the nuts and the wine. Simmer, stirring well, for 2 or 3 minutes. Beat up the egg yolks with the cream and, just before serving, remove soup from heat and stir them into it. Stir well so that it is smooth and creamy, but do not let it boil or it will curdle.

Place a slice of toast in a warmed bowl for each person, pour on the soup, sprinkle with parsley and thyme, and serve quickly.

Mock Turtle Soup

As prepared in a great London house in the nineteenth century for a dinner for the Russian ambassador. The slightly glutinous texture of the calf's head, delicious in soup, is reminiscent of turtle, but the flavour is quite distinct.

For 6–8

half a calf's head
1 quart (1 l.) beef stock
8 shallots
3 oz. (90 g.) butter
2 oz. (60 g.) flour

½ pint (3 dl.) madeira
  or sherry
1 tablespoon each chives and parsley, finely chopped
salt and pepper
a pinch of cayenne pepper
2 teaspoons soy sauce
1 tablespoon mushroom ketchup
lemon juice
croûtons of fried bread
  or very small forcemeat balls

Wash the calf's head, boil it for half an hour and then remove all the meat and cut it in small neat pieces (like the pieces of turtle in turtle soup). Reserve these. Put the bones of the head into the beef broth and boil them for an hour. Fry the shallots in the butter without browning, stir in the flour to make a roux and stir in to it the strained broth. Bring to the boil and add the reserved meat, the wine, chives and parsley, salt and pepper, cayenne, soy, mushroom ketchup and a squeeze of lemon juice. Taste and season a little more if necessary. Serve very hot with croûtons or forcemeat balls.

Mulligatawny Soup

Mulligatawny comes from the Tamil word *milagn-tannir*, which means 'pepper-water'. A highly and subtly spiced soup from East India, it was so popular with the East India Company merchants that they tried to get it made at home in England. The results were often a greasy soup flavoured only with stale curry powder, but the following recipe for a thick mulligatawny, which comes from a nineteenth-century Edinburgh manuscript is very good, though probably less spiced than it would be in India.

Serves 6
1 small chicken, about 2½ lb. (1 k.), or 6 joints
1 oz. (30 g.) flour
1 large onion, peeled and sliced finely
2 oz. (60 g.) butter
2 teaspoons curry powder *or*
  ¼ teaspoon cayenne
½ teaspoon paprika
1 teaspoon turmeric
½ teaspoon mace

½ teaspoon ground ginger
1½ pints (9 dl.) good stock, white or brown
6 cloves
20 peppercorns
salt
3 oz. (90 g.) rice
1 apple, peeled, cored and chopped (this replaces the mango juice in
    Indian recipes)
2 teaspoons lemon juice
2 tablespoons single cream (this replaces the coconut milk in some
    Indian recipes)
mango chutney

Joint the chicken, and rub the pieces well with seasoned flour. Brown very
lightly with the onion in the butter in the bottom of a large saucepan. Stir in
the curry powder, or, preferably, mix all the spices in a cup and stir them in.
Gradually stir in the stock. Add the cloves, peppercorns and salt. Simmer
gently for 1 hour. Meanwhile cook the rice, wash and drain well, and keep
hot, covered: it should be very dry. Remove the chicken joints, cloves and
peppercorns from the stock, strain the liquid, and rub the onion and apple
into it through a sieve. Remove all bone and skin from the chicken meat,
chop it finely, and stir it in to the soup. Add the lemon juice and stir well,
and finally the cream. Check seasoning and add a little more cayenne and
ginger if you want the soup more fiery. Serve in bowls, and offer rice and
chutney separately. Each helping only requires about 1 tablespoon of rice.

A Very Simple Mushroom Soup

1 lb. (½ k.) mushrooms
1 onion
3 oz. (90 g.) butter
1½ oz. (45 g.) flour
1½ pints (9 dl.) milk
seasoning
½ pint (3 dl.) cream (half of this to be whipped)
1 rasher of bacon per person fried crisp, broken to pieces, and mixed
    with the croûtons
croûtons

Cook the finely sliced mushrooms and chopped onion gently in the melted butter in the bottom of a deep saucepan for 3 minutes or until tender, without allowing them to become coloured. Sprinkle in the flour, stir well, and simmer for 3 minutes over a very low heat. Gradually add the boiling milk and stir and simmer a further 5 minutes. Finally add half the cream and season well. Serve very hot with fried diced croûtons and crisp fried bacon and a large spoonful of whipped cream on top of each bowl.

Creamed Onion Soup

1 lb. (½ k.) onions	1½ oz. (45 g.) flour
cloves	½ pint (3 dl.) milk
1½ pints (9 dl.) white stock	croûtons
2 oz. (60 g.) butter	cheese

Cut the onions into eighths vertically. Put in a saucepan with two or three cloves. Add the stock and onions. Bring to the boil and simmer for 1 hour. Pour into a bowl and make a roux with 1 oz. (30 g.) butter and the flour in the saucepan and bring to the boil. Stir in the milk till all is boiling again. Add 1 oz. (30 g.) of butter, and serve very hot with fried croûtons and grated cheese.

Mrs Frazer's Onion Soup (1804)

4 oz. (120 g.) split peas
2 oz. (60 g.) butter to brown the onions and 2 oz. (60 g.) to fry the bread
3 large onions, peeled and thinly sliced
6 tiny onions, peeled but left whole
a slice of bread for each person
salt and pepper

Soak the peas overnight. Next day simmer in a quart (1 l.) of water with a teaspoonful of salt until tender. Put them through a moulin or liquidizer with their liquid. Lightly brown the sliced onions and the small onions separately and add to the peas. Season, and simmer till the onions are quite tender, 30 to 40 minutes.

Fry the slices of bread slightly in butter and float one on each bowl when serving.

Orange and Tomato Soup

This is an unusual and very stimulating soup, especially good if the main course is rather rich and heavy. My own recipe.

329

1 tin of beef consommé
   or 1 pint (½ l.) of cleared beef stock
6 oranges
1 pint (½ l.) tin tomato juice
   or 1 lb. (½ k.) tomatoes stewed in
   1 pint (½ l.) water sieved through a
   fine moulin
juice of half a lemon

2 teaspoons sugar
salt and pepper
¼ pint (1½ dl.) cooking
  sherry
1 tablespoon brandy
croûtons
chopped mint

Squeeze all the juice from the oranges and put it in a saucepan with the tomato juice and the beef consommé. Stir in sugar, salt and pepper and lemon juice. Bring to the boil and stir in the sherry and brandy. Stir boiling for 1 minute. Serve at once with fresh chopped mint sprinkled in the bowls and fried croûtons.

Oxtail Soup

half an oxtail
2 carrots
1 large onion with 3 cloves in it
bouquet garni
2 oz. (60 g.) butter

3 oz. (90 g.) flour
1 large glass sherry
1 teaspoon red-currant jelly
2 teaspoons tomato purée
seasoning

Put the half oxtail, cut through by your butcher into joints, into a large saucepan with carrots, onion, bouquet garni and 2 quarts (2 l.) of water. Bring to the boil, skim and simmer for 2 hours. Remove the oxtail and take off all the meat, and cut into dice. Remove the vegetables and herbs. Allow the stock to become quite cold so that every vestige of fat can be removed. Make a roux with the butter and flour, and add the oxtail stock, stirring till it boils. Simmer 2 or 3 minutes and stir in tomato purée, red-currant jelly and sherry, season well, and add the diced meat. Serve very hot.

Green Pea Soup

Recipe of about 1750 from Somerset. The flavours of the lettuces and cucumber with the peas and mint are distinctive and very good.

For 6–8

1½ lb. (¾ k.) (after shelling) of green peas (quite large and old ones
  will do)
½ lb. (240 g.) fine young peas

3 pints (1½ l.) water
6 or 7 sprigs of fresh mint
   and 2 sprigs of thyme
1 or 2 sticks of celery
2 Cos lettuces
5 oz. (150 g.) butter
2 onions

1 cucumber
pepper and salt
1½ oz. (45 g.) flour
croûtons of fried bread
finely chopped mint and
   parsley to garnish

Put the old peas with the mint, thyme, celery and one lettuce, washed and shredded, into the boiling water with a dessertspoon of salt. Boil for 20 minutes. Pour off the soup into a large bowl and put the vegetables through a moulin into it.

Melt 3 oz. (90 g.) of butter in a frying pan, peel, seed and cut up the cucumber, and peel and slice the onion, and fry gently till almost tender but not coloured. Shred the other lettuce finely, add to the vegetables in this pan and fry another minute or two. Stir into the soup in the bowl.

In your original saucepan melt the remaining butter and stir in the flour. Stir the soup gradually on to this roux, which should just thicken and bind it. Add the uncooked green peas and simmer, stirring occasionally, for ten minutes or until they are tender.

Check seasoning and serve with mixed mint and parsley sprinkled on each bowl and crisp croûtons of fried bread.

Mrs Wight's Recipe for Pea Soup
'A Good Soup'

Serves 6
From the same anonymous unpublished nineteenth-century manuscript as Soop Meagre, but Mrs Wight's name is given for this recipe. A very good vegetable soup, much improved if a tablespoon of cream is floated on each bowl.

2 lb. (1 k.) old peas boiled in their shells in a quart of water, which is
   reserved and the cooked peas put through a moulin into it
1 lb. (½ k.) young peas, shelled
2 lettuces, washed and shredded
a few sprigs of thyme
8 or 9 spring onions, washed and chopped
a carrot cut in thin slices

a large potato, peeled and cut in small cubes
1 tablespoon each chervil, parsley, sorrel and mint, finely chopped
pepper and salt
¼ lb. (120 g.) butter

Bring the purée of old peas to the boil and put into it all the prepared ingredients except the butter. Boil gently for 40 minutes. Add the butter and bring to the boil again. Check the seasoning and serve.

Pea Soup

Serves 6–8
This soup, which uses dried peas, was served at a manor house in North Cornwall in April, when the mint was just shooting and the grass had come on so that cream was being made, but long before the fresh peas were ready. A large spoonful of clotted cream was floated on each bowl at the last minute.

1 lb. (½ k.) dried peas	1 leek
1 bay leaf	1 pint (6 dl.) milk
thyme and mint	croûtons
1 carrot	chopped mint
1 onion	clotted cream
1 rasher of bacon	

Soak the dried peas in cold water overnight. Place the soaked peas in a saucepan with 2 pints (1 l.) of water and the bay leaf, a sprig of thyme and mint, the chopped onion, sliced carrot, finely chopped rasher of bacon and a chopped leek. Bring to the boil and cook until tender (about 2 hours). Sieve the peas and other vegetables, and return to the liquor, and add to this purée 1 pint of hot milk. Garnish with croûtons and chopped mint and a large spoonful of clotted cream.

Poachers or Gypsies Soup: i.e. Game Soup

This recipe was first published in the nineteenth century. While the game laws were in force unreformed, no one would have dared to admit that such a dish was ever made.

It is a stew or pottage rather than a soup in our terms and is a complete meal.

This recipe is given by Mrs Johnstone, who published *The Cook and*

Housewife's Manual in 1826 under the pseudonym Meg Dods of the Clerkum Inn, taken from Scott's novel *St Ronan's Well*.

1 lb. trimmings and bones of venison (or carcases of birds can be used)
2 or 3 carrots
2 or 3 turnips
3 large onions
4 pints (2 l.) water
peppercorns
a bunch of parsley
1 small or part of a large bird (or rabbit or hare) for each person
6 small onions
1 head of celery
6 large potatoes
small white cabbage or about 1 lb. (½ k.) of a large one
½ lb. (240 g.) mushrooms

'Boil up a pound or so of trimmings and bones of venison with 2 or 3 carrots, 2 or 3 turnips, and 3 large onions. Add a bunch of parsley and 12 peppercorns. Boil for 3 hours and strain, keeping the liquid. Into this stock put any game you can get, allowing a small bird or half a larger or part of a hare or rabbit for each person – pheasants, pigeons, partridges, grouse, half a hare, a young rabbit or a wild duck; add 6 small onions, a head of finely sliced celery, 6 large potatoes, peeled and sliced. Boil for 20 minutes and then add about ¾ lb. of finely sliced white cabbage and ½ lb. of mushrooms [field if possible] cut in quarters. Simmer a further half hour or till the game is tender.'

Potato Soup

For 4

2 leeks
1 lb. (½ k.) peeled potatoes
1 oz. (30 g.) butter
seasoning

1 pint (3 dl.) milk
2 tablespoons cream
2 oz. (60 g.) grated cheese
croûtons

Cook the finely shredded whites of the leeks in the butter for a minute in a large saucepan. Add the peeled and quartered potatoes. Cover with 2 pints (1 l.) of water. Season and cook until tender. When the vegetables are cooked, put them through a moulin or into a blender without draining. Add the hot milk. Add a good piece of butter and the cream just before serving. Serve with grated cheese and croûtons.

Potato and Watercress Soup

For 6–8

2 lb. (1 k.) potatoes	pepper and salt
2 large onions	large bunch of watercress
thyme, rosemary, parsley	¼ pint (1½ dl.) double cream
½ pint (3 dl.) milk	

Boil the peeled and cut up potatoes and onions in 2 quarts (2 l.) of water with a bouquet of thyme, rosemary and parsley. When soft (30 minutes) remove the bouquet and put the vegetables through a fine moulin with the water in which they cooked. Add the milk and bring to the boil. Season highly and stir in the watercress, washed and finely chopped – all of it except the pieces of root and very hard stalk. Add the cream and serve at once. The watercress gives a delicious tang to the soup. Dilute with a little more milk if too thick.

An English Pottage

Sir Kenelm Digby (1603–65) did not consider his book *The Closet of the Eminently Learned Sir Kenelm Digby Knight Opened* worth publication in his lifetime, and it was published 'by his Son's Consent' four years after his death. His recipes make fascinating reading, and a few are worth reviving today.

His English pottage, which is really in our terms a fine stewed chicken, is splendid because of the consistency of the cream-coloured sauce and the unusual flavour of the endive with the chicken. It should be served as a main course and not as a soup.

Serves 6

2 pints (1 l.) very good veal or mutton or chicken broth
1 roasting chicken (3–4 lb., 1½–2 k.)
a bunch of sweet herbs or bouquet garni
1 teaspoon powdered mace
2 oz. (60 g.) fine breadcrumbs
1 large onion, peeled and quartered
the boiled marrow of 2 or 3 bones (this may be omitted)

1 lb. (½ k.) white endive (chicory)
1 oz. (30 g.) of butter
yolks of 6 eggs
1 glass white wine
¼ pint (1½ dl.) cream
salt and pepper
24 triangular toasts of white bread

Put the chicken into the broth (veal or chicken broth is more to our taste today than mutton) with the herbs, mace and onion, and the breadcrumbs (which boil away to nothing, thickening the broth slightly). Boil gently for 1 hour.

Boil the marrow bones separately for 30 minutes if you are including them, and extract the marrow. Sprinkle with salt and pepper and keep hot.

Wash the endive, cut into 1-inch (2½-cm.) lengths and poach gently in boiling salted water for 20 minutes. Drain, dot with butter and keep hot, covered.

Just before the chicken is ready, beat the eggs with the wine. Lift the chicken on to a large dish and keep hot. Make sure that the broth is just, but only just, off the boil and slowly pour in the eggs and wine, stirring all the time. Stir for 2 minutes. On no account must it boil again. It should be of a very thin creamy consistency, and at this point you may stir in a quarter of a pint of cream, much improving the sauce, though Sir Kenelm does not suggest this. Pour it all over the chicken and pile the endive on and around the bird, dotting it with the marrow if you have included this. Set the sippets of toast all round the edge of the dish and serve quickly.

To make a fyne pottage

This comes from an anonymous cookbook, beautifully written though very difficult to read because it is not all one hand; it runs from the seventeenth to the eighteenth century. The recipe for a fine feast-day stew would serve about 40. It calls for a whole leg of beef, a large piece of veal, half a pound of bacon, 4 ox palates, four sweetbreads, 2 dozen cockscombs, several fowls, and 24 pints of water, apart from various herbs and spices. Curiously no ale or wine is required.

Translated into quantities for 8–10, and replacing the palates and cockscombs which are not in general use today, it is a most excellent stew, strong, rich and subtly flavoured, very good for a summer party. The rich thickened gravy is inimitable.

2 lb. (1 k.) rump steak, cut in thin slices
½ lb. (240 g.) fillet of veal, also cut in thin slices
2 rashers of bacon, finely cut
1 veal sweetbread, washed, skinned and sliced
3 veal kidneys or ¾ lb. (360 g.) ox kidney, skinned, cored and sliced
1 chicken, about 2½ lb. (1¼ k.)
2 onions, peeled and cut in rings
2 lemons
2 blades of mace
a little thyme, dried or fresh
salt and pepper
peas
carrots
mushrooms
artichokes
new potatoes
2 oz. (60 g.) flour
2 oz. (60 g.) butter

Put all the meat in layers on top of the onions in a very large saucepan. If you have none large enough, use two; it does not matter that only one has the chicken; when dishing the meats, stir the two stocks together. Place the chicken whole on top of the meat. Add a dessertspoon of salt, a teaspoon of pepper, juice of 1 lemon, mace and thyme, and fill up with water just to cover the chicken: there should be at least 4 pints. Stew very gently, closely covered, for 1½ hours. Meanwhile prepare and separately cook 3 or 4 vegetables. Remove from the heat, lift out the chicken and take all the flesh from the bones, keeping the pieces as large as possible. Lift out all the meat from the saucepan and arrange with the chicken on a very large flat dish and keep hot while you thicken the gravy, as follows:

Make a roux in a 3-pint (1½-dl.) saucepan with the butter and flour. Stir in a little of the gravy and bring to the boil, gradually adding more until you have about 2 pints (1 l.), of the consistency of thin cream. Check the seasoning, adding the juice of half a lemon and some fresh black pepper. Pour all over the meats on the dish and serve at once with a border of small heaps of any of the vegetables available.

Queen Henrietta Maria's Morning Broth
(Bouillon de Santé)

Sir Kenelm Digby* tells us that the Queen drank the following simple chicken broth every morning in order to keep her good health.

1 'Brawny Hen or Young Cock'	'½ a great onion'
1 handful of parsley	pepper and salt
1 sprig of thyme and 3 of spearmint	1 clove
a little balm	

All these were put in as much water as would cover them – probably a little more than a quart (1 l.) – and boiled until they were reduced to 'less than a Pint for one good porringerful'.

No doubt someone else ate the chicken.

The broth made with this combination of herbs is very good and is strong and well flavoured if reduced to a quart (enough for 4–6) and served with the breast of the chicken laid in thin slices in each bowl. Of course the herbs should be strained away.

Lady Tillypronie's Scotch Broth (1880)

'A breast of mutton trimmed of fat and boiled with vegetables in at least 3 qts (3 l) of water. Any trimmings of fresh meat or bone improve it. Boil up at first, covered; then draw it to one side, and simmer 2½ hours. When cooked, take out the breast of mutton (you can crumble and broil that for servants' dinner); strain off the soup to get cold and remove the fat; then boil new vegetables in the soup 3 or 4 hours, but if you use rice it should be boiled *alone*, or if barley be used, it should be swelled in cold water 1 hour or more first, and then boiled, covered, with the broth till tender, 3 or 4 hours.

'A little boiled beef stock, if not too salt, improves this soup, cream also at the last, or you may warm but not boil the ½ gill of cream, and add it to the soup in the tureen itself, mixing it well with soup 10 minutes before serving, and it must not boil after cream goes in.

'The best of all Scotch broth is made of sheep's head when the sheep's head is cooking for table with scrag of mutton; you may also make it of shoulder of mutton, add good stock, and pass all, when cooked, through a strainer.'

Lady Tillypronie's recipe is not very clear or well set out. However, translated as follows, it ties up with many earlier recipes for Scotch broth and makes a very good soup.

* *The Closet of the Eminently Learned Sir Kenelm Digby Knight Opened*, 1669.

Serves 6

2 lb. (1 k.) breast of mutton or scrag end of the neck	2 large carrots
	3 pints (1½ l.) water
3 onions	salt
3 turnips	12 peppercorns

Stew all together for 3 hours and allow to get quite cold. Remove every vestige of fat, pour off the broth and reserve.

Take all the best meat from the bones and reserve separately. Meanwhile cut in dice:

1 carrot	1 leek
2 small turnips	2 sticks of celery
2 onions	

Put these in the broth with a handful of pearl barley and stew for 40 minutes. Add the meat, boil for another 5 minutes and serve.

The turnips in the recipe are very important as they give the broth its characteristic flavour.

Spinach Soup

Serves 6–8

A very good Suffolk recipe, 1823.

2 lb. (1 k.) spinach
1 turnip
2 onions
2 carrots
1 stick of celery
1 tablespoon chopped parsley and thyme
2 oz. (60 g.) uncooked rice
3 pints (1½ l.) good stock
1 oz. (30 g.) butter
12 very small suet dumplings (see p. 96)

Wash and shred finely all the vegetables and herbs and cook in a pint (6 dl.) of the stock with the rice till tender and quite thick (30 minutes). Stir well from time to time. Put them through a moulin with their liquor into the remaining stock. Stir in the butter. Season and boil 3 or 4 minutes. Have the dumplings ready, drop them in and serve at once.

Tomato Cream Soup

Serves 6–8

1½ lb. (¾ k.) tomatoes
2 teaspoons sugar
1 teaspoon salt
a good sprinkling of pepper
1½ oz. (45 g.) butter
1½ oz. (45 g.) flour

1 pint (6 dl.) milk
¼ pint (1½ dl.) cream
croûtons
2 tablespoons chopped
    parsley, mint and basil

Quarter the tomatoes, put them in a saucepan with the salt, pepper, sugar, and ½ pint (3 dl.) of cold water. Cover and cook over gentle heat until they are a soft pulp; rub them through a fine moulin. Melt the butter in the saucepan, add the flour and stir over gentle heat until it is a smooth paste; then very gradually stir in the milk, being careful to keep the mixture smooth. Slowly add the tomato purée and stir until it just comes to the boil. Do not let it quite boil. Stir in the cream and serve with chopped parsley, mint and basil sprinkled on each helping, and fried croûtons as an accompaniment. The basil is important as it brings out the flavour of the tomatoes.

Fine Clear Vegetable Soup

Nineteenth-century Scottish recipe.

Serves 4–6

1 quart (1 l.) stock, brown or
    white, well flavoured and clear
1 teaspoon sugar
1 large carrot
1 small turnip
1 piece of white celery
1 leek

1 onion
1 oz. (30 g.) butter
salt
3 sprigs tarragon, finely
    chopped
heart of a small lettuce

Shred all the vegetables very finely and fry them (except for the lettuce) in the butter until lightly browned. Bring the stock to the boil and pour over the vegetables, seasoning to taste. Simmer gently, skimming occasionally. When the vegetables are tender, after about 20 minutes, add very finely chopped lettuce and tarragon, and serve at once.

Mrs Penn's White Soup

This delicately flavoured soup, pure white and velvety in texture, comes from a manuscript of 1750–90 of Sir Peter Wyche's family.

Serves 8

        2 lb. (1 k.) knuckle of veal
        3 oz. (90 g.) lean bacon or gammon
        4 pints (2 l.) water

Bring these to the boil and skim. Then add:

        bunch of sweet herbs   1 blade of mace
            (or a prepared bouquet garni)   2 teaspoons salt
        2 onions peeled and quartered   1 teaspoon white pepper
        6 sticks celery

Boil for 2 hours. Strain off the stock and leave to stand till quite cold. Take off all the fat.

        1½ oz. (45 g.) butter   ¼ pint (1½ dl.) milk
        1½ oz. (45 g.) flour   1 tablespoon finely chopped
        ¼ pint (1½ dl.) double cream   parsley

Make a roux with the butter and flour and gradually stir the jellied stock, milk and cream into this. Allow to boil 2 or 3 minutes, check seasoning and serve in bowls sprinkled with finely chopped parsley.

Winter Soup

From a manuscript of 1800.

Serves 6–8

'Five pints of mutton broth, three or four pounds of windfall apples, cut up but not peeled or cored. Simmer the apples in the broth till soft, and press all through a strainer; season with a very small pinch of ginger (better in this than pepper), salt and reheat with a handful of pearl barley and cook gently till the barley is soft.'

        2 pints (1 l.) mutton broth   salt
        2 lb. (1 k.) cooking apples   2 oz. (60 g.) pearl barley
        ginger

Cook exactly as above. It is a delicious and heartening soup for a winter's night. A glass of brandy makes it superb, as it improves the apple flavour. It makes a perfect supper served with toast and Cheddar cheese.

Fish Soups

A Good Traditional Fish Soup from Yarmouth

Serves 6

2 lb. (1 k.) any white fish	1 glass white wine
1 cod's head	2 tablespoons flour
1 onion	¼ pint (1½ dl.) milk
1 leek	a little fennel, finely chopped
1 stalk celery	lemon peel
3 tablespoons tomato purée (concentrated)	1 clove of garlic
	2 tablespoons of chopped parsley

Put the fish and vegetables into a pan and cover with water up to 3 pints (1½ l.). When the fish is cooked, remove it carefully, taking out any bones and all skin, and keep it aside, divided into quite large pieces. Cook the stock for 20 minutes more with the bones and skin from the fish returned to it. Then strain it through a sieve and return to the pan. Add the white wine and tomato purée; thicken with the flour stirred into the milk. Pour the soup on this, stirring all the time and simmer for 3 minutes. Then add the pieces of cooked fish, and the parsley, fennel, garlic and finely grated lemon peel. The soup may be thickened by making a roux with butter and flour, if this method is preferred.

A Very Fine Fish Soup

A nineteenth-century recipe.

Serves 8

- 3 oz. (90 g.) butter
- 3 oz. (90 g.) flour
- 1 pint (6 dl.) milk
- 1 quart (1 l.) very good fish stock
- 2 large Dover soles (or brill or lemon sole), filleted each into 4, each fillet cut through again in 6 pieces

341

the trimmings and bones of the fish
1 teaspoon anchovy essence
6 cloves and a pinch of mace
2 bay leaves, a sprig or two of fennel and some thyme
12 peppercorns
salt
4 tablespoons finely chopped parsley
½ pint (3 dl.) double cream

Melt the butter in a large saucepan, stir in the flour, and cook for 2 or 3 minutes without browning. Slowly stir in the milk and then all the stock. Add the trimmings and bones of the soles, the anchovy essence and all the herbs, spices and seasonings except the parsley. Let it boil quite briskly for 10 minutes, stirring often. Strain and gently lower all the small fillets of sole into the liquid with the parsley and allow to simmer another 5 minutes, stirring gently from time to time. Finally stir in the cream and serve immediately, making sure that each person gets some of the little pieces of sole. Hot dry toast should be served with it.

Rich Lobster Soup

An Edwardian recipe.

Serves 6–8

1 small lobster or half a large one	1½ oz. (45 g.) cornflour
2 oz. (60 g.) butter	2 teaspoons lemon juice
1 bay leaf	1½ pints (9 dl.) good fish stock
1 sprig of parsley	½ pint (3 dl.) cream
seasoning	

Remove the lobster from the shell and keep the claw pieces for garnish. Wash the shell and pound it with the butter and put into a saucepan with the bay leaf, parsley, seasoning, lemon juice and cornflour. Cook very gently, stirring well, without allowing it to colour, for 10 minutes. Add the stock and roughly chopped lobster with its coral and simmer gently for 40 minutes. Pass through a fine moulin or blend and then strain again to make sure the gritty shell pieces are cleared, stir in the cream and garnish with the diced claw meat. Do not allow it to boil again.

The fish stock must be strong and well flavoured, made from a cod's head, say, and the bones and trimmings of any white fish, with a bouquet garni, a carrot, onion and celery.

Mussel Soup

Serves 6

2 pints (1 l.) mussels	¼ pint (1½ dl.) milk
1 small onion	1 clove of garlic
1 stick of celery	1 glass white wine
a bouquet garni	salt
2 tablespoons flour	1 tablespoon finely chopped parsley
2 oz. (60 g.) butter	

Cook the well-washed mussels in 2 pints (1 l.) of water with the chopped celery and onion and bouquet, and when they have opened, take them out of their shells and keep them aside. Strain the liquid in which they have cooked through a very fine sieve. Make a roux with the butter and flour. Stir in the milk and boil for 3 minutes. Gently add the stock and 1 clove of garlic, crushed, with the salt and the wine. Simmer for 5 minutes, stirring continually. Add the mussels and the parsley and serve at once.

Oyster Soup

Serves 6

1 dozen oysters	2 egg yolks
2 oz. (60 g.) butter	¼ pint (1½ dl.) milk
1½ oz. (45 g.) flour	¼ pint (1½ dl.) cream
1¼ pints (7½ dl.) fish stock	squeeze of lemon juice
seasoning	

Cut the oysters into quarters *after removing their beards*. Melt the butter, stir in the flour, and cook for a few minutes without letting it colour. Add the stock, oyster beards and liquor and seasoning, and simmer for 15 minutes. Sieve through a fine moulin, add the well-beaten egg yolks, milk and cream, oysters and lemon juice, and cook until thickened, stirring all the time and never letting it boil, when it would curdle at once.

Serve with thin dry toast or very thin brown bread and butter.

As with Lobster Soup, the fish stock must be strong and well flavoured.

8 · VEGETABLES AND SALADS

Vegetables

It is fairly generally believed that vegetables were not appreciated in England (and therefore rarely carefully cooked) until our own century, and only in the last two decades of that. 'The English have only three vegetables and two of them are cabbage' is an aphorism of the 1920s that we almost believed to be true until after the Second World War. We can see and smell the awful grey rags of 'landladies' cabbage' dumped on plates with stained boiled potatoes full of eyes, leathery meat and unspeakable dark brown gravy. We shudder and congratulate ourselves on our own conservatively cooked bright green cabbage, well drained and buttery, the variety of vegetables we serve, with the aid of frozen packs, and the delicious sauces in which we put them or which we serve with them. We are, however, unjust to our forebears. Vegetables were taken very seriously; in seventeenth-century cookbooks, recipes abound, and precise instructions are often given as to when to add the vegetables to a carbonade or a ragôut so that they shall not be overcooked.

William Harrison wrote in the sixteenth century:*

Such herbs, fruits and roots also as grow yearly out of the ground, of seed, have been very plentiful in this land in the time of the first Edward and after his days; but in process of time they grew to be somewhat neglected, so that from Henry Fourth till the latter end of Henry VII and beginning of Henry VIII there was little or no use of them in England.

Whereas in my time their use is not only resumed among the poor commons I mean of melons, pompons, gourds, cucumbers, radishes, skirrets, parsnips, carrots, cabbages, navews, turnips and all kinds of salad herbs – but also fed upon as daintie dishes at the tables of delicate merchants, gentlemen and the nobility, who make their provision yearly from new seeds out of strange countries, from whence they may have them abundantly.

It must be remembered that it is a meteorological fact that the summers were considerably hotter in England than they are now and that therefore melons would probably have ripened quite well under a wall in a cottage garden. Navews are field cabbage or Swedish turnips, which are sometimes found growing wild, though probably a naturalized plant.

Harrison, writing of prosperous houses and high living, also tells us that the first dish served at the evening meal throughout the summer was always a salad.

It is obvious, however, that root vegetables and the leaves, shoots and fruits which could easily be grown or gathered wild were of a greater and more desperate importance to the poor. Each labourer grew what he could for his family on his own plot of ground, probably mostly carrots, kale and onions, until, in the second half of the eighteenth century, potatoes, particularly in the north of England 'above the coal line', became popular and greatly improved the poor man's winters. He also grew and dried peas and beans, but in most years all were used up long before the earliest new shoots of sorrel, chives and dandelions could appear. William Langland in the *Vision of William concerning Piers the Plowman* crystallizes for us, in extraordinarily few words, the starvation-level diet of a farm-worker, in this case a small-holder, so by no means in the worst case, in the fourteenth century:

> 'I have no penny' quoth Piers
> 'Pullets† to buy,
> Nor neither geese nor pigs,
> Only two fresh cheeses

* *Description of England in Shakespeare's Youth*, Wm. Harrison, 1577. Ed. F. J. Furnival, 1877.
† If he had this would have been for their eggs and not to eat. The pig would have been fattened for bacon.

345

A few curds and whey
And an oat-cake
And two loaves of beans and bran
Baked for my infants . . .
I have no salt bacon
Nor no egg by Christ
Collops* for to maken.
However I have parsley and leeks
And many cabbage plants
And also a cow and calf†
And a cart mare
To draw to the field my dung
While the drought lasteth
And by this state of life we must live
Till Lammasstime‡
And by that I hope to have
Harvest in my croft.'

During the seventeenth century, market gardening began seriously in the south of England, particularly around London, which was growing rapidly. Sir Richard Weston, in a treatise of 1742 says that in the north and west gardening and hoeing were scarcely known, 'in which places a few gardeners might have saved the lives of many poor people who starved these last dear years'. He also says that in a market-gardening area of Surrey gardeners from Holland were remembered as having come over many years before to plant cabbages and cauliflowers and to sow turnips, carrots, parsnips, kale and peas, all of which, at that time, were rare in England.

By the eighteenth century specific vegetables were mentioned as a desirable accompaniment to certain meat dishes, such as Calf's Head with Cabbage, Boiled Beef with Carrots, Duck with Green Peas, Bacon and Sprouts, or Rabbit with Onions, and, at a Bedford inn, the dinner was noted in the Torrington Diaries as a 'Roasted Fillet of Mutton with Cabbage, Cucumbers and Sallad' in June 1789.

In the nineteenth century vegetables became a duty. Nanny insisted that

* Collops, in this form, were bacon and eggs, and this must be one of the earliest references to them as a specific dish. Markham gives a recipe for collops of eggs and bacon.
† He could not kill the animals for food or he would have had no milk and therefore no cheeses and not even his curds and whey. No one would buy the calf in the winter; he could only sell it when the grass came.
‡ Lammass was on 1 August. The term comes from the Old English *hlafmaesse*, i.e. Loaf Mass: the feast of the wheat harvest.

the children should eat up their cabbage, carrots would 'make their hair curl' – the last not much further from the truth than the idea prevalent one hundred years later in the Second World War that they increased night sight. Various vegetable dishes of a rather solid and plebeian kind became popular, such as Bubble and Squeak, Cauliflower Cheese and Vegetable Pie. Seakale, salsify and very young carrots and turnips and french beans, as well as asparagus and peas, were treated with proper deference as 'dinner-party' vegetables, and served carefully, cooked with delicate sauces or elegantly arranged to set off a rich main dish.

At the present time the quality and variety of vegetables are better than they have ever been before. Frozen vegetables are far better than tinned ones: we can eat green peas all the year round, and though it is no good pretending that the frozen peas are as good as those fresh picked in June they are not to be despised. Imported fresh vegetables vastly extend the season of new potatoes, celery, asparagus and artichokes. Cultivated mushrooms are always obtainable. We take it for granted that we can have salad vegetables, imported or grown under glass, throughout the year.

What would our forefathers have said to a fresh green salad of lettuce and watercress on Christmas Day? To fresh mushrooms in the stuffing of the turkey? To green peas on Boxing Day or to recognizable if not entirely satisfactory asparagus? We are extremely lucky, and we should cook our vegetables as if we recognized this. I am going to give here only traditional recipes and special recipes from manuscripts and family collections. If you make a salamagundy or Mrs Glasse's Green Peas with Cream in January, remember as you do so that she would have been amazed if she could have come suddenly into your kitchen. Indeed, she would have had no doubt that you were a witch.

TO DO HARTICHOCK BOTTOMS

Globe artichoke bottoms and the hearts of very young artichokes were used a great deal in cooking from medieval to Victorian times. They were put into pies, carbonados, ragoûts, fricassées and other made dishes with cockscombs, ox palates, sweetbreads, oysters and mushroom. It is clear that they were grown in the kitchen gardens of most great houses. For some reason they were little grown in English gardens between the world wars, but they are no trouble to grow, flourish exceedingly, and are ornamental as well as delicious.

Mrs Ann Blencowe's Recipe of 1694

'Cut all the leaves and chock off and sok them in cold water. Then change the water once or twice and after that stew them in a little water with gravey and butter and serve them up so: or fry them, which you please.'

If you grow your own artichokes it is probable that twenty or so may be ready at the same time. If the leaves are not fleshy they are not worth eating and only the bottom should be kept, but it is much easier to boil the whole artichoke for about 35 minutes, drain, pull off all the leaves and then trim away choke and stalk, than to cut these off raw. The neat round bottoms can then be stewed as she suggests, or dipped in batter or in seasoned flour and fried or added to a fricassée or a pie. Three or four, lightly fried in butter and cut in dice, are delicious served on buttered toast with scrambled egg on top.

The hearts must be obtained when the artichoke buds are very young and small, so that the choke has not begun to form. The buds should be about 1½ inches in diameter. They should be boiled for about 15 minutes, drained, and the bottom of the stem and all the leaves but the little cone of pale yellow green tipped with violet should be stripped away. This little heart can then be eaten in its entirety.

Jerusalem Artichokes Soufflé

This is not an artichoke soufflé but the artichokes themselves served in soufflé form. Hence the high proportion of the vegetables to the eggs.

For 4

1 lb. (½ k.) artichokes	seasoning
¼ pint (1½ dl.) good white sauce (p. 277)	2 oz. (60 g.) breadcrumbs
	2 oz. (60 g.) grated cheese
1 egg yolk	2 egg whites

Prepare and boil the artichokes till tender. Drain and put through moulin or blender to make a purée. Stir into this the white sauce, egg yolk (well beaten) and half the grated cheese and breadcrumbs. Season well and blend all together. Fold in the stiffly beaten egg whites, which should hold a peak. Put into a buttered fireproof dish, sprinkle with remainder of cheese and breadcrumbs and bake in a hot oven, 425° F., gas mark 7, for 20 minutes till risen and golden brown. Serve at once.

This makes a very good starting course instead of soup, or a supper dish, or is delicious and unusual with roasts or grills if a green salad is served as well.

Asparagus

Perhaps the most prized of all vegetables, asparagus in general requires only careful poaching in salted water, and then to be served hot with melted butter or hollandaise sauce, or cold with a good dressing, or with a delicate mayonnaise. However, Mrs Glasse's Asparagus Forced in French Rolls is so elegant and unusual that I have included it.

For 6

> butter
> 50–70 asparagus stalks, not too thick
> 3 small French loaves (half a loaf for each person)
> lettuce
> 1 pint (6 dl.) double cream
> 6 eggs
> nutmeg, salt and pepper

Cook all the asparagus till just tender. Cut off all the inedible stalks. Leave two thirds whole and chop one third into small bits.

Cut a long lid off each loaf. Scoop out all the crumb. Cut holes through the lid with a pointed knife, large enough to take the shortened asparagus stems – 15 or so in each lid. Fry the rolls and lids very crisp in butter, and leave to drain well.

Beat the eggs and cream with the nutmeg, salt and pepper and stir over low heat or over a saucepan of boiling water till it begins to thicken. Add the chopped asparagus and when about the consistency of mayonnaise, quickly fill the fried loaves with it. Put on the lids, stick the asparagus through the holes as if it were growing, stand in a large flat dish in the oven for 3–5 minutes to make quite hot. The oven should be moderate or the asparagus will dry. Cut each loaf in half when serving; if divided earlier, the cream filling may run out.

BROAD BEANS

Early English recipes often suggest skinning broad beans and making them into a purée and Mrs Glasse suggests a dish where alternate layers of purée and whole skinned broad beans are put together and baked. In fact they make a rather sticky purée and are much better served very young with their skins on. George III went to inspect the progress of the building of Woolwich Arsenal and ate *al fresco* with the workmen. They were having Beans and Bacon and he liked it so much that he instituted an annual beanfeast.

Beans and Bacon

This was a traditional English cottage dish, but it was also a favourite in the great houses, where in the early summer a side dish known as Beans and Collops often featured at sixteenth- and seventeenth-century feasts.

For 4

> 4 lb. (2 k.) very young broad beans shelled
> 2 thick gammon rashers or a piece of gammon for boiling
> 2 glasses red wine
> 1 tablespoon brown sugar
> 6 cloves
> ½ pint (3 dl.) good parsley sauce *or* 3 oz. (90 g.) melted butter with a little chopped parsley and savory in it

Cook the rashers or piece of gammon till exactly tender in the wine, sugar and cloves, with water added just to cover.

20 minutes before you think it will be ready put the beans into boiling salted water and cook till tender. Drain well, pile in the middle of a flat dish and keep hot while you cut the rashers into eight neat pieces or carve the piece of gammon. Arrange these round the beans and pour over the previously heated parsley sauce or, if you prefer it, the melted butter with parsley and savory. Savory is particularly good with broad beans, as it enhances their flavour.

Butter Beans

Particularly good with roast goose or pork.

For 4

> 1 lb. (½ k.) cooked butter beans (canned are good if well drained)
> 1 onion, finely chopped
> 2 blanched tomatoes, cut in slices
> 2 sticks of celery, finely chopped
> 3 oz. (90 g.) butter
> 1 dessertspoon finely chopped parsley
> 1 teaspoon finely chopped thyme and rosemary mixed

Sauté the onion, tomatoes and celery in 2 oz. (60 g.) of butter until just soft, mix in the thyme and rosemary and half the parsley, and lightly mix all with the beans. Turn into a fireproof dish, dot the remaining butter over the top and bake for 20 minutes at 350° F., gas mark 4. Serve sprinkled with the remaining parsley.

French Beans or Young Runner Beans

Mrs Rundell's excellent recipe, 1819.

> 2 lb. (1 k.) french beans, strings removed and beans cut into 4
> ¼ pint (1½ dl.) very good white or brown stock
> 1 oz. (30 g.) butter
> 1 oz. (30 g.) flour
> 2 tablespoons double cream
> salt and pepper

Put the beans into boiling, salted water and boil for 10 minutes. Drain, put into the boiling stock and boil a further 5 or 10 minutes, or until tender. Make a roux with the flour and butter in another saucepan, and pour the stock from the beans into this, stirring to make a smooth sauce. Add the beans, stir in the cream, check the seasoning and serve.

DRIED HARICOT BEANS

Various kinds of beans were grown and dried for winter in all households, rich and poor, throughout the English countryside. All dried beans require overnight soaking before being cooked.

Baked Beans

For 4

> ½ lb. (240 g.) dried haricot beans, soaked overnight
> 1 lb. (½ k.) gammon (or 2 large gammon rashers) cut in ½-in. (1-cm.) cubes
> salt and pepper
> 1 onion, finely chopped
> 1 lb. (½ k.) tomatoes, blanched
> 1 tablespoon golden syrup
> 1 oz. (30 g.) butter

Drain the beans and add to them the bacon, onion, tomatoes and 1 pint (6 dl.) salted water. Stew gently for 1 hour or until the beans are soft. Add the golden syrup and boil a few minutes more. Check the seasoning. Turn into a flat fireproof dish, dot with butter and bake at 400°F., gas mark 6, uncovered, for 10 minutes before serving.

Pot Baked Beans

For 6

    1 lb. (½ k.) haricot beans, soaked overnight
    ¼ lb. (120 g.) fat bacon cut in ½-in. (1-cm.) cubes
    2 tablespoons black or brown treacle
    onions
    1 teaspoon dry mustard
    salt and black pepper

Put the beans into a pan of water, bring to the boil and boil for 3 minutes. Strain into a deep pot with all the other ingredients. Fill the pot with water just to cover the beans. Cover closely and cook all night or at least 4 hours at 250° F., gas mark ½.

Half water, half cider, gives the beans a delicious flavour.

Brussels Sprouts with Chestnuts

For 4–6

    2 lb. (1 k.) brussels sprouts
    ½ lb. (240 g.) cooked and skinned chestnuts
      (good whole canned chestnuts may be used)
    1½ oz. (45 g.) butter
    salt and coarse black pepper

Prepare the brussels sprouts by removing all the outside leaves and hard stem ends, drop into about 2 inches (5 cm.) boiling salted water, stir several times and boil gently till tender (about 20 minutes). Melt the butter in a pan and heat without allowing to brown. Toss the chestnuts in it, breaking them up into pieces as they fry for 2 minutes. Add the sprouts and toss with the chestnuts 2 minutes more. Mix all lightly together, season highly with salt and coarse black pepper, and turn on to hot dish and serve.

Brussels Sprouts Gratinée

For 4–6

> 2 lb. (1 k.) brussels sprouts
> 3 rashers of bacon, rather fat, and cut in small pieces
> 2 oz. (60 g.) cheese, finely grated
> 1 oz. (30 g.) breadcrumbs

The sprouts must be firm and hard, not leafy and not too large.

Boil as in the previous recipe. Drain well. Meanwhile fry the bacon, drain and keep hot in a fireproof dish. Toss the sprouts in the bacon fat for 2 or 3 minutes, so that they are lightly fried all round – do not have the fat too hot when doing this. Lift them out with a slice or perforated spoon and add them to the chopped bacon, lightly mixing all together. Sprinkle thickly with the cheese and crumbs, brown under a hot grill and serve as a starting course or as a supper dish, with croûtons of fried bread. Also very good served with cold meat.

Brussels Sprouts with Green Grapes

For 4–6

> 2 lb. (1 k.) small firm sprouts
> ¾ lb. (360 g.) green grapes
> 1 oz. (30 g.) butter

Boil the sprouts as in the previous recipes. Meanwhile, blanch and seed the grapes. Drain the sprouts, toss in the butter for 2 minutes, lightly mix in the grapes, turn into a hot serving dish and serve at once very hot.

This is delicious served in individual dishes as a hot hors-d'œuvre, with fried croûtons to eat with it. It is also a perfect vegetable to serve with any roast bird, particularly game birds, and is very good with veal in any form.

Baked Cabbage

Serves 4–6

> 1 white drumhead or savoy cabbage about 3 lbs
> 2 large cooking apples
> 2 oz. (60 g.) sultanas
> 1 large onion
> 2 oz. (60 g.) butter

This is best made with a white drumhead cabbage, but a hard savoy may be used.

353

Shred the cabbage very finely. Peel, core and slice the apples finely. Peel the onion and cut into fine rings. Mix the apple and onion with the cabbage, add the sultanas, and place in a well-buttered fireproof dish. Add 2 tablespoons of water, cover closely, and cook in a moderate oven, 300° F., gas mark 2, for 1½–2 hours. When the cabbage is quite tender it may be uncovered and left to crisp slightly in the oven for 15 minutes before serving.

Baked Red Cabbage

A recipe of 1820.

Serves 4–6

1 red cabbage	6 peppercorns
¼ pint (1½ dl.) vinegar	salt
¼ pint (1½ dl.) water	2 onions
¼ pint (1½ dl.) red wine	1 bay leaf
2 apples, diced	sprig of thyme
1 rasher of bacon, diced	2 oz. (60 g.) sultanas

Shred the cabbage finely, removing the stem, and marinade for an hour or two in the vinegar, wine and water. Place it in a saucepan with the liquid together with all the other ingredients and boil for 10 minutes. Then turn into fireproof casserole, cover, and finish cooking in oven, 300°F., gas mark 2, for 1½ hours. Serve with hot ham or game, mutton or pork.

Cauliflower Cheese

For 4–6

1 firm cauliflower	2 oz. (60 g.) crumbs
1 oz. (30 g.) cheese	¾ pint (4½ dl.) cheese sauce (p. 283)

Put the cauliflower into enough boiling salted water to come about half-way up the vegetable. Put on the lid and cook 20–30 minutes according to size. It should be tender but still firm. Meanwhile, make your cheese sauce. Butter a fireproof dish or individual dishes and arrange the cauliflower, broken carefully into sections. Pour over the hot cheese sauce. Sprinkle with grated cheese and top with fine breadcrumbs. Dot with pieces of butter. Brown under a hot grill and serve. It will keep hot for 30 minutes or so in a cool oven or warming drawer, but must not boil.

Cauliflower, Fried

For 4–6

    1 cauliflower, boiled for only 10 minutes and divided into flowerets
    ½ pint coating batter (p. 412)
    oil for frying

Dip each well-drained floweret into coating batter and drop into very hot deep fat, and fry for 2 minutes only, till golden brown and crisp all over. If shallow frying, have the fat (olive oil is best) really hot and at least ½ inch (1 cm.) deep in pan. Drain the flowerets well.

Onions, quartered downwards, divided into leaves and dipped in the same way, are very good mixed with the cauliflower fritters. Fry the onions for a little longer as they are raw when you start. If served with bacon and sausages and a green salad, this makes a very good luncheon or supper dish.

CELERY

In eighteenth-century England, celery was treated with respect. It was carefully grown in prosperous kitchen gardens with no shortage of labour, where it was trenched and well blanched, and when it reached the kitchen it was considered a delicacy. These two recipes prove that it can be.

Fried Celery

Serves 6

    about 2 dozen inside stalks of celery, all strings scraped away, cut into
    3-in. (7-cm.) lengths, boiled for 20 minutes in salted water and
    well drained

For the batter:
2 glasses white wine
yolks of 2 eggs
salt and pepper   all well beaten together
1½ oz. (45 g.) flour
6 oz. (180 g.) butter

Dip each piece of celery in this batter and fry gently in the butter until golden brown. Drain and pile on a flat dish. Just before serving pour 2 oz. of clean melted butter over them.

A variant on this recipe, from a book called *Adam's Luxury & Eve's Cookery*, of 1744, makes the batter with one egg yolk and white separately beaten, the white very stiff and folded in so that the batter is crisper and more spreading and each piece of celery forms a fritter instead of being closely coated. The recipe suggests serving in a good brown gravy or a sharp sauce instead of the melted butter.

Celery and Cream

This is from an eighteenth-century manuscript in a Scottish collection. Serve as a separate course with triangles of hot puff pastry.

For 6

> 2 heads of celery
> yolks of 4 eggs, well beaten
> ⅓ pint (2 dl.) double cream
> salt and pepper and a little nutmeg

Use only the best and whitest of the celery and scrape away all the strings. Cut into 3-inch (7-cm.) lengths and boil in water to cover until tender (about 20 minutes). Take off the heat and pour off all the water. Beat the eggs well, stir them into the cream, season with salt, pepper and nutmeg. Pour over the celery, stirring gently. Hold the pan over low heat, shaking constantly and lightly stirring from the bottom. As soon as it begins to thicken pour on to a hot dish and immediately serve. It must not boil or it will curdle.

Celery and Tomatoes

For 6

> 2 heads of celery
> 2 oz. (60 g.) chopped onions
> 1 lb. (½ k.) tomatoes
> 1 pint (6 dl.) any good stock
>   (a bouillon cube may be used)
>
> 1 oz. (30 g.) butter
> 1 clove of garlic
> 1 bay leaf
> salt and pepper
> 2 rashers bacon, chopped

Prepare and cut the celery into 1-inch (2-cm.) lengths. Melt the butter in a saucepan and add the celery, bacon, chopped onions, garlic, bay leaf, and skinned, seeded and chopped tomatoes. Fry gently for 5 minutes. Season with salt and pepper, and add stock. Poach gently on low heat for 35–40 minutes until tender.

Good served with boiled or grilled ham or bacon.

Colcannon

A traditional Irish peasant dish; I have not been able to discover the origin of the name. It is very good and comfortable with cold meat. There are two secrets to success in making this extremely simple dish. First the cabbage must be *green*, dry and finely chopped; it is horrible made with white cabbage. Secondly, the cake must have a crisp dark brown crust on both sides.

Serves 4–6

2 oz. (60 g.) butter
1 lb. (½ k.) cooked mashed potatoes
1 onion finely chopped
½–¾ lb. (240–360 g.) cooked *green* cabbage (savoys or broccoli are good)
salt and pepper

Fry the onion very gently in the butter so that it is melted but not browned. Lift and mix with the cabbage and potatoes and season highly, using plenty of black pepper. Fry gently in the butter, shaking well in the pan to prevent sticking, until brown on the bottom. Place a plate over the pan and turn the colcannon on to it. Reheat the pan a little, put in a little more butter if dry, and turn the colcannon into it again, browned side uppermost. Fry until the bottom is brown. It may be kept hot in the oven for half an hour or so without harm.

Hot Cucumbers in Cream

2 cucumbers
lemon juice
2 oz. (60 g.) butter
½ pint (3 dl.) fresh cream
salt and pepper
1 tablespoon finely chopped parsley

Peel the cucumbers and split them lengthwise. Remove the seeds. Cut them into pieces about 2 inches (5 cm.) long and squeeze a little lemon juice over them. Melt the butter and slowly fry the cucumbers in it for 3 minutes. Pour in the cream and boil for 2 minutes. Season to taste with salt and pepper. Pour into a shallow dish, sprinkle with parsley, and serve at once.

Stuffed Cucumbers

This is a very fine eighteenth-century dish intended as one of the side dishes at a grand dinner. It is very good as a vegetarian main dish or accompanied by a piece of hot boiled gammon, or by hot cippolata sausages and croûtons of fried bread.

For 4 to 6

> 2 large cucumbers
> ½ pint (3 dl.) good well-seasoned stock, with tomato purée or fresh tomatoes if liked
> parsley, capers and lemon for garnish

For the filling:

> ½ lb. (240 g.) white cabbage, finely chopped, boiled and drained
> 1 small onion chopped very fine
> 2 oz. (60 g.) mushrooms, chopped very fine
> 1 tablespoon parsley, chopped very fine
> 2 hard-boiled eggs, chopped very fine
> salt, pepper, and a little nutmeg
> 3 oz. (90 g.) butter

Peel the cucumbers thinly and cut off the stalk ends. With a long thin knife, scoop out all the centres. Well mix all the ingredients for the filling and stuff the cucumbers. Replace the stalk ends and tie in place by winding thread round.

Fry gently in a large pan in butter, turning all the time so that they are lightly browned all over. Pour off surplus butter, pour in the stock and simmer very gently for 15 minutes.

Lift the cucumbers on to a dish and keep warm, while you season and thicken the stock, adding tomato purée or fresh, strained tomato pulp if liked. Pour over the cucumbers and serve garnished with chopped parsley, capers and thin slices of lemon.

To Make a Delma (Dolmadis)
(Stuffed Vine or Cabbage Leaves)

Mrs Ann Blencowe's recipe of 1694.

This dish must have come originally from Greece or Turkey. It is an excellent recipe and it has been preserved for us by Mrs Anne Blencowe, née Wallis, daughter of a mathematician and cryptographer, and married at nineteen to the M.P. for Brackley, Northamptonshire. Her spelling was erratic even for her era but she was an accomplished housewife who kept a good table. Who brought this famous Greek dish to Northamptonshire in the late seventeenth century?

To serve 8 (about 24 rolls)

> 1½ pints (9 dl.) good well-flavoured stock of any kind – if necessary make up with a bouillon cube
> ½ lb. (240 g.) lean mutton, finely minced (the butcher will do this)
> ¼ lb. (120 g.) prepared suet
> ½ lb. (240 g.) cooked rice
> pinch of nutmeg
> 1 tablespoon finely chopped thyme, chives and parsley
> 2 shallots or a small onion, finely chopped
> 1 egg, well beaten (another may be needed)
> 24–30 fine tender vine leaves or inside cabbage leaves, carefully chosen

Mix all the ingredients but the stock and leaves well together and stir in the egg a little at a time to bind. The mixture must not be too wet to form into rolls, so a second egg should only be added if it seems dry.

Dip each leaf separately into boiling water for a second so that it becomes limp. Form the forcemeat into rolls about 2 inches long and 1 inch thick (5 by 2½ cm.) and roll each as neatly and completely as possible in a leaf. Tie round lightly with thread in two or three places. Lay the rolls neatly in a wide pan and pour over the stock; bring to the boil and simmer very gently for 30 minutes. Lift out the rolls and cut all the thread away. Keep warm while you slightly thicken the stock, check seasoning, pour over the rolls, and serve.

I have reduced the quantity of suet given by Mrs Blencowe to prevent any greasiness of texture (which was more acceptable in the seventeenth century than today).

Leeks and Cheese Sauce

For 4

> 8 leeks
> 2 oz. (60 g.) grated cheese
> 1 oz. (30 g.) butter
> ½ pint (3 dl.) cheese sauce
> 2 oz. (60 g.) breadcrumbs

Cut off roots and green tops and wash the leeks very carefully, removing all grit. Boil them gently until tender. When cooked, press well as they hold a good deal of water. Cut into small pieces. Butter a fireproof dish, pour in a little sauce, then lay in the chopped leeks and pour in the rest of the sauce. Sprinkle the top thickly with cheese and breadcrumbs and dot with butter.

Stand the dish in a tin with a little cold water in it, and bake for about 10 minutes in a hot oven, 450° F., gas mark 8.

Braised Leeks

For 4

8 leeks, or 12 if very small	salt, pepper
2 oz. (60 g.) butter	¼ pint (1½ dl.) stock

Wash the leeks well and cut them in half lengthwise, being careful to remove all grit. Butter a fireproof dish, arrange the leeks in it, season them with salt and pepper, and pour over the stock. Dot them with butter, cover tightly and bake in a hot oven, 400° F., gas mark 6, for 20 minutes. Uncover and allow to brown slightly for a further 5 minutes.

MARROWS

Marrows were grown in the sixteenth century, though they were probably not very common. By the beginning of the nineteenth century every walled kitchen garden had them sprawling on the remains of the manure heap in a warm corner, along with outdoor melons and cucumbers, and cottagers grew them outside their pig sties. Unfortunately, their food value is not high.

Braised Marrow with Sweet Herbs

Serves 4–6

    1 small marrow (allow 2 rings per person)
    1 oz. (30 g.) butter
    2 tablespoons finely chopped parsley
    2 tablespoons finely chopped thyme
    2 tablespoons finely chopped marjoram
    2 tablespoons finely chopped olives

Peel the marrow, remove the seeds, cut in half lengthways and cut each half in four. Butter a fireproof dish well. Lay the marrow in it, dust with pepper and salt and sprinkle thickly with the herbs. Put dabs of butter in each piece of marrow. Closely cover the dish with its lid or with foil. Bake in a moderate oven, 350° F., gas mark 4, for 25–30 minutes. Serve in the dish in which it was cooked.

Vegetable Marrow Duck

So called because the marrow lying whole on the dish, smothered in sauce, looks rather like the long shape of a duck and the sage and onion stuffing is much the same as that generally used for duck.

This is a very old recipe. There is a sixteenth-century version, and it occurs in various eighteenth- and nineteenth-century books and MSS. A different type of forcemeat with veal or other meat is sometimes given. One nineteenth-century MS has a note that the children do not like this wholesome dish. They must have complained very loudly (perhaps there were a round dozen of them), as children were rarely consulted as to what they disliked.

Serves 4-6

1 vegetable marrow about the size of a duck	¼ lb. (120 g.) breadcrumbs
2 large Spanish onions	2 oz. (60 g.) butter
6 leaves sage	1 egg
	pepper and salt

Peel the marrow, cut a slice off one end, and scoop out the seeds, being very careful not to break or pierce the flesh. Parboil the onions, chop them up, add to them the sage, very finely chopped, and the breadcrumbs, season with pepper and salt; add the egg, well beaten, and 1 oz. (30 g.) of melted butter. Mix well and fill the centre of the marrow with this mixture, then put the end on again and tie round with tape. Put the marrow on a baking tin, and pour remaining butter all over. Bake in a moderate oven, 350° F., gas mark 4, till tender, about 40 minutes. Serve with white sauce or cheese or tomato sauce.

Stuffed Marrow Rings

(allow 2 rings per person)
    1 small marrow
    salt and pepper
    2 heaped tablespoons grated cheese
    forcemeat

Peel the marrow and cut into eight rings. Remove seeds by cutting out centres. Put the slices in a steamer, sprinkle with salt and steam over boiling water for barely 19 minutes.

Well drain the rings and arrange on a buttered fireproof dish or individual dishes. Pile the hot forcemeat into the centre of each ring, sprinkle with cheese and put under the grill for a few minutes to brown. They may be kept hot for half an hour or so in cool oven or warming drawer.

The Forcemeat

The following is a good vegetarian filling but any minced meat, chicken or game mixture is very good.

    2 oz. (60 g.) butter
    1 onion finely chopped
    2 oz. (60 g.) mushrooms, finely chopped
    2 tomatoes, skinned and cut up
    ¼ lb. (120 g.) cooked rice or breadcrumbs
    seasoning
    1 dessertspoon chopped parsley

Melt the butter in a saucepan. Stir in the onion, mushrooms and tomatoes and fry till just cooked. Add the rice or crumbs, seasoning and parsley. Mix well and keep hot.

Mushroom Circles

This recipe comes from a Welsh farm. It is very good served with gammon rashers or, using smaller mushrooms and croûtons, as a savoury.

    2 fairly large, flat mushrooms per person
    2 thick slices bread per person, cut into rounds with a cutter,
      approximately to fit each mushroom
    a little French mustard
    2 oz. (60 g.) butter

Fry the mushrooms in butter very gently, until tender. Keep hot. Butter the bread on one side and spread mustard thinly over the butter. Fry it on the plain side only in the pan in which mushrooms cooked, so that the bottom is crisp and the mustard and butter on the soft top have soaked in a little. Place a mushroom on each croûton and serve very hot.

Mushrooms in Cream

A nineteenth-century recipe from Somerset.

Serves 6

¾ lb. (360 g.) mushrooms	salt and pepper
2 oz. (60 g.) butter	¼ pint (1½ dl.) milk
2 oz. (60 g.) flour	¼ pint (1½ dl.) double cream

Wash, dry and slice the mushrooms. Allow them to simmer in butter for 5 minutes. Sprinkle them with flour, stir, and cook for 2 minutes more. Season with salt and pepper, then add the milk, heated, and simmer for 3 minutes more. Stir in the cream. Reheat well and serve with croûtons of fried bread.

Scalloped Mushrooms

A Wiltshire recipe.

For 4

      1–1½ lb. (½–¾ k.) mushrooms (field mushrooms are good for this)
      6 oz. (180 g.) breadcrumbs
      2 oz. (60 g.) butter
      salt and pepper

Slice the mushrooms and arrange a layer in a very thickly buttered fireproof dish. Season well. Put a layer of crumbs and repeat layers alternately, ending with a layer of crumbs. Dot each crumb layer with butter, and put plenty on the top. Cook in a moderate oven, 350° F., gas mark 4, for 30–35 minutes. Make sure the mushrooms are tender, and brown the top under a hot grill if necessary.

Strips of cooked bacon may be added to each layer if liked and the dish served as a supper dish. Or it is very good as an accompaniment to a grill of sausages, kidneys and bacon.

ONIONS, ROAST AND STUFFED

Both these are traditional farmhouse recipes, very good for lunch on a cold winter's day.

Parsley was thought to take the smell of onion from the breath and a bowl of it, finely chopped, was sometimes passed round in grander houses after the onions were eaten.

Roast Onions

      1 large onion per person
      1 oz. (30 g.) butter per onion
      a little flour and salt

Choose large onions, Spanish are the best. Peel and cut off the roots and tops. Arrange them in a baking tray, which has been well greased with butter. Dredge with flour and salt. Put a piece of butter on top of each onion and bake in a moderate oven, 350° F., gas mark 4, for 1–1½ hours until soft and tender. Baste fairly frequently.

Stuffed Roast Onions

 1 large onion per person
 1–2 oz. (30–60 g.) minced meat, game or poultry, or any forcemeat, per onion
 chopped sage, thyme and parsley
 a little flour and salt and pepper
 about 1 oz. (30 g.) butter per onion

Choose very large onions, preferably Spanish. Prepare as above and parboil for 15 minutes. Drain well. Scoop out with a pointed knife a good deal of the inside. Fill the cavity with any mixture of minced meat, game or poultry or any good forcemeat. Season the onions and sprinkle with a very little chopped sage, thyme and parsley. Roast exactly as in previous recipe, but as they are partly cooked they will need only 40–45 minutes.

 Serve with tomato sauce or a good brown gravy, plain boiled rice and green peas.

Creamed Parsnips and Cheese

Parsnips played a much more considerable part in sixteenth- and seventeenth-century cooking than they do in modern recipes because of their sweet taste. This is often disliked in our own times but in the past there was no objection to mixing sweet and savoury in the same dish. They were also liked when potatoes were hardly used because they roast and mash easily and make a fine smooth purée.

 This eighteenth-century recipe is excellent with hot home-cooked ham.

Serves 6
 2 lb. (1 k.) parsnips
 2 oz. (60 g.) butter
 2 tablespoons double cream
 salt, pepper and a pinch of dry mustard
 3 oz. (90 g.) grated cheese
 2 tablespoons fine breadcrumbs

Peel and boil the parsnips until tender, then mash them until quite free from lumps. Beat into them half the butter, and the cream, also a good seasoning of salt, pepper and dry mustard. Butter a fireproof dish, put in half the mashed parsnips and sprinkle with grated cheese. Add the remaining parsnips and cheese, cover with fine breadcrumbs, put small pieces of butter on the top, and bake until brown in a fairly hot oven, 400° F., gas mark 6.

Green Peas with Cream

This is Mrs Glasse's excellent recipe, and it needs no modification except that if the peas are young 15–20 minutes stewing is enough.

Quantities for 6 would be
1½ lb. (¾ k.) shelled green peas
2 oz. (60 g.) butter
1 oz. (30 g.) flour
a pinch of powdered nutmeg
½ oz. (15 g.) sugar
1 tablespoon finely chopped parsley (mint may be substituted for parsley if the flavour is preferred)
¼ pint (1½ dl.) double cream

'Take a quart of fine green peas, put them in a stewpan with a piece of butter as big as an egg, rolled in a little flour, season them with salt and nutmeg, a bit of sugar as big as a nutmeg, a little bundle of sweet herbs, some parsley chopped fine, a quarter of a pint [1½ dl.] of boiling water. Cover them close, and let them stew very softly half an hour, then pour on a quarter of a pint of good cream. Give it one boil and serve it up for a side plate.'

Grandmother's Peas with Bacon

A Cornish recipe of the early nineteenth century.

For 4
2 lb. (1 k.) peas
4 rashers lean bacon cut in fine strips
2 oz. (60 g.) butter
2 medium onions or 4 shallots, chopped finely
3 or 4 lettuce leaves
salt
sugar
a little chopped mint and parsley

Shell the peas. Fry the bacon in butter in a saucepan. Add the chopped onion and fry another minute. Do not allow the butter to colour or the onions to brown. Put in the peas and shake so that they are coated with the butter. Add 1 teaspoonful sugar and 1 of salt. Put in the lettuce leaves. Add ¼ pint (1½ dl.) of boiling water. Cover closely and cook for 15 minutes, stirring from time to time. Add a little more water if it is all absorbed. When the peas are tender serve without draining, sprinkled with chopped mint and parsley.

Summer Peas

An eighteenth-century Somerset recipe. It was served in bowls as a separate course.

For 4–6

> 1½ lb. (¾ k.) (after shelling) small young peas
> 2 oz. (60 g.) butter
> 12 spring onions
> salt and pepper
> sugar
> 12 lettuce leaves (not outside leaves, but need not be hearts)
> 2 sprigs of parsley and 2 sprigs of mint, finely chopped
> 1 tablespoon mint and parsley chopped together

Shell and place the peas in a saucepan with the butter and toss them a little. Add the shredded lettuce leaves, spring onions, sprigs of parsley and mint and ½ pint (3 dl.) of water. Season with salt, pepper and a pinch of sugar. Cook gently for about 15 minutes until tender. Serve sprinkled with chopped parsley and mint and without draining, as the liquid which the peas have not absorbed has become a delicious thin sauce.

Excellent as a starting course for a summer dinner.

Almond Potatoes

For 4

> 2 lb. (1 k.) potatoes
> 3 oz. (90 g.) grated cheese
> salt and pepper
> 2 oz. (60 g.) chopped blanched
>   almonds

> a little butter
> 1 egg
> ½ pint (3 dl.) milk

Peel and slice the potatoes finely and sprinkle them with salt and pepper.

Take a rather flat fireproof dish, butter it well and place a thin layer of sliced potatoes in it. Sprinkle with grated cheese, then cover with another layer of potatoes sprinkled with cheese, and continue in alternate layers until the casserole is full. Mix the beaten egg with the milk and pour this mixture over the potatoes. Sprinkle with a few nuts of butter, cover tightly and cook in a moderate oven, 350° F., gas mark 4, for 40 minutes. Sprinkle the top with the almonds and brown for 2 minutes under a fairly hot grill. Watch all the time, as almonds blacken very quickly.

An Elegant Mould of Potatoes

From an anonymous nineteenth-century MS. in the Macadam collection, Edinburgh.

For 4

    2 lb. (1 k.) new potatoes   seasoning
    8 oz. (240 g.) butter

Wash and scrape the potatoes, slice into thin, even slices. Butter a round mould or a soufflé dish well. Put a layer of potatoes at the bottom, placing them evenly. Season with pepper and salt. Melt the rest of the butter and pour a little over the layer of potatoes. Then add another layer of potatoes, butter and seasoning, and continue until the mould is nearly full. Put the mould into a hot oven, 425° F., gas mark 7, and bake for 1 hour. Then turn mould upside down on a plate, leave for a moment to let excess butter run out, remove mould and the potatoes will be light brown and hold the shape of the mould.

The Duchess's Potatoes

For 6

    2 lb. (1 k.) potatoes   ¼ pint (1½ dl.) milk
    2 oz. (60 g.) butter   2 eggs

Peel and boil the potatoes. Drain and put through a fine moulin or blender. Put the butter and milk into a saucepan and heat, add the sieved potato and stir it until it is hot and creamy. Remove from the heat, add the beaten eggs and beat or blend well. Butter a flat oven tray well; place the potato mixture on the tray in tablespoonfuls, working each up to a high point. Put into a moderate oven, 350° F., gas mark 4, for 20 minutes or until the separate shapes are golden brown and beginning to crisp.

Scalloped Potatoes

For 4

2 lb. (1 k.) potatoes	¼ pint (1½ dl.) milk
pepper and salt	2 oz. (60 g.) butter

Peel and thinly slice the potatoes. Butter a shallow fireproof dish and fill with the neat slices and sprinkle over a little pepper and salt. Fill up with milk so that the potatoes are not quite covered. Dot with plenty of butter, cover with foil, and place in moderate oven, 350° F., gas mark 4, for 35 minutes. Remove foil and brown on top for a further 10 minutes, or place briefly under a hot grill.

Stuffed Baked Potatoes

For 4

4 large potatoes	2 oz. (60 g.) butter
4 oz. (120 g.) minced lean ham	salt and pepper
or 4 oz. (120 g.) grated cheese	breadcrumbs
1 tablespoon finely chopped parsley	grated cheese

One large potato for each person, well scrubbed but not peeled. Make a little hole in each to let out the air. Bake them on the middle shelf of the oven at 400° F., gas mark 6, for about 45 minutes or till soft when pressed.

Take them out and allow to cool enough to handle. Cut in half long ways and scoop out all the inside into a bowl without breaking the skins. Mash the potato in bowl and add about ½ oz. (15 g.) butter and a teaspoon of finely chopped parsley for each potato, and 4 oz. (120 g.) of grated cheese or finely minced lean ham. Mix well and season. Replace in the halved potato skins and smooth the tops over. Sprinkle with crumbs and grated cheese and dot with butter. Bake for 10 minutes to reheat and brown the tops under a hot grill. Serve with green salad and French dressing. They can be kept hot or reheated 10 minutes or so before they are wanted.

SALSIFY

Salsify used to be known as the 'vegetable oyster' or 'oyster plant'. It was regarded as a great delicacy, particularly appreciated because it is eaten in winter. It was frequently served with a rich cream sauce at Edwardian dinners, but nowadays does not find a place in many kitchen gardens and is available only at rather grand greengrocers. The roots must be scrubbed, scraped and cut into neat pieces, each being dropped into water in which the juice of a lemon has been squeezed. More lemon juice should be added to the water in which it boils, as it very easily blackens.

Fried Salsify

For 4

1 lb. (½ k.) salsify	2 or 3 oz. (60–90 g.) butter
¼ pint (1½ dl.) coating batter	

Boil the salsify in salted water with lemon juice (about 20 minutes) until tender and leave it until cold. Cut in pieces of a convenient size, dry them. Dip each piece in batter and fry a golden brown in boiling fat.

Salsify au Gratin

For 4

1 lb. (½ k.) salsify	2 oz. (60 g.) grated cheese
½ pint (3 dl.) white sauce	2 oz. (60 g.) breadcrumbs
1 oz. (30 g.) butter or margarine	

Cook the salsify as above until tender (about 20 minutes). Drain well. Lay in a buttered fireproof dish, pour the hot white sauce over. Cover with crumbs and grated cheese. Dot with dabs of butter. Brown under hot grill and serve.

Salsify in Cream

This is the best and simplest recipe of all.

For 4

1 lb. (½ k.) salsify	salt and coarse black pepper
2 oz. (60 g.) butter	½ pint (3 dl.) double cream

Toss the tender, boiled salsify in butter for 2 minutes. Shake some coarse black pepper over it and pour in the cream. Shake and stir for a further 2 minutes and spoon into warmed, individual dishes and serve at once.

Seakale

Seakale is described in *Gerard's Herbal* in 1597. He writes: 'The sea colewert groweth naturally upon the bayche and brissies of the sea, where there is no earth to be seene, but sand and rowling pebble stones. I have found it growing between Whytstable and the Isle of Thanet neere the brincke of the sea and in many places neere Colchester and elsewhere by the sea-side.'

Cut off the root and open up the seakale; wash very well in plenty of running water to remove sand and grit. Tie in even-sized bundles and place in boiling salted water with the juice of a lemon squeezed in to keep the colour. Boil for 20 minutes. Drain and place in hot dish. Serve with melted butter and white sauce.

Spinach and Eggs

From an unpublished manuscript in the Edinburgh collection.

Serves 6

3 lb. (1½ k.) leaf spinach	½ pint (3 dl.) milk
3 oz. (90 g.) butter	4 hard-boiled eggs
3 oz. (90 g.) flour	18 triangular croûtons of
6 oz. (180 g.) grated cheese	puff pastry

This dish makes a good main course for lunch or supper served with croûtons of puff pastry, but it is also particularly good served with any kind of cold meat.

Frozen spinach may be used, allowing one large packet for two people. Cook the spinach, well washed, without added water, for 10 minutes, stirring occasionally and adding a teaspoonful of salt when it is nearly done. Put it through first a coarse and then a fine sieve or moulin. Make a roux of the butter and flour in a saucepan, gradually add half of the grated cheese, and then the milk, stirring well until a thick cheese sauce is formed. Stir the spinach purée into this sauce, and cook gently until it is really hot. Pour the mixture into a large buttered fireproof dish. Cut the hard-boiled eggs into eighths longways, and arrange them around the edge of the spinach mixture. Cover the whole dish, including the eggs, with the remaining grated cheese, scatter with nuts of butter and put it under a very hot grill until the cheese has melted and just begun to brown. Stick the croûtons in by one corner round the edge of the dish. Serve as soon as possible.

TOMATOES

The tomato was introduced into England from the Americas early in the seventeenth century. It was for a time grown mainly for decoration and known as the love apple, it was thought to be highly aphrodisiac. In the eighteenth century there were various recipes for 'tomata' or 'love apple' sauces, but it was not until the mid nineteenth century that it became popular and not until our own century that it came into common use. During the Second World War it naturally disappeared from the shops and on its reappearance in the forties its refreshing taste and brilliant colour cheered the dull, rationed food of Britain and ensured its now enormous popularity.

Tomatoes Gratinée

For 4

1 lb. (½ k.) tomatoes	1 oz. (30 g.) butter
2 oz. (60 g.) grated cheese	2 oz. (60 g.) breadcrumbs
salt, pepper, sugar	

Blanch the tomatoes, slice them, and place in a well-buttered fireproof dish, sprinkle with salt, pepper and a little sugar, cover the top with breadcrumbs and sprinkle with grated cheese. Cook in a moderate oven, 350° F., gas mark 4, for 20 minutes, then brown the top quickly under a hot grill just before serving.

For a *Tomato Charlotte* use 3 oz. (90 g.) breadcrumbs, 3 oz. (90 g.) cheese and 2 oz. (60 g.) butter, and arrange in layers with the tomatoes, finishing with crumbs and cheese as above.

Surprise Tomatoes

Serves 4

4 very large firm tomatoes	2 oz. (60 g.) mushrooms,
4 eggs	chopped finely
salt and pepper	*or* 2 oz. (60 g.) shrimps
butter	2 oz. (60 g.) butter
a little parsley	

Wash and then cut a slice off the top of each tomato and scoop out the inside. Be careful not to break the skin anywhere. Sprinkle the inside of the tomato with salt and pepper. Break an egg into each, top each egg with a sprinkling of parsley, some mushrooms or shrimps, and two or three dabs of butter. Replace the top slices of the tomatoes and stand them in a thickly-buttered fireproof dish and bake for 10–15 minutes at 350° F., gas mark 4. Spoon the

371

butter and juice from the dish over the tomatoes at least three times during cooking and add a little more butter if necessary. The eggs should be soft and the tomatoes just wrinkled when served.

Stuffed Tomatoes

4–6 very large firm tomatoes	breadcrumbs
salt	2 oz. (60 g.) butter
forcemeat	

Cut off the tops of the tomatoes and discard. Remove the pulp and seeds and fill with the forcemeat, being very careful not to break the skins. Sprinkle the tops with breadcrumbs and dot with butter.

Place in a buttered oven dish and bake in a moderate oven, 375° F., gas mark 4, for 20–25 minutes.

For forcemeat for 4–6 tomatoes:
¼ lb. (120 g.) minced cooked meat, ham, chicken or a mixture
¼ lb. (120 g.) breadcrumbs
2 oz. (60 g.) mushrooms, finely chopped and sauté
2 teaspoons finely chopped onion, lightly sauté with the mushrooms
a little tomato purée
salt and pepper
a little paprika
1 oz. (30 g.) currants, well washed

Mix all the ingredients well together with the tomato purée. Season highly and fill the tomatoes.

Serve with creamed potato or plain boiled rice and green peas or a green salad.

Turnips au Gratin

For 4–6

12 young turnips	2 oz. (60 g.) grated cheese
3 oz. (90 g.) butter	salt and pepper
1 oz. (30 g.) flour	2 tablespoons breadcrumbs
½ pint (3 dl.) milk	

Peel the turnips and boil them for about 25 minutes or until tender. Cut them in slices and put them in a buttered dish. Make a cheese sauce with 2 oz.

(60 g.) of the butter, the cheese, flour and milk (see p. 283). Pour this over the turnips, cover with breadcrumbs, dot with remaining butter and bake in a moderate oven, 400° F., gas mark 6, until the top is brown and crisp.

Turnips with Oranges

For 4–6

> 12 young turnips
> juice of 2 oranges and the rind of 1, finely grated
> 2 oz. (60 g.) butter
> salt and coarsely ground black pepper

Stew the peeled turnips in the orange juice mixed with enough water to cover them. Add half a teaspoon of salt. When tender (about 25 minutes), drain and put them whole in a buttered dish. Put a dab of butter on each and sprinkle all over with the grated orange peel and some coarse black pepper. Put under a hot grill for 2 minutes to melt the butter and slightly crisp and dry the orange peel and the tops of the turnips.

They are particularly good with duck or pork.

Vegetable Pie

For 6

> ½ lb. (240 g.) puff pastry
> 1 large cauliflower
> 12 small onions or shallots
> 2 oz. (60 g.) flour
> a little curry powder
>
> 4 hard-boiled eggs
> peas, broad beans or french beans
> young carrots thinly sliced
> 4 oz. (120 g.) butter

Break the cauliflower into flowerets, and put a layer in a pie dish. Add some of the small onions or shallots, peeled and rolled in flour mixed with curry powder, and any other young vegetables available. Arrange the vegetables in layers with the quartered hard-boiled eggs and 3–4 oz. butter. Put on a pastry lid. Bake for 20 minutes at 400° F., gas mark 6, and then for a further 20–30 minutes at 300° F., gas mark 2.

Creamed Spring Vegetables

For 4

> 6 small young carrots, cut in rings

> 12 very small new potatoes
> 12 small spring onions, cut in rings
> 2 oz. (60 g.) butter
> bouquet of thyme, parsley and mint
> 1 tablespoon flour
> salt
> 1 teaspoon caster sugar
> ¾ pint (4½ dl.) of white stock (or stock up make to ¾ pint with a glass
> or two of white wine)
> heart of 1 medium-sized lettuce
> 1 lb. (½ k.) shelled young peas
> ¼ pint (1½ dl.) double cream

Just melt the butter and toss all the vegetables except the peas and the lettuce in it together with the bouquet. Stir in the flour very gently. Add the stock and white wine and sugar. Cover and simmer for 10 minutes. Add the heart of the washed lettuce cut into strips and the peas, and simmer for another 10 minutes or till all the vegetables are tender. Remove from heat and stir in the cream. The sauce should be only a little thinner than the cream.

Serve as a separate course with croûtons or as an accompaniment to chicken, sole, veal, or any delicate meat or fish.

Salads

Salads, which are sometimes thought only to have been seriously appreciated in recent times and to have owed much of their popularity to America, were in fact longed for by our ancestors through the hard winters of salt meat, bread and sparse roots. The first shoots of a wide variety of herbs, wild and cultivated, were eagerly awaited, and a far wider variety of leaves, roots, buds, flowers and shoots were used than we ever consider today. Indeed, in the sixteenth and seventeenth centuries the salads were considered most important 'at great Feasts and upon Princes' Tables', as Gervase Markham points out, and he devotes a full section of his treatise on cookery to the making of them.

Some 'Sallets', he says, 'be simple, some compounded, some only to furnish at the Table and some both for use and adornation; your simple sallets are Chibols [spring onions], peeled, washed clean and half the green tops cut away and so served on a fruit dish, or Chives, Scallions [shallots] Rhadish roots, boyled Carrots, Skirrets [water parsnips] and Turnips . . . also all young lettuce, Cabbage-lettuce, Purslane and divers other herbs which may be served simply without anything but a little vinegar, sallet oil and sugar; onions boiled and stripped from their rind and served up with vinegar, oil and pepper, is a good simple sallet; so is Camphire . . . Bean-cods [whole young broad beans] Sparagus and Cucumbers . . . with a world of others too tedious to nominate.' Compound salads were often extremely elaborate. An 'excellent Sallet' described by Markham as fit for a Prince's Table contains:

blanched and shredded almonds	spinach
raisins of the sun	oranges and lemons in
dried figs, shredded	thin slices
capers	red colewort
olives, black and green	pickled cucumbers
currants	hearts of lettuce
red sage leaves	

These are all very carefully ordered in layers of different colours and dressed with oil, vinegar and sugar. Salamagundy, for which I give several recipes, was an elaborate compound salad, very popular for more than two hundred years because it was not only good to eat but extremely ornamental. Markham instances as a 'compound boiled sallet' spinach which is first boiled in water, finely chopped and well drained and then sauté in butter, mixed with about half its quantity of washed currants, seasoned with vinegar to make it 'reasonable tart' and then with sugar 'according to the taste of the Master of the house' and then served on sippets of toast. This does not seem promising in either taste or appearance.

Salads made mainly for show were made from pickled and preserved roots, fruits, flowers and leaves, which were cut and arranged on dishes in the shape of roses, houses, trees and so on. Naturally, these were to be eaten as well as admired, but others, made from carrots, turnips and other vegetables dyed to various colours and carefully cut into elaborate knots, scutcheons, heraldic birds and beasts, were entirely for show, though Markham speaks of them as being seasoned with vinegar, oil and pepper.

Joan (christened Elizabeth), the wife of Oliver Cromwell, served at her table a Grand Salad which consisted of equal parts of almonds, raisins, capers, pickled cucumbers, shrimps and boiled turnips, a conglomeration which does not sound attractive.

American salads which combine fruit with lettuce, cheese and ham, are much nearer to the English 'compound' salads of the seventeenth and eighteenth centuries than is generally realized. Most of the grandest salads of the seventeenth century contained thinly sliced oranges and lemons as well as raisins and nuts, usually almonds, but walnuts were used occasionally. Pickles of all kinds, particularly gherkins, were used too.

Salad dressings were much as a good 'French' dressing is made today. In 1699 *Evelyn's Acetaria*, a discourse on salads, was published, and in it seventy-two salad herbs and vegetables were listed. Evelyn gives a recipe for the dressing referred to as *oxoleon*: ¼ pint olive oil; 1 tablespoon of vinegar or lemon juice (Evelyn also suggests orange as an alternative but it is not sharp enough); a few slices of horseradish to marinate in this mixture for a time with a little salt and pepper (a dessertspoon dried horseradish can be used and strained out); as much mustard as will lie on a half-crown piece; all to be beaten with the yolks of 2 hard-boiled eggs. This is an excellent dressing and will keep for two or three weeks in the refrigerator.

For all other dressings and for mayonnaise, see pp. 304–307.

Salads were in general intended as dishes in themselves and, unless they were 'simple sallets', i.e. a single vegetable, raw or boiled, they frequently contained meat, chicken or fish. The idea of a salad as an accompaniment to a separate dish of meat or fish is comparatively recent. No doubt at a table on which a whole 'course' of dishes was arranged at one time, the guests helped themselves from pretty little side dishes of salad and ate them with other meats on a trencher or platter.

It is pointless here to give recipes for green and 'mixed' salads. These depend on very good fresh ingredients (and our lettuces today are far better than any our ancestors grew) or a good dressing. The point that needs making today is that a good salad, no matter what it is made of, or how many ingredients, cooked or raw, it contains, needs a sprinkling of finely chopped herbs, mixed according to taste, or what is available. Of course, fresh herbs are really needed, but dried are better than none. Most greengrocers sell a few, and many grow well in pots on windowsills.

If you live in the country or visit it in spring, it is worth picking very young dandelion leaves and sorrel leaves to add to a salad. If you can, grow a plant or two of the true French sorrel, for the large leaves are both tenderer and sharper than the wild variety, except when this is just springing in April and May. The sharpness of sorrel is delicious with lettuce. Never be afraid of garlic in salad unless you definitely dislike it. Rub the inside of a large bowl with a peeled clove before mixing a green salad in it. Any of the salad recipes given here may have a little garlic added with advantage, but it should be a suspicion only unless it is specifically included in the recipe.

Raisins and currants are excellent added to a watercress and orange salad or a mixed green salad, but should always be soaked for a short time first.

Four Salads: White, Red, Black and Yellow

An anonymous household book of the early nineteenth century suggests four salads, each of a separate colour, set out at the four corners of a table or in a line down the centre. Each salad should be arranged on a green ground of lettuce, watercress, or other green salad vegetables sprinkled with parsley and finely chopped chives and thyme, and this ground, as well as the coloured ingredients, should be lightly dressed with a French dressing.

White Salad   blanched almonds
finely chopped celery
chicory
young boiled turnips cut in fine strips
if possible boiled seakale
white-fleshed eating apples, peeled, sliced and dipped in lemon
    juice to keep colour
chopped white of eggs

Red Salad   cooked carrots, cut in matchsticks, rosettes or fine rings
cooked beetroot in strips or dice
sliced peeled tomatoes
finely sliced or grated red cabbage
red sage, finely chopped and sprinkled over

Yellow Salad finely sliced oranges
finely sliced grapefruit
cooked young swede or parsnips, diced or cut in matchsticks
marigold petals or cowslip flowers sprinkled over
chopped egg yolks

Black Salad mushrooms, lightly sauté
stoned black olives
prunes, soaked, stoned and cut in halves
currants, soaked

Salads in Aspic

These were often served to accompany cold joints or game at Victorian summer luncheons. They are very ornamental and make a good starting course, served on a bed of lettuce on individual plates.

For 6

> 2 pints of aspic jelly
> ¼ lb. (120 g.) cooked green peas
> ¼ lb. (120 g.) cooked young carrots, cut in fine rings
> 2 oz. (60 g.) cooked sweetcorn
> ¼ lb. (120 g.) prawns or diced chicken
> 2 hard-boiled eggs
> 1 crisp lettuce
> French dressing
> 2 tablespoons mayonnaise in which a tablespoon of heavy cream has been mixed

The aspic jelly may be made from 2 packets, using half water and half dry white wine. Season it highly.

In six moulds or small soufflé dishes, put a slice of hard-boiled egg and 2 prawns. Pour on a little cooked but liquid jelly and leave to set enough to hold in place the egg and prawns. Then mix the peas, carrots and sweetcorn, half fill each mould and pour on jelly, not quite to cover. Allow to set, and then arrange the rest of the egg, the prawns and on them the vegetables. Fill up the moulds with jelly and chill in refrigerator. Turn out and serve on crisp lettuce which has been lightly dressed. Put a spoonful of the mayonnaise (which should be fairly stiff) on top of each jelly.

A 'Boiled Salad' of 1840

This grand salad is particularly good served with home-cooked ham or gammon.

> boiled onions, beetroot, cauliflower or broccoli heads, celery, french beans
> 2 oz. (60 g.) currants, soaked for half an hour or so in cold water
> 1 crisp lettuce
> 2 teaspoons chopped parsley
> 1 teaspoon finely chopped mixture of thyme, marjoram, chives, tarragon – any or all of them
> a good oil and vinegar dressing

Take a small quantity of all of the vegetables or 3 or 4 of them and cook them separately, using little water and plenty of salt and being careful not to overcook them. Drain well and allow to get cold. Cut and divide all the cooked vegetables into neat pieces. Arrange half the lettuce on the bottom of a very large flat dish and pour over a little of the dressing. Pile all the cooked vegetables on it, but put the beetroot in four separate heaps around the central pile as it stains the cauliflower. Pour over some more dressing. Arrange the remaining lettuce round the edge of the dish and pour on remainder of the dressing. Drain the currants and sprinkle all over and then sprinkle the parsley and mixed herbs. The currants are important as they give just a touch of sweetness.

Chicken Salad

A Victorian recipe; this looks very fine indeed when arranged and is extremely good as a cold main dish.

Serves 8

> a large crisp lettuce with well-rounded leaves
> ½ lb. (240 g.) potato salad (see p. 384)
> all the meat of a 2½–3 lb. (1–1½ k.) cooked chicken, diced with 8 slices of breast saved
> 3 fl. oz. (1 dl.) double cream
> 2 bunches of watercress
> French dressing
> a touch of garlic
> 1 tablespoon finely chopped parsley and chives
> 2 oz. (60 g.) blanched and shredded almonds
> ½ lb. (240 g.) cooked green peas, well minted
> salt and pepper

Choose eight large deeply rounded leaves from the lettuce. They must be firm and crisp, so do not take them from too near the outside.

Put a spoonful of potato salad in each leaf. Mix the chicken with the cream and season highly. Put a spoonful on top of the potato salad. Place the filled leaves on a bed of watercress dressed with a French dressing to which a suspicion of garlic has been added on a flat round dish which has been sprinkled with parsley and chives. Arrange the leaves to form a large flower on the dark green watercress. In each leaf stick a slice of chicken breast at the end near the centre, leaning inwards to form the cone-shaped middle of the

379

flower. Sprinkle each leaf with shredded almonds. Put little heaps of green peas between the outer ends of the leaves.

A Fine Salad

An eighteenth-century recipe.

For 4

1½ lb. (¾ k.) cooked asparagus	1 clove of garlic
2 large or 4 small artichoke bottoms, cooked	French dressing
1 very crisp lettuce	3 dozen cubes of bread fried crisp

Rub a large plate with the garlic and put the cubes of fried bread on it. Leave at least half an hour.

Put the lettuce in a very large, fairly shallow bowl and dress. Dice the artichoke bottoms, dress them lightly, mix them with the bread cubes and pour among the lettuce. Cut off any inedible stem from the asparagus, shortening it uniformly to about 4 inches (10 cm.), take four or five together and stand the little sheaves among the lettuce. Pour over any remaining French dressing. The fried bread will have taken up just the right amount of garlic.

A Grand Cabbage Salad

This is a seventeenth-century recipe and is very good as a starting course. It comes from a Scottish MS., where it was proposed as a side dish.

Serves 6

about 2 lb. (1 k.) hard white salad cabbage coarsely grated
1 medium onion very finely chopped
24 anchovy fillets, each cut in 2 (*or* herring fillets may be used)
1 tablespoon finely chopped parsley
2 teaspoons finely chopped chives (if possible)
a very little thyme fresh or fried, finely chopped
3 hard-boiled eggs, cut in slices
¼ pint (1½ dl.) mayonnaise in which 1 teaspoon of freshly made mustard has been mixed

Mix the cabbage, onion, half the parsley, the chives and the thyme and lightly mix the mustard mayonnaise into them. Pile on to six small plates and arrange the anchovy or herring fillets and the sliced eggs over the mounds. Sprinkle each salad with the remaining parsley.

A 'Simple Salad' of Celery

A nineteenth-century recipe. Very good as a starting course piled on separate plates with a hard-boiled egg cut in quarters on each pile.

Serves 6
>1 lb. (½ k.) prepared celery *or* celeriac
>2 teaspoons mustard
>½ teaspoon sugar
>salt and pepper
>about ¼ pint (1½ dl.) olive oil
>1 egg yolk
>a few drops of wine or tarragon vinegar
>lemon juice
>2 tablespoons cream
>2 tablespoons finely chopped parsley

Use only the best parts of the celery, trimmed and well washed with all the strings removed. Peel and very finely shred into matchsticks or coarsely grate it. Mix a tablespoon of lemon juice with the celery to keep it white. Place the mustard, sugar, salt and pepper in a basin, and whisk or blend vigorously while adding the olive oil. When the sauce begins to thicken add the egg yolk and continue whisking. Finally, mix in the vinegar, and when this is well amalgamated stir in the cream. Stir this into the celery, and allow it to stand for 1 hour before serving. Garnish with chopped parsley.

A Fourteenth Century Recipe for a Green Salad

Take Psel, Sawge, garles, chiboli, oynons, leek, borage, mynt poneet, fenel, and ton tresses, rew, rosemarye, purslayne, lave, and waishe them we clene, pike him, pluk he small wipe thine hand and myng hem wel with rawe oile, lay on vynegar, and salt and serve it.

Translated in terms of the herbs and vegetables we know and which are easily available, it is delicious (though suitable only for someone with a herb garden), as long as everything is 'pluked small', or finely chopped, as some of the herbs tend to be rather hard in texture.

½ handful of young sage leaves	2 or 3 sprigs of fennel
1 handful of chives	2 or 3 leaves of rue
1 dozen spring onions	1 dessertspoon young rosemary
2 leeks	leaves pulled from the stems
2 leaves of borage	1 handful of parsley
1 tablespoon mint	2 handfuls of watercress

Chop all this very small. A herb may be omitted here and there and another substituted. Use a little wine vinegar, plenty of oil, a teaspoon of sugar and one of salt and a good shake of fresh black pepper for the dressing. Mix very well. The resulting herb salad is very strong, aromatic and slightly bitter, but if mixed with a crisp lettuce, of which all but the larger leaves are left whole, it is very much to our taste today and, eaten with ham, cold salt beef or a fine game pie, it is delicious.

Lobster Salad

'A lobster salad is not a great dish but it is very particular. It wants only the simplest crispest green to set off the lobster and the mayonnaise. I will not have cucumber or parsley added as some do. I prefer to see lettuce only or at most with a few sprigs of watercress picked fresh from our stream. Tomato is anathema in this salad both for its flavour and its colour which takes off from that of the lobster. I like some hard boiled eggs and do not mind a little tarragon: it is a dish suitable for luncheon.' From the family papers of Lady Pipon, writing from Cornwall to advise her daughter on her housekeeping in London in 1890.

Her recipe:

For 4–6

1 large lobster, all meat removed and coral saved
2 large crisp lettuces (Iceberg or Webbs are best)
3 hard-boiled eggs
a bunch of good watercress
a few sprigs of fresh tarragon
¼ pint (1½ dl.) good mayonnaise
4 tablespoons French dressing
salt and pepper

Arrange the best of the lettuce, lightly broken up, in a pile in a large glass dish and dress with the French dressing. Reserve one lettuce heart. Dice all the meat from the lobster claws. Season lightly and arrange this up the sides of the piled lettuce. Chop finely the rest of the lobster meat and mix it with the coral and the mayonnaise and place on top of the mound of lettuce. Slice the hard-boiled eggs and arrange up the sides of the lettuce. Cut the reserved lettuce heart into 8 thin slices without letting it fall apart. Pour French dressing over them and put them round the lobster in the bowl. Chop the tarragon finely if you are using it and sprinkle all over.

Macedon of Spring Vegetables

¼ pint (1½ dl.) cooked green peas
¼ lb. (120 g.) each boiled young carrots and turnips
½ lb. (240 g.) cooked new potatoes
2 tablespoons mayonnaise
1 tablespoon double cream
2 teaspoons chopped chives
2 teaspoons chopped parsley

Cut the carrots, turnips and potatoes into small cubes. Mix them with the peas, toss in mayonnaise to which the cream has been added, sprinkle with the chives and parsley.

Frozen mixed vegetables make quite a good (but not so good) macedon, particularly if some sweetcorn is included or added: in the late sixteenth century this last combination was known as 'turkey wheat', though Gerard says that it came to Europe via Spain from the Americas and not from Turkey.

Mushroom Salad

A delicious starting course. A few shrimps or prawns may be laid on top of the mushrooms, but they are very good without.

Serves 6

1 lb. (½ k.) button mushrooms, finely sliced, very lightly sautéd in butter and well drained
½ lb. (240 g.) diced cooked potatoes, well seasoned
1 crisp lettuce
1 clove garlic, very well crushed
1 tablespoon of chopped parsley
French dressing

Arrange the lettuce on individual plates. Dress. Put a layer of potatoes on each plate and pour on a little more dressing. Lightly mix the mushrooms and the garlic, and put on the potatoes. Sprinkle with parsley.

Raw Mushroom and Orange Salad

> ½ lb. (250 g.) mushrooms
> 3 oranges
> 1 lettuce
> 2 oz. (60 g.) very finely chopped walnuts
> French dressing
> salt, pepper

Wash the mushrooms, lightly dry in a cloth and very finely slice. Squeeze the juice of an orange over them, sprinkle with salt and pepper and leave while you peel 2 oranges to each half-pound of mushrooms, removing all pith and slicing them very thinly. Lay crisp lettuce leaves in the bottom of a dish. Put on them a layer of orange slices and a layer of mushrooms, then more orange slices and a sprinkling of mushrooms on top. Pour over a French dressing and sprinkle with very finely chopped walnuts.

Potato Salad

> 2 lb. (1 k.) boiled potatoes
> French dressing
> 1 tablespoon finely chopped parsley
> 1 tablespoon very finely chopped chives or shallots
> 1 teaspoon finely chopped mint

The potatoes should not be floury; new potatoes are excellent. Make the salad while they are just warm, and cut them into neat slices or small cubes.

Mix the potatoes and herbs well together, reserving a little parsley to garnish, pour over the dressing and very lightly mix again. Leave to chill slightly in the refrigerator and sprinkle with remaining parsley before serving.

Mayonnaise may be used instead of French dressing, or lightly whipped cream may be preferred: it should be seasoned with pepper and salt and with a little garlic and plenty of chives.

Mrs Glasse's Salamongundy

The name became shortened to Salamagundy in later recipes. The dish, which was really a delicious salad elaborately laid out, was intended to form a centrepiece for the supper table. It was always set out on a large flat dish with the separate ingredients all minced or shredded very small in rings of contrasting colours. Sometimes a bowl or large cup was inverted in the middle of the dish and the rings of ingredients built up over this with an ornament made of butter, a sprig of parsley, or some edible flowers, stuck on top. An acceptable alternative was to lay out the ingredients in little heaps or in separate small saucers on the large dish, the centre one being slightly raised. Mrs Glasse emphasizes that 'you may always make Salamongundy of such things as you have, according to your fancy'. The great dish which Soyer invented for the generals of both sides of the Crimean War to celebrate the peace, and which he surmounted with an ornamental label reading 'Soyer's Culinary Emblem of peace . . .', was in fact a form of Salamongundy, and in it he had to use everything he could get hold of in the Crimea or get sent out in time for the dinner.

Mrs Glasse's Recipe, 1747

For 4–6

> 1 cold roast chicken
> 1 crisp lettuce – Webb's or Iceberg are splendid
> 18 anchovy fillets
> 4 hard-boiled eggs
> 1 tablespoon finely chopped parsley
> 12–18 small white onions, tinned or frozen
> French dressing
> ¼ lb. (120 g.) white grapes, skinned and pipped
>   *or* ¼ lb. (120 g.) whole cooked french beans
> 1 lemon

Carve the chicken and cut all the white meat into very thin strips about 3 inches (7½ cm.) long and ¼ inch (½ cm.) wide. Cut all the dark meat into dice. Peel the lemon and chop it very small, removing all pith and pips. Mash the yolks of the hard-boiled eggs and chop four anchovies. Wash and shred the lettuce very finely, Mrs Glasse says 'as fine as a good, big thread'. Spread it, about ½ inch thick, all over the dish. Mix the chopped chicken meat, the chopped lemon, the parsley, the egg yolk and the chopped anchovies all together, and pile in a sugar-loaf shape in the middle of the dish. Decorate with a white onion on top. Lay a circle of the white chicken slivers all round the edge of the dish, leaving spaces between, in each of which put an anchovy fillet cut in half. Inside these, nearer to the central pile, put a ring of the whites of the eggs, finely chopped. Then put another ring of chicken slices if you have them, this time without anchovies. Put the white onions evenly spaced round the rim of the dish. Pour French dressing over all and decorate with the skinned grapes or with the french beans.

A variation

> minced cooked veal or chicken
> duck or pigeon, cooked and chopped small
> fillets of pickled herring, chopped small
> cucumber, chopped small
> apples, peeled and chopped small
> onions, peeled and chopped small
> chopped parsley
> chopped celery
> hard-boiled eggs, yolks and whites chopped separately

Use the minced veal or chicken, mixed with the cucumber and onion and well seasoned, for the central pile.

Decorate with pickles, slices of lemon 'nicely cut', and if possible with nasturtium flowers.

The Thatched House Tavern's Salamagundy (1833)

For 4–6

'Invert a china basin or small dish on a larger one.

'Lay out in circles to cover the large dish and the sides and top of the inverted bowl:

> 'chopped white chicken meat or veal
> chopped yolks of 4 or 5 eggs
> chopped whites of 4 or 5 eggs
> chopped parsley – a handful
> chopped 18 anchovy fillets
> chopped pickled red cabbage
> chopped white cabbage cut in very fine strips
> chopped tongue
> chopped beetroot

Decorate the top of the inverted dish with worked butter or with sprigs of parsley.'

Tomato Salad with Basil

    1 lb. (½ k.) firm tomatoes
    1 tablespoon chopped chives or shallots
    1 tablespoon of Mr Evelyn's oxoleon with an extra pinch of fresh
       black pepper added (see p. 376)
    1 teaspoon of sugar
    2 teaspoons chopped basil
    2 teaspoons chopped parsley
    1 teaspoon chopped thyme

The tomatoes for this salad may be blanched or not, according to taste. Slice the tomatoes as thinly as possible with a sharp saw knife. Arrange them in overlapping rows in the serving dish, sprinkle with the chives and then with the sugar, and pour on oxoleon dressing an hour before serving. Mix together the herbs and sprinkle them over the salad just before serving.

If the herbs are fresh, particularly the basil, this tomato salad is the best in the world. Basil brings out and complements the flavour of tomatoes.

9 · EGG AND CHEESE DISHES

Eggs

The English have always been poultry fanciers, and very fine birds they bred in the past, birds which laid perfect eggs, dark brown, light brown, speckled and all the shades of buff to chalky white. Now we have to stipulate 'free-range eggs' if we are unwilling to accept the chalk-white objects laid by battery-reared hens. Such eggs when cooked have tough whites and tasteless yolks, and omelettes or batters made with them never seem as light or as rich as we hope and expect. It is worth getting free-range eggs whenever and wherever they are available.

The poultry yard and the dairy were traditionally run by the mistress of the house, and the farmer's wife was supposed to obtain her 'pin money' from her profits on selling surplus eggs, butter and cheese at the market.

Early cookery books have some curious recipes by which eggs could be made interesting or ornamental. 'To make an Egg as big as Twenty' says Mrs Glasse, 'part the yolks from the whites, strain them both separate through a sieve and tie the yolks up in a bladder in the form of a ball. Boil them hard. Then put this ball (having removed its bladder) into another bladder and the whites round it and tie it up in oval fashion and boil it. These are used for grand salads. This is very pretty for a ragoo, boil five or six yolks together and lay in the middle of the ragoo of eggs: and so you may make them of any size you please.'

She follows this with a recipe for 'a Grand Dish of Eggs' too long and complicated to quote, but it amounts to two 'Great Eggs' cut in halves and filled with a stuffing of yolks, truffles, morels and pickled mushrooms, with a whole 'great egg' in the middle, the whole covered with a cream and mushroom sauce and decorated with lemon. It does not seem worth the great amount of careful work involved, when twenty separately stuffed eggs, served on a flat dish would have been equally good to eat and could have been garnished to make the dish look very pretty.

Gervase Markham, in 1615, gives an early recipe for Bacon and Eggs:

To have the best Collops and Eggs, you shall take the whitest and youngest Bacon . . . cut the Collops into thin slices, lay them in a dish and put hot water into them, and so let them stand an hour or two for that will take away the extreme saltness; then . . . set them before the heat of the fire so as they may toast . . . which done take your eggs and break them into a dish and put a spoonful of venegar into them: then set a clean skillet with fair water on the fire and as soon as the water boileth put in the eggs . . . and then dishing up the Collops, lay the Eggs upon them and so serve them up . . .

Eggs were lavishly used in all good English cooking until the nineteenth century, when attempts at economy became fashionable even where this was not strictly necessary. In the seventeenth and eighteenth centuries eggs were used in dozens to thicken and bind soups, sauces and gravies, and force-meats: they were beaten in quantity into custards and puddings. 'To make a fine plain pudding,' says Mrs Glasse, 'get a quart of milk . . . flour, half a pound of butter, a quarter of a pound of sugar . . . and twelve yolks and six whites of eggs . . .' They were hard-boiled and flung into pies; they were used in half-dozens in tansies (a sort of omelette).

Occasionally there is a recipe for a pudding specifically without eggs, but it was not until the nineteenth century when urban life had greatly increased and as a result not every household produced its own eggs that their free use in dishes which they would greatly improve was counted an extravagance.

In 1861, Mrs Beeton's 'Common Cake, suitable for sending to Children at School' has not an egg in it: her Economical Cake uses the whites of 4 eggs to a pound of flour, her Common Plum Cake has no eggs at all, nor has her 'Nice Plum Cake', the one using yeast as a rising agent and the other bicarbonate of soda. It is a relief to find that her Pound Cake uses 9 eggs to 1¼ lb. flour.

The records of Ingatestone Hall in Essex in the middle of the sixteenth century give some interesting facts about the use and price of eggs. In 1552 the cook used 2,657. The average used per week seems to have been about 40, but in this year there was a grand wedding feast in the house and 600 (or more probably 720, since 'a hundred' probably meant the long hundred, which was 120) were used in the week of the wedding feast. These extra eggs are referred to as costing 15s. 7d. for 693 – the odd 27 (to make up the 720) probably coming from the hen yard. In 1550 240 eggs had been bought for 3s 10d, so it seems that prices had risen between 1550 and 1552. Since the wedding eggs were bought in June when there would have been no scarcity.

Most of these eggs were used in the preparation of sauces, soups, ragoos, quelquechoses and other made dishes. One hopes that perhaps some Great Eggs were made for the grand salads of the wedding feast, and that perhaps some were blown and the shells filled with 'sweet waters' which ladies might break in their fingers, releasing delicious aromas in the crowded hall (see p. 462).

Eliza Acton (1845) suggests hard-boiling bantams' eggs as a decoration for salad and adds that guinea fowls' eggs are 'much esteemed by epicures' and that turkeys' eggs 'though large . . . are delicate in flavour'. Finally, she says that of swans' eggs only those of young birds should be used. 'They are much more delicate than from their size might be supposed; and when boiled hard and shelled, their appearance is beautiful, the white being of remarkable purity and transparency.'

I can find no recipes for soufflés in published cookery books or in MS. collections earlier than 1830, when Dolby has a couple of curious recipes. A steamed ginger soufflé seems to have been served at the Thatched House Tavern. I think that soufflés cannot be taken as part of the English tradition of cooking, so I have reluctantly omitted them from this section.

General Egg Dishes

A Fricasy of Eggs

From *The Complete Family-Piece*, 1737, second edition

'Boil your Eggs hard, and take out a good many of the Yolks whole, then cut the rest in Quarters, Yolks and Whites together. Set on some Gravy, with a little shred Thyme and Parsley in it; give it a Boil or two, then put in your Eggs, with a little grated Nutmeg; shake it up with a Bit of Butter, till it be as thick as another Fricasy; then fry Artichoke Bottoms in thin Slices, and serve it up. Garnish with Eggs shred small.'

This is a splendid dish which we have lost, since nowadays eggs are very rarely served with a meat gravy or sauce. However, the combination of eggs and artichoke bottoms is well known to be delicious, and with chicken, beef or veal gravy the dish is excellent and distinctive.

For a main dish for 4–6

    12 eggs, hard-boiled
    1½ pints (9 dl.) well-flavoured veal, beef or chicken stock
    1 dessertspoon finely chopped parsley and thyme
    pinch of nutmeg
    2 oz. (60 g.) butter
    2 oz. (60 g.) flour
    6 or 8 artichoke bottoms, tinned or previously cooked, and thinly
        sliced
    pepper and salt
    1 dessertspoon parsley for garnish

Take out 6 yolks from the eggs and cut the remaining 6 whole eggs in quarters. Finely chop the remaining whites to use as garnish. Make a roux with the butter and flour and stir the stock into it, adding herbs and nutmeg. Season rather highly. Put in the whole egg yolks and the quartered eggs and stir gently so that the quarter eggs are not broken up. Simmer for 2 minutes only. Add the artichokes and simmer 3 minutes more. Pour gently into a serving dish and sprinkle with the chopped egg whites and the parsley.

Croûtons of crisp fried bread or puff pastry or plain boiled rice are better with this than potato.

Mirrored Eggs

Mirrored Eggs are supposed to have been cooked by the great Soyer for a dawn breakfast in a London ballroom on his newly invented portable stove. It seemed like a miracle to the guests, hungry from dancing, to see the hot eggs being cooked in those elegant surroundings with no coal, smoke or dirt. Hundreds were cooked in large flat copper pans by the great chef and his assistant, lifted two at a time with a spatula on to small hot plates and handed direct to the guests to eat with crisp rashers of bacon and fresh rolls.

    1 oz. (30 g.) butter
    1 or 2 eggs per person
    pepper and salt

In a flat fireproof dish, earthenware or enamel, melt the butter over a very low heat. Break in 1 or 2 eggs per person. Sprinkle a little pepper and salt on each egg and spoon a little of the melted butter over the yolks. Place the dishes on low heat for 1½ minutes, then finish under the hot grill or on the top shelf of the oven for another 2 minutes or until the whites are just set. They should form a thin film over the yolk which looks like a mirror. The eggs should not stick to the dish, or show any sign of browning or crisping.

Alternatively, heat 2 oz. butter for 6 eggs in a heavy frying pan, break the eggs into it, sprinkle with pepper and salt and spoon the butter over the yolks till they film over. Do not let the butter colour or get too hot.

Eggs and Sausages

A Farmhouse recipe.

For 4

    8 eggs
    a little grated cheese
    butter
    3 pork sausages, skinned and cut each in 6 rings
    1 onion, cut very fine
    2 tomatoes, skinned and quartered
    a little cooked celery and carrots in small pieces
    a few olives or sliced gherkins
    a few cubes of cooked vegetable marrow or cucumber
    some chives and parsley, finely chopped
    a little thyme, finely chopped
    salt and pepper

Fry the sausages and all the vegetables and herbs gently in butter or oil. Transfer to a large flat fireproof dish, sprinkle with salt and pepper and flatten the surface. Carefully break 2 eggs per person on top of the mixture, so that it is covered with eggs. Sprinkle with grated cheese and dot with pieces of butter. Put in a hot oven, 450° F., gas mark 8, till the eggs are just set. Finish them under the grill if the tops seem slow in setting.

Spinage with Eggs

From *The Complete Family Piece*.

'Boil your Spinage well and green, and squeeze it dry, and chop it fine; then put in some good Gravy and melted Butter, with a little Cream, Pepper, Salt, and Nutmeg; then poach 6 Eggs and lay over your Spinage, fry some Sippets in Butter, and stick all round the Sides; squeeze one Orange so serve it hot.'

Translated for present-day use:

For 4

> 2 packets chopped frozen spinach
> 2 oz. (60 g.) butter
> 2 tablespoons double cream
> pepper and salt and a pinch of nutmeg
> 4 to 8 eggs
> 12 triangular pieces of fried bread

Defrost the spinach and cook in butter for 3 minutes. Stir in the cream and seasoning. Poach 1 or 2 eggs per person. Pour the spinach on to a fairly flat dish and carefully lift the eggs on to it. Stick the croûtons round the sides and serve immediately. Neither the gravy nor the orange juice seem to me a good idea, but slices of cooked ham are excellent very lightly fried and placed under the eggs.

Hot Stuffed Eggs

For 6

> 12 hard-boiled eggs cut in half lengthways and all yolks removed and pounded
> all the inside crumb of a small loaf soaked in ½ pint (3 dl.) milk
> 6 oz. (180 g.) butter
> 1 tablespoon finely chopped parsley
> a little chopped thyme
> 3 shallots, finely chopped
> 2 raw egg yolks to bind (reserve the whites)
> pepper and salt

Press all the milk out of the bread (this is a panada) and put it with ¼ lb.
(120 g.) butter, the hard-boiled and the raw egg yolks, the herbs, shallots and
plenty of pepper and salt in a blender, or mix very well by hand. Press about
half of it into the bottom of a buttered fireproof dish, spreading it about
½–1 inch (1–2 cm.) thick. Set 12 half whites of egg on this bed and fill with
the remaining farce, pressing a second half white down on to each, after
brushing the edges with raw white of egg so that they will stick. Dot the farce
and the eggs with butter. Cover closely and bake in a slow oven (250° F.,
gas mark ½) for 15 minutes. Serve with a fresh tomato or cheese sauce
(pp. 283, 291).

Egg Tart

A seventeenth-century recipe from an anonymous Scottish MS. The recipes
are rich and fine in this MS.; it must have come from a great household, but
its provenance is unknown.

For 4

>   an 8- or 9-in. open tart of short pastry, baked blind
>   8 hard-boiled eggs
>   2 raw eggs
>   parsley, thyme, tarragon, marjoram and chives, any or all, finely
>   chopped
>   2 oz. (60 g.) butter
>   2 tablespoons cream
>   pepper and salt
>   ¼ pint (1½ dl.) good white sauce to which grated cheese and a little
>   cream have been added

Beat the herbs into the butter and season with pepper and a little salt. Spread
this on the pastry bottom. Cut the hard-boiled eggs in quarters and arrange
them on the butter to cover it. Beat the raw eggs well with the cream and
pepper and salt and pour over the hard-boiled eggs.

Bake at 350° F., gas mark 4, for 20 minutes or until egg mixture is just set
and nicely brown on top. Serve the sauce separately.

Eggs à la Tripe

This seems to have been a favourite recipe from the fifteenth to the mid
eighteenth century. It is, in fact, excellent as a lunch or supper dish or as a

starting course at dinner. The onion sauce is exactly the same as that made for tripe served in the English manner. This recipe is dated 1833. A variant suggests taking a 'well dried omelet', cutting it in strips and putting them in the sauce: this would really simulate tripe but could hardly be good eating.

For 6

> 12 hard-boiled eggs, kept warm and cut in quarters just before they are wanted
> 6 medium onions, finely sliced
> 3 oz. (90 g.) butter
> 1 oz. (30 g.) flour
> ¼ pint (1½ dl.) double cream
> ¼ pint (1½ dl.) milk
> pepper and salt

Fry the onions very gently in butter so that they become quite soft but do not colour. Stir in the flour, then the milk and cream, bring to the boil, and boil for 2 minutes. Season. Cut the eggs in quarters and lay them in a shallow serving dish. Pour the boiling sauce over them and serve very hot.

Hard-boiled Egg Dishes

Stuffed Eggs with Anchovies

> 1 or 2 eggs per person
> 2 anchovy fillets per egg
> 1 shallot for 4 eggs
> pepper
>
> ½ oz. (15 g.) butter per egg
> fine inside lettuce leaves
> a few capers or olives

Hard-boil the eggs and cut in half crossways. Remove the yolks and cream them with butter, half the anchovy fillets and the very finely chopped shallot. Season with pepper – no salt as the anchovies are salt.

Cut a little piece from the bottom of each half egg so that it will stand firmly. Fill and pile each half high with the anchovy mixture and stick a caper or a stoned olive on top. Set each filled half in the centre of a crisp lettuce leaf and curl an anchovy fillet round it on the lettuce.

Green Stuffed Eggs

> ½ oz. (15 g.) green butter (see p. 303) for each hard boiled egg

395

Cream the egg yolks with the butter, season well and stuff the egg whites with the mixture, piling it well up. Serve on a bed of green mixed salad, lettuce, watercress, cucumber, celery or endive and sprinkle the whole with finely chopped parsley.

Very good and ornamental with cold salmon and green mayonnaise.

Curried Eggs

1 or 2 eggs per person

For 4 eggs:

½ oz. (15 g.) butter
1 small onion, finely cut
1 small apple, finely cut
1 teaspoon flour
1 teaspoon curry powder
½ pint (3 dl.) stock

1 teaspoon lemon juice
a pinch of cayenne
a pinch of paprika
2 teaspoons chutney
plain boiled rice

Hard-boil the eggs and keep them warm. Fry the onion and apple in the butter. When soft, stir in the flour and curry powder. Cook for a minute. Stir in the stock and lemon juice. Add the cayenne, paprika and chutney and stir well. Cut the eggs in half and cut a slice from the bottoms so that they will stand. Arrange in a fireproof dish with a border of plain boiled rice. Pour the curry over the eggs and serve. A few prawns added to the eggs are very good.

Jellied Eggs

1 or 2 eggs per person
1 pint aspic jelly, jelly consommé or jellied stock
6 to 8 eggs
garnishings (see below)
crisp lettuce

Make up 1 pint (6 dl.) aspic jelly from the packet and season highly, or use 1 pint from a tin of good jellied consommé or your own jellied first stock, well seasoned.

The eggs should be soft. Boil them for 4 minutes and then at once hold under cold tap and peel very gently and carefully. Hard-boiled eggs can, of course, be used if preferred or soft poached eggs can be used but are not such a good shape.

Put a little liquid jelly into small moulds or dishes (individual soufflé dishes are good for this). Allow it to cool so that it is almost set. Then put in the egg and arrange garnishings round it. These may be cooked asparagus tips, green peas and tiny strips of lean ham, sliced cooked artichoke bottoms, finely sliced sauté mushrooms, chopped chives and parsley, etc. Fill up the moulds with the jelly and chill to set. Serve very cold turned out on a bed of crisp lettuce.

Eggs in Jelly in Tomatoes

A very easy and ornamental summer hors-d'œuvre. This is a Victorian recipe.

> 1 hard-boiled egg for each person
> 1 very large firm tomato per person
> watercress
> ½ pint (3 dl.) highly seasoned savoury jelly
> mayonnaise
> pepper and salt

Aspic made half with water and half with white wine or good chicken stock with gelatine dissolved in it makes a good savoury jelly. In either case season highly.

Have a very large tomato for each person. Carefully blanch it. Cut off the top, remove the inside, season with salt and black pepper and pour in a little jelly. Put in the egg. Fill up with jelly and allow it to run over the tomato, so that the outside is glazed with jelly. Serve the tomatoes on a bed of watercress, with mayonnaise separately.

Masked Eggs and Asparagus

Served as an hors-d'œuvre at summer dinner parties in a Cornish household. It depends on a very good home-made mayonnaise to which cream is added. Everything may be prepared ahead, including the eggs, but should not be put together until half an hour before it is served.

For 6

> 6 soft poached eggs, left to drain
> 6 croûtons fried bread, trimmed to the size of the eggs
> 6 cooked bundles of tips of small asparagus and the rest of the edible part chopped
> ¼ pint (1½ dl.) home-made mayonnaise into which 2 tablespoons of double cream have been stirred

Place the croûtons on a flat serving dish or in individual dishes or on small plates and the eggs on them. Lay an untied asparagus bundle beside each egg and sprinkle a few small pieces around. Just before serving pour over the mayonnaise so that the egg is hidden but the tips of the asparagus bundle show.

Omelettes

English recipes through the ages claim that to make a good omelette (which Mrs Glasse spells amulet and makes with beans) it is wise to:

beat egg yolks and whites separately	add cream
add water	beat eggs whole but very foamy
add milk	hardly beat them at all.

You can, in fact, do any or all of these things and you will still make a good omelette provided that you have a thick heavy pan and that you make it very hot.

Basic Recipe

Take 3 or 4 eggs for two people. Break them into a bowl and beat them till the whites and yolks are well amalgamated and foaming a little. Season with pepper and salt. Grease the pan with butter and make it smoking hot. Pour in the beaten, seasoned eggs and work them away from the edges with a palette knife or spatula. Shake the pan and gather the omelette in towards the centre a little. In 2 minutes it is done. Fold it with a shake of the pan or with your palette knife and serve on a hot plate at once.

1. For an omelette really wet inside, cook only about 1½ minutes and do not beat the eggs very much.
2. For a dryish omelette, beat the eggs fairly well and cook a little more before folding.
3. For a foamy, light omelette beat very well and cook 2 minutes
4. For a soufflé omelette beat the whites separately from the yolks until they hold a peak, then beat the yolks till just foamy and fold the beaten whites into them.
5. A two-egg omelette is done in 2 minutes, a three-egg in 3–4 minutes, and so on. Do not try to cook more than a six-egg omelette in one pan. If you want more than this, make two.

Everything must be done quickly. If you are slow in cooking (pan not hot) or folding and serving, the omelette will be hard and leathery and more like a badly-made pancake than an omelette.

Mrs Rundle, giving a recipe for 'Omlet' in 1807, uses flour: she stipulates that it should be a small quantity but even so this is sacrilege where omelettes are concerned, and the result would be a kind of pancake.

Dr Kitchiner, in 1840, has some strange views on omelettes: he says that they are often considered too rich and may be lightened by the addition of potato flour to the eggs; he also says that in general only half the number of whites to yolks should be used. His basic recipe, however, is quite conventional except for the high proportion of butter.

Asparagus Omelette

Reheat some cooked asparagus tips in butter and lay on the omelette just before folding over.

Onion Omelette

Cut an onion in very thin rings, cook gently until quite soft and light brown and then add to the omelette before folding.

Omelette with Sweet Herbs

Finely chop parsley, chives, a little tarragon, thyme or marjoram, mixed together and stir into the omelette mixture before beating and cooking.

Mushroom Omelette

Cut the mushrooms in thin slices, cook them slowly in butter, and add them to the omelette mixture.

Ham Omelette

Cut some lean cooked ham in matchstick slices and add to the omelette mixture with a teaspoon of chopped parsley.

Haddock Omelette

From a Scottish nineteenth-century manuscript in the Macadam collection, Edinburgh.

For 2

        1 fillet smoked haddock
        2 oz. (60 g.) Cheddar or Cheshire cheese
        4 eggs
        pepper

Cook and skin the fillet of haddock and flake. Grate the cheese, mix with the well-beaten eggs and haddock, add pepper, but very little, salt, if any (the fish and cheese are already salty).

Mix well and cook as in the basic omelette recipe (p. 398).

Omelette Arnold Bennett

This is reputed to have been the writer's favourite omelette; the recipe originally came from the Savoy Grill, London.

For 2

        1 fillet smoked haddock, cooked, skinned, and finely chopped
        4 eggs
        1 tablespoon double cream
        freshly ground black pepper
        very little salt
        ½ oz. (15 g.) butter
        2 oz. (60 g.) hot cheese sauce
        1 oz. (30 g.) finely grated cheese

Beat the chopped haddock, eggs, cream, pepper and a pinch of salt together. Make the butter hot and cook this omelette mixture only till it is just set and still wet in the middle. Have the grill very hot. Quickly pour and spread over the omelette the hot sauce, sprinkle with the grated cheese and brown for a minute or two under the grill. Slide on to a hot dish and serve very quickly.

Potato Omelette

A Devonshire recipe.

For 3

 2 rashers lean bacon, chopped finely
 1 onion cut very fine
 ½ lb. (250 g.) parboiled diced potatoes
 2 slices bread, white or brown, cut in small cubes
 4 eggs
 pepper and salt and chopped parsley if liked
 2 oz. (60 g.) butter

Make the butter, or some bacon or pork fat, smoking hot in a thick pan. First fry the onion for a minute or two till golden, but not dark brown. Lift it out with a perforated spoon and keep it hot on a plate while you fry the bread cubes till crisp and golden in the same way. Add them to the onion and fry the bacon. Add this to the onion and bread, put a little more fat in the pan if necessary, and put in the potatoes. Fry for a minute, then mix all the other ingredients into them, stirring them gently in the pan. Pour in the well-beaten and seasoned eggs, stir and cook for 2 minutes. Hold the pan under a hot grill to firm and set the top, turn out on to a hot dish and sprinkle with chopped parsley. Do not attempt to fold. The crisp bread cubes are very good.

The Returned Hunter's Omelette

A nineteenth-century Edinburgh recipe. The original uses a few slices of the liver of the just-killed deer.

Serves 2 or 3

 4–6 eggs
 2 chicken, duck or pheasant livers or 2 oz. (60 g.) venison liver
 6 medium mushrooms, finely sliced
 1 small onion or 2 shallots, finely sliced
 a little chopped thyme and chives, and a touch of garlic
 1 teaspoon chopped parsley
 1 tablespoon sherry
 1 oz. (30 g.) butter

Fry the mushrooms, onion or shallots, liver and herbs gently in butter. Stir in the parsley. Add the sherry, stir all together and keep hot. Make your omelette as the basic recipe and lightly spread the hot mixture over it before folding, keeping back any juice. Fold over and serve on a hot dish with the juice poured over outside.

Soufflé Cheese Omelette

For 2

>   4 eggs
>   2 oz. (60 g.) grated cheese
>   salt and freshly ground black pepper
>   ½ oz. (15 g.) butter

Beat the whites till they hold a peak and the yolks separately. Add the cheese to the yolks and season well. Lightly fold the whites into the yolks and proceed as usual, except that the omelette should not be folded. Either turn it over and cook the second side for half a minute or hold the pan for half a minute under the grill.

Kidney Omelette

An Edwardian recipe; this omelette was served at the Reform Club with the famous Reform Sauce. It is best with this, if you have some or have time to make it, but it is also very good with gravy to which a little sherry has been added.

For 2

>   4 eggs   1 tablespoon sherry
>   2 sheep's kidneys   1 oz. (30 g.) butter
>   a little brown gravy   a little flour

Skin and trim the kidneys. Cut into small pieces and fry them in a little butter for 3 minutes; heat the gravy and stir in the sherry. Sprinkle with a little flour, stir again, cook for 1 more minute. Make the omelette as usual, and lightly spread the kidney mixture into it just before folding. Pour the gravy round it.

Cream Omelette

Richard Dolby's recipe, 1830. This is quite unlike an ordinary omelette. Once tried, it will be asked for again.

For 4 or 5

>   6 eggs
>   1 pint (6 dl.) cream
>   3 oz. (90 g.) fine white crumbs
>   1 tablespoon finely chopped parsley

3 shallots, very finely chopped
salt and freshly ground black pepper
1 oz. (30 g.) butter

Bring the cream to the boil and stir into it the crumbs, parsley, shallots and seasoning. Stir, simmering, until it is quite thick. Remove from the fire and allow to cool a little. Beat the eggs well and stir into the cream; beat this mixture. Melt the butter in a large frying pan and when smoking hot pour in the mixture and fry as usual, stirring as it cooks. It will take a little longer than an ordinary omelette. It can be folded or finished under the grill.

Little Anchovy Omelets

An early nineteenth-century recipe.

For 4

4 eggs
1 tablespoon finely chopped parsley, thyme and chives
pepper and salt
olive oil to fry
2 slices of bread cut in very small cubes, fried crisp and kept hot
1 tin anchovy fillets
1 oz. (30 g.) butter

Beat the eggs well, add herbs and seasoning and make two omelettes using a large pan so that they spread out flat. Cut each of these in 4 pieces. Lay cubes of bread and 2 or 3 anchovy fillets on each of 4 pieces. Cover them with the other 4. Put a piece of butter on each and put in the oven for 2 minutes to warm again. Serve quickly.

Edward VII's Favourite Omelette

This is a very rich omelette, typical of the luxurious dishes favoured by wealthy upper-class Edwardians. Edward VII ordered it for private suppers, sometimes following a clear soup and followed by a simple dish of cutlets. The secret of the dish is the unexpected and subtle flavour imparted by the port.

For 2 or 3

the meat of a cooked lobster, about 1 lb. (½ k.), neatly sliced
and the claw meat diced

½ lb. (250 g.) button mushrooms, sliced very thin
glass of *good* port
¼ pint (1½ dl.) double cream
6 eggs
2 oz. (60 g.) grated Parmesan cheese
salt and pepper

Have the grill very hot. Sauté the mushrooms in butter, then stew in the port till the liquid is reduced a little. Add the cream and the lobster to the mushrooms and allow just to simmer while you beat the eggs and make the omelette. When just setting put the lobster mixture down the centre, fold over, lift on to a hot dish, sprinkle with Parmesan cheese and brown under the grill. Serve at once.

SWEET OMELETTES

Sweet omelettes were very popular in Edwardian times. The cook could make them while the butler or parlourmaid was clearing the last course. Nowadays for most of us it is necessary to leave the table and make the omelette from prepared ingredients, but 5 minutes is the most this should take.

Jam Soufflé Omelette, 1

4 egg yolks and 6 whites
1 oz. (30 g.) butter
1 oz. (30 g.) sugar

jam
a pinch of salt

Beat the sugar and egg yolks together. Whisk the egg whites with a pinch of salt until quite stiff and holding a peak. Stir them lightly into the yolks. Melt the butter in an omelette pan, and when very hot pour in the mixture. Allow to cook for 3 minutes, then finish cooking by holding the pan under a hot grill for another 2 minutes until risen and turning golden. Turn the cooked omelette on to a sugared paper and spread it lightly with hot jam before folding in half by folding over the paper. Pull the paper from under the omelette and serve very hot.

Jam Omelette, 2

Prepare the eggs as for an ordinary omelette but without salt and adding a teaspoon of caster sugar. Just before folding the omelette in the pan put in a layer of whatever jam you like. Fold in the usual way and dish the omelette in a fireproof dish. Sprinkle with caster sugar and glaze it quickly under a hot grill.

Fresh Raspberry or Strawberry Omelette

For 3

> 4 egg yolks and 6 whites
> ¼ lb. (120 g.) raspberries or small strawberries
> 1 oz. (30 g.) butter
> 1 oz. (30 g.) caster sugar
> cream

Very lightly crush the raspberries or strawberries with the caster sugar. Make a soufflé omelette as in Jam Soufflé Omelette. Lay the fruit in it instead of the jam. Quickly sprinkle a little caster sugar over the fruit, fold the omelette, sprinkle with sugar again and hold 2 minutes under a hot grill. Serve at once, with plenty of cream.

Rum Omelette

For 3 or 4

> 6 eggs
> 1 oz. (30 g.) butter
> 1 oz. (30 g.) caster sugar
>
> 1 tablespoon rum
> double cream

Prepare the eggs in the ordinary way and add the sugar, beating the eggs well. Put in the pan a little more butter than for an ordinary omelette. Make the omelette, fold it, sprinkle with sugar and glaze for a minute under a hot grill. Meanwhile warm some rum, pour it over the omelette and light it. Carry flaming to table and serve with cream.

Surprise Omelette

Very popular for Victorian dinner parties. This is a slightly simplified version which I find works very well and which can be made in 5 minutes between courses if the ingredients are left ready.

For 4

> a block of vanilla ice cream, kept very hard in freezer but with 4 slices
>   cut almost but not quite through

    4 egg yolks
    6 egg whites
    2 teaspoons caster sugar
    2 tablespoons raspberry or apricot jam

Prepare to make a soufflé omelette as in Jam Soufflé Omelette. Have the warmed but not very hot jam ready to hand and the grill hot.

When you leave the table put the soufflé omelette in the pan. Get out the ice cream. Finish the omelette under the grill, without folding. Quickly pour and spread jam over it. Slide the ice cream on to a warmed flat dish. Turn the omelette right over it jam side down so that it is completely covered, sprinkle with caster sugar. Rush to the table and serve at once, cutting down the divided slices of ice cream. Success depends on doing everything very fast.

Tansies and Pamperdy

TANSIES

This dish, so popular from the Middle Ages until the late eighteenth century, has gone out of use. Nevertheless, the tansy, after it had dropped its connexion with the rather strong and bitter herb, the juice of which was generally included in early recipes, was a very good pudding: really a very delicate kind of sweet omelette.

Markham says that 'To make the best Tansey' you must take 'Eggs according to the bigness of your frying pan . . . abating ever the white of every third egg . . . then with a little cream beat them together . . . then take of green wheat blades, violet leaves, strawberry leaves, spinage and succory and a few walnut tree buds . . . strain out the juice and mixing it with a little more cream put it to the eggs and stir . . . then put in a few crumbs of bread fine grated. . . .' After this the tansy is fried brown in butter and thickly sprinkled with sugar. He mentions that the walnut buds replace the tansy and give a better flavour.

Izaak Walton gives a recipe for minnow tansies, quoted on p. 251, but in general the tansy was sweet. This flowery tansy, which contains no tansy juice, is from the late eighteenth century.

'Take half a pint of cream, 7 eggs, a quarter lb. of amonds, blanch and beat very well with a little cream. You take a good handful of cowslips shred very small mingle them all together and sweeten it with rosewater and sugar to your taste and a little grated nutmeg. So fry it as you do other tansys. You may make it with primroses and a few violets in want of cowslips or with fresh roseleaves.'

The Apple and the Apricot Tansies which follow are delicious light hot sweets. The fruit and the omelette mixture may be prepared ahead, and the final cooking takes only a few moments.

Apple Tansy (1736)

For 6

6 good eating apples (Cox's are excellent)
2 oz. (60 g.) butter
yolks of 6 eggs and whites of 4
2 tablespoons double cream
2–3 oz. (60–90 g.) caster sugar
2–3 oz. (60–90 g.) fine white breadcrumbs
pinch of cinnamon
pinch of nutmeg
cream to eat with it

Peel and core the apples and cut them in thick rings. Using a large heavy pan, fry them very slowly in the butter, turning them so that they become soft and transparent but do not colour or burn at all.

Meanwhile beat the eggs, cream, crumbs, spices and 1 oz. of sugar very well together. Sprinkle the remaining sugar on the hot cooked apples and pour the egg mixture over them, stirring them into it. When brown underneath, turn on to a plate, put a little more butter in the pan and fry on the other side. Dish quickly when fairly solid right through and serve sprinkled with plenty of sugar, and cream served separately.

Apricot Tansy (1736)

Serves 4

1 lb. (½ k.) fresh apricots
butter
caster sugar

4 eggs
2 tablespoons double cream
a very little nutmeg

Stone the apricots, quarter them, and gently fry in butter until they are quite soft. Sprinkle with about 2 oz. (60 g.) sugar and set aside in the pan.

Beat well together the eggs, cream, 1 tablespoon caster sugar, and the nutmeg, and set aside. Just before serving, make the pan with the apricots hot so that they are just sizzling. Put a little more butter in the pan if at all dry. Stir the egg mixture and pour it over the apricots; stir it very gently among them. After 2 minutes it should have set at the bottom. Turn it on to a plate. Melt a little more butter in the pan and slide it back, the unbrowned side (which has the most egg) downwards. Fry 2 minutes more and serve at once. It should be a little soft but not liquid in the middle.

Sift sugar over it and serve thick cream separately.

Sir Kenelm Digby's Tansy (1699)

This is worth making if tansy is grown in your herb garden; the flavour is strange to us, rather strong, but entirely acceptable. The spinach juice serves merely to make the omelette pale green.

Serves 4

> 1 teaspoon tansy juice, obtained by moistening a dozen leaves and stems and rubbing them through a fine sieve or strainer
> ½ pint (3 dl.) double cream
> 4 eggs, (use only 3 whites)
> ½ lb. (240 g.) spinach boiled in 2 tablespoons of water without salt
> 1 oz. (30 g.) caster sugar
> pinch of salt and of nutmeg
> 1 oz. (30 g.) butter
> juice of 2 oranges

Drain the spinach, pressing it well. Discard the spinach, but reserve the liquid. Stir the tansy juice and the sugar into the green liquid. Beat the eggs, cream, salt and nutmeg well together and then beat the green liquid into them. Warm the orange juice and keep hot. Make the butter hot and fry the tansy as an omelette but turning so that both sides are quickly and lightly browned. Serve immediately, pouring the warm orange juice over it.

PANPERDY

Panperdy or pain perdy (originally pain perdu) was a well-known dish for which recipes go back to the fifteenth century in the Harleian MS. and probably much earlier. The two recipes given here, one predominantly sweet and the other savoury, are from the seventeenth century.

A Savoury Panperdy

This recipe is from *The English Hus-Wife*, by Gervase Markham, published 1615.

The bread is 'lost' because, delicately crisped, it is inside the omelettes.

> 2 eggs per person
> 1 slice of crustless bread, about 3 by 2 in. (7 by 5 cm.), per person
> seasoning
> 3 oz. (90 g.) butter

The seventeenth-century recipe suggests cloves, mace, cinnamon, nutmeg and some sugar as well as salt, but for present-day tastes salt and pepper and either a little finely chopped parsley, thyme and chives or some grated Parmesan cheese would make a better savoury omelette.

Beat the eggs well together with the herbs or cheese and salt and pepper. Melt the butter in the pan until it is foaming but not colouring. Put in the slices of bread, fry lightly and turn. Pour some of the egg mixture over each: the egg will spread around the bread. Cook for 2 minutes, then turn with a slice so that the fried bread is upwards and quickly pour on the rest of the egg. Cook for 1 minute only and turn once more to set the omelette, or finish under a preheated grill. Serve immediately.

Panperdy as a Sweet Dish

This is Gervase Markham's recipe for 'the best Painperdy'. The bread, lightly fried and impregnated with butter, is 'lost' in the light fluffy sweet omelette. This is a delicious pudding, hardly ever seen nowadays. It is very quick to make, but the ingredients must be prepared and left ready before the beginning of the meal and the cook must leave the table and make the omelette after the first course. It takes only about 7 minutes.

For 4

> 6 eggs
> a pinch each of cloves, cinnamon and nutmeg *or* 1 teaspoon of vanilla
>   essence
> a pinch of salt
> 1 tablespoon caster sugar
> 4 slices of bread without crust, about 3 by 2 in. (7 by 5 cm.)
> 3 oz. (90 g.) butter

Beat the eggs, spices or vanilla flavouring, sugar and salt very well together.

Make 2 oz. (60 g.) of the butter hot but not brown in a heavy frying pan and lightly fry the slices of bread on one side. Turn them and pour over them half of the beaten eggs and fry for 2 minutes, working away from the sides of the pan. Turn out of the pan on to a large plate. Put in the remaining butter and pour in the remaining egg, and at once slide the omelette back, brown side uppermost. Work to free the edges from the pan and cook till puffed and golden brown, about 3 minutes. Slide on to a hot dish, sprinkle with caster sugar and serve immediately.

The whole dish must be made very quickly or the omelette toughens.

A hot jam or orange sauce served with it is very good.

Batters, Pancakes and Fritters

BATTERS

A batter is a mixture of flour, milk or milk and water, and generally egg. The batter must be beaten well in order to incorporate air into the mixture. When the mixture becomes hot, the air in it expands and so lightens its consistency. It is not necessary to mix a batter some hours before it is needed and then allow it to stand in a cool place, as old-fashioned cooks used to advise. It will not hurt it to do so, but it will not improve it either. If you do mix it ahead, leave it in a cool place; a batter mixture should be as cold as possible before being quickly cooked. For this reason a batter is always dropped into hot fat, whether in frying or baking, and if baked, is cooked in a quick oven. If the batter has stood at all, it is wise to give it a last beating just as you are going to use it.

Pancake Batter

Pancake batters can be very plain if they are to be eaten immediately, straight from pan to plate, with lemon and sugar, or jam and cream, but if they are to be kept hot and filled with a sweet or savoury mixture the batter must be richer or it will not remain crisp. Three basic recipes, one from the eighteenth century, one from the nineteenth, and the third from the end of the seventeenth century, are given here, the plainest first.

Basic Recipe 1

Plain pancakes to be eaten as soon as ready, a nineteenth-century recipe. These quantities make 4 pancakes, about 8 inches (20 cm.) in diameter.

3 oz. (90 g.) flour   pinch of salt
½ pint (3 dl.) milk   3 eggs
1 oz. (30 g.) butter, just melted

Add the salt to the flour, break in the eggs and mix well together. Slowly stir
in the cold milk. Beat well until of a smooth consistency, about the thickness
of thin cream. Grease a heavy frying pan with butter, and when smoking hot
pour 2 tablespoons of the mixture into the centre of the pan, tilting it to ensure
that the liquid covers the whole pan surface. When cooked on one side, toss
and brown the other. If you can't toss the pancake or are afraid to try, simply
slip a palette knife or spatula under it and turn it. This is just as good. The
results are not in any way improved by tossing. When cooked on both sides
(about half a minute a side) roll it up with a palette knife, place on a hot dish
and either serve at once or keep hot for a few minutes.

Basic Recipe 2

This eighteenth-century recipe is much richer than the last. The pancakes
will not become leathery if kept hot while several are made, and then filled
before serving. Makes 8 pancakes about 4–5 inches (10–13 cm.) in diameter;
excellent as a coating batter.

¼ lb. (120 g.) flour
2 tablespoons caster sugar (for a sweet batter; omit for savoury)
a pinch of salt
4 eggs
1 oz. (30 g.) butter, just melted
¼ pint (1½ dl.) milk
2 tablespoons double cream (optional)

Mix the flour, sugar (if required) and salt together, stir in 2 whole eggs and
2 yolks and the butter and beat well. Add the milk and cream and beat again.
(A little extra milk may be used if the cream is omitted or the batter seems
too thick.) Finally fold in 2 stiffly beaten egg whites. The consistency should
be about that of thin cream. Cook as in the first basic recipe.

Brandy or orange curaçao may be beaten in as flavouring. The eighteenth-
century original suggests orange-flower water or rosewater, and a different,
but similar, recipe of the period substitutes beer for the milk when making
savoury pancakes.

Basic Recipe 3

This recipe, adapted from one of 1694, makes particularly good, all-purpose pancakes: 4, about 8 inches (20 cm.) in diameter.

2 oz. (60 g.) butter, melted	½ pint (3 dl.) milk
2 eggs	2 tablespoons cream
3 oz. (90 g.) flour	

Beat the flour, eggs and butter well together. Stir in the milk and beat again, and finally beat in the cream. Cook as in the first recipe.

Coating or Frying Batters

Coating batters are used for dipping fillets of fish or meat, minced mixtures or fruit or vegetables. It is best to deep-fry batter-coated food in oil, but other fats can be used and the food can be shallow-fried. Coating batters are used for all fritters, for which various recipes and suggestions follow.

Basic Recipe 1

¼ lb. (120 g.) flour	1 oz. (30 g.) melted butter
a pinch of salt	¼ pint (1½ dl.) milk, *or*
1 egg	milk and water

Milk alone will make a fairly solid batter; milk and water, half and half, a crisp outside but a slightly soft inside; and water only, a very crisp batter.

Mix the salt and flour and sift them into a bowl. Add the egg and beat until smooth; stir in the butter. Continue beating while you add the liquid gradually. Beat until smooth and covered with air bubbles. It should coat the beater when you lift it out if the mixture is correct in texture. All ingredients may be put into a blender instead of being beaten.

Basic Recipe 2

4 oz. (120 g.) flour	1 oz. (30 g.) butter
salt	¼ pint (1½ dl.) water
2 egg whites and 1 yolk	

Sieve the flour and a pinch of salt into a basin containing the egg yolk. Add the melted butter and warm water and beat until a smooth paste is obtained. Beat the mixture very well indeed. Allow to get perfectly cold. Just before using stir in the whisked egg whites. This gives a crisp casing which stands away from the filling and is very fluffy. Some traditional recipes omit the yolk and use stiffly beaten egg whites only. It is best cooked in oil, which must be really hot.

Savoury Pancakes

Serves 4

Have ready ¼ pint (1 ½ dl.) very good brown sauce – Reform Sauce (see p. 290) is the best of all. Cook on skewers under grill, one for each person:

    4 sheep's kidneys each cut in 4
    12 small mushrooms
    12 very small bacon rolls
    4 chipolata sausages, each divided into 2

When almost ready, make 4 large but very thin pancakes (Basic Recipe 3). Do not roll them but lay them flat, overlapping on a hot dish.

When the skewers are ready, spoon a very little sauce on to the topmost pancake in the middle, and slide all the things from one of the skewers so that they lie on it. Roll that pancake tightly and push it out of the way on the dish, so that another one is freed. When all are filled, return to the oven for 3 minutes to make sure they are hot. Bring the remainder of the sauce to the boil and serve separately.

Stuffed Savoury Pancakes

A Worcestershire recipe: collected from an elderly cook who said she 'had always made them'.

    ½ lb. (240 g.) finely chopped cooked chicken or veal *or* very lean home-
        cooked ham *or* a mixture
    2 oz. (60 g.) finely sliced mushrooms, lightly sauté
    1 oz. (30 g.) finely sliced onion, gently fried in butter till quite soft
        but not brown
    ½ pint (3 dl.) well-flavoured, rather thick white sauce
    about 1 pint (6 dl.) pancake batter
    2 oz. (60 g.) grated Parmesan cheese

Stir the meat, mushrooms and onions into the sauce. Check the seasoning and heat till not quite boiling. The mixture should be quite thick.

Make the first thin pancake, put a tablespoonful of the mixture on one half

413

and roll up as tightly as possible. Lift on to a hot dish and keep hot while you make the rest. Lay them in a row on the dish. When all are done sprinkle with the cheese and brown for a moment under the grill.

Winter Pancakes

Use Basic Recipe 3.

Put a piled teaspoon of hard sauce (see p. 308) on the cooked side of the pancake while the second side is still browning. Spread it a little and roll the pancake as usual. Serve at once, before the sauce completely melts and runs out.

Apple Pancakes

Make pancakes according to Basic Recipe 2. Have ready about ¼ pint (1½ dl.) apple purée, which should be hot and fairly thick and dry, well sweetened and containing some raisins. When the pancake is turned, place a dessertspoon of the apple mixture in the centre, fold the pancake over this, sprinkle with sugar, and lift on to a hot dish with a palette knife.

Chestnut Pancakes

Use pancake batter Basic Recipe 2 or 3. Prepare a thick purée of chestnuts, fresh or canned (p. 298). Sweeten it well instead of seasoning and stir in 1 tablespoon rum to about ¼ lb. (120 g.) purée.

Spread the pancakes thickly with this, roll up, sprinkle with caster sugar and a little more rum, place for 2 minutes under a hot grill and serve with whipped cream handed separately.

A few 'raisins of the sun' were sometimes mixed into the chestnut purée in early recipes.

Christmas Pancakes

When snow was lying, a large piece about 3 × 4 × 3 inches (7 × 10 × 7 cm.) was brought in just as the pancakes were to be cooked, and quickly stirred into the batter. As the batter cooked, the snow began to melt, leaving holes, which made the pancakes light and delicious. This does work, and naturally gives great pleasure to helping children. One or two early recipes say that if snow is used fewer eggs are required.

Use Basic Recipe 2 or 3 for the pancakes. Spread lightly with mincemeat and add a few coarsely chopped almonds. Roll and serve.

Orange Pancakes

Use Basic Recipe 3 and add the grated zest of 1 orange to the flour before beating. The zest flavours the whole of the batter. Serve with fresh orange quarters and caster sugar.

Yorkshire Pudding

This recipe comes from a Yorkshire cook. Recipes vary very much but this gives excellent results.

> 6 oz. (180 g.) flour
> 1 pint (6 dl.) milk
> 2 eggs
> pinch of salt

Mix exactly as for pancake or coating batter. Pour off about 2 tablespoons of the dripping from the roasting beef into a baking tin (Yorkshire pudding is better cooked in a tin than in a glass or earthenware dish). Make smoking hot in the oven. Remove the tin and quickly pour in the batter all at once. Immediately put in the oven, at 400–450° F., gas mark 6–7, on a low shelf below the joint, so that it gets bottom heat to start with. After 10 minutes move it to a higher shelf, above the joint, and cook another 10–15 minutes.

Traditionally, the pudding was cooked under the spitted joint. This can be done in the oven if the beef is put on a stand or grid in a roasting tray and the batter poured in 20 minutes before the beef should be ready; gravy in this case must be made separately, using stock.

Sausage Toad-in-the-Hole

Use the Yorkshire pudding mixture recipe. Fry a pound (½ k.) of sausages which you have first made into halves by twisting the skins in the middle and cutting the joins. Place the cooked sausage halves in a baking tin containing ¼ inch (½ cm.) hot butter or very good dripping and pour the batter gently round them so that they are not pushed out of position.

Cook for 25–30 minutes at 425° F., gas mark 7. Serve at once. Tomato sauce or brown gravy is traditional with toad-in-the-hole.

Toad-in-the-Hole

Recipe from an unpublished eighteenth-century MS. This is much grander than the usual sausage toad-in-the-hole.

For 4

> 1 pint (6 dl.) batter (pancake batter Basic Recipe 1) into which an extra ½ oz. (15 g.) melted butter has been beaten
> 4 small fillet steaks, cut in half again
> 2 tablespoons brandy
> salt and black pepper
> 2 oz. (60 g.) finely chopped almonds fried to a light brown
> ½ pint (3 dl.) very good brown gravy, highly seasoned and fairly thick
> 2 oz. (60 g.) butter

Put the 8 little steaks on a plate, season them with salt and pepper, pour the brandy over them and leave them while you make the batter.

Put the butter in a baking tin in a hot oven (400° F., gas mark 6) and melt till smoking hot. Pour in the batter, bake for 10 minutes. Take it out, preferably not right out of the oven, and very quickly drop in the steaks, spacing them evenly. The batter should be just enough set to hold them. Spoon a little of the brandy over each and put back in the oven for 15 minutes. The steaks should just show above the batter but may be totally covered: in either case they should be exactly done.

Meanwhile fry the almonds and sprinkle over the batter before you carry it to table. Serve brown gravy separately.

Sausage Fritters

This is a West Country dish, which was served for high tea on the farms in winter. It is very filling and very good.

Take half a cold cooked sausage skinned and cut longways for each fritter. Coat in batter (Basic Recipe 1) and fry 3 or 4 minutes in deep, hot oil or in shallow fat, turning once. Drain well and serve with rashers of bacon and fried potatoes.

Apple Fritters

Apple Fritters were very highly esteemed by our ancestors. 'To make the best Fritters,' says Markham in 1615, 'take a pint of cream, 8 eggs, only aboute 4 of the whites . . . put in cloves, mace, nutmeg and saffron and stir them well together: then put in 2 spoonfuls of the best Ale barm [brewer's yeast] and a little salt . . . then make it thick according unto your pleasure with wheat flour. . . .' This very rich batter was then put before the fire to rise, beaten again and 'a penny pot of Sack' stirred into it. After this thick slices of apples were dropped in, fished out and fried in boiling fat in the ordinary way.

A great eighteenth-century gourmet said that the meal he would choose above all others would be simply whitebait, woodcock and apple fritters.

Markham's recipe would give large, very puffed out fritters but it involves so much time to prepare and uses so much cream and so many eggs that it would not often be attempted today.

The following much simpler recipe gives excellent fritters. Use the second recipe for coating batters.

Peel and core 2 or 3 cooking apples, cut into rings. Sprinkle with caster sugar and squeeze lemon juice over. Leave a few minutes. Drain and dip in the batter, so that each ring is well coated all over. Drop into deep boiling fat and allow to fry for about 3 minutes. Lift out with a perforated slice or spoon and drain well on sugared greaseproof paper. Transfer to a hot dish and serve. If you must fry in shallow fat, make sure it is really hot and at least ¼ inch deep all over the pan. Cook the fritters 2 minutes one side, then turn and cook 2 minutes on the other.

Apricot Fritters

Allow 2 apricots per person, fresh and not too ripe. Halve and stone. Sprinkle with sugar and brandy or lemon juice. Leave a few minutes. Drain. Use coating batter Basic Recipe 2, coat each half, and proceed as for apple fritters.

Custard Fritters

This is a very early dish for which recipes recur frequently.

For 4

Make a custard with 2 egg yolks, ¾ pint (4½ dl.) milk and a teaspoon of sugar. Butter a small pie dish, pour in the custard, cover with foil, stand in a baking dish with water and bake at 350° F., gas mark 4, for 30 minutes or until firm to touch. Take it out and let it get cold.

Make your batter as in coating batter Basic Recipe 1, using an extra ounce (30 g.) of flour.

Cut the cold custard into 12 neat pieces. Dip them in the batter and fry. Serve with jam and cream or with a fruit sauce.

417

Elder Flower Fritters

Never made today but traditional since the fifteenth century at least. They are unique in flavour and texture and entirely delicious. The elder blossom must be freshly picked and just fully opened. Cut the big flat head as close as possible to the stalk, or divide into flowerets as you sometimes do a cauliflower. Wash the flowers, shake them dry and marinate for 2 or 3 hours in a little brandy, the juice of half a lemon and a good tablespoon of caster sugar. Drain the flowers and save the liquid.

Make a thick coating batter, using Basic Recipe 2 but using a little extra flour so that it is really thick, and beat the remaining marinade liquid into it. Dip the flowers into this and fry in very hot deep fat. Drain well, sprinkle with caster sugar and serve very hot.

An Apricot Froise

A froise, or frayse, seems to have been a large round double fritter. Recipes go back to the fifteenth century, and occur frequently until the nineteenth. Though variable, the froise was generally made with fruit, bacon, small pieces of meat or vegetables, lightly fried in butter and kept hot. Batter was then fried in butter, the prepared food laid on it as it cooked, and more batter poured over. As soon as the bottom was brown, the froise was turned over, and browned on the other side.

For 4–6

      1 lb. (½ k.) fresh apricots, stoned and halved
      1 pint (6 dl.) batter
      3 oz. (90 g.) butter
      2 oz. (60 g.) caster sugar

Make a batter as in the pancake batter Basic Recipe 2.

Fry the apricots gently in butter for 2 or 3 minutes till beginning to soften. Remove apricots from pan, stir in the sugar and keep hot. Add some more butter to that in which the apricots were cooked, and make it very hot. Pour in half the batter. As it begins to cook and solidify, spoon the apricots on to it. Pour on the remaining batter. As soon as the bottom of the froise has browned, turn it right over (if necessary, slide it on to a plate), add a little more butter to the pan if required, and put the froise back to brown on the other side.

Scotch Pancakes or Dropped Scones

½ lb. (240 g.) self-raising flour	milk to mix
½ teaspoon salt	2 teaspoons sugar
1 egg	oil to grease girdle
½ oz. (15 g.) butter	

Mix together the flour and salt. Add the egg, well beaten, and the butter, melted. Mix with the milk to make a batter that will just drop from the spoon, like thick cream. Drop in tablespoonfuls on to a hot girdle, greased with oil, a little distance apart, and cook for 2 to 3 minutes, then turn and cook on the other side. Serve hot or cold.

A heavy frying pan can be used instead of a girdle.

Cheese and Cheese Dishes

A cantle of Essex cheese
Was well a foot thick
Full of maggots quick:
It was huge and great
And mighty Strong meat
For the devil to eat.
It was tart and punicate.
JOHN SKELTON

Such cheese was indeed strong meat: it was also one of the chief sources of protein of the lower classes, always available in great houses in Tudor days to the servants at the lower tables in the great hall, so that even if the daintier viands ran short before all were served they could be sure of having full bellies. F. G. Emmison in his *Life at Ingatestone Hall* has found from surviving records that two or more great cheeses a week were eaten in the winter of 1551 and later, when the amount was recorded by 'leads' (a lead weighing 56 lb.), between 20 and 160-odd lb. were eaten.

Essex cheeses were, as Skelton makes all too clear, abnormally hard, large and strong and were, in general, made from ewe's milk. Camden, who wrote late in the fifteenth century, was surprised by the vast size of the cheeses made from ewe's milk in the marshes of south-east Essex. At Ingatestone in 1548, 150 'great and huge cheeses' were eaten, and in 1602 about 2,600 lb., the equivalent of more than 200 whole cheeses. More than 100 were generally in store at one time.

Smaller, and presumably more highly esteemed, perhaps milder cheese was sometimes bought outside, for a record of food bought for a wedding feast mentions 'Cheeses: a lead containing 6 cheeses'.

As early as the fifteenth century, other parts of England were producing the cow's milk cheeses which are famous throughout the world, such as Cheddar, Stilton, Cheshire (of which red, white and blue varieties are obtainable) and Double Gloucester. However, there are many fine English cheeses which are very little known and sometimes obtainable only by visitors to the counties where they originate. I give a short list as it is worth enquiring for them when travelling in the provinces.

Caerphilly	Originally Welsh but also made in the West Country. Easy to get, mild. The cheeses weigh about 8 lb. Eaten fresh, whereas farmhouse Cheddar, for example, is kept for some months.
Cottenham	Double cream, with blue veins. Fairly hard: very like Stilton. Rare nowadays.
Derby	Sage Derby is rather like Cheshire but marbled with the dull green of the sage which is worked into it in making.
Dunlop	Scottish cheese. Very good. Rather like Cheddar. Easily obtainable in Scotland and sometimes elsewhere. Cheeses weigh about 60 lb.
Lancashire	Hard. Rather like Cheshire.
Leicester	Hard. Again rather like Cheshire. Can be very good indeed. Cheeses weigh about 40 lb.
Slipcote	Made at Wissenden. Soft and delicious. Made in small cheeses – about ½–1 lb. Originally ripened for a week or so between cabbage leaves. When ready its skin loosens and can be slipped off. Very hard to get now.
Suffolk	The hardest cheese known. Exactly as Essex cheese described on p. 419.
Wensleydale	A Yorkshire cheese, rather white and semi-soft. Apt to be a little chalky. Very easy to obtain. There is a blue-veined type also.

Cheddar is, of course, the most famous of English cheeses. A vast Cheddar cheese was made from the milk of 750 cows as a wedding present to Queen Victoria. It weighed 11 cwt. and was over 9 feet in circumference and 20 inches deep.

Cheese Aigrettes

A Victorian dinner-party savoury. They are very good indeed, but it is a little tricky to get the mixture just right.

It is interesting that Mrs Glasse, in 1747, gives a recipe for what are generally known as aigrettes, calling them 'water fritters'. The recipe, when worked out, is almost exactly as given here except that her aigrettes are of unflavoured paste, fried 'a fine brown' and served with sugar and orange-flavoured water.

1 oz. (30 g.) butter	pepper, salt and cayenne
¼ pint (1½ dl.) water	2 oz. (60 g.) very finely
3 oz. (90 g.) sifted flour	grated Cheddar cheese
3 egg yolks	2 egg whites

Put the butter and water into a saucepan and bring to the boil. Shake the flour quickly into the water when boiling. Reduce heat and stir for 2 minutes, remove from the heat, add the egg yolks, beating them in one by one. Add seasoning and cheese, then fold in the stiffly whisked egg whites. Drop the mixture by teaspoonfuls into very hot deep fat, and fry until golden brown. They will take about 3 minutes to cook. Drain on paper and serve at once.

Gloucester Cheese and Ale

This recipe goes back to the Middle Ages: the dish was sometimes served like this to travellers arriving at Gloucestershire or Oxfordshire inns when the meat and birds were finished. It was originally, of course, a farmer's winter supper dish, but at least one Cotswold manor house still makes it, though cut in neater and smaller portions than those served by earlier farmers' and innkeepers' wives, and made at table in a chafing dish.

For 4

½ lb. (240 g.) coarsely grated Gloucester cheese
2 teaspoons made mustard
1 pint (6 dl.) brown ale, less 3 tablespoons saved and heated separately
4 large slices of rather thick fresh hot brown toast with crusts removed

Put the cheese in a flat fireproof dish or skillet. Daub and spread the mustard over it and then pour on the ale. Stir it over low heat until it is all amalgamated and bubbling. Put the toasts on plates and spread the cheese mixture on them, allowing it to run over. Spoon a little of the hot ale on each piece and serve immediately, very hot.

Macaroni Cheese and Cauliflower Cheese

These two very excellent dishes have been heartily disliked by many an Englishman because they are abominably made at schools and by boarding-house landladies. They are good luncheon or supper dishes, and the following rather grand recipe should bring many converts.

1 pint (6 dl.) good cheese sauce (p. 283)
4 oz. (120 g.) finely grated Cheddar cheese
¼ pint (1½ dl.) double cream
freshly ground black pepper
½ oz. (15 g.) butter
¾ lb. (360 g.) (when cooked) of macaroni *or* spaghetti (just tender but not overcooked) *or* 1 large cooked cauliflower, tender but not over-cooked, broken into flowerets

Prepare or heat up the cheese sauce and add an extra 2 oz (60 g.) of grated cheese to increase the flavour. Stir, just boiling, for 2 minutes: the cheese should not be quite melted. Stir in the cream and the pepper. Taste for seasoning. The sauce should be very little thicker than the cream which was added to it. Lightly butter a wide, open fireproof dish. Put in half the macaroni or all the cauliflower sprigs, arranging the latter flower upwards. Add the almost boiling sauce. In the case of the macaroni stir it gently in to what is in the dish and then put in the rest and stir again. In this way all the pieces of macaroni are separate and coated. Don't stir the cauliflower, as the sauce will penetrate and it is a pity to squash the flowerets. There should be a certain amount of free sauce in the dish, so that it cannot be stodgy. Cover the top thickly with grated cheese and dot with butter. Put in a hot oven, 400° F., gas mark 6, for 10 minutes and then under a hot grill, so that the top is really crisp and golden brown all over.

It will reheat quite well but is better freshly made, as the sauce is apt to boil and reduce and the macaroni becomes stodgy and the cauliflower mushy.

Hard-Boiled Eggs in Cheese Sauce

These may be made exactly as Macaroni Cheese, above, allowing 1 pint (6 dl.)

of finished sauce for 4 eggs. They are usually cut in half longways and laid yolk sides up in the bottom of a dish and the sauce poured over them. They are then finished in the same way as Macaroni Cheese.

Mock Crab

For each person:

2 oz. (60 g.) cheese   cayenne and paprika
2 oz. (60 g.) butter   bread
anchovy essence or paste

Work the grated cheese into the butter. Cream well and then stir in a pinch of cayenne, a pinch of paprika, ½ teaspoon of anchovy essence or a teaspoon of anchovy paste. Season with salt if necessary and a little lemon juice if liked. Spread on fresh toast and serve cold, or put under hot grill for 1 minute only. The paprika and anchovy give the mixture the faint pink colour of crab and a suspicion of its flavour, but the dish is really a very good variant of toasted cheese.

Cheese Pasties

Traditional in various counties and extremely good for picnics or summer lunches with salad.

Recipe from Lancashire

For 8–10 pasties

1 lb. (½ k.) flaky or short pastry (pp. 94, 93)
¾ lb. (360 g.) Cheddar or Cheshire cheese, coarsely grated
¼ lb. (120 g.) butter
egg to gild and milk to moisten
cayenne, salt and black pepper
chives or shallot, very finely chopped

Roll out the pastry ⅛ inch thick and cut in approximate rounds about 5 inches (13 cm.) in diameter.

Break the butter into small pieces, mix with the cheese, put a tablespoonful into the middle of each pastry round and sprinkle with a pinch of cayenne and very little salt, plenty of black pepper and a little of the chopped chives or shallot. Moisten the edges of the rounds with milk, fold over and press well together with a fork to make a patterned edge. Brush over with beaten egg yolk. Bake at 400° F., gas mark 6, for 20 minutes. Serve very hot.

Recipe from Cornwall

Exactly as above except that diced cooked potatoes are added to the cheese filling, and the pasties are made rather larger.

Cheese Straws

A traditional after-dinner savoury, served in tiny 2-inch (5-cm.) long strips which are gathered before being baked into a bundle of 6 or 8, ringed round with another strip and baked so that they look like little sheaves of corn.

For 4

    ¼ lb. (120 g.) puff paste (frozen is good)
    2 oz. (60 g.) finely grated Cheddar or Cheshire cheese
    a pinch freshly ground black pepper
    a pinch cayenne pepper

Roll the pastry thin and sprinkle half of it evenly with the cheese and pepper. Fold the other half over and roll out towards the folded edge, to seal in the cheese. Fold and roll again, so that it is about ⅛ inch (⅓ cm.) thick. Cut into straw-thin strips and make into sheaves as described above. Lay them on a very lightly floured baking tin and cook for 5–7 minutes at 450° F., gas mark 8. Serve very hot. They will reheat perfectly.

Cheese Tart with a Separate Sauce

For 4

    a small packet of frozen puff pastry   ½ pint (3 dl.) milk
    ½ lb. (240 g.) Cheddar cheese   2 oz. (60 g.) plain flour
    2 eggs   seasoning
    2 oz. (60 g.) butter   2 tablespoons double cream

Roll the pastry very thin to make a 9-inch (22-cm.) round case. Bake blind at 425° F., gas mark 7–8. After 10 minutes remove from the oven and with a sharp knife cut round and lift out the puffed part of the centre, being careful not to cut through the bottom layers. The part cut out can be turned upside down and baked for 5 minutes and used as a lid for the tart or to fill as a separate tart. Bake another 5 minutes at a slightly lower heat to crisp the underlayers. While the pastry cools, make a good cheese sauce, rather thicker than usual, with the butter, flour, milk and cheese. Reserve half. Beat 2 eggs and stir into one half when slightly cooled. Pour into the pastry case and bake for 20 minutes at 350° F., gas mark 4. Meanwhile reheat the remaining cheese sauce and thin with the cream. Serve hot with the tart, which may be served as soon as it is baked or set aside and reheated.

A Mild Rarebit

> ¼ pint (1½ dl.) thick, well-seasoned cheese sauce (p. 283), hot but not boiling
> 2 slices toast
> ½ oz. (15 g.) butter
> 1 oz. (30 g.) finely grated cheese

Butter the toast and then pile on the sauce, allowing it to spread outwards. Sprinkle with the grated cheese and put under a hot grill to bubble and brown.

'English Rabbit' (1830)

For 2

> 2 thin slices of bread, soaked in a glass of red wine for a few minutes
> ¼ lb. (120 g.) cheese, coarsely grated
> 1 oz. (30 g.) butter
> 2 tablespoons white wine (or more of the red)
> 2 teaspoons made mustard

Put the soaked bread, dotted with butter, under a hot grill (turning once), while you butter a shallow fireproof dish, lay the cheese on it, dab on the mustard and pour over it the wine. Cover with foil. Set the pan on moderate heat for 2 or 3 minutes, then stir hard until all is smoothly mixed. Spread it quickly on the toasted bread and brown lightly. The large proportion of wine with the cheese in this 'rabbit' gives a delicious flavour.

Welsh Rarebit, 1

> 1 slice of toast per person
> 2 oz. (60 g.) cheese per person
> 2 oz. (60 g.) butter per person
> 1 teaspoon made mustard
> 1 tablespoon of beer } optional
> 1 egg yolk
> salt and pepper

Grate the cheese – use Cheddar or Cheshire. Melt the butter in a small thick saucepan, stir in the cheese with a teaspoon of made mustard and the seasoning. Stir over gentle heat until the cheese melts. This mixture may be spread on hot toast and toasted under the grill as it is or an egg yolk may be stirred in to bind. A tablespoon of beer may also be stirred in before grilling. Serve very hot.

Buck Rarebit

As Welsh Rarebit, but with a poached egg placed on each portion.

Welsh Rarebit, 2

From a Warwickshire manuscript of the eighteenth century.

2 tablespoons ale	1 teaspoon made mustard
4 oz. (120 g.) grated cheese	1 oz. (30 g.) butter
pepper and salt	2 slices of toast

Put the ale in a saucepan, add the cheese and melt it in the ale over low heat. When hot and soft, stir in the mustard, butter, salt and pepper. Heat and stir till you have a rather liquid paste. Pour on to the middle of each slice of toast so that it can spread outwards without running over, and brown under the grill.

Roast Cheese, to come up after dinner

This is Mrs Rundle's recipe of 1807, and very good it is as a supper dish or in tiny quantities as a savoury.

For 4 or 5, or to make 12 to 14 savouries
    3 oz. (90 g.) Cheshire cheese, finely grated
    yolks of 2 eggs
    3 oz. (90 g.) breadcrumbs
    1 teaspoon made mustard
    a little salt and plenty of pepper
    4 or 5 slices of toast

Beat all the ingredients well together (or put them in a blender). Well cover the slices of toast (cut into small strips if to be used for a savoury) with the resulting paste, lay on a baking tin, cover with foil and put in hot oven,

400° F., gas mark 6, for 10 minutes. Remove the foil and allow to brown slightly but not too much.

Stewed Cheese (1830)

As served to the gentlemen of St James's. This is one of Dolby's recipes from the Thatched House Tavern and is simply an English version of the famous Swiss fondue.

> ¼ lb. (120 g.) Cheshire cheese
> ¼ lb. (120 g.) Gloucester cheese
> 1 wineglass red wine
> 1 teaspoon made mustard
> ½ teaspoon freshly ground black pepper

Stir all together over a low heat until the cheese is melted: do not let the mixture get too hot or the cheese may separate. Serve in a fireproof dish over a light, with plenty of fresh toast.

Toasted Cheese

The oldest hot supper in England. Two great slices with a pint of ale made a supper for a hungry man who had worked all day in the fields. A tiny strip, 1 inch by 2, made an elegant finish to a fine dinner for a gentleman who was about to drink some vintage port and maybe a glass or two of brandy.

This recipe is from Yorkshire.

Per person
> 1 slice of bread
> ½ oz. (15 g.) butter
> 2 oz. (60 g.) cheese

Cheddar or Cheshire cheese is best. Cut a slice about ⅛ inch (⅓ cm.) thick to fit a piece of bread from which the crust has been removed. Make the grill very hot. Toast the bread on both sides if wanted very crisp, on one side only if wanted softer. Butter thinly, lay the cheese on the buttered side and toast it for a moment, then turn it over on the toast just as it begins to melt, and toast it for 1½ minutes. Remove and sprinkle lightly with pepper and very little salt and serve at once. If liked, spread thinly with made mustard before serving. Ale should be drunk with this but red wine is also very good.

Painter's Toasted Cheese

Michael Ayrton's recipe.

For 2

> ¼ lb. (120 g.) Cheddar cheese
> 2 oz. (60 g.) butter
> a little milk
> fresh black pepper
> salt
> 2 slices of toast

Chop the cheese roughly into ¼ inch (½ cm.) pieces. Work these into the butter till the mixture is fairly soft. Work in about a tablespoon of milk, very little salt and plenty of black pepper. Spread direct on the toast, covering it all over ¼–½ inch thick. Place under a hot grill until it bubbles and begins to brown (3 to 5 minutes).

This is very much better than simple toasted cheese as the mixture is more creamy.

When the painter was in funds he put fried mushrooms, tomatoes or eggs on top of the cheese; being very young when he evolved this recipe, he often smothered the cheese with fried onions, but this would be too much for most digestions.

10 · HOT PUDDINGS

'Blessed be he that invented pudding, for it is a Manna that hits the Palates of all Sortes of People,' wrote Monsieur M. Misson in his Memoirs on his visit to London at the beginning of the eighteenth century.

Sugar had been a luxury too expensive for many until the beginning of the eighteenth century, when the price dropped to about 6d. per pound. Once it had done so, the practice of 'scraping' the conical sugar-loaf over the crust of a pie and of supplementing sugar in the contents with raisins, was enlarged to a fuller use of sugar in pies and tarts and to its use with 'flower' to make puddings.

At first the puddings formed part of the second or third course, which might also consist of fish, some lighter meat dishes, pies, tarts, vegetables or fruit. By the beginning of the nineteenth century they often, though not invariably, followed the savoury dishes as a separate course. In the first part of the eighteenth century a 'pudding' almost always meant a basis of flour and suet with dried fruit, sugar and eggs added. As the century went on, hundreds of variations were evolved, recipes multiplied; even the plainest dinner served above the poverty line was not complete without its pudding.

Hot puddings, cold puddings, steamed puddings, baked puddings, pies, tarts, creams, moulds, charlottes and bettys, trifles and fools, syllabubs and tansys, junkets and ices, milk puddings, suet puddings: 'pudding' used as a generic term covers so many dishes traditional in English cookery that the mind reels as it dwells on these almost vanished splendours of our tables.

For vanished they almost are. Our grandfathers, even our fathers, expected a 'pudding' at least once a day, sometimes twice; once a day a different pudding was made for the nursery, so that the cook in a middle-class household, before the Second World War, would certainly make at least seven and maybe a dozen different puddings in every week of the year. When there was a children's party she would add two or three jellies, maybe a trifle or two, perhaps blancmange and some tarts; and when there was a dinner party she would make two or three cold sweets. In a poorer household the mistress would make a pudding once every day, if it were only stewed-fruit-and-custard.

But how many puddings do we make in a week today? Often none at all: fearing an excess of carbohydrates and animal fats and jealous of our time, we serve fruit and cheese and coffee after one or two savoury courses. Sometimes we make a tart or stew some soft fruit to make a purée or perhaps a fool. We may make pancakes or a chocolate cream or jelly for the children. For a dinner party we make a chocolate mousse, an orange cream or meringues; sometimes a chocolate or an almond cake. And this, I think, is as it should be: our attention and our energy should be expended on the main course of the meal and perhaps a starting course, and the pudding should be an occasion, almost a 'happening', served for a treat or because the first course of the meal seemed light or because there are guests and the meal is to be more formal than usual, or sometimes purely for nostalgia because someone has mentioned the puddings of his childhood.

Sometimes the puddings of youth are recollected not with nostalgia but with horror: who does not remember steamed ginger pudding (and I have always hated ginger anyway), which had little shiny bits of suet visible in its ugly yellow-brown texture? Who doesn't remember apple or dried apricot hat, with the fruit very sour and the suet pastry gone white and slimy where the water had got in?

However, many of the hot puddings are not only very good if they are properly made but are cheap and easy to make. All those given here are traditional, the recipes going back at least to the nineteenth century and some much earlier.

It is assumed that self-raising flour is used in all recipes for hot puddings unless plain flour is specifically recommended. Extra baking powder or bicarbonate of soda is occasionally recommended for use with self-raising flour.

Light Steamed, Boiled or Baked Puddings

There are literally hundreds of recipes for this type of pudding, all basically much the same and often called by the names of the district or city where they originated or where they were most frequently served. A very full range is still served by the merchant navy at middle-day dinner.

The following are examples:

Snowdon pudding
Buxton pudding
Chelsea pudding
Birmingham pudding
Helston pudding
Madeira pudding
Canary pudding
Black cap pudding
Cabinet pudding
Seven cup pudding
Manchester pudding

Newcastle pudding
New Market pudding
Portland pudding
Guards' pudding
Orange pudding
Lemon pudding
Golden pudding
Railway pudding
Eve's pudding
West Riding pudding

Recipes for a few of the most interesting are given here.

There are three basic methods, and only three, by which such puddings are made:

For light recipes, butter and sugar are creamed together and beaten eggs and flour, with flavourings or fruit, added to the mixture, which is then well beaten.

For rather more solid recipes, flour is rubbed into the butter until the mixture has the consistency of crumbs, and sugar, eggs, flavourings, fruit, are stirred into this mixture.

Lastly, the most solid puddings are made with suet (now almost always bought prepared in a packet). This is simply stirred into the flour, all other ingredients are added and the mixture is moistened with eggs (if the recipe calls for them), milk or water. The plainest of all suet puddings simply consists of flour, suet, a little salt and water, mixed to a stiff dough, made into a roll, floured, tied in a cloth, boiled two or three hours, and served with jam or golden syrup. When currants were added it was called Spotted Dick. This is the easiest, the simplest, cheapest and most filling type of pudding known.

Variations on these methods use oatmeal or breadcrumbs.

Small Almond Puddings

Mrs Rundle* tells us that:

'Very good puddings may be made without eggs . . . a few spoonfuls of fresh small beer or one of yeast will answer instead of eggs.

'Or snow is an excellent substitute for eggs, either in puddings or pancakes [see p. 414]. Two large spoonfuls will supply the place of one egg and the article it is used in will be equally good. This is a useful piece of information, especially as snow often falls at the season when eggs are dearest . . . The snow may be taken up from any clean spot before it is wanted and will not lose its virtue, though the sooner it is used the better.'

Very strange information, but not without foundation, since the snow forms air pockets in a light batter by leaving small holes as it melts, making the batter light and well risen. However, eggs are required for their flavour, fat and protein content and not only as a rising agent, and puddings without eggs tend to have a poor, watery taste. Small Almond Puddings are very good if made with four eggs, and it is my view that there is no satisfactory substitute for them. I have here adapted the recipe:

8 oz. (240 g.) ground almonds	4 oz. (120 g.) butter
1 oz. (30 g.) whole almonds, chopped	2 oz. (60 g.) sugar
	2 tablespoons double cream
4 eggs	1 tablespoon brandy

Mix the almonds all together with the butter melted in a tablespoon of water. Well beat the eggs (having separated and kept back two whites) and stir them together with the sugar, cream and brandy into the almond mixture. Place in small buttered soufflé dishes or ramekins and bake, standing in a tray of water, for 15 minutes at 350° F., gas mark 4, when they should be just firm to the touch. Turn out and serve with any sweet sauce.

* In *A New System of Domestic Cookery*, 1807.

Mrs Rundle suggests 'pudding-sauce', i.e. sweet white sauce (see p. 308), but they are better with a sharp orange or lemon sauce (see p. 308).

Cabinet (or Chancellor's) Pudding

Serves 4

4 sponge cakes *or* 12 sponge fingers	2 oz. (60 g.) currants
2 eggs	2 oz. (60 g.) sultanas
2 oz. (60 g.) caster sugar	12 glacé cherries
½ pint (3 dl.) milk	12 small pieces angelica
vanilla essence	

Cut the sponge cakes and crumble lightly. Whisk the eggs with the sugar. Heat the milk slowly. Add the hot milk and the flavouring to the eggs and sugar. Pour gently over the cake and stir in currants and sultanas. Cover and leave to soak until quite cold. Grease a plain mould and put a round of greased paper or a piece of foil in the bottom. Decorate with pieces of cherry and angelica. Pour the soaked mixture on to this. Cover tightly with foil and place a saucer over it. Steam gently until firm – about ¾ to 1 hour. Turn out of the mould and remove the paper from what is now the top. Serve with a Jam or Hard Sauce (p. 309).

College Puddings

These are always served as individual baked puddings. A few recipes suggest butter instead of suet, but traditionally butter was used in castle puddings and suet in college puddings.

2 oz. (60 g.) currants or other dried fruit	2 oz. (60 g.) sugar
	a pinch of salt
1 oz. (30 g.) candied peel, if liked	1 teaspoon grated nutmeg
3 oz. (90 g.) shredded suet	2 eggs
4 oz. (120 g.) breadcrumbs	1 tablespoon milk
2 oz. (60 g.) self-raising flour	

Grease 6 cups or cocotte moulds well. Shred the peel (if used). Mix the shredded suet, fruit, breadcrumbs, flour, sugar, nutmeg, salt and peel together. Beat the eggs and stir them into the mixture. Add the milk. Pour the mixture into the cups.

Bake in the oven at 350° F., gas mark 4, for 20–25 minutes, standing the cups in a baking tray in which is an inch or so of water. When ready, turn out and serve with hard sauce or custard sauce (see pp. 308, 309).

New College Pudding, traditional at New College, Oxford, consists of spoon-fuls of the same mixture dropped into a pan of very hot butter, which must not colour, fried fast for 3 minutes on each side and served dusted with caster sugar.

Castle Puddings

These are lighter and richer than college puddings, which were traditionally made for 'poor scholars' on feast days, whereas castle puddings were made for the great.

Serves 6

4 oz. (120 g.) sugar	6 oz. (180 g.) self-raising flour
4 oz. (120 g.) butter	2 tablespoons milk
2 eggs	jam sauce or hard sauce
½ teaspoon grated lemon zest	

Grease 6 or 8 cocottes or dariole moulds. Cream the butter and sugar; add the eggs and lemon zest and beat well. Fold in the sifted flour and then add the milk. Half-fill each mould with the mixture and bake for 10–15 minutes at 400° F., gas mark 6.

Turn out and serve with jam sauce or hard sauce. (See p. 308.)

Newcastle Pudding

This recipe comes from a Newcastle household where it is still made almost every week.

Serves 4–6

4 oz. (120 g.) butter	6 oz. (180 g.) self-raising flour
4 oz. (120 g.) caster sugar	a little milk
2 eggs	12 glacé cherries

Grease a bowl, halve the cherries and press them round the bottom and sides.

Cream the butter and sugar, add the eggs and beat well. Fold in the flour and beat again, adding a little milk if the mixture is too sticky. Turn into the bowl, which should be about two thirds full. Cover closely with foil and steam 1½ hours.

Turn out and serve with jam sauce (see p. 308).

The following dish is also known as Newcastle Pudding in at least one manor house in Northumberland:

> 12 slices of fairly thin bread and butter without crusts (bread should not be new)
> 3–4 oz. (90–120 g.) caster sugar
> grated rind of 2 lemons
> 3 eggs
> 1 pint (6 dl.) milk
> a little extra butter
> lemon sauce

Butter the inside of a pudding basin. Sprinkle the sugar and lemon zest on each slice of bread and butter and pile them into the basin. Beat the eggs into the milk and sweeten with a little of the sugar. Pour over the bread and butter. Dot the top with a few little bits of butter and cover closely with foil. Steam for 1 ½ hours. Serve with lemon sauce (p. 309).

Both these puddings are light and very good.

Quaking Pudding

This is the lightest and most delicious of all boiled puddings. When it is turned out it is almost solid, but quakes and shakes like a jelly when moved. Cracks appear on the surface, and it must be moved gently to prevent its cracking into several parts. From the sixteenth century onwards, recipes appear in the majority of cook books. Mrs Rundle in 1803 and Richard Dolby in 1830 give the same traditional recipe, using only flour. The earlier recipe of Mrs Anne Blencowe (1680), which uses flour and breadcrumbs, seems to me to give the best results.

'*A Quakin Puding*'

1 pint (6 dl.) double cream	1½ oz. (45 g.) flour
3 eggs plus one extra white	2–3 tablespoons very fine white
a pinch of mace and of nutmeg	breadcrumbs
¼ lb. (120 g.) caster sugar	

For the sauce:

2 glasses white wine or claret	1 oz. (30 g.) sugar
3 oz. (90 g.) butter	

Bring the cream slowly to the boil and boil for half a minute; allow to cool a little. Well beat the eggs and stir them into the cream, beating well. Allow to get quite cold. It will be fairly thick. Beat in the flour, nutmeg, mace, sugar and breadcrumbs. Use only the amount of breadcrumbs required to bring the cream to the consistency of butter; this may be less than 2 table-spoonfuls or a little more. Flour the whole pudding lightly, tie it in a greased and floured cloth and boil it for an hour and a half. Never let it go off the boil, and fill up with boiling water if necessary.

If preferred, a large pudding basin can be buttered and the pudding steamed, well covered with foil, for an hour and a half.

For the traditional sauce, stir 2 glasses of white wine or claret and a tablespoon of caster sugar into 3 oz. (90 g.) of melted butter.

Sponge Pudding

Also called *Canary pudding* when served with apricot jam sauce; *Golden pudding* when served with golden syrup; and *Black cap pudding* when the bottom of the bowl is covered with currants before the pudding mixture is put in.

Serves 3 or 4

2 oz. (60 g.) currants, apricot
jam or golden syrup
2 oz. (60 g.) butter
2 oz. (60 g.) caster sugar

¼ lb. (120 g.) self-raising flour
2 eggs
4 tablespoons milk

Grease a pint basin, then put a thick layer of currants, jam or syrup at the bottom. Beat the butter and sugar to a cream. Sift the flour and stir into the mixture alternately with the beaten eggs and milk. Beat well for a moment or two, then turn into the prepared basin, cover with foil and steam for 1 hour.

Suet Puddings

Steamed Apple Dumplings

1 large cooking apple per person
½ oz. (15 g.) sugar per apple

suet pastry (p. 95)

Peel and core the apples, being careful not to break them. Roll out the pastry ¼ inch (½ cm.) thick into rounds the size of a tea plate. Place each apple on a round of pastry. Fill the core-hole with sugar. Draw up the edges of the pastry, wet them and press on to the apple.

Tie each one in a cloth lined with greaseproof paper, drop into boiling water and boil briskly for half an hour.

CHRISTMAS PUDDING, I

The greatest of all the suet puddings is, of course, Christmas pudding. King George I, sometimes unkindly called the 'Pudding King', was served with a pudding made from the following recipe on Christmas Day 1714, which was his first Christmas in England.

King George I's Christmas Pudding

For 1 large and 2 small puddings
    ¾ lb. (360 g.) shredded suet
    6 eggs
    ½ lb. (240 g.) stoned prunes
    ½ lb. (240 g.) mixed peel, cut in strips
    ½ lb. (240 g.) small raisins
    ½ lb. (240 g.) seedless sultanas
    ½ lb. (240 g.) currants
    ½ lb. (240 g.) sifted self-raising flour
    ½ lb. (240 g.) demerara sugar
    ½ lb. (240 g.) brown crumbs
    ¼ lb. (120 g.) dates
    ¼ lb. (120 g.) glacé cherries
    1 teaspoon mixed spice
    ½ nutmeg, grated
    1 teaspoon salt
    ¼ pint (1½ dl.) milk
    juice of half a lemon
    a large wineglass brandy

Mix the dry ingredients, stir in the eggs, beaten to a froth, and the milk, lemon juice and brandy mixed. Stand for 12 hours in a cool place, then turn into buttered basins. Boil for 6 hours. On Christmas Day, boil for 2 hours or more before serving.

To boil, cover the basins with buttered greaseproof paper or foil and then tie each one with a cloth. Stand in a fish kettle or bath or separately in large saucepans, so that the water comes half-way up each bowl. Renew water by adding more boiling water from time to time. The puddings will keep for 2 years.

Christmas Pudding, 2

This recipe produces a blacker pudding than George I's. It is one of the earliest recipes I have found which is for a boiled Christmas pudding rather than for mincemeat served in a 'coffin' and called Christmas Pye, which was the earlier form. It dates to about 1700 and comes from Edinburgh.

For 4 large puddings

> 1½ lb. (¾ k.) fine white breadcrumbs
> 1½ lb. (¾ k.) currants
> peel of 1 large lemon
> a little nutmeg or mixed spice
> ¾ lb. (360 g.) candied peel, *or* stoned chopped dates and prunes, if preferred
> ½ pint (3 dl.) milk
> 1 lb. (½ k.) sultanas
> 1½ lb. (¾ k.) seedless raisins
> 1 lb. (½ k.) suet
> ¼ lb. (120 g.) almonds
> ½ lb. (240 g.) dark sugar
> 8 eggs
> 1 wineglass brandy and 1 wineglass of rum *or* 2 glasses brandy

Well mix all the dried fruit with the suet and breadcrumbs. Add the almonds, blanched and finely chopped, nutmeg, mixed spice and sugar. When all are thoroughly blended, stir in 8 well-beaten eggs, the rum and brandy, and half a pint of milk. Stand for 12 hours and then put into bowls as for the previous recipe, and boil 6 hours before and 2 hours on Christmas Day.

These puddings will also keep for 2 years.

Fruit Hat

Serves 8

> 1 lb. (½ k.) self-raising flour
> 6–8 oz. (180–240 g.) chopped suet
> a good pinch of salt
> cold water
>
> *For the filling:*
> 1–1¼ lb. (½ k.) fruit: cooking apples, plums, apricots (fresh or dried), cherries, rhubarb, etc.

2–4 oz. (60–120 g.) sugar, depending on tartness of fruit
about 3 tablespoons cold water

Prepare the fruit as for stewing.

Sieve the flour and salt into a bowl, add the suet, and mix to a firm dough with water. Grease a 1½-pint (1-l.) pudding basin and line with the dough, leaving a quarter for the top. Fill with fruit and sugar, add the water, and mould the remaining dough into a round the size of the top of the pudding. Damp the edges and fit on to the pudding. Cover with greased paper and steam for 1½–2 hours. Turn out and serve.

Ginger Pudding

Serves 4–6

3 oz. (90 g.) plain flour	3 oz. (90 g.) fresh breadcrumbs
1 level teaspoon bicarbonate of soda	1 egg
a pinch of salt	2 tablespoons golden syrup
2 level teaspoons ground ginger	2 tablespoons milk
2–3 oz. (60–90 g.) suet	1 oz. (15 g.) chopped preserved ginger

Sieve together the flour, soda, salt and ground ginger. Mix in the suet and add the breadcrumbs. Mix to a soft consistency with the beaten egg, syrup and milk. Turn into a greased 1-pint (6-dl.) basin, cover with greased paper and steam 1¼–1½ hours. Serve with a custard sauce (see p. 309), to which chopped preserved ginger has been added.

Jam or Treacle Roly-Poly Pudding

Serves 6–8

½ lb. (240 g.) self-raising flour	jam or golden syrup
4 oz. (120 g.) finely chopped suet	a pinch of salt
1 teaspoon baking powder	

Put the flour into a basin, add to it the suet, salt, and baking powder. Mix it with a little cold water, roll it out and wet the edges. Spread it with jam or syrup, leaving 1 inch all round, and roll it up in the form of a bolster. Seal the ends well. Flour a cloth and tie the pudding securely in it. Drop into a large saucepan of rapidly boiling water and boil for 2 hours. Do not allow the pudding to go off the boil, or it will be soggy and heavy. If water is boiling away, add more *boiling* water. Lift the pudding on to a dish, unwrap the cloth quickly, and serve at once with more jam or jam sauce (see p. 308).

Spotted Dick

For 6

> 8 oz. (240 g.) self-raising flour
> 4 oz. (120 g.) suet
> a pinch of salt
> 2–3 oz. (60–90 g.) currants, sultanas or raisins
> milk

Mix all the ingredients together and moisten with a little milk to make a stiff dough. Tie tightly in a floured cloth, drop into boiling water and boil briskly for 2 hours. Serve with caster sugar or with hard sauce (see p. 308).

If preferred, the pudding may be put into a well-greased pudding basin, covered with foil and steamed for 2–2½ hours: but traditionally it was always boiled, usually in a big pot in which other things were cooking.

Plain Suet Pudding

Serves 6–8

> 8 oz. (240 g.) self-raising flour *or* half flour and half breadcrumbs
> a pinch of salt
> 4 oz. (120 g.) shredded suet
> cold water

Sift the flour and salt. Add the suet and just enough cold water to make a stiff paste. Dip a pudding cloth into boiling water, wring it out and flour it well; put the paste into it, roll up and leave enough room for the pudding to swell. Tie up the ends very securely, plunge it into a pan full of fast-boiling water and boil for 2 hours, being careful not to let water go off boil. Fill the pan up with *boiling* water if there is danger of the pudding boiling dry.

Plain suet pudding was traditionally served with butter and brown sugar, but it is also good with jam, treacle, or hard sauce (see p. 308).

Sultana or Raisin Pudding

Serves 4

> 2 oz. (60 g.) sugar

3 oz. (90 g.) self-raising flour
½ level teaspoon baking powder
3 oz. (90 g.) fresh breadcrumbs
3 oz. (90 g.) chopped suet
2 oz. (60 g.) sultanas or raisins
1 egg
¼ pint (1½ dl.) milk
grated rind of ½ lemon

Mix the sugar, flour and baking powder together and stir in breadcrumbs, suet, and prepared fruit. Mix with beaten egg and milk, adding lemon. Pour into a greased 1-pint (6-dl.) basin and cover with greased paper or foil. Steam for 1½ hours.

For a *Steamed Jam Pudding*, use the same mixture without the fruit. Put 2 tablespoons of jam in the greased basin, and pour the pudding mixture on top of it. Turn out when cooked and serve with jam sauce (p. 308).

Treacle Pudding

Serves 6

2 oz. (60 g.) breadcrumbs
4 oz. (120 g.) flour
½ teaspoon baking powder
3 oz. (90 g.) shredded suet
1½ oz. (45 g.) sugar
   (preferably brown)

1 egg
2 tablespoons golden syrup
¼ pint (1½ dl.) milk

Put all the dry ingredients in a bowl. Mix well together. Beat the egg and pour it, with the syrup slightly warmed, into the middle of the dry ingredients. Beat them in gradually, adding sufficient of the milk to make a dropping consistency. Grease a pudding basin and pour the mixture into it. Cover with foil. Put into a pan with boiling water rising about half-way up the basin. Steam for 1½ hours. Turn out and serve with warmed golden syrup to which a tablespoonful of lemon juice has been added.

Kentish Well Pudding

This is a traditional farmhouse recipe which has pleased hungry men and delighted children since the seventeenth century and probably earlier. It is almost never made now, and this is a pity. It is too heavy for the urban and sedentary lives most of us lead for most of the time today, but it is splendid for a cold day in the Christmas holidays.

Serves 8

> 1 lb. (½ k.) self-raising flour
> 6 oz. (180 g.) shredded suet
> 6 oz. (180 g.) currants
> ½ lb. (240 g.) unsalted butter
> ¼ lb. (120 g.) soft brown sugar

Mix the flour, suet and currants with water to form a soft dough. Roll out about 1½ inches (4 cm.) thick and press into a large well-greased pudding basin, reserving a quarter of the suet crust for the top. Put the butter in one piece in the centre and the sugar round the butter to fill up the well. Cover with the remaining crust, pinching the edges firmly together. Cover closely with foil and steam for 2 hours. Turn out carefully. When cut, melted butter and sugar should run out, though part will have been absorbed, making a rich and delicious centre.

Milk Puddings

Rice pudding is by far the best of the farinaceous milk puddings served by tradition in Victorian nurseries. I have included the standard simple traditional recipes for semolina, ground rice, pearl tapioca and sago puddings and three recipes for rice puddings of increasing richness.

Rice Pudding

Serves 3

> 1½ oz. (45 g.) Carolina rice
> 1 oz. (30 g.) sugar
> 1 pint (6 dl.) milk
> ½ oz. (15 g.) butter

Put the rice in a well-buttered pie dish with the sugar. Pour on the milk. Bake in a slow oven at 200–250° F., gas mark 2. After 10 minutes, stir with a wooden spoon to prevent the cream rising to the top and the rice coagulating. Stir again 10 minutes later. Then leave for about 2 hours. If you require a hotter oven for other dishes, stand the pudding in a tray of water.

Rich Rice Pudding

This is a much richer version. Sultanas are often added, or the pudding is served with a jam sauce (see p. 308).

For 3–4

1½ oz. (45 g.) Carolina rice   2 eggs
1 pint (6 dl.) milk   vanilla essence
1 oz. (30 g.) sugar

Boil the rice in the milk with the sugar and cook over very low heat, preferably in a double saucepan till the rice is tender. Allow to cool. Stir in 2 well-beaten eggs and a teaspoon of vanilla essence, pour the whole into a buttered pie dish, and bake for 1 hour at 250° F., gas mark 2.

Richard Dolby's Rich Rice Pudding

As served at the Thatched House Tavern in St James's. Dolby thought that his recipe originated in Holland and was first made in England for the court of William of Orange. It is a kind of rich rice soufflé.

Serves 6

¾ lb. (360 g.) puff pastry
2 oz. (60 g.) Carolina rice
¾ pint (4½ dl.) milk
a pinch of cinnamon and a pinch of nutmeg
4 eggs
4 oz. (120 g.) sugar and a little more
2 oz. (60 g.) butter
2 oz. (½ dl.) double cream

Simmer the rice quite gently in the milk with the cinnamon, stirring from time to time to separate the grains. When tender but not mushy, set aside till cold. When cold add the eggs well beaten, the sugar and the nutmeg. Melt the butter in the cream and beat this while hot but not boiling in to the mixture. Line a pie dish with the puff paste rolled out thinly, and make an ornamental edge round the rim of the dish. Pour in the rice mixture. Sprinkle with sugar and bake in an oven preheated to 400° F., gas mark 6, for about 20 minutes. The pastry should be golden brown round the edge of the dish, and the rice mixture, also golden brown, should puff up like a well-baked soufflé. Serve with cream or with a jam sauce (p. 308).

Semolina, Ground Rice, Pearl Tapioca and Sago Puddings

Serves 4

> 1½ oz. (45 g.) cereal: semolina, ground rice, pearl tapioca or sago
> 1 pint (6 dl.) milk
> 2 teaspoons granulated sugar
> 1 egg

Heat the milk in a rinsed saucepan and sprinkle in the cereal; stir till boiling, and simmer until the grain is soft (about 10 minutes for semolina or ground rice and 20 for tapioca or sago). Remove the pan from the fire, add the sugar, and allow the mixture to cool a little. Break the egg and separate the yolk from the white; beat the yolk, add to the cooled cereal and mix well. Beat up the white to a stiff froth, and mix lightly with the other ingredients. Pour into a greased pie dish, and bake in the oven at 350° F., gas mark 4, for about 20 minutes.

Pies, Tarts and Tartlets

These can, in almost all cases, be served hot or cold.

Short Sweet Pastry

Very good for all sweet open tarts where puff pastry is not called for. When the filling itself is very sweet, a good short pastry may be preferred. (For all other pastries, see pp. 90 ff.)

These quantities will make 1 large open tart.

> ½ lb. (240 g.) plain flour
> 4 oz. (120 g.) butter
> 1 egg
> 2 oz. (60 g.) caster sugar
> a pinch of salt

Mix the salt with the flour and sift them into a basin. Rub in the butter, add the sugar. Now stir in the well-beaten egg, and add enough cold water to form a rather stiff dough. Roll out and bake in oven about 425° F., gas mark 7.

A quarter of a teaspoon of grated lemon or orange rind added to the dry ingredients makes a delicious pastry for lemon or orange tartlets.

GERVASE MARKHAM'S COLOURED TARTS BLACK, RED, GREEN, YELLOW AND WHITE

For a great feast, one or two tarts of each colour were served.

'A Prune Tart. Take of the fairest Damask Prunes you can get . . . when they are stewed then bruise them all to mash in their syrup . . . then boyl it over again with Sugar, Cinamon and Rose water, till it be as thick as Marmalade . . . fill the Coffin according to the thickness of the verge – and serve . . . at the second course; and this Tart carrieth the colour black.

'Take Apples and pare them . . . and cook with white wine, good store of Sugar, Cinnamon, a few Saunders [red colouring material] and Rosewater and so boyl till it be thick: . . . and it carrieth the colour red.

'Take good Store of Spinnage, boyl it in a Pipkin with white wine . . . then put to it Rose water, great store of Sugar and Cinnamon and boyl till it be thick as Marmalade: . . . and this carrieth the colour green.

'Take the yelks of Eggs . . . and beat them well with a little cream . . . then take of the sweetest and thickest cream that can be got and set it on the fire . . . put into it Sugar, cinnamon and Rosewater . . . stir in Eggs and so boyl till it curdle: then let the thin whey run away . . . strain and beat well . . . and put it into the Tart Coffin . . . and this carrieth the colour yellow.

'Take the Whites of Eggs and beat them with Rose-water and a little sweet cream . . . then boyl till it curd and this carrieth the colour white . . .'

The filling for all these tarts when finished had become a smooth paste, as stiff as a 'cheese', and it seems likely that only the apple (red) and the custard (yellow) would be at all acceptable to us today. The chief flavour of all of them must have been cinnamon and rosewater.

However, there are delicious recipes for pies and tarts a little later in date. The following apple pie (referred to in the original recipe as apple pudding) and in fact a version of the dish known as apple amber, dates from 1700 and is excellent.

Apple Pudding

'Peel and quarter eight gold runnets, or twelve golden pippins; cast them into water, in which boil them as you do for Apple sauce; sweeten them with loaf sugar, squeeze in them two lemons, and grate in their peels; beat eight eggs, and beat them all well together; pour it into a dish, cover with puff-paste, and bake it an hour in a slow oven.'

It can be made with any cooking apples but is particularly good made with any of the orange-flavoured eating apples, such as Cox's or Ellison's. Use 2½ lb. (1¼ k.) and for present-day tastes, only one lemon. Sieve or blend well when cooked. Frozen puff pastry is excellent. It is also very good with a rich short pastry. A large packet will be needed, as the finished pudding will serve 8.

All English fruit pies (which in America are called 'deep-dish pies'), are made in the same way, the fruit being suitably prepared and extra sugar used if very sour, as in the case of gooseberries.

Apple Pie

Serves 4

     ½–¾ lb. (240–360 g.) short or rough puff pastry
     1½ lb. (¾ k.) cooking apples
     1 tablespoon cold water
     3 oz. (90 g.) sugar
     1 teaspoon grated lemon rind, if liked

Peel, core and slice the apples, and put them in a pie dish just moistened with the water, adding the sugar and lemon rind. Make sure the top layer of apple is not sugared, as if the pastry touches the sugar it will be soggy. Place a pie funnel or an egg cup in the middle to support the crust.

Roll out the pastry. Cut an oval a little larger than the pie dish. From the remaining pastry cut a strip ½ inch (1 cm.) wide; dampen the edges of the pie dish and cover with the strip. Moisten the strip and place the pastry covering over it. Do not stretch the pastry. Pinch the edges firmly to the dish, and decorate with a fork. If no pie funnel is being used slit the pastry with the point of a knife in two places in the middle so that the steam can escape while it is baking. Place in the oven, preheated to 400° F., gas mark 6, for 1–1½ hours.

Dredge with caster sugar before serving.

If the pastry is cooked before the fruit is soft when tested with a knife through the slits in the pastry, move to the lowest shelf and continue cooking. If the pastry still browns too fast, cover lightly with foil or grease-proof paper.

Apple Turnovers and Apple Pasties

The great value of these is that they are not very fragile and can be wrapped and carried on picnics. Cornish fishermen would take a meat and an apple pasty in the boats with them; the Cornish could never have too much pastry. There is no technical difference between a turnover and a pasty.

Make exactly like Baked Apple Dumplings (below) except that the apple should be cut very small and placed in a heap well in the middle of the pastry square, with the sugar in the centre of the heap. The pastry can be folded to make an oblong (traditional for pasties) or corner to corner to make a triangle. Damp the edges with milk and seal well together, crimping with a fork. Glaze with beaten egg yolk and milk or white of egg and sugar.

Jam Puffs are made in the same way, but traditionally are always triangular and smaller, and should be made with puff pastry.

Baked Apple Dumplings

A general favourite for at least the last 100 years, but in particular a speciality given on the farms in Norfolk for shooting luncheons.

 1 apple per person
 3 oz. (90 g.) rough puff or short pastry per person
 ½ oz. (15 g.) sugar per apple
 a pinch of nutmeg and a clove and a few sultanas may be put in each
  apple with the sugar if liked

Roll out the pastry about ⅛ inch (⅓ cm.) thick. Cut into large squares each big enough to gather over an apple. Peel and core the apples and set one in the centre of each square of pastry. Fill the core hole with sugar, sultanas and spices. Gather the pastry over the top, brushing the edges with milk so that the apple is securely encased. Set them smooth side uppermost on a floured baking tray and bake for 10 minutes at 400° F., gas mark 6, and then lower heat to 300° F., gas mark 2, and bake for a further 20 minutes. Serve hot or cold, preferably with cream.

At a Cornish house where I used to go as a child, apple dumplings were served hot on a flat silver dish; the top of each had had a small hole cut in it just before serving and clotted cream spooned in, with a blob left on top. Into each blob was stuck a stoned date. This seemed to me the height of luxury. Ours at home were served plain with the cream separate.

Bedfordshire Apple Florentine Pie

An eighteenth-century recipe, traditionally made at Christmas.

Serves 4

1 lb. (½ k.) short pastry	1 pint (6 dl.) pale ale
4 large cooking apples	¼ teaspoon grated nutmeg
a little butter	a pinch of cinnamon
3 tablespoons demerara sugar	3 cloves
1 teaspoon grated lemon peel	

Peel and core the apples, place in a deep buttered pie dish. Sprinkle with 2 tablespoons of sugar and a teaspoon of grated lemon peel. Cover with a rather thick crust of short pastry and bake for 30 minutes at 450° F., gas mark 6. Carefully lift off the pastry and pour over the apples, after heating together but not boiling, 1 pint of ale, ¼ teaspoon nutmeg, a pinch of cinnamon, 3 cloves and a tablespoon of demerara sugar. Cut the pastry into four pieces and place one on each apple. Serve very hot in bowls, giving each person plenty of the mulled ale.

Some recipes leave the skin on the apples but they are better peeled as they will then absorb some of the spiced ale.

Apricot Pie

This recipe comes from *Adam's Luxury and Eve's Cookery*, 1744, but is there taken from *A Proper Newe Booke of Cokerey*, 1545. I have translated it here as follows.

Serves 3–4

½ lb. (240 g.) puff pastry
12 large apricots
3 oz. (90 g.) caster sugar
4 egg yolks and 2 whites, well beaten together
2 tablespoons double cream
1 egg white to glaze

Steam rather than boil the apricots with some of the sugar until very soft. Then mash them with the rest of the sugar, removing any large bits of skin, and allow to get cold. Line a large tin or plate with half the pastry. When the apricots are cold beat in the eggs and cream, fill the tart, put on the lid, brush with white of egg and sugar, and bake at 450° F., gas mark 8, for 10 minutes and then reduce heat to 350° F., gas mark 4, for a further 10. Place foil lightly over the pastry if it begins to brown too much.

Bilberry or Blackberry Pie (1867)

This recipe comes from a manor house near Haworth, Yorkshire.

Serves 6

    1 lb. (½ k.) short pastry
    1 pint (6 dl.) or 2 large packets frozen bilberries
      or the same of blackberries
    5 oz. (150 g.) caster sugar
    2 large apples, previously baked in the usual way
    white of an egg

Line a large flat tin or plate with the pastry, reserving a round of the right size for a lid, which should not be too thick. Scrape all the pulp from the baked apples (if they are baked the flavour is better and the pulp stiffer than if they are stewed). Mix it with the sugar and the berries. Pour and spread on the pastry and cover securely with the lid, pinching the two rounds well together at the edges. Brush all over the lid with white of egg and then sprinkle with caster sugar. Bake at 400° F., gas mark 6, for 10 minutes and then turn down to 250° F., gas 1–½, and cook for a further 20 minutes. Serve hot or cold with cream.

Bakewell Tart

The Bakewell tart came originally from Bakewell in Derbyshire. Some early nineteenth-century recipes suggest using half flour and half ground almonds, which makes a richer mixture. The tart was intended for high tea and is in fact a cross between a cake and a pudding.

Serves 6

    1 lb. (½ k.) short or rough puff pastry
    2 tablespoons strawberry jam
    1 egg, and its weight in butter and sugar
    2 oz. (60 g.) self-raising flour
    ¼ lb. (120 g.) glacé icing (p. 530)

Line a tin or enamel plate 9 inches (22 cm.) in diameter with the pastry, work up the edges, and spread the middle with jam. Cream the butter and sugar well together, add the egg and a little of the flour, beat well, then add the rest of the flour. Spread the mixture over the jam. Bake for 20–30 minutes at 350° F., gas mark 4. When cold pour the glacé icing over the top and allow to set. Serve cold.

Chestnut Tart

This recipe, which comes from *The Compleat Housewife* of E. Smith, 1727, is there headed: 'To make a Chestnut Pudding'. It requires 2 quarts of cream and 18 egg yolks apart from sack, orange-flower water and rosewater, marrow or fresh butter, and puff paste. The quantity is vast, but reduced to make one large open tart and with the rosewater omitted, it is easy and splendid.

Serves 6

1 lb. (½ k.) chestnuts, puréed, or ½ tin chestnut purée
4 oz. (120 g.) caster sugar
¼ pint (1½ dl.) double cream
1 tablespoon orange juice
1 tablespoon sherry
2 egg yolks, well beaten
½ lb. (240 g.) puff paste or ¾ lb. (360 g.) short pastry
2 oz. (60 g.) butter

Line a large flat tin with the pastry and weight it down in the usual manner for baking blind. Be careful that the sides adhere to the tin so that you have a depth of ½–¾ in. (1½–2 cm.) all round. Bake for 10 minutes at 400° F., gas mark 6.

Meanwhile mix the chestnut purée with all the other ingredients except the butter. Remove the case from the oven, allow to cool for 5 minutes and then pour in the chestnut mixture. Do not allow to overflow. If any is left over, make up some small tartlets. Dot all over with small pieces of butter. Bake at 300° F., gas mark 2, for about 20 minutes, or till just firm. Sprinkle the top with caster sugar while hot. Serve cold with whipped cream.

A Flan of Cream and Eggs

Flans, spelt flathons or flawns, were always made with cream and eggs, and go back at least to the fifteenth century, and probably earlier. Two recipes are given in the Harleian MSS., which translate, with almost no adaptation, as follows. The resulting flan is excellent.

about ½ lb. (240 g.) short pastry
1 tablespoon jam
½ pint (3 dl.) milk
2 eggs
3 oz. (90 g.) sugar
¼ pint (1½ dl.) double cream
almond essence or lemon juice
1 tablespoon butter
caster sugar

Line a tin with pastry. Put a piece of greased paper in the centre, with a few haricot beans or crusts to weight it down and prevent the pastry rising. Bake blind in a hot oven (400° F., gas mark 6) for 10 minutes. Take the pastry case out of the oven, remove the paper, and spread a thin layer of strawberry or apricot jam on the bottom.

Warm the milk. Beat the eggs and sugar together in a bowl. Pour the warmed milk slowly on to the egg mixture, stirring carefully while pouring. Mix in the cream, and flavour with almond essence or lemon juice. Pour this into the pastry and sprinkle the butter, cut into little pieces, over the top. Replace in the oven turned down to 300° F., gas mark 2, until the custard is set (about 40 minutes). Remove and allow to get cold. When cold make the grill as hot as possible, sprinkle the tart about ⅛ inch (⅓ cm.) thick with caster sugar and place under the grill until the sugar begins to colour and bubble. This only takes a minute and should not burn the pastry edge, but for safety this can be protected by a ring of foil placed over it. When cold again, the flan will have a crisp sugar top.

Kentish Pudding Pie

Pudding pies were evolved originally for Lent, when meat pies could not be served and everyone was tired of pies with fish.

For 6–8

1 lb. (½ k.) short pastry	1 oz. (30 g.) sugar
3 oz. (90 g.) ground rice	2 eggs
1½ pints (9 dl.) milk	2 oz. (60 g.) currants
5 oz. (150 g.) butter	

Boil the ground rice in the milk for 6 or 7 minutes stirring well. Beat 4 oz. (120 g.) of butter to a cream, add the sugar, then beat in the eggs, one after the other. Now mix all with the ground rice and milk. Line a pie dish with short crust, pour in the mixture and sprinkle into it the currants. Dot liberally with the remaining butter. Bake in a moderate oven, 350° F., gas mark 4, for ¾ hour or until top is golden brown and the rice custard just firm to the touch.

A Very Ancient Recipe for Lemon Tarts

This came from a Devonshire house, where it had been handed down from mother to daughter or daughter-in-law. They sometimes used ¼ lb. melted butter and ¼ lb. clotted cream.

For 12–15 tarts

1 large lemon	½ lb. (240 g.) butter
¼ lb. (120 g.) caster sugar	1 teaspoon brandy or sherry
3 eggs	¾ lb. (360 g.) puff pastry

Pound the grated rind of the large lemon with the caster sugar. Add the yolks of 3 eggs, and half the whites whisked to hold a peak. Continue whisking while adding the just melted butter, and then add the juice of the lemon and a teaspoon of brandy. Beat or blend till very smooth and solid. Line patty-pans with very fine puff paste, fill with the lemon mixture, and bake.

Lemon Meringue Pie

A traditional North Country recipe.

For 4

½ lb. (240 g.) short sweet pastry or short pastry
4 oz. (120 g.) caster sugar
1 lemon
2 eggs
2 oz. (60 g.) melted butter

For the meringue:
2 egg whites
4 oz. (120 g.) caster sugar

Line a flan tin with the pastry. Line the centre with greaseproof paper, weight it down with crusts or dried beans, and bake at 425° F., gas mark 7, for 10 minutes.

For the filling use a double saucepan – or a basin or saucepan which will fit into a large one containing boiling water. Put the sugar into the small saucepan or basin. Grate the lemon rind into it, then squeeze in the juice. Beat the eggs lightly and add with the melted butter. Stir continually, keeping the basin or small saucepan in the gently boiling water until the mixture thickens. The curd is ready when it has the consistency of thick cream. Allow to cool. Then pour it into the pastry case, filling it not more than three quarters full.

Whip the egg whites until they are stiff enough to hold a peaked shape when dropped from the whisk. Gently fold in the caster sugar. Spread the meringue on top of the lemon pie, and place in a very cool oven, 200° F., gas mark ½–¼, for about 30 minutes or until the meringue is firm.

Serve hot or cold.

TO MAKE MINCE PIES

From the Reading manuscript of 1760.

The earliest mince pies were boat shaped, with flattened lids, to represent cradles. In the Reformation they were forbidden, as they were thought popish since they represented the cradle of the Christ Child and the spices of the filling the gifts of the three kings.

'Take a pound of tongue, a pound of beef suit, 2 pounds of currants, a pint of clarret, 10 john apples, season it with sugar, nutmeg, mace, cloves and a little salt, you may put some dryed sweet meats when you bake them if you please.'

Early versions of mincemeat usually contained either tongue or lean beef. Mrs Beeton, writing almost exactly 100 years later than the author of the Reading MS., gives one recipe using lean beef and another without, the second being almost identical with the recipe which follows, which comes from Yorkshire.

Mincemeat

1 lb. (½ k.) raisins	1 large glass brandy
¼ lb. (120 g.) sultanas	½ lb. (240 g.) currants
½ lb. (240 g.) dark chunky marmalade	¼ lb. (120 g.) candied peel
½ lb. (240 g.) suet	½ lb. (240 g.) demerara sugar
½ lemon	1 lb. (½ k.) good cooking apples
½ teaspoon mixed spice	¼ teaspoon nutmeg
	a good pinch ground ginger

Wash all the dried fruit. Grate the rind of the lemon. Peel, core and slice the apples. Put all the dry ingredients through the mincer. When minced, stir well, add lemon juice and brandy, stir again, fill into jars and tie down so they are airtight. Keep in a dry cool place.

All mincemeat should be prepared at least a fortnight before Christmas, and to make it in November is better still. Mincemeat keeps almost indefinitely, and some people prefer it when it has been kept from the year before. If it is last year's, it may be a little dry and crumbly-looking. In this case turn it into a bowl and mix it with a little brandy, which will restore the consistency and improve the flavour.

For 24 mince pies, 1 lb. (½ k.) puff pastry or 1½ lb. (¾ k.) short or rough puff will be needed. Roll out very thin; cut rounds at least ½ inch (1 cm.) larger in diameter than your patty pans and lids exactly their size. Use glasses if your cutters are not of the right sizes. Moisten the pastry edges with milk after you have filled the lower cases, and press on the lids, crimping the upper and lower edges well together. Brush each one over with beaten egg and bake at 400° F., gas mark 6, for 8–10 minutes.

Queen Charlotte's Tart

This unhappy Queen, wife of George III, seems to have been enthusiastic about puddings. Her tart, which is very rich and good, is less well known than Apple Charlotte.

Serves 4–6

¾ lb. (360 g.) short crust pastry	5 oz. (150 g.) sugar
2 oranges	5 eggs, whites and yolks
1 lemon	separated

Grate all the peel from the oranges and lemon and mix with all the juice. Stir in 4 oz. (120 g.) of the sugar and the beaten egg yolks. Line a round flat baking tin with the pastry and pour in the mixture. Bake for 40 minutes at 300° F., gas mark 2. Meanwhile beat the egg whites with the remaining sugar till they hold a peak. Quickly pile on top of the hot tart and return to the oven for 10 minutes. The meringue should be biscuit-coloured and crisp on top but soft inside. Serve hot.

Treacle Tart

Treacle tart in the nineteenth century was made with brown treacle and contained currants, peel and spices. The taste of the further refined golden syrup, however, is delicious in itself and needs nothing but a little butter, the crumbs to thicken it, and the pastry and cream.

Serves 4

½ lb. (240 g.) short pastry	about 1 oz. (30 g.) fine breadcrumbs
golden syrup	1 oz. (30 g.) butter

Line a tin in the same way as for jam tart. Sprinkle half the crumbs on to the pastry, then add a layer of treacle, and top with the remaining crumbs. This mixture should not more than half-fill the tart. Dot with small pieces of butter. Bake at 400° F., gas mark 6, until the pastry is golden brown. Serve either hot or cold, preferably with cream.

Apple Charlotte

There is some doubt about the tradition of the 'charlotte', for which a special 'charlotte mould' was used in great kitchens in the eighteenth and nineteenth centuries. However, the name 'charlet' (also 'charlette') appears in several fifteenth-century recipes. There is 'charlet enforsed' and 'charlet a-forcyd ryally' in the Harleian MSS.

The recipes are always for pork or veal, chopped small and cooked in milk: in fact, the dish was simply *chair* = flesh, laitée = milked: i.e. meat cooked in milk, often milk of almonds. Plenty of sweetening was always recommended, and somehow the dish seems to have been translated into a pudding where a smooth, sweet purée was filled into a crisp crust of bread or biscuits.

Apple Charlotte and Charlotte Russe are the most common forms, but other fillings and flavourings were used. Some writers depart altogether from the medieval dish and hold that George III's Queen gave these puddings her name, some that they were German in origin, and called after the heroine of Goethe's *Werther*. Yet another view is that charlotte is a mis-spelling of the Hebrew *schaleth*, which was a sweet spiced purée with dried fruit, and with a lid of crisp crust: in fact, an apple pie. André Simon claims that Carême, most creative of all the great chefs, but for a long time almost illiterate (because of the extreme poverty of his early upbringing, which included no schooling), evolved the charlotte from this dish, and that the more familiar female Christian name was the nearest he could get to schaleth.

Serves 4

1 lb. (½ k.) apples	rind and juice of 1 lemon
6 oz. (180 g.) sugar	about 8 thin slices of bread
a little butter	4 oz. (120 g.) clarified butter (see p. 126)

Stew the apples with the sugar, lemon rind and a very little butter until tender and a thick pulp; stir constantly to prevent burning. Add the lemon juice and beat a little. Dip one side of the bread in the clarified butter and line the bottom and sides of a small fireproof dish. Put in the apple and cover with remaining slices of bread, dipped in the melted butter. Bake for 20 minutes in a hot oven, 400° F., gas mark 6, until brown and crisp. Just before it is ready, sprinkle with caster sugar and return to the oven. Turn out and sift more sugar over.

Other recipes use finely cut uncooked apples, in which case the pudding should cook for 35–40 minutes at 350° F., gas mark 4, and should be served in the dish in which it cooked, rather than turned out.

Apricot Charlotte and Pear Charlotte are also very good. In all these, the fruit is soft and well cooked, but not puréed.

Apple Betty

This differs from Apple Charlotte only in that crumbs are used instead of slices of bread and butter, and spice is generally added. There is no tradition relating to the name Betty as used here.

For 6

> 1½ lb. (¾ k.) peeled, cored and sliced cooking apples
> 1 oz. (30 g.) butter
> 2 tablespoons melted butter
> 6 oz. (180 g.) breadcrumbs
> 1 lemon
> 2 oz. (60 g.) caster sugar
> ¼ teaspoon grated nutmeg ⎫
> ¼ teaspoon ground cinnamon ⎬ if liked
> 2 tablespoons water

Mix the melted butter with the crumbs. Grate the lemon rind and mix with the caster sugar, nutmeg and cinnamon. Cover the bottom of a buttered fireproof dish with a quarter of the crumbs, then with half the apples. Sprinkle with the sugar and spice mixture, then with another quarter of the crumbs. Add the remainder of the apples, then the rest of the sugar and spice mixture. Pour in water and lemon juice. Cover with the remainder of the crumbs and dot liberally with butter. Bake in a moderate oven, 350° F., gas mark 4, for 35–40 minutes. Turn out and serve upside down with cream.

A GOOD BREAD PUDDING, AND BREAD AND BUTTER PUDDING

These are economy puddings intended to use up stale bread, but they are, in fact, very good, very quick and easy to make. Mrs Beeton's recipe for Very Plain Bread Pudding, however, takes boiling water before very small quantities of fruit, sugar and butter are added. At the end she observes that milk substituted for water 'would very much improve the pudding'. It would take eggs as well to make it worth eating and double quantities of butter, sugar and fruit, as in the following recipe.

Bread Pudding

Serves 4–6

1 pint (6 dl.) milk	1 tablespoon melted butter
3 oz. (90 g.) breadcrumbs	2 eggs, beaten with a pinch
2 tablespoons caster sugar	of salt
2 oz. (60 g.) currants	1 teaspoon vanilla essence
2 oz. (60 g.) sultanas	butter

Pour the milk over the crumbs, and stand for ½ hour. Stir in the other ingredients. Pour into a greased pie dish. Place small dabs of butter over the top. Place in a baking tin containing an inch of hot water. Bake in a moderate oven at 300–325° F., gas mark 4–5, for 30 minutes, till set in the centre and golden brown on top.

Bread and Butter Pudding

8 thin slices of bread	2 eggs
2½ oz. (75 g.) butter	½ pint (3 dl.) milk
2 oz. (60 g.) currants and sultanas	vanilla essence
2 oz. (60 g.) caster sugar	

Cut some thin slices from a sandwich loaf or take slices from a cut loaf, butter each slice on one side and cut it diagonally but do not remove the crust. Soak the dried fruit in warm water for 2 or 3 minutes and then spread some of it on the bottom of a buttered pie dish. Put a layer of bread and butter on it, butter side down. Sprinkle a few currants and sultanas on top, then put another layer of bread and butter, butter side up, and so on until the dish is full. Take care not to press the bread down. Mix the sugar and eggs with a whisk in a basin, and gradually add the cold milk and a few drops of vanilla essence. Pour the egg mixture into the dish, a little at a time to allow the bread to absorb the custard. Sprinkle the top with sugar and dot with pieces of butter. Place the pie dish in a tray with an inch of water and bake in a moderate oven at 350° F., gas mark 4, for 35 minutes. It should be crisp and golden brown on top, and will turn out, sides and bottom being also brown and buttery.

Poor Knight's Pudding

Recipes for this pudding go back to the seventeenth century, though I have not found its name before the nineteenth century. The poor knight, though he could not afford a rich plum pudding, could at least do a little better than a plain bread pudding.

Serves 4

    4 slices of bread, crusts removed, cut in quarters
    1 egg
    ¼ pint (1½ dl.) milk or a little more
    1 teaspoon caster sugar
    2 oz. (60 g.) butter
    jam or golden syrup

Beat the egg, milk and sugar. Soak all the quarters of bread so that they are wet through. Make the butter hot in a frying pan but do not let it colour, and fry each piece of bread golden brown on both sides. Lift out on to flat serving dish, spread 8 pieces with jam or a little golden syrup and sandwich with remaining pieces, sprinkle each sandwich with plenty of caster sugar and serve very hot.

Queen of Puddings

For 4

1 pint (6 dl.) milk	2 oz. (60 g.) butter
a strip lemon rind	2 oz. (60 g.) sugar
a pinch of salt	2 eggs
4 oz. (120 g.) breadcrumbs	2 tablespoons strawberry or apricot jam

Put the milk into a saucepan, add the lemon rind and salt, and bring to the boil. Remove the rind. Put the breadcrumbs, butter and most of the sugar into a bowl, and pour the boiling milk over them. Cover the bowl and leave to stand for about 10 minutes. Beat up the egg yolks and add them to the bread mixture. Pour the mixture into a buttered fireproof dish and bake in a medium oven at 350° F., gas mark 4, for 10 minutes. When baked, spread the jam over the top. Whip up the egg whites and fold in a little sugar. Pile on top of the pudding. Brown lightly in the oven for a few more minutes.

Thunder and Lightning

For 4

    8 oz. (240 g.) long-grain (Patna) rice
    6–8 oz. (180–240 g.) clotted cream
    golden syrup

This is a Cornish pudding which delighted us in childhood.

Plenty of long-grain rice is boiled in water with a very little salt. When cooked every grain should be separate, and it should be piled on a large flat dish.

A helping is put on each plate and each person adds golden syrup (the lightning) and a lot of clotted (scalded) cream (the thunder).

11 · COLD SWEETS AND 'BANQUETING STUFF'

Apart from subtleties, which in the fifteenth and sixteenth centuries were renowned all over Europe, 'banqueting stuff', to use Gervase Markham's term, was one of the chief glories of English high cooking. The jellies and creams, tarts, tansies, flummeries, syllabubs, junkets, trifles, hedgehogs and tipsy-cakes which surrounded the centrepiece on the table and soothed the palates of our ancestors were most carefully and beautifully made and decorated in kitchen, stillroom and pantry. They were intended for royal and noble feasts where the feasters had already had their fill and more. Only the smoothest, softest cream, the most totteringly delicious jelly could tempt them. Not for them the hot puddings which sustained children and farm-hands. Not very often for us either (though a section of nostalgic recipes for hot puddings is given here), because today we are conscious of the dangers of overweight: we count our calories and fear carbohydrates. Also, we are generally single-handed in the kitchen, and short of time.

The aristocratic cold sweets of the banquet are of much greater interest to us, in spite of their alarming content of sugar, eggs and cream, because they can usually be made at least a day before they are wanted. When the single-handed cook has prepared two courses she is apt to feel that she has done enough, and that cheese and fruit will be adequate for the end of a good dinner. However, if the first two courses have been well chosen and the second accompanied by a green vegetable or a salad, a cream, trifle or syllabub or an old-fashioned tipsy-cake are delightful and soothing to the palate; the good dinner becomes an excellent one, and gentlemen who say that they never eat sweets and would prefer some cheese are apt to break their rule.

The term 'banquet' seems originally to have applied only to the course at the end of a feast or sometimes a separate sitting, at which elaborate sweets, creams and fruit dishes were set out. The most important of all according to Markham* were the dishes made of marchpane (marzipan):

Thus, having showed you how to preserve, conserve, candy and make pastes of all kinds, in which four heads consists the whole Art of banquetting dishes, I will now procedd to the ordering or setting forth of a banquet, wherein you shall observe that March-panes have the first place, the middle place and the last place [i.e. at the head, the foot and in the centre of the table], your preserved fruits shall be dished up first, your pastes next, your wet suckets after them [i.e. any form of cream, syllabub, etc. though the term as used by Markham is rather obscure and the recipe he gives very peculiar], then your dried suckets [probably the term here included tarts, small cakes and biscuits], then your marmalades and cotiniates [fruit pastes], then your Comfets of all kinds . . . Thus you shall order them in the closet, but when they go to the table, you shall first send forth a dish made for show only, as Beast, Bird, Fish, Fowl according to invention; then your Marchpane . . .

The 'dish made for show only' was known as a soteltie or subtlety and is mentioned for the first time in a fourteenth-century MS: 'At the second course was a soteltee Seint-Jorge on horsebak and sleynge the dragun . . .'

The subtlety, in England which excelled in such things, took on great importance, and it seems that the number and elaboration of these was a mark of the grandeur and importance of the occasion. A feast given by Cardinal Wolsey offered 'a second course with so many dishes, subtelties and curious devices, which were above 100 in number, of so goodly proportion and costly, that I suppose the Frenchmen never saw the like . . .' (George

* The English Hus-wife, 1615.

Cavendish: *Life of Cardinal Wolsey*). One of the Frenchmen present was given the subtlety, which was in the form of a chess board and men, made of 'spiced plate' (a kind of stiff paste of sugar often boiled with apples or quinces) to take home with him, 'because that Frenchmen be very expert in that play. . . . My lord [Wolsey] . . . commanding that a case should be made for the same in all haste, to preserve it from perishing in the conveyance thereof into his country.'

Markham says that the subtleties were for show only, but it is clear that they were made entirely of edible materials. They were the highest form of the cook's art, his chance to please and amaze a great company, and part of their interest lay in the fact that in making them he used only the same materials as were being served in other dishes around the table. No doubt there were plenty of humorists who would cut off St George's head and eat it or seize and devour the lovely sugar lady who leaned out of the castle window. The materials seem to have been chiefly marzipan and the stiff fruit pastes for which many recipes are given in early manuscripts. Marchpane (marzipan) took a very long time to make, when almonds had to be shelled, blanched and then pounded. Today, since we can buy ground almonds, it is no trouble at all, but it is used much less and is disliked by many people.

Gum-dragon (a harmless edible gum) was used to stiffen and set sugar and water to make 'sugar-plate' and 'spice-plate'. 'Leaches', which were a sort of fondant, were used, and spun sugar and various forms of icing. The cook had a variety of sets of 'prints' and 'cutters' in different forms. Many vegetable colourings were used; such as spinach water, 'turnsole' and 'grain' to give red and purple, and saffron. Markham gives optimistic directions for 'setting out' a tart 'in the proportion of a beast' using different coloured preserves, pastes and marmelades, and says that coats of arms of hosts and guests were often laid out in their correct colours on a white tart (the filling made of cream, sugar and white of egg boiled to a curd and then strained and beaten).

Robert May explains how to make a subtlety in his book *The Accomplish't Cook, or The Art and Mystery of Cookery*, 1660. The sub-title seems particularly appropriate to the following:

Make the likeness of a ship in paste-board and cover it with paste, with Flags and streamers, the guns belonging to it of Kickses [i.e. Kickshaws, derived from French quelque chose, sometimes almond paste or marzipan, sometimes stiff jelly, but could be made of almost anything. See Markham's recipe, which follows] with such holes and trains of powder that they may all take Fire; place your ship firm in a great Charger [i.e. dish]; then make a salt round about it, and stick therein egg shells filled with rose-water.

Then in another Charger have the proportion of a stag made of course [*sic*] paste, with a bread arrow in the side of him and his body filled with claret wine.

In another Charger have the proportion of a Castle with Battlements, Percullises, Gates and Drawbridges made of paste-board, the guns of Kickses, and covered with course paste as the former; place it at a distance from the Ship, to fire at each other, the Stag being placed between them . . . At each end of the Charger, wherein is the Stag, place a pie made of course paste in one of which there be live Frogs, in the other live Birds. Make these Pies of course paste filled with Bran, and yellowed over with Saffron or Yolks of Eggs, gild them over in spots, as also the Stag, the Ship and the Castle; bake them and place them with gilt bay-leaves on the turrets and tunnels of the Castle and Pies; being baked, make a hole in the bottom, take out the bran, put in your Frogs and Birds and close up with course paste.

Fire the trains of powder, order it so that some of the Ladies may be persuaded to pluck the Arrow out of the Stag, then will the claret follow as blood running from a wound. This being done with admiration to the beholders, after some short pause, fire the train of the Castle, that the pieces all of one side may go off; then fire the trains of one side of the Ship, as in a battle, and by degrees fire the trains of each other side as before. This done, to sweeten the stink of the powder, let the ladies take the egg-shells full of sweet waters, and throw them at each other. All dangers being over, by this time you may suppose they will desire to see what is in the pies; where, lifting off the lid of one pie, out skips some Frogs, which makes the Ladies to skip and shreek; next after the other Pie, whence comes out the Birds, who by a natural instinct flying at the light, will put out the Candles, so that what with the flying Birds and skipping Frogs, the one above, the other beneath, will cause much delight and pleasure to the company: at length the candles are lighted and a banquet brought in, the music sounds and everyone with much delight and content rehearses their actions in the former passages. These were formerly the delights of the Nobility, before good-housekeeping had left England, and the sword really acted that which was only counterfeited in such honest and laudable Exercises as these.

The centrepieces with which the great chefs in England and France graced royal tables in the eighteenth and nineteenth centuries derive from these early subtleties. Carême was the greatest master of the centrepiece, but every tolerable chef or master cook was expected to be able to produce a fine architectural model for competitions or great occasions.

Mrs Glasse, in her book *The Compleat Confectioner*, published in 1760, gives elaborate instructions for setting out a dessert, showing how the dishes should be arranged at the table:

Giving direction for a grand dessert would be needless, for those persons who would give such grand desserts, either keep a proper person, or have them of a confectioner . . . though every young lady ought to know both how to make all kind of confectionery and dress out a dessert . . . But for country ladies it is a pretty amusement both to make the sweetmeats and dress out a dessert, as it depends wholly on fancy and but little expense.

These are two of the desserts which she suggests:

(1)	Whipped Syllabubs	
Bloomange [blancmange] stuck with almonds [i.e. a Hedgehog]		Ice Cream
	Two salvers, one above another, on the bottom are jellies, the top a	Dried Cherries
Chestnuts	large glass cup covered with raspberry cream	
Ice Cream		Almond Flummery
(2)	Whipped Syllabubs	
	Ice Cream	
Stewed pippins		Little pot oranges
Compôte of pears	A Grand Trifle	Compôte of chestnuts
Postatia Nuts [pistachio]		Nonpareil
	Ice Creams Different colours	

All these should be 'intermixed' according to your fancy with all sorts of little biscuits, almonds, knick-knacks 'throwed in the middle of the salver' or 'wet sweetmeats', i.e. creams and syllabubs, in little glasses.

The central salver on which the jellies and creams or the grand trifle stood could further be 'adorned' with flowers, images, grass, moss and other ornaments. These desserts followed two other courses and were for ten or twelve people. Mrs Glasse implies that the housewife should be able to prepare them single-handed, but by this she probably meant that the housewife would be the only skilled cook but would have a daughter or two and several maids to help her; and she would have needed them all. Let us assume that we may provide flowers, cheese and fruit, but never more than one sweet per dinner per single-handed cook.

KICKSHAWS

This is Gervase Markham's recipe, 1615, for the mysterious quelquechoses or kickshaws which were such an important feature at sixteenth- and seventeenth-century feasts.

The extraordinary ingredients seem, in this recipe, to have been bound together in a kind of stiff and solid omelette. No doubt the form of the dish changed before its name disappeared. Mrs Glasse in 1760 gives them as small pies of apples, gooseberries, raspberries or other fruit completely enclosed in pastry and then either baked or fried.

The kickshaw in any of the forms Markham mentions would hardly be to our taste today. 'Pettitoes' generally meant the feet, heart and liver of a sucking pig or hen's young all boiled together.

'To make any Quelquechose

'To make a Quelquechose, which is a mixture of many things together; take the eggs and break them, and do away one half of the whites, and after they are beaten, put them to a good quantity of sweet cream, currants, cinnamon, cloves, mace, salt and a little ginger, spinage, endive and marygold flowers grosly chopt, and beat them all very well together; then take Pigs Pettitoes slic'd and grosly chopt, mix them with the eggs, and with your hand stir them exceeding well together; then put in sweet butter in your frying pan, and being melted, put in all the rest, and fry it brown without burning, ever and anon turning it, till it be fried enough; then dish it upon a flat plate, and so serve it forth. Onely here is to be observed, that your Pettitoes must be very well boyled before you put them into the Fry-case.

'Additions to the Housewife

'And in this manner as you make this Quelquechose, so you may make any other, whether it be of flesh, small birds, sweet roots, oysters, muscles, cockles, giblets, lemmons, oranges or any fruit, pulse, or other sallet herb whatsoever; of which to speak severally, were a Labour infinite, because they vary with mens opinion. Onely the composition and work is no other than this before prescribed: and who can do these, need no further instruction for the rest. And thus much for Sallets and Fricases.'

Creams, Fools and Flummeries

Cambridge Burnt Cream

Serves 6
> 1 pint (½ l.) double cream
> 8 well-beaten egg yolks
> 4–6 oz. (120–180 g.) demerara sugar

Bring the cream to boiling point and keep it boiling for exactly 1 minute (this timing seems to be important). Then pour it rather slowly and stirring constantly into the well-beaten egg yolks. Beat for a minute and return to the heat, but stirring over boiling water (or above very low direct heat) until it thickens well – naturally never allow to boil again. On no account add sugar to this cream – the whole point of the traditional dish is that the cream is unsweetened. Pour into a wide, shallow fireproof serving dish. Chill well – overnight is preferable. Cover the cold cream with a ¼-inch (½-cm.) layer of demerara sugar. Put it under a preheated grill, not too close to the top heat. Simply watch it and move it further from the heat if the sugar begins to darken and burn. As soon as all the sugar is melted together so that you can't see the separate grains, remove it. Chill it again before serving. You should be able just to tap the crust with a spoon to crack it. Very good made in individual soufflé dishes. Keeps in the refrigerator for 4 or 5 days perfectly.

Mrs Rundle, writing in 1819, gives this recipe exactly, but it is also a speciality of two or three of the Cambridge colleges. Almond biscuits are good served with it. I was once given a variant which had muscat grapes, peeled, stoned and well drained, laid in a layer in the bottom of the dish under the cream. Their flavour with the cream is most elegant.

Caramel Cream

Caramel cream was made just like this in the fifteenth century (though the recipe is in very different language).

> *For the caramel:*
> 4 tablespoons sugar   2 tablespoons water
>
> *For the custard:*
> ¾ pint (4½ dl.) milk   3 eggs
> 1 oz. (30 g.) sugar

Make the caramel by pouring the sugar and water into a small saucepan and heating over a low flame. Stir all the time to dissolve the sugar. Bring to the boil, then, without stirring, simmer until it turns a rich brown. Pour into four individual moulds. Swish them around until the sides are well coated.

To make the custard, heat the milk in a saucepan. Put the sugar into a basin and add the eggs. Beat together. Pour the hot milk on to them gradually. When ready pour at once from the pan into the caramel-coated cups or basin. Place the moulds in a baking tray of hot water and cook in the oven at 350° F., gas mark 4, till set (about 20–30 mins.). Chill and turn out to serve.

Little Pots of Cream

For 4 or 5 little pots
>   2 eggs
>   2 extra yolks
>   4 oz. (120 g.) sugar
>   1 pint (½ l.) boiled milk
>   a few drops vanilla *or* a dessertspoon coffee essence *or* 1 oz. (30 g.) melted chocolate

Beat the eggs and yolks together with the sugar. Pour in the warm, but not hot, boiled milk. Stir the flavouring in well. Pour into cocotte dishes or individual moulds. Place these in a baking tray with hot water coming half-way up the little pots and bake in the oven at 350° F., gas mark 4, for 20–30 minutes till they are just set. Chill before serving. Do not turn out. Decorate with whipped cream, cherries, almonds, or angelica, if liked.

Double Cream

Double cream was made in various forms and versions for Edwardian dinner parties. It requires a ring mould.

For 4 or 5
>   *First cream:*
>   ½ pint (3 dl.) milk   3 eggs
>   3 oz. (90 g.) caster sugar   vanilla essence
>   ¼ lb. (120 g.) chopped almonds

>   *Second cream:*
>   ½ pint (3 dl.) double cream
>   2 oz. (60 g.) caster sugar
>   brandy *or* any liqueur *or* orange *or* almond essence

For the first cream, mix the eggs and sugar together with a whisk and add the vanilla and the cold milk gradually. Sprinkle a ring mould with a hollow centre with chopped, blanched almonds and fill it with the mixture. Place the mould in a baking tray and bake at 300° F., gas mark 2, for 40 minutes or till set. Chill in the refrigerator, and when cold turn out and fill the centre with the second cream. For this you whisk the cream stiff, stir in the caster sugar, and flavour with a few drops of almond essence, brandy, any liqueur, or orange essence. The centre may be decorated with crystallized fruit, angelica, violets or rose leaves.

Fruit Fools

A fool is simply a fruit cream, which should contain nothing but fruit purée, sugar and thick cream. Unfortunately, economical Victorian housewives saved cream by making it up with cornflour custard, which made it almost inedible.

Green gooseberries, young rhubarb and fresh apricots make the best of all fools.

> 1 pint (½ l.) well-sweetened sieved fruit purée
> 1 pint (½ l.) double cream
> extra sugar to taste

Simply blend the fruit, cream and sugar, chill and serve in bowls or glasses, preferably with some kind of light, rich biscuit such as almond fingers.

Boodle's Orange Fool

A traditional recipe at Boodle's Club.

> 4 oranges
> 2 lemons
> 1½ pints (9 dl.) cream
> 8 sponge cakes
> ¼ lb. (120 g.) caster sugar

Mix the juice of all the fruit with the grated rind of a lemon and 2 oranges. Stir in the sugar, and beat in 1 pint (6 dl.) of the cream. Blend well. Cut each sponge cake into 4 pieces and pile into a bowl. Pour the mixture over the cakes. Chill for several hours and pile the remaining whipped cream on top before serving.

FLUMMERY

Flummery was really a kind of rather stiff and solid, slightly acid jelly made from a cereal. Occasionally, however, as in the following recipe from the Reading MS., 1765, the jelly was made with hartshorn (or in some instances with isinglass). This recipe is not a true flummery at all, and since it is stuck with almonds, it becomes a 'hedgehog' (see p. 478).

To Make Almond Fflomery

'Make a stiff hartshorn jelly sweeten it to the taste put into it a little orange flower water take some blancht almonds and beat them with a little of the jelly to keep them from oyleing squeese the white from them and soe put it to the jelly when the jelly is just warm make it very white with the almonde juyce and put it into a bason and when it is cold turn it out and stick it with sliced almonds.'

True Oatmeal Flummery

A recipe of 1760, which is included several times in later collections.

Serves 6–8

Soak 3 handfuls of fine oatmeal in cold water for 24 hours. After this time add an equal quantity of water and leave another 24 hours. Strain through a fine sieve, add a heaped tablespoon of caster sugar and the strained juice of an orange.

Boil till very thick.

Pour into shallow dishes and serve with honey and cream.

Jellies

Jellies were very important cold sweets until they began to be sold ready flavoured, when they lost caste and became a sweet for children, liked only for their appearance and their innocuous mild flavours. However, made with wine or real fruit juice, they are well worth reconsidering.

Originally, jellies were set by using either hartshorn or a calf's foot, or isinglass. Isinglass was made from the bladders of fish. Gelatine was manufactured a good deal later and was sold in flat sheets, very useful for glazing dolls' house windows but difficult to melt and stir into the liquid for the jelly.

Nowadays we use only powdered gelatine, and I can find no difference in the results if a calf's foot is boiled and the resulting jelly strained and flavoured. Jellies in the fifteenth and sixteenth centuries were often made in moulds of elaborate castles, so that they stood high on proud salvers, turreted and castellated, coloured with various vegetable colourings and touched here and there with pure gold leaf which caught the light of the many candles whose heat endangered them.

Port Wine Jelly, 1878

For 4–6

1½ oz. (45 g.) gelatine	pinch nutmeg, grated
¼ lb. (120 g.) loaf sugar	pinch cinnamon, grated
1 pint (6 dl.) good port	2 teaspoons lemon juice

Soak the gelatine for a few minutes in a little of the port and the lemon juice till swollen and soft. Then stir this in to half the remaining port, add the sugar and spices and bring almost, but not quite, to the boil, still stirring. Strain into a bowl and gently stir in the remaining port. Pour into wetted individual moulds.

It is a very good dinner-party sweet served with whipped cream and almond biscuits. The jelly has extra flavour because half the port has not been subjected to heat.

The Orange Jellies of Charles I

They were supposed to have been served to him like this, perhaps in compliment to Nell Gwynne.

For 4–6

1 oz. (30 g.) gelatine soaked in a little water
¼ lb. (120 g.) loaf sugar
juice of 4 oranges and 1 lemon
2 tablespoons sherry

Carefully cut the oranges round, taking off the peel cleanly in two halves. Reserve.

Soak the thinly sliced peel of one of the oranges in the sherry for at least an hour. Then strain off the peel and put the sherry to the fruit juice in a saucepan. Add the sugar and gelatine and stir till all is dissolved. Pour into the halved orange skins and allow to set. When firmly set cut through again so that you have little boats of orange jelly.

Syllabubs

Charles II was so fond of syllabubs that he had cows kept in St James's Park so that when he was walking there and became thirsty he could have them milked into a bowl of sweetened wine. Milk warm from the cow directly milked into the bowl was considered best for liquid syllabubs.

Syllabubs were of two kinds. They were a mixture of spiced and sweetened wine and new milk or cream. A large deep bowl, a ladle and tall narrow glasses were made in sets on purpose for syllabubs of this kind. Sometimes a spoonful of whipped cream was put on top of each glass. Sometimes the syllabub was whipped and the foam piled on top of the liquid in each glass. The following two recipes are examples of these liquid syllabubs, and the next two of solid syllabubs.

A West Country Syllabub Recipe of 1800

In a large glass or pottery bowl put ½ pint of port and ½ pint of sherry (or a bottle of any good white wine): the bowl should be about a third full. Stir in 2–3 tablespoons caster sugar according to taste. Milk the bowl full direct from the cow if possible: if not, fill up with a pint of ordinary milk but stir a little. Leave to stand for 20 minutes, when the curd will have separated from the wine. Pour into glasses, spooning the curd on top, and put a spoonful of whipped or clotted cream on each.

A Whipped Syllabub

This is Mrs Glasse's recipe (1760) for 8 or 10.

> ½ bottle claret ⎫
> 3 oz. (90 g.) caster sugar ⎬ for the glasses
> 1 pint (6 dl.) cream ⎭
> ½ pint (3 dl.) sherry
> juice of 2 oranges
> grated peel of 1 orange and 1 lemon
> ½ lb. (240 g.) caster sugar

Mix all but the claret and 3 oz. (90 g.) caster sugar together in a wide bowl, beat well and skim off the froth as it rises, placing it in a sieve to drain. Fill some small glasses with sweetened claret, pile the drained froth on to these and serve immediately.

Mrs Glasse suggests setting the liquid which remains in the bowl after sufficient froth has been taken off with a calf's foot to make jelly.

SOLID, OR EVERLASTING SYLLABUBS

These are still the best and simplest of all cold sweets, and patient of infinite variations.

Lemon Syllabubs (1741)

Serves 6-8

       1 pint (6 dl.) double cream
       ¼ lb. (120 g.) sugar
       ⅓ pint (2¼ dl.) white wine
       juice of 2 lemons, and grated rind of 1

Put all these together and beat as fast as you can till the mixture is thick. Then pour it into glasses and let it stand for 5 or 6 hours: it can be made overnight, and with a blender it takes only 2 minutes to make.

Solid Syllabub

A nineteenth-century recipe which is the one I generally make myself.

Serves 8–10

       6 oz. (180 g.) caster sugar
       grated rind of 2 lemons and their juice
       3 tablespoons brandy
       3 tablespoons sherry
       1 pint (6 dl.) cream

Grate the lemon peel or slice it off very finely, with as little of the white as possible. Leave it to soak in the juice of the lemons for 2 or 3 hours. Strain it over the sugar. Stir in the brandy and sherry. Pour in the cream. Beat till stiff. It should just hold its form when piled up. Pile it into small glasses and chill. It tastes better if it is made the day, or at least some hours, before it is wanted.

Replace the lemon juice, brandy and sherry with 6 oz (180 g.) sieved raspberry or strawberry purée in season, or with a purée of fresh apricots (in which case retain the lemon juice).

Trifles

Traditionally English recipes for 'a pretty trifle' go back to medieval times. Here I give Mrs Glasse's Grand Trifle, and the Dean's Trifle, which is an eighteenth-century recipe from Cambridge, 'Whim Wham', another eighteenth-century trifle and Floating Island.

A Grand Trifle

Very slightly adapted from Mrs Glasse's recipe.

Serves 10–12

- 2 packeted orange jellies *or* the recipe for Charles II's Orange Jellies (p. 470) (double quantity) (much improved if the juice of 4–6 oranges is used with water)
- 18 small macaroons
- 12 sponge fingers
- 24 ratafias
- ½ lb. (240 g.) raspberry jam
- ½ lb. (240 g.) red-currant jelly
- ¼ pint (1½ dl.) sherry
- 1½ pints (9 dl.) double cream
- 1 lemon
- 1 orange
- 3 oz. (90 g.) caster sugar

In a very large bowl (traditionally glass) make up the two jellies, making a little less than 1 quart (1 l.). Allow the jelly almost to set and then push into it half the macaroons and sponge fingers, each broken into 3, and half the ratafias. By this method the biscuits keep their consistency. If the liquid jelly is poured over them, they absorb too much and become flabby. The jelly should be full of them. Pour over ½ pint (3 dl.) cream, and into it put alternate heaps of raspberry jam and red-currant jelly all over the surface. Soak all the remaining biscuits in the sherry (breaking up the sponge fingers) and arrange over this. Beat up 1 pint (6 dl.) cream with the lemon and orange juice and sugar until it just holds a peak and pile all over, raising it high above the sides of the bowl. Decorate with crystallized fruits, violets, rose leaves, toasted almonds, etc.

Mrs Glasse says, 'This is fit to go the King's table, if well made, and very excellent when it comes to be all mixed together.'

The Dean's Cream

This is a Cambridge college recipe of the eighteenth century and is really a trifle.

Serves 8

6 sponge cakes
raspberry jam
apricot jam
¼ lb. (120 g.) ratafia biscuits
  or macaroons, broken up
½ pint (3 dl.) sherry

1 wineglass brandy
1 pint (6 dl.) cream
2 oz. (60 g.) caster sugar
angelica, cherries and crystallized
  pineapple to decorate

Cut the sponge cakes in half lengthways and spread 6 halves thickly with raspberry jam and 6 with apricot jam. Arrange them in a large glass or china bowl, jam sides upwards: they can be piled two or three deep. Among them put 18 or so ratafias or 3 or 4 macaroons broken up. Pour over the sherry and leave at least 20 minutes to soak.

Meanwhile whip the cream, sugar and brandy as for a solid syllabub. Pile over the wine-soaked cake, decorate, and chill for at least an hour before serving.

A Whim-Wham

A delicious name (probably referring to its very high alcohol content) for an absolutely delicious and very quickly made eighteenth-century trifle.

Serves 6

18 sponge fingers, broken in halves
¼ pint (1½ dl.) fairly sweet sherry
glass of brandy
juice of 2 oranges, sweetened with a tablespoon of sugar
¾ pint (9 dl.) whipped cream
¼ lb. (120 g.) blanched almonds
1 oz. (30 g.) butter
1 tablespoon sugar

Fry the almonds in the butter until just biscuit colour. Throw the sugar over them, shake, and turn on to a plate to cool. They will have a toffee coating.

Put the sponge fingers in a large bowl about half an hour before you start dinner, and pour the sherry and brandy and orange juice over. Leave to soak while you eat (do not prepare it too early, or the alcohol is partly lost, and the biscuits become too soggy). Whip the cream just before dinner. It should be light, and should just hold a peak; it must not be at all buttery. Leave the cream apart until you are ready to serve the whim-wham, then give it a quick stir and pour and pile it over the sponge, which should have absorbed all the liquid. Sprinkle the almonds all over, and serve at once.

Floating Island

This was very often served as a side dish at feasts and great dinners in the seventeenth century and was still made for Victorian dinner parties, though it is scarcely ever seen today. It is a kind of floating trifle. Many variants exist; most recipes build one large island to float in its lake of cream, but some suggest small individual islands. In either case, the dish used must be large and fairly flat.

> ¾ pint (4½ dl.) purée of raspberries or strawberries (frozen will do)
> a large sponge cake
> 2 tablespoons sherry
> ¼ lb. (120 g.) apricot jam
> 3 oz. (90 g.) finely chopped blanched almonds
> 1 pint (6 dl.) double cream
> ¼ lb. (120 g.) caster sugar
> ½ teaspoon vanilla essence

Mix the fruit purée with half the cream, beat well together or blend, and pour on to a large rather flat dish. Cut the sponge cake through into three thin layers, spread each with a little apricot jam, and sprinkle with almonds. Lay the first layer lightly on the purée in the centre. Put the other layers, always lightly, one above the other. It should be floating, supported on the purée. Pour into the cake a little sherry. Whip the remaining cream with the sugar and vanilla and pile high on the island cake.

Chill for an hour if possible, and serve. If the island does not float the dish is still delicious, but it should move freely on its purée.

Early recipes floated the island on a whipped syllabub, using the foam to top it, instead of whipped cream, and French bread instead of cake. A thin egg custard can also be used instead of the fruit purée.

Other Notable Cold Sweets

Bombard Apples

A seventeenth-century recipe. These are really grand apple dumplings, intended to be eaten cold. Mrs Blencowe (1694) says that 'they make a very pretty side-dish'.

> 1 large apple for each person
> 2 or 3 crystallized apricots or some good apricot jam
> puff pastry (allow 2 oz. (60 g.) for each apple to be enclosed)
> white of eggs (allow 1 to every 2 apples)
> about 6 oz. (180 g.) caster sugar
> 2 teaspoons orange juice

Peel and core the apples and fill with the cut-up apricots or apricot jam. Roll the puff pastry very thin, cut in large squares, one for each apple, and enrobe them. Bake for 10 minutes at 450° F., gas mark 8, then reduce the heat to 350° F., gas mark 4, and place a piece of foil lightly over the apples, to prevent further browning; cook a further 15 minutes. Meanwhile, beat the egg whites with the orange juice and sugar until they hold a peak. As soon as you take out the apples, pile this meringue over them, so that it runs down the sides. They should look like snowballs. Put them in the warming drawer of your cooker, to set the meringue without colouring, and after about 2 hours, take them out and let them get quite cold before serving. They should be eaten with cream.

Charlotte Russe

The rich cold cousin of Apple Charlotte: both use a smooth sweet purée to fill a frame of crisp bread or cake. I cannot find out why this version is known as Russian: it may have been made for a distinguished Russian visitor to the court or the recipe may have come from Russia.

Serves 4

> 12–18 sponge fingers
> 2 oz. (60 g.) pistachios, almonds or walnuts
> ½ oz. (15 g.) gelatine
> 4 tablespoons water
> 1 oz. (30 g.) sugar
> 1 pint (6 dl.) double cream
> vanilla essence
> 12 crystallized cherries
> 12 small pieces of angelica

Line a straight-sided round dish with the sponge fingers (casino fingers are the best). Sprinkle chopped nuts thickly over the bottom. Melt the gelatine in 1 tablespoon water, add the remainder and stir over the heat until it is thoroughly dissolved. Remove from the heat and add sugar. Whip ¾ pint (4½ dl.) cream stiffly, flavour it with a few drops of vanilla essence and stir into the gelatine mixture. Stir until nearly set, then carefully pour into the biscuit-lined mould. Allow to set, then turn out. Decorate with ¼ pint (1½ dl.) of plain whipped cream and crystallized cherries and angelica.

A solid syllabub or fruit-flavoured cream may be used as a change from the vanilla; or any fruit purée, to which gelatine is added and into which cream is stirred.

Fruit Salad

This eighteenth-century recipe came from Mr John Roper, whose grandmother had had it from her grandmother and who always insisted on the use of a fine scented China tea for the juice. She was right: it is far finer and more refreshing than any ordinary fruit salad, even one which has been refreshed with a liqueur. Mr Roper says that his grandmother preferred a dark red juice, but the pale salad is equally good.

Dark Red Fruit Salad

½ pint (3 dl.) jasmin tea; or scented Earl Grey or scented orange pekoe
¼ lb. (120 g.) caster sugar

For four people about ½ lb. (240 g.) of any 3 or 4 of these:
dark cherries
raspberries or loganberries
a few mulberries
dark grapes or cherries
strawberries
a few sliced really sweet dark plums

First make ½ pint (3 dl.) tea at 1½ times ordinary strength and allow to get quite cold.

Grapes and cherries must be stoned and halved and plums stoned and cut up. Pile all the fruit in a large bowl and pour over it the cold tea. Pour in the sugar. Leave to macerate for at least an hour but not all night.

Before serving in individual bowls, lightly mix a little, so that the sugar penetrates everywhere and the juice becomes evenly red: a few raspberries, loganberries or mulberries should always be included in order to colour the juice. Frozen raspberries are quite good for this.

Pale Fruit Salad
    white grapes
    fresh pineapple
    fresh pears (never use apple, which is too crisp)
    tinned or fresh lichees (a very elegant flavour with the tea)
    apricots
    peaches
    nectarines
    greengages or gage plums
    ½ pint (3 dl.) tea

Make up exactly as above. If you use orange scented pekoe, the juice of half an orange added to the fruit is very good.

Hedgehog

A very popular traditional dish because it was ornamental and representational, and the split almonds delicious with the jelly and cream. In the earliest recipes hedgehogs were made with ground almonds, eggs, sugar and butter, so that the resulting paste was almost like marzipan and could be modelled to a hedgehog shape, stuck with blanched almonds and surrounded either by a rich cream or a jelly.

However, this Edwardian recipe gives a prune mould for the hedgehog, standing on a green jelly, which is piled with whipped cream for snow.

Serves 6
    1 lb. (½ k.) prunes
    ½ lb. (240 g.) blanched almonds
    1 lemon jelly
    1 lime jelly
    ½ pint (3 dl.) double cream

The prunes should be soaked, sweetened, stewed, stoned and cut in quarters. Reserve the juice.

Make up the lemon jelly in an oval mould using the prune juice made up with water to ¾ pint (9 dl.). Stir in the prunes and leave to set. When nearly set make up the green jelly and reserve. When the lemon jelly is quite stiff, turn it out on a flat dish and stick it all over with the almonds, each split into

2 or 3 narrow strips; leave one end near the bottom without almonds, to represent the head. Pour the half-set green jelly all round and put the dish back in the refrigerator. Just before serving, cover most of the green jelly with the cream whipped with a little sugar, to represent snow on grass.

Hedgehog Tipsy Cake

This eighteenth-century recipe is more sophisticated.

> 1 large madeira or sponge cake *or* 8 small sponge cakes
> ½ bottle sweet sherry or marsala or madeira or rum
> apricot jam
> ½ lb. (240 g.) blanched almonds
> 2 raisins
> 3 oz. (90 g.) caster sugar
> 1 pint (6 dl.) double cream
> juice of 2 oranges

Cut the cake to an oval shape roughly representing a hedgehog. Use a separate piece for the head and stick it on at one end at the bottom with apricot jam. If separate sponge cakes are used, build up and stick together with apricot jam. Cut out a cup in the middle of the back. Reserve the piece of sponge to replace later and fill the cup with wine. Pour more wine all over. Place in the refrigerator overnight and spoon the wine over from time to time.

Next day split the almonds into 2 or 3 pieces, brown them slightly on a tray in the oven, and stick the hedgehog with them. Give him raisin eyes. Whip the orange juice, sugar and cream till stiff enough to hold a peak and pile all round the hedgehog.

JUNKET

Junket was the most common festive sweet dish from the Middle Ages to the eighteenth century. It was served on holidays, at feasts and fairs, so universally that they were often called 'junket-days' and people spoke of going 'a-junketing'. The name comes from the word 'junci' or wild rushes, on which the curds were laid to drain, and on which, when drained sufficiently, they were served. Markham refers to a junket as a 'wet sucket': in fact, it is simply 'curds and whey'.

For 4

    1 pint (6 dl.) milk
    1 teaspoon rennet (can be bought at a chemist)
    pinch of cinnamon   } an improvement, but not essential
    1 tablespoon brandy }
    2 teaspoons sugar
    a little nutmeg

Warm the milk to blood heat only, and stir in the rennet, cinnamon, brandy and sugar. Turn into a wide flat bowl or into individual dishes, and sprinkle lightly with nutmeg. Leave to stand until cold and set, but not in the refrigerator.

Many people dislike junket, but eaten with clotted or thick cream, it is good, if rather insipid.

Meringues

For 12–14 halves

    3 egg whites   pinch of salt
    6 oz. (180 g.) caster sugar

Beat the separated egg whites until stiff enough to hold a peak or to remain in the bowl if it is reversed. Fold in the sugar, one spoonful at a time, with the salt, disturbing the mixture as little as possible. Pipe or place in small spoonfuls on a flat, well-buttered baking tin. Cook at 200° F., gas mark ½, for 2–2½ hours or until crisp and a pale biscuit colour.

No attempt should be made to remove the meringues from the tin until they are perfectly cold. They are best served sandwiched with plain whipped cream, and are also a good accompaniment to any fruit cream or fool.

Negrita

A nineteenth-century recipe for chocolate mousse. There are various versions, but this is particularly rich in flavour and consistency and easy to make.

Serves 4

    4 oz. (120 g.) bitter chocolate   3 eggs
    a pinch of salt   1 small glass brandy
    a little whipped cream

Melt the chocolate in a basin over a saucepan filled with boiling water. When the chocolate has melted add the egg yolks and a pinch of salt and whisk well over the heat until it thickens like very stiff custard. Flavour with the brandy. Allow to cool, then fold in the stiffly beaten egg whites. Serve in individual glasses with whipped cream on top. It may be flavoured with rum instead of brandy.

Orange or Lemon Mousse

This is a very fine eighteenth-century recipe because it sets perfectly without the use of gelatine, which so many recipes for a fruit mousse require. If gelatine is used the mousse is much more likely to separate so that there is a layer of jelly at the bottom.

To serve 6 or 7

    8 large oranges or lemons   4 oz. (120 g.) caster sugar
    8 eggs

Separate the yolks and whites of the eggs and beat the yolks thoroughly. Grate the yellow part of 4 rinds finely, then squeeze the juice from all the fruit. Heat the juice, grated rind and sugar together, stirring until the sugar is dissolved. Allow to cool. Now pour the mixture on to the egg yolks, beat well and stir over a saucepan of boiling water till the mixture thickens. Allow to cool to blood heat. Meanwhile, beat the egg whites until they will hold a peak when dropped from the whisk. Add the orange mixture to the egg whites slowly, and fold in, disturbing the whites as little as possible, but making sure that the whites and the orange are mixed right through. Pour the mixture into the serving dish and place in the refrigerator for several hours, stirring two or three times during the first hour.

Summer Pudding

A traditional pudding always served on the farms when there was a glut of soft fruit. Best of all with scalded cream.

Serves 4–6

    8–9 slices white bread from a thin sliced loaf (crusts removed)
    1 lb. (½ k.) fresh raspberries *or* ¾ raspberries and ¼ red currants,
        stalked
    ½ lb. (240 g.) caster sugar
    ½ pint (3 dl.) whipped or clotted cream

Line a 1½-pint (1-l.) pudding basin with the slices of bread, fitting them carefully with no gaps. Cut them smaller if necessary and leave slight overlaps. Stir all the sugar into the fruit and beat up a little. Pour about half into the bowl. Lay another slice or two of bread over the fruit and then put in the remainder. Cover neatly and closely with bread, cutting slices to fit the round top.

Put a plate on the top of a size which presses down on the bread and does not rest on the bowl. Place a weight on this and put the whole in the refrigerator and chill for an hour or two. Turn out carefully just before serving. The pudding should be a rich even raspberry colour, and should be piled with whipped or clotted cream. Extra sugar should be available as the uncooked fruit is apt to be sharp. Some people also like this pudding made with fresh blackcurrants.

Sorbets, Water Ices and Ice Puddings

Sorbets, which are half-frozen water ices and generally orange or lemon, though sometimes flavoured with rum or liqueur, were often served in Victorian and Edwardian days at large dinner parties with long menus, to provide a welcome pause between the roast and the entrée. Twenty elegant ladies and gentlemen, heated from eating soup, fish and entrées and drinking the appropriate wines while the candles on the table and behind them in sconces on the walls gave out heat as well as light, found a cold, sharp lemon sorbet so refreshing that they could continue to eat and drink their way through the remaining courses of the menu.

Lemon Sorbet

Serves 8

8 lemons	2 oz. (60 g.) caster sugar
2 oranges	2 egg whites
8 oz. (240 g.) loaf sugar	1½ pints (9 dl.) water

Boil the loaf sugar and water for 5 minutes, skimming well. Add the finely grated rind of 2 lemons and the orange and lemon juice. Bring just to the boil again and then strain and cool. Put into the freezing compartment till half-frozen, and then beat in the stiffly whisked egg whites and caster sugar and put back into the ice trays till the consistency is as you like it.

For *Orange Sorbet* use 8 oranges and 2 lemons.

Lemon Ice

A Victorian recipe. I do not think the use of both loaf and granulated sugar has any effect. I have made the ice with 1½ lb. (720 g.) of caster sugar, and it was perfect. The ice comes out as white as snow.

Serves 8–10

5 lemons	4 oz. (120 g.) loaf sugar
1 pint (6 dl.) cold water	2 egg whites
1¼ lb. (600 g.) granulated sugar	

Rub the loaf sugar on the lemon rind so that it soaks up the fragrant lemon oils.

Put the strained lemon juice and the granulated and loaf sugar into the cold water, stir till the loaf sugar is dissolved, and set it to freeze. When nearly set, add the beaten egg whites.

Lord John Russell's Pudding

An iced pudding of 1860. It makes a quart mould.

Serves 8–10

6 egg yolks
finely grated peel of 1 lemon and 1 orange
1½ pints (9 dl.) milk
1 oz. (30 g.) powdered gelatine melted in a little water
1 wineglass brandy
1 pint (6 dl.) double cream
2 teaspoons orange curaçao
2 oz. (60 g.) crystallized pineapple
2 oz. (60 g.) soaked raisins
2 oz. (60 g.) crystallized cherries
2 oz. (60 g.) caster sugar

Beat or blend the egg yolks with the milk, grated lemon and orange peel, sugar and softened gelatine. Beat over slow heat, preferably in a double saucepan, until it thickens. It must not, of course, boil or it will curdle. When thick, stir in half the cream and then the brandy, curaçao and fruit and allow to thicken again without boiling. Pour into a mould and stand in the freezing compartment of the refrigerator for 4 hours. Turn out and cover with the remaining cream whipped with the caster sugar.

Surprise Pudding
Serves 6–8

> sponge or victoria sandwich cake (p. 522)
> large block vanilla ice cream
> rum
> 3 egg whites
> 6 oz. (180 g.) caster sugar } to make meringue top

The cake can be any shape, but if you make one slightly larger than your ice-cream block it is easier to manage. Set the cake on a fireproof dish and sprinkle it with rum. Prepare the meringue (see p. 480), making sure it is really stiff. Put the *hard frozen* block of ice cream on the cake and cover completely with the uncooked meringue. (Some people use a forcing bag for this.) Dust with caster sugar and put in a hot oven at 500° F., gas mark 9, for 2 or 3 minutes to set and colour the meringue. The plate can be stood in a tray of crushed ice while it is in the oven. Remove and serve immediately. A tablespoon of rum may be poured over the meringue when you remove the pudding from the oven; light it quickly and serve it flambé, but everything must be done very fast.

Turkish Pudding

This comes from the collection of Lady Clark of Tillypronie (about 1909). It is very good hot, or chilled for an hour in the refrigerator; it can also be frozen in the deep-freeze compartment and served as iced pudding. In a 3-star deep-freeze allow only about an hour, and check after 30 minutes that it is not becoming too hard to eat.

I have no idea why she called it Turkish Pudding: it is a typically English nineteenth-century recipe for a fairly elaborate pudding.

Serves 8

> 1 large sponge cake in a ring shape   nutmeg
> 2 glasses white wine   ½ lb. (250 g.) caster sugar
> 1 lb. (½ k.) cooking apples   1 oz. (30 g.) butter
>
> *For the custard:*
> ¼ pint (1½ dl.) milk   8 egg yolks
> ¼ pint (1½ dl.) double cream   almond flavouring

8 egg whites for meringue
cherries, angelica, chopped crystallized fruits to garnish

Peel, core and quarter the apples and bake them in the butter with half the sugar in a fireproof dish at 400° F., gas mark 6, until quite tender and transparent. If possible, the quarters should just remain separate. Sift a little more sugar and a very little nutmeg over them and allow to cool.

Meanwhile soak the sponge cake in the wine.

Make the custard by beating the yolks of the eggs well and pouring on to them the milk and cream at boiling point, all the time stirring well. Hold above low heat and stir in ½ teaspoon almond flavouring just as it begins to thicken, and go on stirring till it is of the consistency of thick cream. Allow the custard to cool, and fill the sponge cake with alternate spoonfuls of custard and apple, allowing some of the custard to overflow and pour down the sides a little. Whisk the egg whites and remaining sugar to hold a peak. Pour all over the pudding. Allow to 'dry' a few minutes in the warming drawer and decorate with cherries, chopped crystallized fruit, just before serving. Chill, freeze, or serve hot.

12 · SAVOURIES

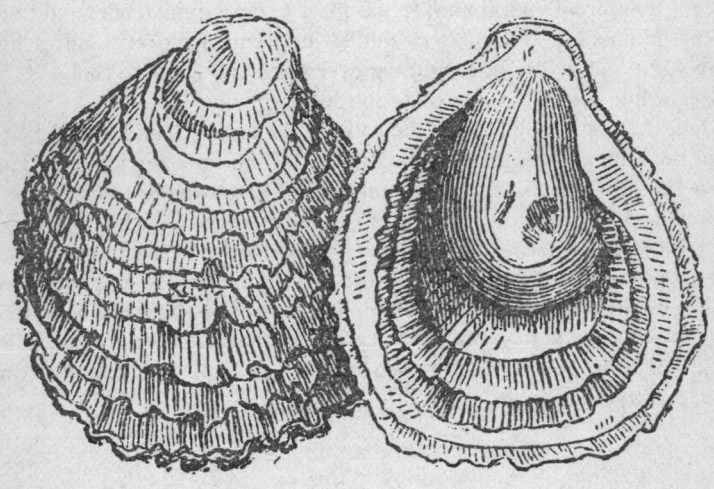

The savoury is an end to a long dinner, a kind of exclamation point following the sweet and preceding the dessert and the port; an entirely English invention. It forms no part of any other cuisine, although it has occasionally been borrowed by the French in anglophile mood. Its original intention was to cleanse the palate after the delicious but cloying sweet and prepare it, in the case of gentlemen, for the port. Ladies very often missed the savoury, their delicate appetites already sated on the seven or so courses which might have preceded it. Gentlemen, on the other hand, sometimes missed the sweet, and this was considered rather discerning and manly.

The earliest references to the savoury, in this sense, seem to be Victorian. In our own time, when a dinner rarely consists of more than three (occasionally four) courses, a savoury is sometimes offered instead of a sweet. Many people welcome this as an interesting change, and it is convenient for the single-handed cook as almost all savouries take only three or four minutes to grill or fry: if the ingredients have been prepared and placed ready, this should take her just the right length of time while someone else clears away the main course.

The savoury should always be very small and strongly flavoured and served very hot, except for a small number of chilled summer savouries.

Almost all the recipes for savouries are good for supper or light luncheon dishes if made in double or treble quantities on whole rounds of toast.

Welsh rarebit, soft roes on toast, mock crab and cheese straws, all given in other chapters, were often served, in very small quantities, as after-dinner savouries.

Anchovies on Toast

For 4

> 1 tin anchovy fillets
> 1 oz. (30 g.) anchovy butter (p. 302)
> 4 strips of toast, 1 × 3 in. (2 × 6 cm.)

Make the toast and spread with the anchovy butter. Lay 3 anchovy fillets longways down each strip. All this may be done in advance. Just before serving, place for 3 minutes under a medium hot grill.

Asparagus

For 4

> 4 strips of hot toast
> 1 tablespoon cold hollandaise sauce (p. 285)
> about 48 tips of small green asparagus, cooked and hot

A small helping of asparagus, with melted butter or hollandaise sauce, is often served in summer as a separate and final course, followed only by fruit. However, strips of hot toast, spread with cold hollandaise sauce and sprinkled with small green asparagus tips, very hot, so that the sauce begins to melt, make a delicious savoury.

Angels on Horseback

For 6

> 6 fingers of bread   3 rashers streaky bacon
> 2 oz. (60 g.) butter   lemon juice
> 6 oysters   cayenne

Fry the bread lightly in the butter, and keep hot on a fireproof dish. Trim the beards from the oysters, sprinkle with lemon juice and cayenne and roll each in half a rasher of streaky bacon. Fry quickly in butter just long enough to cook the bacon, turning the rolls so that they are cooked on all sides. This should only take about 2 minutes, during which time the bacon protects the oysters, so that they are not overcooked. Place one on each piece of fried bread and serve immediately.

Devils on Horseback

For 6

2 chicken livers	black pepper
3 rashers bacon	cayenne
6 fingers hot buttered toast	paprika

Wash, dry and cut each liver into three. Remove the rind from the bacon and cut each rasher in half. Wrap each piece of liver in bacon and fry or grill for 2 or 3 minutes. Serve one roll on each finger of toast. Sprinkle with fresh black pepper and a little paprika and cayenne. Serve very hot.

Devilled Ham Toasts

For 4

2 oz. (60 g.) finely minced lean cooked ham
2 teaspoons Worcester sauce
a pinch of cayenne
½ tablespoon French mustard
½ oz. (15 g.) butter
4 circles of well-buttered toast each 2 in. (5 cm.) in diameter
1 tablespoon finely chopped parsley

Thoroughly mix the ham, Worcester sauce, cayenne and mustard. Melt the butter in a small saucepan and stir the mixture into it, stirring until it is very hot. Pile on to the circles of toast, sprinkle with parsley and serve immediately.

Kipper Fillets on Toast

For 4

2 kipper fillets, each cut in half, or half a large kipper, cooked and filleted, to give 4 small fillets
4 strips of toast
butter
cayenne

Proceed exactly as in Sardines on Toast (see p. 491).

Marrow on Toast

Marrow is very rarely served nowadays, but it was very popular in England, both as an ingredient and served separately, until the First World War. Several gentlemen's clubs specialized in serving excellent marrow bones, and marrow on toast was a favourite savoury. When Francatelli was chef to Queen Victoria, she ate marrow toast prepared in this way as a savoury at dinner whenever she dined alone or en famille.

For 4
> marrow from 4 marrow bones (get the butcher to break the bones)
> 1 tablespoon chopped parsley
> salt and pepper
> 1 finely chopped shallot
> 4 3-in. (6-cm.) squares of hot dry toast

Remove all the marrow from the bones, cut into pieces about ½ inch (1 cm.) square, and cook these for 1 minute in boiling salted water. Drain and keep hot. Season with salt and pepper and add the parsley and the very finely chopped shallot, mixing all together lightly. Serve at once on the hot *dry* toast.

Mushrooms on Toast

> *Per person:*
> 3 medium mushrooms
> 1 strip of hot buttered toast, 1 × 3 in. (2 × 6 cm.)
> salt and fresh black pepper
> ½ oz. (15 g.) butter

Fry the mushrooms very gently and keep hot while the toast is made and buttered. Arrange three on each strip and sprinkle with salt and plenty of fresh black pepper.

This very simple savoury is best made just before it is to be eaten. It will take about 5 minutes to fry the mushrooms.

Pear and Stilton

This is a very fine cold savoury belonging to the English autumn. It depends on excellent pears, fine Stilton and new walnuts.

> *For each person:*
> half a fine ripe dessert pear
> 1 oz. (30 g.) Stilton cheese
> 1 oz. (30 g.) butter
> fresh black pepper
> 2 half kernels of a freshly shelled walnut
> 1 inside leaf of crisp lettuce
> lemon juice

Peel, halve and core the pears very shortly before eating, and squeeze a little lemon juice over them to keep them white. Lay each half on a crisp lettuce leaf. Cream the Stilton with the butter and a good pinch of coarsely ground black pepper. Pile 2 or 3 teaspoonfuls in the centre of each half of pear, and stick the walnut halves to the pile.

If the pears are very large, quarters can of course be used.

Very good indeed with claret or port.

Scotch Woodcock

Many Victorian gentlemen considered this the best of all savouries.

For 4

> 4 slices of toast, 3 × 2 in. (6 × 4 cm.), without crust and well buttered
> 12 anchovy fillets
> 4 egg yolks
> ¼ pint (1½ dl.) double cream
> pepper and salt
> ½ oz. (15 g.) butter for eggs

Arrange the buttered toasts on a fireproof serving dish. Pound the anchovy fillets well, add a little pepper and spread them on the toasts. Keep hot. Beat the egg yolks well with the cream and season with salt and pepper. Melt the butter in a small saucepan, stir in the eggs and stir, holding just off the heat, until they begin to thicken. They should not boil and should only be a little thicker than double cream. Pour over the toasts and serve immediately.

Scotch Woodcock with Ham

Make exactly as the preceding recipe but the anchovies are replaced by 2 oz. (60 g.) finely minced lean cooked ham.

Sardines on Toast

> *Per person:*
> 1 medium-sized sardine
> 1 strip of hot buttered toast, 1 × 3 in. (2 × 6 cm.)
> 1 oz. (30 g.) butter
> cayenne

Keep the strips of toast hot while you place the sardines under a hot grill turning them once and grilling for 1 minute on each side. Place one on each strip of toast. Sprinkle with cayenne and serve very hot.

Devilled Sardines on Toast

Proceed exactly as in the preceding recipe but, before grilling, spread each sardine with a little of the following mixture, and a little more when you turn them.

> 2 teaspoons made mustard
> pinch of cayenne
> pinch of paprika   all well
> pinch of turmeric   amalgamated
> 1 tablespoon lemon juice   to a paste
> piece of soft butter the size of a walnut

Skuets

Tiny silver skewers (or skuets) were used to serve small savoury tit-bits in the sixteenth century. These were generally stuck decoratively through the crust of a raised pie (the Gloucester Royal Pie was ornamented with crayfish on gold skewers), or sometimes surrounded a ragoût or a dish of birds, in which case they were generally filled with the cut livers of the birds, and cockscombs or small pieces of breaded sweetbreads.

Tiny skewers filled with fried and sliced chicken or duck livers and two or three small mushrooms are often served as savouries, each lying along a strip of buttered toast.

491

The skewers may also be filled with prawns or with breaded oysters and tiny rolls of bacon. In either case, melted butter is poured over the contents of each skewer; they are then grilled for four or five minutes and served very hot, sprinkled with paprika and a very little cayenne.

Cheese Soufflé

I do not think the soufflé is truly part of the tradition of English cooking. I cannot find any dish nearer to it in early recipes than various forms of more or less soufflé omelettes. However, a cheese soufflé is, in many ways, a perfect savoury, and since every form of cold and hot soufflé graced Edwardian tables, I have fallen to the temptation of giving my own favourite recipe here.

Serves 4

¼ pint (1½ dl.) cheese sauce (p. 283) made with an extra 2 oz. (60 g.)
    very finely grated cheese
1 oz. (30 g.) grated Parmesan cheese
5 yolks and 6 whites of egg
pepper and salt
a little butter

This may be made either as one large soufflé or in individual soufflé dishes. A large soufflé will take 15 minutes to bake in an oven preheated to 450° F., gas mark 8. Small ones will take 8 minutes at the same temperature. The large one can be put in as you finish serving the previous course; the small ones just as you finish eating it.

Beat the egg yolks and mix into the warm cheese sauce, blending well. Season rather highly with pepper but only a little salt (because the cheese is salt). Set aside. Well butter the soufflé dish or small dishes and put ready.

The egg whites can be beaten a little before the soufflé is to be cooked, and given a final beating just before they are combined with the cheese mixture. They must hold a peak and be perfectly stiff throughout. Just before the soufflé is to go into the hot oven, fold them into the cheese mixture, lifting and stirring rather than beating, and making sure that they are evenly mixed in. Pile into the dish or dishes, so that they are two thirds full. Put them quickly into the oven about half-way up, and do not open it again until they should be ready. Carry the beautifully puffed and risen golden-brown soufflé quickly but smoothly to the table and serve. If it is waved about it may begin to sink. Start to eat it immediately.

13 · BREAD AND CAKES

Bread and Rolls

From time immemorial until late in the nineteenth century baking day, usually a Friday or a Saturday, was the hardest day of the week for the English farmer's wife. Laundry, until the eighteenth century at least, was often done only once a month, in some houses once every three months, not because dirty linen was endured but because home spinning and weaving had resulted in dower chests of linen which lasted the household from generation to generation: everything from sheets to embroidered petticoats was counted in dozens, and grandmother's and mother's linen sheets were handed down, often as good as on the day they were hemmed and embroidered. But baking had to be done every week, in some large households twice a week, and though it was pleasant work in winter, it was exhausting on a hot summer's day. In the really great households, a baker was kept who often baked daily so that the mistress of the house was always served with a fresh fine manchet and even the coarser bread for the servants was new.

F. G. Emmison has clarified the records from Ingatestone Hall in the middle of the sixteenth century. They show that between twenty and thirty servants and, later, about fifty, had to be catered for, apart from the family and guests, guests' servants, visiting tradesmen and unexpected travellers, and that the baker produced three kinds of bread, the 'manchet' being fine white bread and the others coarser wholemeal bread. Some households mixed rye with the wheat, but this does not seem to have been the case at Ingatestone.

The Harleian MS. of 1526 refers to the 'manchetta' allowed to the queen's maids at Eltham Palace. With a gallon of ale they received one in the morning along with a coarser loaf, another later, with more ale, and 'after supper' a third with a coarser loaf, two gallons of ale and half a pitcher of wine.

Baking was measured by the 'cast', which equalled two or three loaves according to size. In 1552 at Ingatestone Hall, 1,900 casts of manchet were baked, 5,560 casts of yeoman's bread and 1,480 casts of carter's bread. This means that at least 20,000 loaves were baked in the year.

In the smaller household of perhaps six or eight to twenty people, a large cake or two and some pies and tarts were usually baked with the bread if the household was prosperous. Certain early recipes say that a cake or pie should be 'bread baked', simply meaning that it should be put into the bread oven with a batch of bread.

In the deep country up to the First World War, bread ovens in the sides of chimneys were often still used and were heated by being filled with faggots of brushwood, which were lit and replenished till the oven was burnt clean except for white hot ash in the bottom. This was raked out and the bread and cakes put in, those to go at the back being slid into position on a long-handled 'peal'. Such an oven, which is reputed to have produced beautiful bread with a specially fine crust, was not opened until it was thought that the bread would be ready, as heat was lost very quickly. A smaller cake or some pastry might be slipped in or pulled out after the baking had begun, but a raised pie with well-protected sides, or a large plum cake, would take at least the same time as the loaves, and experienced housewives made them in sizes to do so.

As the cities grew, the making of bread at home declined, until today very few housewives make bread more than two or three times in their lives and many never do. This is a pity, because home-made bread is an entirely different food from baker's bread, and it is interesting to eat on occasion the staple food of our ancestors through so many centuries. Apart from this, making bread is satisfying and very pleasant. It is, however, essential to have most of a day free, because the different operations are spaced by periods dough must be left to 'rise' or 'prove', and it is not worth making one small loaf. A pound of flour, in general, makes two fair-sized loaves.

Plain flour should be used for bread making.

Yeast is a living micro-organism which needs warmth and food to make it grow. It 'lightens' the bread dough by producing bubbles of carbon dioxide (the chemicals in baking powder produce the same gas). The right warmth is just below blood heat, 80–83° F. If the dough is heated above 95° F., the yeast is killed, and if the temperature is below 77° F., it is dormant and gives off no carbon dioxide. When the dried yeast is mixed with sugar and warm water it begins to 'work' and give off bubbles of carbon dioxide. Then when it is mixed with the flour and when the dough is placed in a warm place to 'sponge' or 'prove', the gas makes it spongy and full of air. This takes about 20 minutes. It is then kneaded to make a smooth elastic dough, and the bread left again in a warm place for 1½ hours to double its original size. When the dough is finally put in the oven, the yeast is killed, so no more gas is produced. It is therefore important to make sure a yeast dough has been 'proved' thoroughly before baking, or the bread will be close and heavy. On the other hand, over-rising can stretch and weaken the dough, so that it collapses in the oven, which again results in heavy bread. If you remember that the yeast is alive and must always be kept warm and handled gently, using it is not difficult. It should not be put in a cold mixing bowl, or mixed with cold liquid. Always warm all the things you are going to need, and use warm sugar and warm milk or water to mix into it. One part boiling and two parts cold water mixed together is just right. The dough must be put in a warm place to rise, not too hot, and not in a draught. The plate rack over a stove or an airing cupboard are good places, or the warming drawer of your cooker, left open.

It is assumed that dried yeast, bought in a packet from any grocer, is to be used, as this is excellent and saves a great deal of trouble. Mix according to the directions on the packet. If, however, you can arrange to get fresh baker's yeast, you may consider that your bread has a sweeter, fresher taste, and some cooks say that it rises more quickly than when dried yeast is used.

White Bread

3½ lb. (1¾ k.) best plain flour (*not* self-raising)	1½ oz. (45 g.) yeast
1 tablespoon salt	2 level teaspoons caster sugar
	1½ pints (9 dl.) milk and water

3 2-pint (1-l.) bread tins or round cake tins 2 inches (5 cm.) deep and 9 inches (20 cm.) in diameter will be required for these quantities.

Warm all the utensils before you begin to make the bread. Make up the yeast as directed on packet, if dried is used. If fresh is available, mix in a cup with 1 teaspoon caster sugar and 2 tablespoons tepid water.

Put flour, salt and remaining sugar into a mixing bowl and mix lightly so that the salt and sugar are evenly distributed throughout.

Make the water and milk just lukewarm – one part boiling and two of cold mixed together give the right temperature. Add the prepared yeast. Then with a wooden spoon make a hole in the centre of the flour and pour all the liquid gently into the hole. The hole must not go to the bottom of the bowl, as there must be a layer of flour under the liquid. Now, with the spoon, stir a little of the flour into the liquid, and sprinkle a little of the dry flour which remains round the edge over the batter and leave the remainder of the dry flour in a wall round it. If the liquid overflows the flour in places, no harm is done.

Cover the bowl with a cloth and stand it in a warm place for the 'sponge', as it is called, to rise. This will take about 20 minutes. When the yeast has risen through the flour and is a mass of bubbles, it is ready to knead.

To do this, just mix the dry flour into the central batter, then turn it on to a board. Knead with your knuckles, lightly but firmly, turning and gathering the dough for about three minutes.

When the dough is smooth and elastic, put it back in the bowl and cover again with the cloth, which should have been sprinkled with flour on the side nearest the dough to prevent sticking. Leave it in a warm place for one and a quarter hours to rise. It should then have doubled its original size.

If you are baking the bread in tins, make them warm and do not grease. Knead the dough again for at least 3 minutes: divide it by cutting and half-fill each tin with the dough. Put the tins in a warm place to 'prove' them for at least half an hour. Then put in a hot oven – 425° F., gas mark 7 – and reduce the heat to moderate after 10 minutes. Bake for about 45 minutes. Reduce the heat a little half-way through cooking, if the bread is darkening too much.

The loaf should sound hollow when tapped if it is done. If you like, test with a skewer, which should come out clean.

To make rolls, divide the dough into small evenly sized pieces. Knead each piece lightly and shape into balls, twists, etc. Place on a greased baking sheet, score with a knife and prove for about 10 minutes in a warm place. Glaze with egg or milk and bake until the rolls sound hollow when tapped – about 10 minutes.

Very Fine White Loaves

The following recipe comes from the unpublished eighteenth-century Reading manuscript.

'Beat 2 eggs with a little salt lay to them half a pint of ale barme or more then put to it three pounds of fine flower and pit it in as much bloodwarm milke as will make it soft and light then make it into loaves or Rowles. When they be baked and cold rasp or grate all the outside.'

Translated, it works out as follows and makes perfect loaves and rolls. I do not know why the outside of the rolls should be rasped, or grated. This is suggested in various early recipes and one can only assume that people disliked the crisp crust.

1 lb. (480 g.) flour	1 egg, well beaten
1 teaspoon salt	½ oz. (15 g.) yeast
about ½ pint (3 dl.) milk	1 teaspoon caster sugar
1½ oz. (45 g.) butter	

Make up the yeast with the sugar. Sieve the flour and salt into a basin. Melt the butter, add the milk and make it tepid. Pour the tepid milk over the prepared egg, add to the yeast and pour into the flour and make a soft, smooth dough. Beat well. Cover with a cloth and put to rise in a warm place for about 1 hour. Form into loaves, place on a greased baking sheet and prove for about 15 minutes.

Bake in a quick oven, 425° F., gas mark 7, for about 40 minutes.

Small Milk Loaves

1½ lb. (¾ k.) flour	1 teaspoon caster sugar
1 small teaspoon salt	½ oz. (15 g.) yeast
2 oz. (60 g.) butter	¾ pint (4½ dl.) milk

Make the milk lukewarm. Cream the yeast and sugar in a basin, add the milk to it, also the egg, well beaten.

Put the flour into a bowl, add the salt and mix well. Rub in the butter until evenly mixed. Pour in the yeast mixture and beat to a dough. Put it in a warm place to rise for 1¼ hours, then form the dough into little cottage loaves, horseshoes or twists. Leave them in a warm place for 10 minutes. Brush over with beaten egg and bake in a hot oven, 425° F., gas mark 7, for 20 minutes.

Wholemeal Bread

2 lb. (1 k.) wholemeal flour	2 teaspoons sugar
1 teaspoon salt	½ pint (3 dl.) water
1 oz. (30 g.) yeast	½ pint (3 dl.) milk

Prepare the yeast. Put the meal and salt into a warm basin and make a well, leaving a thick layer of meal at the bottom. Add the milk and water, which should be at a lukewarm temperature, to the yeast and pour in to the centre of the meal. Work in some of the meal gradually with the tips of the fingers until a batter is formed. Sprinkle a little dry meal over the top and cover the basin with a folded towel. Set the basin in a warm place for about 20 minutes or until the yeast begins to work and form bubbles on the top of the batter. Then mix in the meal from the sides of the basin and make a dough, using a little more warm milk or water if necessary. Give this 3 or 4 minutes' kneading and put back in the bowl in a warm place for 1¼ hours (it should double its size). Then divide the dough into two or three small greased bread tins, half filling each of them. Cover again with a clean cloth, and set the dough to rise in a warm place for a further 15 minutes. Bake the loaves in a hot oven, 425° F., gas mark 7, until they sound hollow when tapped on the bottom (from ¾ to 1 hour). When sufficiently cooked, turn out the bread on to a wire rack, and allow free circulation of air round it while cooling.

Wholemeal Splits

1 lb. (½ k.) wholemeal flour	1 oz. (30 g.) yeast
1 lb. (½ k.) white flour	½ oz. (15 g.) lard
1 teaspoon salt	½ pint (3 dl.) tepid water
2 teaspoons sugar	1 tablespoon milk

Mix thoroughly in a basin the wholemeal and white flour and the salt. Make a well in the middle and into this put the sugar and prepared yeast. Melt the lard and mix this with the tepid water and milk, and pour over the yeast.

Allow to stand till the batter rises and bubbles (about ¾–1 hour). Do not knead, but mix with a knife or spoon to the consistency of a soft paste, adding more warm water if necessary. Dust over with flour and set in a warm place to rise well (about 30 minutes). Then turn out on to a well-floured board, and lightly roll out about 1 inch (2½ cm.) in thickness. Place on a warmed greased tin and set to rise once more. Bake in a moderately hot oven,

400° F., gas mark 6, for 15–20 minutes. When cold, cut into squares, split and butter to serve.

Treacle Loaf

1 lb. (½ k.) wholemeal flour	2 oz. (60 g.) butter
1 large teaspoon salt	2 tablespoons treacle
1 oz. (30 g.) yeast	½ pint (3 dl.) boiling water
1 teaspoon caster sugar	

Make up the yeast. Put the treacle in a basin with the butter, pour in the boiling water, stir well to mix and leave it until it is just lukewarm. Put the flour in a bowl and well mix the salt with it. Pour the yeast into the treacle mixture and stir well. Then add this to the flour to form a rather soft dough. Cover with a cloth and put in a warm place for 1 hour to rise.

Turn the dough on to a well-floured board and knead for 3 or 4 minutes. Put the dough into 2 well-greased tins, which should be about three-parts full. Leave in a warm place for 20 minutes, then bake in a hot oven, 425° F., gas mark 7, for about 40 minutes.

¼ lb. (120 g.) stoned and chopped raisins or dates or walnuts may be added to the flour.

A few traditional yeast recipes for teacakes, buns and fruit breads follow. Now that it is possible to buy dried yeast they are as quick and easy to make as any others.

Home-made Crumpets

This nineteenth-century recipe gives something between drop scones and bought crumpets. They are so good that they should be better known.

1 lb. (½ k.) flour	1 teaspoon caster sugar
a pinch of salt	rather more than 1 pint
2 eggs	(7 dl.) milk
1 oz. (30 g.) yeast	

Make up the yeast and when ready add the warmed milk. Make a hole in the flour, add the salt, pour in the liquid and mix well; then add the beaten eggs and beat the batter well for 10 minutes if by hand. Alternatively, beat very well with electric beater or blend. Put in a warm place to rise, which will take about 1 hour, then cook.

If the crumpets are to be cooked in the oven, preheat it to 425° F., gas mark 7. Heat a baking tin and brush it over with melted butter. Put individual large tablespoonfuls of the mixture at equal distances on the greased tin, turn them once when holes have formed on the surface, bake a further 5 minutes. Butter them and serve hot.

To cook over the fire, generously grease a large frying pan or make very hot and grease a gridiron or girdle. Then drop the mixture in tablespoonsful at equal distances on the hot surface. Turn over and brown the other side, when well risen. Grease a little more if they start to stick or burn.

Devonshire Teacakes

1 lb. (½ k.) flour	3 oz. (90 g.) caster sugar
a pinch of salt	3 tablespoons milk
½ teaspoon cinnamon	½ oz. (15 g.) yeast
2 oz. (60 g.) butter	2 oz. (60 g.) sultanas

Mix the salt and cinnamon with the flour, rub in the butter, stir in the sugar, mix well. Warm the milk and dissolve the yeast in it. Make a hole in the middle of the flour, pour in the yeast and milk, and form into a dough. Add a little more milk if necessary. Stand it in a warm place for 1 hour.

Then knead·in the sultanas. Divide the dough into small pieces. Form into buns and leave to rise for half an hour before baking in a hot oven, 425° F., gas mark 7, for 15 minutes.

Serve hot with butter.

Sally Lunn

Eighteenth-century recipe for this traditional Yorkshire teacake.

1 lb. (½ k.) flour	1 oz. (30 g.) yeast
1 oz. (30 g.) granulated sugar	1 teaspoon caster sugar
a good pinch of salt	½ pint (3 dl.) lukewarm milk
6 oz. (180 g.) butter	3 egg yolks and 2 whites

Mix the granulated sugar and salt with the flour. Rub in 2 oz. (60 g.) butter until the mixture has the consistency of coarse breadcrumbs. Cream the yeast with the caster sugar, add a tablespoonful of milk to it and let it stand in a warm place for 10 minutes. Then make a hole in the centre of the flour and pour in the yeast. Mix a little of the flour with the yeast. Then add the beaten eggs and mix to a soft dough with milk, using a little water, or, as in some recipes, a little beer, if necessary to increase liquid.

Stand in a warm place for 1 hour to rise before kneading. Knead the dough for a few minutes, then divide it in 2 and make 2 large flat rounds. Leave them in a warm place until nearly twice their original size and then bake for 20–30 minutes at 425° F., gas mark 7.

When cooked split the first loaf across the middle and fill with butter – about ¼ lb. (120 g.) – and spread a little more over the top. Return it to the oven for 5 minutes for the butter to melt and penetrate the cake. The second cake can be reheated the next day.

Some recipes include currants, sultanas and a little spice.

Chelsea Buns

> 12 oz. (360 g.) flour
> a pinch of salt
> 4–5 oz. (120–150 g.) currants and sultanas, mixed
> 2 oz. (60 g.) sugar
> 1 oz. (30 g.) yeast
> 3 tablespoons warm milk and water
> 1½ oz. (45 g.) lard
> 1 egg
> a little melted butter
> 1 tablespoon sugar to glaze

Sieve together the flour and salt and put to warm. Mix the currants and sultanas with 2 teaspoons sugar. Cream the yeast with ½ teaspoon sugar and add it to the liquid. Add this to one third of the flour and set to sponge. Rub the fat into the remaining two thirds of flour, add another 6 teaspoons of sugar and gradually beat in the egg. Mix in the sponged mixture. Beat all thoroughly and put in a warm place to rise. When double its size, knead lightly on a floured board and then roll into an oblong strip about ¼ inch (½ cm.) thick. Brush over with melted fat and sprinkle evenly over it the fruit and 2 teaspoons sugar. Roll up tightly and cut into 12 even-sized slices. Place lightly on a greased tin. Allow to prove for 25 minutes, then bake in a hot oven, 425° F., gas mark 7, for 15 to 20 minutes. Glaze with sugar and water syrup or with melted golden syrup.

Christmas Fruit Loaf

An eighteenth-century recipe from an Edinburgh manuscript.

> 1 lb. (½ k.) flour
> ½ teaspoon salt
> ½ oz. (15 g.) yeast
> ½ pint (1½ dl.) warm milk and water
> 4 oz. (120 g.) butter
> 6 oz. (180 g.) sugar
> 8 oz. (240 g.) currants
> 8 oz. (240 g.) raisins
> 1 oz. (30 g.) mixed peel (*or* dates *or* sultanas)
> 1 teaspoon mixed spice

Sieve the flour and salt together. Mix the yeast with a very little of the warm milk and water. Rub the fat into the flour, make a well in the centre, pour in the yeast and allow to sponge for 20 minutes. Add the rest of the ingredients, beat very thoroughly until a soft dough is obtained. Grease and warm 3 loaf tins and half-fill with the dough. Put to rise in a warm place until the dough comes to the top of the tins (about 1 hour), then bake in a moderate oven, 375° F., gas mark 5, for ¾ hour. Turn out and cool on a rack.

The loaves can be iced with royal or boiled icing (pp. 528, 531).

Jam Doughnuts

My Cornish aunt's recipe for inimitable doughnuts.

> ½ oz. (15 g.) yeast — 1 oz. (30 g.) sugar
> ¼ pint (1½ dl.) milk and water — 1 egg
> 10 oz. (300 g.) plain flour — jam
> ¼ teaspoon salt — deep fat for frying
> 1 oz. (30 g.) butter — 1 oz. (30 g.) sugar

Mix the yeast to a smooth paste with a little of the milk, and gradually stir in the remaining milk and water. Place 4 oz. (120 g.) of the flour in a warmed bowl. Gradually add the milk and water mixture, and stir in. Whisk or beat well, cover with a cloth, and leave in a warm place for about 20 minutes, until well risen, with bubbles appearing.

Sieve the remainder of the flour and salt together, and rub in the butter. Stir in the sugar. Make a well in the centre of the flour, and pour in the yeast mixture and the slightly-beaten egg. Mix well, cover with a cloth, and leave in a warm place for half an hour. Press the dough down with the knuckles until it is reduced to its original size, and again cover and leave in a warm place for a further half-hour.

Turn out on to a floured board, shape into a round or roll, and divide into 12 or 16 equal portions, according to the size required. Form each portion into a ball, flatten out, place about a teaspoonful of jam in the centre, brush half-way round the edge with a little milk, fold over and press the edges securely together so that the jam cannot ooze out, then place on a floured baking sheet and set aside in a warm place for a further 20 minutes.

Have ready the boiling hot fat. Drop in as many doughnuts as the pan will hold conveniently, and cook for 5–7 minutes. When one side of each dough-nut is cooked, it will, if the correct mixture has been used, turn over to the other side automatically without being touched. When cooked, lift out, drain on kitchen paper, and roll in sugar and cinnamon.

Hot Cross Buns

A nineteenth-century recipe from a great Suffolk house where they were made like this on Good Friday morning fresh for breakfast.

1 lb. (½ k.) flour	2 oz. (60 g.) currants
a pinch of salt	2 oz. (60 g.) yeast
1 level teaspoon powdered cinnamon	2 tablespoons caster sugar
	about ½ pint (3 dl.) milk
1 level teaspoon mixed spice	1 egg
2 oz. (60 g.) butter	

Sieve the flour with salt and spices, rub in the butter and add the prepared currants. Cream the yeast with a little of the sugar, add a little warm milk and pour in the centre of the flour, sprinkle lightly over with flour and leave for 10 minutes. Then mix to a stiff dough with the beaten egg, adding a little milk if required.

Allow to rise until the mixture doubles itself in size. Divide into portions, mould into small buns, mark with a cross, cutting fairly deeply, and place on a greased and floured tin. Allow to rise until half as large again. Bake in a hot oven, 425° F., gas mark 7, for 5 to 8 minutes. Melt a little sugar in 1 table-spoonful of milk and brush over the buns.

BREAD AND ROLLS WITHOUT YEAST

This bread is so much quicker and easier to make than yeast bread that it can be produced without trouble when bread runs short or becomes very stale over a holiday weekend. It is quite different from yeast bread but extremely good.

Soda Bread

> 1 lb. (½ k.) flour
> 2 teaspoons cream of tartar ⎫
> 1 teaspoon bicarbonate of soda ⎬ or 3 teaspoons baking powder
> 1 teaspoon salt
> 1 tablespoon of sugar
> ½ pint (3 dl.) milk

Alternatively you may use self-raising flour and add 1 small teaspoon of baking powder.

Mix all together with the milk to a soft dough. Knead a little.

Bake on a greased tin as a flat cake, or in a bread tin, for half an hour, at 400° F., gas mark 6.

For wholemeal soda bread use one-third wholemeal to two-thirds white flour.

Quick Rolls

> ½ lb. (240 g.) flour   2 teaspoons sugar
> 2 teaspoons baking powder   ½ pint (1½ dl.) milk
> a pinch of salt

Put the flour, baking powder, sugar and salt in a basin, pour in the milk gradually, and mix into a firm dough. Knead a little. Divide into small-sized rolls and brush over the tops with milk. Prick the rolls with a fork and place them on a greased baking tin. Bake for 10 minutes in a good oven, 425° F., gas mark 7.

Potato Cakes

The recipe originates in Ireland. The cakes are very good not only for tea but served on side plates with a plain grill.

½ lb. (240 g.) cooked potatoes   3 oz. (90 g.) butter
½ lb. (240 g.) self-raising flour   a little milk
a pinch of salt

Cold cooked potatoes can be used and passed through a moulin; or dried potato, made up according to directions and allowed to cool, is good for this purpose.

Sift the flour and salt in a basin. Rub in the butter with tips of fingers. Add the sieved potatoes and mix to a fairly soft dough, adding a little milk if necessary. Roll out very lightly to about ¾ inch (2 cm.) thick; cut into rounds 2 inches (5 cm.) in diameter or make into a large flat cake, and bake in a moderate oven, 350° F., gas mark 4, until golden brown (about 10 minutes). Split and butter generously, or in the case of a large cake simply butter the top.

Serve very hot.

Scones

Plain Scones

½ lb. (240 g.) flour   2 oz. (60 g.) butter
2 teaspoons caster sugar   a little milk to mix
1 teaspoon salt

Rub the butter into the flour and mix in the sugar and salt. Mix to a stiff dough with a very little milk. Knead for a minute on a floured board and then roll out ¾ inch (2 cm.) thick. Cut into rounds with a cutter or into triangles with a knife. Place on a floured tin and bake in a hot oven, 400° F., gas mark 6, for 10–15 minutes.

Eat hot with plenty of butter or with clotted cream and jam. May be split and toasted the day after they were made.

Cheese Scones

½ lb. (240 g.) sifted flour   ¼ pint (1½ dl.) milk
2 oz. (60 g.) grated cheese   a pinch of salt

Mix together the dry ingredients. Form into a dough with the milk, mix well, and cut into rounds. Bake in a hot oven at 425° F., gas mark 7, for 10–15 minutes.

Wholemeal Scones

¾ lb. (360 g.) wholemeal flour   1 oz. (30 g.) caster sugar
1 saltspoon salt   4 tablespoons milk and
2 oz. (60 g.) butter   water mixed

Mix the salt and flour. Rub in the butter, stir in the sugar and add the water and milk to make a stiff dough. Knead this for a few minutes. Roll out, form into scones and bake on hot tins in a good oven for about 20 minutes at 425° F., gas mark 7.

Cakes

The English cuisine early developed a style in cakes which is quite unlike that found anywhere else in the world. The earliest cakes were really spiced and sweetened breads, with or without the addition of dried fruits, raised by the use of yeast and generally made while the main batches of bread were 'proving' and baked in the bread oven. 'Cakes and ale' really meant 'sweet fruit bread and ale' and in the eighteenth century what we mean by cake was known as 'sweet cake'.

It was with the introduction and establishment of afternoon tea among the gentry that the English cake reached its full grandeur. Lady de la Warr claimed that afternoon tea originated with the Duchess of Bedford and first took place at Belvoir Castle when she was visiting there. She had brought some tea with her and used to invite the other female guests to drink it with her in her room in the afternoons. When she went back to London she continued to serve tea in the drawing-room of her town house.

Mrs Humphrey in *Etiquette for Every Day*, 1902, gives an Edwardian 'high life' tea menu which shows how the simple cup of tea in the drawing-room developed. Written entirely in menu French, 'tea' comprised: tea, coffee, bread and butter, 5 kinds of sandwiches, vol au vents of oysters and cutlets of chicken; 4 kinds of jelly, 2 creams and an ice; soft drinks and claret cup. Such a meal was considered suitable refreshment after 'carriage exercise' before the rigours of dressing for dinner. Ladies returning from their carriage exercise changed into long, loose, elaborately decorated dresses called tea gowns; there is a mention of this habit as early as 1877.

In the country, on the farms, and in the more prosperous cottages, large solid fruit cakes, gingerbreads, and 'plain' cakes had long been a tradition at the high tea or early supper which was eaten as soon as work finished in winter or before a final spell of work in summer. Children in all walks of life, probably always a little short on sugar, were devoted to cake: the best schools sometimes provided it on Saturdays; schoolrooms and nurseries two or three times a week, never more than two pieces allowed, generally only one, and always after bread and butter. Poor children tasted it only at school treats. A very old Suffolk farm labourer was recently quoted as saying that the children of his village, when he was a child, would go anywhere for cake; no matter how dreary the occasion. Quality was not in question: cake was cake and you never got it at home.

And what cake it was that was sometimes given to children! From an anonymous MS. recipe book of 1887 comes this recipe for a

> *Plain Cake for School Children*
> One stone flour [14 lb, 7 k.] 10s.
> One stone currants [14 lb, 7 k.] 11s.
> Quarter stone sugar [3½ lb., 1¾ k.] 2s. 7½d.
> Eggs and spice only to be added
> Made at home, and price of baking 1s. 6d.
> > Total cost: £1 5s. 1½d.

Sufficient for *ninety* children to have three good-sized pieces each. The total weight would have been about 34 lb. (17 k.). This particular recipe is attributed by the writer to a Mrs Bozle. It was certainly a very plain cake indeed.

Mrs Beeton neatly sums up the whole question of tea, its definition and proper serving as follows:

There is Tea and Tea, the substantial family repast in the house of the early diner, and the afternoon cosy, chatty affairs that the late diners have instituted. Both are eminently feminine; both should be as agreeable and social as possible. The family tea-meal is very like that of breakfast, only that more cakes and knickknackery in the way of sweet eatables are provided. A 'High Tea' is where meat takes a prominent part and signifies really, what it is, a tea-dinner. A white cloth is used, and two trays, one for tea, and one for coffee prepared, as at breakfast. Hot buttered cakes, plain and sweet, are chiefly used at tea. And there is the mere cup of tea that the lady or ladies of the house take after their afternoon drive as a kind of reviver before dressing for dinner. The afternoon tea signifies little more than tea and bread-and-butter, and a few elegant trifles in the way of cake and fruit. This meal is simply to enable a few friends to meet and talk comfortably and quietly, and, therefore, there is never a large party asked. There are proper services for these afternoon teas, exceedingly pretty and good.

When, however, there is really a veritable tea-party, such as our grandmothers delighted to give – and these are far from unfashionable – the repast differs little from the family one just mentioned; only that there would be extra provision made and, probably, more attention bestowed upon it.

Certain cakes were traditional on various feast days or special occasions: every child above the poverty line was entitled to a birthday cake; christening cakes, wedding cakes and Christmas cakes were inevitable; a simnel cake was proper at Easter; and a ring cake with a cone and a bean in it was often made for Twelfth Night. Ladies and gentlemen sometimes offered a madeira or a seed cake with a glass of madeira to callers, and various cakes were traditional at suppers given to workers in the course of the farm year.

In his *Five Hundred Pointes of Good Husbandrie*, *c*. 1580, Thomas Tusser says:

> Wife, sometime this weeke if that all things go cleare,
> An ende of wheat sowing we make for this yeare,
> Remember you therefore though I do it not
> The Seede Cake, the Paties and Furmenty pot.

American cakes derive from English recipes (there is a tradition that a copy of Gervase Markham's *The English Hus-wife* was taken to America in the *Mayflower*) but have developed into something very different. The basic American mixtures are smoother and lighter, and the fillings and frostings an essential part of the cake rather than merely additional sweetening and decorations which can well be omitted, as is the case with most English cakes.

The English rich fruit cake, such as pound cake, rich Genoa or Dundee, is accepted as a masterpiece of culinary invention and may be bought in tins as a speciality all over the world. Most of our other cakes seem to be a national taste only.

The following recipe, from the unpublished Reading MS. of 1760, shows the expensive ingredients used in a really rich cake, the vast size of the great cake (containing at least 10 lb. of raw ingredients) and the time spent on it and its icing. The actual baking time is short for such a large cake but it is in fact a 'bread' cake, using a great deal of yeast as well as many eggs and is partly risen before the fruit is added and it is put in the oven.

'To make a Plumb Cake

Take 4 pound of fine flower rub in half a pound of butter, one ounce of mace finely beaten, half a pound of fine sugar one quart of good cream boyled cut into it 2 pound of butter let it stand till it is pretty cold then take a large pint of good barm 12 eggs take out half the whites strain all through a white cloath and put in half a pint of sack then beat it up till it comes clear from the bottome of the thing you beat it in set it before the fire covering it with a warm cloth for a quarter of an hour or till you see it rife you must have ready 4 pounds of currants wel washed rubbed picked and dryed the oven must be pretty hot then beat it up you may put in what sweetmeat* you please haveing your hoope† buttered put it in and prick it with a silver pin, one hour and 3 quarters bake it.

To Ice It

Take 3 quarters of a pound of double refined sugar pound it and sift it very fine put it in a silver bason and let it be very drye then take the whites of 2 eggs with a spoonful of sack or brandy and beat it for a full hour till it comes up to a thick froth and when the cake is baked draw it out and put it upon it then put it in the oven againe for a quarter of an hour.'

A splendid recipe for 'A Great Cake' from a south Cornish manuscript dated 1763 uses the following ingredients: 5 lb. butter, brought to a cream, 5 lb. flour, 3 lb. white sugar, 7 lb. currants, 2s. 6d. worth of perfume, peel of 2 oranges, a pint of canary wine, ½ pint of rosewater, 43 eggs (half ye whites) and 1 lb. citron. These quantities could not have been baked in one great vessel, though a bread oven might have contained a great tin bath. It seems more likely that the cake was baked in 3 or 4 large tins and set up in tiers. The perfume is a strange addition. It presumably replaced brandy, spreading a slightly alcoholic and flowery aroma through the cake.

The days of afternoon tea are gone: even after-school tea for the children does not see a home-made cake every day; most of us make them a simple 'sponge' or a 'quick chocolate' once a week or so, or when we have forgotten to buy their proper quota of biscuits, crisps and buns. Many of us order birthday cakes from shops and buy a ready-made Christmas cake. However, since to make a good cake four or five times a year is a pleasure, and any rich cake is excellent served with coffee after dinner instead of a sweet, I shall give a few traditional recipes, but shall not give a full range covering the whole of the British Isles because very few today would have time to make even a fair

* The 'sweetmeats' would have been crystallized fruits, comfits, preserved ginger, etc.
† The 'hoope' was a circle of tin which was placed on a flat tray to contain the cake as it baked. In the nineteenth century with the coming of the kitchen range it was replaced by the cake tin.

selection, and even fewer the proper occasions to eat them if they were baked.

NOTE: All cake mixtures must be well beaten to give good results. An electric beater or a blender not only saves time but tends to give a lighter cake. Old recipes often demand that mixtures should be beaten for anything up to one hour. Nowadays we have neither the time nor the patience for very long hand beating, and if such things as cakes, mayonnaise, meringues and soufflés are often made, an electric beater is certainly desirable.

All flour in the cake recipes given here is self-raising unless otherwise stated.

FRUIT CAKES

Cherry Cake

10 oz. (300 g.) flour	4 oz. (120 g.) halved glacé
5 oz. (150 g.) butter	cherries
5 oz. (150 g.) sugar	milk and water to mix
3 eggs	sugar to sprinkle on top

Use an 8-inch (20-cm.) round tin.

Put the flour into a mixing bowl and rub in the butter with the fingertips until no lumps can be felt. Add sugar, and then the well-beaten eggs. Roll the cherries lightly in a little dry flour and beat them into the mixture, reserving about six for decorating the top of the cake. Use sufficient milk to mix just to dropping consistency but be very careful not to make the mixture slack. Put into a greased cake tin, put the rest of the cherries on the top of the cake and dredge with a little caster sugar. Bake in a moderate oven, 375° F., gas mark 5, for about 1¼ hours.

Mrs Raffald's Bride Cake (1769)

This is a superb dark fruit cake, which keeps for months and is well suited for occasions other than weddings. The quantities given by Mrs Raffald for a wedding make a cake of just over 20 lb.: they are reduced here to make a cake of about 3½ lb. (1¾ k.).

A very large cake tin is required – about 15 inches (38 cm.) in diameter.

¾ lb. (360 g.) flour	½ lb. (250 g.) sugar
¾ lb. (360 g.) butter	½ teaspoon nutmeg

½ teaspoon mace
7 eggs
¾ lb. (360 g.) currants
3 oz. (90 g.) chopped
   blanched almonds

4 tablespoons brandy
8 oz. (250 g.) candied peel,
   chopped
8 oz. (250 g.) sultanas
8 oz. (250 g.) raisins

The sultanas and raisins replace a vast quantity (3 lb.) of peel, which is less popular nowadays than it was.

Cream the butter and sugar. Beat the egg whites to a stiff froth and mix with butter and sugar. Beat the yolks till creamy and then add them. Put in all the dry ingredients, always beating, and finally beat in the brandy. Put in a lined and greased tin and bake 3½ hours at 300° F., gas mark 2. Test with a skewer and cook a further 10 or 15 minutes if it does not come out clean.

Dundee Cake, 1

A very good traditional recipe from a nineteenth-century Edinburgh collection. The quantities given make a cake of about 2½ lb. (1¼ k.).

3 oz. (90 g.) candied peel
2 oz. (60 g.) chopped almonds
10 oz. (300 g.) flour
½ teaspoon salt
6 oz. (180 g.) sultanas

4 oz. (120 g.) currants
6 oz. (180 g.) butter
6 oz. (180 g.) sugar
3 eggs
milk to mix

Grease and line a cake tin 8 or 9 inches (about 20 cm.) in diameter. Finely chop the peel and almonds, leaving about ½ oz. (15 g.) of nuts whole for the top of the cake. Sieve the flour and salt, and stir in the fruit, nuts and peel. Cream the butter and sugar, beat in each egg separately, then stir in the dry ingredients, adding a little milk if required. Put into the prepared tin, place the remaining nuts on top, and bake for approximately 1½ to 2 hours in a moderate oven, 350° F., gas mark 4. If the top begins to brown too much, cover lightly with foil.

Dundee Cake, 2

This is a really rich cake, a treasure chest of fruit and nuts. The recipe comes from Exeter.

8 oz. (240 g.) butter
6 oz. (180 g.) brown sugar

juice of 1 lemon and 1 orange
a little orange and lemon rind, grated
5 eggs, beaten
6 oz. (180 g.) each of currants and sultanas
4 oz. (120 g.) chopped raisins
2 oz. (60 g.) candied pineapple
2 oz. (60 g.) almonds (blanched and chopped)
2 oz. (60 g.) chopped ginger
8 oz. (240 g.) flour
blanched almonds to scatter on top

Use a cake tin about 8 inches (20 cm.) in diameter.

Cream the fat and sugar. Add juices, eggs and grated rinds and beat well. Mix together the dry ingredients and fold into the mixture; beat well again. Fill the tin, prepared with two layers of buttered paper, not more than two thirds full, make a deep depression in the centre and scatter blanched almonds, previously dipped in milk, on top. Bake for 2 hours, the first hour at 350° F., gas mark 4, and the next at 300° F., gas mark 2.

Guards' Club Luncheon Cake

Placed on the sideboard at the Guards' Club in Victorian days, to be eaten after a quick luncheon of bread and cheese and beer.

½ lb. (240 g.) butter
1 lb. (½ k.) plain flour
1 lb. (½ k.) brown sugar
½ lb. (240 g.) sultanas
½ lb. (240 g.) currants
2 oz. (60 g.) peel
2 oz. (60 g.) cherries
2 oz. (60 g.) almonds
1 teaspoon mixed spice
1 teaspoon bicarbonate of soda
1 teaspoon black treacle
½ teaspoon tartaric acid mixed with 2 tablespoons of milk (this improves lightness and colour)
2 tablespoons milk
2 tablespoons beer

Use a tin about 12 inches (30 cm.) in diameter.

Rub the butter and flour together very finely until like fine cake crumbs. Add all the dry ingredients, then the beer, eggs, treacle and milk. Put in a double-papered tin and have a small pot of water in the oven to make a moist heat. Cook for 2½ hours starting at 350° F., gas mark 4; after 40 minutes lower the heat to 300° F., gas mark 2.

Rich Pineapple and Walnut Cake

My own recipe: particularly good served with coffee after dinner instead of a sweet. These quantities make a 2½-lb. (1¼-k.) cake.

¼ lb. (120 g.) shelled walnuts	½ lb. (240 g.) caster sugar
½ lb. (240 g.) glacé pineapple	5 eggs
¾ lb. (360 g.) flour	a little milk
½ lb. (240 g.) butter	

Chop the walnuts, but not finely. Cut the glacé pineapple into small pieces. Sieve the flour. Cream the butter, add the sugar, then the beaten eggs, and beat thoroughly. When the mixture has been well beaten, stir in the flour very lightly. Mix carefully, adding a little milk if necessary to bring it to the right consistency which should be creamy but firm. Add the prepared walnuts and pineapple, and turn the mixture into an 8-inch (20-cm.) cake tin that has been greased and lined with paper. Bake in a slow oven, 300° F., gas mark 2, for 1½ to 2 hours, according to size. This cake may either be left plain or decorated with a coating of glacé icing (see p. 530) and pieces of thickly cut glacé pineapple on the top.

Rich Pound Cake

This recipe makes a good rich fruit cake and is excellent for a Christmas cake. The quantities given here make a cake between 2 and 3 lb. (1–1½ k.) in weight.

8 oz. (240 g.) butter
8 oz. (240 g.) caster sugar
4 eggs
8 oz. (240 g.) flour
1 teaspoon salt
¼ teaspoon mixed spice (optional)
8 oz. (240 g.) currants and sultanas
8 oz. (240 g.) seedless raisins

> 4 oz. (120 g.) glacé cherries
> 1 tablespoon brandy
> milk if necessary
> a few halved walnuts to decorate

Grease and paper a 10-inch (25-cm.) cake tin.

Cream together the butter and sugar very thoroughly and add the beaten eggs, a little at a time. Fold in the flour, salt and spice and add the fruit. Mix to a soft dropping consistency with the brandy and a little milk if necessary, turn into the tin, and place the walnuts on the top of the mixture. Bake in a slow oven (250° F., gas mark 1–1½) for 4–5 hours, or until, if a skewer is introduced, it comes out clean. Allow to cool slightly before turning out.

Plum Cake

This unusual nineteenth-century recipe gives a very light cake mixture which just supports the chopped fruit. Ice with royal icing (see p. 531). The quantities given make a cake of about 3 lb. (1 ½ k.).

8 oz. (240 g.) raisins	4 eggs
4 oz. (120 g.) currants	1 teaspoon almond essence
2 oz. (60 g.) glacé cherries	1 teaspoon grated orange rind
4 oz. (120 g.) sultanas	1 teaspoon cinnamon
4 oz. (120 g.) ground almonds	12 oz. (360 g.) plain flour
4 oz. (120 g.) peel	2 teaspoons baking powder
8 oz. (240 g.) butter	1 oz. (30 g.) whole almonds
4 oz. (120 g.) caster sugar	(blanched)

Chop all the fruit fairly finely, as the cake is very light and it would otherwise sink. Cream the butter and sugar very thoroughly, then beat in the egg yolks and the flavourings. Add the flour to the mixture, a little at a time, alternating it with handfuls of the fruit. Beat well after each addition. The baking powder should be sifted in with the last spoonful of flour. Then whip the egg whites very stiffly and fold in gently. The mixture must be poured at once into a well-greased and papered 9 inch tin, which should not be more than three quarters full.

Cook at 350° F., gas mark 4, for ½ hour and then for 2 hours at 300° F., gas mark 2.

Do not open the oven before the cake has been in for at least an hour or it may sink. Half an hour before it should be cooked, open the oven and quickly sprinkle the almonds over the top. Leave in the tin until cold.

Raisin Cake

This is a rather plain cake but very good and well flavoured. It keeps well. These quantities make a 2-lb. (1-k.) cake. Use a 10-inch (25-cm.) tin.

¾ lb. (360 g.) flour	rind of half a lemon
6 oz. (180 g.) butter	½ lb. (240 g.) sugar
6 oz. (180 g.) raisins	2 eggs
¼ lb. (120 g.) currants	¼ pint (1½ dl.) milk

Rub the butter into the sieved flour. Add the fruit, lemon rind and sugar. Mix well together, make a well in the centre, add the well-beaten eggs and the milk gradually. The mixture should be stiff enough to hold a spoon upright. Beat well. Bake in the greased and lined tin in a moderate oven, 350° F., gas mark 4, for about 1½ hours, covering the top lightly with foil if it becomes too brown.

Saffron Cake

Saffron cake is still made in Cornwall today. It is really a saffron-flavoured currant bread, very good with plenty of butter.

2 oz. (60 g.) butter	2 eggs
¼ lb. (120 g.) lard	warm milk to mix
1 lb. (½ k.) flour	1 teaspoon saffron
¼ lb. (120 g.) caster sugar	¼ lb. (120 g.) currants
a pinch of salt	¼ lb. (120 g.) sultanas
1 oz. (30 g.) yeast	

Use an oblong tin about 10 inches (25 cm.) in length.

Rub the butter and lard into the flour and add the sugar and salt. Prepare the yeast and put in a hole in the centre of the rubbed flour, turning a little flour into the yeast. Beat the eggs with the just warm milk. When the yeast sponges through, mix into a soft dough, using the milk and egg mixture and working in the fruit and the saffron. Knead a little and leave in the bowl in a warm place, covered, until it has doubled its size. Knead again and place in a greased tin. Allow a further rising time of 20–30 minutes. Then bake for about 30 minutes at 400° F., gas mark 6.

Sherry Cake

This is perhaps the best of all fruit cakes. It used to be made in the Cotswolds and served to those who had just come in from hunting. It can be made with brandy instead of sherry.

¼ lb. (120 g.) butter	2 oz. (60 g.) cherries
¼ lb. (120 g.) caster sugar	2 oz. (60 g.) shredded whole
3 eggs	almonds
½ lb. (240 g.) flour	2 glasses sherry
½ teaspoon salt	1 teaspoon sodium bicarbonate
¼ lb. (120 g.) ground almonds	2 teaspoons vinegar
¼ lb. (120 g.) currants	sherry for pouring over cake
¼ lb. (120 g.) peel	

Use an 8-inch (20-cm.) cake tin.

Cream the butter and sugar, add the egg yolks one at a time, beating well in. Add the dry ingredients gradually, then pour in a wineglass of sherry and beat well. Fold in the stiffly beaten whites, and finally the sodium bicarbonate dissolved in the vinegar. Beat well again. Bake in a greased, papered tin, with a piece of paper on the top. Place in a hot oven, 425° F., gas mark 7, then after 10 minutes lower the heat to 325° F., gas mark 3. Bake for 2 hours.

When cooked and still very hot, pour over a glass of sherry, by spoonfuls, and leave the cake, covered with a cloth, in the tin till it is quite cold.

Simnel Cake

Traditional at Easter. These quantities are for a 2½–3 lb. (1¼–1½ k.) cake.

5 oz. (150 g.) butter	1 oz. (30 g.) candied peel
4 oz. (120 g.) sugar	½ teaspoon mixed spice
2 teaspoons golden syrup	½ teaspoon ground cinnamon
3 eggs	¼ teaspoon ground cloves
8 oz. (240 g.) flour	milk if necessary
12 oz. (360 g.) mixed dried	1 lb. (½ k.) almond paste
fruit	

Grease and line a 10-inch (25-cm.) cake tin.

Cream the butter and sugar until white and fluffy. Add the warmed syrup to the beaten eggs and stir in. Mix the dry ingredients together and fold in, keeping a fairly stiff texture throughout. Use a little milk to blend if necessary. Put half the mixture into the tin, then a layer of almond paste which you have rolled to a thickness of about ¼ inch (½ cm.). Press down to make sure there are no air bubbles underneath, then add the remainder of the mixture. Bake at 300° F., gas mark 2, for about 2¼ hours or until well risen and firm to the touch. Cover with the remainder of the almond paste when quite cold, and brown slightly under the grill.

Twelfth Night Cake

Twelfth Night (6 January) was the last night of the Christmas Feast and was celebrated often with a masque or a play before the work of the New Year started in earnest the next day. Traditionally, there was always a special cake, which contained a bean. Whoever got it was called King of the Bean and had good luck in the coming year. The actor Robert Baddeley, who started out as a cook, left a legacy to Drury Lane Theatre for a cake to be eaten and a Port Wine Negus drunk, every Twelfth Night in the Green Room there.

This is a traditional nineteenth-century recipe: earlier recipes often use yeast. An eighteenth-century version gives 6 lb. flour and 1 lb. butter, with 4½ lb. currants, a great deal of spice, yeast and no eggs, which would give a kind of currant bread.

½ lb. (240 g.) butter	a pinch of cinnamon
½ lb. (240 g.) caster sugar	½ lb. (240 g.) currants
4 eggs	½ lb. (240 g.) raisins
3 tablespoons brandy	¼ lb. (120 g.) sultanas
½ lb. (240 g.) flour	2 oz. (60 g.) blanched chopped
a pinch of nutmeg	almonds

Use a 12-inch (30-cm.) cake tin.

Cream the butter and sugar and stir in the well beaten eggs and the brandy. Stir in the flour and spices gradually, then add the fruit and nuts. Beat well. Line the cake tin with buttered paper, put in the mixture and bake at 300° F., gas mark 2, for 3 hours. Cover the top lightly with foil if it becomes too dark. When quite cold, ice with royal icing (see p. 531).

Traditionally the cake was decorated with cherries, angelica and other crystallized fruits.

Cornish Heavy-Cake

A delectable flat cake, neither cake nor pastry. Sometimes eaten hot with butter and sometimes with clotted cream.

½ lb. (240 g.) flour	a pinch of salt
½ lb. (240 g.) butter	a little milk and sugar
3 oz. (90 g.) currants	

Rub a third of the butter into the flour, add the currants and salt and mix with a little cold water to a stiff dough. Roll it out on a floured board and dot all over with dabs of butter, using about half of what remains. Fold over and roll out, and repeat using all the remaining butter. Roll to a neat oblong shape 1 inch (2 cm.) thick, and lay on a baking tray. Mark the surface in diamonds, brush over with milk, sprinkle with caster sugar and bake for 30–35 minutes at 400° F., gas mark 6.

LIGHT CAKES AND SPONGES

Cider Cake

This recipe is from Somerset. The cake has a subtle flavour of cider and is particularly good served with a purée of apples with plenty of cream; or at a picnic with apples and with cider to drink.

4 oz. (120 g.) butter	1 teaspoon bicarbonate of soda
4 oz. (120 g.) sugar	1 teaspoon grated nutmeg
2 eggs	¼ pint (1½ dl.) cider
8 oz. (240 g.) flour	

Cream the butter and sugar, add the beaten eggs, then half the flour, sifted with the bicarbonate, and the nutmeg. Pour the cider over and beat it thoroughly until the acid of the cider acts on the alkali of the bicarbonate and makes it froth. Then stir in the remaining flour and put quickly into a square well-greased cake tin. Bake at 350° F., gas mark 4, for 40 minutes.

Rich Chocolate Cake

2 oz. (60 g.) butter	2 level teaspoons cocoa
2 oz. (60 g.) sugar	1 level teaspoon salt
1 level teaspoon syrup	1 level teaspoon bicarbonate
a few drops vanilla essence	of soda
3 eggs	3 fl. oz. (1 dl.) milk and water
6 oz. (180 g.) flour	

Use 2 8-inch (20-cm.) sandwich tins.

Cream the butter and sugar together and beat in the syrup and vanilla. Add the eggs and beat again. Sift the dry ingredients, except the soda, and stir into the creamed mixture. Dissolve the soda in the milk and water and stir in to give a soft consistency. Spread evenly in the 2 well-greased sandwich tins and bake in a moderate oven, 350° F., gas mark 4, for 25–30 minutes.

Leave the cake in the tins to cool for a few minutes before turning out. Fill with chocolate butter cream filling (p. 529) and ice with any white or chocolate icing.

Chocolate Cake to keep well

This is a particularly good chocolate cake: it will keep 3 or 4 weeks in an airtight tin and also deep-freezes very well. The recipe comes from the Macadam collection in Edinburgh.

4 oz. (120 g.) butter	vanilla essence
4 oz. (120 g.) caster sugar	2 oz. (60 g.) grated chocolate
2 eggs	6 oz. (180 g.) flour
2 oz. (60 g.) ground almonds	salt

Line an 8-inch (20-cm.) cake tin with buttered greaseproof paper, covering the bottom with a double thickness.

Cream the butter and sugar and add the well-beaten eggs. Stir in the ground almonds and vanilla, and the chocolate which has been melted in a basin over hot water. Sift in the flour and a pinch of salt. Mix and beat well. Bake for 30 minutes at 350° F., gas mark 4, and then turn down the oven to 300° F., gas mark 2, and bake a further 30 minutes. Test with a skewer, which will come out clean when the cake is done.

Rich Madeira Cake

This is the best of all fruitless cakes if eaten fresh. When stale it should only be used up in trifle. Delicious eaten in a sunny garden in the middle of the morning with a glass of sherry or madeira. This is from an eighteenth-century collection. The recipe was headed 'Madeira or Sweet cake'.

8 oz. (240 g.) butter	pinch of salt
8 oz. (240 g.) sugar	grated rind of a lemon
4 eggs	2 tablespoons lukewarm milk
8 oz. (240 g.) flour	

Use an 8-inch (20-cm.) cake tin.

Cream the butter and sugar very well. Add the beaten eggs a little at a time. Sift the flour with the salt and add gradually. Stir in the lemon rind. Beat in the just-warm milk and bake for 1½ hours at 325° F., gas mark 3.

Sweet Cake

From the unpublished Reading manuscript, this recipe is dated 1776. It is for a very large cake, so half-quantities are given here.

6 oz. (180 g.) butter	8 oz. (240 g.) flour
4 oz. (120 g.) caster sugar	a small glass of brandy
5 eggs, omitting 2 whites	a small glass of sherry

Grease and line a tin (about 8 inches, 20 cm.) with greaseproof paper. Cream the butter and sugar, beat in the eggs, add the flour, little by little, beating all the time, and pour in the brandy and sherry, also a little at a time. Put into the prepared tin and bake at 350° F., gas mark 4, for 1 hour. Lightly cover the top with foil if the cake is becoming too brown.

Marble Cake

Made in my family to please various children, which it invariably does.

Make a double quantity of Victoria sandwich mixture (p. 522) and divide the batter in four bowls. Colour one with cocoa, one with cochineal, and one with green colouring and leave one plain. Put in a well-greased 10-inch (25-cm.) tin in spoonfuls alternating from bowl to bowl. Bake for 45 minutes at 350° F., gas mark 4, and test with a skewer.

When cut each slice of cake is 'marbled' in the four colours.

Seed Cake

Enormously popular from the sixteenth century to the end of the nineteenth century, or even up to the First World War. Thomas Jusser, writing in 1580, mentions 'The Seede Cake' as traditional for the feast which marked the end of the spring wheat sowing. Now it is almost universally disliked; very few people can stand the taste of caraway seeds. Recipes abound. This is a typical but fairly simple one, given in case anyone cares to reconsider the strong flavour of caraway seeds.

8 oz. (240 g.) flour	1 oz. (30 g.) caraway seeds
a pinch of salt	2 eggs
4 oz. (120 g.) butter	2–3 tablespoons milk
4 oz. (120 g.) sugar	

Thoroughly grease and flour an 8-inch (20-cm.) cake tin. Mix the flour and salt in a basin. Rub in the fat with the tips of the fingers until the mixture resembles fine breadcrumbs. Add the sugar and caraway seeds and mix well. Make a well in the centre, stir in the beaten eggs and just sufficient milk to mix. Beat well. Put into the prepared tin and bake in a moderate oven, 350° F., gas mark 4, for 45 minutes or until a skewer inserted in the cake comes out clean.

Simple Sponge Cake

This is a traditional fatless sponge, the pride of the Victorian cook. It should puff up enormously. Delicious to eat quite fresh but very dull after a few hours except as a basis for trifle or if baked in a ring mould to be filled with whipped cream and fruit.

| 3 eggs | 3 oz. (90 g.) flour |
| 3 oz. (90 g.) sugar | |

Break the eggs into a large bowl. Add the sieved sugar and whisk until the mixture is thick and creamy. Now add the sieved flour and fold in lightly with the whisk. Pour into a well-buttered and papered 8-inch (20-cm.) tin and bake in a moderate oven at 375° F., gas mark 5, for the first 10 minutes, and then lower the heat to 350° F., gas mark 4, for 15 to 20 minutes. Invert the tin and leave to cool on a wire tray. Ease the cake out gently, running a knife blade round the sides.

Sponge Cake

This recipe, adapted from a manuscript of 1750–90 of Sir Peter Wyche's family, which I found in a Scottish collection, gives the lightest of true sponge cakes (which contain no fat).

| 7 eggs, leaving out 2 whites | ½ lb. (240 g.) flour |
| ¼ lb. (120 g.) caster sugar | ¼ pint (1½ dl.) water |

Put the eggs in the blender and beat a little, or beat in a bowl. Bring the sugar to the boil in the water and when boiling, pour immediately on to the beaten eggs, beating hard all the time, and continuing for several minutes. Add the flour and beat again till you have a light, smooth batter.

Put the batter in a large, high, well-greased sponge tin (about 10 inches, 25 cm.), or two small ones, and bake 1 hour in a moderate oven (350° F., gas mark 4). Do not open the oven until the sponge is cooked, as it may fall. A very good recipe for a ring sponge, which is to be filled with fruit and cream, as it is extremely light.

Swiss Roll

Presumably this well-known nursery cake came to us from Switzerland, but it has been a favourite in England for so long, and when made at home is so different from the factory-produced roll, that I give a recipe here.

3 eggs	2–3 tablespoons hot water
3 oz. (90 g.) sugar	some very good jam
3 oz. (90 g.) flour	

Grease and line with paper a shallow baking tin about 8 by 9 inches (20 by 22 cm.). Brush the paper all over with melted butter. Put the eggs into a bowl with the sugar and 2 oz. (60 g.) of the flour, and whisk over boiling water. Continue whisking until the mixture is light and spongy and thick: this will take about 15 minutes. (It may be mixed in a blender instead.) Remove from the heat and fold in the remaining flour, adding a very little hot water to keep the mixture slack. Put at once into the tin and bake in the top of a hot oven, 475° F., gas mark 9, for about 8 minutes or until well risen, brown and firm to the touch. Turn upside down on a piece of sugared paper and carefully strip off the paper lining. Trim off the crisp edges, spread with warm jam, and roll up immediately.

Victoria Sandwich

4 oz. (120 g.) butter	4 oz. (120 g.) flour
4 oz. (120 g.) sugar	a little milk if necessary
2 eggs	

Cream together the butter and sugar until very light and creamy. Beat the eggs and add them a little at a time to the creamed mixture. Fold the flour lightly into the mixture, together with a little milk to give a soft dropping consistency. Turn into 2 well-greased 8-inch (20-cm.) sandwich tins and bake in a moderate oven at 375° F., gas mark 5, for 25–30 minutes, until well risen, golden brown and firm to the touch. Cool on a cake rack and, when cold, sandwich together with jam or other filling, dusting the top lightly with icing or caster sugar.

This is a very good basic mixture and may be flavoured with lemon or orange peel and a little juice, or with half cocoa and half powdered chocolate, and iced appropriately.

Rich Butter Sponge

This is a very rich sponge cake, smoother and lighter than a Victoria sandwich mixture, excellent for strawberry shortcake or to cut in small squares to be iced and decorated.

3 large eggs	2½ oz. (75 g.) flour
4 oz. (120 g.) caster sugar	½ oz. (15 g.) cornflour
3 oz. (90 g.) butter	

Whisk the eggs and sugar in a basin over a saucepan of hot water for about 10 minutes. They should be thick and smooth, the eggs being partly cooked, but of course they must never boil. The water should not cool, but should be kept a little below boiling point throughout. Clarify the butter and add to the eggs with the sieved flour and cornflour, folding in very lightly. Pour into a shallow baking tin lined with greased paper. Bake in a moderate oven, 375° F., gas mark 5, for about 45 minutes. This can be baked in an oblong tin or used for little cakes.

GINGERBREADS AND SMALL CAKES

Old-fashioned Gingerbread from Yorkshire

10 oz. (300 g.) flour
1 teaspoon ground ginger
½ teaspoon ground cinnamon
a pinch of salt
4 oz. (120 g.) chopped dates
5 oz. (150 g.) treacle *or* golden syrup
3 oz. (90 g.) butter
1 egg
4 oz. (120 g.) dark brown sugar
¾ teaspoon bicarbonate of soda, dissolved in 3 teaspoons of milk

Well grease and dust with flour a square tin (about 10 inches, 25 cm.). Sieve together the flour, ginger, cinnamon and salt. Add the dates. Melt the treacle and butter together in a pan over gentle heat, and leave to cool slightly. Meanwhile beat together the egg and sugar. Add the melted butter and syrup to the flour alternately with the beaten egg and sugar. Lastly add the dissolved bicarbonate of soda and beat well to a soft consistency, adding a little water if necessary. Pour into the prepared tin and bake in a slow oven – 325° F., gas mark 3 – for 1½ to 2 hours. Cool on a cake rack.

Gingerbread

This is a traditional recipe from the West Country.

8 oz. (240 g.) flour	2 oz. (60 g.) brown sugar
½ teaspoon salt	2 tablespoons syrup
½ teaspoon cinnamon	¼ pint (1½ dl.) milk and water
1 teaspoon ginger	1 teaspoon bicarbonate of soda
3 oz. (90 g.) butter	1 oz. (30 g.) almonds (blanched)

Grease a 10-inch (25-cm.) square tin thoroughly.

Mix the flour, salt and spices together. Melt the butter, sugar and syrup with the milk and water in a saucepan, taking care not to boil them. Stir the warm liquid into the flour mixture and mix very thoroughly. Lastly, add the bicarbonate of soda dissolved in a little water. Pour into the greased tin, and bake in a slow oven, 300° F., gas mark 2, for 1½ hours. About 10 minutes before it should be cooked, pull out the tray a little from the oven and quickly scatter with almonds. If possible, keep a few days before cutting, as this will improve the flavour.

Almond Macaroons

An eighteenth-century recipe.

3 egg whites	1 tablespoon ground rice or fine
a pinch of salt	semolina
6 oz. (180 g.) ground almonds	18 blanched almonds
8 oz. (240 g.) caster sugar	2 or 3 sheets of rice paper

Whip the egg whites and salt until stiff enough to hold a peak. Fold in the ground almonds, sugar and ground rice or semolina. Put in little mounds or roll into balls and then flatten on rice paper on a well-greased baking tray.

Place an almond on each, bake in a slow oven at 300° F., gas mark 2, till crisp – about 30–40 minutes.

They can be baked on buttered greaseproof paper, which can be peeled off, but there is danger of breaking the macaroons, and the texture of the rice paper is good.

Jumbles

Jumbles were made by Richard II's cook and recorded in a rather incomprehensible recipe in the *Forme of Cury*. Recipes occur in many later cookery books, as jumbles seem to have been an almost essential part of the banquet which followed the main feast. In fact they seem to have been no more than a simple almond biscuit, the paste rolled out and cut into intricate shapes, 'Whatever forms you think proper,' says Richard Dolby. A manuscript recipe suggests that they be made in the form of the letter S.

6 oz. (180 g.) butter	¼ pint (1½ dl.) cream
½ lb. (240 g.) flour	½ lb. (240 g.) ground almonds
½ lb. (240 g.) caster sugar	well–beaten whites of 3 eggs

Rub the butter into the flour; stir in the sugar and cream. Add the almonds and incorporate the fluffy egg whites. Work into a paste. Knead on a floured board, roll out and cut out. Bake on greased flat trays at 300° F., gas mark 2, for 20 minutes or a little more if they are not set and firm.

They seem to have been served sometimes hot with melted butter and sugar and sometimes cold as biscuits.

Orange Jumbles

4 oz. (120 g.) ground almonds	a pinch of salt
4 oz. (120 g.) flour	4 oz. (120 g.) caster sugar
2 teaspoons finely grated orange rind	3 oz. (90 g.) butter
	well–beaten whites of 2 eggs

Mix the flour, almonds, salt, sugar and orange rind. Rub in the butter. Bind with the egg, place on a lightly floured board and knead till smooth and free from cracks. Roll out into a long thin sausage, about 1 inch (2 cm.) in diameter. Divide evenly into 20 pieces. Roll out each piece till 3 inches (6 cm.) long, place in 'S' shapes on a greased tin, and bake at 350° F., gas mark 4, till golden brown, 12–15 minutes.

Wafers

Wafers are recorded in England as early as the twelfth century, and were made in special irons, as waffles are made today. They were always very light and crisp and preferably eaten hot. The following fifteenth-century recipe, called simply 'Wafers', is very good. Bake them in the oven.

8 oz. (240 g.) flour
a pinch of salt
4 oz. (120 g.) butter
1 oz. (30 g.) double cream
2 level tablespoons honey

Rub the butter into the flour and salt. Add the honey and cream, and work into the dry ingredients with a knife until the mixture holds together. Roll out to ⅛ inch (2 mm.) thick, and cut into small rounds with a glass or a cutter. Bake on a greased baking sheet for 15–20 minutes at 300° F., gas mark 2. Eat hot, or cool on a wire rack.

GAUFFRES

Like wafers, these were made from very early times. They were sticky and pliable and were cooked on one side only, peeled off a flat iron or tray, and rolled. They survive today as brandy snaps.

Brandy Snaps

4 oz. (120 g.) butter
8 oz. (240 g.) flour
8 oz. (240 g.) brown sugar
2 teaspoons brandy
2 well-beaten eggs

Rub the butter into the flour, add sugar, eggs and brandy, and beat very well. The batter should be of a soft, dropping consistency. Heat a girdle or a very large frying pan so that a piece of butter dropped on it sizzles and smokes at once. Drop small spoonfuls on to the buttered pan, well apart, and allow them to spread to the size of saucers, becoming full of holes as they do so. Quickly lift, roll each on a skewer or a stick and place on a rack to become dry and crisp.

Serve filled with whipped cream.

Parkin

Traditional in Yorkshire and in much of the north of England.

> 1 lb. (½ k.) fine oatmeal   2 teaspoons ground ginger
> 2 teaspoons baking powder   1 teaspoon mixed spice
> ¼ lb. (120 g.) lard   ½ lb. (240 g.) golden syrup

Rub the lard into the oatmeal and mix in the spices and baking powder. Warm the syrup and mix it into the oatmeal till you have a stiff mixture.

Grease a flat baking tin, pour in the parkin and bake for 1–1¼ hours at 300° F., gas mark 2.

Ratafia Cakes

These small flat almond biscuits were traditional in England from the sixteenth century if not earlier. They are good eaten alone or used in trifles or to accompany creams or jellies. This recipe is from the *Court and Country Confectioner* of 1772. It is particularly easy and successful.

> ½ lb. (240 g.) whole blanched almonds
> 5 egg whites
> 1 lb. (½ k.) sugar

Beat the egg whites until they hold a peak. Put the almonds through a mouli or blender into the egg whites. Stir in the sugar a little at a time and mix all well together. Shape into small flat rounds and bake on a greased or paper-lined tin in a slow oven, 300° F., gas mark 2, for 40 minutes or until dry and beginning to crisp at the edges.

Richmond Maids of Honour

Apparently these small rich cheesecakes were invented at Queen Elizabeth's palace at Richmond, to tempt the queen's capricious appetite: the story goes that her maids of honour liked them so much and ate so many that the cakes received their name.

The original recipe passed to a shop in Richmond, which for many years had the sole right to make them: they could still be bought there until about twenty years ago when the shop was pulled down. The following recipe comes from a fifteenth-century manuscript and, if it is not the original palace recipe, it must be very like it.

1 lb. (½ k.) good puff pastry
½ lb. (240 g.) curd mixed with 6 oz. (180 g.) fresh butter
4 yolks of eggs beaten with a glass of brandy and 6 oz. (180 g.) sugar
2 oz. (60 g.) very fine white breadcrumbs, mixed with 2 oz. (60 g.)
    ground almonds and a little nutmeg
juice of 1 lemon and the grated zest of 2

Line 2 dozen or more tartlet tins with the puff pastry. Work all the other ingredients into the curd and butter, beating well. Fill each tartlet and bake for 10 minutes at 400° F., gas mark 6.

Icings and Fillings

Almond Icing or Marzipan

Quantity for an 8–9 inch (20–22 cm.) cake.

½ lb. (240 g.) ground almonds	1 teaspoon lemon juice
½ lb. (240 g.) icing or caster sugar	2 teaspoons water
1 egg	

Caster sugar enhances the slightly rough texture of the ground almonds; icing sugar makes the paste smoother.

Lightly mix the almonds and sugar together in a mixing bowl. Stir in the beaten egg and lemon juice and water. Dust a pastry board with icing sugar and knead the almond paste on it till it is smooth and coagulated.

Roll out about a ¼ inch (½ cm.) thick. Brush the cake over with warm apricot jam. Fit the almond paste over and press gently on to the cake, being careful not to break it. Cut away the surplus from the bottom edges of the cake. If small breaks occur, gently fill them.

Alternatively, cut a circle the size of the top of the cake. Roll out the remainder to the length of the circumference of the cake (measure it with string) and trim to a strip the depth of the cake. Then brush the sides of the cake with jam and lay on the strip and roll so that the strip adheres. Brush the top with jam and apply the circle. Gently press cut edges together.

Boiled Icing

This icing is very good. It is much easier to make if you have a sugar thermometer.

6 oz. (180 g.) sugar

2 teaspoons golden syrup

3 tablespoons boiling water

1 teaspoon of lemon juice

2 egg whites

Boil the sugar, water, syrup and lemon juice together to 240° F. or until a ball forms when dropped in cold water. Do not stir while boiling or it will crystallize. Beat the egg whites until stiff, then pour over them the boiling syrup in a thin, slow stream, beating all the time. Continue beating for 7 minutes, or until cool and easy to spread.

Plain Chocolate Icing

3 oz. (90 g.) grated chocolate

a few drops of vanilla essence

1½ tablespoons of water

8 oz. (240 g.) icing sugar

a teaspoon of fresh butter

Put the chocolate, water and butter into a saucepan and melt together until smooth, then allow to cool a little. Add the vanilla and sifted icing sugar and beat well. If the icing gets cold, stand it over a saucepan of warm water and beat again until smooth and of a coating consistency. Spread over cake with a hot, wet knife.

Chocolate Butter Cream

1½ oz. (45 g.) plain chocolate

3 oz. (90 g.) fresh butter

6 oz. (180 g.) icing sugar

2 teaspoons water

Melt the chocolate in 2 teaspoons of water over low heat and cool a little. Cream the butter with the sieved icing sugar, and when creamy beat in the soft chocolate. This can be used as a filling or on the top of a cake.

Chocolate or Coffee Butter Cream Filling

3 oz. (90 g.) butter

6 oz. (180 g.) sieved icing sugar

1 teaspoon coffee essence *or* 2 teaspoons cocoa *or* chocolate powder

Cream the butter, adding the sugar by degrees, beat till smooth and creamy, then add the flavouring. Chopped nuts or cherries may be stirred into the finished cream for variety.

529

Fondant Icing

A sugar thermometer is essential for this kind of icing.

> 3 tablespoons water
> 6 oz. (180 g.) caster sugar
> ¼ teaspoon cream of tartar
> 1 egg white

Put the water in a saucepan, rinsing it up the sides. Add the sugar and cream of tartar and dissolve over low heat. When dissolved bring to boiling point (240° F.) and boil *without stirring* for 3 minutes or until a thread forms from a spoon (255–260° F.). Leave to cool slightly and beat the egg white stiffly. Pour the sugar syrup in a thin, slow stream over the egg white. Beat until it starts to thicken. Pour quickly over cake.

Fudge Filling

> 4 oz. (120 g.) soft brown sugar
> 2 oz. (60 g.) butter
> 1 teaspoon coffee essence
> 1 tablespoon golden syrup
> 1 tablespoon milk

Bring all the ingredients slowly to the boil and stir all the time while gently simmering for 10 minutes. Remove from the heat and allow to cool for 10 minutes. Then beat until thick and creamy. When quite cold use to fill a cake. Excellent if chopped nuts are added.

Glacé Icing

A soft icing to be put straight on the cake instead of almond paste, and covered with royal icing.

> ½ lb. (240 g.) icing sugar
> 1 tablespoon water
> 1 teaspoon lemon juice

Sieve the icing sugar into a saucepan in which you have already put the water and lemon juice. Stir it over a low heat, holding it off the fire, until the sugar is melted and the temperature is just above blood heat. Pour it over the cake and allow it to run down the sides, smoothing it with a hot knife.

Royal Icing

This is the icing to use for the final coating and for piped decorations.

> 1 lb. (½ k.) icing sugar
> 2 egg whites
> 2 teaspoons lemon juice
> 1 teaspoon glycerine (this keeps the icing from setting too hard and may be bought from any chemist)

Sieve the icing sugar, making sure that it is quite free from lumps and lying slightly fluffed in the bowl. Stir in the lemon juice and the glycerine. Whip the whites of eggs to a medium stiffness, not until they will stand in peaks. Stir in gently, and then beat with a wooden spoon, or with an electric beater or in a blender, till you have a perfectly smooth, very white cream. If there is any delay before using, cover the bowl with a damp tea-towel tightly stretched across the top to prevent air entering and hardening the icing. If the icing seems too thin, more sugar may be beaten in.

Part of the icing may be put in a separate bowl and colouring beaten into it.

Uncooked Icing

This is the quickest of all icings to make.

> ½ lb. (240 g.) icing sugar
> 1 tablespoon water
> few drops of lemon juice
> colouring if desired

Sieve the icing sugar into a bowl, stir in the lemon juice, then add the water a few drops at a time until the mixture is just thick enough to coat the back of the spoon. Lastly, add any colouring, and beat well.

BIBLIOGRAPHY

Accessions, Medical & Household Recipes, Late 17th–early 18th century.

Acton, Eliza, *Modern Cookery in all its Branches reduced to an Easy Practice*, 1845

Adams, Samuel & Sarah, *The Complete Servant*, 1825, Macadam Collection, Edinburgh

Allen (Mrs A. Macaire), *Breakfast Dishes*, 1896, J. S. Virtue & Co, Ltd

Allen, Elliston, *British Tastes*, 1896, Hutchinson, London

Andrew, Kirwan, *Host and Guest*, 1864, Macadam Collection, Edinburgh

Anon, *The Family Receipt Book*, 1820, Macadam Collection, Edinburgh

Anon, *The English Hus-wife*, 1615

Anon, *The Complete Family Piece* (7th edition), 1737

Anon, *The Court and County Confectioner*, 1772

Anon, *A Proper New Book of Cookery* (recension from Book of Cookery, 1500), 1546

Anon, *The Court and Kitchen of Elizabeth, commonly called Joan Cromwell, the wife of the late Usurper, truly described and represented*, 1664

Anon, *The Babees Book*, late 15th century MS

Apicius, *The Roman Cookery Book*, Trans. Barbara Flower and Elisabeth Rosenbaum, 1958, Harrap

Austin, Thomas, Two 15th century Cook Books, the Harleian MS, the Ashmole MS, 1888, Early English Text Society

Aylett, Mary, and Ordish, Olive, *First Catch your Hare*, Macdonald, 1965

Beeton, Mrs, *Household Management*, facsimile, 1968, Cape

Bellows, Albert J., *The Philosophy of Eating*, Hurd & Houghton, NY, 1868

Bennett, Curtis, *Food of the People*

B. H., *The Housekeepers' Assistant*, 1847

Blencowe, Ann, *Receipt Book*, 1694, published 1925, Guy Chapman

Boorde, Andrew, *A Compendyous Regymen or a Dyetary of Healthe* 1562

Braithwaite, *Rules and Orders for the Government of the House of an Earl*, c. 1615, MS

Brett, Gerard, *Dinner is Served*, 1968, Hart Davis

Burnett, John, *Plenty and Want*, 1968, Penguin Books

Clark, Lady, *Lady Clark of Tillypronie's Cook Book*, 1909 Edinburgh
Cooper, Charles, *The English Table in History and Literature*, 1929, Sampson Low
Cooper, Joseph (head cook to Charles I), *The Art of Cookery Refined and Augmented*, 1654
Culpeper, Nicholas, *The Complete Herbal*, 1952, Foulsham

Digby, Sir Kenelm, The Closet of the Eminently Learned Sir Kenelm Digby, Knight, Opened, 1669
Dodds, Mistress Margaret (Mrs Johnstone), The Cook and Housewives Manual, 1824
Drummond, J. C., and Wilbraham, Anne, *The Englishman's Food*, 1958, Cape

Edden, Helen, *County Recipes of Old England*, 1929, Country Life
Ellwanger, C. H., *The Pleasures of the Table*, 1903, Heinemann
Emmison, F. G., *Tudor Food and Pastimes*, 1964, Benn
Evelyn, Sir John, Diaries, 1959, OUP

Furnivall, F. J., Editor, *Description of England in Shakespeare's youth* by Wm. Harrison (1577), 1877

Furnivall, F. J., *Early English Meals and Manners*
Furnivall, F. J., Editor, the Harleian MS, the Ashmole MS, Early English Text Society
Gerard, *Gerard's Herball*, 1597
Girth Inventory, Household Management, Macadam Collection, Edinburgh
Glasse, Mrs Hannah, *The Art of Cookery Made Plain and Easy*, 1747
Golding, Louis, and Simon, André, *We Shall Eat and Drink Again* 1944, Hutchinson

Hall, Augusta, *Good Cookery Illustrated*, 1867, Macadam Collection, Edinburgh
Hardy, *The Gourmet's Book of Food and Drink*, Bodley Head
Hartley, Dorothy, *Food in England*, 1962, Macdonald
Hartman, *Excellent Directions for Cookery*, 1682
Hayward, Abraham, *The Art of Dining*, 1883, John Murray
Hazlitt, Wm. C., *Old Cookery Books and Ancient Cuisine*, 1886, Elliot, Stock
Heaton, Nell, *Traditional Recipes of the British Isles*, 1951, Faber
Heritage, Lizzie, *New Universal Cookery Book*, 1896, Cassell
Hill, Brian, *The Greedy Book*, 1966, Hart Davis
Hill, B. E., *The Epicure's Almanac*, 1841
Holinshed, ed. Nicoll, *Chronicles*, Dent, Everyman's Library

Jeffreson, T. C., *A Book About the Table*, 1875, Hurst & Blackett

Kettner, Auguste, *Kettner's Book of the Table*, 1877, Dulan
Kitchiner, Dr. Wm., *Apicius Redivivus, The Cook's Oracle*, 1804, enlarged in 1831

Lamb, Charles, *Letters of Elia*, Dent, Everyman's Library
Lamb, Patrick, *Royal Cookery, or The Complete Court Cook*, 1710
Lemery, Louis, *A Treatise of All Sorts of Food*, 1745, Macadam Collection, Edinburgh

Markham, Gervase, *The English Housewife*, 1649
Marshall, Mrs A. B., *Mrs A. B. Marshall's Cookery Book*, *c.* 1880, Robert Hayes
Marshall, Mrs A. B., *Fancy Ices*
May, Robert, *The Accomplish't Cook*, 1671
W. M., *The Queen's Closet Opened*, 1655

Napier, Mrs, *A Noble Boke of Cookery* edited from an early MS in the Holkham Collection, *c.* 1480, published 1882

Ozell, Mr, *M. Misson's Memoirs. Observations on his travels over England*, 1719

Patterson, Miss S. J., MS from Colchester
Pennel, *Guide for the Greedy*
Pullar, Philippa, *Consuming Passions*, 1970, Hamish Hamilton

Quennell, Nancy, *The Epicure's Anthology*, 1936, Golden Cockerel Press

Raffald, Elizabeth, *The Experienced English Housekeeper*, 2nd edition, 1771
The Reading MS
Reavely, Thomas, *A Book of Choice Receipts*, Edinburgh MS
Rundell, Maria Eliza, *A New System of Domestic Cookery*, 1840, John Murray

Simon, André L., *A Concise Encyclopaedia of Gastronomy*, 1952, Collins
Smith, Elizabeth, *The Complete Housewife*, 1736
Soyer, Alexis (Chef to the Reform Club), *The Gastronomic Regenerator*, 1846

Tillinghast, M., *Rare and Excellent Receipts in Cookery*, 1690
Torrington Diaries
Tusser, Thomas, *500 Points of Good Husbandrye*, 1580 (the last edition published in his lifetime)

Ude, Louis Eustache (Chef to the Earl of Sefton, the Duke of York, Crockfords Club and the United Services Club), *The French Cook*, 7th edition, 1822

Venner, Tobias, *Via Recta ad Vitam Longam*, 1620 MS, British Museum

Walton, Izaak, The Compleat Angler, Dent, Everyman's Library

Ward, E., *The London Spy*, 1703

Warner, The Rev. Dr, *Antiquitates Culinariae* (contains the Forme of Curye), 1791

White, Florence, *Good Things in England*, 1932, Cape

White, Florence, *Good English Food*, 1952, Cape

Wither, George, *The Englishman's Table*

Wolley, H., *The Queen-Like Closet*, 1670

Wynkeworthe de Worde, *The Book of Kervynge*, Quarto 1508, reprinted 1513 and 1613

M. W., *The Queen's Closet Open'd*, 1671, Macadam Collection, Edinburgh

GENERAL INDEX

INDEX OF RECIPES

MORE ABOUT PENGUINS
AND PELICANS

Penguinews, which appears every month, contains details of all the new books issued by Penguins as they are published. From time to time it is supplemented by *Penguins in Print*, which is our complete list of almost 5,000 titles.

A specimen copy of *Penguinews* will be sent to you free on request. Please write to Dept EP, Penguin Books Ltd, Harmondsworth, Middlesex, for your copy.

In the U.S.A.: For a complete list of books available from Penguins in the United States write to Dept CS, Penguin Books, 625 Madison Avenue, New York, New York 10022.

In Canada: For a complete list of books available from Penguins in Canada write to Penguin Books Canada Ltd, 41 Steelcase Road West, Markham, Ontario.

SPICES, SALT AND AROMATICS IN THE ENGLISH KITCHEN

ELIZABETH DAVID

In this volume, the first in an original study of English cooking, Elizabeth David presents English recipes which are notable for their employment of spices, salt and aromatics. As usual, she seasons instruction with information, explaining the origins and uses of such ingredients as nutmeg, cardamom and juniper. Mrs David stresses the influence of centuries of oriental trade on the English kitchen, where spices and indian curry, kebabs and yoghurt are now perfectly at home, along with immigrant dishes such as rissotto, paella and pepper steak.

This book, with its brawns (or pig's-head cheese), briskets and spiced beef, its smoked fish and cured pork, its old-fashioned curd dishes and sweet fruit pickles, sounds a welcome, if uncommon, note in the English kitchen.

'Has all the characteristic qualities of her earlier books. There is that same precise evocation of how food should look and smell and the same lack of pretentiousness, the same scholarly approach, combined with forthright opinions and suggestions' – Lucia van der Post in the *Sunday Times*